Charles Spielman

REDEEM THE TIME

A Publication of the
Center for the Study of the History
of Liberty in America
HARVARD UNIVERSITY

HARVARD UNIVERSITY PRESS

CAMBRIDGE, MASSACHUSETTS, AND

LONDON, ENGLAND • 1977

REDEEM
THE TIME

The Puritan Sabbath
in Early America

Winton U. Solberg

Library of Congress Cataloging in Publication Data

Solberg, Winton U
  Redeem the time.

  (A Publication of the Center for the Study of the
History of Liberty in America, Harvard University)
  Bibliography: p.
  Includes index.
  1. Sabbath—History.   2. Sunday—History.
3. Puritans.   I. Title.   II. Series: Harvard Univer-
sity. Center for the Study of the History of Liberty
in America. Publication.
BV111.S64   263'.0973   76-26672
ISBN 0-674-75130-2

To Connie

Foreword

by Oscar Handlin

BY THE TIME of the American Revolution most of the problems involved in the relationship of church and state had been amicably settled in practice. In the decades that followed it was only necessary to effect the legal changes that incorporated the understandings already worked out pragmatically.

One exceptional issue lingered through the nineteenth century and, indeed, well into the twentieth. The law in New England and, to a lesser extent in other states, used the instruments of governmental coercion to impose a particular conception of the Christian Sabbath on the whole population. The Sunday blue laws led to prolonged political controversy that had not yet ended in the 1970s. No great economic or social issues were involved. Yet any effort to alter the existing arrangement evoked bitter conflict. At stake were important religious and emotional considerations that were the product of a view of the Sabbath unique in the Christian world.

Winton Solberg's perceptive study reaches back to sixteenth-century England to trace the evolution of the Puritan conception of the Sabbath and the means by which it became involved in the mechanism of state sanctions. By a comparison with the other colonies the analysis shows why the Sabbath took the particular form it did in the Puritan settlements. The book thus contributes to the understanding of important aspects both of the relationship of church and state in the United States and of Puritanism.

vii

Preface

THE PURITAN SABBATH exerted a powerful influence on the life of the American people from the time of the initial settlements until well into the twentieth century, a fact which led a naturalized French citizen in the early nineteenth century to write that Sabbath observance was the only truly American and national characteristic. The foundations of this development were laid in the colonial period of the United States, and yet, strange to say, the history of Sabbatarianism in these years has never before been written. No phase of our early history, as Professor Charles H. McIlwain said of another topic years ago, exhibits a greater discrepancy "between the importance of the subject to contemporaries and the indifference to it of most historians."

The present volume is intended to repair that long-standing deficiency. It analyzes the emergence in America of the Sabbatarianism which remained so prominent in this country for more than three centuries. My original intention was to use the weekly day of rest and worship as a means of studying religious pluralism in the United States after 1800, a task that necessitated a firm understanding of the septennial festival in early America. Since no work of that type could be found and the subject proved highly significant in its own right, what was originally envisaged as a chapter has become a book.

Redeem the Time focuses on the origins of Sabbatarianism in the colonial period, but one simply cannot comprehend that development without transcending the local frame of reference. The Sabbath and Sunday question has occupied some of the best minds in Western civilization since antiquity, and a central problem in writing this book has been to explain how a new and powerful Sabbatarian impulse emerged in England on the eve of colonization and proved so significant in molding the United States in its most formative years.

Part One deals with the English inheritance. After a brief discussion of certain distinctive ways of thinking about and observing holy days during the long pre-Reformation period, the three main expressions of the Continental Reformation are analyzed with a view to showing that the Sabbath flowered best in an environment of Reformed theology and even better still in alliance with covenant theology. English Puritans under Elizabeth developed the idea of the Sabbath with new thoroughness and rigor. The theological grounds of the new theory were in the Reformed tradition, but economic and social forces peculiar to England at the time were also instrumental in bringing about a fresh outlook on the matter. Proper Lord's Day observance constituted an important part of the Puritan program for the spiritual renewal of England, and the practice spread rapidly after 1595. But Sabbatarianism became a badge of controversy between Puritan and Anglican under the early Stuarts, and it was most closely identified with Puritanism by the time the settlement of America began.

Part Two analyzes the impact of this revitalized Sabbatarian impulse in early America. A problem in writing this portion of the book was that of striking a proper balance between the general history necessary to show the institutional and intellectual context in which Sabbatarianism arose in a given time and place and the specific details that explain the evolution of the weekly observance. I have dealt with the matter as seemed best warranted in each particular situation. The sources convince me that contemporaries attached tremendous importance to proper Sabbath observance, and to demonstrate the point I have offered evidence of different types from the various colonies. But enforcement instances are illustrative rather than comprehensive, and they could easily have been multiplied. To be sure, the Puritan Sabbath always prospered best in New England, but the emergence of Sabbatarianism in many different "social laboratories" on this side of the Atlantic demonstrates the widespread influence of Puritanism in early America. There was a close interaction between ideas imported from England (and from places to which English Puritanism was carried such as Holland and Scotland) and the realities imposed by the environment of the New World, and yet religious theory was always pragmatically adapted to special circumstances and from generation to generation. To tell the complete story it has been necessary to treat those English (and Dutch) developments that most influenced the colonies in the years under review. The post-Restoration period is especially significant in this respect, for it was in these years that the revolutionary Quaker testimony on the observance of times and days and the Old Testament legalism of Seventh Day Baptists became important in America. As this genetic study makes clear, the Sabbath was ever a dynamic rather than a static institution. The Puritan theory on the subject influenced practice in all of the colonies in the century after it was first adumbrated, and hence this book offers evidence on the extent to which American culture was "puritanized" at its very inception.

As used in the following pages, the term "early America" means from the beginning of settlement to that point in time when the reciprocal interaction between tradition and design had succeeded in creating an indigenous pattern of Sabbatarianism in each colony. This varied from locality to locality depending on circumstances, but everywhere the task was essentially complete before the commencement of the Great Awakening. The year 1740 therefore serves as a convenient terminal date for this study. The book considers all of the American colonies founded in these years and later part of the United States except Georgia, which was established too late to figure here.

The present volume points to the future in saying that the pattern of Sabbatarianism which had arisen in the different colonies by the early eighteenth century remained essentially unaltered until the Revolutionary period. This was clearly the situation with respect to laws regulating observance of the Lord's Day, although closer study may show that other, more subtle changes occurred during these years of ferment. In any event, the evidence suggests that after 1740 the periods of greatest significance in the history of Sabbatarianism in the United States were the late eighteenth century and the decades from the 1820s through the 1880s. But that is another story, and I may be able to tell it in another volume.

All quotations are given as in the original, with the spelling and, as far as feasible, the capitalization and punctuation of the original retained. But superscript letters have been lowered to the line, contractions and abbreviations have been expanded where necessary for clarity, the thorn *y* has been changed to *th*, the ampersand has been replaced with *and*, modern usage has been followed with respect to the letters *i* and *j*, *u* and *v*, and the purely typographical peculiarities of the printing of an earlier age have been disregarded. Titles are generally given in brief form, but fuller or complete titles are sometimes furnished to illustrate a point. The Revised Standard Version is followed for all biblical quotations unless otherwise indicated. All dates are given Old Style (Julian), but the years are modernized and given New Style (Gregorian), with 1 January as the beginning of the new year.

I have accumulated numerous obligations in preparing this volume, and it gives me great pleasure to thank those who provided encouragement and assistance along the way. Conversations with the late Arthur M. Schlesinger led me to undertake the original project that eventuated in this book, and the late Wallace M. Notestein fortified my subsequent resolve to concentrate on the Puritan Sabbath. My research and writing were facilitated by a Morse Fellowship from Yale University, a Summer Fellowship from the Henry E. Huntington Library in San Marino, California, the Wallace Research Fund of Macalester College in St. Paul, Minnesota, and a Fellowship from the Center for the Study of the History of Liberty in America at Harvard University.

The original materials on which this study rests are in libraries scattered throughout the country, and the collections on which I have drawn most heavily are at the following places: Harvard University Library, Boston Public Library, Boston Athenaeum, Massachusetts Historical Society Library, American Antiquarian Society Library, John Carter Brown Library at Brown University, Yale University Library, New York Public Library, Union Theological Seminary Library, Historical Society of Pennsylvania Library, Library Company of Pennsylvania, Presbyterian Historical Society Library, Library of Congress, Folger Shakespeare Library, University of Illinois Library, and the Henry E. Huntington Library. My thanks to the directors and staffs of these institutions for many courtesies, and also to the reference librarians at the University of Illinois at Urbana-Champaign who cheerfully and skilfully obtained interlibrary loans for my use.

I am grateful to Professor Oscar Handlin of Harvard University not only for a critical reading of an earlier draft of the manuscript but also for wise and patient counsel in the preparation of this volume. He deserves praise for such merits as the work may possess, but I alone assume responsibility for any defects. The dedication is but a small token of appreciation for my wife, who made it possible for me to write this book, and (silently) for our children, Gail, Andrew, and Kristin, who each know better than anyone else how they contributed to *Redeem the Time*.

In releasing this study, I am reminded of the words of the incomparable Augustine, who ends his great classic by treating the eternal felicity of the city of God and the perpetual Sabbath and then adds, "I have now . . . discharged my obligation in writing this large work. Let those who think I have said too little, or those who think I have said too much, forgive me; and let those who think I have said just enough join me in giving thanks to God. Amen."

W.U.S.

Contents

Illustrations on pages 4, 81, and 82 from *Divine Examples of God's Severe Judgments upon Sabbath-Breakers* (London, 1671); courtesy of Houghton Library, Harvard University.

REDEEM THE TIME

Prologue:
The Structure of Time

SAINTLY THOMAS SHEPARD considered his flight from England providentially arranged. A hunted man who could not freely exercise his faith in his native land, he set out from Harwich for Massachusetts in the autumn of 1634. For three days after embarkation a violent wind assaulted the *Hope* and drove it to Yarmouth Roads. Here, on a day later remembered as Windy Saturday, the ship broke from its anchors and was cast upon the sands. Shepard and his fellow passengers committed their bodies and souls to God, whereupon the tempest immediately abated.

Some of the company left the vessel during the calm on the morning after, but the Puritan divine feared they did so "a little soon." For Shepard revered the Sabbath as the very bulwark of his faith and thought his companions should have spent the day on board praising their Lord and Savior.[1] "Its easie to demonstrate by Scripture and argument as well as by experience," he contended, "that Religion is just as the Sabbath is, and decayes and growes as the Sabbath is esteemed: the immediate honour and worship of God which is brought forth and swadled in the three first Commandements, is nurst up and suckled in the bosome of the Sabbath."[2] Shepard's conviction was common among Puritans, and it registered a deep and lasting impression upon early America.

This belief originated in England on the eve of American colonization, a product of fresh speculation aroused by the Reformation. "England was

1

at rest," wrote Shepard, "till they troubled Gods Sabbath."[3] Certain that the Bible justified Puritan doctrine and practice, he regarded the opposing view as a prime source of the discord that culminated in the English Civil War. The reasons for that upheaval were far more complex, but the Sabbath controversy did play a critical role in the England that spawned the first American settlements.

The Protestant Reformation animated several new theories of the Lord's Day. The two most important in seventeenth-century England were the Sabbatarian and Ecclesiastical ones.[4] The former emerged late in the Elizabethan era and became identified with Puritanism. According to its tenets, God instituted the Sabbath at the Creation, the Patriarchs from Abraham to Moses kept the day, and the Fourth Commandment reenacted it. Thus, the Sabbath was so deeply engraved on man's heart that its obligation was a matter of natural or moral law. Since "the seventh day" and "one day in seven" obviously mean the same thing, mankind was fairly entitled to transfer to the first day of the week whatever Scripture says of the seventh day. Hence the Christian Sabbath was to be observed as strictly as the Jewish Sabbath.

The Ecclesiastical or Dominical view was reconstructed by seventeenth-century Church of England writers on older foundations. According to their teaching, the Sabbath was not enjoined on man at the Creation but was first revealed to the Jews when God gave the Decalogue to Moses. This theory made the Sabbath a Jewish ceremony that expired with the Jewish dispensation and almost completely divorced the Lord's Day from the Fourth Commandment. In no sense a Sabbath, the Lord's Day was a purely Christian institution, an appointment of the Church in apostolic or post-apostolic times. Observance of the festival should recognize man's compound nature and provide for the body as well as the soul.

Sabbatarian and Ecclesiastical opinions furnished grounds for a heated controversy in early Stuart England. The argument got caught up with other pressing issues—economic, political, social, and constitutional. According to Shepard, King Charles I and his bishops considered Sabbatarianism as a recent and fanatical Judaizing novelty, another stratagem designed to advance the program of religious dissent, and altogether "a superstitious seething over of the hot or whining simplicity of an over-rigid, crabbed, precise, crack-brain'd, Puritanicall party." To Puritans like Shepard, however, God himself had established the solemn days of his worship; the Lord Jesus, not the lord bishops, a government of his house, not the house of Stuart, must reign; and heaven and earth would pass away "before one tittle of the Law (much lesse a whole Sabbath) shall perish."[5]

The resulting crisis drove Englishmen to migrate, and on American soil Sabbatarian theory began to shape the pattern of life. Shepard preached on the subject and, encouraged by a favorable reception, expanded and published his sermons as *Theses Sabbaticae: Or, The Doctrine of the Sabbath* (1649). It was these views that prompted the spiritual children of Israel, Shepard's own breed, to trouble England's rest.

Sabbatarianism became a distinctive characteristic of Puritanism before Shepard fled, and it made its strongest impress upon America through New England. But the Puritan Sabbath exerted a profound influence in nearly all of the colonies and remained a vital aspect of national life well into the twentieth century. The reason is readily comprehended. The Lord's Day had no meaning other than as a link in a perfect chain.[6] At stake was not simply the religious observance of a stated day of the week, but a whole way of life involving man's relations with God and the entire realm of work and play. Moreover, since the American colonies used the power of the state to foster religion and morality, Sabbatarianism brought theology and religion into contact with politics and law, with lasting consequences for American culture.

Numb 15.36

Remember that thou keepe holy yᵉ Sabboth Day
The profane Iſralite, that durſt aſſay,
In gathering ſticks, to breake the Sabboth day,
Is ſtonde to death, for like Contumacy
The Lord hath ſworne, that every Soule ſhall dye.

A Woman and her two Daughters pill and dry
flax on the Lords day, are all burnt

Part One

THE ENGLISH
BACKGROUND

1

The Judeo-Christian Inheritance

FOR ALL ITS apparent novelty, the Puritan Sabbath actually fell into the tracks of an ancient institution. Yet the septenary method of marking time did not prevail in antiquity. Mankind has measured periods of existence in various ways, and many ancient peoples counted time by decades, nundines (our eighth day), or calends, nones, and ides, that is, the first day of the month, the ninth day before the middle of the month, and the middle of the month (which was the fifteenth of March, May, July, and October, and the thirteenth of other months). But the seven-day week was not general at the dawn of history. It prevailed only in the Near East, primarily among Jews, Egyptians, and Persians.

As biblical scholars began to argue in the nineteenth century, there was no need to ascribe the origin of the seventh-day Sabbath to a divine revelation. James A. Hessey declared that man's reason might have discovered the seven-day week. The appearance of a new moon would suggest a division into roughly twenty-eight days, a full moon would lead to two weeks, and half of that would approximate a perfect septenary division of time.[1] S. R. Driver thought it more than possible that the Sabbath was ultimately of Babylonian origin, although there was no evidence that a continuous succession of "weeks," each ending with a day marked by special observances, was a Babylonian institution. The Hebrews probably adopted the Babylonian rest day and gave it a new character. They detached it from its connection with the moon, extended and generalized the abstinence associated with it, stripped it of superstitious and heathen associations, and made it subservient to ethical and religious ends. The first creation story in the Bible ends by declaring (Gen. 2:2-3) that "on the seventh day God finished his work which he had done, and he rested on the seventh day from all his work which he had done. So God blessed the seventh day and hallowed it, because on it God rested from all his work which he had done in creation."

This account does not name the Sabbath or lay down any law for its observance. According to Driver, the sanctity of the seventh day is here explained unhistorically and antedated. Instead of the Sabbath's closing the week and being sacred because on it God desisted from his six days' work of creation, the work of creation was distributed among six days, followed by a day of rest, because the week ended by the Sabbath already existed as an institution, and the writer wished to adjust the work of creation to it artificially. "In other words, the week, ended by the sabbath, determined the 'days' of creation, not the 'days' of creation the week."[2] Yet, in the first creation story there is an institutionally motivated purpose: the Sabbath. This is absent in the second creation story, Gen. 2:4b-24.[3] In the first, the Sabbath exists in the Garden of Eden; thus, one can argue that the obligation to observe it is part of the divine and moral law and binding upon mankind forever.

However, the Old Testament also describes the Sabbath after Yahweh made Israel a covenant people and delivered them from Egyptian bondage. The doctrines of election and covenant are the master keys to understanding Israel's existence and the Jewish Bible. The covenant was the device for explaining the nature and meaning of Israel's election as the one family of the human race to receive God's blessing. At Mount Sinai, Yahweh made known his will, the Decalogue, to the other party of the covenant, Israel. The Decalogue reduces to its most significant essence a comprehensive body of instruction for the Chosen People. The Fourth Commandment in Exod. 20:8-11 enjoins Israel to "Remember the sabbath day, to keep it holy. Six days you shall labor, and do all your work; but the seventh day is a sabbath to the Lord your God; in it you shall not do any work, you, or your son, or your daughter, your manservant, or your maidservant, or your cattle, or the sojourner who is within your gates; for in six days the Lord made heaven and earth, the sea, and all that is in them, and rested the seventh day; therefore the Lord blessed the sabbath day and hallowed it." This statement validates the Sabbath institution in terms of the pattern of creation described in Gen. 1:1-2:4a.[4]

The form of the Decalogue as preserved in Deuteronomy presents considerable deviation, and in Deut. 5:12-15 the Fourth Commandment rests upon a different foundation. "Observe the sabbath day, to keep it holy, as the Lord your God commanded you. Six days you shall labor, and do all your work; but the seventh day is a sabbath to the Lord your God; in it you shall not do any work, you, or your son, or your daughter, or your manservant, or your maidservant, or your ox, or your ass, or any of your cattle, or the sojourner who is within your gates, that your manservant and your maidservant may rest as well as you. You shall remember that you were a servant in the land of Egypt, and the Lord your God brought you out thence with a mighty hand and an outstretched arm; therefore the Lord your God commanded you to keep the sabbath day." Here Sabbath observance rests upon not a primeval but a historical event. Yet the fundamental sanction of the Sabbath in both statements is creation—in Exodus, of the world; in Deuteronomy, of a people. To remember and keep the day is to acknowledge Yahweh as Creator-Sustainer and to affirm that life continues under his Providence.

The place of the Decalogue in the life of ancient Israel cannot be overemphasized. It was understood and celebrated as a major event, on a par with and inseparably linked to Israel's deliverance from Egypt. The Decalogue disclosed the fact, meaning, and purposiveness of Yahweh's Word in Israel and the world. The Sinai covenant and therefore the obligation of the Fourth Commandment was absolute rather than conditional or reciprocal. As Bernhard W. Anderson writes, "the Sinai covenant was in no sense a parity contract in which both parties were equal and mutually dependent. It was a relationship between unequals, between God and man. . . . The covenant was *given* by God; the relationship was conferred upon the people by their sovereign. Yahweh was not legally bound to Israel, for his sovereignty was not limited by the covenant. He had freely initiated the relationship and . . . he was free to terminate it." The Exodus story emphasized what Yahweh had done on Israel's behalf. Therefore Israel's pledge of obedience, as expressed in the covenant ceremony, was based on gratitude for what Yahweh had already done on their behalf, on the realization that Israel's whole life depended upon his sovereign grace and promise.[5]

As Exod. 31:12-17 in particular makes clear, the Sabbath was a perpetual covenant or sign between Yahweh and the Chosen People. It required strict rest from ordinary labor and the performance of religious exercises on the seventh day of the week, and keeping the covenant was so important that the penalties for disobedience were severe. A number of Old Testament passages specifically warn that whoever profanes the Sabbath by working on it shall be put to death, and that desolation awaits the land that pollutes the Sabbath.[6]

But the sacred festival was also a pleasure and a delight, and at first Israel celebrated it joyfully. Its observance honored the heavenly Lawgiver. In time, however, a narrow legalism and ceremonialism triumphed. Pharisees exalted the Law, rabbinical writers surrounded the observance with prohibitions, forbidding as many as thirty-nine principal classes of work on the day, and an excessive reverence arose for the rules which formed a "hedge about the Law." Jewish Sabbath restrictions eventually became a "byword for extravagance and absurdity."[7]

Out of Israel came Jesus Christ, and with him the New Covenant that made perfect the ancient bond between God and man. Jesus came to fulfill rather than to abrogate the Law, but he found that human inventions had set aside what was essentially divine and spiritual in it. He interpreted the Fourth Commandment in relation to his whole life and mission, sometimes keeping and sometimes breaking the Sabbath. He defended his disciples for plucking ears of corn in cases of necessity and justified his own healing of the sick and lame on the holy days. Rejecting Jewish legalism and striving to break down completely the "hedge about the Law," Jesus reminded critics that in cases of conflict even they violated the rest day, as when they put the law regarding circumcision above that of the Sabbath. "The sabbath was made for man, not man for the sabbath"; Christ said, "so the Son of man is lord even of the sabbath."[8]

A question as to how far the authority of the Old Testament obligated Christ's followers arose during his life on earth. This query led to the central problem of biblical interpretation during the Christian era, that of establishing the proper relation between the two Testaments. What is the link between the Chosen People of the Old Testament and the Christian Church of the New Testament? Is there but one covenant and one people of God, or are there two? Do the ceremonial, judicial, and moral aspects of the Mosaic Law all remain in effect for Gentiles after the coming of Christ? Is Sabbath observance binding upon Christians after the Resurrection of the Lord?[9]

In dealing with the basic question, Christian exegetes have immemorially treated the whole Bible as one unified testimony. The Epistle to the Hebrews early exemplified this approach, declaring (Heb. 1:1-2) that "in many and various ways God spoke of old to our fathers by the prophets; but in these last days he has spoken to us by a Son." Yet if Christian interpreters regarded the Old Testament as of equal authority with the New, they developed several exegetical methods in extracting full meaning from the richness of the Bible, and these influenced how people thought about the sabbatical institution.

One system of hermeneutics is allegorical exegesis. Introduced early in the Christian era by the Alexandrian School, it offered an escape from what many saw as unhistorical and literally false statements and facilitated reconciliation of contradictory accounts in Scripture. Allegorists could find deep Christian content in Jewish texts by interpreting them as meaning something different from what they actually said. The use of symbolism and imagery to read hidden significance into difficult passages offered great freedom. In the hands of Augustine and others, the Sabbath rest was made to signify not the literal cessation from work on the seventh day but spiritual rest from sin at all times. Although allegory freed the Church from simple literalism, it raised the danger of theological chaos.

Another system of interpretation is typological exegesis. Its practitioners drew a system of parallels between the two Testaments, making Old Testament types stand as models for New Testament antitypes. Jewish circumcision prefigures Christian baptism, for example, and Adam, Christ. Whether the Jewish Sabbath was a type of the Christian Lord's Day was a question on which opinion divided.

Still another interpretive method was that of the literalists. Although not a sixteenth-century innovation, literal exegesis became newly important when Protestant reformers, seeking emancipation from Catholic interpretive traditions, made the Bible the standard by which to judge the Church. Luther and Calvin both emphasized a literal, historical, and grammatical interpretation of the text, though differing significantly on matters of exegesis. Their seventeenth-century followers, notably the Puritans, entertained an even more rigid view of biblical interpretation. Fearing subjectivism, they came to regard all parts of the Bible as equally true and directly inspired, and literal interpretation provided fertile soil for modern Sabbatarianism.

AT THE DAWN of the Christian era the Lord's Day replaced the Sabbath as a positive institution of the Church. The Resurrection invested it with special character as a symbol of redemption in Christ. Thereafter the festival gradually established firm root. For practical reasons the Apostles and other followers of Jesus needed a periodically recurring day that would allow them to assemble for worship and distinguish them from the Jews. The First Day celebration resulted. It was analogous to and yet entirely distinct from the Jewish ceremony; its observance in no way depended on the Fourth Commandment. Although Jesus had not directly ordained the memorial day, the Church, which was still believed to possess special inspiration, had instituted it before the canon of the New Testament was finally confirmed in the fourth century. Christians therefore considered the Lord's Day divinely constituted.

On Sundays the faithful gathered for the Eucharist, treating the remaining hours like an ordinary working day. Nothing sabbatical, neither commanded rest not strict prohibitions against labor, characterized the early Lord's Day, an institution under the law of liberty. The Jewish Sabbath and the Christian Lord's Day coexisted for a time, and only by degrees did the first day of the week achieve a position of honor. The Church treated the lingering Jewish ceremony with forbearance but declared the Ebionites heretical when, interpreting the Old Testament literally, they insisted upon viewing the old institution as a day of universal obligation. The Lord's Day remained at the end of the third century the same simple ordinance which the Apostles had bequeathed to the Church.[10]

A new era opened in A.D. 321, when the emperor Constantine issued his edict concerning Sunday observance. At a time when many religions had spawned a diversity of festivals, Constantine decreed the establishment of one weekly holiday. "On the venerable day of the sun," he ordered, "let the magistrates and people residing in cities rest, and let all workshops be closed. In the country, however, persons engaged in the work of cultivation may freely and lawfully continue their pursuits; because it often happens that another day is not so suitable for grain-sowing or for vine-planting; lest by neglecting the proper moment for such operations the bounty of heaven should be lost."[11]

Some have interpreted this declaration as an approximation of Sabbatarianism, while others have regarded it merely as a means by which the state aided a church custom and not a divine ordinance to prevail. Steering a middle path, Hessey concluded that Constantine dared not offend pagans, even though he might want to encourage Christians, whom he had recently granted toleration in the Edict of Milan (313). Thus he selected as a rest day one which Christians regarded as divine, and gave it a civil name, Sunday, which Christians both knew and employed and which did not offend heathens. Moreover, he made an exception for rural districts, where paganism predominated. But Constantine's deed was in no way Sabbatarian; it contained no reference to the Fourth Commandment, and it did not discourage the cheerfulness associated with the Christian festival. The edict neither gave Christians a permission to labor which they had not previously enjoyed nor imposed upon the urban faithful an unwelcome rest from ordinary labor on Sunday. For their spiritual welfare Christians had already ceased working and prosecuting legal proceedings on that occasion. Nevertheless, the decree provided Christians with state authority for observing a day that from the time of the Apostles had been revered solely as a religious ordinance.[12]

Meanwhile, a tendency to confuse the Sabbath and the Lord's Day had arisen. The Lord's Day stood alone as a festival in the Christian year until the Council of Nicaea (325), after which the Church developed a liturgical calendar which celebrated historical events in the life of Christ and witnesses to his truth, thereby stamping a Christian impress upon the rhythm of nature. Although the numerous holy days designated to honor saints and martyrs resembled the Lord's Day, their foundation was inferior to that of the scriptural festival since the Church established them at a time when it no longer possessed special inspiration. The reverence accorded to saints' days obscured the singularity of the divinely appointed Sunday. Christians occasionally apologized for the abundance of their holidays by analogy to Jewish practices, thus blurring the distinction between Jewish and Christian observances. And the Church tried to invest some Sundays and holy days with special obligation by simply asserting its authority. As a result men were in danger of forgetting that the Lord's Day was entirely different from the Sabbath and that its apostolic origins placed it above all merely ecclesiastical ordinances.[13]

In the fourth and fifth centuries both ecclesiastical and civil authorities began to circumscribe the liberty of the Lord's Day. Church councils, imperial edicts, and individual writers promulgated rules which intruded Judaism into Christianity. A strict rest on Sunday and attendance at public worship gradually became required. Councils at Eliberis and Sardica in the early fourth century announced penalties for absence from church on three Sundays, for example, and in 436 the Fourth Council of Carthage discouraged Lord's Day attendance at games or circuses. Civil officials proscribed the payment of debts and legal proceedings, and in 386 Emperor Theodosius the Great forbade the transaction of business on Sunday. Despite these restrictions, there was no compulsory ban on such recreations and necessary duties as were permitted on other days, so long as they did not interfere with divine worship and the things appropriate to the weekly day of worship. At the end of the fifth century the Lord's Day had not yet been transformed into a Jewish Sabbath dependent upon the Fourth Commandment.[14]

In the millennium that followed, however, Christian Sabbatarianism became a well-developed aspect of medieval religion. During these centuries the Roman Catholic Church established numerous fasts and festivals which in effect lowered the Lord's Day to the status of the other ceremonies that rested upon ecclesiastical rather than divine authority. Then Rome surrounded Sundays and holy days with a mountain of restrictions. Because the people could not celebrate all the ceremonies appointed in the Church calendar, authorities devised sanctions to insure the observance of festivals of special obligation and of the Lord's Day. They declared the new Christian ceremonies to be the legitimate successors of the old Jewish ceremonies. The Church justified Lord's Day observance by reference to the Old Testament Sabbath, and in doing so relied upon the Fourth Commandment, which Christian writers had traditionally assigned a place inferior to the other nine. The Fourth Commandment now became a moral law binding all mankind rather than a ceremonial law binding only the Jews.

Roman Catholic legalism elaborated a system which required a precise rest like that of the Jewish Sabbath and an exacting sanctification of Sunday. Both church and state issued minute regulations to further the ideal. Bishops and princes enjoined rest from servile labor and commercial activity and prohibited travel and recreation on the Lord's Day. In England the first Sunday statute dates from the late seventh century, when the West Saxon King Ina forbade all work, a prohibition that the Archbishop of York incorporated into his Constitutions of 743. Two centuries later a law of Edgar the Peaceable ordered the Lord's Day to commence at three o'clock on Saturday afternoon and to last until dawn on Monday.[15] After the Norman Conquest the tendency to compel great strictness continued. The term "Christian Sabbath," which early Christians would have found self-contradictory, was apparently first used in the twelfth century on the Continent,[16] whence the abbot Eustace of Flay set out in 1201 to crusade in England for a strict and Judaic Sunday observance.[17]

The obligations of this Ecclesiastical Sabbatarianism were constantly being heightened. Both Germany and England in the late thirteenth century afford examples of scrupulous observance of regulations, and in the fourteenth century the Spanish Bishop of Avila, Tostatus, declared it a mortal sin to do any unnecessary labor on Sunday.[18] This negativism obscured the ideal of a Sunday employed solely in worship and good works.

A literature of warning developed as a means of securing obedience to these levitical rules. Clergymen taught that divine judgments awaited those who transgressed the strict injunctions concerning Sabbath observance, and fear of incurring God's wrath gained a firm hold on the popular mind. Stories were told of people who worked or played on the Sabbath being stricken for their impiety and dropping dead during the week. In the nineteenth century some Americans were still drawing from this treasury of horrors in an attempt to save the perishing Puritan Sabbath.

Although the medieval Church formulated a demanding theory of Christian Sabbatarianism, it failed to secure general compliance with its expressed ideal. Many laymen found it impossible to observe Sundays as well as the numerous obligatory feast days. Some took their morning sleep on the Lord's Day and spent the remainder of Sunday in various innocent or vicious pastimes. They enlivened the frequent festival days with pageants, carnivals, processions, and folk dances and by drinking lots of ale at parish celebrations. Mother Church indulgently winked at these lapses as long as offenders did not question her precepts.

Nevertheless, sporadic dissatisfaction with the prevailing theory manifested itself in sectarian movements that attempted to reform medieval Christianity. In the Pyrenees in the twelfth century the ephemeral sect of Petrobrussians rejected all fasts and festivals. In southern France at the end of the thirteenth century the Waldensians disparaged all distinction of days. And in the fourteenth century the English Lollards extended their antipathy for holy days to the Lord's Day as well. These scattered protests, the harbingers of a new era, ineffectively challenged the Ecclesiastical theory of the Catholic Church. The Christian Sabbath was one of many nonscriptural elements present in late medieval religion, and it thoroughly obscured the original meaning of the Lord's Day.[19]

THE PROTESTANT REFORMATION liberated powerful forces that revitalized Christianity and fostered a new Sabbatarian doctrine. The sixteenth-century religious upheaval contained both negative and positive tendencies. Protestant leaders on the Continent preoccupied themselves with destroying their Sabbath inheritance but were weak in constructive accomplishment. The reformers wrote comparatively little about the Sabbath because they were still influenced by Roman Catholic doctrines and because they stressed Pauline strictures against the observance of days. The theological and social climate which favored a creative new departure appeared in England more than a half-century after Luther posted his Ninety-Five Theses. Preachers within the Church of England during the reign of Elizabeth I adumbrated a positive alternative to the Ecclesiastical view. Significantly, they were in the Reformed theological tradition, and an analysis of three aspects of the Continental Reformation will show why Reformed theology prepared the soil in which the unique Puritan theory of the Sabbath arose.

The attitude of the reformers toward Scripture went far in determining their position on the Lord's Day. The main expressions of Continental Protestantism—Lutheranism, the Reformed religion, and the Radical Reformation—all rejected the Roman Catholic reliance upon ecclesiastical tradition and papal authority and recovered the Bible as the ultimate rule of Christian life. But they differed over biblical interpretation and the relation between the two Testaments, and their views led to distinctive positions on the holy day.

Luther made Scripture the sole authority in breaking from Catholicism.

He emphasized the literal sense of the text and understood the whole Bible in the light of the Pauline doctrine of justification by faith alone. The German reformer emphasized the New Testament over the Old and stressed the antithesis between Law and Gospel. He feared legalism as the path to salvation. Man could not gain credit with God by "works righteousness" or strict obedience to the Law. The laws of Moses were binding only on Jews, and even the Ten Commandments applied to Christians only insofar as they agreed with the New Testament and the law of nature. Luther found it hard to distinguish moral from ceremonial elements in Old Testament law, and in combatting the legalistic element in Roman Catholicism he held that the Fourth Commandment was a Jewish ceremonial law abrogated by the New Testament. With faith in the Gospel, the sinner had to depend solely on God's mercy.[20]

The Radical Reformation, the left wing of the Protestant upheaval, possessed both inner coherence and great diversity. Of its subdivisions, the Anabaptists and the Spirituals are of central importance here. These groups differed over the ultimate source of divine authority, and none of their views stimulated the growth of modern Sabbatarianism. Anabaptists interpreted Scripture in ways that tended either to abolish the Lord's Day altogether or to revive a strict Jewish Sabbath. One branch that included Hutterites, Swiss Brethren, and Mennonites relied on the New Testament as normative and interpreted the Old Testament typologically and allegorically. Another branch, the revolutionary group containing Melchior Hoffman's followers and the Munsterites, considered both Testaments normative. It relied on Jewish models in reconstructing the Church. Spirituals were in the mystical tradition. The religion of inward experience espoused by the Zwickau prophets, Andreas Carlstadt, and Thomas Muntzer stressed the inspiration of the Holy Spirit, a position unsympathetic to stated religious observance. Though Luther opposed legalism, he perceived the dangers inherent in a mystical approach and severely criticized these heavenly prophets for sailing up into "cloud cuckoo land" by holding that the Holy Ghost acted directly upon believers' hearts without being able to indicate precisely how individuals came by their subjective experience of the Inner Word.[21]

The Reformed interpretation of Scripture contributed most directly to a new theology of the Sabbath. Zwinglians and Calvinists shared a common outlook, but Calvin exerted the most far-reaching influence on Anglo-American religion. John Calvin (1509-1564), the preeminent biblical theologian of the Reformation, lacked Luther's remarkable freedom in handling the Bible. He adumbrated his theological system in the *Institutes of the Christian Religion* before completing his twenty-sixth year, and that work changed surprisingly little between the thin first edition of 1536 and the thick final edition of 1559. The Genevan differed from Luther in emphasizing the basic unity of the Old and New Testaments. The infallible Word teaches the sovereignty of God, the corruption of human nature, and a divine plan of redemption revealed in Jesus Christ. This scheme of redemption unfolds in one unbroken sequence throughout the two Testaments. One covenant unites the people of God; it varies only in the mode of administration, not in substance. The Christian Church rather than the Jewish nation is the society adopted by the Lord, and both were federally connected with him by the same law and doctrine. Using the same exegetical method as that of the Epistle to the Hebrews, Calvin Christianized the Old and Judaized the New Testament in order to make them appear as one unified covenant.

This master conception led Calvin to abandon the Pauline and Lutheran antithesis between Law and Gospel and to assimilate the Mosaic religious code into Christianity. God had given Israel and the world the Decalogue when knowledge of the law of nature, which was rooted in the divine law, had become indistinct. The *Institutes* stressed the perfection of the moral law summarized in the Ten Commandments. Salvation lay in strict obedience to the Law, though it was impossible for the sinner to fulfill its demands. Christian liberty meant deliverance from the constraint of the Law as a means of regeneration, although it required voluntary submission to its moral influence as a guide and stimulus to practical religion. Calvin charged the saint with finding his proper relation with God and the universe through precise adherence to the Decalogue. Calvin's scriptural interpretation was of the greatest importance in providing a foundation for Puritan Sabbatarianism.[22]

A second influence in the development being traced was the Continental Reformation's assault on the inherited Sabbath. Derived from attitudes toward the authority of Scripture, the attack cleared the way for a new departure. Lutherans and Radicals, however, proved less able than Reformed to offer grounds for a substitute Sabbath theology. Luther attacked the multiplicity of saints' days and regarded the Catholic Sabbath as perpetuating the Jewish ceremonial ordinance. He thought the literal, outward observance of the Fourth Commandment (in the Lutheran division of the Two Tables, the Third) did not concern Christians. When Carlstadt, whose internal religion ultimately became very legal, resurrected the Sabbath in order to afford men relief from mundane tasks, Luther strongly criticized him and with characteristic vigor denounced the Anabaptist minority that observed the Sabbath after the Jewish fashion. He once told his followers that if Sunday were anywhere made holy merely for the day's sake or its observance set on a Jewish foundation, "then I order you to work on it, to ride on it, to dance on it, to feast on it, to do anything that shall remove this encroachment on Christian liberty."[23]

But Lutheran formularies took low doctrinal ground on the subject. The Saxon reformer's sermons, catechisms, and commentaries taught that the proper use of the Lord's Day required both rest for the sake of bodily need and the service of God at home and in church by hearing and discussing his Word. The Augsburg Confession (1530) arraigned Rome for exercising human authority in instituting new ceremonies and introducing a new legalism by requiring observance of the ceremonies as a condition of salvation. But since the welfare of Christianity necessitated some time for worship, the Church acted lawfully in appointing the Lord's Day for a weekly observance. The Confession insisted on Christian liberty rather than bondage to the Law. Luther's noblest affirmation of this theme came in a 1544 sermon at Torgau in which he accepted Sunday as the Sabbath, as long as Christians insisted they were lords of the Sabbath and did not attribute special holiness to a particular day.[24]

The impulses motivating the Radical Reformation were both more primitive and more modern than those within the Protestant mainstream. As a consequence, two radical theories on the observance of holy time arose. One taught that the Decalogue was completely moral and that the Sabbath enjoined therein was still in force. Jesus had come to fulfill rather than destroy the Law. The Sabbath therefore ought to be observed on the seventh day and with all the rigor prescribed in the Old Testament. Beginning in 1528, Oswald Glait and Andrew Fischer successfully propagated this idea among Anabaptists in Silesia and Moravia. Five decades later the followers of Francis David among the Unitarians in Transylvania also became Judaizing Sabbatarians. These views later received a fresh impetus in England and North America in the Seventh-Day Baptist and Seventh-Day Adventist churches.[25]

The second Radical theory held that the New Covenant replaced the Law with a ministry of Grace. The whole Mosaic dispensation had been fulfilled and passed away. Christ himself neither instituted nor authorized others to institute any special day of rest or worship in place of or in succession to the Jewish Sabbath. The immediate operation of the Spirit on the heart of believers made external religious discipline unnecessary. No special day was binding for there existed either no Sabbath at all or a perpetual spiritual Sabbath. Here lay the main legacy of the Radical Reformation on the matter. Anabaptists and Antinomians introduced this view in England, Quakers and leftist Puritans gave it vitality, then it passed to the American colonies. Years later Mennonites, Hutterites, and other denominational progeny of the Protestant left wing again carried this antilegalist approach to America.[26]

The Continental Reformed churches joined with other Protestant groups in attempting to destroy saints' days and the Catholic Sunday. Their conception of one enduring covenant along with their strong Hebraizing and legalistic tendencies laid a path that pointed toward the Puritan Sabbath. Zwinglians contributed only slightly to this achievement, and even Calvin's intellect met a supreme challenge in the effort to make the Mosaic Law and the Gospel of Grace parts of one unbroken covenant. The Sabbath is one of the few subjects on which the Swiss reformer significantly revised the *Institutes*. In the 1536 edition he Christianized the Law and partly spiritualized the Fourth Commandment. A new edition three years later went further in leveling distinctions between the two Testaments. Now Calvin portrayed the Decalogue as a summary of a perfect code of morals. In treating the Sabbath, he acknowledged the divine institution of a special rest day and arbitrarily substituted the first day for the seventh. The final edition of the *Institutes*, drawing on these formulations, regarded the external observance of the Sabbath rest as a Jewish ceremonial ordinance and no longer binding on Christians. For Christians the Fourth Commandment possessed a spiritual meaning: they were to desist from evil works and find rest in God. Christians ought to cease all superstitious observance of days, and those who thought that the ceremonial part of the Commandment (the appointment of the seventh day) had been abrogated but that the moral element (observance of one day in seven) still remained, "surpass the Jews three times over in a crass and carnal Sabbatarian superstition."[27]

Nevertheless, Calvin wanted to retain a stated day for rest and worship as a practical necessity. It afforded servants a weekly remission from labor and the faithful an opportunity for religious exercises and meditation. The ancient Church had wisely substituted the Lord's Day for the Sabbath. When Spirituals taunted Protestants as Judaizers for still keeping Sunday, Calvin replied that they celebrated it not scrupulously but "as a remedy needed to keep order in the church."[28] The Genevan, however, did not require observance every seventh day or only on Sunday. In this respect he offers a precedent for the present-day practice of conducting the main weekly worship service at a time (Thursday evening, for example) that permits Christians to attend church before the start of a long weekend. In Calvin's Geneva, citizens were free to amuse themselves after Sunday worship, and they did so with military drill and bowling. Calvin himself bowled on Sunday and was buried on a Lord's Day afternoon.[29]

In the Heidelberg Catechism (1563), Zacharius Ursinus and Casper Olevanius gave expression to Calvin's practical and spiritual interpretation of the Fourth Commandment. They declared that God required believers to attend church diligently and engage in other religious exercises on the day of rest and to rest from evil works at all times so as to begin in this life the everlasting Sabbath. Reformed churches in Germany, Switzerland, Holland, and New Netherland adopted this statement.[30]

Heinrich Bullinger, one of the most influential Rhineland reformers during his long incumbency (1531-1575) as Zwingli's successor at Zurich, led the German-speaking wing of the Reformed faith. The Second Helvetic Confession (1566), authored by Bullinger and the accepted standard of most Swiss Reformed, declared that every church needed a time for religious exercises. The Lord's Day had been appointed for this purpose since apostolic times. The Reformed churches observed the day with Christian freedom rather than Jewish superstition. They did not account one day holier than another or consider mere rest of itself acceptable to God. Bullinger's *Decades* (1575), a summary of Reformed theology, viewed the Jewish Sabbath as an abrogated ceremony and denounced all festival days except those appointed to honor God. Yet he regarded the Christian Sabbath as perpetual. The outward rest of the Sabbath was commanded so that bodily business would not hinder the spiritual work of the day. He called upon magistrates to enforce this means of maintaining true religion. Leading Protestant divines in England looked to Bullinger for doctrinal guidance. In 1586 Convocation required all English clergymen to buy the *Decades* and study it constantly.[31]

The Reformed religion triumphed in Scotland after John Knox returned there from the Continent in 1559, but neither he nor his co-workers were Sabbatarians. The Scots Confession of Faith (1560) condemned the keeping of holy days but contained no trace of Sabbatarianism. It described the work reputed good before God by paraphrasing the Two Tables and presented the obligation to keep the Sabbath holy as one of hearing and believing God's Word and communicating with his sacraments. The first *Book of Discipline* (1561) underscored the idea that the Fourth Commandment required participation in worship when it equated the strict observance of Sunday with the freeing of time for religious services. The Scottish kirk found the only objectionable feature in the Second Helvetic Confession to be its approval of certain festival days in addition to the Lord's Day. Scots of this period banqueted, traveled, and engaged in sports on the Lord's Day; and Knox himself attended Sunday dinner parties. It was the Puritan theory imported from England that made Scotland famous for Sabbatarianism.[32]

The third aspect of Continental Protestantism that conditioned the soil for the growth of Anglo-American Sabbatarianism was the reformers' views on church and state. On this subject the Radical Reformation was not conducive to the Puritan theory. Spirituals wished to assemble a church that was externally free but inwardly disciplined by the covenant written on the heart by the Holy Spirit, and an antinomian tendency often led them to repudiate all organized religious life. Anabaptists stressed the covenant relation between God and man, but regarded the church as a voluntary association of adult believers and made baptism of adults upon confession of faith the constitutive principle of the church. Anabaptists were convinced that the state had been ordained because of sin. True Christians, like the early martyrs, would always suffer persecution from a wicked world. Hence the gathered community of saints had perforce to withdraw from the larger society in order to live in purity. The church could have nothing to do with the state. The Radicals separated on principle from territorial and churchly forms of Christianity. They developed new organs of ecclesiastical self-discipline and repudiated religious coercion by civil authority. Their attitude significantly advanced the modern principle of separation of church and state but precluded the growth of a complete Sabbatarianism.[33]

The mainstream Protestants contrasted sharply with the left wing of the Reformation in their views on church and state. Luther and Calvin subscribed to the idea of a Christian society within which there were two divinely grounded orders, the political and the ecclesiastical. These great reformers were significant in the birth of the modern world because they attempted to overcome the medieval dualism between the sacred and secular. They wished to reconcile the world with the Spirit and bring every aspect of life under a divine standard through the Christian doctrine of vocation. Salvation was to be attained in the world by saints who found their proper place in a providentially governed universe.

To Luther the Church was grounded in God's Word, and he emphasized its spiritual and invisible nature. He also believed there was a Church visible, though he lacked Calvin's constructive genius for organizing it. Luther wanted both a confessional church based on the believer's faith in the Word and a territorial church that included everyone in a given locality. He considered the secular order divinely grounded and ultimately came to invest the ''godly'' prince with the organization and administration of territorial churches. He enjoined subjects to obey their rulers but did not slavishly exalt the authority of the magistrate, and he allowed for disobedience where the civil power forced individuals to violate the commandments pertaining to man's relations with his Creator. Luther's

teaching made for profound religious piety but led to a quietistic aban-
donment of worldly initiative.[34]

Calvin agreed that the Church was essentially the mystical body of
Christ. For him the doctrine of election formed the basis for distinguishing between the invisible and visible Church. God's elect of all ages,
known only to him, constituted the former; all believers in specific
churches the latter. Although God alone could distinguish saints from
sinners, professing Christians were presumably among the elect; their
children were heirs of the covenant by hereditary right, the line of election running in the loins of the saints. Infant baptism was the Christian
equivalent of circumcision for the Jews. Calvin had the noblest conception of the Church as the organ of religious and ethical life based on its
inherent divine rights and powers. Along with Luther he laid great emphasis on the pulpit. Effective preaching and hearing of the Word were
tangible proofs of a true church, and he stressed ecclesiastical discipline as
a means of insuring its purity.

In Calvin's view the state was divinely instituted and subject to the
sovereign rule of God. He found it impossible to create the type of church
and society he envisioned without the protection of the state and regarded civil authority as a nursing father of the church. The ruler was to
maintain the honor of God and preserve public worship, even though
this required coercing men to lead Christian lives. The reliance of the
Lutheran and Reformed churches on the prince prompted George H.
Williams to label these expressions of Protestantism the "Magisterial
Reformation."[35] But Calvin went beyond Luther in charging the civil
government with enforcing the duties of the First as well as the Second
Table. The Gallican Confession of 1559 declared that God had put the
sword into the hands of magistrates to suppress offenses against the First
Table. In addition, Calvin inspired in his followers a furious worldly ac-
tivism, and he was buoyantly optimistic about the capacity of the elect to
build a holy commonwealth in collaboration with the magistrate.[36]

ON THE CONTINENT the Reformed churches, with their method of interpreting the Bible, their assault on the inherited theory and practice of the
Sabbath, and their ideas about church and state, cleared the way for a
new doctrine of the Lord's Day. But Reformed theologians left the task of
devising a new doctrine of the Sabbath to others. England escaped much
of the doctrinal ferment that agitated the Continent during the early
Reformation. Henry VIII broke with the papacy in the 1530s and established a national church with the crown as its head; but he refused to
allow Lutheran and Reformed teachings a foothold and mercilessly punished Protestant heretics.

Nevertheless, the religious upheaval led to efforts to improve the use of Sunday. The early English reformers were vigorously anti-Sabbatarian. Robert Barnes contended that people were no more bound to serve God on Sundays or holy days than on other days. "For the Christian," he said, "every day is a Sabbath day and a festal day and not only the seventh day." John Frith described Christians who observed Sunday superstitiously as "much madder" than Jews who observed Saturday superstitiously. Although William Tyndale regarded the Old Testament moral law as still binding, he tried to liberate believers from Jewish ceremonial laws. "We be lords over the Saboth," he wrote, and might change it to any other day of the week, to every tenth day, or have two Sabbaths every week. The only reason to change the day from Saturday was to distinguish Christians from Jews. And no holy day whatsoever would be necessary, "if the people might be taught without it."[37]

The Crown added its voice to the growing chorus of opposition to saints' days. This hostility reflected a new attitude toward work and leisure which attended the birth of modern industrial society. Religious festivals were richly plentiful early in Henry's reign; Sundays and holy days together totaled 217 days annually, over half of the year.[38] Although many went unobserved, dissatisfaction with them was growing. The petition of the Commons in 1532 protested the excessive number of holy days, charging that they resulted in "execrable vices" and "wanton sports." In 1536 Henry directed the clergy to abrogate certain holy days during the harvest time on the grounds that they perpetuated superstition, fostered idleness and riot, and led to the decay of industrial crafts.[39]

The two formularies of faith designed to safeguard doctrine treated this subject while also demonstrating how slowly the Church of England emancipated itself from Roman Catholic Sabbatarian beliefs. When the bishops discussed the Decalogue in *The Institution of a Christian Man* (1537), they distinguished between the Fourth Commandment and the other nine. The latter were moral commandments and pertained to all peoples at all times; the former was partly ceremonial. Concerning rest from bodily labor on the seventh day, the Sabbath precept pertained only to Jews. Concerning spiritual rest from sin, however, the Fourth Commandment was binding on Christians. Besides the spiritual rest required, Christians were bound on Sundays and holy days appointed by the church to cease from bodily labor and to worship and do good works. But *The Bishops' Book* warned against superstitious abstention from bodily labor on holy days. A person might work at such times if necessary in order to save his corn or cattle; indeed, failure to do so for scruple of conscience offended God. Yet the formulary denounced idleness and offered no sanction for Sunday amusements or recreations. It was better to plow or spin on Sundays than to waste time in leaping, dancing, or wantonness.

The King called for revision of this statement, but in *A Necessary Doctrine and Erudition for any Christian Man* (1543) the section on the Fourth Commandment remained essentially unaltered. Beyond allowing work in times of necessity such as harvest, however, *The King's Book* also permitted labor on Sundays and holy days, "for the speedy performance of the necessary affairs of the prince and the commonwealth, at the commandment of them that have rule and authority therein."[40]

In these formularies the Church of England refused to insist that the Fourth Commandment was literally binding on Christians. The will of the monarch was supreme. As a result, the Henrician Reformation raised a problem of religious authority which proved significant in the development of the Sabbatarian movement. Henry erected an independent national church headed by the Crown and laid foundations for a comprehensive Anglicanism designed to embrace the entire country. But the Protestant reformers wanted a Christianity ruled by some principle other than the divine right of kings. In making their bid, England's first Protestants borrowed first from Luther and then from Rhineland reformers— Zwingli, Oecolampadius, Bullinger, and others. They were unable to reconcile the primacy of the Crown over religion with that of the Bible. The former issued in uniform worship, the latter in moral living. The reformers increasingly depended upon the concept of the covenant for their doctrine of authority.[41]

William Tyndale, the key figure in this development, moved through three stages in the evolution of his ideas. Initially he relied upon Luther in translating the New Testament (1526). The Gospel freed believers from legalism and moralism. Good deeds counted for nought in justification. The Law was theologically useful only as a schoolmaster to drive sinners in guilt to Christ. Then, in translating the Pentateuch and other Old Testament writings, Tyndale freed himself from Luther and made the Law a pillar of his theology. The moral but not the ceremonial law of the Old Testament provided a divine prescription for righteousness. Yet faith remained prerequisite to the Christian life, for the Gospel promises enabled men to love the Law and to fulfill its demands. Finally, Tyndale borrowed ideas from the Rhineland and made covenant theology the basis of his religious outlook. Now he regarded the encounter between God and man as mutually binding. Scripture declared the terms of the covenant, which was first made with Adam after the Fall and is entered by Christians at baptism. The scriptural promises are conditional: God covenants to bestow certain blessings on the understanding that the recipient will obey the Law. Rewards await the righteous, punishments the faithless.

The English reformer parted with Luther in viewing the entire Bible as a divine code for Christian life and in treating God's action toward man legalistically, but he never compromised the doctrine of justification by faith alone. Without this gift one could neither believe the promises nor obey the Law. Tyndale impressed upon England the idea of Christianity as a system of rewards and punishments for moral action, and that conception influenced Sabbatarianism. His achievement in combining this notion with that of solafideism, according to William A. Clebsch, makes him "the real if unacknowledged founder of the type of English-speaking Christianity that is commonly called Puritan."[42]

After the death of Henry VIII, the English Reformation first advanced and then retreated before Elizabeth I came to the throne. Protestantism tightened its hold upon the nation during the reign of Edward VI (1547-1553), with the influence of Luther giving way to that of Calvin. The religious innovations of these years demonstrated the Anglican spirit of compromise; they concerned themselves less with what people thought than with how they acted. Although the two versions of the Book of Common Prayer (1549, 1552) were masterpieces of compromise on disputed theological points, the Act of Uniformity (1552) ordered everyone to attend his parish church on Sundays and holy days but provided no penalty for offenders.[43]

The Edwardian policy on holy and festival days broke some new ground. The Royal Injunctions of 1547 declared that just as the people were commonly occupied on work days with labor for their bodily sustenance, "so was the holy-day at the first beginning godly instituted and ordained, that the people should that day give themselves wholly to God." But in our time, God is "more dishonoured than honoured upon the holy-day, because of idleness, pride, drunkenness, quarrelling, and brawling." People think they have sufficiently honored God if they go to church, "though they understand nothing to their edifying." Thus, the king's subjects shall henceforth "celebrate and keep their holy-day according to God's holy will and pleasure; that is, in hearing the word of God read and taught; in private and public prayers," in good works and acts of mercy, "and godly conversation." Here, Sunday, which seems to be singled out as the holy day, is set aside as a day for spiritual nourishment. Yet the clergy are to teach people that they may with a quiet conscience in time of harvest "labour upon the holy and festival days." Any superstitious abstention at such times is a grievous offense to God.[44]

The distinction between Sundays and saints' days became sharper in these years. The continued observance of the festival days abrogated by Henry drew laborers and artisans away from work and encouraged idleness. The second Book of Common Prayer, approved by Parliament in the Holy Days and Fasting Days Act (1552), further reduced the plethora of festal days.[45] The number retained was seventy-nine, about a third of the former superfluity. Only on holy days, which included all Sundays and other designated feasts, were people to refrain from ordinary labor, devoting the entire day to religious exercises and good deeds. The law permitted everyone in time of harvest or necessity to ride, fish, or work on the specified holy days. The statute gave Sunday a preferred position in the week and introduced an unprecedented austerity. Labor now took on larger proportions in life. Englishmen suddenly found that they had few free days a year—fewer than present-day Americans enjoy.[46] Contemporary accounts understandably complain that practice fell far short of the ideal.

Mary recommitted the nation to Catholicism, and in her brief reign (1553-1558) the tide bringing in a new kind of English Sunday was temporarily reversed. The Queen repealed the legislation on holy days along with other acts concerning the Church passed in the reign of Edward VI. The Royal Injunctions of 1554 directed people to observe holy and fasting days as they had in 1547. This reinstated a large liberty for idleness. Sunday games resumed with greater freedom, though the nation still accepted an obligation to serve God on holy days, whether Sundays or church-appointed festival days.[47]

Perhaps more significant for the future of English Sabbatarianism was the experience of the religious refugees. Nearly eight hundred Protestants, at least a quarter of whom were ordained clergymen or theological students of Cambridge and Oxford, fled to the Continent upon the accession of the Catholic queen. These Marian exiles took up residence in the German Rhineland and Switzerland, where they came under Reformed influences. Conservative and radical factions arose, with the former trying to put an "English face" upon their refugee churches and the latter adopting local practices. Calvin may have been the strongest single influence on the thought of the exiles, but perhaps only a quarter of the whole group came under Genevan influence.[48]

The Marian exiles gained no close familiarity with Sabbatarianism while away from home, for the Continental Reformation, including Calvin, produced nothing resembling the Puritan doctrine of the Sabbath. But Reformed theology was highly conducive to the development of such a theory, especially when coupled with covenant theology. The English refugees were imbued with these ideas during their foreign residence. When they returned, wanting a Christianity ruled not by the power of the king but by the Word of God alone, their beliefs stimulated the development of a new doctrine of the Sabbath.

2

The Puritan Sabbath

SABBATARIANISM ESTABLISHED ITSELF in England during the long reign of Elizabeth I. In the mid-1580s three clergymen—Lancelot Andrewes, Richard Greenham, and Nicholas Bownde—adumbrated theoretical foundations for a practice that was rapidly gaining favor among English Protestants. Bownde published their results a short time later in *The Doctrine of the Sabbath* (1595). Although he did not initiate the Sabbatarian movement in England, certainly not single-handedly, he did put the current elements of thought into a single book, and that book provided a theological rationale for the precise Sabbatarianism which became characteristic of mature Puritanism.

The new doctrine was the product of forces that were transforming England at the dawn of the modern era. Though basic to what occurred, Calvinism was by no means solely responsible. Had it been, a similar development should have taken place in Reformed centers on the Continent, whereas such was never the case. Holland and Switzerland imported the English doctrine but applied it less rigorously, and in France and Hungary the Reformed minorities lacked the capacity to impose the English Sunday upon their countrymen. Not Calvinism alone, then, but Calvinism interacting with basic economic and social forces accounts for the rise of the Puritan Sabbath.[1]

The religious question demanded attention when Elizabeth came to the

27

throne in November 1558. On the Continent the ruling Catholic powers were engaged in suppressing Protestant revolt and in rivalry for European mastery, and control of the English Crown seemed imperative to each. By choosing the Protestant side and establishing a national church the Tudor monarch hoped to steer clear of foreign entanglements. Moreover, the course of the English Reformation had left the country divided over religion, and Elizabeth wished to accommodate her subjects in one household of faith. Thus, she made the Church of England a *via media* between Rome and Geneva.[2]

The religious legislation of 1559 laid the legal foundations for this policy. The Act of Supremacy established an independent national church under the Crown and made obedience to the sovereign the one religious test. The Act of Uniformity made England Protestant by reestablishing the Book of Common Prayer (the second, more Protestant book of Edward VI's reign, with certain amendments) as the service book. Although the act allowed wide latitude of belief, it demanded uniformity in practice. Everyone having no lawful or reasonable excuse was ordered to attend public worship in his parish church on Sundays and other days ordained holy, upon penalty of ecclesiastical censure and a twelvepence fine. Reasons of state rather than solicitude for souls underlay this insistence upon conformity, a provision aimed at Roman Catholic and radical Protestant alike.[3]

The Queen rejected Rome but was in no haste to embrace Geneva, and therein lay the roots of Elizabethan Puritanism. A host of clergymen and a core of zealots in the House of Commons entertained high hopes that the new ruler would carry the Reformation to completion. These Protestants wanted a national church ruled by a godly prince and dedicated to the religion of the Word as opposed to the religion of the Mass. When the religious settlement rudely shattered their hopes, they set out to achieve a more complete break with the past. The result was English Puritanism, which as a historical movement lasted a century, from its rise under Elizabeth until its rapid disintegration after the Restoration.[4]

This complex phenomenon passed through several stages, and the Sabbath runs through them like a red thread. The initial protest centered upon externals of worship, with the innovators appealing to Scripture and the teachings of Calvin as the standard by which to judge. Puritans demanded complete purification of the Anglican church of all relics of Catholicism, regarding the ornaments, rites, and vestments retained as biblically unwarranted on the principle that Scripture forbids whatever it does not command. Puritans feared that if authorities could require the use of one popish relic they could dictate everything in matters of doctrine and practice, and what then of obedience to God and the future of the English Reformation? Nonconformists criticized the Book of Common Prayer for retaining holy days; in the Convocation of 1563, which agreed on the Thirty-Nine Articles, a proposal to abrogate all holy days except Sundays and the principal feasts of Christ, after great debate, lost by only one vote.[5]

This Vestiarian Controversy intensified after 1563, as the role of authority increasingly became the issue. Dissenting clergymen challenged the sovereign in challenging the bishops, so Elizabeth required Archbishop Parker to compel conformity. His Advertisements of 1566 drove the malcontents further left, and Puritans realized that they would have to fight to have their way.[6]

A second stage in the Puritan movement witnessed an attack on episcopal government as well as the Prayer Book. Nonconformists viewed the religious establishment as unreformed and based on erroneous principles. For them God was the sovereign over all creation and Christ, not the civil magistrate, the only true head of the church. The obedience he exacts from men is voluntary. Hence the church is a community of the elect in which the Word is preached by a minister chosen by the congregation and not imposed by the hierarchy. These beliefs inspired a search for new forms of ecclesiastical polity, and both Independency and Presbyterianism had their origins at this time.

Led by Robert Browne, some insisted upon immediate reformation. These separatists, who began to form their own congregations in the 1570s, believed that each church was autonomous and ruled democratically under the immediate leadership of Christ. Though eager for improved use of the Lord's Day, they had no hand in formulating a theory for it.[7] Far more important were those clergymen who remained within the church while demanding its reform along presbyterian lines. Thomas Cartwright, their leader, initiated a campaign against episcopal church government in 1570, and two years later the Puritans in Parliament introduced bills designed to advance a presbyterian form of polity. Near the end of the session John Field and Thomas Wilcox published an anonymous attack on the liturgy, polity, and discipline of the Anglican church. Entitled *An Admonition to the Parliament*, it demanded that "al[l] popish remnants both in ceremonies and regiment" be replaced by "those things only, which the Lord himself in his word commandeth."[8]

Cartwright subsequently debated these issues with John Whitgift, a Cambridge academic and Anglican leader. The impetuous Puritan contended that the Word of God contained the direction of all things pertaining to the Church and any part of man's life and enunciated a two-kingdom theory designed to subordinate the civil magistrate to the church in civil as well as ecclesiastical affairs. Whitgift, demonstrating that Cartwright interpreted the Bible in the light of rational preconceptions derived from various sources, including post-apostolic writers and Geneva practice, charged him with turning Scripture into a "nose of wax" to suit his own purposes.[9]

In these years Cartwright and Walter Travers collaborated in outlining a presbyterian polity for the Church of England, and during the 1580s the conference or classis movement became the backbone of an embryonic presbyterianism. Field tried covertly to unite the various classes, and the fledgling organization, though confined to clergymen to avoid detection, enjoyed considerable support among country gentlemen, in Parliament, and even in the Privy Council and at court.[10]

Elizabeth was determined to crush the clandestine classical movement, and in Whitgift, elevated to Canterbury in 1583, she found an ecclesiastic equal to the challenge. A staunch anti-Puritan, the Queen's "little black husband" immediately began to demand conformity to the constitution of the church and subscription to test articles. He brought rebellious clergy before the Court of High Commission, while his administrative assistant, Bishop Richard Bancroft, publicly exposed the pattern of secret subversion with its implied denial of the royal supremacy from the Disciplinarians' own letters and papers. By 1593 nearly all of the Puritan leaders had been silenced and the faction routed; a decade passed before they regathered their forces to renew the offensive under James I.[11]

Puritanism was far more than a matter of church government, and the spiritual preachers who desired above all a revitalization of personal religion based on the Word constituted the most influential element in Elizabethan Puritanism. Refusing to tie their hopes to the reorganization of the church, these moderates were willing to compromise with authorities for the sake of peace and unity. Molded by the tradition of the English popular pulpit and the Reformation stress on preaching, they used the pulpit and the press as vehicles for indoctrinating the people in the authority of Scripture, the reality of sin, and salvation by faith alone.

The Puritans were concentrated in the more economically advanced south and southeast of England, which included London and Cambridge, their intellectual center. About 1570, at Cambridge University, moderate Puritans devised spiritual preaching with a view to effecting a moral reformation. Its practitioners acquired an immense popular influence by ministering to troubled souls in a time of rapid change. The spiritual preachers constituted an informal group, united by personal ties and a common purpose. They were instrumental in transforming the moral outlook and code of conduct of the English-speaking people.[12]

In addition, the spiritual preachers were inspired by the belief that England was an elect nation whose providential mission was to build the New Israel. John Foxe did not originate this legend, but he fused its current elements into an integrated whole during his Marian exile. He set his Book of Martyrs in the framework of the Christian philosophy of history outlined a millennium earlier by Augustine in *The City of God* and given a Protestant twist in the sixteenth century. According to this interpretation, God governs the world by his Providence and history is the story of the ceaseless warfare between good and evil which fills all time. Foxe defined the Catholic Church as the antichrist and identified the Protestant faith with the cause of the national state. English rulers responsible to God and their people had always kept alive the pure faith in battles with alien intruders, and it was the Protestant Elizabeth's duty to promote national redemption. From English-language editions of Foxe's Book of Martyrs published in 1563 and 1570, Puritans learned to regard England as God's New Israel.[13]

Richard Greenham (1535?-1594?) was the patriarch of the spiritual brotherhood and one of the first formulators of the new doctrine of the Sabbath. Indeed, the Puritan theology of the Sabbath was largely the handiwork of this circle, whose founders included Laurence Chaderton (1536?-1640), master of Emmanuel College, Cambridge, founded in 1584 as a Puritan seminary of learning; John ("Decalogue") Dod (1549?-1645), the husband of Greenham's stepdaughter; and Arthur Hildersam (1563-1632). These early luminaries inspired a younger generation of Cambridge Puritans, notably William Perkins (1558-1602), a leading spokesman of Elizabethan Puritanism; William Ames (1576-1633), who fled to Holland and exerted great influence on New England Puritanism; and many who later became prominent clergymen in New England: John Cotton (1584-1652), Thomas Hooker (1596?-1647), John Davenport (1597-1669), and Thomas Shepard (1605-1649). Little is known about Nicholas Bownde (d. 1613), who first published the new Sabbatarian theory, but his mother's second husband was Greenham, and Bownde must surely have been affiliated with the brotherhood. The new theology of the Sabbath was an integral part of the spiritual brotherhood's program for revitalizing personal religion and building a holy commonwealth.

ELIZABETH'S ACCESSION BROUGHT no immediate change in official policy toward Sabbath observance. The Act of Uniformity and the Royal Injunctions of 1559 required observance of Sundays and holy days by public and private worship. The Injunctions permitted labor after divine service in time of harvest, however, and they warned that superstitious abstention from work on festival days displeased God. The bishops set forth their ideas on the subject in the second Book of Homilies, prepared by Convocation in 1563 to be read from in parish churches in the absence of preaching. The homily entitled "Of the Place and Time of Prayer" cautioned that God sent plague and punishment for neglect of Sunday worship, and it distinguished between the ceremonial and moral elements in the Fourth Commandment. The former, which bound Jews, made the Sabbath the time for assembling in church. The latter, which pertained to the law of nature and obligated Christians, meant having one day a week for rest and sanctification. Since the Ascension, this had been the Lord's Day.[14]

Church and state cooperated in an endeavor to realize official policy. The visitation articles framed to guide inspections of ecclesiastical jurisdictions demonstrate a lively concern for keeping the Lord's Day, as does the Register of sermons delivered at Paul's Cross. And the depositions in ecclesiastical courts demonstrate that churchwardens, who bore the brunt of the enforcement battle, presented offenders for servile labor and unlawful pastimes on Sundays (and holy days). In archidiaconal and diocesan courts the ordinary could impose penalties that included admonition, penance, fines, and, as a last resort, excommunication. Individuals unamenable to church censure could be turned over to civil authorities, who shared responsibility for maintaining religious discipline. Local officials admonished offenders for traveling or playing before noon on Sunday. Constables presented to courts of assize persons who absented themselves from public worship, and justices levied the authorized fine which churchwardens spent on the parish poor. The system produced a substantial revenue to support relief for the indigent.[15]

Nevertheless, practice fell far short of the ideal. "Of the Place and Time of Prayer" castigated two kinds of Englishmen who profaned the Sabbath. First were those who used all days alike and refused to rest even when extraordinary circumstances did not require Sunday labor. Much worse were those who rested not in holiness but "in ungodlinesse and filthinesse, . . . in excesse and superfluitie, in gluttony and drunkennesse, . . . in brawling and rayling, in quarrelling and fighting: . . . in wantonnesse, in toyish talking, in filthy fleshlinesse, so that it doeth too evidently appeare that God is more dishonoured, and the devill better served on the Sunday, then upon all the dayes in the weeke besides."[16] The Queen's conduct, too, left much to be desired. She not only licensed the use of plays and games on Sunday but also enjoyed these and other entertainments herself. In 1586 a certain William Fuller told Elizabeth he feared that she "hath to[o] litle used so to sanctifie the Lords Sabaothes;

for if you had, things could never have gone as now thei doe''; when people "without punishment offend God more at that daie than in anie other daie in the weeke."[17]

Dissatisfaction with the official attitude mounted rapidly under Elizabeth, and midway through her reign a number of interrelated forces worked together to bring about a voluntary change in practice and a new theory. Marshaling the data about a complex phenomenon, we can identify four factors which produced the Puritan Sabbath: the impact of the vernacular Bible upon the English people; the influence of covenant theology in shaping Puritan piety; a new attitude toward economic action (the work ethic); and the condemnation of Sunday recreations.

The Reformation made the Bible the supreme guide to the life of righteousness. This development coincided with the shift from Latin to the vernacular as the chief instrument of expression in the countries of Europe. The way people thought and felt about religion was more important to England's earliest Protestants than any dynastic reformation, so they directed their energies to getting the Bible translated, printed, and circulated in the popular language. Though Henry VIII authorized the English Bible for reading in churches, for many years the editions available were bulky, expensive folios.

During the reign of Elizabeth the Bible finally became accessible to the people. A group of Marian exiles produced the first Bible whose size, price, and apparatus made it well-adapted to private use. The Geneva Bible, published in 1560, far surpassed in circulation any other edition of the period, going through sixty editions before 1603 and ten later. It "set before the reader in comprehensible terms keyed to the Scriptures a statement in the common tongue of the conception of man's inner life derived from Paul by way of Augustine and Calvin. It enabled the reader to discover for himself from the text before him . . . the essentials of the great doctrine of salvation by the election of divine grace alone."[18] As a result, Elizabethans became the people of the Book. Men with earnest minds "would not be blinded with those vain shadows of fathers, times and customs," John Stockwood wrote in 1578, "but would measure the truth of religion by the square of the Word."[19] This determination soon produced a change in the thought of the people. "A new conception of life and of man superseded the old," according to J. R. Green. "A new moral and religious impulse spread through every class. . . . The whole nation became, in fact, a Church."[20]

Yet within the household of the faith men differed in interpreting Scripture. Puritans emphasized the total corruption of the natural faculties by the taint of original sin and adhered strictly to the pattern of righteousness contained in the Bible. For Anglicans, however, original sin had not totally destroyed the natural faculties. Reason, though subordinate, remained a necessary complement to grace. Richard Hooker, the Anglican apologist who answered Cartwright in the *Laws of Ecclesiastical Polity* (1597), argued that God was the author of man's rational faculty as well as the Bible. If all Elizabethans agreed that the Bible was an authoritative revelation, Puritans were distinctive in demanding specific scriptural warrant for their system of thought and code of conduct.[21]

The discipline of the Word figured prominently in the rise of English Sabbatarianism. Anxious people were searching the Bible for the rule of life. They believed Scripture to be divinely inspired in all its parts, a conviction affirmed by the Reformed tenet that the Old and New Testaments constitute one unbroken covenant. The Thirty-Nine Articles taught that the Old Testament was not contrary to the New, and the Decalogue was more familiar to Elizabethans than to previous generations.[22] The Queen had ordered Catholic ornaments in chancels replaced by the Two Tables of the Law, and recitation of the Ten Commandments had become part of the litany. In these same years William Perkins weighed the extent to which Old Testament law was binding in practical affairs, while Thomas Cartwright envisioned an entire scheme of jurisprudence based on the Ten Commandments and attempted to revive Mosaic Law as a basis for obedience.[23]

Little wonder that many seized upon the Fourth Commandment as the source of binding authority for observance of the Lord's Day. To be sure, there is a momentous theological confusion in identifying the Christian holy day with the Sabbath of the Decalogue. Yet the confusion is understandable. Learned Puritans believed that Scripture was self-illuminating, even to the uneducated. Searching the Book intensively to discover the way to salvation, individuals found in the Fourth Commandment the only explicit scriptural warrant for keeping the holy day. The equating of the Lord's Day with the Sabbath occurred in diverse places and at various levels of sophistication during Elizabeth's reign. Three examples in as many decades illustrate how bibliolatry was laying English Sabbatarianism on ancient foundations.

In June 1567 some Nonconformists hired Plumbers' Hall in London upon the pretense of conducting a wedding but actually to hold a religious meeting. These early Separatists were strict in their own observance of the Sabbath and opposed the keeping of saints' days. Sheriffs interrupted the assemblage and arrested several leaders whom they charged with doctrines denying the authority of the Crown to appoint for use in the church any practice not expressly provided for in Scripture. To the ecclesiastical commissioners who questioned them, the Separatists replied that God gave man clear commands in the Bible. Exodus (20:10) appointed the Sabbath for rest and worship, and it was the Queen who broke a divine law by requiring the observance of holy days. Their defense was: "We ought to do that [which] God commandeth."[24]

A decade later John Northbrooke cited the Fourth Commandment as the basis for strict Sunday observance. A moderate Puritan clergyman, who searched for a scriptural rule as he pondered the subject of weekly rest, Northbrooke finally settled on the confused doctrinal ground provided by the Old Testament. Many other clergy and laity were traveling this same road, but Northbrooke merits attention as the first person known to have enunciated the distinctive tenet of later Puritan thought, that "the whole keeping of the lawe standeth in the true use of the Sabboth."[25]

By the 1580s the Puritan conviction that one should give primary obedience to the divine law was bringing about voluntary change in Sabbath observance. So staunch was the commitment to the Fourth Commandment that it led to extremes. A scholar named John Smith demonstrated the logical outcome of the tendency to insist upon rigorous application of the Old Testament rule. At Cambridge University he preached a doctrine of keeping the Christian Sabbath according to the Jewish practice, wanting the festival observed for twenty-four hours from evening to evening and with the strictest kind of rest. When cited before authorities in 1585, however, he retracted most of his views.[26]

In sum, a Calvinistic approach to the Bible prompted Elizabethans to discover in the Fourth Commandment a divine foundation for observance of the Sabbath. And yet an uncritical biblical literalism was insufficient to account for Sabbatarianism. "The real reason why the Puritans held many of their distinctive tenets was not necessarily because Scripture enjoined them"; A. F. Scott Pearson writes, "they sought Scriptural support because they already believed in or were inclined to such tenets."[27] His point is exaggerated with respect to the Sabbath, for the Decalogue offered compelling sanction of the institution.

A second and closely related factor affecting the Puritan Sabbath was the doctrine of covenant theology and its offspring, an attitude toward salvation which made proper keeping of the Lord's Day essential to a life of righteousness. The Puritan differed fundamentally from other Englishmen in his outlook on redemption. Searching the Bible, he rediscovered sin and salvation as the essence of the drama of the human soul. His was an experiential religion in which he felt the love and wrath of God immediately and directly. Man, having inherited Adam's depravity, was spiritually dead, and only Christ could redeem him. Overwhelmed by a sense of sin as an obstacle to divine favor, the Puritan agreed with William Perkins, for whom the greatest question of conscience was how a man might know whether he is the child of God.[28]

Just as the eagerness to experience a new birth in Christ made Puritanism a religion of the heart, so too the search for a doctrine of redemption in Scripture made Puritanism a religion of the head. Men were never saved without being exposed to the Word. The Bible revealed the righteousness of God and the iniquity of man, thus demonstrating the need for conversion. Puritan theologians explained the process of conversion in the late sixteenth century by fashioning a highly intellectual framework for an intensely personal piety. They did so by incorporating the quest for the assurance of salvation within the doctrine of covenant theology.

Covenant thought deals with the relation between divine initiative and human responsibility in the process of regeneration. The idea of a covenant between God and man runs prominently through the Old Testament and is found also in Christianity, although in discussing salvation pre-Reformation writers did not develop the biblical idea of covenant. The theological tradition associated with Paul and Augustine taught that man sinned necessarily and could not turn toward the good without the aid of grace, which preceded and created faith. In the Middle Ages, Thomas Aquinas and other ecclesiastical writers accorded man's reason a larger role in the process of human endeavor. Man's hope was grounded on human merit as well as divine aid.[29]

The sixteenth-century reformers revolted against their late medieval inheritance, reviving the Pauline doctrine of justification by faith alone. Luther, a profound pessimist on the nature of man and on the capacity of the human reason, denied the value of good works to salvation. He treated nature and grace within the framework of the antithesis between Law and Gospel which constituted the normative element of his soteriology or doctrine of salvation. Although man's reason still rules in the realm of nature after the Fall, unregenerate reason could never arrive at belief. Human reason was actually arrogant, always ready to ally with the Law, thus producing a religion of works, a scripturally unwarranted legalism which affords a false security of salvation while undermining Christianity. To keep the Law, even the Decalogue, as a means of salvation was sinful. Man is saved by the righteousness of God, by grace through faith.[30]

The Reformed churches firmly believed in justification by faith rather than works, but in contrast to Luther they made the covenant the master principle governing relations between God and man. Swiss and Rhineland Reformers originated the doctrine of covenant theology about 1525, and over the next half-century Continental Reformed theologians developed the concept more fully. Initially they formulated the notion of the covenant of grace, later adding the idea of the covenant of works. Wherever Reformed theology struck roots, covenant theology flowered. It played a significant part in the doctrinal teaching of Calvin, who discussed the subject in his *Institutes,* his commentaries on the Bible, and his sermons.[31]

According to double covenant theology, a covenant of works bound all men and constituted the basis of the moral life. God established a covenant of works with Adam in Paradise, promising life eternal in return for obedience to the divine law (which Reformed theologians equated with moral law or the law of nature). But Adam disobeyed, thereby rendering the whole human race incapable of fulfilling the divine commandments and bringing mankind under judgment of damnation. After the Fall, however, the Lord established a covenant of grace, promising salvation, the life forfeited, in return for faith and obedience. God first made the New Covenant explicit with Abraham, through whom Israel became an elect nation. He renewed the covenant at Mount Sinai in giving Moses the Decalogue and singling out the Fourth Commandment for special attention: the Sabbath was the sign of the perpetual covenant between God and his Chosen People. The New Covenant was rooted in the promise that God would send a Redeemer, and eventually Christ had come to fulfill the promise. He offered faith to the elect of all nations. Though men are saved by faith, they must fulfill the covenant by keeping the Law.[32]

Covenant thought was carried to England in the morning of the Reformation. It attracted followers during the reign of Henry VIII and subsequently; Protestants exiled on the Continent became familiar with the concept during the Marian supremacy; and after 1560 the marginal comments in the Geneva Bible popularized the idea. However, Elizabethan Puritans were free to choose between two different ways in which Reformed theologians understood the covenant relation between God and man.[33] One was the conditional covenant derived from the Rhineland reformers. Tyndale introduced it into England. In his earliest writings Tyndale, following Luther, emphasized the dialectic between the bondage of the Law and the freedom of the Gospel. Later, adopting the covenant scheme of Rhineland theologians, he held that the divine promise is given to man on condition that he keep the covenant containing the Ten Commandments. Reciprocity is the keynote: God's promise elicits a responding promise, creating a mutual pact. Although Tyndale never lost sight of the Reformation principle of justification by faith alone, he increasingly stressed the ethical element and put the burden of responsibility on man. "If we meek ourselves to God, to keep all his laws, after the example of Christ," he wrote in 1534, "then God hath bound himself unto us, to keep and make good all the mercies promised in Christ throughout all the scripture."[34] All of the vernacular versions of the Bible which Henry VIII authorized for reading in churches were based in some measure on Tyndale's translations. Hearing these texts, Englishmen gained a conception of Christianity as a system of rewards and punishments for moral actions.

A second option was the absolute covenant taught by Calvin.[35] A sovereign God is free to deal with man as he wills, and the Lord does not make reciprocal binding agreements. Yet the Almighty does want to save sinners; and in the covenant of grace, faith is bestowed upon the elect without regard to human merit. "The Kingdom of Heaven is not servants' wages but sons' inheritance," Calvin remarked, "which only they who have been adopted as sons by the Lord shall enjoy, and that for no other reason than his adoption."[36] Thus, Calvin preserved the doctrines of divine sovereignty and predestination. "Calvin's covenant-God certainly offered grace and demanded obedience," as Jens G. Møller writes, "but he did not recompense obedience by offering grace."[37]

The Genevan nevertheless made human responsibility a complement to divine sovereignty. His teaching on the Law obligated those in the covenant of works and those in the covenant of grace to obey the Word of God voluntarily. The Law for Calvin meant primarily the moral law, "the true and eternal rule of righteousness, prescribed for men of all nations and times, who wish to conform their lives to God's will."[38] The Law was contained in the covenant, and the covenant, founded in Christ, was substantially the same in the Old and New Testaments. The function of the Law remained the same throughout the entire history of salvation: to lead men to Christ.

Calvin described three uses of the Law. The first was as a mirror revealing God's perfection and man's imperfection. For ancient Israel as for Christians, the Law set forth a pattern of perfect righteousness and promised eternal life in return for complete obedience. But man lacked the natural capacity to fulfill its demands; he could never merit salvation by doing good works. The Law was therefore a schoolmaster to bring men to Christ, a ministry of damnation which drove despairing sinners to implore divine help.[39]

The covenant of grace offered freedom from the bondage of the Law. The saints were granted the gift of faith in accordance with predestined decree rather than individual merit. Nevertheless, the covenant of redemption, though solely the fruit of sovereign grace, did obligate the regenerate. For Calvin the third and principal use of the Law was as a guide to the elect. They must continue to keep the covenant, not in the hope of reward but out of thankfulness for divine mercy and to ratify their membership in the covenanted community. In its third use the Law provided the saved a better understanding of the divine will and an exhortation to obey. Even for the converted, "the law is to the flesh like a whip to an idle and balky ass, to arouse it to work." Calvin made his most important contribution to covenant thought by bringing the requirements of the Law within the context of the promises of the Gospel.[40]

Scholars differ as to how Puritan divines drew on Reformed covenant thought, and despite considerable attention given it over several decades, we lack a satisfactory general account of this development. It seems clear that covenant theology was highly conducive to a type of piety which encouraged a rigorous Sabbatarianism. According to the late Perry Miller, whose writings on the doctrine of covenant thought shaped the minds of an entire generation, the Puritans were post-Calvinists who found it psychologically imperative to close the vast gulf between God and man bequeathed by Genevan doctrines. Seeking grounds for urging moral obedience and for assuring individuals that works counted toward salvation, Puritan preachers in the first half of the seventeenth century elaborated the notion that God had voluntarily limited himself by establishing a covenant with man which bound both parties. The covenant of grace became a conditional covenant: the condition is faith, and faith has in the Law a prescribed rule of righteousness. The perfection required was best stated in the Decalogue. On these theoretical foundations, Miller concluded, Puritan clergymen became shamelessly pragmatic in urging preparation for salvation.[41]

Such views obviously would have exalted the importance of Sabbath-keeping, but Miller concentrates on a later period than that in which covenant thought arose, and other weaknesses of his interpretation have been indicated in the preceding discussion.[42] Norman Pettit has shown that starting in the late sixteenth century spiritual preachers devised covenant theology in the light of Scripture, which describes conversion as God's turning man to himself and as man's voluntary return to God, and in the light of their Reformed intellectual heritage. These Elizabethan clergy addressed themselves to numerous questions. Granted that divine activity must precede human activity in regeneration, could man do anything to prepare himself for the initial movement toward salvation? What was the relation between human merit and divine grace in conversion? Is the influence of the Law in preparing man for redemption God's work or man's? How close can the Law bring sinners to Christ? What is the normative pace in the restoration of man to rapport with God? Does grace come gradually or suddenly? Salvation, admittedly, was for the elect; it required the intervention of grace, and without grace, repentance, which permitted the rise of faith, was impossible. But what was the temporal relation between repentance and faith? Did repentance precede or follow faith, or come simultaneously?[43]

English covenant thought was still fluid and plastic when Puritans began dealing with these questions in the 1580s. Their search for a sound scriptural basis on preparation for conversion led to many different results. Some preachers apparently emphasized legalism while others stressed the role of the Holy Spirit.[44] Perhaps those who developed a doctrine of preparation for conversion which united a religion of personal experience with the doctrine of covenant theology represented a happy medium and attracted the largest following. Among the leading formulators of the concept of "the heart prepared" were Richard Greenham, Arthur Hildersam, and William Perkins. Their teaching shows the strong influence of Calvin. They set within a scriptural framework their notion of gradually preparing the heart for grace in the period before justification and devised a scheme to explain the process of conversion. In the first stage, which consisted of several steps, saving grace was not at work. At this point the offering of Christ came through the use of means and applied to all men: a sinner could gain a legal conviction of sin by attending the ministry of the Word, reading the Bible, and judging himself by the standards of the Law. In the second stage, again comprising several steps, saving grace was at work through the will of the individual and with his active participation. Now the Holy Spirit brought about a desire to believe, leading the soul to battle doubt and despair, then to a feeling of imperfect assurance, later to evangelical sorrow for sin, and finally, for the elect, to communion with Christ.[45] The preparationists reduced to its essence a body of instruction on how men should act to be saved and made proper Sabbath observance a key element in that code of conduct. In sum, the Puritan doctrine of the covenant and the Puritan theology of the Sabbath were born twins.

As Protestantism was advancing, economic and social forces were transforming England into a modern capitalistic-industrial society. Sabbatarianism emerged within an environment of interaction between new religious ideas and new forms of economic organization and conduct. Of various attempts to relate the Protestant Reformation and capitalism to the formation of the modern world, the thesis announced by Max Weber in the early twentieth century was the most influential and the most controversial.[46] *The Protestant Ethic and the Spirit of Capitalism* reflected his effort to link the contribution of prophetic religion to the rationalization of the whole of Western life. Reversing Marx's formula, Weber emphasized intellectual factors in explaining the origins of modern capitalism, which he defined as the rational organization of formally free labor. What most interested him was the spirit of this capitalism, the new ethos that made it a duty to seek profit for its own sake by systematic and continuous hard work.

The origins of this spirit of capitalism Weber traced to the Protestant ethic, in particular to a set of ideas associated with Calvinism. The dogma of predestination created an unprecedented feeling of inner loneliness, and the Calvinist conception of the calling spurred the individual, anxious about the certainty of salvation, to prove his faith by strenuous activity in his worldly vocation. Though admitting that good works were no means of attaining salvation, Weber argued that the Calvinist regarded them as indispensable signs of election. Thus, the follower of Calvin rationalized his pattern of conduct in terms of an inner worldly asceticism. The economic virtues of industry, diligence, frugality, sobriety, and prudence became spiritual ends, and a spirit of lust for gain triumphed. Treating ascetic Protestantism as a single whole, Weber found its best expression in post-Restoration Puritanism, especially the writings of Richard Baxter (1615-1691).[47]

England underwent a fundamental material transformation between 1500 and 1800, and the late sixteenth century was a critical phase in the transition from the medieval to the modern era. At the start of the period the nation was still frozen in the pattern of the past, an economic backwater in relation to European centers of commerce and industry. Capitalism existed elsewhere in Europe, but not in England, or in insignificant degree. Under the Tudors, however, new forces rapidly expanded economic life in a capitalistic direction. A steady growth in population, a sharp price inflation, and the powerful impetus of the sale of confiscated monastery lands contributed to changes in landownership and a restructuring of classes. A new group of profit-hungry landowners, employing capitalistic methods, revived the enclosure movement, evicting thousands from the soil to make way for a more productive agriculture. The agrarian upheaval created vagabondage. Masterless men roamed the countryside and swelled the cities in search of employment. Reduced to begging and stealing in order to live, they aggravated the problem of poverty and struck terror into the established classes. Tudor governments tried repeatedly to eliminate these sources of social instability by laws designed to check rural depopulation and establish a system of poor relief.[48]

The Tudor policy of encouraging discovery and overseas expansion bore fruit under Elizabeth, and with Spanish maritime supremacy successfully challenged, England's foreign commerce became brisker than ever. Merchant adventurers opened trade to exotic places, accumulating capital which enhanced their position in society and provided a base for other economic undertakings.

Industry also expanded. According to John U. Nef, an industrial revolution occurred in England between 1540 and 1640, with the rate of change becoming most rapid after 1580 (the decade in which Sabbath theory emerged). Nef, wishing to account for the origins of industrial civilization, contends that it was called into being not only by the development of private capitalist enterprise but also by a novel emphasis on quantity production and scientific methods of investigation and measurement. In modern society, whether Protestant or Catholic, capitalist or socialist, mass production and rationalization of the economic process become ends in themselves. He is, therefore, less interested in what the Reformation did to stimulate capitalism than in what it did to stimulate the quantitative outlook and scientific method, and as much concerned with the scientific revolution which accompanied the industrial revolution as with the Reformation.[49]

The classic industrial revolution occurred more than a century after 1640, but the process of industrialization brought substantial material transformation to England starting in the late sixteenth century.[50] A tremendous expansion of output occurred in older industries, large-scale industry controlled by private capitalists became common in mining and many manufactures, and technological innovation led to the introduction of new as well as the transformation of old industries which had to be conducted on a large scale or not at all. These undertakings, producing such commodities as brass, cannon, paper, and sugar, required unprecedented amounts of capital, and the entrepreneurs who provided it rationalized the industrial process, making quantity production and large-scale labor distinguishing features of their mines, factories, and workshops. Scores of such industries appeared before 1640. The great majority of workers continued to labor in their homes or village cottages, but the proportion so employed was notably reduced in this period and "tens of thousands" were "swept from the country dwellings and town shops of their forefathers or from a ragged existence of vagabondage into hundreds of new, capitalistically owned enterprises." By 1640 London was the leading industrial city and England the most advanced industrial nation in the world.[51]

Tension arose between the old ethical theory and the new realities. Elizabethan divines were prominent in applying Protestant ideas to the changing conditions of life, and the Puritans who ransacked Calvin for the purpose were the most advanced social thinkers of the day. They developed a body of doctrines which offered ethical guidance for economic conduct, and the theory of the Sabbath was one outcome. The first treatises on the subject, while elaborating many themes, recognize man's connection with the world of work. They treat the moral issues raised by novel forms of economic organization and action in terms of such concepts as vocation (work and idleness), holy days, wealth, stewardship, and poverty.

The doctrine of the calling, though a constituent element of Sabbatarian theory, was not a product of the Reformation. For early Protestants the notion was "nothing but a new expression of the old belief . . . that different men were 'called' to their several occupations and estates by a divine providence." Mid-sixteenth-century Puritans made the teaching an integral part of their ethical system, employing it on the side of conservatism rather than to encourage capitalism. In their view the concept meant ordered status and taught men to be content with the position in life assigned by Providence.[52]

Elizabethan Puritans reoriented the doctrine of vocation, as we see in the earliest writings on the Sabbath and in more concentrated form in William Perkins' *Treatise of the Vocations, or Callings of Men.* A systematic theologian who applied Calvinist ideas to practical affairs, Perkins wrote no separate essay on the Sabbath but had much to say on the subject in his *Treatise of Callings* and other writings. He enormously influenced Anglo-American thought on ethical economic conduct just as modern society was coming into being.[53]

The calling is a "certaine kinde of life, ordained and imposed on man by God, for the common good." There are two kinds of callings, the general and the particular. The former is "the calling of Christianity, which is common to all that live in the Church of God." Its duties include furthering the welfare of the church, serving others, a daily renewal of repentance, and a constant "indeavour to performe new obedience in respect of all [God's] commandements." Such a description restates Puritan ideas on divine election and the voluntary obedience of the saints.[54]

The personal calling is "the execution of some particular office, arising of that distinction which God makes betweene man and man in every society." In discussing the rules on individual vocation, Perkins expressed a viewpoint on the order of society commanded by God. First, every person must have a particular calling. This appears plainly from the Word of God as revealed to Adam in Paradise and to all men after the Fall. Moreover, the calling must be lawful, one that upholds church, state, or family. Second, everyone must see that his personal calling is best fitted to his individual interests and talents. Third, the Christian must join the practice of his general and particular callings "as bodie and soule are joyned in a living man." Though God could rule mankind otherwise, his "pleasure is, that men should be his instruments, for the good of one another." Hence men profane their callings when they devote them to the accumulation of worldly possessions. Perkins denounced covetousness as the root of nearly all evil and emphasized the perils of riches. Men could of course expect a reward for their labor, although neither wealth nor poverty is an index to divine favor. The true end of life is not to serve ourselves but to serve God by serving mankind in the works of our callings. Thus a particular calling must give way to the general calling when both cannot stand together.[55]

The affirmation of labor in the *Treatise of Callings* represents a new view of society. Work had long enjoyed an honorable place in Christian ethics, although the medieval church had made a sharp distinction between the spiritual and material realms and applied different ethical standards to the clergy and the laity. Catholics exalted the life of prayer and contemplation associated with religious vocations and monastic discipline, attaching a penal quality to servile labor. The Reformation introduced a fresh departure. Protestants sought to regenerate the world by uniting the two realms and rejecting the double standard of morality. Elizabethan Puritans, like Perkins and the writers on the Sabbath, contributed by regarding all callings as equal in their religious aspects and emphasizing the positive value of mundane work. They spiritualized the economic process by teaching that all men glorified God by serving others in the works of their callings.[56]

Thus, the work ethic became a vital part of the Puritan code of conduct Industry evidenced a proper understanding of how to realize God's true order. "Every man must doe the duties of his calling with diligence," Perkins advised, for only by diligence could they glorify God in this world. Time was fleeting and precious, a supreme value, and God held men strictly accountable for using it wisely. *"Redeeme the time,"* urged the Puritan spokesman, employing a Pauline injunction to define Christian stewardship.[57]

Censure of idleness accompanied praise of work. True, the medieval Church had condemned idleness as morally dangerous. But Puritans, associating it with the feudal and Catholic past, brought a fresh intensity to the attack. Perkins castigated idleness and slothfulness as contrary to God's order and the cause of many damnable sins. He singled out four groups wherein lack of a particular calling led to idleness: rogues, beggars, and vagabonds; monks and friars; rich gentlemen who "spend their dayes in eating and drinking, in sports and pastimes''; and serving men. Convinced that it was a ''foule disorder'' for any commonwealth to tolerate persons without a calling, Perkins praised the Elizabethan Poor Law of 1598 for the restraining of beggars and rogues as ''an excellent Statute . . . being in substance the very law of God.''[58]

Closely related to industry and idleness was the Puritan assault on holy days other than the Sabbath.[59] These festivals were very numerous in premodern England, totaling about 165 days a year. The Reformation and the rise of capitalistic-industrial society fed an appetite for change, and, as we have seen, in 1552 authorities reduced the number of holidays to 79. Puritans included the suppression of holy days in their demand for reform, and in the Convocation of 1563 came within one vote of achieving their purpose.[60]

The issue remained a live one. A decade later the first *Admonition* cited in opposition to holy days God's command, ''Sixe dayes shalt thou laboure,'' and in the ensuing Admonition Controversy, Cartwright argued that holy days were remnants of popery which encouraged superstition. He insisted that the Fourth Commandment gives men a liberty to work six days a week which no earthly authority could destroy. Whitgift replied that the Church of England had removed the superstitious element from the holy days retained and regarded them as a profitable means of edifying the people. To rest one day is commanded, to labor the other six only permitted. Both Scripture and custom give to the church and the prince the authority to appoint times other than Sunday for the service of God. But Cartwright was not convinced. The plethora of holy days was ''a thing which breedeth idleness and consequently poverty, besides other disorders and vices, which always go in company with idleness.''[61]

Thus, Sabbatarianism incorporated the new gospel of work and the critique of idleness, and these attitudes, according to Michael Walzer, ''formed the concrete basis of the Puritan repudiation of the old order.'' In his view the transition from traditional to modern society raised fresh problems which ''can be summed up most sharply in the appearance of the 'masterless man,' '' and Puritans dealt with this situation by attempting to impose a godly discipline. They ''discovered in work the primary and elemental form of social discipline, the key to order, and the foundation of all further morality.'' The work ethic was ''at least as much a response to the overriding problem of social order as it [was] to the individual's anxiety with regard to his fate in the life to come.''[62] Perkins showed no conscious awareness of the social dimensions of vagabondage and poverty, but he called upon Parliament to require weekday work and prohibit Sunday labor.[63]

Sabbatarianism facilitated the emergence of modern society by rationalizing time and the productive process. Large-scale industry and labor, quantity production, and an attempt to reduce labor costs led to a demand that factories, mines, and workshops operate on a fixed and uniform schedule. Time became a matter of precise measurement by exact recording instruments; a greater use of clocks and watches was made. The concentration of religious observance on one day a week admirably suited the rhythm of new forms of economic organization. Sabbatarianism held workers to their tasks six days a week and allowed them to rest on the seventh. Then, strength restored, they could start the cycle over again. Thus, the theological convictions of English Calvinists and the environment of an incipient capitalistic-industrial society reinforced each other.[64]

Elizabethan Puritans did not consciously intend to sanction capitalism. Salvation and material success were still regarded as unrelated. It may well be that entrepreneurs eager for profit were inclined toward Sabbatarianism on economic grounds. Economists soon realized that holy days represented a costly loss in national output. Nevertheless, Puritan preachers stressed the hazards more than the attractions of material prosperity and were quick to criticize merchants and industrialists who violated God's laws. In 1583, for example, the Dedham Classis expressed concern over clothiers' setting their wood vats on the Sabbath. Moreover, Sabbatarianism protected workers from exploitation by employers who demanded Sunday labor. It also prevented small shop owners from having to remain open on the Lord's Day or lose out to competition. These were liberalizing rather than repressive effects of English Puritanism. But the new doctrine worked a hardship on the poor who depended upon daily wages for their bread.[65]

The Puritan attitude toward work's opposite also was a stimulus to Sabbatarianism. If work is purposeful activity put forth in doing or making something, its antithesis is inactivity or idleness. Though Puritans condemned idleness, they directed their antagonism mainly against the vices it generated. Play transformed idleness, "the mistresse of wanton appetites," into wickedness.[66]

Elizabethans engaged in the three basic kinds of play which are a part of human culture. One was simple physical activity such as leaping, running, and dancing aimed solely at diversion or amusement. Another was a more developed type of bodily exercise or sport in the form of athletic contests and ball games. Third was the acting out of something, including ritual or sacred drama and secular drama.[67] All but the simplest kind of play took place at times regulated by the church calendar, which was geared to the rhythm of nature and the Christian liturgical year. The calendar released people from work on major seasonal feasts celebrating events in the life of Christ, on lesser festivals commemorating saints and martyrs, and on Sundays; the multitude seized upon these occasions as their prime opportunity for revels as well as rituals.

Puritans opposed the keeping of all holy days other than the Lord's Day and regarded the manner of observing such church-appointed festivals as pagan and popish. Ritual had originated in primitive society when man performed rites at periodical intervals associated with the change of agricultural seasons in order to insure the food supply or as acts of worship or propitiation of the divine powers. Sports and games, which had arisen as part of the magicoreligious rites or been added as they became more secular, were closely allied to ritual. Later, when Christianity established a liturgical calendar, the Church superimposed its own observances upon the existing seasonal festivals. But it never completely succeeded in suppressing survivals of magic and superstition in the old folk practices.[68]

Elizabethans still celebrated the festal days with pagan and Christian customs. The Feast of the Nativity coincided with the season of the winter solstice, and the Epiphany Eve custom of wassailing the fruit trees with a view to securing an abundant crop as well as the popular practice of Christmas masking had their origins in rituals marking the renewal of fertility processes and the rebirth of the sun. In the latter folk festival, parties of rustic mummers clad in uncouth garb went from village to village, sometimes merely singing or dancing but commonly performing a crude drama which represented a fight, slaying, and revival of the victim. These plays, with their death and resurrection theme, had a comic side which served for amusement, but the pagan mummery occasionally turned into burlesque and even invaded the sanctuary.[69]

Folk games were frequently associated with a particular seasonal festival. Football, a rough and violent sport of mass participation, was often only an annual event, as in the Haxey Hood game played on Epiphany Day in Lincolnshire. Opposing teams fought fiercely to capture the Hood, some encased rope, and carry it several miles through town and country to their captain's home. The game was the vestigial observance of a supernatural rite in which contestants scrambled for the prize, originally the head of a bull sacrificed to fertilize the fields, to increase their crops. Shrovetide held first place for boisterous and barbarous outdoor sports, including cockfighting, cockthrowing, and games of football involving hundreds of players.[70]

In the May Day festivities the symbolism lay even closer to the surface. This spring celebration had its origins in ancient myth and ritual in which the rebirth of nature was believed to depend upon the veneration of a phallic image. Customarily, English young people went into the woods after midnight on May first to engage in fun and games, cut down a tree, and take it back to the village at dawn. With great ceremony they erected the Maypole in a central place and then danced and made merry around the object of devotion. The Maypole festivities were to Puritans heathen idolatry and a source of debauchery. "Of fortie, threescore, or a hundred maides going to the wood over night," the critic Stubbes reported, "there have scarsely the third part of them returned home again undefiled."[71]

Numerous other church festivals provided opportunities for merriment. Whitsunday was the principal time for church ales to raise funds for general parish purposes and the favorite season for morris dances. Moreover, each church celebrated an annual wake or feast in honor of its dedication. People loved to sing and dance and drink at these affairs, and those who bought the most ale were often accounted the godliest. Traditional customs appealed to man's physical nature and touched the irrational and unconscious side of his being. This accounts for the people's stubborn attachment to the old ways and Puritan opposition to them. English Puritanism was the cutting edge of the Protestant revolt against pagan and Catholic popular superstitions and profane customs, and its adherents strove to impose a rational standard upon life by bringing conduct into strict conformity with the Word of God.[72]

Closely related was the Puritan crusade to suppress Sunday recreations. The forms of play used on that day had fewer pagan associations, but Sunday was a favorite occasion for gaiety, since it was the only non-work day other than the medieval holidays, which had been reduced in number in 1552. Elizabethans worked more than their fathers had and made the Sabbath a day for reveling. In rural areas, where few other entertainments were available, traditional country sports and pastimes were deeply entrenched, although sport itself was undergoing change. In London and the provincial towns familiar sports were less important than various kinds of dramatic presentations, especially the Elizabethan stage. Puritans found many reasons for opposing sports and the stage, but they particularly objected to the fact that both took place more often on Sunday than any other day. This was the crux of the matter, and under the circumstances the Puritan criticism was equivalent to condemnation of sports and the theater.[73]

The Puritan attitude toward sport was a creative response to contemporary conditions rather than a legacy from the past. Continental reformers offered little guidance on the subject, and there was little conscious thought about it at the time of Elizabeth's accession. Anglican theologians seldom expressed themselves on sportive recreations, although Richard Hooker wrote that the body had its occasions for the enjoyment of feasts and festivals, and Bishop Gervase Babington held that amusements in moderation were justifiable. Puritans, however, took sports seriously because of their implications for the life of righteousness. Starting about 1580, several writers dealt with the problem, including Samuel Bird, an Ipswich clergyman; the Sabbatarian theorists; Phillip Stubbes, a layman with the moral outlook of the Puritan preacher; and William Perkins. In *The Anatomie of Abuses* (1583), Stubbes expressed views which were becoming widespread among Elizabethan Puritans. We know little about the man. He began his book intending to condemn only the abuse of recreations, but ended with harsh strictures on their use as well. However, he had traveled throughout England for seven years before 1583 and was familiar with his subject; he thought the abuses were serious, especially the abuse of the Sabbath; and he struck a popular chord. His book went through five editions in thirteen years.[74]

Persons inclined to Puritanism were fundamentally hostile to sportive play,[75] and theological conviction was the wellspring (though not the sole source) of their attitude. They offered numerous reasons for their views. In the first place, sportive play was essentially frivolous. Man's chief end was to glorify God in the duties of his calling. Work was the means by which man furthered the divine purpose, and it gave needed physical exercise. Work was serious, earnest, a material necessity. Play was altogether different. Puritans could have agreed with Huizinga, who defined play as "a free activity standing quite consciously outside 'ordinary' life as being 'not serious,' but at the same time absorbing the player intensely and utterly. It is an activity connected with no material interest." Such a position enabled the Puritans to approve some play. William Perkins argued that God in commanding man to labor allowed the means to make him fit for work; thus God admits recreations. He warned, however, that recreations must be moderate lest they draw man away from his calling, they must be lawful, and they must take place on days of labor, not on the Sabbath. Even Stubbes endorsed certain physical exercises when practiced in moderation on weekdays for "Godly solace and recreation." But if a bit of play was justifiable to rejuvenate the tired laborer, anything more was an indulgence and a waste of time. Man should redeem the time, not "idely and vainely spend his golden dayes" pursuing his "owne fantasies and delights."[76]

In the second place, sports and games conflicted with proper observance of the Sabbath. Even innocent diversions such as running, jumping, stoolball, kit-cat, marbles, handball, archery, hunting, and fishing were devilish pastimes because they lured people away from church and kept them from spending the entire day in spiritual edification. Other recreations disturbed public worship. Boisterous activities like bowling were played in the churchyard during time of service, and the Lord of Misrule festivities, a popular Sunday "sport" as well as a Christmas revel in the great halls of nobles, spilled over into the sanctuary itself. According to Stubbes, the Lords of Misrule, with their large retinues of colorfully attired retainers, their pipers piping, drummers thundering, bells jingling, hobbyhorses and dragons skirmishing, danced into the church while the congregation was at prayer, after which these "lustie Guttes" went into the churchyard to feast and frolic for the remainder of the Sabbath.[77]

In the third place, several sports were brutal and barbarous. Football was becoming a Sunday game as well as a seasonal festival, and for Stubbes it was neither sport nor recreation but a "bloody and murthering practise" in which the players tried to do maximum violence to each other. Serious bodily injuries and even deaths resulted, to say nothing of lasting rancor and enmity. Cockfighting and the baiting of bulls and bears were equally offensive. These spectator sports attracted large followings in the cities as well as the countryside. In London, crowds of gentlemen and commoners alike flocked to the Bear Garden on the Bankside on Wednesdays and Sundays to watch dogs tear at flying fur. A tethered bear—the baiting of bulls remained largely a rural pastime—was attacked by several mastiffs, the bloody encounter lasting until the poor creature was killed or the badly mauled dogs pulled away. Bearbaiting was considered worthy entertainment for distinguished foreign visitors, and at Kenilworth in 1575 the Queen herself watched dogs set upon thirteen bears at one time. Puritans refused to countenance such a brutalizing sport.[78]

In the fourth place, sports and recreations constituted a moral danger. Sunday was an occasion for gambling. Elizabethans gathered at the gaming tables for cards and dice and enjoyed betting on athletic contests—bowling, pitching the bar, races, and the like. To the Puritan, all gaming mixed with covetousness was equivalent to theft and to play games of chance for stakes made a mockery of the conviction that nothing happens by chance in a world governed by Providence. In addition, sport was an incentive to vice because it afforded pleasure. The player ran the risk of forgetting his religious duties by abandoning himself to the rapture generated by exhilarating physical exercise and sportive competition. Play might open the door to sensuality by appealing to man's physical nature. Feasting, drinking, and dancing were seen as the path to perdition. The Reverend Samuel Bird thought Christians should condemn the kinds of dancing popular in England, and Stubbes strongly denounced mixed

dancing because he feared carnality. Dancing stirred up the flesh, encouraged ribaldry, and fired Venus's coal. "For what clipping, what cull-
ing, what kissing and bussing, what smouching and slabbering one of
another, what filthie groping and uncleane handling is not practised every
wher in these dauncings?"[79] J. W. Allen argues that the Puritan went to
extremes in avoiding the world and the flesh because he equated the fear
of pleasure with the fear of damnation. Carnal delight was of course all
the more sinful on Sundays because it violated the Fourth Commandment. Strict adherence to the Word of God was the only way to develop
an assurance of salvation. Thus, according to Allen, the Puritan "dare
not be anything but Sabbatarian. . . . He dare not dance and make merry;
he dare not enjoy cakes and ale, not because he thinks himself virtuous,
but because . . . they are 'seasoned and salted with sin.' He dare no more
take part in forms of worship not enjoined in Scripture than he dare play
tip-cat on Sunday. . . . For, above all, he needs to convince himself that
he . . . has no portion with the unbelievers. He dare not partake of the
loves and hopes and enjoyments of the profane multitude. . . . He dare
do nothing that might make him doubt his hard-won assurance."[80]

In the fifth place, Sunday recreations were socially as well as personally
damaging. They attracted crowds and provided an opportunity for rogues
and ruffians to practice trickery and deceit. Permit Sabbath recreations,
and what followed was sexual immorality, crime, drinking and gambling,
brutal sports, quarreling and brawling, and scenes of wild disorder. In
many places the magistrates wanted strict Sabbath observance to maintain the peace, and in the late sixteenth century local officials were more
ready to act than were higher civil or ecclesiastical authorities.[81]

The crusade against Sunday sports was an important element in the
break with the past. Not content with eliminating the pagan folk customs
and popish practices of the old medieval holidays, the Puritans insisted
upon suppressing all Sunday amusements so that people could sanctify
the entire Sabbath. Though their attitude ran counter to human nature,
the Puritans constituted a pressure group to advance a radical message
which a large segment of the population found increasingly attractive.
Since Puritanism made its greatest headway in urban and settled communities, while traditional sports retained their strongest hold in rural
and backward areas, the attack on Sunday pastimes may be interpreted as
an attempt to impose the ethos of an urban civilization upon the "dark
corners of the land."[82]

The new morality met stubborn resistance from the partisans of "ye
olde merrie England" led by the Queen herself. She often enjoyed games,
jousts, and interludes on the Lord's Day, and when the Earl of Leicester

entertained Elizabeth with the Princely Pleasures at Kenilworth in 1575, he provided fireworks, sports, dances, and stage plays on two successive Sundays. The upper classes were unwilling to fit their sportive play into a Puritan mold. They avoided the rustic amusements of the common people and engaged only in certain sports, and then in highly stylized ways associated with social status. And the lower classes were not to be denied their familiar pastimes. In 1588, for example, when Shrewsbury authorities, urged on by the town preacher, prohibited the Maypole, several shearmen were sent to jail for defending this symbol of their simple pleasures. Struggles over Sunday sports became increasingly bitter and political under the early Stuarts.[83]

In the cities, animal-baiting, minstrels, and interludes attracted Sunday crowds, but here plays and playgoing became the focus of criticism. Various kinds of dramatic performances had long been popular on holy days, but not until the late sixteenth century did acting become professionalized and the public theater emerge in England. London's first permanent playhouses were erected in the suburbs in 1576, a new school of dramatists came to the fore in the 1580s—Shakespeare made his appearance about this time—and soon the Elizabethan stage became the great glory of the English Renaissance. Although Calvinists followed the church fathers in their hostility to dramatic presentations which did not serve didactic religious purposes, England had experienced little opposition to the stage before these developments occurred. At that time the Puritans and the theater became deadly antagonists.[84]

A literature of complaint, which culminated in the 1640s with the legal closing of the stage, began. John Northbrooke sounded the alarm in 1577 with a treatise against Sunday plays; John Stockwood raked the stage in 1578 and 1579 with sermons from Paul's Cross, the outdoor London pulpit; Stephen Gosson, a reformed playwright and Puritan clergyman, delivered harsh invective in *The School of Abuse* (1579); Anthony Munday, a quondam playwright, published a similar diatribe the following year; and Stubbes furthered the onslaught in *The Anatomie of Abuses* (1583).[85]

Hostility to the theater took many forms. There were theological objections. Ministers did not welcome doctrinal challenge. By holding up a mirror to nature, playwrights offended those who believed that Scripture affords all that man can know of God's will. "The whole world," said the Puritan Richard Sibbes, echoing Calvin, "is a theater of the glory of God." Plays, Stubbes wrote, were "sucked out of the Devills teates to nourish us in ydolatrie, hethenrie, and sinne."[86] Clergymen resented economic competition from a new profession whose evolution out of wandering companies of minstrels, tumblers, conjurers, and the like was very recent. Players sucked up the honey without working. "Wyll not a fylthye playe, wyth the blast of a Trumpette," Stockwood asked, "sooner call thyther a thousande, than an houres tolling of a Bell, bring to the Sermon a hundred?" He charged companies of actors with taking in substantial sums of money that might otherwise have gone to ministers and respectable merchants.[87] The theater encouraged idleness and waste. Professional actors were numerous by 1570, but their lack of a lawful calling and of settlement in the community made them seem guilty of vagrancy. In addition to being rewarded for their own idleness, players compounded the offense by enticing craftsmen, apprentices, and servants away from work and worship. Northbrooke raided classical and Christian learning to prove that "more idlenesse can there not bee, than where such playes and enterludes are."[88] The stage was a threat to civic welfare. The new mixed audience contained many base elements. Cutpurses and pickpockets wishing to practice their craft made theaters the scene of crime. Plague manifested itself repeatedly in London after 1563, and the City fathers, fearing that crowds magnified the danger of the spread of disease, forbade playing at least five times during these years.[89] The theater was an incentive to vice. The plays of the period dealt freely with sex, and the literature of complaint emphasized the "filth" associated with the stage. Northbrooke charged that players stirred up "fleshly lusters, unlawfull appetites and desires, with their bawdie and filthie sayings and counterfeyt doings." Gosson described the theater as degrading and immoral, and Munday termed it a brothel house of bawdry. Critics depicted the theater as a human flesh market. Young, unescorted women were avid playgoers, and men made aggressive sexual advances at the playhouses. Authorities expressed concern over sexual dalliance at the theater and what followed the performances in taverns and houses. So too did Puritans: Gosson reported great toying, smiling, and winking in theatrical audiences, as every John and his Joan cheapened the merchandise which they paid for elsewhere; and Stubbes, always imagining the worst, added that after the pageants "in their secret conclaves (covertly) they play *the Sodomits,* or worse."[90]

Above all, according to E. K. Chambers, a leading student of the Elizabethan stage, "there was Sabbatarianism to be taken into account." Sundays were a favorite time for plays, and by conflicting with public worship, plays constituted a flagrant offense to the divine law and an impediment to the type of society desired by the spiritual preachers. "No feeling was more common than this of the profanation of the Lord's day," E. N. S. Thompson wrote. Starting abut the 1570s, "the feeling grew that playgoing on the Sabbath was a sin certain to call down the curse of God upon the offenders. To this, perhaps, more than to any other one of these causes, the clear-cut opposition to the stage was due.''[91]

DURING THE FIRST half of the reign of Elizabeth, mighty forces were converging to bring about a climate favorable to Sabbatarianism. Not everyone accepted the new attitude which, with Puritan encouragement, the passing of the old order was calling into being. But by the mid-1580s, except among the upper and lower classes, the conviction that England needed an improved Sabbath observance must have been fairly common. The fear that profanation of the Sabbath provoked divine punishment, an inseparable part of the belief in a providentially governed universe, gathered momentum in these years. After the earthquake of 6 April 1580, someone quickly published *A Discourse of God's Judgments against Great Sins,* which interpreted the tremor as an expression of God's displeasure that Englishmen spent Sundays and holy days "full heathenishly in taverning, tippling, gaming, playing, and beholding of bearbaiting and stage-plays." (Since the earthquake was on a Wednesday and the only casualties were two children who had been hearing a sermon at Christ Church, Newgate, the pamphlet obviously pointed the wrong moral.) Three years later, on Sunday, 13 January 1583, the scaffold of the bearbaiting ring at the Bear Garden collapsed, killing eight persons and injuring hundreds. Within a week, John Field, the Puritan organizer, rushed into print *A Godly Exhortation,* portraying the disaster as divine retribution for abuse of the Lord's Day. Many shared the belief expressed by the versifier who wrote:

> If he were slain which on the Sabbath day
> For need did gather sticks: Oh! how shall they
> Escape God's wrath, which for base pelf or pleasure
> Profane God's Sabbaths in most frequent measure.[92]

The growing demand for more reverent observance of the Lord's Day inspired Parliament to act. The very first bill introduced in the House of Commons which met in November 1584 aimed at this end. We know little about its origins. Perhaps some of the bishops, acting through Sir Walter Mildmay, a prominent Puritan, rather than the presbyterian faction, introduced the measure. As passed by the house, the bill banned markets, fairs, unlawful games, bearbaiting, and wakes on Sundays; and it prohibited hunting, hawking, and rowing with barges during the time of church services. The Lords resisted until the following March, when the Commons prevailed. Speaker of the House John Puckering gave the bill priority in requesting royal assent to legislation. All good statutes ought to be grounded upon the eternal law of God, he said, and in providing for the right use of the Sabbath, Parliament wished the Queen to legislate on the Fourth Commandment. Elizabeth vetoed the bill, however, perhaps determined not to allow Parliament to interfere with religion, but perhaps also because she preferred a merry England to a Puritan England.[93]

Nevertheless, the groundswell of opinion favoring better use of the Lord's Day required appropriate intellectual justification, and between 1585 and 1588 three ministers—Lancelot Andrewes, Richard Greenham, and Nicholas Bownde—effectively collaborated in setting forth the Puritan doctrine of the Sabbath. In all likelihood Andrewes (1555-1626) was the first to formulate the new theology. Entering Pembroke Hall at Cambridge in 1571, he remained a student and fellow there for nearly twenty years. Many of his associates in this Puritan stronghold were Nonconformists. An indefatigable and excellent scholar, Andrewes took holy orders in 1580, having earlier been appointed Catechist of his college. In this capacity he lectured on the Ten Commandments in the Pembroke chapel every Saturday and Sunday afternoon, and his lectures attracted a wide following from within the University and beyond. In 1585, treating the Fourth Commandment, Andrewes enunciated the doctrine of the Sabbath which later became identified with Puritanism. His views spread by means of hundreds of copies of student-transcribed notes which passed from hand to hand. Years later Andrewes, now a bishop and an ornament of Anglicanism, dissociated himself from the Sabbatarian theology of his Cambridge years. At this time, according to Peter Heylyn, he destroyed his original lecture notes and authorized one of his chaplains to disown anything attributed to them. Although his lectures were not published until after his death, their content had been well known since 1585.[94]

Greenham had been well acquainted with Andrewes at Cambridge, although we lack detailed knowledge about their relationship. He resigned his fellowship at Pembroke in 1570 to become rector in nearby Dry Drayton. A spiritual preacher with a zeal for reviving piety, his learning was great and his sermons among the most valuable of the day. Notes on his pulpit utterances circulated briskly, and the young men who studied with the minister formed a "school" which further extended his influence. Perhaps about 1586 Greenham wrote *A Treatise on the Sabbath*, though it was not published until later. His treatment of the Fourth Commandment closely resembles that of Andrewes.[95]

Little is known about the life of Greenham's stepson Bownde, a moderate Puritan who gained fame as the author of the new doctrine of the Sabbath.[96] He too attended Cambridge University, where he was a fellow of Peterhouse before becoming rector in Norton, Suffolk. There his zeal for godliness met a favorable response, and no later than 1586 parishioners entreated him to publish his sermons on the moral law. Bownde chose to emphasize the Fourth Commandment, believing the Sabbath was for educated people the most controversial point in religion. After finishing his manuscript about 1588, however, he discovered that Greenham had already completed a similar work. Greenham, the more learned of the two, asked Bownde to combine the discourses for publication. Bownde declined, wishing Greenham to publish first, but the latter died in 1594 before doing so, whereupon Bownde brought out *The Doctrine of the Sabbath* the following year. It may be true, as Bownde says, that he had "never read a leaf" of Greenham's treatise before sending his own manuscript to press, but the two men probably had discussed their common concern.[97]

Bownde's large quarto volume marked the emergence of a new phase in the history of English Sabbatarianism. The work is similar in structure and content to the treatises by Andrewes and Greenham, although more detailed and stricter in outlook. All three begin by discussing the theory of the Sabbath. They make the Fourth Commandment part of the moral rather than the ceremonial law. The Sabbath existed in the Garden of Eden before the introduction of the ceremonies, and the Patriarchs observed the day until its reinstatement at Mount Sinai. The Ten Commandments as a whole constitute a moral code, and each commandment must therefore be of the same moral character. Thus, the Sabbath is binding on Christians. The Lord's Day is the occasion to be observed. The Fourth Commandment required man to devote one full day in every seven to religious observance. But the Sabbath was transferred from Saturday to Sunday in New Testament times in order to commemorate the Resurrection. This weekly festival should be called the Lord's Day, a name used during apostolic times and one which conferred an honor lacking in both the Jewish term "Sabbath" and the heathen word "Sunday."[98]

Dispatching theory quickly, the three authors pay more attention to proper practice. They begin by describing the need for rest—Bownde contends that the "most *carefull, exact and precise rest*" required did not impose a Jewish yoke because Christians rested for different purposes from those of ancient Israel—and listing the activities prohibited on the Lord's Day.[99] Labor and travel on the Sabbath are forbidden. Bownde follows Andrewes, and both stick closely to the Old Testament in proscribing such employments as gathering or preparing manna; building, sowing, or harvesting; attending fairs or markets; buying and selling; burden-bearing; and journeying. Bownde also describes what teachers, students, lawyers, court officers, and physicians are not to do, and is stricter than earlier writers. Northbrooke had thought it legitimate to gather hay on Sunday and Greenham and Perkins permitted harvesting under certain stipulated conditions. Bownde denied it without exception: "for though the corne be in danger, yet better were for us, that it should rot on the ground, than for us by carying it in with the breach of the Sabbath, *to treasure up . . . unto our selves wrath against the day of wrath.*"[100] Man's obedience is greatest when he observes the Lord's Day despite many worldly reasons for doing otherwise.

Bownde permits the travel necessary to attend public worship, the ringing of one bell to give notice of religious assemblies (more are considered popish), and the liberty of preparing food and cooking hot meals. Although he discourages feasting on the Sabbath, he allows the servants of noblemen and great personages to prepare bountiful tables on that day, provided they do so without loss to religion. This evidence of class bias may have been an attempt to make Sabbatarianism palatable to the powerful. He allows works of mercy, but distinguishes between acts immediately necessary, such as quenching a fire and tending the sick, and those of imagined necessity. A good Sabbath rest requires careful advance planning.[101]

Sunday sporting and playing are banned. The prohibition includes "honest recreations" such as shooting, hunting, hawking, fencing, and bowling; and unlawful pastimes such as gaming, drinking, dancing, whoring, attending stage plays, bull- and bearbaiting, cockfighting, and dancing around Maypoles. Bownde also forbids the use of Sunday to discuss worldly business or to plan the duties of the forthcoming week.[102]

These negations were designed to serve affirmative purposes, and over half of the book describes the positive duties of the weekly celebration. The chief part of sanctifying the Lord's Day is to attend public worship, the "school of God," both morning and afternoon, and Bownde endorses the use of the magistrate's authority to enforce this duty. The remainder of the day is to be spent in praying privately, reading Scripture, meditating, discussing religion, singing Psalms, and doing works of mercy. The author recognizes the difficulty of attaining this ideal, but he reminds readers that divine punishment awaits Sabbath-breakers.[103]

The Sabbatarian doctrine devised by Andrewes, Greenham, and Bownde was a creative theological response to the changing conditions of English life. It represented a major theoretical achievement, one which Professor Knappen went so far as to call "the first and perhaps the only important English contribution to the development of Reformed theology in the first century of its history."[104] None of the constituent elements was entirely novel, and yet the theory as a whole marked a significant break with the past.

Sabbatarianism was to prove highly influential in Anglo-American history. For Bownde the Sabbath was "a tower to mount on high," and its proper observance was an index to the vitality of religion.[105] The conviction was gaining ground, apparently a part of the growing millennialism of the period, that well-kept Sabbaths were essential to the realization of the New Jerusalem. The Sabbatarian ideal emphasized a way of life in which duty to God outweighed the claims of Mammon, and in the context of the times the doctrine contained many progressive features. It refused to allow the necessity of physical survival or the desire for material prosperity to deny man his dignity and humanity. Sabbatarianism made for the highest moral standards, and nowhere would its beneficial effect on individual character and community life be more felt than in British America.

3

Good Sabbaths
Make Good Christians

THE EMERGENCE OF a unique attitude toward the Sabbath was a landmark in the transition from the medieval to the early modern age in England. The climate of opinion was receptive to the new outlook, and "one of the most striking and significant facts of the history of England during the seventeenth century," J. W. Allen wrote, "was the development and spread of what is known as Sabbatarianism. Many degrees of it appear, and we cannot say that, at any time, all Sabbatarians were Puritans. Long before 1640, however, all Puritans seem to have been Sabbatarians."[1]

None of the Continental countries possessed anything like Sabbatarianism (clergymen in Holland termed its underlying doctrine a *Figmentum Anglicanum*), but it struck deep roots in England on the eve of American colonization.[2] Two closely related events combined to insure that it would flower luxuriantly in the New World. Although the Church of England was a national institution commanding broad allegiance when *The Doctrine of the Sabbath* was published, Sabbatarianism met growing acceptance by middle-class Englishmen. Organized Puritanism had recently been broken up by Whitgift and Bancroft, but the moral temper of the nation was becoming more Puritan. All but the highest and lowest classes found it easy to conclude that good Sabbaths make good Christians.

Sabbatarianism became a distinguishing characteristic of Puritanism as early as the 1590s. Bownde's treatise initiated a quarrel over the question, which became entwined with other leading issues of the day. "It is almost incredible how taking this doctrine was," Thomas Fuller wrote of Bownde's volume, "partly because of its own purity, and partly for the eminent piety of such persons as maintained it."[3] This response sprang from religious and rational convictions. The economic argument against saints' days made a strong appeal to employers and employees in an emerging industrial order. The industrious poor found the compulsory observance of church-appointed holy days a "very high Burthen," since they were forced either to forego a day's wages or to risk ecclesiastical penalty for working.[4] Economists came to realize that church festivals were costly. Enforced idleness deprived the nation of an increment of wealth equal to the loss of wages from productive employment. Toward the end of the century John Pollexfen estimated the national loss at £500,000 for every holiday kept.[5] The use of Sunday for sports and pastimes created grave social problems, and magistrates made a good case for Sabbatarianism as a means of promoting morality and order.

The Lord's Day began to be precisely kept after the appearance of Bownde's book, especially in towns and areas where Puritanism was strongest. People became a law to themselves, rejoicing at their restraint in forbearing such sport as still permitted by statute. The stoutest fencer laid down his buckler; the most skillful archer unbent his bow, and May-games and morris dances were no longer sought. Some individuals were ashamed of their former pleasures; others gave them up for fear of their superiors; and many "left them off out of a politic compliance, lest otherwise they should be accounted licentious."[6]

At the same time Bownde's book aroused strong opposition. The hierarchy felt that the Sabbatarian doctrine showed a dangerous contempt for church authority by emphasizing the Lord's Day with the express intent of eclipsing all other holy days. They thought that Sabbath theology rested upon the wrong foundation: it reestablished a Jewish yoke which endangered Christian liberty. The teaching was also unchristian in regarding Sabbath-breaking as the principal procurer of God's wrath. Hence authorities suppressed *The Doctrine of the Sabbath*. In 1599 Archbishop Whitgift called it in; a year later Sir John Popham, the Lord Chief Justice of England, forbade any more copies to be printed. Bownde's volume became extremely scarce. Though it doubled in price, transcribed copies enjoyed great favor.[7]

A new reign seemingly offered Puritans a fresh opportunity and their leaders lost no time in seizing the occasion. Soon after James I arrived in London in early 1603, a group of Puritan ministers presented him with

the Millenary Petition, which stressed the need for further reform in relation to cermonies and liturgy, the ministry and preaching, and church
discipline. It also included a request "that the Lord's Day be not profaned; the rest upon holy days not so strictly urged."[8]

Although no Puritan, James was eager to win the approval of his subjects. He knew that Bownde's treatise had not eliminated Sunday abuses
and on 7 May issued a proclamation which acknowledged great neglect in
keeping the Sabbath and commanded that "no bear-baiting, bull-bait-
ing, interludes, common plays, or other like disordered and unlawful
exercises and pastimes" be allowed at any time upon the day. This proclamation failed to satisfy the Puritans.[9]

The King enjoyed theological argument and was quite willing to play
the role of arbiter in church affairs, so he agreed to summon a conference
to discuss ecclesiastical reform at Hampton Court early in 1604. He first
met with representatives from the episcopate, and later with two bishops
and the Puritan spokesmen. The request for a more reverent observance
of the Sabbath met the general approval of those present, but James saw
no reason for any major alteration in the liturgy or government of the
church. He particularly distrusted the political implications of Puritanism, knowing presbyterianism to be incompatible with the claims of absolute monarchy. He epitomized his opposition by declaring, "No Bishop, no King," and warned the Puritans to conform or he would harry
them out of the land.[10]

Hampton Court set the pattern for Stuart Erastianism by stressing the
identity of interest between the Crown and the Church. The conference
widened the breach between Anglican and Puritan and marked a significant step in linking the Puritans with strict control over Sunday conduct.
When James insisted upon ruling by prerogative, responsible only to
God, he precipitated a battle over the locus of sovereignty. Puritans and
common-law lawyers held that supreme authority in the realm lay in the
fundamental law, which comprised the divine law revealed in Scripture,
the common law, and statutory enactments; the monarch as well as the
subject was bound by the divine commandment with respect to the Sabbath. On such grounds they were ready to do battle with the king.[11]

After Hampton Court, in its first codification of the rules and regulations of the Anglican church since the Reformation, the government officially opposed Sabbatarianism. Bancroft, who presided over the Convocation of 1604, appreciated the need to reconstruct the church and provide
a new legal and administrative basis for checking Puritans and papists.
The assembly devised a body of 141 canons which the King confirmed in
September. The first 12 made belief in Anglican doctrines prerequisite to

membership in the Church of England. Canon 13 required everyone within the Church of England to "celebrate and keepe the Lords day, commonly called Sunday, and other Holy dayes according to Gods holy will and pleasure, and the Orders of the Church of England prescribed in that behalfe" by hearing the Word of God in private and public prayers, acknowledging their offences to God, reconciling themselves charitably to their neighbors, frequently receiving Holy Communion, visiting the poor and sick, and using all godly and sober conversation. These directions incorporated Elizabethan policy on the proper celebration of Sundays and holy days.

But a new posture had arisen since 1559 and Puritans objected to the canons because they failed to reflect current realities. Canon 13 and others directly countered the Puritan theory of the Sabbath by equating the Lord's Day with saints' days and holy days, thus putting human institutions on a par with divine ones. Yet Bancroft accommodated his adversaries in part. He knew that the Puritans strongly opposed Sunday labor, and Canon 13 did not grant permission to work on Sundays or saints' days, even under special circumstances. But the canons made no mention of Sunday sports or recreations; people therefore assumed that they were permitted.

The Canons of 1604 met strong disapproval in various quarters, but they furnished a weapon with which to enforce conformity and under Bancroft, elevated to Canterbury in late 1604, the bishops used it. The number of Nonconformists actually deprived of their spiritual charges has long been a matter of dispute and uncertainty, with estimates ranging from a low of 49 to a high of 300 or more. Babbage's study concludes that at least 80 and possibly 90 ministers in fifteen different dioceses were deprived. Once again Bancroft had decisively checked the Puritans—at least temporarily.[12]

At this point Bownde reentered the lists by publishing *Sabbathum Veteris et Novi Testamenti: Or the True Doctrine of the Sabbath* (London, 1606). He dedicated this book to John Jegon, Bishop of Norwich, who was notorious for the rigor with which he enforced conformity. Perhaps Bownde hoped by this means to secure better treatment for dissenting ministers. The revised and enlarged volume tightened and amplified the earlier argument, countered objections, and made the duties of the Lord's Day even more rigorous.

Thomas Rogers, Bancroft's chaplain, replied the following year. According to him, after the Puritans failed in their effort to introduce innovation in doctrine and to subvert the episcopacy, they abandoned that course and, in 1595, "set upon us afresh again by dispersing in printed books . . . their sabbath speculations, and presbyterian . . . directions for the observation of the Lord's day.'' Rather than attack the bishops they attacked holy days, charging that the church had no authority to sanctify to holy uses any day other than the Lord's Day. This opened a wide gate to ''licentiousness, liberty, and profaneness'' on the holy days, which all sorts of people used to the dishonor of God and the gross contempt of the orders of the church. Rather than build up presbyteries the Puritans set up a new idol, ''Saint Sabbath.'' This introduced a ''new, and more than either Jewish or popish superstition into the land . . . and therewith doctrine most erroneous, dangerous, and antichristian.''

Rogers feared the consequences of these faulty tenets, ''so plausible are they to men either popularly religious, or preposterously and injudiciously zealous.'' He cited several examples of clergymen who equated Sabbath-breaking with adultery or murder to illustrate the horrible heresies spawned by the doctrine and took pride in having been the man who called these impieties to the attention of authorities. Rogers was the first person publicly to criticize Bownde's publication, and the battle of the books over the Sabbath question grew in intensity in later years.[13]

DESPITE EXPRESSED OPPOSITION, Sabbatarianism *was* gaining favor. Steady growth of the Puritan spirit made people exceedingly exact in the performance of religious duty. ''I like you and your company very well,'' someone told the Puritan Richard Rogers, ''but you are so precise.'' ''O Sir,'' replied the Essex clergyman, ''I serve a precise God.''[14] Sabbatarianism admirably suited men of this temperament, and it grew during the reign of James I.

Parliament came close to enacting a bill on the subject. Elizabeth vetoed the Sabbath bill passed by both houses in 1585, and only in 1601 did the Commons, inspired by a Puritan element, again try to secure a bill for the better keeping of the Sabbath. We know nothing about its contents, but the house wanted it divided and one of the bills subsequently introduced prohibited the holding of fairs and markets on Sunday upon penalty of ten pounds and forfeiture of the goods. The bill used the word ''Sabbath,'' but in committee ''Sunday'' was substituted. This terminological dispute indicates that ''Sabbath'' was now associated with a Puritan mentality or strict Sabbath observance based upon the Fourth Commandment. The bill passed the Commons and went through two readings in the Lords, then nothing more was heard of it. A second bill, introduced by Sir Robert Wroth and Sir Francis Hastings, two Puritan worthies, aimed at enforcing regular attendance at church on Sundays by improving the collection of the shilling fine for willful absence. The bill aroused considerable controversy and eventually lost by one vote.[15]

Under James, the Commons, which contained a Puritan element but was not yet a Puritan body, had much to say about the Sabbath. James's first Parliament sat in five different sessions from 1604 to 1610, and in January 1606 a member introduced a bill to improve Lord's Day observance. Few details of the debate have survived, but two members observed that cessation from labor on Sunday was sufficient recreation for people. The bill passed the Commons and reached the committee stage in the Lords.[16]

Puritans were quick to introduce the Sabbath question in James's second Parliament, which met for only two months in 1614. Soon after the session opened, both Nicholas Fuller, a prominent London Puritan, and an unidentified member introduced bills urging improved Sabbath observance. The debate indicates that the main concerns of the Commons were use of the day for transacting ordinary business, "wherein the Lawyers most faulty," Sunday sports, and Sunday drinking. The bill finally passed the lower house, and in the upper house the Archbishop of York reported that the committee thought its "Drift and Purpose" good but that some amendment was still needed. But the Addled Parliament was dissolved without further action on the bill.[17]

Meanwhile, clergymen were urging Sabbatarianism by pulpit and press. The treatises of Greenham and Bownde had won a following, and other divines took up the subject, enabling a contemporary to write that the doctrine was "found in the hands of the whole kingdome." The sermons preached at Paul's Cross seem to have denounced Sabbath profanations with increasing frequency during the early reign of James.[18]

An Anglican bishop, Lewis Bayly (d. 1631), exerted wide influence in advancing Sabbatarianism during these years. Although he demonstrated Puritan leanings soon after completing his education at Oxford, Bayly was consecrated Bishop of Bangor in 1616. His *Practise of Piety*, a devotional guide for householders published early in the century, won an extraordinary popularity in and beyond Puritan circles. Bayly lacked originality in treating the Sabbath. He paid scant attention to theory but eloquently affirmed that the whole sum of religion lay in proper observance of the Lord's Day: "The *conscionable* keeping of the Sabbath, is the *Mother* of all Religion, and good discipline in the Church. Take away the Sabbath . . . and what will shortly become of *Religion* . . . ? *The Sabbath day is* Gods *Market day*, for the weekes provision, wherein *hee* will have us to come . . . and *buy of him, without silver or money*, the *Bread* of Angels, and *Water* of life, the Wine of the Sacraments, and *Milke* of the Word, to feede our Soules: . . . Hee is not *farre* from true *Pietie*, who makes conscience to *keepe* the *Sabbath* day: but he who can *dispense* with his conscience, to *breake* the *Sabbath* for his own profit or pleasure:

his *heart* never yet felt, what eyther the *feare* of God or *true* Religion meaneth."[19] *The Practise of Piety* required rest from servile labor, recreations, and sports on the Sabbath and consecration of that rest wholly to the service of God.

The spread of Puritan ideas inspired churchwardens and civil magistrates to work for improved Sunday observance. The Church still exercised its ancient discipline, keeping close watch over private lives. Churchwardens in each parish presented offenders to the ordinary at his annual visitation, and the ordinary cited those charged to appear in spiritual courts. Wrongdoers who persisted in evil ways after receiving ecclesiastical censure could be punished in civil courts. The ecclesiastical court records, which supply the best evidence of contemporary religious and social conditions in the early seventeenth century, contain many cases involving the Lord's Day.

Holy Trinity in the town of Ely was a typical parish, according to Roland G. Usher, its story "an epitome of the record of all England." Neither Catholicism nor Puritanism tainted the jurisdiction, whose records are complete, well kept, and unusually full for the time. The number of presentments for Sabbath-breaking there was one in 1582 and none in 1584; but after Bownde's book appeared the number shot to twenty-five in 1601, six in 1603, twelve in 1604, and twenty-two in 1607. More than Bancroft's administrative vigor was apparently at work here. And in Littleport parish in the same diocese, thirty of fifty-one presentments in 1606 were for breach of the Sabbath.[20]

Sunday labor constituted one of the major abuses of the rest day. Evidence from widely scattered areas shows that most of the presentments for servile work involved agricultural pursuits, and local magistrates were more willing to enforce the Sabbath rest than were central government authorities. Women seem to have been charged rarely. But merely to be cited meant the loss of a day to attend court, and dismissal with an admonition cost fourpence in court fees. On occasion a humiliating public penance was imposed.[21]

Sunday sports gave rise to serious misbehavior. Recreations as well as drinking in alehouses were strictly prohibited during time of divine service, and the church records contain many cases of individuals presented for tippling, bowling, morris dancing, and playing football, tennis, or "fives" (hitting a ball with the hands, usually against the church) during public worship. At Crewkerne in Taunton the wardens presented Alexander Howell for "that hee did Catch birds with his nett on the Saboth day being the forenoone"; he was condemned to do penance. At Wells in Somersetshire in 1610 and at Yorkshire in 1613 and 1615 men who bowled or played games upon Sunday were presented before civil courts.[22]

The crux of the problem of Sunday sports came from their use after the second religious service of the day. Neither the Royal Proclamation of 1603 nor the Canons of 1604 explicitly prohibited most Sunday pastimes, so people felt free to engage in them. The government encouraged archery and the development of healthy bodies for reasons of state, and the Church of England opposed strict suppression of amusements on the Lord's Day because of its teaching that man consisted of body as well as soul. E. R. Brinkworth found no convicions for Sunday sports, so long as they were not during service time, in Oxford archdeaconry during the period he studied.[23] But Puritans insisted upon a complete sanctification of the rest day. Like Augustine, they thought it better to plow than to dance on the Sabbath, but they even opposed plowing.

England was not yet receptive to such an outlook, but both religious and rational convictions were leading that way. The faithful maintained that Sunday recreations kept people from the service of God, and the magistrates held that Sunday merrymaking often led to drunkenness, immorality, and violence. Many authorities concluded that nothing short of a total ban would eliminate abuses. In 1607, for example, the Devonshire justices suppressed church-ales and similar revels. Eight years later the assize court at Exeter in Devon returned to the matter because of the ''infinite number of inconveniences daily arising'' from such activities, including several manslaughters committed at two church-ales within the county in less than a month. The justices ordered the utter suppression of all revels, church-ales, and bullbaitings.[24]

In the last analysis the successful establishment of the Puritan theory of the Sabbath depended upon public acceptance, and countless persons shouldered its demands in these years when the Reformation was being consolidated in England. The diary of Lady Margaret Hoby, the earliest known British woman diarist, shows the influence of Sabbatarianism on the life of an upper-class woman of the period. In 1596, Lady Margaret, already twice-widowed, married Thomas Posthumous Hoby and took up residence on a country estate at Hackness in Yorkshire. Three years later she began keeping a daily personal record, largely to assist herself in religious self-examination. This spiritual ledger reveals a deeply religious person. She was reading Bownde's treatise on the Sabbath and practicing its precepts when she started her diary in 1599, at the age of twenty-eight. She regarded Saturday as a vestibule to the Lord's Day, planning her entire round of activities so as to be able properly to celebrate the weekly festival and examining the state of her soul more carefully on Saturdays than on other weekdays. At the same time she allowed herself some liberties on the Lord's Day which Puritans would later forbid.[25]

In 1611 John Brerewood provoked a controversy over Sunday labor which revealed much about contemporary attitudes toward the subject. The young man was apprenticed to Thomas Shipton, a London grocer, who sent him to Chester on business. Upon returning home, he refused to work on the Sabbath when his master ordered him to do light duties such as bidding guests and fetching wine. The apprentice was nephew to Edward Brerewood, professor of astronomy at Gresham College in London, who concluded that John was suffering from an acute case of conscience brought on by learning from the Reverend Nicholas Byfield of Chester that to perform such work was a sinful transgression of God's commandment. John talked of refusing to obey Shipton or leaving his service, and such talk troubled his uncle, who had previously found it hard to steer his orphaned and errant charge in the right path. Fearing an act of folly which might ruin John and make himself liable to damages, since he had gone surety on his nephew's indenture of apprenticeship, Professor Brerewood wrote to Byfield, refuting his seductive doctrine.[26]

Christopher Hill has seized upon this case to support his conclusion that "Sabbatarianism might stimulate a critical independence in prentices and journeymen."[27] So it might, but not in this instance. According to Nicholas Byfield and his brother Richard, John had misled his uncle about the reasons for his unsettled mind; the real reason was a woman.[28] Love-struck, he had feigned a wounded conscience in order to escape service before his apprenticeship was half-completed.[29]

The controversy illuminates the social and political ramifications of a religious idea. In his *Learned Treatise of the Sabbath,* Professor Brerewood argued that the law of nations binds servants to their masters and that this law had not been dissolved by the law of God. The Fourth Commandment was given only to masters. God did not want to put servants, who were but their masters' living instruments, in a position where they would have to choose between God and man in rendering obedience. A servant's duty was to obey his master unquestioningly; any sin incurred in doing exacted work was the master's and not his own. Brerewood maintained that the Fourth Commandment prohibited only servile work and not light duties. He also contended that Sunday work was not in violation of the divine law, since the Jewish Sabbath of the Fourth Commandment had expired and the Lord's Day was not divinely established. The church and the prince regulated Sunday observance, and they did not require complete abstention from labor. The dregs of Byfield's doctrine, the Professor warned, would lead to "nothing but disturbance and sedition both in Church and Commonwealth."[30]

Brerewood's argument was authoritarian politically and socially. His views would permit authorities to command Sunday work, and as servants of the state the people would be bound to submit even if they regarded the labor as sinful. It would enable masters to exploit servants, the consequences of which can readily be imagined in an emerging industrial society.

Richard Byfield, who later served in the Westminster Assembly, responded for his dead brother. He reasserted the perpetual morality of the Lord's Day. The Fourth Commandment is a law of nature, obligatory upon servants as well as masters. A servant is not the animated tool of an earthly superior, but a human being responsible to his maker. As God's servant he is free from his master's work on the Sabbath, although his master may enjoin him to do the Lord's work then. All works were forbidden on the rest day, not only heavy toil or the pursuit of riches.

Byfield refuted the charge that Sabbatarianism inspired insubordination. He insisted that Brerewood's own doctrine endangered society and religion and put servants and inferiors under an unsupportable burden, "which hath alwaies (through mans corruption) caused rebellion and disturbance." It took servants from under the command of their rulers, "for if God may not command them to his Service, because as you say, it is against the law of nature; How may Princes command them to their occasions." The law of nations, a positive law, could not annul the Fourth Commandment. As for servants and masters, Sabbatarianism at most empowered the servant submissively to refuse unlawful commands, not to cast off subjection to his master's authority. As a responsible being, "the servant is not to fulfill the boundlesse and unlawfull puttings forth of that [his master's] power." Any master "by nature is ready to preferre his humour, pride, and profit, before the feare of sinne: and will not easily bee persuaded there is sinne in that which is no breach of any divine commandement, as you wickedly have taught, which is no lesse than *to teach rebellion against the Lord.*" Thus, the consequences of Brerewood's doctrine must be the triumph of atheism and profaneness.[31]

Byfield was historically correct in observing that loyalty to the nation-state replaced submission to the feudal lord and then the Puritan belief in obedience to God challenged all existing loyalties. Byfield based his demand for a Sunday free from work on the Fourth Commandment, and he took this stand at a time when Sunday was the workingman's only rest day. In advancing this principle the Puritan minister conferred political and social benefits upon his own and all succeeding generations.[32]

John Winthrop affords a fine example of growing reverence, on the eve of American colonization, for the Lord's Day. The future governor of the Massachusetts Bay colony and the doctrine of the Sabbath appeared on the scene almost simultaneously: Winthrop entered this world at Suffolk in 1588, at the time clergymen were fashioning the Puritan theory. He felt the powerful stirrings of religion in his heart when he was about eighteen and, under the "strong excersises of Conscience," forthwith determined that he "could no longer dally with Religion." But for more than a decade he continued to experience spiritual turmoil, until he "concluded there was no way to help it, but by walking more close with God and more strict observation of all dutyes." Perhaps the precise Sabbath observance of Winthrop's young manhood reflected this legalism. In 1607, for example, he discovered that if he deferred reading and prayer till three o'clock Saturday afternoon (the hour when good Puritans began their Sabbath observance) for the performance of a needless task, his "herte was verie muche unsettled." In 1613, when Winthrop (temporarily) found his spiritual condition much improved, he resolved to give himself totally to his Savior. "I will diligently observe the Lords Sabaoth," the young man promised, "bothe for the avoidinge and preventinge worldly busines, and also for the religious spendinge of suche tymes as are free from publique exercises, viz. the morninge, noone, and evening."

But bondage to the Law with its ceaseless cycle of sin and repentance made him melancholy, and at this point Winthrop perceived the difference between the covenant of grace and the covenant of works, the latter "onely held forth in the law of Moses to drive us to Christ." The sinner could never earn salvation by keeping the commandments, and Winthrop fixed his eyes on the covenant of grace. While acknowledging that his own efforts counted for naught, he nevertheless continued to stress the importance of Sabbath observance to the Christian life. Though we are saved by grace we must keep the Law.[33]

As shown in the *Experiencia,* his own account of his spiritual development, Winthrop equated good Sabbaths with good Christians before the Puritan exodus to New England began. Christians were bound to make use of their "Sabaothe businesse all the weeke after," working to stir up in themselves on weekdays the "speciall affections" afforded by the religious exercises of the Lord's Day. "For certainly," he declared, using a figure of speech popular at the time, "the Sabaothe is the markett of our soules."[34] On this day the person who loved the world with unweaned affections found his way back to God. At times, however, worldly thoughts engulfed even Winthrop on Sunday. His heart getting loose one Sabbath in 1616, through lack of watchfulness and resolution, "it gate so deepe into the world as I could not get it free," thus making itself "utterly unfitt for dutye all the week followinge." But at its best, the Sabbath was a joyful festival.[35]

Despite growing middle-class acceptance, Sabbatarianism aroused hostility from other elements in English society during the early seventeenth century. James I, who conducted affairs of state, traveled, and enjoyed plays and recreations on Sunday, was not eager to restrict the Sunday liberties of the people. The Privy Council met and witnessed public spectacles on the Lord's Day, and the Church of England threw its weight against Sabbatarian docrine. Aristocrats, unwilling to sacrifice their pleasure for the sake of middle-class morality, took their cue from the king and court, and some conscious defiance of Sabbatarian principles appeared in the more exalted walks of life.[36]

The lower classes had little taste for an austere Sunday. Thomas Shepard, born in 1605, described the Northamptonshire town of his youth as profane and ignorant, a "sink and Sodom"; so, too, was neighboring Adthorp, where even children were taught to sing and sport and dance at Sunday ales. Richard Baxter, born in 1615 in Shropshire, recalled ignorant and immoral ministers who read prayers but lacked religion and did not preach on Sunday. He also remembered shepherds' stirring up popular demand for a hasty Sunday service so that people could spend the rest of the day dancing around the Maypole on the village green. Baxter's father, a conforming Anglican, refused to take part in order to read the Scriptures to his family, an exercise which street noises made impossible. The unregenerate masses and the "dark corners of the land" were not yet ready for Sabbatarianism. Even in such a godly household as John Winthrop's the servants presented a problem. When Thomasine, Winthrop's second wife, lay dying in 1616, she summoned family and servants to her side to close earthly accounts. "Thou hast been in badd servinge longe in an Alehouse etc," she told Anne Adams, "thou makest no conscience of the Sabaothe; when I would have had thee gone to Church thou wouldst not, etc." "Thou art a good woman," she told Mercy Smith, "bringe up thy children well, you poore folks commonly spoyle your children, in suffering [them] to break Gods Sabaothes, etc."[37]

Nevertheless, the tide was running with the Sabbatarians. They stood to gain by patiently waiting for the spread of Puritan ideas to win additional recruits, just as they stood to lose by trying to impose a doctrine drawn from the Old Testament upon unwilling compatriots. But zeal overbalanced wisdom, and the pressure to make actual practice accord with right theory became an important factor in the ensuing crisis.[38]

A NEW PHASE in the development of English Sabbatarianism opened in 1618 with publication of the Book of Sports. This royal declaration applied to the entire nation a policy devised a year earlier to settle a conflict over Sunday recreations in Lancashire. That conflict dated back to Elizabethan times and was aggravated by the fact that popish recusants abounded in the county. In the late sixteenth century local magistrates had attempted to suppress both the brutal and innocent forms of Sunday sports, acting for reasons of prudence and religion as well as from a belief that Roman Catholics especially profaned the Lord's Day. County authorities continued to present Sabbath-breakers in the first part of the seventeenth century, but perhaps less rigorously after the worst danger from recusancy passed. In any event, empty churches and Sunday disorders were soon common, and on 8 August 1616 the Lancashire justices of the peace issued orders to secure general attendance at church and otherwise enforce proper Sabbath observance. Their orders for the most part reaffirmed existing laws and canons in an effort to bring actual practice up to minimum national requirements. But the local magistrates wished to prohibit all Sunday recreations, not just the unlawful ones. On their own authority they went beyond current legislation to ban piping, dancing, or any other profanation upon any part of the Sabbath or upon any festival day during divine service.[39]

This repression of Sunday sports deepened the antagonism between Puritans and papists, with the result that "both parties, by a kind of mutual repulsion, were equally distinguished for their superstitious practices." Many believed that Roman Catholic leaders encouraged the people to dance and sport rather than attend established worship on Sunday, and in the autumn of 1616 the new bishop, Thomas Morton, attempted to redress this gross abuse.[40]

Such was the tense situation James encountered when he stopped in Lancashire on his return homeward from Scotland in August 1617. Two days after his arrival, a delegation of servants prompted by Catholic gentry presented the monarch with a petition in which they asked for greater freedom for Sunday sports. James responded with a speech about liberty to "pipeing and honest recreation," and rural folk disturbed a neighboring church the following Sunday with piping and dancing. Bishop Morton caused the piper and the chief offender to be punished, thus antagonizing prominent Roman Catholics, who denounced the impositions as tyrannical and pleaded with the King to allow innocent Sunday recreations to those whose callings prohibited them during the week. James disavowed any intention of encouraging such profanations and asked Bishop

Morton how he might satisfy the complainants by permitting liberty without licentiousness. Despite his disavowal, the King and his court indulged in loose revelry that afternoon at Hoghton Tower. He witnessed rushbearing and piping, feasted sumptuously, and enjoyed a masque in the garden followed by witty speeches, gay frolics, and fashionable Lancashire dances. The next day Bishop Morton submitted a list of limitations to be imposed upon all who enjoyed Sunday sports. The King approved Morton's draft after minor amendment, and on 27 August the secretary of state signed the Declaration of Sports for Lancashire.[41]

The situation in Lancashire was basically a microcosm of that in all England, so James published the declaration in somewhat fuller form and applied it to the entire nation on 24 May 1618. *The Kings Majesties Declaration to His Subjects concerning Lawful Sports to Be Used* first explained the reasons for the royal rebuke of "some puritans and precise people" in Lancashire. Their unlawful prohibition of Sunday sports produced two evils. It hindered conversions in a heavily Catholic county by enabling priests to persuade people that "no honest mirth or recreation" is lawful on Sundays. It also barred "the common and meaner sort of people from using such exercises as may make their bodies more able for war, whenever we or our successors shall have occasion to use them; and in place thereof, set up filthy tiplings and drunkenness, and breed a number of idle and discontented speeches in their alehouses." Since the common people must labor on weekdays in order to live, when shall they exercise if not on Sundays and holidays?

The Declaration of Sports ordered that people were not to be "disturbed, letted, or discouraged from any lawful recreation" after the end of divine service on Sunday afternoon. The lawful recreations included dancing, for either men or women; archery for men; leaping, vaulting, "or any other such harmless recreation"; May-games, the setting up of Maypoles, "and other sports therewith used"; Whitsun-ales; and morris dances. Women were free to carry rushes into church for decorative purposes. Games designated as unlawful and prohibited on Sunday were bearbaiting, bullbaiting, and interludes; bowling was prohibited to "the meaner sort of people" at all times. The Book of Sports made attendance at divine service in one's own parish church prerequisite to participation in Sunday sports and permitted gaming only within one's own parish. No offensive weapons were to be carried or used during time of recreation.[42]

The King may well have thought that the Book of Sports would steer between excessive piety and corrosive irreligion. But making church attendance a test of eligibility to participate in sports was disliked both by the ungodly, who opposed compulsory worship, and by the pious, who resented the employment of a bribe to secure the performance of a religious duty. The freedom granted in the Declaration, which permitted rather than commanded Sunday sports, sprang from no altruistic motive. James designed the Book of Sports less to advance religious and social welfare than to condition men's bodies for the service of the state and to reconcile conflict.[43]

The significance of the Declaration lies in its reactionary character. James simply reiterated what had long been the law of the land; he did not enunciate new policy. Failing to appreciate how much public opinion had changed since the early seventeenth century, he seriously misjudged a potentially explosive situation. Hence the Declaration stood little chance of doing good. The unregenerate element in society had never voluntarily attended church or kept the Sabbath holy. The religious element in society, whether Anglican or Puritan, together with magistrates who had seen at first hand the harmful social consequences of misspent Sundays, had been struggling to secure a stricter Sabbath observance. Neither group was likely to change its attitude merely because the King reaffirmed the old ways.

The chief result of the Book of Sports was to widen the breach between Anglican and Puritan. The King attempted to associate improved use of the Lord's Day with Puritans alone. The Declaration spoke of "puritans and precise people" as instigators of the trouble and charged their policy of curbing Sunday sports with causing drunkenness and seditious speeches. In each respect, James libeled the Puritans. Anglicans and civil magistrates also wished to eliminate Sunday abuses; drunkenness and riots on Sunday predated the movement to suppress Sunday sports; and everyone knew that Puritans refused to countenance tippling and idle gossip in alehouses. Peter Heylyn called the Declaration "the first Blow, in effect, which had been given, in all his [James's] time, to the new Lord's-day-Sabbath, then so much applauded."[44] Its publication greatly accelerated the process of equating Sabbatarianism with Puritanism: henceforth advocacy of Sabbatarianism opened one to the charge of puritanism, implying an attitude inimical to the state as well as a desire for a loftier moral standard. By making no allowance for their views, James inspired in Sabbatarians a new determination to press their demands more insistently.

The monarch transmitted the Declaration to his bishops with an order that it be read from pulpits, but resistance was immediately forthcoming. Some clergy, including the Archbishop of Canterbury, determined to refuse compliance, while a few bold spirits preached against the royal proclamation. James prudently withdrew his order, but the Declaration had already begun its divisive work. In Worcestershire in 1619, parishioners maliciously accused Gerard Prior, Vicar of Eldersfield, of having preached a sermon in July 1618 against Sunday sports, and also of immoral conduct. The bishop suspended Prior not because of immorality, whether true or not, but because of his Puritan attitude toward the Sabbath. And in 1621 Bishop Bayly, famous for *The Practise of Piety*, was ''sent to the Fleet, for disputing malapertly with the King on the Sabbath.''[45]

Publication of the Book of Sports, which occurred the same year as the outbreak of the Thirty Years' War and the meeting of the synod at Dort to reformulate Calvinist doctrine, imparted new urgency to the vital question of the locus of sovereignty in England at a critical time. Although James claimed the law of the land and the canons of the church as authority for his proclamation, he never once cited a specific statute or canon and repeatedly offered ''our express pleasure'' as the basis for the statement. This assertion of the royal prerogative alarmed Puritans and common lawyers, and both groups were eager to press their views.[46]

As a result, the Sunday question was much to the fore when Parliament met in 1621. Soon after the House of Commons settled down to business, Sir Walter Erle, a Puritan member from Dorsetshire, introduced a bill for punishment of ''divers Abuses on the Sabaoth-day, called *Sunday.*'' Presumably this was the measure passed by the house in 1614, now amplified with prohibitions of the recreations allowed by the Book of Sports. At the bill's second reading, on 15 February, Thomas Shepherd of Shaftesbury, a Lincoln's Inn lawyer (not the Puritan Thomas Shepard), assaulted Erle's measure. He first attacked the title, arguing that the law understood the Sabbath to be Saturday. He next took exception to the prohibition of dancing and other exercises on Sunday; the lawfulness of such recreations was for divines rather than legislators to determine. Even more important, the bill countered the Declaration of Sports. King James, like King David in the Old Testament, bade us to dance, and the house ought not legislate to the contrary without royal approval. Lastly, Shepherd charged that the bill ''growes from a kind of Cattle that will not submitt themselves to the Ceremonyes of the Church.'' Its spirit was Puritan, ''refractorie to good order.'' The critic denounced justices of the peace for favoring Puritans, taxed members for making snares to catch papists but not so much as a ''Mouse-trappe to catch a Puritan,'' and denounced the author of the bill as ''a perturbator of the Peace.'' A hostile Commons interrupted Shepherd's outburst and brought the offender to the bar.[47]

The members who debated the matter the following day included Sir Edward Coke and several Puritan leaders. John Pym made his first recorded speech in the Commons on this occasion. He attacked Shepherd for denouncing a measure that the house had passed in 1614 and wished to pass again and lamented the effort to set King against Commons and Commons against itself. The will of God was best interpreted by the lower house, which wanted no Declaration of Sports. Pym demanded harsh penalties for Shepherd, and the chamber, judging him unworthy to sit as a member, ordered a new election to fill his vacancy.[48]

Now the King spoke. He thought the censure of Shepherd just, but wished that the lower house would strike Puritans as it had papists. He had published the Book of Sports after mature deliberation and advised Commons not to enact a bill diametrically opposed. Still eager to preserve good relations with the Crown, the members passed and sent to the Lords in early March a bill that harmonized in every respect with the royal proclamation. Gone were Erle's prohibitions against church-ales, dancing, May-games, and the like. In their place were bans on the baiting of bulls and bears, interludes, and gaming outside one's own parish. The Lords accepted this measure on 28 May, substituting "Lord's Day" for "Sabbath" in the title to discourage the Judaism to which many were inclined. Passage of "An Act for the punishing of divers Abuses committed on the Lord's Day, called *Sunday*" culminated years of legislative effort. But on that same day the King communicated his intention to adjourn Parliament speedily. He refused to accept the bill, and it never became law. James himself prevented Parliament's wishes on Sabbath observance from becoming state policy.[49]

At the opening of Parliament in 1624 a member of Commons introduced "the Bill of the Sabaoth" with a reminder that it had passed both houses in 1621 and had ever since 1585 passed the House of Commons. Bearing the same title as in 1621, the bill sailed through both chambers within two weeks and only required the royal assent to become law. The only point upon which discussion is reported was referred to judges for an opinion, and they ruled that the exercise of arms after evening prayer was not a sport forbidden by law and so not within the act. Evidently the bill pleased those who found the king's Book of Sports inadequate. But James declined to approve the measure "on the ground that it contradicted his own allowance of lawful recreations, and that this act would give the Puritans their way, who think religion consists in two sermons a day."[50]

SABBATARIANISM WAS HIGHLY divisive when James died in 1625, and under Charles I the dispute became more bitter. He governed arbitrarily, forcing people to choose sides; under the circumstances the King strengthened his alliance with the Church and the Puritans drew closer to Parliament. William Laud, an Arminian of High Church views who was translated to London in 1628 and elevated to Canterbury in 1633, threw the weight of the religious establishment behind divine-right monarchy and uniformity in worship. In 1628 the King required all clergy strictly to conform to the doctrinal articles of the Church of England. Commons responded by declaring that whoever advanced religious innovation or sought to introduce popery or Arminianism ''or other opinions disagreeing from the true and orthodox Church, shall be reputed a capital enemy to this kingdom and the commonwealth.'' The bishops' disciplining of Nonconformists and the birth of an heir to the throne stimulated the flight of religious exiles to New England.[51]

The Sabbath question was one of the issues between rival camps in the years preceding the Civil War. Parliament was still determined to assert its initiative in the matter of Sunday observance, and in 1625 the very first item introduced in the House of Commons was the 1621 bill. It quickly passed through all legislative stages in both houses, received the royal assent on 11 July, and became law. The King found it prudent to accept a measure which Parliament had long desired. The act prohibited people within the realm or any of its dominions from gaming out of their own parishes on the Lord's Day or from participating in bearbaiting, bullbaiting, interludes, common plays, or other unlawful pastimes within their own parish, on penalty of three shillings and fourpence for every offense.[52]

In 1627 a bill ''for the further Reformation of sundry Abuses committed on the Lord's Day'' made its way through both houses and received the royal assent. This legislation for the first time proscribed certain types of labor on Sunday. It forbade carriers, wagoners, carters, wainmen, and cattle drovers from traveling in pursuit of their callings on the Lord's Day upon penalty of twenty shillings for every offense, and it prohibited butchers from exercising their trade on Sunday upon pain of six shillings and eightpence for each offense. Two years later the King adjourned Parliament and ruled without it for eleven years.[53]

Work was still done on Sunday after 1627, though authorities attempted to stop it. In the Puritan stronghold of London two successive lord mayors strictly enforced the statute, with one of them exceeding its requirements. In 1629 Lord Mayor Raynton prohibited an old woman from selling apples on Sunday in the churchyard. Bishop Laud protested civil enforcement of this kind as an infringement upon his ecclesiastical jurisdiction. Work on Sunday would undoubtedly continue as long as state policy permitted play on Sunday, and Sunday recreations led to renewed controversy.[54]

In Somersetshire and neighboring western counties, Sunday wakes and ales remained prime incentives to disorder. In 1627 the judges at the summer assizes revived an order, originally issued for Devon in 1615, forbidding such festivities. The judges directed the ministers to publish this order thrice yearly and the county magistrates to enforce it. But trouble continued. Alarmed at the numerous indictments in the county for murdering bastards begotten at wakes and ales, in 1632 local authorities appealed to Sir Thomas Richardson, the Lord Chief Justice. He reissued the 1627 order and directed ministers to publish it from their pulpits. But Laud complained to the King that this civil edict impaired ecclesiastical jurisdiction; Charles directed Richardson to revoke his order; and the Lord Chief Justice reluctantly did so.

Local justices of the peace then petitioned Charles for support, but Laud, now Archbishop of Canterbury, appealed to him to end the strife by issuing a declaration on the subject. The primate asked the bishop how church feasts were conducted, and seventy-two diocesan clergy testified to the beneficial influence of the feasts of dedication in promoting church attendance and concord. On 18 October, before receiving this report, Charles reissued his father's Declaration of Sports under the same title as in 1618. He prefaced the Declaration of 1633 with an account of the circumstances which led to the earlier document and added, "Now our express will and pleasure is, that these feasts with others shall be observed." Local authorities were to see that people were not troubled for their lawful recreations, while bishops were to see that the order was published in all parish churches.[55]

The second Book of Sports widened and deepened the cleavage between the King and the Laudian church on the one hand and Puritan Sabbatarians on the other. The pattern of clerical reactions was similar to that in 1618. Laud does not seem to have punished refusals to read the Declaration with particular severity, but Archbishop Richard Neile was a strict disciplinarian and some bishops enforced the requirement vigorously. Rightly or wrongly, Puritans held their "malignant adversary," Laud, chiefly responsible.[56] Emigration to New England greatly quickened as a result of the Book of Sports. Many clergymen, including John Cotton, John Davenport, Thomas Hooker, and Thomas Shepard, fled at this time.[57]

Reissue of the Book of Sports also intensified the literary warfare over the Sabbath. The ablest theologians brought their learning to bear on complex problems in dense polemical tomes that fell rapidly from the press.[58] "So thoroughly was the subject exhausted by these writers," James Gairdner concluded, "that in all the literature of the last two centuries it would be impossible to point out a single fact or argument bearing upon the authority of the Sabbath which has not been fully discussed by the divines of Charles the First's time."[59]

Defenders of King and Church rushed apologias into print. Francis White, Bishop of Ely, and Peter Heylyn, Laud's chaplain and future biographer, assumed major responsibility, dividing the task of correcting Sabbatarian errors and bringing Puritans to the truth. White, taking the theological argument, published *A Treatise of the Sabbath-Day: Containing, A Defence of the Orthodoxall Doctrine of the Church of England against Sabbatarian Novelty* (London, 1635). Heylyn, taking the historical and practical argument, published *The History of the Sabbath* (London, 1636).[60] He contended that Sabbatarianism was unknown until discovered by Puritans during the reign of Elizabeth and that the recreations authorized by the Book of Sports were inconsistent with neither Mosaic nor Christian law. Richard Byfield (or perhaps William Prynne) answered White in *The Lords Day, the Sabbath Day: Or, A Briefe Answer to Some Materiall Passages, in a Late Treatise of the Sabbath-Day: Digested Dialogue-Wise Betweene Two Divines A. and B.* (London, 1636). Bishop White replied with *An Examination and Confutation of a Lawlesse Pamphlet, Intituled "A Briefe Answer to a Late Treatise of the Sabbath-Day"* (London, 1637), and his answer called forth a rejoinder. The opening phase of the battle, in which defenders of the Declaration of Sports took the initiative, ended about 1637. Puritans countered with many defenses of their doctrine during the 1640s.

An unconscious hypocrisy pervaded the entire conflict, according to Henson, and the determining influences throughout the debate were more political than religious. Men took this means to align themselves for or against the king, and logic was allowed to count for more than it was worth. "No portion of the vast mass of dead literature which the seventeenth century has bequeathed to us," Henson wrote, "is more incapable of resuscitation than the storehouse of perverted erudition and grotesque reasoning which the sabbatarian conflict created." He is persuasive, but religious influences weighed heavily, and the debate, for all its defects, exhibits genuine erudition and cogent reasoning on the question of man's obligation to set aside time for spiritual purposes. Henson concluded, "yet it is not less certain that the conflict made an abiding impression on the national life."[61] And English emigrants carried that impression to America.

The controversy over the Sabbath fed the flames of fanaticism and superstition. Strict adherence to the Fourth Commandment often led to Judaizing the observance. Beginning about 1618, John Traske, after taking holy orders, began to preach that the Fourth Commandment obligated Christians to keep a Saturday Sabbath with a scrupulous legalism. He forbade the preparing of food, the sweeping of houses, and the kindling of fires on the Sabbath. Considering this tendency dangerous to true religion, the Star Chamber brought pressure to bear on Traske and he recanted in *A Treatise of Liberty from Judaism* (1620).[62]

In 1628 Theophilus Brabourne, a minister, revived Traske's heresy by stealthily publishing *A Discourse upon the Sabbath Day*. The Fourth Commandment required Christians as well as Jews to observe Saturday, he held, and the Lord's Day was an ordinary working day. Brabourne affronted Charles I by dedicating to him a second edition of his book in 1632, whereupon the High Commission induced him to abandon his Judaical views and conform to the established church. But not all of Brabourne's followers would recant, and one of the reasons Charles I reissued the Declaration of Sports was to dampen such fanaticism.[63]

A literature of warning was harnessed in the service of Sabbatarianism in the Elizabethan period, and in the early seventeenth century other works, notably those by Thomas Beard and John Reynolds, popularized the theme. By 1633 the climate was ripe for a sudden flowering of Sabbatarian superstition. Samuel Clarke, who refused to read the Book of Sports and preached on the Fourth Commandment instead, boasted that this conduct pleased God to show "remarkable Judgments" on profaners of the Lord's Day.[64] Nehemiah Wallington, a turner by trade and an intense Puritan, as a young man began to collect biblical examples of God's judgments against the wicked. During the reign of Charles I he started cataloguing similar recent events, and in 1632 initiated a separate work entitled *God's Judgements on Sabbath Breakers*. Wallington busily collected examples until 1633 and then had to slow his pace, since after the Book of Sports "there were so many of them in so short a time . . . the like, I think, was never heard of."[65]

Henry Burton, an anti-Laudian minister, went even further in *A Divine Tragedie Lately Acted: Or A Collection of Sundry Memorable Examples of Gods Judgements upon Sabbath-Breakers, and Other Like Libertines, in Their Unlawfull Sports* (1636).[66] This treasury of fifty-six purportedly true stories showed that severe punishments followed profanations of the Lord's Day. For example, fourteen youths playing football on Sunday on the river Trent near Gainsborough scuffled, and eight of them drowned when they fell through the ice. A party at Stoke quarreled after playing fives on Sunday and one was stabbed. Divine retribution was particularly visited upon participants in Sunday wakes and ales and Maypole-dancing. This type of crude superstition made a strong impression on the national mind at the time America was being settled.

The most famous work of Richard Brathwaite, country gentleman and poet, appeared in 1638 with the title *Barnabae Itinerarium, or Barnabees Journall.* A record of provincial travel in parallel Latin and English doggerel verse, the English part is best remembered by the often quoted lines in which the author relates that at Banbury he saw a Puritan

Hanging of his Cat on Monday,
For killing of a Mouse on Sonday.[67]

The religious institution of the Sabbath became a vital part of English middle-class culture under the early Stuart rulers. A whole generation was nurtured in the belief expressed by George Herbert in writing that

Sundaies the pillars are,
On which heav'ns palace arched lies:[68]

Sabbatarianism became a distinctive characteristic of Puritanism. All religion, as Gilbert Ironside wrote, is for Puritans "reduced to this one head, the observation of the Sabbath."[69] Accordingly, at a time when the Anglican priest and poet George Herbert observed that

Religion stands on tip-toe in our land,
Readie to passe to the *American* strand,[70]

Puritans were excessively if not fanatically devoted to maintaining the pure Sabbath, and fear that profanations of the day called down divine vengeance was widespread.

Severall young men playing at foote-ball on the Ice upon the LORDS-DAY *are all Drownd*

A Millers House and Mill Burnt etc.

Part Two

THE AMERICAN
EXPERIENCE

4

The Chesapeake
Colonies

THE NEW DOCTRINE of the Sabbath which emerged in England at the
turn of the seventeenth century was influential throughout various strata
of society at the time the colonization of America began. Englishmen carried the theory to all the original American settlements, and the growth
of Sabbatarianism in many different geographical areas and social struc-
tures demonstrated the powerful force of Puritan ideology in molding
early American culture.

The Chesapeake colonies are a case in point. In religion Virginia was a
daughter of the Church of England, and the first settlers intended to
make the church a focal point in their life. Maryland was religiously
mixed. The presence of Catholics and Protestants prevented the official
establishment of any religion and gave the church a lesser role than in
Virginia. In their material environment the areas were similar. Geography
and climate made both agricultural, and an economy devoted to tobacco
spread out settlement and precluded the establishment of closely knit societies like those in old and New England. Yet, on either side of the Potomac, Sabbath theory conditioned human behavior. For several decades
differing circumstances in the two Chesapeake colonies created contrast-
ing patterns of religious observance, but as time passed they came to share
a similar type of Sabbatarianism.

PERRY MILLER ONCE wrote that religion was "the really energizing propulsion" in the settlement of Virginia.[1] Although he overstates the case, there can be little doubt that a desire to advance the kingdom of God as well as to accumulate earthly riches underlay the venture. From the beginning, the Church of England was the established religion, as the Virginia Company's charter, the King's instructions of 1606, and custom all acknowledged, and the Lord's Day was observed, though not with Puritan precision.[2] The first immigrants arrived in Chesapeake Bay on a Sunday in April 1607 and did not hesitate to debark at a place they named Cape Henry. Pushing ahead, they erected a cross at their settlement on the James River on a Sunday in May. The Reverend Richard Hunt subsequently conducted public worship there according to Anglican rites. John Smith recalled how the whole company except for guards assembled twice daily for common prayer and gathered every Sunday under an awning or in an old tent for two sermons.[3] The respect accorded religion was further revealed by an episode involving Edward Maria Wingfield in 1607. As president of the colony, Wingfield canceled the sermon as a concession to fatigue and hunger on a few Sundays when Indian attacks on Jamestown unduly lengthened divine worship. His foes helped secure his downfall by charging that he had forbidden preaching.[4]

Nevertheless, the colony experienced grave disorders during the first two years of settlement. Much of the trouble arose from the profane and unruly persons recruited for the undertaking. Contemporaries also attributed the misfortunes to the transplantation of custom without the sanction of law, which departed from the accepted teaching that church and state should cooperate closely to restrain wickedness and promote righteousness. They concluded that temporal affairs would prosper if the authorities established religion on a firmer basis. Accordingly, the Virginia Company was reorganized in 1609, and its new charter gave ample power to the council. The directors planned to send out a large expedition to revitalize the colony and to establish stern discipline under military rule. As an initial step they appointed Sir Thomas Gates lieutenant general and dispatched him with eight ships and a pinnace in June 1609. The following April a second party sailed under Lord De La Warr, who had been named governor and captain general. In a sermon on the latter's departure, William Crashaw advised De La Warr not to look at the gain but "at those high and better ends that concerne the Kingdome of God." He urged the governor to "let the Sabboth be wholly and holily observed, and publike praiers daily frequented, idlenesse eschewed, and mutinies carefully prevented." Laws wisely made must be obeyed, "and let none stand for scarre-crowes; for that is the way to make all at last to be contemned."[5]

The *Sea Adventure*, which carried Gates and other officials, was separated from the fleet in a storm and landed in Bermuda. The company spent ten months on the bountiful island before pushing on to Virginia; upon arriving there the following May conditions were found to be so deplorable that Gates decided to evacuate the colony. But at the mouth of the James River the party met the expedition under De La Warr, who turned them back to Jamestown. Gates immediately laid down a strict code of laws, which William Strachey, historian and first secretary of the colony, later published in England under the title *For the Colony in Virginea Brittania: Lawes Divine, Morall and Martiall*.[6] Strachey wrote that Gates promulgated the laws on 24 May 1610, De La Warr approved them on 12 June, and Sir Thomas Dale enlarged them in June 1611.

The *Laws Divine, Moral and Martial* contained a total of ninety pages, by far the largest part of which regulated military duty. Dale, an experienced soldier and disciplinarian, authored this military code after landing in Virginia in the spring of 1611, and it is of no further concern here.[7] The smaller part of the *Laws,* a preface and thirty-seven statutes governing civil and criminal offenses, is relevant to this study. Drafted by Gates, the measures were extremely harsh. They imposed the death penalty for major crimes and certain sexual wrongs, and also for misdeeds that had led the colony to the brink of disaster, such as robbing stores, stealing from gardens, killing domestic animals without official approval, unauthorized trading with Indians, and price-gouging.[8]

The *Laws* attempted to end disorder by promoting righteousness and safeguarding religion. The code made death the penalty for deriding God's Word or denouncing the Christian faith, it punished disrespect to the ministry with public confession and whipping, and it insured religious uniformity by requiring all residents to give acceptable account of their orthodoxy to a clergyman. The statutes directed colonists to prepare themselves at home with private prayer for attendance at public worship. Every colonist was compelled to assemble twice each workday to hear divine service and on Wednesday for an additional sermon, and to attend morning worship and afternoon catechism on Sunday. The penalty for failure to observe the Sabbath by attending church was graduated: for the first offense it entailed loss of a week's provision and allowance, for the second, whipping, and for the third, death.[9]

Gates made ample provision to insure that everyone would attend public worship on the Sabbath. Military guards were to shut the gates of the settlement and place sentinels a half-hour before the service began. After the bell tolled they were to search houses to see that everyone had gone to church. Then the captain of the watch was to proceed with the guards to the house of God, lay the keys to the portals before the governor, and join the entire community in worship. To educate people in their duty, the ministers were to read the "divine and politique" statutes to the congregation each Sunday afternoon.[10]

The *Laws* banned profanation of the Lord's Day. No person "shall dare to violate or breake the Sabboth by any gaming, publique, or private abroad, or at home." The ministers were to choose four reliable men to gather information as to how people served God on Sunday, and the captains of the watch were to see that the Sabbath was not profaned by disorderly gaming, drunkenness, or intemperate meetings.[11]

When Strachey published the *Laws* in England in 1612, he made it appear that Gates had established the civil and criminal code upon landing in 1610. In reality, many of the thirty-seven statutes arose gradually in response to practical needs. The religious features alone seem to have been proclaimed at one time. Gates had been sent to restore discipline and make a success of a venture designed for both worldly gain and God's glory. He may have devised the statutes protecting religion on the outward voyage in 1609, for we know that he forced the colonists shipwrecked on Bermuda to observe the Sabbath along the lines directed by the *Laws*.[12] He drew upon the Bible, English laws, and reason for his code, and its harsh penalty for neglect of public worship demonstrates the conviction that proper Sabbath observance is a bulwark of religion and of civil order.

Strachey's purpose in bringing the *Laws* before an English audience was to promote settlement of the colony. By demonstrating that God's decrees were not scarecrows, he hoped to silence the continuing charge that anarchy threatened to ruin Virginia's prospects. Men who had risked their capital along the James River took pleasure in reading religious provisions which brought Virginia into line with the approved theory of relations between church and state. Alderman Robert Johnson, for example, praised the code because of its care for "the honour and service of God, for daily frequenting the Church, the house of prayer, at the tolling of the bell, for preaching, catechizing, and the religious observation of the Sabbath day."[13] But the *Laws* were harsh; "there was not in western Europe at that day so stern a criminal jurisprudence."[14]

For a decade military governors enforced the Draconian statutes in a manner considered by many "cruell, unusuall, and barbarous."[15] For five years, starting in 1611, Sir Thomas Dale administered an iron discipline. Although he did not hesitate to demand capital punishment for violations of the code, there is no record of the death penalty for neglect of Sabbath worship. The population at the time varied from around three hundred to a thousand souls, and late in the decade there were three ordained ministers and two without orders.[16] Dale's successors ruled somewhat more leniently. Captain Samuel Argall believed that public worship fostered social welfare, but in May 1618 he eliminated the death penalty for neglect of divine worship, while still requiring everyone to attend church on Sundays. The penalty for a first offense was to "lye neck and heels on the Corps du Guard" throughout Sunday night and give service to the colony during the ensuing week. A second violation brought a month of servitude, and a third a year and a day.[17]

We have now seen two stages in the transplantation of the Sabbath to Virginia. During the first the institution rested upon custom alone, while in the second its foundation was military fiat. A third phase began in 1619 when the military regime was replaced by a representative government. Henceforth the development of the Sabbath, along with the welfare of religion in general, depended upon the popular will. In the period to the middle seventeenth century the people of Virginia tried to establish a type of Sabbath observance which approximated that of the Puritan model, but economic forces prevented the realization of this ideal.

The General Assembly which met in the church at Jamestown on 30 July 1619 enacted fifty statutes to replace the *Laws Divine, Moral and Martial.* Several dealt with morals and reflected English middle-class culture. Some laws proscribed idleness, gaming, drunkenness, and excess in apparel; and one ordered all persons to frequent divine service and sermons in the forenoon and afternoon on the Sabbath. Clergymen were made responsible for enforcing attendance, with the fine of three shillings for each transgression going to the church rather than the state. Servants who willfully neglected their master's command to frequent church were to be whipped. The first Virginia assembly did not ban profanations of the Lord's Day.[18]

In 1619 the population of Virginia was contained in boroughs at Jamestown, Henrico, Charles City, and Elizabeth City, and in seven particular plantations. The latter were distinct and contiguous settlements established by private promoters who sent out settlers in return for headrights. These microcosms of the larger society cast light on attitudes toward Sabbath observance in Virginia at this time, and at Berkeley Hundred, a particular plantation north of the James River with nearly two score of inhabitants, the proprietors required that the Lord's Day be kept "in holy and religious order," with all bodily labor, vain sports, and scandalous recreations prohibited.[19]

In the years between the loss of the royal charter in 1624 and the restoration of the General Assembly as a permanent institution in 1639, the people continued to safeguard the sacred character of the First Day. Several laws designed for the purpose emerged in these years. In 1624 the assembly directed every plantation to reserve a house or room for worship only and made unexcused absence from Sunday service finable by one pound of tobacco for the first violation and fifty pounds for a month's absence.[20] The latter was a staggering penalty, amounting to seven and a half pounds sterling at the 1619 rate. In 1626 Governor Yeardley directed the commander and churchwardens of every plantation to see that persons delinquent in attending the service of God were punished according to statute. The assembly which met three years later repeated his order and clarified the rule on Sunday labor by enacting that the Sabbath was not to be "ordinarily profaned by workeing in any imployments or by journeye-ing from place to place."[21] A statutory revision in 1632 ordered religion in Virginia to be made uniform with the canons of the Church of England and declared 22 March an obligatory holy day to commemorate the colony's deliverance in 1622 from an Indian massacre.[22] In this same year the penalty for failure to attend church was reduced from three shillings or one pound of tobacco to one shilling. The legislature also ordered that at the quarter court each June at least one churchwarden from each parish was to join with as many ministers as could conveniently assemble and present Sabbath-breakers.[23]

Here were laws enough to foster piety, and their enforcement remained feasible as long as people were settled compactly, with the church as the focal point of community life. Responsibility for the enforcement of statutes designed to promote religion and morality underwent an evolution in the early years of the colony. In 1619 the legislature had charged the clergy with enforcing its order pertaining to the Sabbath. In following years various civil officials gradually assumed a large share of the burden. Establishment of the county system of government in 1634 enabled local authorities—at first county commissioners and later justices of the peace —to act. Ordinarily the clergy and churchwardens presented offenders, and county officials imposed such punishment as warranted by law.

A few examples illustrate the system in operation. In 1624 Governor Sir Francis Wyatt and his Council ordered Thomas Sulley, who had broken the Sabbath by "goinge A huntinge," to pay five pounds sterling in tobacco to the church and to acknowledge his fault before the congregation. In 1626 Thomas Farley, a gentleman, was presented for not coming to church on the Sabbath for three months. He confessed and Governor Yeardley's court ordered him to pay one hundred pounds weight in tobacco into the public treasury, though the fine was partly mitigated because the offender pleaded special circumstances. But when a churchwarden testified that Farley had hunted hogs on James City Island upon the Sabbath, the court directed him to pay the full amount. In 1629 Gover-

nor John Pott's court sentenced William Capps and James Sipse of Elizabeth City, presented by churchwardens for not regularly attending divine
service, to the full limit of the law. Their fine was to be levied by distraint
at the next crop. This judgment was more rigorous than that usually
given by Puritan magistrates at a similar stage in the development of New
England.[24] Few persons were punished for Sabbath offenses in Accomack-
Northampton County, but two men presented by a churchwarden in
November 1638 for "disordering and abuseing themselves upon the Sabboth day" were ordered to sit in the stocks following church the next
Lord's Day and to pay thirty pounds of tobacco toward public uses.[25]

The people of Virginia remained loyal Anglicans after 1640, when
Puritanism triumphed in England, but they continued to make the
Lord's Day the primary means of rendering external duty to their Creator.
Although the General Assembly omitted compulsory attendance at worship from its 1643 statutory revision—either inadvertently or because of
the situation in England—it passed other measures which established the
special character of the Sabbath. One required masters of families to
bring a serviceable gun with them to church on Sundays on penalty of up
to twenty pounds of tobacco for masters and up to twenty lashes for servants. Another forbade the shooting of guns on the holy day, except to
defend against Indians or to frighten birds away from cornfields. Still
another prohibited voyages on the Lord's Day, except to church or because of extreme necessity.[26] In addition, the assembly extended the powers of vestries, now officially recognized for the first time, and of churchwardens in checking immorality. A law bound the latter by oath to join
with the minister to present to the county court an annual written list of
Sabbath profaners and other evildoers. A 1646 enactment laid a much
wider enforcement net by authorizing churchwardens to present Lord's
Day violators and other ungodly persons upon information supplied by
any person in the parish as well as by their own observation.[27]

The law did not develop in a vacuum, but there is no evidence that
Virginia clergymen influenced it with doctrinal tracts on the Sabbath.
Most likely they pointed the path of duty in their sermons, and the magistrates used the power of the state to advance the Sabbatarian ideal. In
the late 1640s, for example, local officials sentenced Oliver Segar of York
County to build a bridge on a road for profaning the Lord's Day by fishing on a Sunday when the sacrament had been administered; they fined
Thomas Williams of Lower Norfolk one hundred pounds of tobacco for
getting drunk on Sunday. The Lower Norfolk County grand jury presented both Thomas Wright and Mrs. Elizabeth Lloyd for causing their
servants to break the Sabbath by laboring, and George Heigham was

indicted for permitting drunkenness and disorderly company in his house on the Sabbath. A 1650 incident demonstrated the tension between Sabbatarian doctrine and economic realities. Henry Crowe had transferred his tobacco plants to the field on a Sunday, perhaps seizing upon the one good day in weeks to perform the vital task. Although he had clearly done wrong, county magistrates let him escape a heavy fine when he promised not to offend again.[28]

It was easier to punish abuses than to achieve positive sanctification of the Lord's Day, but the community ideal at mid-century was the latter. Some confusion existed as to the legal requirements, however, because the 1643 statutory revision had failed to mention compulsory attendance at divine service and a 1646 law directing masters of families to send their childen and servants to Sunday afternoon instruction and catechism implied that adults were no longer expected to attend more than morning worship. To remove all uncertainty, the burgesses passed a statute in 1658 requiring servants and others to repair to church on the Lord's Day. The law repeated earlier prohibitions against traveling and shooting guns on Sunday and for the first time banned the loading of seagoing vessels on the Sabbath on penalty of a hundred pounds of tobacco or time in the stocks.[29]

Even as the legal foundations of a mature Sabbatarianism were taking shape, obstacles to its realization were arising. Economic development undermined the physical basis upon which proper sanctification of the Sabbath rested. Tobacco cultivation exhausted the soil and sent planters in unending pursuit of virgin land. This forced the tithables left behind to expand parish boundaries in order to support a ministry. The immense size of these made it difficult to attend church and to supervise morality. In Accomack-Northampton County on the Eastern Shore, for example, the population numbered some six hundred and fifty souls spread over about fifty square miles in 1632; by 1640 a thousand people inhabited three times the former area.[30] Attempts to adapt to the changed conditions proved unavailing. One group of Puritans in Virginia wanted to divide their large county into three parts to facilitate public worship and sanctification of the Lord's Day. And by mid-century the grand jury of Lower Norfolk County, complaining of general indifference to Sunday observance, charged the entire population of the county with breach of the day. It attributed the offense primarily to lack of a suitable minister and urged that the vacancy be supplied.[31]

Meanwhile, religious dissidents began to challenge the attempt to establish Sabbatarianism in Virginia. Compulsory-attendance laws were the cutting edge of a policy of religious uniformity, and since Virginia was

Anglican, both Puritans and Quakers created trouble for authorities. Although Puritan influences existed in the colony from the beginning, Puritans as an organized party were never strong there. The Puritans of Nansemond County simply left for Maryland in 1649 to escape the stern rule of the ardently Anglican governor William Berkeley. And eight Puritan residents of Lower Norfolk County were indicted in that year as "seditious sectaries" for refusing to attend their parish church.[32]

The Quakers presented a grave threat to religious uniformity. Their first missionary apparently arrived in Virginia in 1656 and met ready acceptance. That year some adherents of the Inner Light were presented in Lower Norfolk County for traveling and working when they should have been attending authorized worship. Two years later the colony enacted a law demanding conformity to the existing religion and providing for the banishment of Quakers. Most of the ensuing prosecutions under the statute were for holding private assemblies, but often presentments were for absence from constituted worship. To deal with the latter, the General Assembly in 1662 provided a fine of twenty pounds sterling for a month's dereliction and twelve times that amount as well as security for good behavior for absences of a year. Attendance at an unlawful Quaker meeting was punishable by a fine of two hundred pounds of tobacco. In 1663 officials fined three Friends of Lower Norfolk County the legal penalty for refusing to attend the parish church on four successive Sundays and another Quaker three hundred and fifty pounds of tobacco for laboring in his fields on the Lord's Day.[33]

SABBATARIANISM IN VIRGINIA in the period before the Stuart Restoration in 1660 was the product of the interaction between an imported ideal, largely Puritan, and local religious, economic, and social conditions. Across the Potomac a different pattern of Sabbatarianism developed. Religious pluralism conditioned observance of the Lord's Day in Maryland, and that colony anticipated many of the problems regarding the role of church and state in promoting religion and morality which became important in the United States after the American Revolution and the adoption of the Constitution.

From the beginning Maryland promised new possibilities for religious liberty. Although George Calvert, the first Lord Baltimore, may have "entertained no advanced views of human liberty," he sincerely desired to found a colony based on the principle of religious toleration.[34] His personal interests led him to envision Maryland as a "land of sanctuary" for different faiths, because this was the only way a Catholic convert could obtain permission from a Protestant king to establish a haven for fellow

Catholics.[35] The religious provisions of the Maryland charter of 1632 were imprecise. They empowered the proprietor to erect places of worship and cause them to be dedicated and consecrated according to the ecclesiastical laws of England. No interpretation of the charter was to be made whereby God's holy and true Christian religion would suffer prejudice.[36]

Cecilius Calvert, who became the second Lord Baltimore upon his father's death in 1632, faithfully sought to make religious toleration the foundation principle of the colony. He found it imperative in recruiting Protestant settlers to assure them of toleration in a law by which "all sorts who professed Christianity in Generall might be at Liberty to Worshipp God in such Manner as was most agreeable with their respective Judgm[en]ts and Consciences without being subject to any penaltyes whatsoever for their soe doing." Without this guarantee the province would perhaps never have been established.[37]

The exact number of Catholics and Protestants among the nearly three hundred original colonists is unknown. Catholics were a minority, but their ranks included many gentlemen-adventurers, two Jesuit priests, and two lay brothers. The Protestant majority contained men of lower social status but no clergyman of that faith. Calvert ordered his brother Leonard, whom he sent out as lieutenant governor, carefully to "preserve unity and peace" and suffer neither scandal nor offense to be given on sea or land to any Protestant. Roman Catholic rites were to be celebrated privately, and Catholics were not to discuss religion with others. The governor and commissioners were advised to treat Protestants with as much favor as justice would permit.[38] Everything considered, Maryland was a religiously mixed rather than a Catholic colony.

Although the charter presupposed Trinitarian Christianity, the circumstances of the founding prevented any religious establishment in Maryland.[39] The proprietor did not compel attendance at public worship, and the majority of inhabitants had no organized church to minister to their spiritual needs. Lord Baltimore upheld the principle of separation of church and state and used his authority not to restrain freedom of conscience but to restrain those who attempted to restrain freedom of conscience.[40]

Despite this ostensibly unfavorable socio-intellectual climate, the Sabbath became an important institution in early Maryland, but with a character understandably different from that in Virginia or New England. The proprietor and the people shaped its development. Although the charter granted absolute power to the former, it permitted freemen to give their "advice, assent and approbation" to laws ordained by him.[41] This seed of representative government quickly germinated, and a long struggle between the Roman Catholic Baltimores and a rising popular opposition, largely Protestant, ensued. In 1638 the freemen in the assembly imitated the English House of Commons and won the legislative initiative. A year later the assembly exhibited great independence in dealing with religious measures sent out from England.

Lord Baltimore wished to foster religion and morality by law, without using the state for the purpose, since he regarded both church and state as autonomous spheres. Thus, he proposed legislation to punish as breaches of order a variety of offenses ranging from unruliness to drunkenness, fornication, adultery, and "prophane Adjuration by God or some holy creature."[42] Nevertheless, Baltimore was clearly willing to use civil authority to safeguard the Lord's Day, though lack of an established church made it impossible to compel attendance at divine service. He protected the "lesser" half of the Sabbath by commanding a weekly cessation of labor. He ordered that every master, mistress, or freeman who engaged in servile labor on the Lord's Day or on holy days, other than in cases of necessity allowed by a judge, was to forfeit thirty pounds of tobacco or five shillings sterling for every offense and the like sum in addition for every servant who offended by his command or consent.

This draft act was reminiscent of late medieval Catholic Sabbatarianism, and nowhere did Baltimore present a specifically religious justification for the protection afforded the Lord's Day. Instead he offered a civil ordinance to preserve peace by providing a common day of rest, although it is true that such a rest day would facilitate public worship. The assembly ignored his proposal but agreed not to meet on holy days.[43] Despite his failure, Baltimore anticipated a solution which the United States devised in the nineteenth century to reconcile its commitment to Protestantism with the principle of church-state separation and the fact of religious diversity.

The Lord's Day received statutory recognition in Maryland in the 1649 "Act concerning Religion." Its origins are found in the religious struggles of the period. Calvert temporarily lost the colony during the Puritan supremacy in England and feared that Parliament might revoke his charter. Upon regaining possession, the Catholic proprietor tried to silence charges that Maryland was a hotbed of popery. To this end he offered "free liberty of religion" to attract Puritans and appointed officials of the Protestant faith.[44] Some five hundred Puritans of Nansemond County left Governor Berkeley's Virginia to found Providence, near present-day Annapolis, in response to this appeal.[45] Then, in reorganizing the colony, Lord Baltimore found it desirable to translate religious toleration into law. The English Civil War had kindled interest in liberty of conscience, and he thought the principle would appeal to Catholics and Protestants alike and thereby enhance his control over the proprietary. So, in 1649 he sent out sixteen laws as a basis for settling a host of problems. One of these became part of the famous Toleration Act.[46]

At the time there was a delicate balance of religious forces in the colony, with Catholics and Protestants differing over what type of religious toleration or freedom to grant.[47] As a result of this conflict and that between the assembly and Calvert, the "Act concerning Religion" was a curious compromise. The second half gave legal form to Baltimore's proposal for securing peace by granting freedom of conscience. It assured all Trinitarians, or those "professing to beleive in Jesus Christ," free exercise of their religion as long as they were not unfaithful to the lord proprietor and did not conspire against the established civil government. The act provided punishments for those who troubled another's faith or compelled belief against consent. Though admirable, the measure rested on no high principle. Its justification took the low utilitarian ground that "the inforceing of the conscience in matters of Religion hath frequently fallen out to be of dangerous Consequence in those commonwealthes where it hath been practised," and that the enactment would ensure quiet and peaceable government of the province.[48]

The first part of the act narrowed the general principle of freedom of conscience, while giving it specific content. The assembly drafted the four sections of this half in response to pressure from various religious interests in Maryland and with an eye on England. Following the lead of the Puritan Long Parliament, which on 2 May 1648 passed an ordinance punishing heresies and blasphemies with death, the act made the doctrine of the Trinity a religious test by a provision punishing blasphemy with death and confiscation or forfeiture of all property. A Catholic-inspired section prohibited reproachful speeches concerning the Virgin Mary and the Holy Apostles. The Toleration Act also proscribed the use of epithets to revile the holder of any of seventeen named religious viewpoints. (The list described the rich profusion of sects produced by religious upheaval in England rather than those actually present in Maryland at the time.)

The Toleration Act made profanation of "the Sabbath or Lords day called Sunday by frequent swearing, drunkennes or by any uncivill or disorderly recreacion, or by working on that day when absolute necessity doth not require it" punishable by a fine of two shillings and sixpence for a first offense, five shillings for a second, and ten shillings for a third infraction. If the offender lacked the means to pay, he could be compelled in open court to acknowledge the "Scandall and offense" he had given God and the civil government of the province. A poor person guilty of profaning the Sabbath a third time might also be publicly whipped.[49] Puritans were no doubt instrumental in securing this act, and yet the law was not full-blown Sabbatarianism, for it was impossible to require sanctification of the Lord's Day in Maryland. The assembly therefore tried to ensure that compulsory leisure would not have pernicious consequences.

The attempt to balance freedom of conscience with protection of the Sabbath distinguished Maryland from Virginia. The ramifications of the former meant that Maryland had no established church, no tax to support the ministry, and no obligation to attend public worship. The number of churches remained small, therefore, and few residents had the opportunity to attend holy worship regularly or even intermittently. In the early days the Society of Jesus supplied priests to say Mass in a chapel at St. Mary's, where Protestants heard laymen read homilies or the Book of Common Prayer. Three Protestant chapels probably existed by 1642, and on rare occasions a visiting Virginia clergyman celebrated holy communion. But organized Protestant parish life did not commence until the Reverend William Wilkinson, an Anglican, arrived in 1650, and only twenty-two Protestant clergymen are known to have been in Maryland before 1692.[50]

Nevertheless, Puritans were dominant in the Maryland assembly in 1654, and they strengthened legislation affecting the septennial institution. They withdrew the protection of religious liberty from "popery or prelacy" as well as from those who protected licentiousness under the profession of Christ, and enacted a separate law entitled "Concerning the Sabboth Day." This measure of October 1654 tightened the Toleration Act by prohibiting all work, except that done of necessity or charity; "Inordinate Recreations as fowling, fishing, hunting or other"; and the shooting of guns except in case of necessity. The penalty of one hundred pounds of tobacco for violations, half of which was to go to the informer and half to public use, was twice as stiff as that enacted by Virginia in 1662.[51]

Enforcement of the laws regulating Sabbath observance was most vigorous in Kent County, which included the island of that name in Chesapeake Bay and part of the Eastern Shore. Kent had been settled by Puritans who arrived directly from Virginia or indirectly by way of neighboring Providence. In April 1655, shortly after the 1654 enactment, county officials presented five men, including Matthew Read, a commissioner of the local court, and a woman for misbehavior, drinking, profaning the Sabbath, and shooting off their guns unseasonably. Because it was a first offense and they promised amendment, the accused were dismissed upon payment of costs. The following January, Edward Rogers was charged with shooting a turkey on the Sabbath. He was found guilty, but since it was a first offense and Rogers pleaded ignorance of the law, confessed sorrow for his wrong, and promised never to do the like, the justices imposed no penalty other than costs. In late 1656 a constable presented Captain John Russell, himself a Kent County justice, and John Gibson for fighting on the Lord's Day. And in 1660 Henry Clay was presented for "strikinge tob[acco] on the sabath day." He had been observed in the act when the sun was not down, a scrap of evidence which suggests that for Kent County Puritans the Sabbath extended from sunset to sunset. Clay was ordered to pay fifteen pounds of tobacco plus costs, with half to the informer and half to the proprietor.[52]

Despite the lack of an established church, a judicial decision in 1662 gave legal sanction to the contention that attendance at worship was a matter of *religious* obligation. The case involved Francis Fitzherbert, a Jesuit priest, and first came before the provincial court in 1658. Fitzherbert had vigorously proselytized among Protestants and had tried to compel Thomas Gerard, a Roman Catholic and member of the Council, to attend church and bring along his wife and children. Gerard's wife was an Anglican, however, and Gerard refused to obey. Father Fitzherbert then threatened excommunication, for which he was charged with treason, sedition, and rebellious and mutinous speeches that endeavored to seduce people from their religion. He pleaded that his preaching and teaching of Trinitarian Christianity were a free exercise of religion protected by a 1639 ordinance and the Toleration Act. The former declared that "Holy Churches within this province shall have all her rights and liberties," but it had not yet been judicially construed. Now, however, the court concluded that every church professing Trinitarian beliefs was accounted Holy Church in Maryland, and it allowed Fitzherbert's defense. Although the state could not compel attendance at worship, the church could employ the weapons at her disposal to do so.[53]

Maryland perfected its laws regulating Sabbath observance in the 1670s. In June 1674 members of the assembly noted that a deficiency in earlier statutes permitted disorder in ordinaries on the Lord's Day which dishonored God, debauched youths, and increased vice. Accordingly, the assembly passed a law prohibiting ordinary-keepers from dispensing liquor or permitting any tippling or gaming at cards, dice, ninepins, or other unlawful exercises on Sunday on penalty of two thousand pounds of tobacco and loss of their license. Moreover, any person who sold liquor on the Lord's Day was liable to the former fine. When the assembly met at St. Mary's four years later, members thought that a new statute was necessary, since the day was still profaned in various ways to the discredit of

Christianity and the apparent ruin of many inhabitants. To remedy this condition, "An Act for keepeing holy the Lords day" of November 1678 ordered that no person was to work or permit those under him to do any bodily labor upon the Lord's Day; no person was to take fish by any means from any waters or command or permit persons under them to fish on the Lord's Day; and no person was to profane the day by drunkenness, swearing, gaming at cards, dice, billiards, shuffleboard, bowls, ninepins, or horse races, fowling or hunting, or any other unlawful sports or recreations. The penalty was one hundred pounds of tobacco, with fines going to the poor of the place where the offense was committed. This statute incorporated the earlier law prohibiting ordinary-keepers and others from dispensing liquor or permitting in or about their houses on the Lord's Day any tippling, drunkenness, or gaming. It specified that the Lord's Day in Maryland be deemed to begin according to "primitive and Christian usage" at twelve o'clock Saturday night and last for twenty-four hours.[54]

THE DIFFERENT PATTERNS of religious observance that emerged in the Chesapeake colonies by the middle of the seventeenth century shaped life on either side of the Potomac. Both Virginia and Maryland forbade ordinary labor and certain other activities on Sunday, and the available evidence shows that the laws were enforced with some care if not altogether uniformly. The Sabbath served as an important check on the capacity of the frontier to dehumanize the first settlers in the Chesapeake area. In the beginning of a plantation physical survival alone required constant toil, and later the opportunity to build a fortune and establish a family dynasty in the New World offered a temptation to labor incessantly and to drive servants mercilessly. In such a setting the Lord's Day represented an island of rest in an ocean of endeavor.

Yet an enforced weekly rest day constituted a moral danger by freeing individuals from the discipline of work at a time when the level of social development offered few opportunities for the profitable use of leisure time. Maryland especially ran this risk, for it did not require sanctification of the holy day. Town life with its civilizing influence developed slowly because production of an agricultural staple isolated families. Masters of households were patriarchs responsible for their little domains, training their charges to work and presiding over family prayers. Schools were at best rare. Events like weddings, funerals, horse races, monthly court day, and the day of general muster afforded relief from normal routine and transformed individuals into a community. But such occasions were infrequent.[55]

Weekly churchgoing was the most important means of forming character and society. In this respect Virginia had a decided advantage over Maryland. Ideally, the residents of a parish assembled in their spacious churchyard for a goodly part of every Sunday. Here persons of various ages and ranks intermingled, before worship and again while waiting for a second service later in the day. Talk of politics and affairs trained men in the duties of citizenship. In addition, Sabbath worship was a conduit of grace and a source of moral instruction. At the appointed time the parishioners entered church in the order of social precedence. The minister read the service from the Book of Common Prayer, preached, and occasionally administered the sacrament, while the clerk led the responses and doled out, line by line, the Psalms which were sung. The congregation gave glory to God and begged relief for its necessities.[56]

Churchgoing in Virginia must have been the norm about mid-century, for sheriffs customarily apprehended wrongdoers and served papers in churchyards on Sunday rather than going to the homes of individuals. But this practice deterred men from public worship, so in 1658 and 1662 the assembly enacted laws prohibiting the serving of writs and warrants or the making of arrests on Sundays and holy days. The statutes also protected muster and election days, although they permitted arrests on these occasions in cases of riot, felony, or escape. Although Maryland sheriffs could not count on churchgoing to ease their task, the assembly in that colony did make Sunday arrests illegal in 1664. This law, however, was less a response to local need than the imitation of an English statute. Yet a provincial court decision in 1677 indicated that all Sunday legal activity in Maryland was forbidden. Because an undersheriff of St. Mary's County executed a writ of *scire facias* on a Sunday, the court found the return on the writ invalid.[57]

As time passed the differences between Virginia and Maryland with respect to the Sabbath were leveled out by the same environmental forces and English influences at work in both areas, and the Lord's Day gradually assumed a similar character in both colonies. In Virginia the theoretical and legal foundations of the Sabbath remained remarkably stable after the Restoration.[58] The population increased rapidly, from fifteen thousand in 1648 to forty thousand in 1671. Between 1662 and 1680 the number of parishes remained about constant but the number of rectors increased. In all likelihood, not more than ten of less than fifty parishes had resident ordained clergymen in 1662, whereas in 1680 there were forty-eight parishes and thirty-five ministers in Virginia.[59] In 1662 the General Assembly provided that nothing was to be used or done that might tend to profane Sunday. Works of ordinary employment and anything else that might keep one from worship, especially travel, were specifically proscribed. All persons with no lawful excuse were ordered to report diligently to their parish church or chapel on Sundays and on four holy days of the year.[60]

According to Philip A. Bruce, the determination to enforce strict observance of the Lord's Day was stronger during the last quarter of the century than it had been previously. Among the Sabbath profanations which led to prosecution in these years were carrying a gun, hiring a horse, sending a servant to a tannery with a hide, trimming and replanting a nursery, shelling corn, fetching shoes from the cobbler, fishing, killing deer, selling liquor, ordering slaves to bring water in preparation for planting tobacco, picking up tobacco, driving a cart, going on a journey, getting drunk, and playing cards.[61]

Prosecutions of Quakers under the 1662 act reveal an insistence upon enforcing attendance at legally constituted worship. Groups ranging from eleven to thirty persons were presented in a number of counties between 1665 and 1682. The fines imposed on John Plaisants (or Pleasants), a wealthy and prominent Quaker of Henrico County, and his wife for not attending church and for other offenses were so great that Governor Culpeper, acting under royal instructions to grant liberty of conscience, "stopped execution against . . . Plaisants . . . for not coming to church," until he received a report of the affair.[62]

Friends were not alone in refusing to comply with church-attendance laws. In 1678 twenty Virginians preferred drinking in a private house on Sunday to public worship. That same year the grand jury of Lower Norfolk County presented all the ecclesiastical officials in the county for failure to enforce attendance at divine worship, in consequence of which the Sabbath had been profaned by evil persons "who made of the Lord's Day what their pleasures led to." And in 1679 the grand jury of Henrico County presented Joseph Royal for playing cards, John Edwards and another for playing checkers, Henry Martin for swearing, and Charles Fetherstone and Edward Stratton for getting drunk and fighting on the Sabbath. Henry Turner was later tried in Henrico for stripping tobacco on Sunday.[63]

Confronted with laxity, the General Assembly tried to maintain the old Sabbath. Although in 1690 it spurned a suggestion by James Blair, newly appointed by the Bishop of London as commissary of the Virginia church, that ecclesiastical tribunals be established to try Sabbath-profaners, the legislature had to reckon with the English Toleration Act (1689), which allowed dissenters to attend their own churches. In 1691 the assembly acknowledged that its Sabbath observance law of 1662 had not produced the desired effect and reaffirmed that nothing was more acceptable to God than keeping the Lord's Day holy.[64] The legislature's 1691 statute did not explicitly require everyone to attend church but aimed in this direction by prohibiting people from going to meetings outside their own parishes on the Lord's Day and by banning travel and anything that tended to profane a day that was to be kept holy in every respect. The statute carried a stiff penalty of twenty shillings for violations.[65]

In subsequent years the Virginia assembly was divided over the issue of the Lord's Day. The legislature unsuccessfully sought a new Sabbath law in 1693. The lower house, which paced the drive to retain a well-kept holy day, probably reflected public opinion better than the council, as constituents pressed their views on their representatives.[66] In 1696 residents of Northumberland County complained to the House of Burgesses that Saturday horse racing led to profanation of Sunday. Three years later, petitions from the widely separated counties of Lancaster, Gloucester, and Accomack informed the lower chamber that every citizen should be compelled to attend some congregation or place of worship on Sunday. The house thereupon ordered a more effective Sabbath bill prepared.[67]

On 15 May a committee under the chairmanship of Colonel Philip Ludwell of James City introduced a measure that received Governor Nicholson's assent on 8 June 1699. This omnibus statute provided that everyone twenty-one years of age or over should attend his parish church once in two months upon penalty of five shillings or fifty pounds of tobacco. Anyone presented who could furnish a "true and reasonable" cause for absence, however, should not be liable for the fine. In addition, Protestant dissenters were allowed their own religious assemblies, which they were to attend once in two months or be punished. Now the colonial law was much more lenient than the Toleration Act of 1689.[68]

This sudden departure from precedent is hard to explain. Dissenters were a small minority, consisting of three or four groups of Quakers and a few Presbyterian congregations.[69] In addition, evidence of attempts to enforce old and secure new Lord's Day statutes suggests that public opinion supported the established church and also favored a compulsory-attendance law. So far as the legislative history of the 1699 statute is discoverable, it appears that the house wished to permit only one monthly absence but lost out to the council, which wanted to require attendance at church only once every six months.[70] Since the house was an elected and the council an appointed body, it is hard to conclude that the people of Virginia revolted against the legal obligation to attend Sunday worship frequently. It is possible, however, that Virginia liberalized its requirement more than England did because Governor Nicholson and his councillors were intent on introducing the principle of religious toleration into the colony, and that rivalry with the burgesses led them beyond their original objective. Added to this, undoubtedly, was the realization that economic and geographic realities made regular attendance so difficult that it was time to establish a more practical ideal. As a result, Virginia entered the eighteenth century with a greatly relaxed standard of church-going.

Six years later, however, the assembly altered its course and wrote into law what appears to have approximated the community's wishes. Now the legislators required attendance at church at least once a month. They again prohibited Sabbath profanations, which were defined as attending disorderly meetings, gaming or tippling, making a journey, traveling anywhere except to and from church, and performing works of one's ordinary calling.[71] Except for minor adjustments, this law remained in effect until the ferment of the Revolution.

The reorientation that led to more relaxed Sunday observance in Virginia had the opposite effect in Maryland, where a Protestant revolution occurred in 1689. Political and religious forces which had been increasing for decades combined to produce this upheaval. Opposition to the political power of the absentee proprietor intensified steadily in these years, as did antagonism to Charles Calvert's Catholicism and a demand for official establishment of Anglicanism. When the Glorious Revolution brought Protestant William and Mary to the English throne, local dissidents seized control of Baltimore's province. Maryland became a royal colony in 1692, the lord proprietor surrendered all but his property rights there, and the Church of England was legally established.[72]

Poor Sabbath observance was one of the reasons given for erecting a state church. Several parties insisted that the colony suffered low standards of morality which public worship might correct. As early as 1676 the Reverend John Yeo, who lived in southern Maryland and actively clamored for an Anglican establishment, had informed the Archbishop of Canterbury of flagrant delinquencies that should be remedied. Twenty thousand souls, he said, were scattered throughout ten or a dozen counties in Maryland, and although papists and Quakers were provided with priests and speakers, only three Church of England clergymen were present to minister to the vast majority. As a result, "many Dayly fall away either to Popery, Quakerism or Phanaticisme but alsoe the lords day is prophaned, Religion despised, and all notorious vices committed soe th[a]t it is become a Sodom of uncleanness and a Pest house of iniquity." Yeo urged the Archbishop to prevail upon Lord Baltimore, then in England, to secure an able, learned, and established Protestant ministry.[73]

The Archbishop asked that the plan be pressed, and the Bishop of London had it read before the Committee of Trade and Plantations in July 1677. Called to defend himself, Baltimore said that Maryland Anglicans who wanted ministers had them—he knew of four maintained by their flocks. He stressed the voluntary principle, asserting that every county possessed churches built and supported by this means. He also suggested that it would be difficult to obtain consent to an establishment, since three-fourths of the inhabitants were Presbyterians, Independents, Anabaptists, and Quakers, while Anglicans and Roman Catholics were fewest in number. But the committee, accepting Yeo's description as accurate, directed the proprietor to ascertain what each congregation could freely provide and make that sum a compulsory levy by law.[74]

Baltimore ignored the request, however, and dissatisfaction with ungodliness in Maryland remained active. Nearly a decade after Yeo's complaint, Mary Taney, a forbear of the Chief Justice of that name, petitioned the Church of England hierarchy for aid in maintenance of a minister and expressed horror that for ''want of the Gospel our Children and Posterity are in danger to be condemned to infidelity or to apostacy.''[75]

In 1688 Deputy Governor William Joseph spelled out the dangers in his first address to the General Assembly. He related the need for laws designed to improve moral conditions in Maryland to a defense of Jacobite political theory. In describing the sins of drunkenness, swearing, adultery, and Sabbath-breaking in the colony, he tended to create the impression that the people of Maryland spent the Lord's Day in sodden sensuality. Joseph seized upon the Fourth Commandment to recommend that the assembly prevent such unchristian practices as laboring on the Sabbath, spending the day idly, or passing it in drinking, tippling, or gaming.[76]

Although these witnesses probably magnified the evils to gain their objectives, apparently the situation left much to be desired. A careful modern student has concluded that ''the moral condition of the province at this time was notably bad. Drunkenness and the grosser vices were the besetting sins, while such more serious crimes as incestuous marriage, the peril of thinly settled communities, were not uncommon.''[77] Colonists saw failure to sanctify the Lord's Day as a vital part of the problem.

The first act of the Maryland assembly in June 1692, after it recognized William and Mary, was a statute establishing the Protestant religion. Although Anglicans were not in a majority, all Protestants probably supported legal foundation of the Church of England as the only means of creating a moral force in the colony.[78] After stating that the Church of England was to enjoy all her legal ''Rights Liberties and Franchises'' wholly inviolable and that Magna Carta was to be observed, the statute declared that sanctifying the Lord's Day was a principal part of Christian worship but that in most places of Maryland "many wicked Lewd and disorderly people" profaned and neglected it by working, drunkenness, swearing, gaming, and other unlawful pastimes and debaucheries. This was the first official use in Maryland of the word "sanctifying" in connection with the First Day, which was here termed the "Lords Day commonly called Sunday" but not the Sabbath.

To correct the evils cited the law prohibited laboring, except for works of absolute necessity and mercy, and profaning the day by drunkenness, swearing, gaming, fowling, fishing, hunting, and sporting. It made those in authority responsible for restraining their inferiors. The penalty for violation was one hundred pounds of tobacco, twice the amount imposed in Virginia, to be used for the poor. Convictions were to be based upon evidence of one official, testimony of two witnesses, or confession. In addition, neither ordinary-keepers nor masters of households were to sell strong liquors or allow tippling, drunkenness, or gaming on this day.[79]

The act did not require attendance at public worship, though the assembly expressly acknowledged that keeping the Lord's Day holy was a principal part of Christian worship and that a correlation existed between the lack of positive Sabbath observance and abuse of the holy day. Sixty years of provincial tradition counted against any policy of compulsory churchgoing, and by 1692 the time had passed when such laws might be initiated. It was enough to compel non-Anglicans to support the Church of England without also forcing them to frequent it.

After further statutes designed to adjust the religious establishment to the colony, an enactment of 1702 laid the legal foundation of the Church in Maryland that lasted until the Revolution.[80] Counties were laid out into parishes and churches were constructed in the twenty-three parishes lacking them. Five clergymen were resident in 1692, a number that increased to seventeen by 1700.[81] The parishes gradually took on a significance in the life of the colony which approximated that in Virginia, and their vestries became responsible for moral welfare. The Ten Commandments were physically displayed in churches to remind everyone of his duty to God and man, and a 1696 law directed the minister to read the penal laws of the province four times yearly.[82] In 1704 the assembly declared that the "Act for Sanctifying and Keeping holy the Lords day commonly called Sunday" was to be and remain in full force and effect for ever. Apart from an enactment of 1723, which tightened the provisions of 1692 by doubling the penalty for each offense and permitting conviction on proof of one rather than two witnesses, the legal position of Sunday in Maryland had been fixed by the opening of the eighteenth century.[83]

Despite the differences in their early religious foundations, after a century of development the two Chesapeake colonies achieved a strikingly familiar Sabbatarianism. Environment only partly explains the result. If the same economic influences were at work, Puritanism spread its influence throughout the tidewater and inland settlements. Sabbath patterns still differed at the dawn of the eighteenth century, but they were developing along parallel lines and on the basis of statutes that would last essentially unchanged until the Revolutionary era.

5

A Light
to the Nation

THE SABBATARIANISM OF the Chesapeake colonies exemplifies the pervasive influence of Puritanism in early America, but New England deserves the major credit for kindling the Sabbath light to the new nation. Puritans settled this region primarily to put their theological doctrines into practice and raised the Sabbath to a position of prominence because they valued it as the palladium of true religion. This achievement should be seen in relation to the goals of the Reformation. The Puritan movement became the most advanced expression of the Protestant effort to regenerate man spiritually and to reorder society in accordance with the Word contained in Scripture, and the theology of the Sabbath was an integral part of the cluster of ideas employed by American Puritans to justify their immigration and understand their place in universal history.[1]

First and basic in this set of beliefs was the doctrine of divine Providence. Puritans held that Providence governs every aspect of the universe in order to achieve the ends for which God created the world. Men find meaning in their lives by discovering how God acts to save sinners and realize his purposes. Ever since the Reformation, Protestants had insisted that the Protestant rather than the Roman Catholic Church was the proper vehicle for advancing the kingdom of Christ; and Englishmen, identifying Protestantism with the national state, became eager to create the New Israel in their land. Frustrated in their attempt to reform England, some Nonconformists decided to establish the pure church on virgin soil. William Bradford reflected the view of those who saw the establishment of New England as part of God's plan for the redemption of mankind. "Religious men . . . came for religions sake," he wrote in the *History of Plymouth Plantation,* "and the Lord so helped them, whose worke they had in hand" that "he brought things aboute . . . in his devine providence, as they were not only upheld and sustained, but their proceedings both honoured and imitated by others."[2]

Second and closely related was the belief that the Puritans were the people of God. Zealous English Protestants likened themselves to the Chosen People of the Old Testament, and John Foxe's Book of Martyrs reinforced the conviction that they were God's instruments for the reformation of England. The doctrine of covenant theology led Puritans to regard themselves as a peculiar people set apart for a special purpose. According to the tenets of the social or collective covenant, they were called to emigrate not as individuals but as a people with a common end willed by God. American Puritans were thoroughly imbued with these ideas. Governor Bradford often called the Pilgrims "the people of God,"[3] and John Winthrop emphasized that the Massachusetts Bay Puritans had entered into a covenant with God to execute a divine commission.

Third, American Puritans thought that New England was the place for them to erect a religious society based on God's Word as expressed in the Bible. New England was not precisely the land of promise, since the scriptural promise was no longer attached to a specific location after the coming of Jesus. Nevertheless, Puritan immigrants held that God had postponed the opening of the New World until their own time to afford his people an avenue of escape from religious oppression, and that the plague of 1616-17, which decimated the Massachusetts Indians, represented the intervention of a favoring Providence. John Cotton told Winthrop's company in his farewell sermon before their departure in 1630, "The placing of a people in this or that Countrey is from the appointment of the Lord." Winthrop later described Massachusetts as "this good land, which God had found out and given to his people."[4]

Fourth, New England Puritans considered establishment of the pure Sabbath essential to the fulfillment of their divine mission to build a truly reformed society. Though they insisted on the primeval origins of the Sabbath and were themselves engaged in creating a new world, there is no evidence that they justified their activity by virtue of Exod. 20:8-11 (the preferred text for Puritan Sabbatarians), where the Sabbath is validated in terms of the creation of the world described in Gen. 1:1-2:4a. Instead, they identified with ancient Israel, which was the historical model for their New Israel. The archetypal covenant was that made between God and Abraham and renewed with the giving of the Law at Sinai. Deut. 5:12-15, which validates the Sabbath institution in terms of the creation of the Chosen People after their deliverance from bondage, should have been their favorite text. In any event, Scripture teaches that the Sabbath is the symbol of the everlasting covenant between God and his elect nation, and Sabbatarianism set Puritans apart from other people. Duty required them to build the New Jerusalem on the foundations of the Fourth Commandment.

Among early Puritan writers, Edward Johnson, who was more typical of the majority of settlers than were Bradford, Winthrop, and Cotton, best encapsulated the foregoing ideas. A woodjoiner by trade, Johnson emigrated to Boston in 1630, and except for the years from 1631 to 1637, spent back in England, lived in Massachusetts the rest of his life. He knew local conditions well and was religiously orthodox. In 1650 Johnson began the book which he called *The Wonder-Working Providence of Sion's Saviour in New England* to refute the enemies of Massachusetts with evidence of God's sustaining favor. His history of New England was the first to be published. Its opening paragraphs emphasize the centrality of the Sabbath in the planting of Massachusetts: "When England began to decline in Religion, like lukewarme Laodicea, and instead of purging out Popery, a farther compliance was sought not onely in vaine Idolatrous Ceremonies, but also in prophaning the Sabbath, and by Proclamation throughout their Parish churches, exasperating lewd and prophane persons to celebrate a Sabbath like the Heathen to Venus, Baccus and Ceres; in so much that the multitude of irreligious lascivious and popish affected persons spred the whole land like Grashoppers, in this very time Christ the glorious King of his Churches, raises an Army out of our English Nation, for freeing his people from their long servitude under usurping Prelacy; and because every corner of England was filled with the fury of malignant adversaries, Christ creates a New England to muster up the first of his Forces in."

Having identified Anglicans as apostates and Puritans as the Chosen People, Johnson continued by saying that Christ Jesus began with "our English Nation" to manifest his kingly office more fully than before and in martial imagery added that in 1628 a proclamation called "all you the people of Christ that are here Oppressed, Imprisoned and scurrilously derided" to prepare to be shipped "for planting the united Collonies of new England; Where you are to attend the service of the King of Kings." He assured those who questioned whether they should depart that Christ purposely caused his instruments to retreat, so that his adversaries, "glorying in the pride of their power, insulting over the little remnant remaining,'' could be cast down suddenly forever. If earthly princes could pass their armies over the wide seas at need, "How much more shall Christ who createth all power, call over this 900 league Ocean at his pleasure, such instruments as he thinks meete to make use of in this place, from whence you are now to depart, but further that you may not delay the Voyage intended, for your full satisfaction, know this is the place where the Lord will create a new Heaven, and a new Earth in, new Churches, and a new Common-wealth together.''[5]

These passages, although shaped by the religious orthodoxy which had emerged by 1650, offer the best contemporary statement on the relation of the Sabbath to the ideas that inspired the founding of Massachusetts. And Johnson's belief that proper Sabbath observance was essential in creating a new heaven on earth faithfully reflected the views of the vast majority of New England Puritans, the Separatists at Plymouth as well as the nonseparating Congregationalists of Massachusetts Bay, Connecticut, and New Haven colonies.

AS PURITANS STROVE to translate an imported theory into practice in the free air of the New World, the Sabbath was constantly changing. At first they relied on Scripture, custom, and reason to regulate its observance. The unwritten code was enforced by individual conscience and public opinion, and magistrates punished the exceptions. This stage ended with the enactment of positive laws on the Lord's Day.[6]

The Puritan settlers were in nearly universal agreement on the theory of the Sabbath; as a result there was far less controversy over the question in New England than in old England. True, Roger Williams and the Antinomians challenged the emerging orthodoxy, but they were suppressed, and Thomas Shepard's subsequent defense of the orthodox position was the only sustained treatise on the Lord's Day by an American in the seventeenth century. Quakers and an occasional free spirit later criticized the prevailing doctrine. At New Plymouth, when Samuel Hicks questioned scriptural authority for current religious practices, several of the ablest brethren of the church went to some lengths to demonstrate from Scripture that the Sabbath was a divine rather than human institution and to be kept on the First Day, also known as the Sabbath or Lord's Day.[7] After the Restoration some Saturday Sabbatarians became troublesome in New England, but it was not until the early eighteenth century that Jeremiah Dummer seriously challenged accepted theory.

Sabbatarian superstitions apparently declined as a result of the migration. The conviction that God punishes Sabbath-breakers to preserve the sanctity of his commandments was prevalent in England on the eve of American colonization, and Puritans brought it to New England. Winthrop relates several instances which illustrate the point. He told of a Boston man who continued working on a Saturday afternoon after "his conscience began to put him in mind of the Lord's day," and whose five-year-old daughter drowned the next day. Winthrop, seeing "a special hand of God" in the event, reported that "the father, freely in the open congregation, did acknowledge it the righteous hand of God for his profaning his holy day against the checks of his own conscience."[8] Examples could be multiplied, but it seems that the removal to New England curbed such superstition.[9] The explanation is that a people united in support of Sabbatarianism and free to live in accordance with its requirements had little need to believe that divine retribution awaited profaners of the Lord's Day. Sabbatarian superstitions flowered again, however, during New England's spiritual crisis of the late seventeenth century.

From the beginning the Puritan settlers observed the weekly day of rest and sanctification from sunset on Saturday to sunset on Sunday. New England was in all likelihood the only region in Christendom where this custom prevailed. English Puritans devised a rationale for the practice after 1600. The Roman mode of measuring days from midnight to midnight had obtained on the Continent since time immemorial, and in 1595 Nicholas Bownde's Sabbatarian treatise held that the Lord's Day ran from morning to morning. Shortly thereafter, however, several Puritans concluded that Scripture required the observance to begin at the evening because the evening and the morning were the first day. Increase Mather said that before the great Puritan migration only John Dod, Arthur Hildersam, and John Cotton favored this view.[10]

In 1611 the Lincolnshire Nonconformist wrote "A short discourse of Mr. John Cotton touchinge the time when the Lordes day beginneth whether at the Eveninge or in the morninge." Drawing on the Bible, Patristic writings, and recent authorities, he argued that the Jews had kept the evening as part of the following rather than the previous day. God had given no command to change the time of beginning the Sabbath in the Christian era, and Christ's resurrection on Sunday, the Christian Sabbath, was insufficient to make that day holy. His words of institution accomplished this task. The Fourth Commandment required one day in seven to be kept holy perpetually, and since the Jewish seventh-day festival had been abrogated, the Christian Sabbath must begin where the Jewish Sabbath ended. Cotton added that evening-to-evening observance had been the practice of the primitive church and the rule of English ecclesiastical law in the days of kings Edgar and Canute.[11]

Cotton's treatise provided an intellectual justification for a practice that was already attracting followers in Puritan circles. In 1607, as we saw, John Winthrop started his Sabbath observance at 3 P.M. Saturday and thought himself somewhat tardy at that. Others adopted the custom. They wanted scriptural authority for their entire code of conduct, and the Old Testament was more explicit than the New about the duration of the septennial institution. Years later, William Pynchon, a founder of the Massachusetts Bay Company and an amateur theologian who lived in Massachusetts from 1630 to 1652, cited 191 Old Testament as opposed to 46 New Testament references to the subject in his treatise about holy time.[12] And the New Testament stated that Jesus died at the ninth hour, or 3 P.M. Puritans found much practical value in beginning the Lord's Day early; the Sabbath was the most valuable day in the week, and a good preparation was essential to its proper sanctification.

This custom, which affected only a small minority in England, was the norm in New England during the colonial period. The Pilgrims introduced the observance, as Bradford revealed in commenting on an exploring party which sought a permanent habitation for the newcomers in late 1620. The expedition stopped on Clark's Island, a short distance across Plymouth Harbor from the site chosen for settlement, on a Saturday, when so many motives urged haste to set foot on the mainland. "And this being the *last day of the weeke*," Bradford wrote, "they prepared ther to keepe the *Sabbath.*" The Bay colony was influential in disseminating the usage. Its leaders were closely associated in England with the major theorists of the practice, and on 17 April 1629, six weeks after the Massachusetts Bay Company was chartered, the directors "to the end the Saboth may bee celebrated in a religious manner" in their settlement at Salem, ordered "that all that inhabite the plantacion . . . may surcease their labor every Satterday throughout the yeare at 3 of the clock in the afternoone, and that they spend the rest of the day in catichising and preparacion for the Saboth." Some carried the convention to extremes. "On Saturday evening," Winthrop wrote of the Boston church after John Cotton arrived in 1633, "the congregation met *in their ordinary exercise.*"[13]

Observance of the evening before raises the question of whether the American Puritans were an Old or a New Testament people. They were Hebraic, it has been said, and their Sabbath observance is among the items cited to support the assertion. True, the Puritan Sabbath fell into the tracks of an ancient Hebrew institution, and its adherents found a sanction for their observance in the Fourth Commandment. Nevertheless, the Puritans came to New England to plant the Gospel. Because they were in the Reformed tradition, they believed in the basic unity and equal authority of the two Testaments. They were "Old Testament Christians,"[14] who drew on Hebrew writ to serve their needs; proper Sabbath observance was a means of bringing sinners to Christ and a rule of righteousness for the saints.

The Puritan observance of the Lord's Day was holy rather than festive, but the Sabbath was a time for solemn rejoicing. It was a day of rest from incessant toil, a memorial of the Resurrection, a foretaste of heaven. The Sabbath in New England was intended as a day of joy, though the Reverend Samuel Peters created the popular impression that it was a day of gloom. A native of Connecticut and an Anglican clergyman, Peters became an outspoken Loyalist and fled to England during the American Revolution. He published a strongly anti-Puritan *General History of Connecticut* (London, 1781), the most famous part of which treats the blue laws of New Haven.[15] Although a careless author, Peters was not the "mendacious refugee" depicted by Puritan apologists; over half of the forty-five laws discussed did exist in New Haven, either expressly or in the form of judicial customs under the common law, and more than four-fifths existed in the same fashion elsewhere in New England. However, the laws in Peters which are unauthenticated, essentially misstated, or wholly spurious include several on the Sabbath. His "symphony in indigo" maintained that it was forbidden to do such things as cook victuals, make beds, sweep houses, cut hair, and shave on the Sabbath, and he went so far as to write that "no woman shall kiss her child on the Sabbath or fasting-day."[16]

Ideally, the first settlers sanctified the day by laying aside worldly thoughts and activities and devoting themselves to spiritual edification. The Lord's Day was given over to private and family prayer, attendance at public worship, Bible-reading, and acts of charity and mercy. Going to church meetings constituted the most important positive obligation of the day. The beat of the drum summoned people to service at nine in the morning and two in the afternoon.

English Puritans emphasized the divine appointment of the Lord's Day and opposed the multitude of other holy days in the ecclesiastical calendar on the ground that they lacked scriptural warrant and occasioned pagan revelry. Edward Winslow of New Plymouth spoke for fellow immigrants when he said, "wee came from thence to avoid . . . the Hierarchy, the crosse in Baptisme, the holy dayes, the booke of Common Prayer."[17] Upon arrival in New England, the Puritans abandoned the medieval church calendar. They sanctified the day appointed by God, setting it apart from worldly or profane works and devoting it to the works of holiness. "Sanctifycation," the Plymouth laymen told Samuel Hicks, "is when any Creature or time is soe sett apart for holy thinges as it must not be used in Any thinge but that which is holy; and though the same holy actions be don att another time they shall not be accoumpted soe holy as att this time."[18] Hence certain activities, including sexual intercourse, were considered improper on Sunday. Puritans apparently regarded children born on the Sabbath as having been conceived on that day. Ministers inveighed against the practice, and the Reverend Israel Loring of Sudbury, Massachusetts, allegedly refused to baptize children born on Sunday until his wife gave birth to twins on that day. Loring then publicly confessed his error and administered the ordinance to his own children.[19]

At the same time Puritans suppressed church-appointed festivals honoring saints, martyrs, and events in the life of Christ. The first occasion for this radical break with the past came at Plymouth in 1621. Because Puritans no longer celebrated the Feast of the Nativity, Governor Bradford called the people to work as usual on Christmas Day. But most of the thirty-five immigrants who had arrived a month earlier were not in religious sympathy with the Pilgrims and excused themselves from labor on grounds of conscience. Bradford, remembering the incident "rather of mirth then of waight," agreed to respect their consciences until the newcomers were better informed and led the others away. Returning home from work at noon, however, "he found them in the streete at play, openly; some pitching the barr, and some at stoole-ball and shuch like sports. So he . . . tooke away their implements, and tould them that was against his conscience, that they should play and others worke. If they made the keeping of it mater of devotion, let them kepe their houses; but ther should be no gameing or revelling in the streets."[20]

While elevating the Lord's Day and abolishing the feast days retained by the Anglican church, the colonists established their own fast and thanksgiving days. Despite Old Testament precedents, the practice derived mainly from the doctrine of Providence. God's people were in covenant with the Lord to plant the Gospel in the wilderness, and special occasions required special ceremonies. When things went badly, people observed a day of fasting and prayer; when heaven smiled they celebrated a day of thanksgiving.[21] These occasions differed from the old holy days in that they were kept as circumstances dictated, rather than regularly on a fixed or movable schedule, and were ordained by civil rather than ecclesiastical authority. Contemporary accounts indicate that the so-called first Thanksgiving Day at Plymouth colony in 1621 does not qualify. After the first harvest was gathered in, Bradford sent four men fowling "so that we might after a speciall manner rejoice together." The Pilgrims and some ninety Indians then feasted and entertained themselves for three days. This was not a single day set apart for thanksgiving, the records say nothing about a religious service, and Puritans would not have allowed recreations during a religious observance. The Pilgrims were celebrating a harvest festival, and the event marks the beginning of civil religion in America.[22]

A SMALL COMPANY of Separatists introduced the institution of the Sabbath at Plymouth colony in 1620. This group originated in Scrooby, a town on the great road between London and Edinburgh, when Puritans from the surrounding area organized their own church about 1606 under the leadership of the Reverend Richard Clyfton and William Brewster, a layman who had attended Cambridge University. William Bradford, a religious teenager from neighboring Austerfield, became a member. Since separatism entailed penalties, the members of the Scrooby congregation decided to seek asylum in the Low Countries, where toleration existed. Despite extreme hardships in escaping, about 125 persons eventually reached Holland. They sojourned briefly in Amsterdam and in 1609 removed to Leyden.[23]

Here the Scrooby Separatists lived for a decade. Their church flourished under the leadership of Pastor John Robinson, a Cambridge graduate, and Elder Brewster; and the English got along well with the Dutch. The Puritans were in general agreement with the Reformed Church of the Netherlands, but even so, religious differences made life difficult. Not only was there a "great mingle-mangle of Religion" in the Low Countries,[24] but also the Dutch had embraced Calvinism without Sabbatarianism, and their poor observance of the Lord's Day distressed the English exiles. None of the Reformed confessions which were widely received in the Netherlands at the time endorsed anything like the Puritan Sabbath, and as a result a Continental Sunday observance prevailed. "It falls out in these towns of Holland," wrote Sir Dudley Carleton, English ambassador to the Hague from 1616 to 1621, "that Sunday, which is elsewhere the day of rest, proves the day, as always of labour (for they never knew yet how to observe the sabbath)."[25] Worse still was the gaiety, drunkenness, and licentiousness of the Dutch on the Lord's Day.

The Puritan theory of the Sabbath inspired an attempt at reform while the Scrooby Separatists resided in Holland. Dutch ministers and Puritan refugees wrote on the topic, provoking dissension. The imported doctrine became entangled with the conflict precipitated by Arminianism in 1603. Although entirely theological, this controversy became entangled with political issues and shook the entire nation. To deal with the matter the States General called the Synod of Dort, which met from late 1618 through May 1619. Though little interested, the orthodox forces that controlled the gathering could not avoid discussion of the Sabbath. Anglican divines among the many foreign members of the international Calvinist assembly complained of the intolerable abuse of the Sabbath in Holland, and twice the body resolved to ask the government to suppress profanations of the Lord's Day. After the Synod formally closed, members approved six articles on the subject in supplementary sessions, but they were of a conciliatory nature and fell short of the Puritan standard.[26]

As the early historians of Plymouth all testify, poor Sabbath observance in Holland and the fear that the English refugees would become typically Dutch in their sporting and merrymaking on the Lord's Day weighed heavily in the decision to remove to America. Bradford cited four reasons for the migration: economic hardship; a crushing burden of labor necessitated by the economic situation; a desire to advance the Gospel in the New World; and "of all sorowes most heavie to be borne, was that many of their children, by these occasions, and the great licentiousnes of youth in that countrie, and the manifold temptations of the place, were drawne away by evill examples into extravagante and dangerous courses, getting the raines off their neks, and departing from their parents. . . . So that they saw their posteritie would be in danger to degenerate and be corrupted."[27]

In *Hypocrisie Unmasked* (1646) Edward Winslow, who lived in Leyden from 1617 to 1620, mentioned economic hardship as a cause for removal but stressed the danger of losing the English heritage. This led him to make Bradford's anxiety explicit by observing "how little good wee did, or were like to do to the Dutch in reforming the Sabbath."[28]

Nathaniel Morton never lived in Leyden, but after arriving in Plymouth in 1623, at the age of eleven, he had access to the oral tradition about the Pilgrims' past. He became secretary of the colony in 1647 and inherited the manuscripts of his uncle, William Bradford. His *New England's Memoriall* (1669) follows Bradford's *History* closely, often verbatim, though with a narrower spirit. All the reasons Morton gave for the migration appear in the two earlier accounts, but the Sabbath heads his list. After ten years in Holland, he wrote, the English exiles could not bring the Dutch "to reform the neglect of Observation of the Lords-day as a Sabbath, or any other thing amiss amongst them."[29]

America offered new opportunity, and some Scrooby-Leyden Separatists therefore organized their own church out of Robinson's congregation and made preparations to migrate there. In July 1620, 33 persons departed from Delfshaven (in present Rotterdam), and in England they were joined by more than three score of persons recruited out of necessity. The enterprise took the form of a joint-stock company financed by English merchant-adventurers. These undertakers ventured their money and the planters their services with the agreement that all property and profits were to be held in common for seven years. In September the *Mayflower* sailed from Plymouth with 102 souls for the Promised Land.

The Pilgrims made a landfall off Cape Cod in late November and a month later, after scouting out the best site for a permanent habitation, occupied Plymouth. Their civil government arose quickly in this day of small things. Since their patent did not authorize settlement as far north as New England, the adult males made themselves self-governing by means of a compact, and the state took shape during the first winter at Plymouth when the men met to devise laws and orders for the colony government.[30]

The church at Plymouth, organized in Leyden before departure, was based on principles developed by Separatists after they began withdrawing from the Church of England in the late 1560s. To Robinson and the Pilgrims, a church was a company of the faithful joined in a covenant with Christ and among themselves to advance God's glory and the salvation of members. Admission was by a profession of faith, subscription to the covenant, and good behavior. However, the church at Plymouth developed very slowly. A majority of Robinson's congregation remained in Holland, probably intending to come over later if the venture succeeded. Robinson stayed with them and died in 1625. The Plymouth church was without a pastor until 1629, when the Reverend Ralph Smith, a man "of very weake p[a]rtes," became their minister. No formal records of the church survive for the first four decades of its existence.[31]

We know, nevertheless, that the Sabbatarian ideal shaped life at Plymouth from the beginning. The Pilgrims scrupulously devoted every seventh day to rest and sanctification, though the colony passed no law on religion until 1636 and did not legislate on the Lord's Day until 1650. At an early date authorities ordered the compact settlement of families in the town of Plymouth, thereby insuring that everyone would live close to the meetinghouse even before such a structure was built. Elder Brewster preached twice every Sabbath for a decade, and on occasion there was "exercising by the way of prophecy," or extempore sermons and comment by members of the congregation.[32]

The Pilgrims made their first friendly contact with the Indians in March 1621 when Samoset, who spoke broken English, came into their settlement on a Friday. Given hospitality that night and dismissed with gifts the following morning, he returned on Sunday with five companions and several deerskins to trade. The English fed and entertained their visitors, who returned the compliment by singing and dancing "like Anticks." But because of the Sabbath the Puritans "would not trucke with them at all that day," and sent the savages away as soon as possible.[33]

The following July the company sent Stephen Hopkins and Edward Winslow on a mission of peace and friendship to Massasoit, chief sachem of the neighboring Wampanoags. Leaving Plymouth on a Monday morning, they penetrated into the interior as far as the limits of Rhode Island, where they were welcomed by Massasoit and entertained by the tribe with games. "Very importunate he was to have us stay with them longer:" Winslow wrote, "But wee desired to keepe the Sabboth at home." So they departed with Indian guides before daybreak on Friday, spending the night en route. A violent storm arose early Saturday and the Indians entreated them to stay over. But the Pilgrims pushed on, perhaps to arrive home before the Sabbath began at 3 P.M., though the natives "wondered we would set forthe againe in such Weather."[34]

Despite problems, high standards of Sabbath observance were maintained during the 1620s. New immigrants joined the small remnant of the Pilgrims, and by 1624 Plymouth contained an estimated 180 souls. A majority of the new arrivals were more interested in profit than religion, and those who had paid their own transportation costs over—they were said to be "on their particular"—presented the general company a special challenge. Directed by the merchant adventurers to grant these persons land, the Plymouth authorities assigned them home lots and freed them to work for themselves on condition that they be subject to the colony laws and pay a tax. But they denied them a vote in colony affairs and debarred them from the Indian trade.[35]

These "particulars," finding life hard, complained to the adventurers whose opinions differed from those of the Pilgrims, and in March 1624 a letter from James Sherley, treasurer of the Company of Adventurers, brought twelve criticisms of conditions in the colony. Such criticism was intended primarily to stir up trouble. Bradford summarized the points and added his responses. Many complaints were frivolous, but the four heading the list related to serious religious matters. One of these charged "neglecte of familie duties, one the Lords day." To this Bradford replied, "We allow no such thing, but blame it in our selves and others; and they that thus reporte it, should have shewed their Christian love the more if they in love had tould the offenders of it, rather than thus to reproach them behind their baks. But (to say no more) we wish them selves had given better example."[36]

The Lyford episode is revealing on Sabbatarianism and its uses. John Lyford, a clergyman, was sent out by the adventurers to fill the need for a minister. He arrived in March 1624, joined the Plymouth church, and was allowed to teach, though he was not ordained. Assisted by John Oldham, Lyford put himself at the head of the discordant faction and in letters to the adventurers accused colony leaders of mismanagement and unfair treatment of the "particulars." Bradford secretly intercepted these writings, and when Lyford and others withdrew to set up their own church, the General Court arraigned them for conspiracy against church and state. Lyford and Oldham were convicted and sentenced to banishment. Before Lyford departed he wrote again to England, justifying his former conduct by charging that the Plymouth church, a minority in the colony, appropriated the ministry to itself and held to the principle "that the Lord hath not appointed any ordinary ministrie for the conversion of those that are without, so that some of the poor souls have with tears complained of this to me, and I was taxed for preaching to all in generall." "This is a meere untruth," Bradford countered, "for this dissembler knows that every Lords day some are appointed to visite suspected places, and if any be found idling and neglecte the hearing of the word, (through idlnes or profanes), they are punished for the same. Now to procure all to come to hear, and then to blame him for preaching to all, were to play the madd men."[37]

In sum, the Leyden Pilgrims were a minority in New Plymouth by 1624, and at a time when dissension based primarily on economic considerations wracked the colony, the insurgents seized upon religious issues in an attempt to undermine the standing order. The Pilgrim Fathers, thinking that Lyford and his faction "intended a reformation in church and commone wealth," suppressed the threat and retained control. They insured religious uniformity by compelling everyone to attend the authorized ministry of the Word every Sunday. The Sabbath was the keystone in the arch of orthodoxy, and from this time forward "a charge of sedition lay against all innovations in church government or in matters of doctrine."[38]

The Pilgrims "never felt the sweetness of the country till this year," Bradford wrote in 1625, but Thomas Morton soon created bitterness.[39] Although well-educated and a lawyer of sorts, Morton was a disreputable adventurer who had "left his country for his country's good."[40] He took over the trading post at Mount Wollaston in present Quincy in 1626, renaming it Merrymount, and his quest for profit and pleasure soon brought him into conflict with Plymouth. That colony, acting in concert with the straggling plantations around Massachusetts Bay, finally banished Morton because he endangered their existence by giving the Indians rum and guns in exchange for furs. Before his arrest, however, this reckless libertine aroused the bitter wrath of the Puritans at New Plymouth by holding revels in which his Indian companions participated. Spirits flowed freely at these festivities, and perhaps there was sexual dalliance with the "lasses in beaver coats," who were always welcome at Merrymount. The boisterous amusement reached a climax in 1627 when Morton held May Day ceremonies to celebrate the change of the plantation's name. Quaffing the beer and strong waters which flowed freely, Morton's men and the Indians erected an eighty-foot pine tree with an elaborate fanfare provided by drums, guns, and pistols, and then danced around the Maypole singing a song whose refrain goes:

> Then drinke and be merry, merry, merry boyes;
> Let all your delight be in the Hymens ioyes;
> Jô to Hymen, now the day is come,
> About the merry Maypole take a Roome.[41]

Bradford denounced Morton as a "lord of misrule" who maintained "a schoole of Athisme," and the Plymouth elders were outraged at the revival in New England of the "beasly practieses of the madd Bacchinalians."[42] Puritans were determined to destroy this relic of paganism in a virgin land, and in 1628 they cut down the loathsome idol erected by Morton.

Isaack de Rasière, secretary of New Netherland, visited New Plymouth in October 1627, a few months after the scandalous May Day, and was much impressed. His description of the Sabbath Day procession to the public meeting is a classic. On Sundays the people in their long cloaks assemble at the beat of the drum in front of the captain's house, wrote the Dutch visitor, then, followed by the governor, flanked by the minister on his right and the captain on his left, they proceed, each man armed and marching three abreast, up Burial Hill to the fort, the lower part of which they used for their church.[43]

About 1630 the environment began to exert a strong reciprocal pressure on the institution of the Sabbath. The migration of thousands of Puritans to the neighboring colony of Massachusetts Bay raised the prices of corn and cattle, and residents of Plymouth, hoping to increase their production of salable commodities, began to scatter in search of better soil and larger landholdings than their town afforded. Their removal left the original compact settlement "very thine, and in a short time allmost desolate."[44]

Dispersal of the population raised questions about church attendance. In April 1632 some prominent Plymouth residents, who had erected houses across the harbor in Duxbury, promised "to remove their fam[ilies] to live in the towne in the winter time, that they m[ay] the better repair to the worship of God."[45] Apparently they returned home every Lord's Day during the summer. William Wood wrote in *New England's Prospect* (1634) that Plymouth men "no more remove" from their old habitations "than the Citizen w[hi]ch hath one house in the Citty and another in the Countrey, for his pleasure, health, and profit. For although they have taken new plots of ground, and built houses upon them, yet doe they retaine their old houses still, and repaire to them every Sabbath day."[46] However, it became burdensome to return every Sunday, so the people of Duxbury asked permission to establish their own church, and in 1632 Plymouth reluctantly assented.[47]

Bradford feared this dispersal would be "the ruine of New-England, at least of the churches of God ther," but the trend was irreversible. Six new towns existed by the time representative government was established in 1639: Duxbury and Scituate to the north; Taunton on the Narragansett Bay watershed; and Barnstable, Sandwich, and Yarmouth on Cape Cod. Rehoboth, Marshfield, and Eastham were settled shortly thereafter. The scattering of population raised such critical questions about religious and moral welfare that the Reverend John Reyner, the minister at Plymouth, and Elder Brewster sought advice on the matter from the Boston church. Although the use of places of husbandry three or four miles distant from the place of a man's habitation and of the public meeting had value, nevertheless, "seing by means of such farmes a mans famylie is Divided so that in busie tymes they cannot (except upon the Lords day) all of them joyne with him in famylie duties," the writers wondered whether the use of farms "be not to doe evell that good may come of yt." And what about servants or tenants employed at farms on weekdays? Reyner and Brewster presupposed that they "doe report duly before the Lords Day to the famylies they belong too and continue there till the second Day, except some one whoe is necessaryly Detayned there, though not usually from the publike assemblies." But the men of Plymouth remained "Darke and Doubtfull" about these things.[48]

These developments weakened the hold of the church on the people, and the first recorded punishment for profaning the Sabbath dates from 1636. In November of that year the General Court revised the colony laws. None of the revised statutes dealt with religion except for a provision empowering civil authorities to appoint holy days for thanksgiving and humiliation. However, the code of 1636 did provide for punishment of "all such misdemeanors . . . as tend to the hurt and detriment of society Civility peace and neighborhood."[49] Such a law could have been used to punish Sabbath offenses, and in the absence of more explicit enactments the civil magistrates used their discretionary authority to enforce God's commandments.

When John Barnes was presented to the General Court "for Sabboath breaking" on 4 October 1636, he was fined thirty shillings and sentenced to an hour in the stocks. Edward Holman, presented for the same offense "though not guilty in so high a degree," was forced to pay twenty shillings. These fines were exorbitant: since the wages of laborers were set at a maximum of eighteenpence a day without diet in 1638, Barnes was fined the equivalent of over three weeks' pay.[50] We do not know what proportion of Sabbath-profaners ended up in court, but in January 1638 Richard Knowles was acquitted and discharged for bringing a bark from Green Harbor near Marshfield on the Lord's Day. The following June, Web Adey was sentenced to sit in the stocks at the pleasure of the bench for working two successive Sundays and "for disorderly liveinge in idlenesse and nastynes." In addition, he was ordered to find a master for himself or his house and lands would be sold to the highest bidder and Governor Thomas Prence would find a master for him. A month later Adey was again found guilty of profaning "divers Lords dayes by working sondry times upon them." Adey, apparently a sot, was now severely whipped for his offenses. Although Mark Mendlowe had previously been convicted as an accessory to a felony, he was discharged when presented in December 1640 for drawing eel pots on the Lord's Day, because "it appeared to be donn of necessytie meerely." The next recorded cases came in June 1649, when John Shaw, Jr., and Stephen Bryant were presented for profaning the Lord's Day by working at the tar pits. They denied the charge but were found guilty. Shaw was sentenced to sit in the stocks, while Bryant was only admonished. On 5 June 1650 Edward Hunt of Duxbury was fined two shillings for shooting at deer on the Lord's Day, whether for sport or meat we do not know.[51] These are the only cases of this type found in the *Plymouth Colony Records* through 1650, and many of those convicted appear to be from the margins of society.

New Plymouth enacted its first Sabbath laws in 1650 and 1651. No sudden breakdown in the standard of Sunday behavior accounts for such measures, and the resort to statutes dealing with religious matters after three decades can be explained by other reasons. One was an increase in vice and wickedness which Bradford sorrowfully noted in 1642. Particularly shocking was the case of Thomas Graunger, a Duxbury teenager convicted and hanged in September for bestiality with several animals. The Governor, wondering why so many wicked persons had so quickly found a place among the people of God, questioned "whether the greater part be not growne the worser?''[52] A perceived decline in morality created an environment conducive to religious legislation.

Loss of religious unity was more important. The continued movement of people to new settlements weakened the original church at Plymouth, leaving it "like an anciente mother, growne olde, and forsaken of her children."[53] In addition, religious heterodoxy made rapid headway throughout the 1640s. Early in the decade Samuel Gorton was in Plymouth crying down churches, church ordinances, and the Sabbath.[54] Anabaptism and other forms of dissent later spread here as elsewhere in New England. In October 1645, someone, probably William Vassall, a critic who led in establishing a second church at Scituate, petitioned the General Court "to allow and maintaine full and free tollerance of religion to all men that would preserve the Civill peace, and submit unto Goverment." Governor Bradford, Edward Winslow, and Thomas Prence opposed, while three assistants and a majority of the deputies favored this radical proposal. When Bradford failed to persuade others that liberty of conscience would "eate out the power of Godliness," he refused to put the question to a vote.[55] By 1650 the existence of dissent created a grave situation, and legislation was enacted to restore and preserve religious uniformity. Massachusetts had passed statutes for the same purpose in 1635 and 1646, so Plymouth had a precedent.

In June 1650 the General Court prohibited the establishment of any church or public meeting without government approval and the denigration of any church, minister, or ordinance; and the law ordered a ten-shilling fine or a whipping for profaning the Lord's Day by servile work "or any such like abusses." A year later the court made attendance at public worship compulsory. The statute of June 1651 provided that heads of households and other responsible adults pay ten shillings for not attending authorized worship or for attending unauthorized worship; any who in a lazy, slothful, or profane way neglected public worship were to pay the same or be publicly whipped.[56]

ALTHOUGH NEW PLYMOUTH was settled first, the Massachusetts Bay colony fixed the character of New England. It was founded by people from the mainstream of the Puritan movement, and they were imbued with a keen sense of divine mission. This included a determination to establish scriptural observance of the Lord's Day. The settlement leaders were identified with the spiritual brotherhood which had formulated and propagated Sabbatarian theory, and by the time the migration to Massachusetts got under way Sabbatarianism had become a leading characteristic of Puritanism. Moreover, the Bay contained a large number of Cambridge and Oxford graduates who were masterly in articulating Puritan doctrine and in translating it into practical reality.[57] Massachusetts quickly became the most influential center in New England.

The religious purposes that inspired the planting of the Bay are evident in the evolution of the Massachusetts Bay Company out of two earlier trading companies organized to colonize New England.[58] John White, a conforming Puritan clergyman of Dorchester, took the lead in forming the first of these. Puritanism had made itself felt in the West Country about the time of the first Book of Sports, spurring the town of Dorchester to adopt "stricter rules of conduct in such matters as church-going, preaching, and the observance of the Sabbath,"[59] and White anticipated that a religious refuge abroad might soon be required. Hence he brought together some gentry, merchants, and moderate Puritan clergymen of the area to form the Dorchester Company. In 1623 the Council for New England issued the group a charter in the name of Sir Walter Erle, the Member of Parliament for Dorset who had aroused sharp controversy in the House of Commons in 1621 by introducing a bill to curb the Sunday recreations allowed by the Declaration of Sports. These adventurers colonized at Cape Ann until 1626, when the company curtailed its activities. Roger Conant led southward the "Old Planters" who remained in New England, and they founded Naumkeag (Salem).

White then recruited nearly ninety persons who shared a common religious and commercial interest to continue the work of the Dorchester Company. The New England Company, organized on the basis of a patent issued on 19 March 1628 by the Council for New England, was made up of adventurers from the West Country, London, and East Anglia, the nursery of nonconformity. Many were worthy Puritans, and "all were possessed of strong religious sympathies and a determination to give their undertaking a distinctly religious character."[60] In June the directors sent out a colonizing party to Salem under John Endecott, who replaced Conant in command. One of the first acts of this blunt and forceful Puritan was to visit Merrymount and chop down Morton's loathsome Maypole.

Some members of the New England Company, to strengthen the legal basis of their grant, secured a charter from the Crown which created the Massachusetts Bay Company. The royal patent of 4 March 1629 organized the Governor and Company of the Massachusetts Bay in New England as a trading corporation, confirmed its title to a carefully defined area in Massachusetts, and empowered the freemen or stockholders to legislate for the company and for any plantation that might be established as long as its laws were not repugnant to those of England. Soon this incorporated body, designed for both religious and commercial purposes, was transformed into a vehicle for advancing the glory of God in New England.

The early years under Charles I were unhappy ones for the Puritans. They thought England was overburdened with people, a land where corruption permeated commerce and undermined learning and where the godly perished for want of employment. Worse still was the religious and political situation. Laud, translated to the See of London in 1628, became the rallying point for the High Church party which denied that the Church of England was bound by Calvinist doctrine. When Parliament met in 1629 and complained of the spread of Arminianism and the introduction of new ceremonies, the King dissolved it. Now government was by prerogative only. Laud, who had the ear of the sovereign, suppressed Puritan lecturers and silenced Nonconformist clergy. Edward Johnson portrayed conditions as desperate in his *Wonder-Working Providence,* and they rapidly deteriorated.[61]

A loosely affiliated group of Puritans in the Massachusetts Bay Company concluded that the time had come to build the kingdom of Christ in New England. Although incorporated companies were expected to conduct their business in England, the royal charter did not designate a place of residence. An emigrating element within the company therefore saw an opportunity to use the patent as the basis for erecting a self-governing society in Massachusetts in complete harmony with God's Word. Accordingly, twelve of them, including John Winthrop, met at Cambridge on 26 August and agreed to emigrate by the following 1 March, provided that both the government and the charter were legally transferred. Three days later the General Court or governing body approved.

Winthrop, elected governor of both company and colony on 20 October, immediately took charge of preparations for the migration, assembling seven hundred persons and a fleet of eleven ships by the following spring. Assisted by members of the spiritual brotherhood, he chose a company well suited for its task. After unsuccessful efforts to recruit distinguished Puritan clergymen such as William Ames and John Cotton, he enlisted George Phillips and John Wilson as ministers. Winthrop imposed no religious test in screening lay applicants, but looked for the qualities of godliness and diligence in one's calling and included a variety of needed occupational skills. Twenty counties contributed to this army of the Lord, with East Anglia, especially Suffolk and Essex, and London providing the largest contingent. The company contained about two dozen persons of social rank above artisan or yeoman (with the nobility barely represented) and a large number of apprentices and indentured servants. The great majority were artisans, yeoman farmers, tradesmen, and their wives and children. Nearly all were products of a subculture which insisted that good Sabbaths make good Christians.[62]

On 8 April 1630 the four lead vessels carrying most of the passengers sailed from England, the vanguard of the great Puritan migration which brought some twenty thousand persons to New England during the following decade.[63] On the trip over Winthrop described the Puritan mission in a lay sermon entitled "A Modell of Christian Charity." He gave classic expression to a Christian socialist ideal reflecting the late medieval outlook. Society is composed of mutually interdependent individuals, each with a vocation and rank assigned by God, the whole functioning in accordance with the divine will. Love, which Scripture defines as the bond of perfection, knits society together. That society is a living organism in which the public interest must outweigh the private, Winthrop demonstrated in applying his doctrine. We profess ourselves "fellow members of Christ," and our task is to find a place to live "under a due forme of Goverment both civill and ecclesiasticall." Moreover, "wee are entered into Covenant with [God] for this worke," and if the Lord brings us to the place we desire, "then hath hee ratified this Covenant and sealed our Commission, [and] will expect a strickt performance of the Articles contained in it."[64]

The *Arbella*, bearing Winthrop and the charter, entered Salem Harbor on 12 June, with the rest of the fleet arriving by early July. The Puritans were ready to possess the land, and the guiding spirits immediately began to build a society in which men could live a new life following the commandments of God. But the land also possessed the Puritans, and the results were not quite as anticipated. Winthrop and other leaders undoubtedly intended to establish one tightly knit "Citty upon a Hill,"[65] but the search for favorable places of habitation led to the establishment of several plantations. By autumn the colonists were scattered around the Bay at Salem, Saugus, Medford, Charlestown, Boston, Newtown (Cambridge), Watertown, and Roxbury. In addition, a party of 140 West Countrymen, sent out by John White and associates, had landed on 30 May and founded Dorchester. In all, a thousand persons arrived in Massachusetts in 1630.[66]

While physical settlement was taking place, the leaders were translating religious doctrines into institutional structure. They established a "due form" of government, assigning both church and state a vital role in furthering scriptural observance of the weekly rest day. The foundations of the state were laid by adapting a trading company charter to the requirements of a body politic. The political thought was that of the Middle Ages as modified by the Reformation. Winthrop and his colleagues saw the ideal form of government as one in which the supreme authority was the law of God as interpreted by the civil magistrates with advice from the clergy. This compact group of rulers, which actually possessed all governmental power after landing in Massachusetts, soon consolidated their supremacy on a new basis.[67]

The charter empowered the General Court, consisting of the governor, deputy governor, assistants, and freemen or stockholders, to legislate for the company in quarterly meetings and authorized these persons to elect the officers annually, out of the freemen, at the spring court. However, the charter constituted the governor or deputy governor and seven (of eighteen) assistants a quorum to conduct business. Since all but one of the freemen who emigrated were also assistants, the Court of Assistants was identical with the General Court.[68] Winthrop and a handful of other members of the Massachusetts Bay Company were the governing body of the colony. Yet when the General Court first met, on 19 October 1630, Governor Winthrop, Deputy Governor Dudley, and the six assistants then present in the colony proposed that the freemen should choose the assistants annually and the assistants should select from among themselves a governor and deputy who, with the assistants, should have power to legislate and to appoint officers to administer the laws. This deprived the freemen of their charter right to make laws and select officers from among themselves, leaving them only a vote in the yearly election of assistants. It also conferred exclusive legislative, executive, and judicial power on the assistants. But "the people" present at the meeting, who had no existence in the eyes of the charter, fully assented by raising their hands. When the General Court met again, on 18 May 1631, it admitted 116 persons to freemanship and at the same time ordered that "noe man shalbe admitted to the freedome of this body polliticke, but such as are members of some of the churches within the lymitts of the same."[69]

What accounts for this revolutionary transformation of the charter of a business organization into the constitution of a civil commonwealth? For one thing, Winthrop and his colleagues altered the charter to keep authority in the hands of magistrates determined to enforce God's laws. And then, because 109 residents had indicated a desire to be made freemen at the October court, they admitted a large number of persons to the freemanship in the spring. This violated the charter by transforming the freemen from members of a trading corporation into citizens of a commonwealth. But it strengthened the government by forming a covenant between the rulers and the ruled, thus binding the people to obey the magistrates. Moreover, the franchise was limited to the godly, and in the period to 1641 a very small proportion of the population had any voice in the government.[70] Under the original frame of government the civil magistrates had full power to regulate personal conduct in accordance with the Word of God contained in the Bible.

The church in Massachusetts was an independent sphere which possessed the same Christian vision as the state. Unlike the Separatists at Plymouth, the Massachusetts Puritans went to New England to separate not from the Anglican church but from the corruptions in it. Although the origins of the nonseparatist Congregationalism of Massachusetts have been a matter of scholarly debate, it appears that the Bay colonists were familiar with the broad outlines of congregational polity before departure, though they had not worked out the details. By 1630 they had reached an understanding as to what constituted a true church, borrowing heavily from the Separatists, who had defined the proper form of ecclesiastical organization as they formed their own congregations starting in the late 1560s. In their view a church was first a company of believers united to each other and to Christ by a voluntary covenant. Second, a church was made up of professed believers who demonstrated their faith by good conduct. The profession required was historical rather than saving faith, an understanding and acceptance of the truths of Christianity as opposed to evidence of a conversion experience. Third, a church possessed the power of discipline and could exclude or expel evildoers.[71]

The Massachusetts Puritans, steering between separatism and conformity, established a nonseparatist Congregational form of church organization. The pioneer church in Massachusetts was founded at Salem on 6 August 1629; members of Winthrop's company organized churches at Charlestown and Watertown on 30 July 1630; and the number rapidly rose in later years. The method of gathering a church was everywhere essentially the same. On a fast day several persons (theoretically at least seven) entered into a covenant with God and one another in which they promised to conform to the rule of the Gospel and God's ordinances as prescribed in His Word, after which the congregation elected and ordained a pastor and teacher and two ruling elders and chose deacons. Once formed, a church subsequently admitted other eligible candidates to membership. Saving faith as a requirement for admission was added in later years. John Cotton apparently introduced this innovation in Boston in 1634, and other ministers soon adopted a practice which the General Court seems to have made official in 1636. The new test required candidates to give satisfactory evidence about their experience of saving grace as well as about their knowledge of Christian doctrine. With the insistence that visible saints were the only fit material for constructing a true church, the basic outline of Massachusetts congregational polity was complete. Covenanted believers alone possessed the right to partake of the sacraments of baptism and the Lord's Supper. In this ecclesiastical system each autonomous congregation was independent of the others.

The state and the churches cooperated in carrying out the divine commission which brought the Puritans to Massachusetts. The churches occupied a dual role in furthering proper Sabbath observance. They provided the public worship which everyone was required to attend before any statutes on the subject existed. However, in the early days a shortage of ministers made it impossible for all to sanctify the Lord's Day by attending church meetings. Only five or six clergymen graced the colony during the first year. Francis Higginson and Samuel Skelton were in Salem, having been sent out by the Massachusetts Bay Company in 1629; but Higginson died on 6 August 1630, leaving Skelton the sole pastor there. Of the two preachers who arrived with Winthrop, John Wilson became teacher and later pastor of the Boston church, and George Phillips became pastor at Watertown. Two clergymen, John Maverick and John Warham, accompanied the West Countrymen to Dorchester. For a time many settlements were served either by a neighboring minister or by lay persons who engaged in prophesying. One critic complained in late 1632 "that fellowes which keepe hogges all the weeke preach on the Saboth."[72]

Authorities hastened to bring over more Puritan divines, finding recruitment easy at a time when conditions in New England were improving and Nonconformists were meeting increasing trouble in England. Roger Williams and John Eliot arrived in 1631, followed by Thomas Weld and Thomas James the next year. The flow quickened after Laud became primate and Charles I renewed the Declaration of Sports in 1633. John Cotton, Thomas Hooker, and Samuel Stone escaped in that year, followed by Nathaniel Ward, Thomas Parker, James Noyes, and Zachariah Symmes a year later. Hard on their heels in 1635 came Thomas Shepard, Hugh Peter, John Norton, and Richard Mather. The new clergy made public worship readily available. Required churchgoing was not based on English or Massachusetts law but on Sabbatarian doctrine and ultimately on the Fourth Commandment. Compulsory attendance made the churches vital agencies of education and control in the Bay colony. As preachers of the Word, the ministers played a vital role in molding individual and collective behavior in accordance with their understanding of the Puritans' divine mission.

The churches discharged their second responsibility regarding the Sabbath by disciplining wrongdoers. The punishments available were public rebuke, public admonition, and excommunication.[73] One authority on the disciplinary action of the Congregational churches in Massachusetts demonstrates that they penalized members for profaning the Sabbath and for failure to attend church throughout the colonial period and well into the nineteenth century. His study leaves the impression that the churches were more active in furthering the Sabbatarian ideal than was actually the case, however, and we have few records of church discipline in Massachusetts until the late seventeenth century.[74] If the First Church of Boston is representative, churches rarely imposed penalties for Sabbath offenses. From 1634 to 1652 the Boston church publicly admonished only seventeen persons, and from 1630 to 1720 it excommunicated a total of seventy-two, after which no excommunications are recorded.[75] Punishments for Sabbath-breaking were extremely rare in this church. Members did excommunicate James Mattocke for "Drunkenesse and Outrage" on the Lord's Day in 1649, and in 1653 they cast out Henry Evans for "drunkennes and uncleane adulterous Carages" on Sunday.[76] But Mattocke was a sot, and for both men the sin rather than the time of its commission seems to account for the penalty. In any event, the churches dealt only with their members, a small minority of the entire population.

The major responsibility for securing proper Lord's Day observance fell to the state. As we have seen, a strict ban on weekday idleness was part of Sabbatarianism. By an order of 28 May 1629 the Massachusetts Bay Company had directed every person in the plantation to apply himself to a calling and ordered that "noe idle drone" be permitted to live in the colony. On 1 October 1633 a Court of Assistants reinforced this decree by ordering that all workmen should work the whole day and that no one should spend his time "idlely or unproffitably," upon penalty of such punishment as the court thought appropriate. Constables were diligently to search for offenders.[77] The Massachusetts Bay Company's order of 17 April 1629, as previously noted, called for complete cessation of servile labor one day a week beginning at 3 P.M. Saturday. The Sabbath rest required some sacrifice in material well-being at a time when the settlers had "all things to doe, as in the beginninge of the world."[78]

The evidence indicates a high standard of Sabbath observance in the colony's infancy. One testimony comes from a Master Wells, an otherwise obscure immigrant who landed with his wife and family in 1633 and settled in Charlestown, whence he wrote to Nehemiah Waliington, the English Puritan who collected examples of divine judgments on Sabbathbreakers, announcing his safe arrival and describing religious conditions as follows: "And how hath my heart been mad[e] glad with the comforts of his house and the Spirituall days in ye same wherein all things are done in the forme and patterne shewed in the mount. . . . Fast days and holy dayes and holy fest days and all such things by Athority Commanded and performed according to the precise rule. . . . I am already fully paid for my voyage Who never had so much in the Stormes at Sea as one repenting thoght rested in my heart, praised and thanked be God who moved my heart to Come and made open the way to mee. And I profes if I mite have my wish in what part of the world to dwell, I know no other place on the whole globe of the earth where I would be rather then here."[79] A "precisian" who treasured the pure Sabbath, Wells called New England the New Jerusalem.

Civil magistrates dealt with only two recorded profanations of the Lord's Day before 1635. On 30 November 1630 John Baker was brought before the Court of Assistants at Boston for shooting at fowl on the Sabbath. Baker was a certified Puritan. He and his wife had come out with Winthrop's fleet in June, he was admitted to the Charlestown church in 1630, and he was made a freeman in 1634.[80] In all likelihood he was shooting for meat rather than sport, since starvation was then stalking the settlement. The colonists had arrived too late in the season to plant their seed, and provisions soon ran dangerously low. In July Winthrop acknowledged that "the hand of God" was upon the settlers, visiting them with sickness and death.[81] Some left the Bay, fearing famine, while Winthrop hastened a ship to the nearest port for a fresh supply of victuals. Before it returned "people were necessitated to live upon clams, and muscles, and ground-nuts, and acorns, and these got with much difficulty in the winter time." At least two hundred colonists died by December.[82] Such was the condition of affairs when Goodman Baker went out to shoot at fowl on the Sabbath. Nevertheless, the court ordered the offender whipped. More compelling fidelity to God's laws would be hard to find.

The second recorded breach of the holy day occurred when the Court of Assistants fined James White thirty shillings on 2 July 1633 for drunkenness at Marblehead on the Sabbath.[83] Since the assistants ordinarily imposed lighter penalties for disorderly drinking on weekdays—ten shillings, for example—wrongs were aggravated when committed on the Lord's Day.

The Bay colony enacted its first law concerning the Sabbath in 1635. When the General Court met at Cambridge on 4 March it heard that "complainte hath bene made to this Court that dyvers persons within this jurisdiccion doe usually absent themselves from church meeteings upon the Lords day." No additional details are given, but by 1635 the population had increased to about eight thousand souls, pushing settlement thirty miles beyond Boston and reducing the capacity of custom and opinion to shape behavior; and at this same time the court asked the churches to agree on a uniform mode of ecclesiastical discipline agreeable to Scripture. Thus, the civil authorities enacted a law empowering "any two Assistants to heare and sensure, either by Fyne or imprisonm[en]t, (att their discrecion), all misdemean[o]rs of that kinde," meaning failure

to attend church, provided the fine not exceed five shillings for each offense.[84] This statute brought to an end the first stage in the development
of the Sabbath in Massachusetts.

WITH THE ESTABLISHMENT of Connecticut and New Haven colonies the
foundations of the core area of New England Puritanism were completed.
Three river towns which constituted the nucleus of the Connecticut colony were the direct outgrowth of expansion from the Bay. Trading posts
arose within a few miles along the river at Windsor, Hartford, and Wethersfield as early as 1633; shortly thereafter groups of people from Massachusetts began migrating to the Connecticut Valley, with the great movement occurring in 1636. John Warham emigrated with part of his
Dorchester congregation to Windsor, accompanied by Roger Ludlow, a
trained lawyer and former deputy governor of Massachusetts; a small
Watertown contingent settled at Wethersfield; and in June 1636 Thomas
Hooker and Samuel Stone led a party from their church in Cambridge to
Hartford.[85]

These three settlements shared a common religious faith and looked
upon themselves as one colony. Their original government was under a
commission from Massachusetts, with Ludlow responsible for "the River
of Conectecotte." The first court, held at Hartford on 1 May 1637 with
Ludlow presiding, declared war against the Pequots and dealt with important civil and religious matters. The communities united under one
government when the chief planters of the three towns met at Hartford
and adopted the Fundamental Orders on 14 January 1639. No record
exists of the proceedings, but the evidence suggests that Hooker inspired
and Ludlow wrote the document. Acknowledging that there should be
"an orderly and decent Goverment established according to God," the
people organized a commonwealth "to mayntayne and presearve the liberty and purity of the gospell" and "the disciplyne of the Churches . . .
now practised amongst us," and agreed to be governed in civil affairs according to such laws as shall be ordered. A General Court was provided,
and although church membership was required of the governor, all freemen were authorized to vote without any such test—a departure from
Massachusetts practice which may explain something about the reasons
for departure. The General Court was to administer justice according to
the laws established, "and for want thereof according to the rule of the
word of God."[86]

There is reason to believe that the colonists honored the weekly holy
day from the time of initial settlement. Hooker's party had stopped to
observe the Sabbath on their overland trek, setting a precedent which
California-bound pioneers, even during the gold rush, were still follow-

ing on the overland trail in the mid-nineteenth century;[87] social sentiment dictated respect for the ceremony; and the magistrates had ample
power to enforce the unwritten Sabbatarian code. Hence attendance at
public worship was expected, as indicated by laws requiring men to bring
their firing pieces to church to defend against Indian attack, and the Sabbath was not counted in fixing the time for fulfilling secular duties.[88]

Sabbatarianism spread to the new towns which arose within the jurisdiction by mid-century. Most of the population still lived on or near the
river, but some whose political allegiance ran to Hartford were settled
along the coast at New London, Saybrook, Stratford, Fairfield, and Nor-
walk; on Long Island at Southampton and East Hampton; and in the interior at Middletown, Norwich, and Farmington. Although there was no
recorded breach of the Sabbath prior to 1650, on 30 October 1643 the
town of Hartford ordered that anybody who played or misbehaved in or
around the meetinghouse during time of public exercise should be corrected.[89] In 1650 the river colony adopted a code of laws which explicitly
regulated Sabbath observance for the first time. With that code, to be
discussed in a later chapter, the first stage in the growth of the Lord's Day
in Connecticut came to an end.

The New Haven colony differed from other New England settlements
in carrying Puritan ideas to a logical extreme. Its origins go back to the
parish of St. Stephen, Coleman Street, London, where John Davenport,
Theophilus Eaton, and others were associates. This church, of which Davenport was elected vicar in 1624, was located in a Puritan stronghold, and
several of its vestrymen were interested in trading companies. Davenport
and his boyhood friend and parishioner Eaton, a prominent merchant,
were founding members of the Massachusetts Bay Company, although
they had no plans to leave England with the Winthrop fleet in 1630.
About that time, however, Davenport became a Puritan, and after Laud
became archbishop in 1633, he had to flee. After a short exile in the
Netherlands, Davenport returned home, where he and Eaton organized a
company to begin a plantation in New England. The leaders and their
families comprised the nucleus of a group which numbered some two
hundred and fifty persons. They arrived in Boston on 26 June 1637, intending to stay among friends, but eventually decided to erect their
kingdom of Christ along the shores of Long Island Sound. Eaton scouted
out a site favorable to trade, and an enlarged company sailed from Boston
on 30 March 1638 and entered the mouth of the Quinnipiac in mid-
April.[90]

Here the settlers were free to erect an orthodox Puritan community.
Church worship was available from the beginning. On the first Sabbath
the people met for worship under a spreading oak near the landing. Dav-

enport preached in the morning, Peter Prudden in the afternoon, both choosing texts with wilderness themes.[91] The compact settlement of the town was dictated in part by religious considerations. "Now if we provide not for the sanctification of the Sabbath," the Puritan divine warned, "the will of God will not be done." The Law expressly commanded that the Sabbath be kept as a day of holy rest, said Davenport, who feared that with the farms at a distance from the town's center "we shall live in the breach of the 4th Commandem[en]t." Eaton agreed.[92]

These and other leaders now began to fashion their civil and ecclesiastical institutions on the Bay model. Lacking a charter, the planters purchased land from the Indians, and on a fast day soon after arrival organized their civil government by entering into a plantation covenant in which they promised that in matters concerning both church and civil affairs "we would all of us be ordered by those rules w[hi]ch the scripture holds forth to us." What they had actually done was to adopt "Moses his Judicials."[93] This document was a brief outline of the frame of government and law of Massachusetts. John Cotton presented it to the General Court of the Bay on 25 October 1636 for the consideration of that body. Despite its marginal references to Scripture, Cotton's code was based mainly on the charter and the common law of England. It offered New Haven a valuable pattern, albeit far more complex than needed, for the government of the colony. In addition, Cotton's draft code aimed at insuring the sanctification of the Sabbath. In capital cases the Boston minister drew upon the Mosaic code, and he proposed the death penalty for profaning the Sabbath.

Adoption of the Cotton code terminated the first stage in the evolution of the Sabbath in New Haven. A year later, on 4 June 1639, the proprietors or free planters, seventy strong, gathered according to tradition in Mr. Newman's barn to complete the laying of institutional foundations. They unanimously agreed that Scripture sets forth a perfect rule for the government of all men in the duties they are to perform to God and men as well as in families, the commonwealth, and the church, and then they voted to confine the elective franchise to church members, after which they organized a church. Those assembled chose from among themselves twelve (actually eleven) godly men, who in turn selected seven from their number, and on 21 or 22 August these seven pillars entered a covenant and gathered a church. Davenport was chosen pastor. In October these seven saints and nine others admitted to the church organized themselves as a civil court for New Haven. The court selected Eaton as magistrate and four deputies.[94] The Puritan Sabbath rested on solid foundations in New Haven.

6

Roger Williams
and the Antinomians

THE SECOND STAGE in the evolution of the New England Sabbath was
characterized by a search for a written law on the subject. Massachusetts
led the way. There the quest for positive statutes governing the Lord's
Day was part of a struggle to develop a legal code which went hand in
hand with conflicts over the system of government, the question of power
versus rights, and challenges to an emerging orthodoxy. This stage ended
in 1648 with the adoption of the *Laws and Liberties* of Massachusetts.

Under the first Massachusetts constitution a compact group of Puritan
magistrates ruled by the Word of God. They made case law regarding the
Sabbath in dealing with offenders like Baker and White, relying on Scripture, custom, and reason. The original frame of government came under
attack soon after its completion. The freemen, criticizing the concentration of authority in the hands of the assistants, demanded a share in government. In 1632 the General Court agreed to allow them to participate
in the election of officers (with the governor still to be chosen from among
the assistants), and representative government was established two years
later. The freemen of every town were permitted to elect deputies to the
General Court, which was empowered to make laws and raise taxes.
Though the assistants and deputies sat together in the court until 1644,
no law could be enacted without the approval of a majority of both

bodies. By 1634 Massachusetts had achieved the structure of government which it long retained.[1]

The absence of fixed laws was another source of tension under the original constitution. Winthrop defended the situation by arguing that it was best in an infant plantation for laws to "arise pro re nata upon occasions" and that growth by custom ran no risk of making laws repugnant to those of England. He also held that, except for capital crimes, punishments "ought to be left arbitrary to the wisdom of the judges." His views met with opposition. On the one hand, magistrates like Thomas Dudley and John Haynes regarded Winthrop as too lenient; on the other, the people felt their rights were insecure while so much power was left to discretion. They wanted written laws defining all punishments, and the deputies became champions of popular opinion.[2] Winthrop's stance led to temporary political eclipse. Dudley was elected governor in 1634, and Winthrop was passed over for three successive years.

A drive for a code of laws began in 1635. In March the General Court appointed Winthrop and Richard Bellingham to survey all previous orders and report necessary corrections; and in May the court named Governor Haynes, Deputy Governor Bellingham, Winthrop, and Dudley to frame laws for the colony. This committee progressed slowly owing to divisions among its members and among the people, some adhering to Winthrop and others to Dudley, "the former carrying matters with more lenity, and the latter with more severity."[3] To heal the rift, Sir Henry Vane and the Reverend Hugh Peter called a meeting at Boston in January 1636 to which three leading ministers—Cotton, Wilson, and Hooker— were also invited. Vane, a young man of fickle mind whose father was a privy councillor and comptroller of the king's household, and Peter, a zealous Puritan preacher whom Laud had driven from England, were eager to alleviate the contention they had discovered upon arriving in the colony the preceding October. According to Vane, the purpose of the meeting was to secure unity between Winthrop and Dudley, though Haynes expressed a desire to deal with Winthrop for laxness in treating offenders. The ministers present favored Dudley, saying that "strict discipline . . . was more needful in plantations than in a settled state, as tending to the honor and safety of the gospel." Winthrop then acknowledged overleniency and promised greater severity in the future, and those present formulated rules guiding the magistrates in a policy of rigor.[4]

In May the General Court enlarged the committee of magistrates by adding Vane, the new governor, and three ministers—Cotton, Peter, and Thomas Shepard—and directing the members to present the following year "a draught of lawes agreeable to the word of God, wch may be the

Fundamentalls of this commonwealth."⁵ Courts were in the meantime to determine cases according to existing statutes or as near the law of God as possible. Cotton submitted a code of laws to the court in October 1636. His draft, a summary in ten chapters of the existing frame of government, criminal code, and practices of Massachusetts, was accurately described as *An Abstract of the Lawes of New England* when first published in London in 1641.⁶ Cotton, however, added numerous marginal references to Scripture and closed by quoting Isa. 33:22: "The Lord is our Judge, the Lord is our Lawgiver, the Lord is our King, he will save us."⁷

Winthrop entitled this code "Moses his Judicials." Cotton's reliance on God's Word was most evident in chapters on inheritance and crimes, which contain the document's only remarks on the Lord's Day. Since civil affairs were to be so ordered as to forward the worship of God, the chapter on inheritance held, no one, whatever the location of inherited land, should be permitted to live more than a mile from the meetinghouse. Acts 1:12 on a Sabbath Day's journey was cited as authority. In the chapter on capital crimes Cotton included this provision: "Profaning the Lords day in a carelesse or scornful neglect or contempt thereof, to be punished with death." The reference was Num. 15:30-36, which describes the stoning to death of a man who presumptuously profaned the Sabbath by gathering sticks then.⁸

Did Cotton intend his proposal to be taken literally? The twentieth-century mind revolts at the very thought. The penalty seems disproportionate and inhumane. We take comfort, therefore, in concluding that Cotton included this suggestion for rhetorical effect: the story of the hapless Israelite's death would serve as a reminder of the supreme importance of proper Sabbath observance. Yet, if we try to understand Cotton's draft from within the Puritan ideology, it is probable that he meant precisely what he said. In discussing how far his code bound Massachusetts, Cotton contended that the Ten Commandments are perpetual laws, adding "the more any Law smells of man the more unprofitable."⁹ Massachusetts executed people for violating various commandments, and willful profanation of the Sabbath was a grave offense. The biblical story of divine wrath visited upon bold impiety possessed a horrible fascination for contemporary Puritans. In 1644, for example, the Massachusetts clergy illustrated their belief that penalties must always fit crimes by saying, "so any sin committed with an high hand, as the gathering of sticks on the Sabbath day, may be punished with death, when a lesser punishment may serve for gathering sticks privily, and in some need."¹⁰ A decade later William Aspinwall, a Fifth Monarchy pamphleteer who had lived in New England more than twenty years, drafted a criminal code for England which provided capital punishment for twelve offenses, including adultery, "wilful profaning the Sabbath," and "cursing the Rulers of the people." Cotton's code embodied existing Bay colony laws, and his Sabbath provision probably reflected his understanding as to how authorities should punish the described offense. Nevertheless, Winthrop struck the death penalty for Sabbath-breaking and five other crimes from Cotton's draft, a document never adopted by the General Court. Thus, only Virginia and the jurisdictions that did endorse "Moses his Judicials" earned the dubious distinction of providing capital punishment for Sabbath offenses.[11]

THE CHALLENGE OF Roger Williams (c. 1603-1683) came to a climax soon after the search for a written legal code began. He differed with Bay colony leaders over certain fundamentals of the faith, the most important of which for our purposes and for modern culture was freedom of conscience. Williams denied the authority of the civil magistrate over observance of the Sabbath, expressing his uncompromising opposition to the emerging orthodoxy with the declaration that "forced worship stinks in God's nostrils."[12]

Much about the origins of Williams' thought is still unclear. Born the son of a merchant tailor, he graduated from Pembroke College, Cambridge, and took holy orders in 1627. He shortly became a Separatist and concluded that a wider scope awaited his talents in New England. A man of magnetic personality with a reputation for godliness, Williams reached Boston early in 1631.[13] He quickly became a center of controversy owing to his stand on two issues. Separatism was one. Upon arrival he rejected an invitation to become teacher of the Boston church on grounds that he "durst not officiate to an unseparated people." Williams then went to Salem, where the Separatist-inclined church installed him as teacher, despite a warning from the General Court not to do so without conference. The power of civil authorities was another issue that aroused controversy. Within two months after landing the newcomer "declared his opinion, that the magistrate might not punish the breach of the Sabbath, nor any other offence, as it was a breach of the first table."[14] Thus, Williams broke his first lance for freedom of conscience over the Sabbath question.

Williams removed to Plymouth before the end of the summer. Here he held no religious office but assisted the minister and exercised "by way of prophecy." After two years friction with the Separatists caused him to leave Plymouth. Returning to Salem in August 1633, he was made a minister of the church and immediately became embroiled in fresh controversy with Bay authorities for attacking the validity of the colony charter and the use of oaths to secure the allegiance of freemen and residents and in judicial proceedings. These conflicts were troublesome, but it was not until Williams was installed as pastor at Salem, following the death of Samuel Skelton in August 1634, that he launched the assault that brought banishment a year later. In September he denounced eleven public sins and subsequently compounded his offense by again attacking the charter (thereby breaking a promise) and the use of oaths.[15] What prompted his onslaught at this time is unclear. Perhaps he felt it was now or never in reversing the fatal course on which Massachusetts had embarked.

The authorities tried to reason with their antagonist over a period of several months. Governor Dudley sent for him in April 1635, and fellow ministers "very clearly confuted" the notion that magistrates might not tender oaths to the unregenerate. At the General Court in July, the ministers and magistrates concurred in judging his opinions to be "erroneous, and very dangerous."[16] Given until autumn to recant, Williams was warned to give satisfaction then or be sentenced. But a turbulent spirit and the "heady . . . pursuite" of disturbing doctrines and practices worsened his situation, and in October he showed no intention to submit. Unintimidated by the charge that he was self-willed and pitted his judgment against both church and state, the New England Luther stood firm, dauntlessly praising "one Scripture in the mouth of one simple Mechannick before the whole Councel."[17] The court accordingly ordered banishment within six weeks, and all the ministers except one approved. The offical reason for the sentence was that Williams had "broached and dyvulged dyvers newe and dangerous opinions, against the aucthoritie of magistrates" and that he had written letters defaming the magistrates and the churches before conviction and maintained the same without retraction.[18]

This formula embraced a variety of possibilities. Separatism, though not expressly mentioned, was a main reason for expulsion. At stake was the question of the nature of true worship. Williams, holding that it was an act of worship to teach and to be taught in a church estate, demanded complete separation from the Church of England as the only way of keeping the church pure. The leaders of Massachusetts considered it a Christian duty for all to attend divine service, but only members could participate in church worship. Cotton, for example, contended that an infidel might enter a Christian church to hear the Word preached and be converted; and yet without profession of faith and owning the covenant such a person would not be joined in church fellowship.[19] The state had the responsibility of requiring attendance of nonmembers. Also at stake was the welfare of the colony. Williams' insistence on complete separation invited interference from England.

Soul liberty, though not explicitly mentioned in the sentence, was another reason for banishment. For Williams the individual conscience was inviolable. He contended that man's relations with God were beyond the reach of any third party. Faith was a divine gift and could not be forced by human authority. Hence Williams opposed the direction the province was taking. Almost immediately after landing he opposed civil punishments for breach of the First Table, and subsequently he held that it was unlawful for the unregenerate to call the regenerate to pray. His fears for the future were justified when, in March 1635, the General Court ordered everyone to attend public worship on Sunday and asked the churches to agree on a uniform mode of ecclesiastical discipline and to consider how far the magistrates were bound to interpose to preserve that uniformity. Although Williams acknowledged the state's jurisdiction over breaches of the First Table that disturbed the civil peace,[20] he proposed to limit the power of the magistrate to enforcement of the Second Table, which conerned man's relations with his fellow man. These views, a threat to the foundations on which Massachusetts was being built, were seen as meriting banishment.

After sentencing, Williams returned to Salem with permission to remain until spring on the understanding that he not try to win others to his beliefs. But he violated the agreement and Governor Haynes sent soldiers to deport him to England. Williams, eluding his captors, fled in the winter of 1636 to the Narragansett Bay area. The following summer his antagonist John Cotton wrote to convince Williams that he had banished himself from the fellowship of the Bay churches on weak grounds and that the civil expulsion was ''righteous in the eyes of God.''[21] When Cotton's letter, a needless wound, mysteriously appeared in print in 1643, Williams published a rejoinder. This exchange led to a full discussion in Williams' *The Bloudy Tenent of Persecution for Cause of Conscience* (1644), Cotton's *The Bloudy Tenent Washed in the White of the Lamb* (1647), and Williams' *The Bloody Tenent Yet More Bloody* (1652). Williams set forth his views on freedom of conscience with much repetition in these volumes, which afford the best understanding as to why the critic opposed the pattern of Sabbath observance developing in Massachusetts.

Underlying the wayward Puritan's outlook was a typological interpretation of the Bible.[22] Whereas New England Puritans in general favored a literal reading of Scripture and emphasized the continuity between the Old and New Testaments, Williams interpreted the Bible typologically and stressed the discontinuity between the two dispensations. For him ancient Israel was no model for any state religion but only figuratively a type of the spiritual discipline that the church should exercise over its members. Israel did not recognize any separation between the religious and secular realms. The Old Testament Hebrews comprised both a nation and a church. Abraham's seed were all in the covenant, and kings ruled the national church, wielding the sword against heretics. The Chosen People were unique in being set apart from the world. But Jesus abolished the church of Israel and instituted the church of Christ. Henceforth the people of God were no longer identical with any one nation but elect Christians, the company of the faithful scattered over the face of the earth. Between the Apostasy and the Reformation, however, God's people had "opened a gap in the hedge or wall of Separation between the Garden of the Church and the Wildernes of the world." Christianity fell asleep in Constantine's bosom when the state recognized the church; the faith lost its vitality when the whole world became Christian. Thus, the state churches spawned by the Reformation were not the institutions founded by Jesus. Both history and hermeneutics convinced Williams that civil magistrates were not responsible for matters of conscience.[23]

One key element in his thought was the monstrous character of national religious establishments. The Roman and Anglican churches were filled with corruptions and false worship, and the churches of Massachusetts were unsatisfactory because they had not separated from all anti-Christian pollutions. Although his explanations leave much to be desired, Williams differed from others in the Bay colony as to what constituted fit material to form the church of Christ.[24] He distinguished between personal godliness and godliness of worship. The former was a divine gift and essential to salvation, for the natural man lacked the capacity to comprehend spiritual truth. But personal godliness did not prevent enthrallment to false worship. Godliness of worship was that by which Christ formed a body of worshipers. Williams subordinated it to personal godliness, thereby enabling Cotton to charge that he made "Church-Covenant to be no better than a Covenant of workes: whereas indeed if Church-Covenant be not a branch of the Covenant of grace, the Churches of Christ are not built upon Christ."[25] Williams, however, thought neither type of holiness was sufficient to constitute a true church unless the godly repented "the sinfulness of every sipping of the whores cup."[26] But the Bay offered only what Cotton called the "substance of true repentance" for continued association with the Church of England, and for the Separatist this was not enough.[27]

Williams also differed from his Massachusetts contemporaries as to the nature of the true ministry, an issue directly related to compulsory churchgoing. New England Puritans, although rejecting the validity of

episcopal ordination, allowed members to attend but not to take communion in the Church of England. Cotton argued that a person from
Massachusetts might visit an English parish church as an infidel would,
for his presence constituted only the natural communion of an auditor
with a minister; if a visible saint, actually a hypocrite, were converted by
an English clergyman, it was in respect of the minister's gifts rather than
his exercise of office. Williams, however, contended that the true ministry, overcome by the Apostasy, had not been restored after the Reformation. He rejected Cotton's distinction between attending the worship
of the Word and of the sacraments, holding that there was no ministerial
office except by appointment of the Lord. Williams believed that the
Spirit was always at work stirring up true churches and ministers, although
the multitude of pretenders made it hard to find the real thing. However,
neither Anglicanism nor Massachusetts Congregationalism met his exacting requirements; thus he ceased regularly to attend religious assemblies
in the Bay colony. Neither a humanist nor a rationalist, Williams was a
Seeker who vowed he would readily join any church professing Christ in
which his soul could find rest.[28]

His pilgrimage led Williams to separate from the church but not the
state, and he repeatedly pressed Cotton to explain why voluntary withdrawal from the former necessitated involuntary removal from the latter
unless the two were identical, which Puritans denied. Williams therefore
charged Cotton with that "body-killing, soule-killing, and State-killing
doctrine of not permitting, but persecuting all other consciences and
wayes of worship but his own." His expulsion for religious belief mixed
two spheres that should be kept distinct, and the result was to bring "all
the world into Combustion."[29]

A second key element in Williams' thought was the evil of restraining
the conscience. The decline of Christianity since the Apostasy proved that
pure religion never prospered when mixed with the world, and Massachusetts therefore erred in perpetuating the Jewish polity and making the
state the "nursing father" to the church. Church and state had their own
distinct means and ends, according to Williams, and a strict separation
between them was essential. Each particular church possessed the spiritual
weapons to further its own purpose: the salvation of souls. The Word
should be preached only to those possessing personal godliness and godliness of worship, and hypocrites were to be resolutely banished from the
church. The state possessed the power to promote the temporal good of
society. Civil magistrates need not be church members or profess the religion of their people, for the state lacked jurisdiction over souls and could
thrive without true religion. Society ran no risk of being corrupted by unregenerate or excommunicated persons, because the natural man was spiri-

tually dead. With a strong hedge between them, Christ's lilies could flourish in the Garden though the weeds grew rank in the Wilderness. Let the Word be freely preached in the world for the purposes of conversion and many briars would be turned into roses.[30]

Williams acknowledged that the office of magistracy was given by God to preserve civil harmony. An advanced political theorist who found the origin of civil power in the people, he considered it proper for rulers to enforce the duties mandated by the last six commandments, which involved objectively measurable relations between individuals, but not the first four commandments, which touched the inner recesses of the conscience. Temporal good required that the state be empowered to correct "scandalous livers" who disturbed the civil peace, but the promotion of truth and freedom of conscience required that the state be denied the power to punish "seducing teachers," even those whose ideas might prove socially disruptive.[31]

His defense of soul liberty brought Williams into conflict with the standing order in Massachusetts. Rejecting the distinction between natural and spiritual communion which enabled magistrates to contend that compelling attendance at prayer but not prayer itself forced no conscience, Williams held that both teaching and being taught in a church constituted church worship. The state committed "spirituall rape" in requiring one uniform mode of discipline; compulsory churchgoing forced whole nations to pretend religion. If persons were compelled to forsake their own religion to attend church all their days, Williams queried, would this not be the people's religion? "And if this bee not so, then I aske, Will it not inevitably follow, that they . . . enforce people to bee of no Religion at all, all their dayes?"[32]

The Bloudy Tenent of Persecution elaborates on the evils of violating the individual conscience. Forced worship was presumptuous in that faith was a gift of God; for the state to compel belief exalted free will over divine grace. Civil authorities lacked the theological capacity to judge spiritual matters, and their handling of cases of conscience brought ecclesiastical matters under civil jurisdiction. Forced worship convinced many that religion was untrue. To require all to worship by "setting up that for *godlinesse* or *worship* which is no more than *Nebuchadnezzars golden Image, a State worship,"* was the greatest cause of breach of the civil peace. Compulsory attendance either drove residents to remove or encouraged mass hypocrisy. The sword could produce a nation of hypocrites, soothing people in a formal state of worship to the ruin of their souls and sooner or later kindling the devouring flames of civil war, but the sword could not create one single Christian.[33]

Though orthodox on most doctrines, Williams profoundly differed from other Puritans on church organization and religious liberty. The heretic held that there could be no recovery of the faith until Christ sent new apostles to plant new churches, and he may have believed this was his mission.[34] In any event, when Massachusetts headed on an allegedly destructive course Williams became an aggressive critic, and his challenge brought swift expulsion.[35]

THE VICTORY OVER Williams vindicated the principle of civil jurisdiction in matters concerning the First Table, and on this basis the task of erecting a holy commonwealth went forward. But shortly after the banishment a more far-reaching threat to the emerging orthodoxy arose, when a group holding theological views of an antinomian tendency criticized the manner in which Massachusetts was implementing the Reformation. The upshot was the Antinomian Controversy, which began in October 1636 and ended in March 1638. Antinomianism is the theological doctrine that the Christian is freed from all legalism, even the Decalogue, by faith and God's gift of grace through the Gospel. Advocates of this new light revived complicated questions about the grounds of a sinner's hope for salvation, and the ensuing conflict had an important bearing on the future of the Sabbath in New England.

Who advanced the new opinions, and why did the controversy erupt precisely when it did? *"Dux foemina facti,"* wrote Winthrop, attributing the troubles to a woman. Although Anne Hutchinson (1594-1643) played a prominent part in the crisis, the "American Jezebel" actually took her lead from John Cotton.[36] The daughter of Francis Marbury, an independent-minded clergyman, Anne grew up in the religously charged atmosphere of early seventeenth-century England. She married William Hutchinson, a merchant, in 1612, settled in Alford in her native Lincolnshire, and began a large family. But separatist inclinations and religious uncertainty troubled her, and her soul found comfort in the evangelical preaching of Cotton in neighboring Boston. Mrs. Hutchinson came to rely on him as a religious guide, and when Cotton fled to Massachusetts in 1633, Anne could find no rest until she followed him there. The Hutchinson family emigrated in 1634, arriving in Boston in September.[37]

The two Hutchinsons quickly established prominent positions in the community, with Anne overshadowing her doting and mild-tempered husband. She was intelligent and forceful and won great affection through her skill as a nurse and midwife. Religion was her true métier, and Boston, where religion satisfied every individual and social need, offered full scope for her talents. Though suspected on landing of harboring antinomian views, she was admitted to the Boston church on 2 November

1634. Subsequently she began to hold weekly meetings for religious conference in her house, ostensibly to repeat Cotton's sermons to the younger women. Mrs. Hutchinson also commented on doctrine and made the Scriptures suit her own purposes. A meeting for men and women was later added and the discussion was expanded to include an evaluation of the merits of various preachers and specific sermons. Some sixty to eighty persons from Boston and outlying towns attended these gatherings, which were unprecedented and potentially dangerous because Puritans considered it improper for the laity to judge the doctrine or inspiration of the clergy and for a woman to lead men in such matters.[38]

In the beginning, according to Winthrop, only two issues were involved as Anne Hutchinson spread the new light. She taught ''that the person of the Holy Ghost dwells in a justified person,'' and ''that no sanctification can help to evidence to us our justification.'' It now seems clear that she drew her doctrines from John Cotton, and that he was the chief figure in the Antinomian Controversy. Her second point was the main issue in the debate between Cotton and his fellow ministers.[39] Cotton emphasized that a Christian should not look to any confidence in human ability in the process of regeneration, for this was a covenant of works, and the Hutchinsonians turned his teaching into an insistence that without any evidence of a changed spiritual condition a Christian should rely on an immediate revelation made to the soul. Later, at a crucial juncture, Cotton disavowed the Antinomians and sided with orthodoxy.

The background of the Antinomian Controversy is found in the nature of Puritanism. The central problem of Puritan piety was how a sinner could gain assurance of salvation. Puritans dealt with the matter in terms of covenant theology and the antithesis between Law and Gospel. Men were to prepare for conversion by obedience to the Law, but no conditional promises were made. A Christian could not earn salvation by his own efforts, this being a deadly covenant of works. Justification was by faith alone. God made an absolute promise that he would plant saving grace in the souls of the elect, and the saints, those effectually called and justified, showed their love of God by keeping his commandments. This was Calvin's third use of the Law. Though the covenant theology explained the terms of assurance, Puritans were troubled by uncertainty and developed ways to test their own spiritual estate. They tended to make outward behavior an objective measure of grace: sanctification or personal holiness could be taken as a sign of justification.

Massachusetts operated on these assumptions during its first five years of settlement. Winthrop envisioned the colony as a model of Christian charity. As long as the bond of love united people, sanctification was the common standard of behavior in the colony, the witness of the true life of the New Israel. The Holy Spirit inspired a zeal for perfection, and that impulse underlay a religious revival that began after John Cotton arrived in September 1633. Many new members entered the Boston church in the next six months, and by mid-decade a confession of saving grace was added to the requirements for church membership.

About 1635 a shift from utopia to reality occurred. The revival burned itself out, and from the ashes emerged a fresh and compelling sense of anxiety about the assurance of salvation. Meanwhile, the constitutional revolution of 1634 demonstrated that the law of love did not prevent a conflict of interests. A new politics ensued, and ministers and magistrates began a cooperative search for legal foundations to ensure godliness of conduct so that from outward evidence it could be argued that Massachusetts was still a community of saints. Precisely at this moment the Antinomians denounced the danger of looking to works rather than grace in the salvation of sinners.[40]

The Hutchinsonians became an object of suspicion in the autumn of 1635, after John Wilson returned to Massachusetts and resumed his place as pastor of the Boston church. The Opinionists, as contemporaries called the Antinomians, began comparing Wilson with Cotton to the detriment of the former. They insisted that obedience to the Spirit within rather than observance of community norms gave evidence of justification and labeled Wilson a "legal" preacher, meaning one who saw a connection between man's obedience to external duties, or works, and redemption by Christ. Before long Mrs. Hutchinson charged that all the colony ministers except Cotton were "legal" ministers. They preached a covenant of works, were not able ministers of the New Testament, and lacked the seal of the Spirit.[41] His fellow ministers suspected Cotton as the source of the new light and finally arranged a conference at Boston in October 1636 to sound him out. Mrs. Hutchinson was present, along with John Wheelwright (1592?-1679), her brother-in-law and supporter, a minister who arrived from England that spring. The results were encouraging, for Cotton and Wheelwright agreed with the other clergymen on the essential point, "that sanctification did help to evidence justification."[42] But the harmony was short-lived.

The Antinomian Controversy became a public matter in late 1636. Religious differences in the Boston church erupted into open quarrel when a majority proposed Wheelwright for the ministry, intending to replace Wilson. Winthrop thwarted the election but his strong criticisms brought increased bitterness. Cotton's sermons and the doctrines held by all but four or five members of the Boston church continued to cause alarm, so in

December the other colony ministers propounded sixteen questions and asked Cotton to deliver written judgment on them. He cleared some doubts but gave no satisfaction on others.[43] Cotton feared that the other clergy overemphasized human ability. He held that the promises were absolute rather than conditional and that justification could not be built on sanctification. To think that one could win heaven by effort was to fall into a covenant of works, which was the foundation of popery. His fellow ministers—Bulkeley, Peter, Shepard, Weld, and others—defended the use of sanctification as evidence of justification. Their doctrine provided a foundation for a legal code that would bind the entire community to walk in the path of righteousness and keep good Sabbaths.[44]

This controversy began to wrack the General Court in December. Henry Vane, the young and inexperienced governor and a supporter of Cotton and Hutchinson, submitted his resignation because he feared "God's judgments to come upon us for these differences and dissensions." His gesture was a blow against orthodoxy, and the Boston church persuaded their friend in power to withdraw his resignation. In the debate that followed about the causes of the trouble, Vane pointed to the ministers while John Wilson "laid the blame upon these new opinions risen up amongst us, which all the magistrates, except the governor and two others, did confirm, and all the ministers but two."[45] Wilson's speech gave great offense, so the General Court appointed a general fast for 19 January to reconcile the differences.

The Fast Day only aggravated the conflict. Wheelwright, preaching in the Boston church, "inveighed against all that walked in a covenant of works," meaning "such as maintain sanctification as an evidence of justification." His remarks emboldened members of Boston to spread the new opinions, and the result was much bitterness. Though the new light was concentrated in Boston, where some of the leading men of the colony took sides with the Antinomians, it also divided a number of churches in outlying towns. The Opinionists labored to destroy the reputation of clergymen who maintained commonly received doctrines, calling them "legal" preachers who could not be instruments to bring others to the Gospel. According to Winthrop, "it began to be as common here to distinguish between men, by being under a covenant of grace or a covenant of works, as in other countries between Protestants and Papists."[46]

At this point orthodoxy launched a counterattack. When the General Court met in March 1637 "the greater number far" of magistrates and deputies were sound regarding the new light.[47] Thus, the members voted approval of Wilson's controversial speech and sentenced Stephen Greensmith, who had said that all the ministers except Cotton, Wheelwright, and he thought Hooker, taught a covenant of works, to acknowledge his fault in every church and pay a forty-pound fine. In addition, the court found Wheelwright guilty of contempt and sedition for having "purposely set himself to kindle and increase" bitterness by his Fast Day sermon.[48] These events set the stage for the court of elections on 17 May. Though a tense situation developed in Newtown (Cambridge), where this session was held to minimize the influence of Boston, the people chose Winthrop governor in place of Vane. The standing order now had sufficient power to crush its adversaries, but apart from enacting one law to prevent immigrants from rushing in to swell the opposition ranks, the authorities pursued a course of moderation. The state also decided that ministers and lay representatives from the New England churches should confer about the theological aspects of the controversy.[49]

A general council of churches, the first of its kind in Massachusetts, met in Cambridge at state expense from 30 August to 22 September. Thomas Shepard, pastor of the host church, opened the assembly with prayer. With the magistrates present and the Opinionists free to speak, the delegates discussed the issues for three weeks and concluded by publicly condemning eighty-two errors and some "unsavoury speeches" attributed to the Antinomians. Nearly all the ministers present subscribed to the list of proscribed doctrines. Cotton but not Wheelwright ended in agreement with the majority, and thus the Cambrige Synod restored theological unity.

The catalog of erroneous opinions and their confutations is the most complete guide to the theological issues in the Antinomian Controversy. Several of the eighty-two items overlap, but a few examples demonstrate the nature of the threat to the Puritan doctrine of the Sabbath. As for Law and Gospel, the Synod labeled as erroneous the beliefs that persons united to Christ are not under the Law as the rule of life and that the whole letter of Scripture teaches a covenant of works. The prevailing view emphasized the Decalogue as the perfect summary of the rule of life for Christians. Scripture, the elders replied to the Antinomians, speaks of Christians as under the Law to Christ. Moreover, the letter of Scripture holds forth a covenant of grace rather than a covenant of works. To be sure, the new birth of life was the work of the Spirit as opposed to the Letter, yet many Scriptures make keeping the commandments evidence of a good estate. In short, Sabbath observance was no mere obligation of the Law but a fruit of the Gospel.[50]

On human ability in redemption and personal holiness as evidence of justification, the Synod denounced as erroneous the following beliefs: (1)

to act by virtue of or in obedience to a commandment is legal; (2) all the activity of a believer is "to act to sinne"; (3) there can be no true closing with Christ in a conditional promise; (4) conditional promises are "legal"; (5) "to take delight in the holy service of God, is to go a whoring from God"; (6) one may not be exhorted to duty, because he has no power to do it; (7) one cannot evidence his justification by his sanctification; (8) to do so is a soul-damning error. Grant these propositions and it would have been impossible to urge Sabbath-keeping as a means by which sinners could prepare themselves for regeneration and by which saints could voluntarily express their love of God.[51]

In addition, the Synod designated as erroneous the beliefs that the Spirit may testify to the soul immediately, "without any respect unto, or concurrence with the word"; that there is no true assurance of salvation unless it be without fear and doubting; and that the Spirit acts most in the saints when they endeavor least.[52] These notions, advanced by Anne Hutchinson, John Wheelwright, and their followers, show that antinomianism was radically subversive of the commonly accepted tradition. Edward Johnson thought that the new lights rejected the good old way of Christ. They told him, take a naked Christ and he could attain revelations full of such ravishing joy that he would never have cause to be sorry for sin. Also, that he would find little increase in the graces of Christ through hearing the Word preached and other divine ordinances. Johnson knew better. He had fled to the New Israel to find Christ's presence in the preaching of the Word and to have his own sinful nature fully revealed by the mirror of the Law. For what, he asked, is the whole life of a Christian upon this earth but through the power of Christ to die to sin and live to righteousness? And for that end he should be diligent in the use of means. Johnson spoke for the orthodoxy upheld by the ministers and magistrates of Massachusetts.[53]

Although the Cambridge Synod united the ministers, the colony remained divided after the assembly adjourned. Some Opinionists vented their displeasure by petty disturbances, while Wheelwright and his followers stirred up fresh contention in the churches. So the magistrates, concluding that two parties could not exist together without ruin to the whole, decided to put an end to the matter. At its session beginning on 2 November 1637 the General Court crushed the antinomian movement. The leaders, including Wheelwright and Mrs. Hutchinson, were disfranchised and banished, and their followers were disfranchised or disarmed. Authorities seized upon a March remonstrance by some sixty members of the Boston church protesting Wheelwright's conviction as a pretext for these punishments. The magistrates had difficulty, however, in making a case against Mrs. Hutchinson. Because she had not participated in the political protest, she was charged with holding public lectures in her house and with reproaching most of the colony ministers for not preaching a covenant of free grace.[54] The unyielding witness skillfully parried questions for two days but finally sealed her doom by disclosing that she had received divine revelations.[55] Officials feared that anyone claiming immediate access to divine truth might forcefully oppose those differing from them in judgment. Mrs. Hutchinson was permitted to remain until spring, and on 22 March 1638 the Boston church, after a lengthy trial in which Cotton tried to reclaim her, excommunicated the heretic for persisting in gross errors.[56] Mary Dyer, who later became a Quaker, followed Anne Hutchinson out of the meetinghouse, a gesture that shows the close affinity between the spiritual emphasis in Puritanism and in Quakerism.

The new opinions constituted a potentially serious threat to the Puritan Sabbath from the beginning, and the danger increased as the Antinomian Controversy progressed. At a critical point in the development of the Bay colony, the authorities resorted to new techniques to further the achievement of their original objectives. The ministers exhorted the faithful to the performance of external duties and cooperated with the magistrates in a search for legal foundations to advance the holy commonwealth. The Antinomians, fearing the emphasis on human ability in the process of regeneration as subversive of the Reformation principle of justification by faith alone, resisted the fresh direction. They insisted on evangelical as opposed to legal righteousness and on absolute as opposed to conditional promises. The Christian, without any evidence of a changed spiritual condition, should rely on an immediate revelation made to the soul. A sinner was effectually called and justified by the free gift of God's grace, and those in a covenant of grace were incapable of sin.

According to contemporaries, antinomianism spread rapidly because it offered an easy way to heaven. Puritanism was a demanding religion; antinomianism a bed of ease. It enabled the slothful to escape the hard effort of keeping the commandments by shifting the burden of salvation to the Holy Spirit. Orthodox leaders were convinced that the erroneous opinions of their adversaries led inescapably to degenerate practices, and this conviction became especially strong after the General Court defeated the antinomian movement in late 1637.[57] Shortly thereafter Winthrop noted that many Bostonians were tainted with "foul errors," one of which held "that the Sabbath is but as other days."[58] That proposition was anathema to a people who regarded the perpetual morality of the

Sabbath as a foundation of the New Israel, and it was strangled in infancy. The triumph of orthodoxy insured that the Law would be the rule of life for the Christian in Massachusetts, where a synthesis of moralism and activism came to prevail. With the defeat of the Antinomians the way was clear for the Puritan Sabbath to become a central feature in the New England Way.

7

The Letter
and the Spirit

AS SOON AS the Antinomian Controversy ended the leaders of the Bay colony resumed the task of building the New Israel in America. A number of domestic and foreign influences shaped this work during the ensuing decade, and by 1648 Massachusetts Puritans were splendidly bound to their society by *The Book of the General Lawes and Libertyes,* a legal code which laid the foundations of the civil commonwealth, and the Cambridge *Platform of Church Discipline*, a plan of church government which became part of the laws of the colony. Adherents viewed the system, of which the Puritan Sabbath formed an integral part, as the greatest achievement of the Reformation.

Although the search for written laws initiated by Massachusetts in 1635 brought Cotton's *Abstract* before the General Court in October 1636, the court neither accepted nor rejected it, and the quest resumed when the authorities could again present a united front. In March 1638 the court called upon the freemen to propose laws for revision and abridgment by a committee. Nathaniel Ward (1578-1653), the minister at Ipswich and a trained lawyer, was a member of the group. He prepared a Body of Liberties, and in November 1639 the Cotton and the Ward codes were before the court. Ward's draft was a lengthy bill of rights which limited the arbitrary power of the magistrates. The court sent both proposals to another committee, which formed one document by incorporating Cotton's cap-

152

ital laws into Ward's liberties. The product was then submitted to the towns for the freemen and churches to consider. In December 1641 the court adopted the Body of Liberties, thereby effectively disposing of "Moses his Judicials."[1]

Ward's code, which appears not to have been printed at the time except for the provisions relating to capital offenses, contained both general principles and specific laws. It adapted Scripture as well as English statutory and common law to local needs. Punishments were to be by the Word of God in the absence of specific enactment, and civil authority was to see that the ordinances of Christ were observed in every church so long as this was done in a civil rather than an ecclesiastical way. No injunctions other than those of the Lord were to be imposed upon any church in point of doctrine, worship, or discipline, and every church was to have freedom to celebrate days of fasting, prayer, and thanksgiving according to God's institution. The new code made no crime capital that was not capital in the Mosaic Law, but the death penalty was not provided for everything punishable by death in the Old Testament. The Lord's Day was not expressly mentioned. Scripture, aided by custom and reason, remained the ultimate sanction for Sabbath observance, a situation that continued for several years.[2]

After 1641 the effort to perfect a code of laws was affected by the elaboration of Sabbatarian theory and triumphant Puritanism in England. Though the Antinomians were suppressed, their threat to the emerging orthodoxy in Massachusetts was not forgotten, and other heresies arose. A doctrinal defense of the theoretical foundations of the Puritan Sabbath was in order, and the ministers provided it. Thomas Shepard penned the most masterly discussion of the subject. *Theses Sabbaticae: Or, The Doctrine of the Sabbath* (1649) is the substance of several sermons on the Fourth Commandment which the greatest evangelist of early New England preached to his Cambridge congregation. At the request and for the use of students in Harvard College, Shepard expanded the discussion, while reducing it to the form of scholastic theses or short propositions. Later, at the urging of elders throughout New England, he enlarged and published the work in London the year of his death.[3]

Shepard was convinced that "religion is just as the Sabbath is," and *Theses Sabbaticae* was intended primarily to defend the morality of the Sabbath against Antinomians and advocates of spiritual religion, which flourished during the ferment of the 1640s. He thought that if any state would reduce the people to superstition and impiety, let them have a dancing Sabbath; and if a total immunity from the law of God, then an everyday Sabbath. According to him, many were cold toward the external

Sabbath because they exalted the internal and spiritual Sabbath. By turning the Christian Sabbath into a spiritual Sabbath, they made all days
Sabbaths. This specious doctrine was dangerous, however, for if people
abolished the outward Sabbath in favor of an inward Sabbath of rest in
the bosom of Christ, they might also reject all external New Testament
ordinances by allegorizing and spiritualizing them away.[4] Shepard took
issue with several European writers who had criticized the Puritan doctrine of the Sabbath earlier in the century, including Franciscus Gomarus,
a Dutch theologian, and Francis White, an English bishop whose *Treatise
of the Sabbath* (1635) took an Ecclesiastical view on the subject.[5]

The Antinomian Controversy was presumably the original stimulus for
Shepard's book. Harvard College opened to students probably in July or
August 1638, and the sermons from which *Theses Sabbaticae* evolved
may have begun shortly thereafter, when popular interest and the need to
combat heresy were great. If not then, the sermons may have commenced
in the middle 1640s, when the rapid spread of antinomianism and of
spiritual religion furnished a fresh incentive to defend the morality of the
Sabbath. In all likelihood the sermons continued for some time, after
which they were turned into theses—a total of 373—and prepared for
publication while the busy author was also writing several other works.
The Cambridge pastor took great pains to strengthen his argument and
seized upon the latest books advancing a spiritual interpretation of the
Sabbath. *Sparkles of Glory,* which the English spiritual writer John Saltmarsh published in 1647, came in for special criticism.[6] Shepard consulted fellow ministers in the Bay for advice, and Richard Mather furnished a critique as late as 20 July 1648.[7]

Shepard's treatise discusses the morality, change, beginning, and sanctification of the Sabbath. He devotes the first book, two-thirds of the
entire work, to morality, the most controversial topic at the time. His
complicated argument begins with a definition of the moral law intended
to establish the morality of the Sabbath. According to him, God first
made the divine law good and then established it because it is suitable to
human nature. The law of the Sabbath is moral, perpetual, and universal
because of its intrinsic goodness. The divine determination of something
in a law does not alter its morality; however, moral laws cannot be known
to all because of corrupt human nature. Man's reason could never discover the observance of one day in seven, but it is comely that God have
"some magnificent *day of state.*" "Take away a Sabbath, who can defend us from Atheism, Barbarisme and all manner of devilism and prophaness?"[8]

The entire Decalogue is the moral law, and it is wrong to think that men are not bound to observe the Fourth Commandment. Some hold that only those commandments are good which the Gospel confirms to be so; yet if moral laws need such ratification, the Fourth Commandment has it, for there we read that the moral law is holy, just, and good (Rom. 7) and that Christ came not to destroy the Law (Matt. 5). Some maintain that the law of the Sabbath is ceremonial rather than moral, yet the Decalogue does not mix the two; otherwise one would have to resort to the light of nature to distinguish between them, a remedy worse than the disease. The true question is whether the Sabbath is one of those laws commanded because it is intrinsically good and of perpetual and universal obligation or a Jewish ceremonial precept from which Christians are exempt. All agree that the law of the Fourth Commandment is moral; the real controversy is how and in what respects this is true. The general consent is that the morality is in something general rather than in the particular day mentioned by the commandment, otherwise the day could never be changed. The general characteristic Shepard acknowledged as moral is a seventh day, whereas others recognized merely a day, without noting how frequently it occurs.[9]

Shepard resolves the question through lengthy interpretation of the Fourth Commandment, concluding that a periodically recurring seventh day was moral by that part of the Decalogue. Antinomians and others sin in making all days equally holy under the Gospel. After examining Scripture texts used to justify equality of days (Gal. 4:10, Col. 2:16, and Isa. 66:23), Shepard notes the distinction between the internal and external Sabbath. If all external observances of worship are not to be attended because the kingdom of God consists in internal peace, "then far[e]well all externall Preaching, Sacraments, Profession and Confession of the Name of Christ, as well as Sabbaths." The chief reason some abolish the Sabbath of the Fourth Commandment is that they abandon the Decalogue as a Christian's rule of life. An inward Sabbath may well agree with an external Sabbath, but if there be no set times, "we may then bid *goodnight* to all the publike worship and glory of God in the world."[10]

Shepard next examines the great controversy as to whether the Law is a rule of life to a believer. This material is lengthy (thirty-nine theses) and seemingly a digression. Yet it is central to the author's purpose and a major if neglected source on the Antinomian Controversy. Though justification is by faith, Shepard writes, if sin is a transgression of the Law, then a believer must attend to the Law as his rule. The outward Law revealed in Scriptures is perfect, for it declares God's will. The inward Law written on the heart is imperfect and unfit to be our guide. The faithful receive the Spirit of God by the Word externally preached or written, not by immediate revelation. To renounce the written Law and cleave to an inward and better rule opens a gap to licentiousness.[11]

Certain errors of the Antinomians regarding the rule of law are analyzed. Shepard argues that both the Law and the Gospel require people to act. The difference is that the Law accepts only perfection, the Gospel less. A believer is to act by virtue of a command. Though God works in us, we need to work out our own salvation by attending to the rule. The Law as delivered by Moses was delivered by Christ in Moses, thus the Gospel has us walk according to the Law. Men are freed from it as a covenant of life but not as a rule of life. The new creature is under rather than above the Law, which offers guidance to the saint. Here again Calvin's third use of the Law is apparent. The conditional promises annexed to obedience are in the Gospel, and requiring the condition is the means to work the promise. The Gospel requires activity of a justified person. Since the moral law has a directive use, it is wrong to neglect the preaching of the Law to make way for the Gospel and to deny that sanctification is clear evidence of our justification.[12]

The author then returns to the main argument, the morality of a set time for public worship. He holds that a seventh day is determined generally in the Fourth Commandment. God commanded a seventh day because it was good and set an example by resting on that day. The seventh day which God shall determine is primarily moral, and the church can order neither more nor less time. A particular day of the week is secondarily moral, though men cannot take any day for the Christian Sabbath. The first book of *Theses Sabbaticae* concludes with a diffuse restatement and elaboration of the theme that the law of the Sabbath is part of the moral law which is man's universal rule of life.[13]

The second book treats the change of the Sabbath from the seventh to the first day. This issue was much discussed by New England ministers in the 1640s, when biblicism led many to insist upon the unchangeable time of the original Sabbath. Shepard refuted in particular the English writers David Primrose and Theophilus Brabourne, basing his argument on the light of Scripture rather than on tradition or human authority. The Gospel appoints a new seventh day, but it stands by virtue of the Fourth Commandment and its observance is a matter of Christian duty. The will of God is the efficient cause, the Resurrection the secondary or moral cause for the change. The first day of the week was honored by the primitive church from the commandment of Christ. Thus, the sanctification of the Lord's Day is a divine institution. Shepard supports this conclusion by examining Acts 20:7, 1 Cor. 16:2, and Rev. 1:10.[14]

The third book considers the beginning of the Sabbath. Shepard starts by considering various doctrines on the subject. One set the time according to the civil customs of different nations. Another made the artificial day, the time from sunrise to sunset, the Sabbath. A third allowed God his full twenty-four hours but started it at midnight. A fourth began and ended the Sabbath at sunrise. All of these Shepard rejects as scripturally untenable and in some cases also impractical. He defends the familiar New England doctrine and practice of beginning and ending the Sabbath in the evening as a mandate of God's Word in the Bible.[15]

The fourth book, on the sanctification of the Sabbath, holds that all the nonceremonial holy duties enjoined on the Jews are also exacted of Christians. This entails rest on the Sabbath from all servile works. These include any work done for worldly gain, profit, or livelihood as well as worldly sports and pastimes, which are ordained by God to whet the appetite for ordinary employments and are therefore proper appurtenances to days of labor. However, preparation of food and works done for the preservation of creatures, such as rescuing an animal, quenching fire in a town, saving grain from flood, keeping fire in the iron mills, and steering a ship, are not unlawful. Servile works also comprise worldly labors not done for gain which with provident foresight might be done as well either before or after the Sabbath. Hence bringing in a crop or setting sail upon the Sabbath because of uncertain weather is forbidden, as is sweeping the house, buying at shops, or washing clothes. But works of necessity for comfort of life are allowed, such as watering animals, preparing hot food, putting on comely garments, and washing one's hands and face.

The weekly rest is the means to the holiness required on the Sabbath, and Shepard describes the proper sanctification of the day. He calls for more immediate holiness on this day than on others, for special endeavors unto holiness which would make the Sabbath a delight, for constant holiness throughout the entire day, for a sweet and quiet holiness that refreshes the soul, and for a holiness that communicates itself to others. He urges civil magistrates to enforce Lord's Day observance, for God will certainly revenge the pollutions of his Sabbaths. A single breach of the Sabbath is not as great a sin as murder, but to commit sins upon the day when all the treasures of God's rich and precious love are opened is to double their evil. The Lord has crowned the English nation above all other places on the earth with this "garland of glory," and Shepard is determined that New England shall uphold God's Sabbaths.[16]

WHILE SHEPARD WAS elaborating the doctrine of the Sabbath, the century-long conflict between Puritan and Anglican was reaching a crisis in

England. As the opposing armies took to the field, Parliament began to reconstruct the national church on a presbyterian basis. The Assembly of Divines, summoned to draw up plans for the purpose, sat at Westminster from 1643 to 1649. During these years Parliament enacted Sabbath laws that expressed mature Puritan theory. The first of these, the ordinance of 8 April 1644, relied on the Fourth Commandment. In the interest of seeing that the day was celebrated by worship, it banned the sale of goods, travel, and labor as well as wrestling, shooting, bowling, ringing of bells for pleasure, masques, wakes or feasts, church-ales, dancing, games, and other sports—on penalties of from five to ten shillings. It also forbade Maypoles and ordered that the king's Book of Sports and other writings against the morality of the Fourth Commandment be called in and publicly burned. (The Book of Sports was actually burned in the City of London that year.) The ordinance directed rogues, vagabonds, and beggars to attend worship on Sundays and allowed the dressing of meat in families and inns and the sale of milk between 9 A.M. and 4 P.M. in the winter and from 8 to 5 at other times. This ordinance did not try to curb ordinary domestic work on Sundays, and it did not go as far as strict Puritans desired.[17]

Parliament later abandoned negative prohibitions and imposed a more demanding standard. An ordinance of 4 January 1645 replaced the Book of Common Prayer with the "Directory for the Public Worship of God" drawn up by the Westminster Assembly. The Directory's instructions for sanctification of the Lord's Day simply encapsulated the Puritan theory of the Sabbath. Two years later Parliament implemented one provision of the Directory by abolishing Christmas, Easter, Whitsunday, and other holy days on the ground of superstitious usage. But the ordinance of 8 June 1647 granted scholars, apprentices, and servants the second Tuesday of each month for recreation. Obviously English Puritans objected to Sabbath desecration more than to sports as such, and their enactment introduced a valuable social reform. Sunday work was growing in the seventeenth century, and without protective legislation freedom from Sunday labor would not have survived much longer. In the matter of rest the average Englishman was better off under the Puritans than under the Stuarts. Formerly work was permissible after service on holy days. Now holy days were abolished but Sundays were protected, and a sizable element of the population had a monthly day of recreation.[18]

Meanwhile, the Westminster Assembly was devising doctrinal symbols based on the Word of God. The Confession of Faith, formulated in eighteen months of interrupted debate ending in late 1646, was a clear and strong statement of Christian doctrine according to the Calvinist scheme.

Parliament adopted it in 1648. The chapter dealing with religious worship and the Sabbath Day compactly expressed Puritan teaching on the subject. In addition, two members of the Assembly of Divines, Daniel Cawdrey and Herbert Palmer, published *Sabbatum Redivivum: Or The Christian Sabbath Vindicated* (1645-1652). These two volumes of over a thousand pages, the longest treatise on the matter by English authors, agreed with Shepard and the prevailing view in Massachusetts in all essentials except the time when the Sabbath began.[19]

CONSOLIDATION OF THE Puritan theory of the Sabbath in old and New England was the background of the continued search for legal foundations for Lord's Day observance in Massachusetts in the 1640s. Because the Body of Liberties inadequately checked the discretionary power of the magistrates, every General Court for three years after 1641 weighed it with a view to improvement. Then in May 1645 the court appointed a committee of five, including Thomas Shepard, to draw up bills for positive laws against Sabbath-breaking and other moral offenses, and in response to strong popular demand four successive committees of the court prepared a fuller code of laws. The *Book of the General Lawes and Libertyes* was published in 1648.[20]

This compilation, alphabetically arranged by subject, resulted from judicial interpretation and legislative determination. The magistrates relied upon the Bible, custom, and English and Massachusetts statutes in deciding cases, and the deputies and assistants drew upon this body of precedents as well as other sources in drafting written laws. The two routes converged in 1648. The *Book of Laws,* the first attempt at comprehensive reduction of a body of legislation in an English-speaking country, blended Mosaic, English, and Massachusetts law. The capital crimes contained the only Old Testament references, in the margin. The 1648 code made the Bay colony a government of laws rather than men. It was the basis of all subsequent Massachusetts legislation and influenced the legislation of other colonies, notably Connecticut and New Haven.[21]

The *Laws and Liberties* contained four articles regulating Sabbath observance. One required attendance at public worship; another forbade the undermining of religious belief, including the denial of the morality of the Sabbath; a third prohibited Sabbath-breaking; and a fourth dealt with burglary and theft on the Sabbath and at other times.[22]

The compulsory attendance and antiheresy articles were enacted in 1646 in response to the same set of problems. Massachusetts always emphasized the importance of public worship, and in 1635 the General Court passed a law providing a fine for failure to attend divine service.

The court employed the law in 1638 when it summoned Ezekiel Holli-man, a former cohort of Roger Williams, for not frequenting the public assemblies "and for seduceing many" from orthodoxy. The dissident was referred to the ministers, who could not convince him of his wrong. Holliman subsequently fled to Rhode Island, where in March 1639 he and Williams baptized each other and founded the first Baptist church in America.[23] But the original compulsory attendance law was seldom used in the decade following its enactment, and evidence indicates a generally high standard of church attendance in these years.[24] In relating accidents that befell children left home unattended on the Sabbath, for example, Winthrop takes for granted that parents went to the assemblies that day. He records that when D'Aulney's commissioners from French Acadia spent the Lord's Day in Boston in 1646, he acquainted them "with our manner, that all men either come to our public meetings, or keep them-selves quiet in their houses." As a courteous gesture, Winthrop invited the Catholic delegation to his residence, where they remained until sun-set, reading his Latin and French books and walking in his garden, "and so gave no offence."[25]

The immediate background to the legislation of 1646 was the rise of new threats to the faith. Religious sectarianism flourished in England when traditional authority and the compound of Puritanism disinte-grated during the Civil War, and a variety of strange doctrines made their way to America. The opinions of Antinomians, Seekers, and Anabaptists were being broached in New England after 1640. Rhode Island was a prime source of infectious error. Besides Anne Hutchinson and other Antinomians, it harbored Samuel Gorton, a self-styled "Professor of the Mysteries of Christ," and his spiritualist followers.[26] Gorton came into conflict with the Bay because he took land from Indians and others who put themselves under the jurisdiction of Massachusetts and because of his heterodoxy. In September 1643 commissioners sent from Massachusetts arrested Gorton and others and took them to Boston. A month later they were examined in the General Court for denying all visible and external ordinances of the Bay colony churches and for reviling the magistracy as an ordinance used among Christians. Though Gorton was not above denouncing his adversaries for working and trading on the Sabbath and otherwise profaning it, he charged that the Lord's Day was one of "dark-ness and gloominess" to Massachusetts but of "joy and gladness" to his company, and in various ways attacked the morality of the Sabbath. The Gortonists were found to be blasphemous enemies of the religion of Christ and his holy ordinances and likewise of civil authority. Most of the magistrates favored a death sentence, but finally the seven chief offenders were ordered dispersed to various towns and confined to work, while wearing leg-irons and without maintaining any of their damnable heresies, during the pleasure of the court. The next March, however, after discovering that their captives were corrupting residents with their doctrines, authorities ordered them out of the jurisdiction, with a warning never to return on penalty of death.[27]

That autumn the Massachusetts legislature passed a law authorizing punishment of the Anabaptists (or Baptists) on the ground, among others, that they denied the power of the magistrate to punish outward breaches of the First Table. Conviction brought a sentence of banishment. A year later a small group led by William Vassall of New Plymouth and Dr. Robert Child began agitating to overthrow the existing institutions of Massachusetts. They charged that the colony denied the liberty of subjects both in civil and in ecclesiastical matters, and their Remonstrance of 1646 complained that they were compelled under a severe fine to appear at the congregation every Lord's Day.[28] By the fall of 1646 the authorities were responding to all of these challenges. In September the Cambridge Synod, to be discussed later, took up the problem. At the same time the Commissioners of the United Colonies, except those of Plymouth, recommending to their legislatures some improvement of religion, argued for the suppression of Anabaptism, Familism, Antinomianism, and similar errors which undermined the Scriptures, the Sabbath, or other ordinances of God.[29]

In addition, the General Court on 4 November 1646 enacted a new and more complete statute requiring attendance at divine service. The preamble, noting that the state did not compel any to enter into church fellowship involuntarily, held that public worship was the ordinary means to promote the faith, civil obedience, and social order. Hence the law directed everyone in Massachusetts to attend public worship on the Lord's Day (as well as on fast days and days of thanksgiving appointed by authority) wherever the ministry of the Word was established according to the order of the Gospel. The penalty for failure without just and necessary cause was five shillings.[30]

The statute was little used immediately after its adoption. Massachusetts Puritans were brought up to sanctify the Sabbath, and in small communities social pressure encouraged attendance. Nevertheless, authorities in Essex County presented two offenders before the law, minus its preamble, was incorporated into the *Laws and Liberties* in 1648. A year later the quarterly court at Salem fined William Cantelbury "according to order" for not attending church, though it merely admonished Richard Hollingsworth, a prosperous elderly man, for frequent absence from Sunday afternoon service. That the enactment exerted an influence was testified to by Goodwife Holgrave of Gloucester, who said that "if it were not For the law, shee would never com to the meetinge," since William Perkins was so dead that he was more fit to be a lady's chamberman than the teacher of the church. Nevertheless, she persuaded Goodwife Vincent to come to her house on the Sabbath and read good books.[31]

The antiheresy article of *Laws and Liberties* was originally enacted along with the compulsory attendance statute and in response to the same set of forces. As stated by the General Court in November 1646, laws may not constrain the conscience, since no human power is Lord over it; and yet persons who brought in "damnable heresies" tending to destroy the faith or subvert souls ought to be deterred. Hence the court forbade the broaching or maintaining of various doctrines, including denial of the morality of the Fourth Commandment. The penalty for remaining obstinate after conviction was twenty shillings a month for six months and double the amount thereafter, and five pounds for endeavoring to seduce others to any of the proscribed views.[32] Mary Oliver was presented under this law by a Salem court in 1648. Charged with denying the morality of the Sabbath and other offenses, she was treated leniently on this occasion but later banished.[33] That autumn the *Book of Laws* incorporated this statute, increasing the penalty for remaining obstinate after conviction to banishment.[34]

A third article in the *Laws and Liberties* proscribed "Sabbath-breaking," a term not further defined. Bay magistrates had punished the offense in the absence of written statutes, and in November 1637 the General Court took an additional step by authorizing towns to enact ordinances to restrain neighboring Indians from profaning the Lord's Day.[35] The legislature did not return to the problem until 1646; in the meantime the law on the subject developed by judicial construction.

The courts included labor and travel under the rubric of Sabbath-breaking. In Essex County nine presentments were made between 1642 and 1648 for such Sunday activities as carrying a burden, carrying a fowling piece, "bringing home sticks in both . . . arms," gathering peas, rolling a cask, and brewing. (A man who carried dung in his canoe on Sunday escaped presentment by drowning.) Most of these wrongdoers escaped lightly. The court dismissed the case involving the casks and another involving a ship's safety on the ground that the labor was necessary. Only two of those arraigned were fined for working on the Sabbath, and in each instance they were also charged with other violations of the Fourth Commandment. One offender, Elizabeth Lambert, was admonished because she left some of her Saturday brewing to the next day. Even yeast could not be allowed to work with impunity on the Sabbath![36]

Travel on the Sabbath, except for necessity, was rigidly suppressed. Though he rarely went from his own congregation on the Lord's Day, in 1639 Governor Winthrop journeyed to Cambridge to hear Thomas Hooker of Connecticut.[37] A few years later officials authorized men of Ipswich, Rowley, and Newbury to go and disarm the Indian Passaconamy on the Sabbath, and the armed party sent to arrest the Gortonists advanced after sunset on Saturday. Nevertheless, a quarterly court held at Boston in 1638 ordered Richard Hollingsworth to be set in the stocks at Salem for traveling on the Sabbath; in 1641 two men, condemned to be severely fined and banished on pain of death for criticizing the religious doctrines of Massachusetts, were enjoined to depart immediately after the Sabbath; and the constable of Wenham was presented in 1647 for sending a prisoner to Salem on the Lord's Day.[38]

Other violations of the Lord's Day were punished. The injunction "Six days you shall labor, and do all your work" (Exod. 20:9) was binding, and in early New England, where land awaited the plow and forests the axe, physical survival demanded incessant toil. In October 1633 the General Court passed a law ordering all workmen to work the whole day and not to spend time idly or unprofitably. A quarterly court held at Boston in 1637 sentenced George Barlow to be whipped for idleness (examples of similar penalties could be multiplied), and John Cotton preached that idleness broke the Fourth Commandment, since one cannot honor the Sabbath by resting unless one has first been laboring.[39] Rest from worldly employment was confined to the Sabbath. But sports and pastimes were forbidden, so, lacking wholesome recreations, people used their freedom from the discipline of work for the pleasures of the flesh.

By the middle 1640s magistrates had gained considerable experience in dealing with profanations of this type, and they punished misdeeds more severely when committed on the Sabbath than on other days. At Salem a quarterly court in 1639 directed a servant to be severely whipped for drunkenness, "pilfering from his master, etc." on Sunday. Tom Sams, complained of by Emmanuel Downing for "coming unseasonably on Lord's day and in nights" to court the Downings' maidservant, was given an hour in the stocks. A court held at Ipswich fined a man twenty shillings for striking another on the Sabbath, and a Salem court levied twice that amount for a similar offense. The Salem magistrates also fined two men for disturbing the congregation by hunting and killing a raccoon during time of service.[40]

Knowing the community would be at the meeting, some seized upon the day of worship to perform foul deeds. In 1641 a young Salem servant, William Hackett, "was found in buggery with a cow, upon the Lord's day. He was discovered by a woman, who being detained from the public assembly by some infirmity that day and by occasion looking out at her window, espied him in the very act." After trial and conviction Hackett repented, but he was executed by hanging. A year later Daniel Fairfield, a married man about forty, was convicted by the General Court of having had carnal knowledge of two very young girls, daughters of one of the magistrates, over a period of two years, "especially upon the Lord's days and lecture days."[41]

When the legislature finally addressed itself to the problem it gave constables authority to suppress all manner of Sabbath profanations. The statute empowered these officials to apprehend without warrant certain types of criminals, including Sabbath-breakers, provided the constable witnessed or received firsthand information about the offense. Since the law assigned no specific punishment for a crime that was stated in general terms only, magistrates could still use discretion in imposing sentences. The measure became the article entitled "Constables" in the *Law and Liberties*.[42]

A fourth section of that book dealt with burglary and theft. The Sabbath was prime time for robbers. The problem arose as early as 1636, when Winthrop observed that a Boston servant, a "very profane fellow" who hanged himself when threatened with prosecution, "did use to [go] out of the assembly, upon the Lord's day, to rob his master." Richard Gell, a Salem apprentice, was sentenced to be severely whipped and to sit in public with a paper on his head for "breking a hous, stealing, etc. on the Lord's day." Marmaduke Barton, a Salem servant, was meted out the same punishment for taking half a cheese, a piece of cake, a knife, and a little milk from two houses on the Sabbath. And Thomas Savory, a Boston servant, "for breaking a house in the time of exercise, was censured to bee severely whiped, and for his theft to be sould for a slave until hee have made double restitution." He had previously committed burglary on the Sabbath in Rhode Island.[43]

In June 1642 the General Court passed a law empowering magistrates to punish, according to the nature of the offense, anyone who robbed a dwelling on the Lord's Day when its inhabitants had gone to worship or who committed burglary or robbery at any other time. Records show two additional convictions for Sabbath burglary before 1648. One offender was to be moderately whipped; the other, Richard Gell again, severely. The article on "Burglary and Theft" in the *Laws and Liberties* differed from the 1642 statute in that it prescribed the penalties and gave special protection to the Sabbath. For weekday burglary or robbery a first conviction brought branding on the forehead with the letter *B;* a second conviction meant branding as before and also a severe whipping. These same penalties applied for Sabbath burglary or robbery; in addition, a first conviction resulted in the loss of one ear, a second in the cutting off of the other ear. For a third offense the penalty was death if the act was done presumptuously.[44] Thus, Massachusetts perfected a body of laws empowering the state to enforce a Puritan standard of Sabbath observance.

Meanwhile, the ministers and magistrates were endeavoring to perfect the ecclesiastical polity of Massachusetts and to distinguish between the two jurisdictions. Despite the fact that Congregationalism was in effect the established church of New England, its basic structure and essential unity had received no authoritative statement, a need revealed by the agitation of the Remonstrants in 1645 and 1646. A synod or council of churches was the recognized method for reaching agreement, but opinion was divided as to whether the churches should consult the civil government in holding such an assembly. After much deliberation the ministers applied to the magistrates for a meeting in May 1646, and the legislature resolved its internal differences by inviting rather than commanding the churches to assemble. The General Court intended the representatives of the churches to deal with questions of ecclesiastical policy raised by William Vassall, Robert Child, and others—especially those concerned with baptism and church membership.

The Cambridge Synod met in three sessions: September 1646, June 1647, and August 1648. The problems before the assembly changed during this period. In England the political situation took a new turn when the Independents gained the ascendancy at the expense of the Presbyterians, thereby assuring the autonomy of Massachusetts and the continuation of its existing institutions. Since the Remonstrants were defeated by this turn of events, the Synod passed over the questions of baptism and church membership. The delegates enlarged their scope to include preparation of a confession of faith, but when the Westminster Confession was received the Synod accepted it, bringing New England Puritans into doctrinal accord with English Puritans. The main achievement of the Synod was *A Platform of Church Discipline,* which described the polity of the Congregational churches. The last chapter, dealing with the power of the civil magistrate in ecclesiastical matters, answered a host of critics starting with Roger Williams. According to the Cambridge Platform, it was the duty of the civil magistrate to take care of matters of religion and to enforce the duties commanded in the First as well as the Second Table. Civil authority was specifically directed to punish profanation of the Lord's Day. The document was presented to the General Court in October 1649, and after a three-year period during which it was submitted to the churches and elders for comment and correction, the court finally endorsed it on 14 October 1651.[45] The Cambridge Platform remained the legally recognized standard of ecclesiastical practice in Massachusetts until 1780. The law, both moral and civil, endeavored to insure that the people of Massachusetts would lead Gospel lives.[46]

8

The New England Way

MASSACHUSETTS PIONEERED IN making proper Sabbath observance part of the New England Way, and by mid-century the Sabbatarian ideal regulated the pattern of life in the entire region. The Fourth Commandment enjoined people to work six days a week and to rest and worship on the seventh, and most inhabitants conducted themselves accordingly. Profanations of the Lord's Day were rare.

The conviction prevailed that good Sabbaths make good Christians, and during the Commonwealth period the example of England reinforced that belief. Parliament, having legislated the Puritan theory of the Sabbath into existence in the 1640s, enacted only two new statutes on the subject during the following decade, one in 1650, and another in 1657.[1] (In addition, a law on compulsory attendance at public worship was revised.) An English authority found the saneness and moderation of the legislation passed between 1640 and 1660 remarkable, particularly if one starts with the view that Puritans were killjoys. Parliament's action, he concludes, was the logical development of the thinking of more enlightened legislators and administrators of the previous half-century, and the legislation was socially beneficial and progressive.[2]

Nevertheless, abuses of the Lord's Day remained a problem in the 1650s, and English Puritans divided over the question of strictness in enforcing legislation. Late in 1656, when they concluded that people observed church-appointed festivals more zealously than the Lord's Day, Parliament agreed to suppress Christmas and other holy days which encouraged superstition. When Parliament considered a Sabbath bill the following year, Commons feared the measure went too far. At question was the power to enter private houses to determine if there were disorders on the Lord's Day, as well as a prohibition of "idle sitting, openly, at gates or doors, or elsewhere" and "walking in church-yards, etc." on the Sabbath. The majority repudiated these extreme proposals, and the bill that was passed recapitulated Sabbath legislation since 1640.[3]

IN MASSACHUSETTS DEVOTION to God's day of state, already ardent by 1648, became even more intense in the years following. Increase Mather in later life told how, as a Harvard student in the early 1650s, he brought his copy of a Greek text on Aristotle's moral philosophy to John Norton on a Sunday evening to obtain the assignment for the following day, reminding his tutor that by local reckoning the Sabbath was now over. But Norton thought it unseemly *"so Suddenly* to entertain Meditations or Discourses Heterogeneous to the *work of the Day."*[4] In 1655 Charles Chauncy, president of Harvard College, equated the Puritan Sabbath with civilized society, saying, "there be many in the country, that account it their happiness to live in the vast howling wilderness, without any ministry, or schooles, and means of education for their posterity, they have much liberty (they think) by this want, they are not troubled with strict sabbaths, but they may follow their business at any time."[5]

Michael Wigglesworth offered an excellent picture of the influence of the Sabbath in these years. Graduating from Harvard in 1651, he was a fellow and tutor there from 1652 to 1654, during which time he began preaching occasionally, before settling as minister at Malden. His diary, which runs from February 1653 to May 1657, reveals that the cyclical return of the Lord's Day determined the structure of time for the author. During the week he anticipates the approaching Sabbath, frequently calling Saturday the "Last day" or "Dies ult." The Sabbath itself was a blessed season bringing rest to his troubled soul. True, the morbidly introspective Wigglesworth was often beset with spiritual doubts and guilt for his iniquities on the Sabbath and at times felt that when he was nearest to God in the public ordinances his heart was apt to be furthest away. But he also experienced that God "in the day of his power" came with exceeding grace, quickening his heart, speaking to his needs, and granting sweetly precious communion. Because the Sabbath was a day of delight, Wigglesworth was torn as to whether he should do more "by reproveing lightness and mad mirth on Sabbath Evenings and by visitings." He once tormented himself with the question of whether he should out of duty shut a stable door that beat to and fro in the wind on the Sabbath. Wigglesworth, who was less the typical than the quintessential Puritan, amply demonstrates that for Massachusetts Puritans the Sabbath was indeed a tower to mount on high.[6]

The General Court was little concerned with new legislation on the weekly holy day. Apart from dealing with specific problems, the Massachusetts assembly enacted only one law between 1648 and 1660 designed to strengthen Sabbath observance. This statute, passed on 11 May 1659 and following an English precedent, prohibited the keeping of Christmas or other feast days and the playing of cards or dice on these festivals and at other times on penalty of five shillings.[7]

Most of the colony's effort to advance the Lord's Day went into enforcing existing legislation. In view of the importance attached to the institution, the moderation shown is surprising. Courts in Essex County treated neglect of public worship leniently. In mid-decade they admonished half of the twenty persons presented for this cause, knowing that one of them had not gone to church more than once or twice in a year. For a time, when Baptist doctrines induced withdrawals from Congregational worship—William Witter was charged with absence from authorized meetings for nine months, for example, and Joseph Redknapp for leaving the church during infant baptism—the magistrates were even indulgent with first offenders whose absence sprang from principle.[8]

Courts were generally forbearing with ordinary Sabbath-breakers. Magistrates admonished persons for traveling, serving a warrant, and "profaning the Sabbath" but fined others, including a man who unloaded barley before sunset on the rest day, a man who hunted raccoons during divine service, and a woman who beat another of her sex on Sunday. At Ipswich, James White and Jacob Davis were ordered fined or to sit in the stocks for stealing apples on the Lord's Day, and at Salem Thomas West, convicted on a first offense of Sabbath burglary, was condemned to be branded on the forehead with a B and to have one ear cut off.[9]

The moderation of the courts makes it hard to credit the tale that in 1656 Thomas Kemble, a Boston merchant, was put in the stocks for two hours for "lewd and unseemly behavior" on the Sabbath because he publicly kissed his wife after returning from an absence of three years. This story was probably the invention of John Josselyn, an Anglican who published an account of voyages to New England in 1638 and from 1663 to 1671. He described the body of laws drawn up by Massachusetts to illustrate the harshness of the Puritan regime, and falsely reported that the punishment for "kissing a woman in the street, though in way of civil salute" was a whipping or a fine.[10]

While most Massachusetts Puritans equated the sanctification of the Sabbath with all the duties immediately respecting the service of God in the First Table, two problems intruded during the decade: the restlessness of the younger generation, and the Quaker invasion. When the first complaint that young people were abusing the Lord's Day reached the General Court in 1653, that body passed a statute prohibiting the objectionable activities—playing in the streets or other places, uncivilly walking the streets and fields, traveling from town to town, going on shipboard, and frequenting "common howses" and other places to drink, sport, and otherwise misspend the precious Sabbath—during daylight on the Lord's Day. Penalties were graduated, with monetary fines to be borne by parents. Children over seven and others were to be admonished for a first offense, pay five shillings for a second, and ten for a third offense. Punishment for further misdeeds could be augmented by a county court according to the nature of the crime, and nonpayment brought a whipping by the constable not exceeding five stripes for a ten-shilling fine. This was the first time any Massachusetts statute legislated whipping for profaning the Sabbath, though courts had ordered it on many occasions.[11]

But youthful energies were not easily suppressed. The town of Boston in 1656 ordered that if any young persons or others be found outside the meetinghouse idling or playing during time of public exercises on the Lord's Day, constables were to bring them before authority.[12] Two years later, the General Court, lamenting that young people took liberty to walk and sport on the rest day, often going to taverns after sunset on Saturday and Sunday, enacted a law providing a five-shilling penalty for such transgressors.[13] These youths, born and bred in New England, had not grown up hating the Book of Sports, and in a busy port like Boston it was impossible to maintain intact the faith of the fathers.

The rising generation posed a problem for the future, but the Quakers were a far more immediate threat. The origins of the Quaker movement, their missionary outreach, and their theory of the Sabbath are treated in Chapter 10. Here it will suffice to note that Puritanism contained within itself the seeds of a spiritual interpretation of religion, and many New Englanders were moving in that direction. Yet Puritan and Quaker were basically incompatible, and a focus of conflict was the Sabbath. Friends found compulsory attendance at public worship where a hireling minister preached the written Word a form of legalism from which Christ had freed men. Hence Massachusetts made the institution of the Sabbath a bulwark in its defense of the established ecclesiastical and civil order against the "cursed sect" of Quakers and their blasphemous heresies.

The Quaker invasion of Massachusetts began in 1656, with English Friends often coming by way of Barbados.[14] The first missionaries, Mary Fisher and Ann Austin, arrived in Boston on 11 July 1656, and their coming shook New England "as if a formidable Army had invaded [its] Borders." The women were imprisoned five weeks and then banished. Two days after their departure, on 7 August 1656, a ship sailed in with eight more Quakers, four men and four women. After authorities examined their views, Governor John Endecott offered the significant warning: "Take heed you break not our Ecclesiastical Laws . . . for then ye are sure to stretch by a Halter."[15] The eight Quakers were confined for eleven weeks and then sent back to England. On 14 October 1656 Massachusetts enacted a statute to keep the commonwealth immune by outlawing Quaker missionaries and writings, authorizing imprisonment of Friends who succeeded in landing, and providing punishments, including banishment, for defense of Quaker doctrines.[16] Nevertheless, "Publishers of Truth" continued to come. Massachusetts was the main target of apostles of the Inner Light, and Rhode Island offered a convenient sanctuary. The *Woodhouse* arrived at Newport on 3 August 1657 with a group of Quakers, including six previously expelled from Boston, among them Christopher Holder, John Copeland, and William Brend. William Robinson, a London merchant and a young man of education, successful in his affairs, and Humphrey Norton, who had suffered severe persecution in Ireland, were newcomers.[17]

Salem contained a group of restless souls dissatisfied with orthodox Congregationalism. Lawrence and Cassandra Southwick, an elderly couple, were prominent members, and in July 1657 authorities punished Cassandra for absence from authorized worship. Soon after landing, Holder and Copeland set out for Salem, and on 21 September, Holder arose in the meeting after the Sabbath sermon to declare the Truth. During the ensuing scuffle someone gagged him and Samuel Shattuck came to his aid. As a result the two Quakers and Shattuck were taken to Boston, where the former received thirty stripes each and the latter was imprisoned. The Southwicks and their son Josiah were also sent to jail in Boston. Lawrence was soon released and turned over to the church for correction, but Cassandra was imprisoned seven weeks and heavily fined for possessing a Quaker tract.[18]

At its session in October 1657 the General Court sought to crush the Quaker heresy by passing a law which imposed a fine of forty shillings an hour for entertaining or concealing Friends. It provided corporal punishment for nonresident Quaker preachers; this rose on the third conviction to boring through the tongue with a hot iron and close confinement until the offender could be sent out of the country at his own expense.[19] Nevertheless, Salem residents continued to attend Quaker meetings. William Hathorne, a strongly orthodox local magistrate, invoked the compulsory attendance law of 1646 to deal with them. In late 1657 and 1658 Essex County courts tried several persons under this statute. It was found to be inadequate for the purpose, so a new Sabbath law directed against religious dissent was promulgated. The General Court on 19 May 1658 ordered that every person who attended a Quaker meeting on the Lord's Day was to be fined ten shillings and all who committed blasphemy by speaking at such assemblies were to be fined five pounds. If convicted persons had already been whipped under the law of 1656, they were to be jailed until they furnished security that they would cease their activities or depart from the jurisdiction.[20]

The new measure was put to the test that summer when constables apprehended persons gathered at the house of Nicholas Phelps near Salem to hear William Brend and William Leddra, a Quaker from Barbados. A Boston jailer mercilessly beat the aged Brend, and a score of Salem inhabitants were presented for absence from authorized worship and attendance at unauthorized worship. Five failed to appear in court; ten repented and were released; Phelps, who confessed to being a Friend, was fined forty shillings for entertaining Quakers; and six professed Quakers —the three Southwicks, Shattuck, Samuel Gaskin, and Joshua Buffum— were sent to the house of correction and given ten stripes. The Southwicks, Gaskin, and two others were also fined twenty-five shillings each for five absences from church, but Thomas Brackett, convicted of the same offenses, repented and had half of his fine abated.[21]

About three weeks later some twenty persons, most of whom had attended the Sabbath assembly at Phelps's house, were fined under the 1646 compulsory attendance law for absence from public worship and under the 1657 anti-Quaker statute for frequenting ''disorderly'' Quaker meetings. The six Salem Quakers imprisoned for being present when Brend and Leddra spoke now petitioned for release on the ground that they had been jailed under one law but were being confined under another. They asked to be tried as heretics, but Daniel Denison, a Salem justice, replied that they were to be punished by the General Court not for errors of judgment—this might bring an appeal to England and occasion trouble for Massachusetts—but for neglecting public worship. Accordingly, in late September, Buffum, Phelps, and Shattuck were each fined thirty shillings for violating the statutes of 1646 and 1657. George

Bishop, a contemporary Quaker, wrote that the Salemites were punished until "their Lives (as Men) became worse than Death."[22]

At its session commencing 19 October 1658, the General Court made still another effort to suppress the infectious Quaker heresy. The Reverend Charles Chauncy in a Boston lecture about six ravening wolves who deserved death (a reference to the Salemites) spurred the legislature to its duty of preserving civil and ecclesiastical order. The assembly therefore enacted a statute which ordered nonresidents convicted as Quakers to be banished upon pain of death and residents similarly convicted to depart voluntarily or give bond for appearance at the next Court of Assistants where, upon failure to retract, they were to receive the same punishment. The court also directed the Reverend John Norton to draft a statement showing the evil tenets and dangerous consequences of Quakerism. Then the Salem six were brought from prison, and when they remained obdurate the bench ordered them to depart before 11 May or face banishment upon penalty of death.[23]

That autumn the hounds of orthodoxy were especially active in Essex County. Major Hathorne encouraged a careful watch for forbidden meetings, constables like Edmund Batter and Thomas Putnam zealously pursued offenders, and witness fees provided an incentive for prosecutions. The five-shilling penalty for neglecting public worship was repeatedly exacted. A large number of the victims were women. On 1 December 1658 the wives of Robert Buffum, John Kitchin, Samuel Shattuck, John Smith, and John Southwick as well as Miss Provided Smith were each fined four pounds for sixteen absences, and Mrs. George Gardener forty shillings for eight. The following spring Edward Wharton was fined five pounds, Samuel Gaskin eight, and Mrs. Nicholas Phelps ten for absences ranging from twenty to forty Sundays. In some cases husbands who attended lawful worship were forced to pay fines imposed for the absences of their consorts. Since convicted Quakers lacked the means to pay such heavy penalties, the marshal attached their cattle, houses, and land.[24]

In May 1659 the General Court gave the imprisoned Salem Quakers until 8 June to depart; to avoid martyrdom for the crime of withdrawing from public worship and holding their own meetings, they left the colony.[25] That September three nonresidents—William Robinson, Marmaduke Stephenson, and Mary Dyer—were apprehended in Boston and banished on pain of death. They left but soon returned to plant the Truth in Massachusetts. Norton's treatise appeared on 18 October, calling Quaker doctrines destructive of Holy Scripture as a perfect rule of life and faith.[26] The three Quakers, brought before the court the following day, asserted that they had come "in obedience to the call of the Lord."

Since banishment had failed to protect the established order, the court now sentenced the trio to death. They were marched to the gallows on 27 October, where the two men sealed their fate with their lives. Mary Dyer was reprieved. The authorities intended to scare her away, so they let her stand on the gallows with a rope around her neck until the men were executed and then carried her to Rhode Island. But she returned the following May, was again offered her life if she would return home, and refused: "In obedience to the will of the Lord God I came and in His will I abide faithful to death." The only other capital execution of a Quaker in Boston was that of William Leddra, on 14 March 1661.[27]

Although no one was ever executed in New England for Sabbath-breaking as such, the Quaker martyrs were victims of a determination to uphold the Sabbath and the religious system it exemplified. Puritans had long reminded themselves that the Old Testament sanctioned the death penalty for presumptuous profaners of the Sabbath, and when the enforcement of Sabbath laws failed to crush the heretical sect, Bay colony authorities took sterner measures. Soon after the execution of Robinson and Stephenson, Essex County magistrates, impelled by the hope that the bloody lesson would allay further conflict, suspended the sentences of fourteen Quakers presented for habitual absence from public worship.[28]

THE EARLIEST RECORDED profanations of the Lord's Day in New Haven occurred shortly after the Fundamental Orders were promulgated in the spring of 1638. In the absence of prescribed penalties in either "Moses his Judicials" or Scripture, the town magistrates used their own discretion in awarding punishments. Through 1643 most of the presentments involved burglary, theft, or drunkenness on the Sabbath. In December 1639 the civil court ordered Roger Duhurst and James Stewart to make double restitution and to be whipped for stealing nearly six pounds out of their master's chest during the time of the Sabbath meeting. "Isaiah, Captain Turner's man," was fined five pounds for being drunk on the Lord's Day. Goodman Hunt and his wife encountered difficulty for associating with William Harding, a "lewd and disorderly person" who enticed many maids into "filthy dalliances." Even worse, the Hunts kept company with him on the Lord's Day, and Goody Hunt allowed Harding to kiss her then. The magistrates ordered the Hunts to depart within a month or sooner if they misbehaved again. This episode provides the best evidence for concluding that New Haven's blue laws (and here, judge-made rather than statutory) forbade kissing on the Sabbath.[29]

The jurisdiction of New Haven was formed in 1643 when the New England Confederation was called into existence. With the original town as its nucleus, it included settlements at Milford, Guilford, Stamford, Greenwich, and Branford, and for a time the villages of Oyster Bay, Huntington, Southold, and Southampton on Long Island. A frame of government based on Massachusetts practice as outlined in the Cotton code was devised for the jurisdiction in October 1643. Only church members were to be admitted freemen and have the vote in civil affairs. The General Court was to maintain purity of religion according to their understanding of the Word of God. For some time thereafter the only written laws on the Sabbath were an explicit agreement that Scripture was the perfect rule of life and faith and the provision in "Moses his Judicials" calling for the death penalty for presumptuous profanation of the Sabbath. A judicial system comprising various levels of courts was created, and the General Court, meeting at New Haven on 3 April 1644, ordered that the moral part of the judicial laws of God as delivered by Moses were to be a rule to all courts in the colony, "till they be branched out into perticulars hereafter."[30]

The plantation or particular courts developed judge-made laws on the Sabbath in the dozen years before the colony formulated a legal code. Their treatment of persons delinquent in watching at posts to defend religious assemblies from Indian attack shows care in securing attendance at public worship. On one occasion a court excused two tardy sentinels who explained that they had stopped at home for a little rest after being on watch all the previous night so that they might not sleep during the ordinances. But on another occasion a court fined a man who tried to excuse his absence by stating that he had either to miss worship or to choose between carrying his arms or his children to church. And local judges condemned John Morse to pay ten shillings for staying in the meetinghouse rather than walking the rounds on his Sabbath watch.[31]

Sentences for profaning the Lord's Day varied greatly in the absence of legally prescribed punishments. William Pert, who stole two watermelons on Sunday, was publicly but moderately corrected because he appeared repentant. Nathan Burchall, who finally succumbed to the temptation to steal from the house in which he was living during time of worship on the Sabbath, was ordered to make double restitution—he had stolen thirteen pounds in money and other things valued at thirty-four shillings—and to be given some corporal punishment. William Blayden, who excused his failure to attend public worship (a second offense) by saying that he had got his clothes all wet, was ordered whipped for profane neglect. Steven Reekes, master of a ship from Barbados, was called to account for hauling his vessel, which had been grounded for some days but floated when wind brought a tide, "to or towardes the necke bridge" upon the Sabbath. Reekes explained that his crew had only kept the ship from running on the bank or driving upon its anchor, but the magistrates at New Haven replied that "it is the duty of all men to remember the Saboth, and to provide so beforehand that nothing maye disturbe them upon the Saboth, unlesse it bee in cases of mercy or workes of such necessitie as could not be provided for the day before nor staye till the day after." One Larebe, also a foreign seaman, had gone aboard his ship that same Sunday to prevent it from overturning, which he thought was a work of charity. Earlier that day, however, Larebe had sought advice from Richard Malbon, and Malbon, consulting John Davenport, had been told to "leave it to Gods providence, the Saboth was a day of rest, and therfore hee ought to rest." Malbon therefore urged Larebe to do nothing, but Larebe "went and wrought, contrary to the lawe for the Saboth." Since Reekes and Larebe acted out of ignorance rather than contempt, acknowledged their fault, and promised amendment, they were not punished. "But if any of our owne take libbertie heareby," the court warned, "the sentenc will bee heavier on them."[32]

Soon thereafter New Haven colony enacted a statute regulating Sunday conduct, impelled by a belief that some had recently taken too much liberty in exercising their ordinary employments upon the Sabbath and a desire to see that the law of God was strictly enforced. On 31 January 1648 the General Court ordered that servile labor on the Sabbath from sunset to sunset upon either land or water, extraordinary cases and works of mercy or necessity excepted, was to be punished by particular courts according to the nature of the offense.[33] Apart from laws making Scripture the rule, this was the first written enactment on the Sabbath in the jurisdiction. The records show only a few Sabbath cases in ensuing years, and some were minor, as when magistrates warned persons for failure to attend church and for sending servants to the banks to gather oysters on Sunday. In 1654, however, when Joshua Bradley, a cowkeeper, carried on in a "base, filthy, lustfull way" with a six-year-old girl left at home while her parents attended meeting, a court sentenced him to be whipped, and all the more sharply because it was the Sabbath.[34]

A year later New Haven colony began the first codification of its laws. The General Court requested Governor Eaton to survey all the statutes enacted since 1643 with a view to retaining those considered suitable, to borrow what was profitable from the laws of Massachusetts, and to send for Cotton's *Abstract,* a second edition of which was published in England in 1655. The court approved Eaton's draft and five hundred copies were printed in England. *New-Haven's Settling in New England, and Some Lawes for Government* (1656), which was distributed to the towns the next year, contained an alphabetical arrangement of laws, liberties, and orders, with many marginal references to the Bible.[35]

The Sabbath laws in the New Haven code were drawn largely from the Massachusetts compilation of 1648. The compulsory attendance part, which provided a penalty of five shillings for absence from public worship, was taken with slight variation from the *Laws and Liberties*. An article entitled "Prophanation of the Lord's Day" improved on its Bay model, which empowered constables to arrest Sabbath-breakers. Eaton defined profanations as servile work, unlawful sports, recreations, "or otherwise" and authorized punishment by fine, imprisonment, or corporally according to the nature of the offense. Death was the penalty if any of the proscribed acts were "proudly, presumptuously, and with a high hand committed against the known command and authority of the blessed God," a feature presumably borrowed from Cotton's draft. As for Sabbath burglary, the New Haven code softened the penalties contained in the Massachusetts *Laws*. Branding on the hand and a severe whipping for a first offense were ordered, as opposed to branding on the forehead and cutting off of one ear; and for a second trespass time in the pillory and wearing a neck halter at the pleasure of the court, as opposed to loss of the other ear.[36]

Few violations of the Sabbath laws in *New Haven's Settling in New England* were brought before the bench through 1660. A case involving John Meigs, presented in Guilford in 1657 for the noise his cart made as he came from Athomonossock late on a Saturday, suggests that popular zeal for strict Sabbaths kept the dockets clear. Meigs pleaded misjudgment of the time required for the trip. A heavy burden and slow cattle had prevented his arrival until after the Sabbath began. Since the offender repented and promised to be careful in the future, he was merely reproved and ordered to acknowledge his fault publicly.[37]

However, the jurisdiction experienced the same difficulties encountered by Massachusetts in these years. In 1650 the General Court meeting in New Haven ordered any person found standing or sitting outside the meetinghouse during time of worship on Sabbath or lecture days to forfeit two shillings. That measure was probably intended to deal with the rising generation. The Quakers raised another problem. On 1 March 1658 Humphrey Norton was sent as a prisoner from Southold to a court in New Haven. He had spoken out in the Lord's Day meeting and been found with papers which denounced the established ecclesiastical and civil order. The court thought he was at least guilty of breaking the laws against heresy and disturbing the peace, and since he had attacked the visible church and visible ordinances he was probably feared as a threat to the morality of the Fourth Commandment. The judges ordered that Norton be severely whipped and branded on the hand with the letter *H,* banished upon penalty of the utmost censure of the law, and fined ten pounds.[38]

Three months later a New Haven court of magistrates tried Richard Crabb and his wife on similar charges. A number of witnesses testified that the couple, residents of Greenwich and obviously Quakers, had made speeches reproaching the ministers and magistrates and had for a long time neglected the ordinances and Sabbaths. Governor Newman demanded to know whether Crabb owned the Lord's Day to be the Christian Sabbath; when he equivocated, evidence was introduced to show that Crabb's judgment was against the morality of the Sabbath. Mr. Bishop, pastor of the church at Stamford, noted a great suspicion that Crabb was responsible for the dangerous ideas spreading among the young people at Stamford concerning the Sabbath and the written Word of God. Crabb was told that Greenwich was no place for him unless he reformed. The court ordered him to pay a fine of thirty pounds, to give one hundred pounds as security for good behavior, and to make public acknowledgment in Stamford to the satisfaction of persons he had wronged.[39]

IN CONNECTICUT COLONY the period of reliance upon custom and Scripture in the enforcement of rest and worship on the first day of the week ended in 1650 with adoption of a code of laws that explicitly regulated Sabbath observance. Roger Ludlow was the author of the Fundamental Orders of 1650, an alphabetical arrangement of seventy-seven titles whose Sabbath provisions were heavily indebted to the Massachusetts *Laws and Liberties.* Like its prototype, the Ludlow code made attendance at worship compulsory upon penalty of five shillings; authorized constables to apprehend Sabbath-breakers without prescribing an amercement for that crime; and made burglary and theft on the Sabbath punishable precisely as in the *Book of Laws.* Connecticut borrowed its law on the subject from Massachusetts, but the General Court's enactment of 1653, which prohibited seamen from weighing anchor on the Lord's Day without first obtaining a license, was apparently a response to a specific local need.[40]

The statutory revision of 1650 furnished a basis for maintaining strict Sabbaths, and county courts vigorously suppressed profanations of the Lord's Day. Servile labor drew stiffer penalties than in neighboring colonies. A particular court at Pequot (New London) fined Will Bratlitt ten shillings for unnecessary labor on the Sabbath, and quarterly courts at

Hartford exacted twenty shillings of one Fetchwater for mowing upon the Lord's Day and forty shillings of John Gutteridge for profaning the Sabbath by working on it. (The latter fine was the equivalent of a laborer's monthly wages.) John Bartlitt, for great misdemeanors in frequenting the house and company of Goody Parsons of Windsor, "unseasonably and dissorderly on the Sabath dayes and other times," was fined forty shillings and ordered to find security for his good behavior. The general crime of profaning the Sabbath also led to a ten-shilling penalty, while a court of magistrates at Wethersfield directed Thomas Troughton to pay five shillings for unnecessary withdrawal from public preaching on the Sabbath. When an Indian complained to the quarterly court at Hartford that a Mr. Styles had "shott his body with Swan Shott upon a sabath day," Stiles was ordered to appear in court unless he gave satisfaction to the Indian.[41]

Starting in October 1656, the Connecticut legislature passed a number of laws in the next two years to protect the colony from the contagion of the Quaker heresy. In addition, the court decreed in March 1658 that no one might form a church without official consent or attend an unauthorized meeting for public worship on the Sabbath.[42] To deal with restless young people, the towns of Hartford and Stratford in 1659 appointed a man to command into the meetinghouse persons who stood without during the time of public exercises on the Lord's Day.[43]

PLYMOUTH COLONY ENACTED its first written legislation regulating Sabbath observance after three decades of settlement. A statute passed in June 1650 banned the profaning of the Lord's Day by servile work or similar abuses on penalty of ten shillings or a whipping, and in June 1651 the General Court prohibited neglect of public worship or attendance at any unauthorized assembly on pain of ten shillings and "lazey slothfull or prophane" neglect on punishment of the same fine or a whipping.[44]

The prosecution of ordinary Sabbath-breakers under these ordinances mirrors Plymouth morals during the 1650s. Travel and servile labor vexed the authorities, who used their discretion in awarding sentences. Thus, Gowin White and Zacharie Hick, presented for traveling from Weymouth to Scituate upon the Lord's Day, and John Smith of Taunton, charged with a needless round trip to Nunckatateesett on the rest day, were all cleared. William Chase, Sr., of Yarmouth was presented for driving a pair of yoked oxen five miles during time of worship. The records are silent on the outcome of this case, but Josias Hallott and Thomas Gage were fined "according to order" for putting out to sea from Sandwich Harbor upon the Sabbath.[45]

Pursuit of ordinary employments on the Sabbath brought punishment. Elizabeth Eeddy, presented to the General Court in 1651 "for wringing and hanging out clothes, on the Lords day, in time of publicke exercise," was fined ten shillings, though the penalty was remitted. Authorities sharply reproved Lieutenant James Wiatt in 1658 for writing a note about common business on the Lord's Day, "in the evening somewhat to[o] soone." The records of these years show that six men were charged with failure to attend church for reasons other than principle. Abraham Peirse of Duxbury, presented for "slothfull and negligent spending the Saboth, and not frequenting the publick assembly," was cleared but warned to mend his ways. Ralph Jones, convicted for neglecting divine service, was found liable for the legal amercement.[46]

Religious dissidence troubled the Old Colony. On 2 October 1650 nine residents of Rehoboth were presented for holding unauthorized religious meetings on the Lord's Day contrary to the court order of the previous June. Obadiah Holmes was a member of this group of Anabaptists, and this was the first appearance of schism within Plymouth. The record does not show if punishment was inflicted.[47]

A drift toward a religion of inner experience also made inroads. Thirteen residents of Sandwich were presented to the General Court in October 1651 for failure to attend public worship. The magistrates referred the Cape Cod group to conference and decided to consider the matter further. Early the following year the court fined two of the thirteen, Ralph Allen, Sr., and Richard Kerbey, five pounds apiece for deriding God's Word and ordinances. Three years later Allen and two more of the original Sandwich party were back in court for neglecting the religious assembly. On this occasion one of them, Peter Gaunt, said that "hee knew noe publicke vizable worship now in the world." This manifestation of spiritual religion if not outright Quakerism directly threatened the morality of the Sabbath, but the nonplussed magistrates again left the case for further consideration.[48]

Early in 1657 complaints were made that Nicholas Upsall and many of the Sandwich thirteen were disturbing public worship and holding their own meetings on the Lord's Day. Upsall had been living in Boston when Mary Fisher and Ann Austin arrived to bear witness to the Spirit. He was the first resident of Massachusetts to become a convinced Quaker, and for protesting the anti-Quaker law of 1656 was fined and banished. Now he was ordered to leave Plymouth (he went to Rhode Island), and some of the others were sentenced to be publicly whipped. About this time authorities were also troubled by events at Marshfield, where Robert Huchin, Arthur Howland, and others were actively promoting Quakerism. In addition, Holder, Copeland, Norton, Brend, Leddra, and other Quaker missionaries were swarming over the colony.[49]

On 3 June 1657 the legislature enacted a law to counter the threat. The doctrines and practices of the Friends were subversive of ecclesiastical and civil order, according to the preamble, so no Quaker was to be entertained in the colony under a penalty of five pounds for every offense. Residents were to inform the constable if any Ranter or Quaker entered their town, and the holding of a Quaker meeting was prohibited, with a penalty of forty shillings for the owner of the house and those who spoke, and one of ten shillings for every head of family present.[50]

New Plymouth revised its laws again in 1658. The new code retained the previously enacted regulations governing conduct on the Sabbath. The 1650 law had prohibited servile labor and similar abuses on penalty of ten shillings or a whipping; the 1651 law forbade neglect of public worship (ten shillings) and lazy, slothful, or profane neglect (ten shillings or a whipping), a measure repealed in 1652. The new statute suppressed traveling, bearing burdens, and carrying packs on the Sabbath, all growing problems, on penalty of twenty shillings or four hours in the stocks. Also added were provisions that no Quaker and no opponent of the laws of the commonwealth or the true worship of God could be admitted a freeman, and that any freeman who was a Quaker or spoke contemptuously of the court or its laws was to be disfranchised. Those who refused to take an oath of fidelity were to have no vote in civil affairs.[51]

Plymouth colony was no more liberal in spirit or tolerant in religion than its Puritan neighbors. "New Plymouth saddle is on the Bay-Horse," wrote James Cudworth of Scituate in 1658, and "now we must have a State Religion; a State Ministry; a State way of maintenance. We must all go to the public place of meeting . . . or be presented. I am informed of sixty or eighty last Court presented for not coming to public meetings." Cudworth was deprived of his militia captaincy and disfranchised for his views, and the government made the Sabbath laws a vital weapon in its endeavor to crush heterodoxy.[52] Though George Barlow, marshal of Sandwich, resolutely arrested offenders, nearly the whole town became convinced Quakers, and residents were heavily fined for holding unauthorized meetings on the Lord's Day. By about 1659 the total amount in fines levied on twenty leading Quakers, mainly from Sandwich, for refusing to attend public worship and take the oath of fidelity amounted to over six hundred and sixty pounds.[53]

THUS, THE PURITAN colonies bound their inhabitants to proper observance of the weekly day of rest and worship and defended the theory and practice of the institution against the Quakers. As a result, by 1660 the Sabbath was more deeply entrenched in New England than it had been a decade or two earlier.

During these same years the American Puritans endeavored to bring the Indians and the northeastern frontier to the observance of strict Sabbaths. Though conversion of the Indians was an important aim in the colonization of New England, the task was slow in getting under way. The planters first had to establish their own civil and ecclesiastical government and to fit the covenant theology, which was not conducive to evangelistic outreach, into the larger framework of their belief in the providential plan for the salvation of mankind. According to Puritans, Christ would return to rule after the conversion of the Jews; they also believed that the American Indians were one of the ten lost tribes of Israel. Redemption of the heathens would hasten the advent of the kingdom of God. Such millennial speculations were stimulated after 1642 by the collapse of traditional authority and the spread of sectarianism in England.[54]

Missionary activity in Massachusetts began about this time. In June 1644 the General Court, which in 1637 had empowered towns to keep away all "strange Indians" and to restrain others of their neighborhood from profaning the Lord's Day, ordered that Indians be permitted to come into any English town or house on the Lord's Day to attend public worship. It also announced that all Indians in the jurisdiction be enjoined to meet at conveniently appointed places on the Lord's Day, and that neighboring towns choose qualified persons to instruct them in the knowledge of God. In November the legislature directed county courts to take care that the Indians within their borders be civilized and taught the faith. And in October 1645 the magistrates invited the ministers to advise them about the best way to redeem the lost sons of Adam.[55]

Thomas Mayhew, Jr. (c. 1621-1657) was the first missionary to the Indians of New England. He settled on Martha's Vineyard in 1642 and the following year made his first convert, Hiacoomes. Mayhew continued to evangelize among the natives, learning their language and preaching in their own tongue, until his loss at sea in 1657. John Eliot (1604-1690), minister at Roxbury from 1632 until his death, was the outstanding apostle to the Indians in seventeenth-century New England. He turned his attention to them in 1646, convinced that their conversion would hasten the rule of Christ over the world, learned Algonquian, and labored incessantly to win over the pagans.

The missionary program rapidly gathered momentum. In November 1646 the Massachusetts legislature ordered that the colony laws be made known annually to the Indians through an interpreter to reduce them to civilization, and that two ministers be chosen every year to proselytize among them.[56] To enlist support abroad, Edward Winslow of New Plymouth or an unknown agent secured the publication in London of some pamphlets describing the progress of the Gospel among the Indians. The first of these "Eliot tracts" was issued anonymously in 1647, Thomas Shepard authored the second in 1648, and Winslow the third in 1649.[57] That year Parliament incorporated the Society for the Propagation of the Gospel in New England. The New England Company, whose members were prominent Puritans, and especially Independents, organized support in England, arranging for the publication of four additional Indian tracts by 1655 and collecting over £15,910 by 1660. In New England the Commissioners of the United Colonies received and administered the funds sent over. Additional ministers advanced the work in Massachusetts, Plymouth, Connecticut, and New Haven colonies, and on Long Island. New England was the world center of Protestant missionary activity in the seventeenth century.[58]

To convert the Indians it was first necessary to civilize them; this required a radical transformation of a rude and barbarous people into late Renaissance Englishmen. The Puritan missionaries emphasized the law of God to lead the savages into accepted paths of righteousness, and Sabbatarianism occupied a central place in this effort to civilize and Christianize them. Eliot's work makes this clear. In his first sermon to the natives at Nonantum (near Watertown) in October 1646, he briefly explained the Ten Commandments and told of God's dreadful wrath against transgressors. Before the end of the year individual Indians worried about the strictness of their Sabbath observance and the group declared that it intended to keep the Sabbath.[59]

How was this to be accomplished? The Indians, who knew nothing of the institution, needed instruction in its far-reaching obligations. The Sabbath had no meaning except as a link in a perfect chain. It involved the entire pattern of life, how one spent the six days of the week as well as the seventh. Since language was a formidable barrier between the races, a policy of segregation was decided upon. The Indians would live apart from the whites, organizing their own towns and churches. Missionaries would visit these communities, teaching select natives to help transform the residents into praying Indians and adherents of the New England Way.

The first Indian town was formed at Natick in 1651, but it took longer to gather the first Indian church. The natives were required to give a satisfactory account of their conversion experience in order to become fit material for building a church, and the Bay elders were not satisfied with their attempts until 1660. Five years later the General Court reported that there were six Indian towns in Massachusetts in which the inhabitants professed the Christian religion and kept the Sabbath; other towns were subsequently established.[60]

The Indian towns had a large degree of self-government, and the Sabbath was regulated both externally and internally. Eliot wanted the Indians to be governed wholly by the Scriptures in civil and ecclesiastical affairs, and he echoed Cotton (and Isa. 33:22) in saying that the Lord should be the Indians' Lawgiver, Judge, King, and Savior.[61] To educate the natives, Eliot undertook to translate the Bible into the Indian language. The Book of Genesis, which provided a basis for instruction in the morality of the Sabbath, was published in 1655. Meanwhile, the legislature provided quarterly courts for the Indians and appointed persons to instruct them in civilization and religion. The General Court expressed its desire that "some care may be taken of the Indians on the Lords dayes." Indian sachems were authorized to hold court once a month, and their jurisdiction included such crimes as breach of the Sabbath.[62]

The praying Indians regulated Sabbath observance in their towns. At Concord in February 1647, when the Indians adopted orders for their own government, they included an article which required Sabbath observance and provided for a twenty-shilling fine for profanation of the day. Law was one thing, practice another. The Indians were extremely hard to civilize because they were habituated to idleness and the work ethic was integrally bound up with Sabbatarianism. Puritans believed that the Fourth Commandment required labor six days a week as well as rest on the seventh, and some progress was made in winning these sons of Adam to this view. John Speene, for example, confessed that before his conversion he had greatly loved hunting and hated labor, but afterwards he believed "that word of God, which saith, Six dayes thou shalt labor."[63]

To convince the Indians to rest on the Sabbath was less difficult, as Puritans discovered in 1644 when Cutshamekin and others put themselves under the government of Massachusetts. Advised not to do any unnecessary work on the Sabbath, especially within Christian towns, the Indians replied: "It is a small thing for us to rest on that day, for we have not much to do any day, and therefore we will forbear on that day."[64] Some Indians, however, had to be persuaded to rest. One asked Eliot if his wife sinned in doing housework on the night before and after the Sabbath, and the convert Nishohkou confessed that, though formerly he thought work on the Sabbath was no great matter, he had given it up.[65] To prevent such abuses the General Court at Plymouth in 1652 forbade the Indians to do any servile work on the Sabbath, and four years later ordered that no Indian shoot a gun on the Lord's Day. In 1655 the Commissioners of the United Colonies ordered that the Pequots should not profane the Sabbath, and in May 1667, Connecticut provided that Indians who played or labored on the Sabbath within the English limits be fined.[66]

Indians were taught to sanctify the Sabbath. While realizing that they could not compel belief, the Massachusetts General Court in November 1646 ordered that the Indians forsake their powwows and pagan worship on heavy penalties, and many Indians not only worked six days and rested the seventh but also treasured the Sabbath worship of the Puritans' God. Nishohkou expressed a desire "to reverence the Word every Sabbath day"; an Indian evangelist told his kinsmen, "We enjoy the Lords Sabbath dayes for our Souls good, and communion with God"; and at his death John Owussumug, Sr., said, "I did greatly love to goe to the Sabbath worship. Therefore I now say to all you men, women, and children, love much, and greatly to keep the Sabbath."[67] Sabbath-keeping was a visible symbol of the acceptance of Christianity and English civilization by the Indians of New England, and by 1660 a foundation had been laid for bringing the scattered red men to observe this vital aspect of the New England Way.

THE COASTAL REGIONS of the present states of Maine and New Hampshire constituted the principal New England frontier in the second third of the seventeenth century. These waters were explored by seamen from several European nations during the age of discovery, and the Virginia Company of Plymouth, patented in 1606 and led by Sir Ferdinando Gorges and Sir John Popham, attempted to plant a trading post at Sagadahoc in 1607. After it failed, Gorges, along with Captain John Mason, became the most important English adventurers in the area. Both were staunch royalists and loyal Church of England men, and Gorges especially entertained grandiose visions of vast feudal seignories in America. In 1620 he reorganized the Plymouth Company along proprietary lines, securing a patent for the Council for New England. The forty patentees became the sole proprietors of a domain extending from the fortieth to the forty-eighth parallel and from sea to sea. The New England Council was a land company, and its main activity through 1635 was the making of land grants.[68]

In 1622 Gorges and Mason obtained a charter granting them all the territory between the Merrimac and Kennebec from the sea to the heads of the two rivers. They divided the area in 1629, drawing a line down the middle of the Piscataqua River. Mason called his holding New Hampshire. Colonists went there for economic rather than religious reasons. Originally fishing was the chief attraction and later the fur and timber trade became important. Two organized settlements had been established by the time of Mason's death in 1635: Strawberry Bank (Portsmouth), and the place later called Dover. Although the early arrivals were often attached to the Church of England, the fishermen were hard-drinking and unruly, and religion lay lightly on them.

New Hampshire began to attract Massachusetts Puritans in the late 1630s. Many emigrated for religious reasons, establishing themselves at Exeter in 1638 and Hampton the following year. Though the towns had their own voluntary compacts, the province lacked an effective government. The inhabitants, desiring more orderly rule, turned to Massachusetts, and on 9 October 1641 the General Court annexed all the towns except Exeter. It allowed the people at Piscataqua self-government under local courts, made them freemen without requiring church membership (a great concession), and granted representation in the Massachusetts assembly. Exeter petitioned and was received under the Bay colony's jurisdiction on 7 September 1643. The political conquest of New Hampshire lasted forty years.[69]

The Puritan Sabbath established roots between the Merrimac and the Piscataqua soon after the annexation. The province contained perhaps little more than a thousand souls at the time. The theory of the observance was presumably imported from the Bay, and at first customary rather than written law regulated practice. The Massachusetts Sabbath laws were not well advanced in the early 1640s, and the only local ordinances regulated the sale of liquor on the Lord's Day. The duration of the Sabbath was from the preceding to the following sunset, but with rare exception New Hampshire did not punish Sabbath crimes more severely than weekday crimes.

Court records afford the best picture of local Sabbath observance, though details are often lacking. Through 1660 grand juries presented five persons for neglect of public worship: three men in 1643, John Reynolds and family in 1648 (Reynolds may have been an Anabaptist), and James Rollins in 1656. Only one sentence is recorded: the county court at Portsmouth admonished Rollins and ordered him to pay fees of two shillings and sixpence.[70]

Roughly twice as many presentments for breach of the Sabbath were made in the same period. A few were for servile labor (such as trading with the Indians or carrying wood to the Isles of Shoals) or for traveling (going to the Newichawannock—or Salmon Falls—River on the Lord's Day). Admonishment and payment of court fees was the penalty in each case. Far more presentments involved drinking on Sunday, which often led to quarreling and fighting. Penalties varied, some being as high as twenty shillings. Thomas Gwin was fined ten shillings for being drunk on the Lord's Day in the meetinghouse in time of exercise, and Ralph Hall five shillings for letting his maids serve Gwin the drink. To remedy such abuses, local magistrates in 1657 and 1659 enacted ordinances prohibiting the sale of wine and strong waters on the Sabbath and on either evening of the Sabbath except in special cases. Another presentment involved a woman who cursed and swore on a Sabbath morning and reviled the constable when he appeared. She was ordered to be whipped with four stripes or pay forty shillings and was bound to good behavior by a sum of ten pounds.[71]

In 1629 Gorges became the proprietor of the province of Maine, and when Puritans arrived in Massachusetts the following year he began efforts to annul their charter and gain control of a New England vastly larger than we know today. During these same years the Council for New England granted a number of overlapping grants for the territory of Maine. The situation was further complicated when Sir Ferdinando's plan to perpetuate feudalism in America bore fruit in 1635. To undermine the Massachusetts Bay Company's patent, the Council agreed to surrender its charter on two conditions: that the king establish a general government for New England under Gorges, and that the king confirm the patents of land previously issued by the Council. The New England Council therefore divided its territory into twelve provinces, four of which were in Maine; the charter was surrendered, and Gorges was named governor general of New England. In 1639 the King confirmed Sir Ferdinando's title to the province of Maine and established the Church of England in the area.

As a result of these complicated maneuvers the coast of Maine had four political divisions. One of these was Gorges' province of Maine, which extended from the Piscataqua to the Kennebec (Casco Bay). Another was the province of Lygonia, extending from the Kennebunk (Cape Porpoise) to the Kennebec (Casco Bay). Based on a patent granted in 1630, it overlapped Sir Ferdinando's province. Settlements were found along the coast at a number of points, including Kittery, the Isles of Shoals, Agamenticus, Saco, Black Point, and Richmond Island, and there were fishing stations at Pemaquid and Monhegan Island. Gorges intended to make Agamenticus, a straggling hamlet on the York River, the capital of his province and an episcopal see. He renamed it Gorgeana; it later became York.

Though Sir Ferdinando never set foot in New England, he provided a government for his proprietary. A deputy sent over in 1635 held the first general court in the jurisdiction the following year, and it levied a tax for the support of public worship. In 1640 a more elaborate provincial government was organized, and Sir Ferdinando sent his cousin Thomas Gorges as deputy. After he returned to England in 1643, Richard Vines and Henry Jocelyn served as deputy governors until 1649. During these years the General Court began to regulate Sabbath observance. When that body met at Saco on 8 September 1640, it provided that the court not meet on Sundays and received the presentment of two men for profaning the Sabbath in carrying boards "contrary to his Majesties lawes." Five years later a court at Saco fined two men twenty shillings each for breach of the Sabbath, and another man was presented for breach of the Sabbath and breach of peace.[72] True, Puritanism was gaining the ascendancy in England at the time, but these acts were done by Church of England officials before Massachusetts controlled Maine.

Sir Ferdinando died in 1647, and when the news reached the colony in July 1649, the people met at Gorgeana to regulate their affairs until further authority came from England. With "unius animus Consent" the inhabitants formed a social compact to govern themselves. That October they elected Edward Godfrey deputy governor and ordered that all people were free to form a church, provided they did it in a Christian way, "with the due observation of the rules of Christ revealed in his worde," a statement with a distinctly Puritan flavor.[73]

During the three years of this government local courts maintained the Sabbatarian ideal. William Hilton, a London fishmonger who had settled on the Piscataqua in 1623 and represented Dover in the Massachusetts General Court in 1644, was presented to the General Court at Gorgeana on 16 October 1649 for breach of the Sabbath in carrying wood. A year later the court fined Thomas Donston and wife ten shillings for neglecting God's ordinances upon the Sabbath, warning them they would pay forty shillings upon future complaint. At Kittery in March 1651 Joseph Miles was presented for failure to attend church on Sunday, and at Agamenticus on 14 October 1652 a Miss Batcheller was presented "for entertayning Idle people on the sabboth day."[74]

At this point Massachusetts asserted its jurisdiction over the province of Maine, basing its claim upon a construction of its charter which made the northern boundary of the colony a line drawn east from the headwaters of the Merrimac that came out at Portland. The Bay colony sent commissioners to receive the consent of the inhabitants of the area, and in the autumn of 1652 those in Kittery and Agamenticus (York) were persuaded to submit, with those of Wells falling into line the following July. The northern half of the Isles of Shoals and the area north of the Piscataqua were erected into the county of York, and the political conquest of the province of Maine was complete.

Maine had been settled by men interested in riches rather than grace, and many inhabitants were coarse and hard-drinking, averse to the civilizing influences of religion, government, and law. Massachusetts authorities now imparted a new vigor to corrective action, and to help local officials impose Puritan culture on the area a Bay magistrate sat with county courts. During the rest of the decade these tribunals sought to improve Sabbath observance. The records show twenty-six persons presented for neglect of public worship on the Lord's Day, a high number in the thinly populated jurisdiction. Some, like Thomas Crowley, were riffraff. Hugh Gunnison, an innkeeper, was indicted for allowing his daughter to stay home from church for several months together. Late in the decade it was obvious that several persons, charged with not attending public worship for several months or even years, were infected with Quakerism. The court used its discretion in imposing punishments, with monetary fines ranging from five to twenty shillings and costs. Only a handful of cases of breach of the Sabbath by labor or otherwise were tried in these years.[75]

New Plymouth had a satellite colony on the Maine coast at Kennebec, and in March 1654 the General Court commissioned Thomas Prence to erect an orderly government there. On 23 May the inhabitants met at the home of Thomas Ashley on Merrymeeting Bay and adopted regulations for their jurisdiction. One of these required that willful profanation of the Lord's Day be punished according to the discretion of the magistrates.[76]

After its surveyors drew a line from the headwaters of the Merrimac east to Casco Bay, Massachusetts claimed control over the province of Lygonia as well as that of Maine. Though the local government under George Cleaves stoutly resisted encroachments for a time, on 13 July 1658 the commissioners of the Bay met at the home of Robert Jordan in Spurwink, opposite Cape Elizabeth, and residents of the area subscribed their submission to Massachusetts. Boston's deputies now formed various scattered settlements into the towns of Scarborough and Falmouth, and laws were immediately enacted to extend the religion and culture of the Puritans to this region. At Jordan's house a day earlier, in fact, the local court had declared that since both God's Word and the laws of the country required the people to assemble every Lord's Day for public worship, town rates should be levied to build a meetinghouse and support a minister. This introduced general taxation to support the established church of Massachusetts. A year later at York the county court, informed that the people

of Falmouth were destitute of "any publique meanes for their aedifica-
tion on the Lords day," which gave a great advantage to the "Comman
Enemy," the Devil, and opened the way for Sabbath profanations, ordered the inhabitants to meet for public worship on the Lord's Day.
Other towns received similar orders in subsequent years. And we know
from regulation of the sale of liquor that the duration of the Sabbath
along the Maine coast was from sunset to sunset.[77]

By 1660 the Puritan Sabbath was taking root in Maine. That year some
inhabitants of Wells petitioned the county court for dismissal of their
minister, the Reverend Seth Fletcher, on the grounds that "for near two
years past he had drawn them into neglects relating both to the sanctifying of the Sabbath, and the performance of God's holy work therein."[78]

WHILE THE INSTITUTION of the Sabbath was becoming firmly established
elsewhere in New England, the colony of Rhode Island was taking shape.
Roger Williams, its founder and guiding spirit, intended the Narragansett Bay area to be "a shelter for persons distressed of conscience."[79] In
this corner of New England, Puritanism ripened into spiritual and mystical religion and the principle of religious liberty prevailed. As a result, a
distinctive form of Sabbatarianism arose.

Settlements at Providence, Portsmouth, Newport, and Warwick formed
the nucleus of the province. After his forced flight from Salem in January
1636, Williams spent the winter in western Plymouth colony. Late that
spring he and some associates crossed the Seekonk River, receiving a warm
welcome from the Indians at Slate Rock in what became the town of Providence. The land was scrupulously purchased from the natives, although
the consideration tendered was not money but kindness and service. According to Williams, "Rhode Island was purchased by love."[80]

The civil community began as a simple democracy of the first arrivals.
The eight heads of families ordinarily met once a fortnight and regulated
affairs by mutual consent. They admitted other religious refugees and, as
Winthrop recorded, ordered "that no man should be molested for his
conscience." This attracted a number of young single men who soon
chafed at being denied the franchise. Accordingly, late that summer thirteen signatories established a government by compact, which provided
for rule by consent of the majority.[81]

The church was never established in Rhode Island, and Sabbath observance in Providence differed from that in orthodox New England. There
were two ministers in the colony besides Williams: Thomas James, a Con-
gregationalist, and William Blackstone, an Anglican. Williams held
meetings for worship in his house on the Lord's Day, and in 1639 he and

Ezekiel Holliman baptized each other and formed the first Baptist church in America. But the spiritually restless Williams soon began to doubt the validity of believers' baptism and withdrew from the church.

Social pressure if not law put a premium upon attending divine service in the early days. The first recorded problem concerning the conflicting claims of religious liberty and public worship in Providence occurred on 21 May 1638 when the town disfranchised Joshua Verin, "upon the breach of a covenant for restraining of the libertie of conscience."[82] The young man had refused to attend worship, presumably at Williams' house, the preceding year with impunity, but his struggle about his wife's conscience led to trouble. According to Verin and William Arnold, the principle of freedom of conscience enabled women, children, and servants to claim liberty to attend religious services on weekdays, but Jane Verin used her freedom to shirk domestic duties. According to Williams, however, Verin tried to draw his wife into ungodliness; since the town respected freedom of conscience it patiently tolerated this action and Verin's tyrannical and brutish treatment of his wife for some time. When the authorities finally decided to censure Verin, he and Arnold complained that the town violated its own principles. Obviously Providence refused to consider all claims to liberty of conscience equally valid, and in this case it registered preference for those who attended as opposed to those who neglected public worship.[83]

Nevertheless, forced worship was not permitted in Providence. Though the inhabitants enjoyed freedom in observance of the First Day, Williams had scruples about use of the Sabbath. On occasion he refused to travel then, obliging companions to wait until the rest day ended before commencing a journey. But he probably had commercial dealings at his trading post on Sunday and consulted Indian sachems on that day. Others were freer. Samuel Gorton charged that Robert Cole, one of the first settlers, "usually conversed with . . . the Indians on the Sabbath days," that William Arnold constantly employed himself in servile work on the Sabbath "and professed it to be his excellency above that which his neighbors had attained unto," and that Arnold's son Benedict constantly traded with the Indians on the Sabbath.[84]

Williams pioneered in missionary labors to the Indians of New England. Because he rejected the doctrine of covenant theology, he could deal with them as equals. He learned their language and performed countless acts of generosity, winning great favor among the Indians. Nevertheless, he failed conspicuously as an evangelist, winning not a single convert in nearly a half-century in Rhode Island. An Indian sachem once told John Eliot that the Narragansetts did not care to learn of Williams, "because hee is no good man but goes out and workes upon the Sabbath day."[85] The reality was more complex. Williams believed it would be presumptuous to convert the Indians before God turned them from their idols and made them capable of worship. He contended that he could have brought the entire Narragansett tribe to keep one day in seven but saw no value in securing external observance of a religious ordinance out of respect for himself rather than conviction. Hence the Indians did not become Sabbath-keepers, and in September 1662 the Commissioners of the United Colonies charged Rhode Island with setting a poor example for the Pequots by profaning the Sabbath and selling them quantities of liquor.[86]

Two of the original Narragansett Bay settlements were on Aquidneck or the island of Rhode Island. Pocasset (later Portsmouth) at the north was founded when nineteen persons led by William Coddington and John Clarke signed a compact for government on 7 March 1638. Most of the group were Antinomians from Massachusetts, including Anne Hutchinson and members of her family. The refugees purchased Aquidneck Island and established a theocracy. According to the compact, the government was to be by the Word of God in Scripture; and Coddington, elected governor, was to rule with the powers of Moses, Joshua, and the Judges. The town government appointed a committee to locate the meetinghouse, thus making the state a nursing father to the church.[87]

Internal strife led to the reorganization of the government at Portsmouth and a division of the settlement the next year. Coddington and others went to the south of the island and founded Newport. The two towns were united in 1640, and Coddington was again chosen governor. At Portsmouth the following year the General Court for Aquidneck declared that the power to legislate rested with the freemen and that none be accounted delinquent for doctrine. The court also affirmed the principle of liberty of conscience.[88]

The inhabitants paid some respect to the Sabbath, for at Newport a meeting of the General Quarter Court was changed when it was learned that the appointed time fell on the Lord's Day. Yet John Clarke, who conducted worship at Newport until the first ordained clergyman arrived from Massachusetts, considered the Sabbath a ceremonial institution. He attacked forced worship, and civil authorities never compelled the performance of religious duties on Aquidneck.[89]

The fourth of the original Rhode Island settlements was on the mainland at Shawomet or Warwick, where Samuel Gorton, the mystic, arrived in 1643. As previously noted, Gorton emphasized inward religion and assaulted the institution of the Sabbath. Two Massachusetts Indians who had spent a Sabbath at Warwick and visited Providence told Eliot that the people of Rhode Island differed from those of the Bay in giving a spiritual interpretation to religion. Such a view left no room for observance of the external Sabbath.[90]

The Rhode Island settlements contained no tradition of Sabbatarianism when Roger Williams succeeded, on 14 May 1644, in obtaining from the Commissioners for Foreign Plantations in England a charter empowering the residents to establish a civil government. The patent contained the most complete grant of self-government yet bestowed upon an English colony, and its silence on religion was construed as making liberty of conscience an inviolable right. The four towns established a loose confederation and in the spring of 1647 formed a legal code which adapted English law to the local situation. Without drawing upon the Old Testament, this body of laws provided the death penalty for a number of crimes. But it did not mention religion and concluded with the declaration that apart from the transgressions herein forbidden, "all men may walk as their consciences perswade them, every one in the name of his God."[91]

In 1654 commissioners from the four towns adopted the Articles of Union and renewed the legal code of 1647. A day after the union was effected the legislature enacted the colony's first Sabbath law. On 1 September the General Assembly meeting at Warwick observed that it had received several complaints "against the incivilitie of persons exercised uppon the first day of the weeke which is offensive to divers amongst us." The reason for the difficulty was the lack of an appointed day for recreation. The colony then numbered about twelve hundred souls, primarily farmers and drovesmen who customarily made Sunday their rest day. To deal with the abuse, the assembly authorized each town to allow whatever days they might agree upon for recreation in order to avoid disturbances on the First Day (the words "Sunday," "Sabbath," and "Lord's Day" were avoided).[92] Such an order, unthinkable in Puritan New England, had a precedent in a Puritan Parliament's enactment of 1647. Rhode Island was trying to balance liberty of conscience with the claims of Sabbatarianism.

Williams served as president (governor) of Providence Plantations for the next three years, during which time Quaker missionaries began to arrive. During his tenure of office a paper circulating in Providence contended that it was against the rule of the Gospel to punish transgressors against the public or private welfare. Williams disclaimed support for principles tending toward an infinite extension of liberty of conscience so destructive of civil peace. He likened a religiously pluralistic community to a ship containing Protestants and Papists, Jews and Turks. All the liberty he had ever pleaded for was twofold: no passenger should be forced to attend the ship's worship nor compelled to forsake his own; and the ship's captain should set the course and see that justice and order were maintained, punishing those who transgressed laws designed for the common welfare. On this basis Rhode Island granted liberty to the Quakers, with whose principles Williams profoundly disagreed.[93]

In the last half of the seventeenth century Rhode Island developed a pattern of Sabbatarianism resembling that of more orthodox colonies. The royal charter of 1663 provided the legal foundation. It granted the colony the power to make its own laws, required no oath of allegiance, and confirmed the liberties previously established. It held that no person was to be punished or called in question for any difference of opinion in matters of religion that did not affect the civil peace. This charter guaranteed religious freedom for the first time in American fundamental law.[94]

Like all societies, Rhode Island had to find a proper balance between work and rest and constructive uses for leisure time. Religion traditionally had been the dominant force in organizing the rhythm of life, the cyclical pattern of labor and recreation. Rhode Island, for all its reputed radicalism, was actually conservative in handling this legacy. It did not abrogate the seventh-day rest but fell into the tracks of an ancient institution.

Contemporaries did not always see the situation in this light. Complaints reached the Archbishop of Canterbury about 1670 that the Rhode Islanders were ''a profane people, and do not keep the Sabbath, but some do plough, etc.'' Williams replied that all England, after the formality and superstition of morning and evening prayer, played away the day, and that American Puritans did not keep the original Sabbath, that is, the seventh day. ''You know,'' he added, ''that generally, all this whole colony observe the first day, only here and there one out of conscience, another out of covetousness, make no conscience of it.''[95]

Rhode Island wanted to preserve the wholesome character of the day set apart for rest and worship, and the General Court, meeting at Newport in 1673, expressed concern over tippling, gaming, and wantonness on the First Day. While acknowledging that it could not force worship or the keeping of any day holy, the assembly said that the First Day was the usual rest day in the colony and urged masters and parents to require persons under them to refrain from debased practices. No liquor was to be sold and no one was to entertain in gaming or tippling on the First Day on penalty of six shillings. A constable in each town was to restrain the named offenses so that ''modest assemblys'' might not be interrupted. But all who professed to meet for worship of God, even false worshipers, were to be left undisturbed, for only spiritual weapons could properly be used against spiritual errors.[96]

The free air of Rhode Island inevitably attracted religious radicals, and Stephen Mumford, a Seventh-Day Baptist proselytizer, arrived from New England in 1665. The Saturday Sabbatarians gained a foothold in the colony and, feeling themselves at a disadvantage economically because Saturday was the regular market day, petitioned the legislature in 1667 to change the day of rest and worship. Although the assembly retained Sunday as the jewel in the crown of the week, it ordered an additional market day to be kept on Thursdays. On 3 January 1672 Mumford and six others organized a Seventh-Day Baptist church at Newport, the first in America.[97]

The colony contained over three thousand inhabitants at the time, and Sabbath observance was well enough established to receive statutory authorization. The immediate background to the legislative action of May 1679 was a complaint that more servile labor was being done on the first day of the week than was necessary. The General Assembly therefore prohibited the employment of servants on Sunday on penalty of five shillings, which would aid the poor of the town where the crime was committed. In addition, the Assembly banned a number of Sunday pastimes, including sporting, gaming, shooting, playing at games, and drinking in any tavern more than necessity required, all on pain of five shillings or three hours in the stocks.[98] This enactment was not as prohibitive as similar laws in most other colonies, but the intent was to protect the traditional Christian day of rest and worship.

This law long remained the legislative basis for regulating Sabbath observance in Rhode Island. There is no evidence that enforcement was vigorous, but in December 1679 a court sitting in Newport questioned Samuel Stapleton and Christopher Hargall as to why they had not kept their shops shut on an appointed thanksgiving day. Stapleton replied that he was above the observance of days and times; Hargall answered that his son opened the shop and worked on his own account, "and that he was lame, or else he did not know but that himself might have wrought." In 1688 Francis Brayton of Portsmouth was ordered to pay ten shillings for selling drink to Indians on that day. In 1730 the General Assembly decreed that there was to be no appeal from conviction by a justice of the peace for violating the statute.[99]

A large degree of religious freedom prevailed in Rhode Island. Attendance at church was entirely a private matter, and the "stink of forced worship" never arose in the colony. A good deal of visiting, feasting, and pleasure-taking apparently occurred on the Sabbath, the duration of which was probably from dawn to dusk.[100] To be sure, orthodox Puritans regarded Rhode Island as a sink of iniquity. Cotton Mather described the neighboring colony as a *"colluvies of Antinomians, Familists, Anabap-*

tists, Antisabbatarians, Arminians, Socinians, Quakers, Ranters, everything in the World but *Roman Catholicks,* and *Real Christians.''* Even some residents thought things went too far. When it received complaints in 1725 that the Seventh-Day Baptists of Westerly annoyed their neighbors and scandalized the colony by working on Sunday, the General Assembly cautioned the offenders ''that, although the ordinances of men may not square with their private principle, yet they must be subject to them, for the Lord's sake.''[101]

Thus, Rhode Island balanced its commitments. The colony wrought a reformation in human affairs by establishing the principle of liberty of conscience and refusing to permit forced worship. In time, however, the institution of the Sabbath, revitalized by the Puritans, took hold in the area. The 1679 law regulated Sabbath observance in Rhode Island for three-quarters of a century. In 1750, finally, the assembly, declaring that the penalties in the act were so small that people disregarded them, increased the fines for working and playing on the Sabbath from five to forty shillings for the first offense and double for the second. This stiff penalty testified to the persistent force of the Sabbath in shaping early American culture.[102]

9

New Netherland
and New York

THE DUTCH IN New Netherland were Egyptians compared to the Israelites of New England. With their interest in material values, in improving one's condition in this world, and in assimilating various tongues and faiths, they created a culture more like that of modern America than did any other group of colonists.[1] The Netherlands had embraced Calvinism without Sabbatarianism, and the early settlers of Manhattan and its environs were cast in this mold. The idea of a strict Sabbath made headway in Holland in the seventeenth century, however, and Peter Stuyvesant introduced it to New Netherland in 1647. The English, conquering the province in 1664, built on these foundations, and by the early eighteenth century the province of New York possessed its own brand of Sabbatarianism.

To understand the interaction between Old World attitudes and New World experiences which produced these results we must start with the Dutch religious situation at the time New Netherland was settled. During their revolt against the Spanish yoke starting in the 1570s the Low Countries split along religious lines, with Catholicism prevailing in the southern Netherlands, Belgium, and Protestantism in the northern Netherlands, Holland. The United Provinces of the north declared independence in 1579, and by the early seventeenth century the Dutch Republic ranked among the foremost nations. The country enjoyed an extraordinary degree of eminence in art, literature, science, and commerce.[2]

The Reformed religion was established in the United Netherlands. The Belgic Confession (1561) together with the Heidelberg Catechism (1563) constituted the recognized standards of doctrine, and the church was organized in a system of consistories, classes, synods, and national synods. Although Roman Catholics constituted a majority of the population and radical Protestants were numerous, the Reformed religion alone could be publicly exercised. Dissenters were allowed to worship in private, however, and freedom of conscience was more fully recognized in the United Provinces than in any other country.

The Belgic or Netherlands Confession said nothing about the Sabbath, while the Heidelberg Catechism spiritualized the duties required by the Fourth Commandment. The obligation was not very demanding: men were diligently to attend church on the day of rest and to rest from evil works on all days to "allow the Lord to work in me by his Spirit, and thus begin in this life the everlasting Sabbath."[3] Catholics had a lax attitude toward the Lord's Day, and many Protestant sectarians tended to abjure all distinctions of days. Accordingly, the Dutch worked, played, and drank on the day of rest.

The theory enunciated by Nicholas Bownde in 1595 soon spread to the Low Countries and led to conflict that agitated the Netherlands throughout the seventeenth century. Puritan refugees introduced it into Zeeland, and two Dutch clergymen—Godefridus Udemans, in *Practice . . . in the Christian Virtues* (1612), and Willem Teellinck—became agents of Sabbath reform in and beyond Zeeland. The new views became intertwined with the issues raised by the Arminian Controversy at a time when Reformed theology was being redefined throughout western Europe. This challenge to Calvinist orthodoxy was precipitated in 1603 when Jacobus Arminius and his followers tried to modify Calvinism so as to make God's sovereignty more compatible with man's freedom in salvation. The theory of the Sabbath became a point of dispute as Gomarists and Arminians battled over predestination and election, and open contention erupted by 1618.[4]

The issues were submitted for judgment to the Synod of Dort, which met in 154 sessions between 13 November 1618 and 9 May 1619. The assembly revised and endorsed the Belgic Confession and the Heidelberg Catechism as symbols of the national church, branded the Arminians as teachers of false doctrine, and restated Calvinist orthodoxy in five canons. The Synod resolved that all ministers were to expound the catechism on Sunday afternoons and agreed to call upon the magistrates for assistance in prohibiting Sunday work and other profane practices, especially drinking and gaming, on that part of the day so that people might learn to sanctify the entire Sabbath.

After the foreign representatives departed, local members tried to settle the controversy by entrusting a commission of four deputies with the preparation of articles that the contending parties could accept. These held that the Fourth Commandment contained both ceremonial and moral elements. The former consisted in the seventh-day rest and the rigid observance of it enjoined on the Jews. The latter consisted in the assignment of a "certain and stated day" to divine worship and as much rest as was required for worship and holy meditation. Because the Jewish Sabbath had been abrogated, Christians should sanctify the Lord's Day, which had been observed by the Church since the time of the Apostles. The day ought to be so consecrated to divine worship as to preclude all servile works, except works of charity and urgent necessity, and such recreations as hinder the worship of God. The Synod again petitioned the States General for strict measures to prevent the increasing profanation of the Sabbath and decreed that no one should preach or write against the six articles until another national synod was called.[5]

The controversy soon resumed with greater heat. It passed from the ministers to the professors and agitated the churches intermittently for a century. The Dutch debate was confined within narrower theoretical limits and was more practically oriented than the English debate. The period from 1620 to 1633 set the terms of the ensuing struggle and was influential in molding New Netherland. In these years attention focused on questions of the origins of the Sabbath and the nature of the Fourth Commandment. Had the Sabbath been instituted in Paradise or in the desert? Was the Fourth Commandment binding under the New Covenant? Three positions were taken: a strict Puritan one, a moderately strict Dutch Sabbatarianism, and an anti-Sabbatarian stance. Teellinck and Ames represented the first, Walaeus and to some extent Rivetus the second, and Gomarus the third.

Willem Teellinck (1579-1629) was the most popular preacher and voluminous writer among the Dutch clergymen of his day. He had studied in Scotland and visited England, where members of the brotherhood of spiritual preachers deeply influenced him. On returning home, he became a champion of Puritan pietism and improved Sabbath observance. Shortly after Dort he published *De Rusttijdt: Ofte Tractaet van d'onderhoudinge des Christelijken Rust Dachs* (The Rest Time: Or a Treatise on the Observance of the Christian Sabbath; Rotterdam, 1622).[6] William Ames (1576-1633) lived as a refugee in the Netherlands from 1610 until his death. The most influential Puritan in Holland, his great contribution was to relate dogma to ethics. His famous *Medulla Theologica* (Amsterdam, 1623)—*Marrow of Theology*—began as lectures to Leyden students between 1620 and 1622 and took a Puritan view of the Sabbath obligation. Following lines laid out by Bownde, Greenham, and Perkins, he tried to provide a theoretical basis for improved Sabbath observance in Holland, and his discussion of the Sabbath, the most documented chapter in the *Marrow,* has a distinctively Dutch resonance.[7]

The controversy now deepened. The *Synopsis Purioris Theologiae* (Synopsis of Purer Theology; Leyden, 1625), in which four leading theologians, Professors Polyander, Rivetus, Thysius, and Walaeus of the University of Leyden, discussed the entire field of Reformed dogmatics, included a chapter on the Sabbath. Antonius Thysius (1565-1640), its author, expressed agreement with the six Dort articles on the subject but added two important amendments. These held that the "certain and stated day" required by the morality of the Fourth Commandment was a perpetual seventh portion of time, and that the Lord's Day was of apostolic ordination and consequently of divine authority.

The first attack on Sabbatarianism appeared with publication of Threnos or Lamentation Showing the Causes of the Pitiful Condition of the Country and the Desecration of the Sabbath (Tholen, 1627). Jacobus Burs (1580-1650), minister in a village near Middelburg, was named as author, though Gomarus was understood to have aided in the work. Burs, refuting Teellinck, held that a primitive Sabbath transferred under Christianity to a new day was a novel, erroneous, and dangerous doctrine and that strict Sabbath observance meant a loss of liberty to the church. The book split the churches of Zeeland. Gisbertus Voetius entered the controversy with *Lachrymae Crocodili Abstersae* (The Tears of the Crocodile Wiped Away; 1627), doubting the sincerity of Burs and his supporters; and Teellinck reaffirmed his Sabbatarian creed in a book published shortly before his death.[8]

These preliminaries inaugurated a major literary quarrel between eminent Dutch theologians at Leyden and Groningen that lasted from 1628 to 1633. Friends persuaded Antonius Walaeus (1573-1639) to apply his abundant talents to the settlement of the vexing Sabbath question. His *Dissertatio de Sabbatho, seu Vero Sensu atque Usu Quarti Praecepti* (Dissertation on the Sabbath, Or the True Meaning and Use of the Fourth Commandment; Leyden, 1628), was praised by Sabbatarians and translated into Dutch. But Franciscus Gomarus (1563-1641), a leader of the strict Calvinist party in the Arminian struggle and a professor at Groningen, countered with *Investigatio Sententiae et Originis Sabbati atque*

Institutionis diei Dominici Consideration (Enquiry into the Meaning and Origin of the Sabbath and Consideration of the Institution of the Lord's Day; Groningen, 1628). Gomarus' contention that the Sabbath was an abrogated Jewish ceremony aroused Andreas Rivetus (1572-1651), the most influential member of the Leyden theological faculty in his day, who briefly answered Gomarus in his *Praelectiones* (Lectures) on Exod. 20 (1632). Gomarus replied with a copious *Defensio Investigationis Originis Sabbati* (Defense of the Enquiry into the Origin of the Sabbath; Groningen, 1632)—and Rivetus published a rejoinder, *Dissertatio de Origine Sabbathi* (Dissertation on the Origin of the Sabbath; Leyden, 1633).[9]

At this point a young Englishman published an analysis of the debate since 1628. Nathanael Eaton (1609?-1676) had studied at Trinity College, Cambridge, before going to the Netherlands in 1632. He was briefly a student of Ames at the University of Franeker, where Ames had been a professor of theology since 1622 and rector since 1626. At Franeker, Ames had treated the Sabbath again in *De Conscientia et Eius Iure vel Casibus* (Amsterdam, 1630), *Conscience with the Power and Cases Thereof* (London, 1633).[10] Eager to reform Dutch practice, he probably suggested that his compatriot examine the recent publications from this perspective. Eaton studied the works on one of the hottest issues of the day and presented his results both in the form of a disquisition before a university audience and in a Latin booklet entitled *Inquisitio in Variantes Theologorum Quorundam Sententia, De Sabbato, et die Dominico* (An Examination of the Diverse Opinions Held by Certain Theologians concerning the Sabbath and the Lord's Day; Franeker, 1633).

Eaton started by describing the various views on the origin of the Sabbath. Gomarus held that the festival was instituted in the wilderness and renewed at Sinai and that Gen. 2:3 should be understood proleptically, as anticipating something to come later. Walaeus and Rivetus protested, maintaining that the Sabbath was of primeval appointment; God blessed and sanctified the seventh day because he rested on it after the work of creation. Eaton agreed, reflecting Ames's views.

The *Inquisitio* then analyzed different Dutch opinions on the nature of the Fourth Commandment. Gomarus was the chief advocate of those who interpreted it ceremonially, contending that the precept prescribed a Sabbath only for the Jews. Dutch Anabaptists also inclined to this outlook. The generally accepted doctrine in the Dutch Reformed Church held that it was partly ceremonial and partly moral. Walaeus, a leading exponent of this notion, held that the ceremonial part had passed away but that the moral part was perpetual. The Lord's Day was partly of divine authority, insofar as the Fourth Commandment was moral, and partly of ecclesiastical, yet apostolic institution, since the Apostles had altered the day of rest and worship from the last to the first day of the week. Rivetus, parting company with his Leyden colleague, held that the Fourth Commandment required only the consecration of some day to rest and worship. Although he thought that Lord's Day observance was not necessarily binding on Christians, he recommended that the day be spent in rest, joyfulness, and beneficence. Eaton, who found all of these opinions wanting, followed Ames, who interpreted the Fourth Commandment as purely moral and argued that a perpetual obligation to keep the Sabbath had been transferred by divine authority from the seventh to the first day of the week. The Lord's Day began in the morning because the resurrection of Christ had occurred at that time. The correct observance of the weekly festival required a complete rest from all work which hindered divine worship and sanctification of that rest by public worship and pious activity.[11]

When the Sabbath controversy heated up again in the 1650s, Eaton's *Inquisitio* was republished by Christian S. Schotanus (1603-1671), a professor at the University of Franeker, who erroneously attributed it to Ames.[12] The leaders in the new round of an old battle were Gisbertus Voetius (1589-1676) and Johannes Cocceius (1603-1669). They gave their names to the main theological parties in the Reformed church in the Netherlands at this time. Voetius, professor of theology at Utrecht, was a pietistic and rigidly orthodox Calvinist who buttressed his views with scholastic philosophy. Cocceius, who had studied under Ames at Franeker before becoming professor of theology at Leyden, was more liberal in thought and freer in exegesis. He sought to separate theology from the old Aristotelian philosophy and was identified with Cartesianism, which Voetius considered incompatible with Reformed theology. Totally Bible-oriented, Cocceius unlocked the treasures of Scripture through the central idea of the covenant and developed an extravagant typology or system of parallels between the Old and New Testaments. He understood the Law spiritually and found a place for the Ten Commandments in the covenant of grace. The Fourth Commandment had been abrogated by Christ, according to Cocceius. This teaching aroused the Dutch church to the peculiarities of his doctrine, and Voetius became his chief antagonist. Voetius insisted upon strict Sabbath observance according to Jewish law; Cocceius saw no need to keep special days. The ministers ranged themselves under the Voetian or Cocceian banner, and though the States General intervened in 1659 to suppress it, the controversy wracked the Dutch Reformed church.[13] "As a consequence disorders existed in the church; with one, the least domestic employment on the Sabbath was a sin; with another, the day was no more holy than other days; 'the one village on Sunday was a dead house; the other a house of feasting.' ''[14]

THIS HERITAGE DECISIVELY influenced New Netherland. That colony, unlike New England, was established by a trading company for its own pecuniary advantage. On 3 June 1621 the States General chartered the Dutch West Indies Company. It received for twenty-four years a monopoly of the Dutch trade to the west coast of Africa and all the coasts of North and South America. Within these limits the company had vast power to colonize and govern unoccupied areas. Under the superior authority of the States General, its government was vested in five chambers representing various sections of the United Provinces, each of which had proportional representation on a general executive board, the Committee of the Nineteen. The main purpose of the company was profit through trade and conquest, and its center of interest was Spain's colonial dominions. But the charter included New Netherland, a large, undefined territory between the English settlements at Virginia and New Plymouth, and the company began to colonize there, entrusting the Amsterdam Chamber with the immediate management of affairs.[15]

The first colonists, a company of thirty families, mostly Protestant Walloons, arrived in New Netherland in the spring of 1624. They established a series of trading posts at advantageous locations for prosecuting the fur trade: two on the North (Hudson) River—one at its mouth, the other at Fort Orange (modern Albany)—and a third on the South (Delaware) River at Fort Nassau (near present Gloucester, New Jersey). These forts were strengthened by ships sent from Holland, and the Dutch also settled on the Connecticut River at Fort Good Hope (near Hartford). In 1626 the governor called in all but small garrisons from the outlying forts, and New Amsterdam became the heart of the province. The fortified outpost on the tip of Manhattan Island contained nearly the entire population, numbering two hundred men, women, and children in that year.

New Netherland was slow to develop. The primary duty of the director-general, or governor, was to return a profit; but prior to 1647 three held office for only a year each, while those with longer tenures—Peter Minuit (1626-1632), Wouter van Twiller (1633-1638), and Willem Kieft (1638-1647)—were unfortunate choices. The settlers were employees of a commercial monopoly. Although the beaver trade was profitable, agricultural settlement made slow progress, and the colony operated at a net loss to the stockholders. The population rose to two hundred and seventy souls in 1628 and three hundred in 1630, and the company decided to open the entire province to permanent agricultural colonization. The Charter of Freedoms and Exemptions of 7 June 1629 reserved the fur traffic for the stockholders but offered individual immigrants as much land as they could improve and introduced the patroon system. Members of the company could become large proprietors with feudal privileges in return for planting fifty adults on the land. Although several directors of the Amsterdam Chamber tried to establish patroonships, only Kiliaen van Rensselaer, a dealer in precious jewels, succeeded. He bought vast tracts on both sides of the Hudson around Fort Orange and created the colony of Rensselaerswyck.

New Netherland as a whole still failed to flourish. The charter discouraged individual enterprise, and the governors did little to advance public welfare. Van Twiller brought affairs to a ruinous condition by 1638. That year, therefore, the company sent out Kieft and proclaimed free trade. In 1640 it issued another Charter of Freedoms and Exemptions, which curbed the power of the patroons, established a class of smaller proprietors, and extended to all "free colonists" the commercial privileges formerly restricted to patroons. These changes stimulated growth, and New Netherland attracted immigrants from a variety of places. In 1643, according to Father Isaac Jogues, a visiting Jesuit, Manhattan and its environs contained some four or five hundred persons of different sects and nations, speaking eighteen languages. No religion could be publicly exercised except the Calvinist, but the colony also contained Catholics, English Puritans, Lutherans, and Anabaptists.[16] A commercial spirit prevailed, and the people were a hard-drinking, fun-loving lot.

Although until 1640 no official document makes the point explicit, the Reformed religion was established in New Netherland from the beginning, as indicated by the provisional regulations for colonists drawn up by the company on 30 March 1624. These stated that "they shall within their territory practice no other form of divine worship than that of the Reformed religion as at present practiced here in this country . . . , without however persecuting any one on account of his faith, but leaving to every one the freedom of his conscience." A year later instructions to the governor on the advancement of religion included a directive to see that "the Lord's Sabbath be not violated."[17]

The Sabbath could not have been well kept in the early years of settlement. Under the rule that the direction of ecclesiastical affairs in Dutch colonial possessions fell to the churches within whose bounds the various chambers of the company were located, the Consistory and later the Classis of Amsterdam assumed responsibility for religion in New Netherland.[18] This body sent out two comforters of the sick or lay preachers prior to 1628. Their duties included conducting divine service by leading in prayer and reading from the Bible and Reformed authors, but not exercising such functions of the ordained clergy as administering the sacraments. Bastiaen Jansz Krol, a velours worker who was taught by his wife to write his name, arrived in 1624 with the first colonists. Apart from a brief trip back to Holland, he ministered to the settlers, probably at Fort Orange, until 1 August 1626. Jan Huyghen, a former church elder in the Low Countries, landed in 1626 and ministered to the people at New Amsterdam, where plans called for building a room to accommodate a large congregation over the grist mill which was then under construction.[19]

Isaack de Rasière, secretary of the colony, offered valuable if indirect evidence on the relation of the Sabbath to social conditions. Arriving in the colony in the summer of 1626, he found the people "quite lawless, owing to the bad government hitherto prevailing" and characterized them as "a rough lot who have to be kept at work by force."[20] By contrast, de Rasière was much impressed with the orderliness of New Plymouth which he visited in 1628, when he penned the classic description of the Pilgrims marching to church on Sunday. He reported that the Indians around Plymouth conducted themselves better than those around New Netherland "because the English give them the example of better ordinances and a better life."[21]

The provisional form of worship ended in April 1628 with the arrival of Jonas Michaelius (b. 1584). A graduate of the University of Leyden while Gomarus was teaching there, he was an ordained minister and had been engaged by the company for three years. Michaelius found most of the people "rather rough and unrestrained," but he quickly founded the Dutch Reformed church in America and was optimistic about the future. Fully fifty communicants attended the first administration of the Lord's Supper, the congregation was "pretty large" in proportion to the population, and the church grew "in numbers and piety." A quarrel between Michaelius and Minuit soon dashed these hopes, and the minister denounced the magistrate as a compound of iniquity and wickedness who put private interest over public welfare. Having tried unsuccessfully to remedy the evil by complaining to the directors, Michaelius returned to Holland in 1632. He left no evidence that his faithfulness to the Reformed religion included concern for improved Sabbath observance.[22]

Everardus Bogardus was the second minister sent out by the Amsterdam Consistory under contract to the West Indies Company. He had entered the University of Leyden in 1620 and before his ordination in 1632 had been a comforter of the sick in Guinea. Bogardus came to Manhattan in April 1633 along with van Twiller. That weak and ineffective governor, though he erected the first church building in New Amsterdam the year of his arrival, was no defender of religion. Bogardus, a master of verbal abuse whose invective became worse with drink, made the pulpit a center of contention. Shortly after landing he had the public prosecutor excommunicated and began quarreling with the director-general. The Dutch domine once berated van Twiller as a child of the Devil and promised to assault him strenuously from the pulpit; and the drunken governor chased the offending clergyman in the street with a naked sword.[23]

Willem Kieft became director-general in 1638, and to correct the ruinous conditions he promulgated the first ordinances of record prohibiting immorality and immoderate drinking. In 1641 the director and council ordered that no liquor was to be sold during divine service or after 10 P.M. on penalty of fine. This was the first Sunday regulation in New Netherland. Although a new stone church was erected the following year, Kieft and Bogardus brought the colony to the edge of disaster before being recalled. An Indian war provoked by Kieft's exactions ravaged the settlement from 1643 to 1645. Meanwhile, Bogardus led his flock astray by going into the pulpit drunk and by publicly abusing Kieft. The governor retaliated by encouraging his subordinates to play games and make noise about the church during time of service, which officials refused to attend. In short, for some years before Stuyvesant arrived as governor, authorities at New Amsterdam had trained the people to violate the Sabbath.[24]

At Rensselaerswyck, however, the patroon combined a zeal for profit with a desire to establish the Reformed religion. During the 1630s Kiliaen van Rensselaer ordered his thinly scattered tenants to assemble on Sundays and holidays for Bible readings and prayers conducted by his schout or sheriff, sent out copies of *De Practijcke der Godtsalicheyt* (The Practice of Godliness), and arranged for Bogardus to hold religious services a few times a year. The settlers refused to help provide for a minister, so van Rensselaer contracted with Johannes Megapolensis, a pious and learned convert from Catholicism, who went to Rensselaerswyck in 1642. A church was erected opposite Fort Orange on the east side of the Hudson the next year. The patroon believed "that hardly any semblance of godliness or righteousness" existed in the colony at this time. Seeing a connection between fidelity to divine commandments as well as to worldly contracts, he ordered all to attend church at least once a week upon penalty of a fine. But because members of families living farthest away could only attend church by turns, so as not to leave houses unsupervised, husbands and wives were to be fined only if both stayed away. In order to reach all of the widely dispersed residents, Megapolensis was to preach occasionally at Rensselaers Steyn, a small fort on Beeren Island at the southern entrance to the colony.[25] The patroon's strong hand was removed by death in late 1643 or 1644, and the colony was poorly administered for the next several years.

PETER STUYVESANT ARRIVED in New Netherland on 11 May 1646 amid great rejoicing. He ruled until the British conquest in 1664, and his administration was marked by many progressive accomplishments. Stuyvesant was unique among the Dutch governors in the respect he accorded the Sabbath, and ordinances regulating its observance bulked large among the many laws he issued to promote internal good order. The reasons for Stuyvesant's Sabbatarianism can be ascertained with a fair degree of certainty. The son of a Dutch Reformed clergyman, he was born not in 1592, the date traditionally assigned, but in 1610 or 1611. His father removed with the family to Berlicum in the Classis of Franeker in 1622, and Peter enrolled at the University of Franeker in 1628 or 1629, at a time when the debate over the Sabbath was at fever pitch. A strict adherent of the Dutch Reformed church, he was apparently deeply influenced by the growing demand for improved Sabbath observance. He seems to have avoided the views of Ames as well as of Gomarus, subscribing to the moderately strict Dutch Sabbatarianism of which Walaeus was a spokesman. In any event, Stuyvesant's career took him to New Netherland with a commission from the States General, upon landing he discovered the wretched state of affairs in the land without a Sabbath, and he began to translate his religious convictions into public policy.[26]

Within a year after stepping ashore, the governor promulgated three ordinances regulating Sunday observance. The first, the earliest recorded ordinance of his council (31 May 1647), forbade the sale of liquor on Sunday, except to travelers, before 2 P.M. or 4 P.M., depending on whether there was afternoon preaching, and after 9 P.M. on penalty of loss of license for the innkeeper and six Carolus guilders for the drinker.[27] Despite the heavy fine, this law apparently had little effect.[28] Johannes Backerus, the minister who accompanied Stuyvesant, said that most of the congregation at New Amsterdam were ''very ignorant in regard to true religion, and very much given to drink.'' The temptation was great, since at that time a full fourth of the buildings in the city had been turned into taverns. Accordingly, an edict of 10 March 1648 regulated taprooms and forbade publicans from selling liquor on Sunday before 3 P.M., except to travelers and boarders. A month later, after consulting with Domine Backerus, the director and council ordered everyone to attend divine service on Sunday afternoons as well as in the forenoons. This made church attendance compulsory for the first time in New Netherland, but there is no record of enforcement. The 29 April law also prohibited all tapping (selling of drink), fishing, hunting, ordinary occupations, and trading during divine service upon stiff monetary penalty. Excessive drinking was to be published at the pleasure of the court. In 1648 Stuyvesant demonstrated further respect for the Lord's Day when, in establishing an annual free market of ten days corresponding to the Amsterdam Fair, which always began on a Sunday, he set the first Monday after St. Bartholomew's Day as the opening day.[29]

No fresh legislation regarding the Sabbath in Manhattan was forthcoming for several years. But the weekly rest day took root in other parts of New Netherland. In Rensselaerswyck, Brant van Slichtenhorst arrived as the new commissioner on 22 March 1648. His instructions from the patroon specified that he was to provide regulations for the proper observance of the "Sabbath of the New Testament." This he attempted to do as the presiding officer of the court of Rensselaerswyck from April 1648 to April 1652. Public worship was not always available, since Megapolensis left in 1649 to replace Backerus at Manhattan, and Gideon Schaets, his successor, did not arrive until 1652. Yet on at least one occasion the court ordered a man to go to church rather than the tavern on the Lord's Day, and authorities tried to prevent the desecration of the Sabbath. On 28 May 1648 van Slichtenhorst issued an ordinance prohibiting the serving of beer and wine during divine service, imitating "that of the Manhatans." Although the magistrates acted slowly, the court did fine Jochem Kettelheym, a farmer, and Thomas Chambers, a carpenter, thirty florins each for fighting on a Sunday; Kettelheym was charged six florins more for drinking with others during divine service.[30]

In 1652 a long-standing controversy over the territory around Fort Orange was settled when Stuyvesant took the main settlement of the colony, consisting of about a hundred houses on the west side of the Hudson, out of the patroon's jurisdiction and turned it into the independent village of Beverwyck (later Albany). Henceforth the newly established court of Fort Orange and Beverwyck overshadowed the court of Rensselaerswyck and was more active in dealing with Sabbath-breakers. Most presentments involved liquor, the serving or consuming of which brought fines of six and three guilders respectively. Sunday fighting was a frequent and more serious offense. Men released from work discipline drank heavily, and the bloody brawls of drunken men armed with knives and other convenient tools endangered life. The court imposed heavy penalties on such malefactors. Few inhabitants of the area were presented for other types of Lord's Day violations, although Hendrik Hendricksen was fined twelve florins for carting hay on a Sunday.[31]

Between Albany and Manhattan a settlement began where the Esopus River enters the Hudson, and on 16 May 1661 Stuyvesant chartered the village of Wiltwyck (present Kingston) and established a court with jurisdiction over lesser crimes. In November 1661 the director and council issued an ordinance regulating Sabbath behavior at the frontier outpost. It prohibited servile work and the sale of liquor on Sunday on penalty of one pound Flemish for the first offense, two for the second, and eight for the third. Anyone found drunk on the Sabbath was to be jailed as well as fined. Four days later the court fined Pieter van Allen for selling brandy during divine service. Subsequently it prosecuted inhabitants for transporting a wagonload of beer, discharging a gun, and carrying horse fodder on the Sabbath.[32]

Long Island experienced rapid population growth once the West Indies Company permitted individuals to own private property in New Netherland. Many New England Puritans flooded into the area after 1640, greatly alarming Dutch authorities. After much friction over boundaries, Governor Stuyvesant finally abandoned the attempt to retain Dutch jurisdiction east of a line, established by the Treaty of Hartford (1650), which ran from Oyster Bay south to the ocean. The Puritan Sabbath prevailed in this region. It had been introduced by immigrants, mainly from New Haven and Connecticut colonies, who crossed the Sound and settled at such places as Huntington, Brookhaven, Southold, East Hampton, and Southampton. Southampton, established in 1640 when the Reverend Abraham Pierson led a group of settlers from Lynn, Massachusetts, to Long Island, exemplified the strict Sabbatarianism in existence beyond the Hartford treaty line. Pierson's company brought along a copy of "Moses his Judicials" and made the Cotton code the basis of their plantation covenant. The Sabbath began at sundown on Saturday, attendance at public worship was required, and the death penalty was provided for "prophaning the Lord's daye in a careless or scornfull neglect or contempt thereof."[33]

On western Long Island, between the East River and Oyster Bay, ten villages were within Dutch jurisdiction during most of Stuyvesant's administration. Five were Dutch towns: Breuckelen (Brooklyn), Midwout (Flatbush), Amersfoort (Flatlands), New Utrecht, and Boswyck (Bushwick). Their records reveal little about Sabbath observance. The villages lay somewhat beyond the governor's immediate supervision, and much probably depended on whether their ministers were Walaeites or Gomarists, Voetians or Cocceians. In 1654 the first Dutch Reformed church on Long Island was established at Flatlands (in present Brooklyn), selected for its central location, with Johannes T. Polhemus as minister. Four years later church worship was first held at Brooklyn, with Henricus Selyns called to serve.

The five English villages were Middelburgh (Newtown), Hempstead,

Flushing, Rustdorp (Jamaica), and Gravesend. Puritans were dominant in all but the last-named, and under colony law possessed considerable autonomy in internal affairs. Whether Presbyterian or Congregational in polity, the residents gave the Puritan Sabbath an honored place in both custom and law. In 1650 the General Court of Hempstead made attendance at church on Sunday compulsory, with half of the fine going to the informer. After a third offense, for which the penalty was twenty guilders, corporal punishment and banishment were provided. According to Domine Megapolensis, Gravesend was inhabited by Mennonites, and a majority rejected observance of the Sabbath.[34]

When Quaker missionaries first arrived in New Amsterdam in 1657, the authorities sent them away. Robert Hodgson, a Friend in his early twenties, made his way to Long Island. At Hempstead he was arrested and jailed for holding a religious meeting on Sunday, but when the arresting officer returned from church he discovered Hodgson preaching to a crowd from his place of confinement. So the town fathers reenacted the 1650 ordinance, and now for the first time the governor and council explicitly endorsed it. Subsequently the colony government used Sabbatarian legislation to combat Quaker inroads on Long Island.[35]

North of Manhattan the one village between the Hudson River and Long Island Sound was Oostdorp (East Town in Westchester County), a staunch Puritan settlement established by immigrants from southwestern Connecticut. When a Dutch civil commission sent by Stuyvesant arrived there in 1656 for consultation on a Sunday, its members were informed, " 'Tis our Sabbath morning; the Inhabitants will not come."[36]

New Amsterdam was never so precise. Yet Stuyvesant initiated an effort to improve Sabbath observance there. The growth in the size and the religious diversity of the provincial capital complicated his problem. The population was estimated at seven or eight hundred inhabitants in 1653, and the town was growing rapidly. Dutch Calvinists constituted the largest religious group by far, but Puritans, Lutherans, Jews, Quakers, and persons of other faiths or none at all were swarming into New Amsterdam and Long Island. The Dutch clergy of Manhattan—Megapolensis and Samuel Drisius, who arrived in 1653 to help minister to the growing congregation—regarded all but the Puritan newcomers as a threat to the supremacy of the Reformed church. Their intolerance won the support of Stuyvesant and of the Classis of Amsterdam. But the directors of the Amsterdam Chamber, who wished to attract more settlers, insisted that New Netherland extend freedom of conscience to all.[37]

Under the circumstances the state could not compel attendance at public worship, and there is no record of enforcement of that part of the law

of 1648. Authorities did try to make the Sabbath a day of rest. Not long
after Jews first settled permanently at Manhattan, a member of that faith
was charged with trading on Sunday. When Cornelis van Tienhoven, the
sheriff and public prosecutor, presented Abram de la Sina (Abraham de
Lucena) on 1 March 1655 for retail sales in his store during the Sunday
sermon, he asked that the defendant be deprived of his trade and fined
six hundred guilders.[38] This unreasonable fine, which greatly exceeded
the law, reflected a strong current of anti-Semitism, which Domine Megapolensis demonstrated when he characterized the Jews as "godless ras-
cals" eager only for profit and Christian property. The governor and
council resolved that the Jews must depart from the province, and the
burgomasters and schepens (aldermen) of New Amsterdam agreed. However, the Amsterdam directors overruled Stuyvesant, ordering that the
Jews be permitted to remain. And in 1658 Dutch authorities in New Amsterdam recognized the significance of Saturday to the Jews. When Jacob
Barsimon failed to appear in court on the proper day, no default was
entered against him, "as he was summoned on his Sabbath."[39]

On the grounds that earlier statutes had been disregarded, Stuyvesant
on 26 October 1656 obtained the enactment of a new Sabbath law. It forbade ordinary labor on Sunday under a fine of one pound Flemish;
banned plays, drunkenness, the frequenting of taverns, and various other
recreations during the time of afternoon sermon under a double fine;
prohibited the sale or consumption of liquor during this same period on
pain of the former exactions; and totally proscribed the sale of liquor after
9 P.M. An amendment the following June prohibited ordinary labor, the
sale of liquor, and pleasure parties on Sundays or during divine service.[40]
The intent of the ordinance was to protect the whole rather than merely a
part of the Lord's Day from desecration, although this was not made clear
until later.

Meanwhile, authorities enforced the existing law. For example, in 1658
the council sentenced Andrew Vrydach, a mason, to lose six months'
wages and stand sentinel for a like period for being drunk and fighting
during divine worship; and Ralph Turner, a Lancashire soldier, to stand
sentry for six hours a day on six consecutive days for fighting on the Sabbath. In 1661 the council fined Hendrick Assueros, a publican, for selling
liquor and permitting various persons to play ninepins during public worship. A year later Jan de Wit was fined six guilders "for picking his mill
stones on Sunday." (De Wit's mill was located in present City Hall Park,
and doubtless he worked on the Lord's Day so that he could operate
without loss of profit during the week.) Paulus Turck was penalized one
rixdollar for playing ninepins on Sunday. In 1663, during harvest time,

several farmers were fined six guilders each for working on the Sabbath; the following spring judgment was rendered against several Manhattanites for shooting pigeons on the Lord's Day.[41]

In April 1664 the schout of New Amsterdam was charging men in the local court with furnishing drink at their houses in violation of the Sunday ordinance. Pieter Tonneman demanded 120 guilders of Jan Schryver for entertaining twenty persons after the second sermon, and 132 guilders of Hendrick Janzen for serving twenty-two persons on Sunday. On 27 May, Janzen, brought before the burgomasters and schepens for another violation of the law, was fined 16 guilders and reprimanded. Shortly thereafter he committed suicide by hanging, and the schout asked the court to declare his goods forfeit and to exhibit his corpse as an example to others. But the city court considered Janzen ''an old Burgher'' concerning whom no bad behavior was ever heard and granted a decent burial in the corner of the churchyard.[42]

To dispel confusion over the duration of the Sabbath arising from the 1656 law as amended, the governor and council on 10 September 1663 issued an ordinance which declared that the Sabbath extended ''from the rising to the setting of the sun.'' No customary labor could be performed or drinking parties held during that time, and recreations, dissolute plays, riots, and ''too unrestrained'' playing of children in the streets were forbidden under penalty of forfeiture of the upper garment or six guilders for the first offense, double for the second, and exemplary corporal punishment for the third. This fell considerably short of the more exacting New England standard, but it still went too far for the local populace. Although they judged the ordinance to be ''highly necessary,'' the burgomasters and schepens of New Amsterdam declared on 10 March 1664, that they dared not publish it because many of its provisions were ''too severe and too much opposed to Dutch liberties.''[43]

On this note the history of Sabbatarianism in New Netherland ended. The British fleet sailed into New York Bay late in August, and Stuyvesant surrendered the province on September 6. Finding conditions in New Amsterdam deplorable on arrival, for two decades he had striven to effect moral reform by means of improved Sabbath observance. Experience taught the governor that halfway measures were inadequate, so he insisted on a stricter, more Puritan, observance of the Sabbath.[44] This new rigor leaves no doubt that a momentous social transformation had taken place in the Dutch province within a short span of time.

NEW NETHERLAND BECAME New York when English forces took possession. King Charles II issued a charter in March which made his brother James, Duke of York, proprietor of the entire region between the Connecticut and Delaware rivers. Territorial changes soon reduced the size of this domain. In June the Duke gave New Jersey to others; New York later regained title to all of Long Island but lost its claim east to the Connecticut River. Within these confines the proprietor possessed sole power to make laws and govern as he saw fit, as long as the laws harmonized with those of England. James ruled as duke until 1685 and three years longer as king. He hoped for a financial return, but was also concerned with expelling the Dutch from North America. The governors appointed were unable to fatten the proprietor's purse or satisfy provincial demands for representative government, and the resulting social unrest ripened into rebellion at the time of the Glorious Revolution.[45]

The religious situation after 1664 was very complicated. Although the Articles of Capitulation gave the Dutch freedom in matters of worship and church discipline, the change in political sovereignty raised important questions about the position of the Dutch churches under English ecclesiastical law. The Dutch Reformed church remained for decades the largest in the province; indeed, Dutch Calvinists along with the French Reformed and the Puritans (Presbyterians and Congregationalists) constituted more than 90 percent of the population of the colony for the next half-century. Nevertheless, English ecclesiastical authorities wished to extend the Anglican church to the colony, though the Roman Catholic tendencies of Charles II and the Duke of York hampered such a policy.

The transition to English rule brought no immediate change in Sabbath observance. The provincial capital, renamed New York, contained fifteen hundred inhabitants in 1664, with the Dutch the largest ethnic group. Governor Richard Nicolls (1664-1668) reconstituted the municipal government, appointing a mayor, five aldermen, and a sheriff. But the town fathers issued no new legislation on the Lord's Day for more than a decade, perhaps recalling the popular reaction against the strict Sabbath ordinance of 1663.[46]

The Dutch enclave on the upper Hudson was governed by its own local court under the supervision of the nearest English military commander. Although the court records from 1660 to 1668 are missing, we know that a Sabbath ordinance was promulgated in 1665. In that year Governor Nicolls consolidated existing tribunals into the court of Albany, Rensselaerswyck, and Schenectady. Its minutes testify to a continuing concern regarding desecration of the Lord's Day. For example, the court fined Jochem Wessels, a baker, twelve florins for baking bread on Sunday and forbade barbers to shave Albany residents at that time (though permitting them to shave country people until the second ringing of the bell for divine service).[47]

The Governor combined Long Island, Westchester, and Staten Island into the county of York. He invited delegates from the area's seventeen towns to a convention at Hempstead in February 1665 and promulgated a code of laws for the county. This document, known as the Duke's Laws, was an alphabetical arrangement adapted from the New Haven code of 1656 and the Massachusetts statutory revision of 1660. Although Nicolls refused to allow the people a representative assembly, he gave local communities considerable autonomy. Dividing York County into three ridings (subordinate jurisdictions), he entrusted the administration in each to a court of sessions made up of magistrates drawn from residents of the community.[48]

The Duke's Laws dealt with the question of worship by making each town a parish for ecclesiastical purposes and requiring it to establish and maintain a church of its own choosing. The code thus protected the Dutch Reformed church in Dutch villages and Puritan congregations in English villages. All residents were obligated to support the local church, but no professing Christian was to be molested, fined, or imprisoned for differing in matters of religion. Nicolls did not slavishly copy New England's Sabbath ordinances. The Duke's Laws failed to require attendance at public worship but did prohibit desecration of the weekly rest day. Sundays were not to be profaned by "Travellers, Labourers or vicious Persons," no one was to disturb any congregation on the Lord's Day (a provision aimed at Quakers), and Sabbath-breaking, along with drunkenness, fornication, and adultery, was declared one of the "abominable Sinnes" for which churchwardens could present offenders twice yearly to the courts of sessions. Constables were authorized to apprehend Sabbath-breakers and to search taverns and suspected places for offenders.[49]

During the third war between England and the United Provinces the Dutch recaptured the province, retaining control from August 1673 to November 1674. The burgomasters and schepens of the capital, renamed New Orange, enacted a new Sabbath ordinance on 28 August 1673. It declared that "all sorts of handicraft, trade and traffick, gaming, boat racing, or running with carts or wagons, fishing, fowling, running and picking nuts, strawberries etc. all riotous racing, calling and shouting of children in the streets, . . . unlawful exercises and games, drunkenness, frequenting taverns or taphouses, dancing, cardplaying, ballplaying, rolling nine pins or bowls etc." were "more in vogue on this than on any other day," and prohibited them from sunrise to sunset on penalty of fine. At the same time Governor Anthony Colve and his council enacted ordinances to reestablish and maintain the Reformed church and Dutch authority in other towns on Long Island and west of the Hudson. These statutes safeguarded the weekly rest day by prohibiting servile labor, recreations, the frequenting of taverns, and drunkenness throughout all of Sunday. The Dutch, with their energetic concern for the matter, acted as if their entire welfare depended upon proper Sabbath observance.[50]

The Treaty of Westminster restored the province to England, and during the next half-century a more uniform type of Sabbatarianism gradually developed. In November 1676 the Common Council of New York City issued the first Sunday ordinance for the provincial capital under English rule. It perpetuated Dutch practice by prohibiting trading and unnecessary labor; unlawful playing of cards, dice, and games; and disorderly assemblies of children on the Sabbath, without prescribing penalties. The law also forbade drinking or gaming on the rest day on penalty of ten guilders for the buyer and heavier, graduated fines for the seller.[51]

In the Dutch enclave around Albany, law aided custom in promoting morality. The civil authorities obtained a promise from Domine Schaets never to leave Albany without divine worship and later held him to his pledge when Schenectady requested his services four Sundays a year. In addition, the court dealt with persons presented for such crimes as fighting, drinking, causing an uproar, riding to Schenectady, wife-beating, and going shooting on the Lord's Day. Magistrates fined Jan Clute seventy-five guilders and costs for selling two beavers and sending two servants with wagons to his farm during Sunday worship.[52]

Considering the Sabbath greatly desecrated at Kinderhook, on the east bank of the Hudson several miles below Albany, the court in 1677 appointed a deputy sheriff for the area and empowered him to levy fines below twenty-five guilders and to report more serious Sabbath crimes to the sheriff. Officials also authorized the Albany church to choose a precentor for Kinderhook, whose efforts to suppress Sabbath-breaking the court agreed to sanction. But here and elsewhere around Albany people continued to offend. Convinced that many residents made little distinction between Sundays and weekdays, the magistrates in 1679 and again in 1682 enacted comprehensive ordinances banning all ordinary employments and various named recreations, including drinking in taverns, from sunrise to sunset on the Sabbath. The penalty was set at six guilders for the least fault and more at the discretion of the court.[53]

But in treating Sunday as a *dies juridicus,* a day on which legal business might lawfully be transacted, civil authorities themselves detracted from its special character. In 1678 a defendant said that he often had received warrants on Sunday; and the following year three Kinderhook men were required to appear before the bench in Albany on a Sunday. Moreover, the court allowed two inhabitants to remove their houses from Albany to Schenectady after the Sunday service![54]

Relations with the Indians constituted a special problem in this fur-trading center, for the rest day afforded whites a prime opportunity to get the natives drunk and cheat them. To publicize the measure, the court in 1679 renovated an earlier proclamation prohibiting direct or indirect trade with the Indians upon the Lord's Day upon penalty of fifty guilders and banning the sale of food during the sermon on forfeiture of twelve guilders. But sale of victuals after preaching was allowed in shops osten-sibly closed to business. Two years later the magistrates ordered that on Sunday no Albany resident was to receive in his house or converse with the Indians near his stoop or in the streets under penalty of twenty-five guilders. Bakers who sold bread to Indians were alone exempt. This mea-sure drove Albany inhabitants to the Indians' dwellings to obtain pelts, with the result that racing and riding desecrated the Lord's Day. Hence in May 1682 the court ordered that no whites were to accost Indians directly or indirectly or go to their villages, with punishment at the discretion of authorities. Two years later magistrates fixed the fine at twenty-five guilders and made the act applicable to Albany and also its environs. A man presented in August 1684 for having had two Indians in his house on the Sabbath defended himself by arguing "that the sun had set and that Pieter Schuyler [a deacon and prominent citizen] and Mr. Pretty [the sheriff] said that one was then free to do so." This legalistic attitude toward religion was resented by the Indians, who observed that traders who contributed generously in church on Sunday beat down the price of beaver pelts on Monday.[55]

New York's highest standards of Sabbath observance were still found on Long Island. In 1674, for example, the village of Brookhaven ordered that young people be punished for abusing the rest day.[56] Later, three Huntington men confessed in court that they had traveled to Hempstead on the Sabbath the previous winter; repentant and submissive, they went free. At Southold, however, Nathaniel Baker was fined forty shillings and costs—a total of nearly ten pounds—for searching for a lost ox on Satur-day and bringing it home on Sunday. Brought before the bench, he ag-gravated his offense by minimizing his fault and challenging the law, and the court of sessions in that Puritan stronghold exacted a bond of twenty pounds for good behavior for nine months.[57]

An interesting example of how Sabbatarianism affected personal con-duct occurred in 1682. Robert Kellem departed from Oyster Bay on a Sun-day afternoon, and as he rode into neighboring Huntington, Return Davis caught the sound of a horse breaking the Sabbath stillness. She asked Kellem, perched atop a sack of meal as he trotted by her house, why he had set out for home on the Lord's Day, for the sun was even then still half an hour high. Huntington authorities found Kellem guilty of traveling and carrying a burden on the Sabbath, and he had to pay twenty shillings or make acceptable acknowledgment and pay costs.[58]

In 1679 two representatives of the Labadists, a spiritualist sect in Holland, came to America seeking a site for a colony. One of them, Jasper Danckaerts, kept a detailed journal of their travels in New York and elsewhere over a period of fourteen months. Though Danckaerts was a severe critic whose judgments are not always reliable, his observations on Sabbath observance are instructive. He noted that in New York City he and his companion occasionally went to church to avoid giving scandal, thus revealing the existence of a public sentiment not otherwise readily discernible. This community pressure could not have been too strong, however, for Danckaerts and Peter Sluyter often absented themselves from public worship to rest, write and dispatch letters, and make tours. After hearing Domine Schaets preach in the provincial capital, Danckaerts called him a Voetian, the other clergymen in the colony Cocceians. This comment goes far to explain why the available records furnish no evidence of ministerial as opposed to magisterial demand for improved use of the Lord's Day. The visitors were taken to a tavern, a "low pot-house" which was "resorted to on Sundays by all sorts of revellers." Later they were dissuaded from going to Flatlands for preaching, since the house "was so full of people on Sundays . . . that you could scarcely get in or out." Danckaerts also reported that a man who had attempted suicide, assured of God's grace for repentant sinners, confessed his wickedness, including violation of God's Sabbaths. Advised to take care of his affairs and work when he felt inclined, the man replied, "Work, I have no more work. It is as if it were Sunday."[59]

A new era in the history of the colony opened during the administration of Governor Thomas Dongan (1683-1688). He called delegates to sit with him and his council in October 1683, and this body adopted the Charter of Liberties and Privileges. The charter provided for an elected assembly which was to meet at least once in three years and share the supreme legislative power with the governor and council. It divided the province into ten counties, set up a system of local and county courts, and insured trial by jury. All existing churches in the colony—the Dutch Reformed, the Congregational, the Presbyterian, and the Lutheran—were declared "privileged Churches" with freedom of worship and discipline, "provided allsoe that all Christian Churches that Shall hereafter come and settle within this province shall have the Same priviledges."[60] This last clause was intended to pave the way for Roman Catholicism.

Dongan granted liberal charters to Albany and to New York City. The charter of November 1683 for the provincial capital divided the city into six wards, each of which was to elect an assistant and an alderman, and established a common council consisting of the assistants and aldermen plus a recorder and an appointed mayor. This council, which had full power to enact legislation not contrary to provincial and English laws, issued many Sunday ordinances. In 1684 it tightened the previous city statute (1676) by banning all servile work and trading, children's sports, drinking in taverns during the sermon and excessive drinking at any time, and the assembling of more than four Negro or Indian slaves on the Lord's Day, all on penalty of substantial fines. Constables were directed to take turns touring the wards during Sunday service to secure compliance.[61] The significant fact about this legislation was that the elective council was demanding a higher standard of observance than its appointed predecessor. Dutch Calvinists still constituted the largest element in the population of New York City, although there was considerable religious diversity. "Here bee not many of the Church of England," Dongan reported in 1687, "few Roman Catholicks; abundance of Quakers preachers men and Women especially, Singing Quakers, Ranting Quakers; Sabbatarians; Antisabbatarians; Some Anabaptists some Independents; some Jews; in short of all sorts of opinions there are some, and the most part of none at all."[62] The common council made Sunday observance a common denominator for people of different faiths, and new regulations on the subject were constantly forthcoming. During the next two decades the council issued two ordinances regulating Sabbath observance in the years 1690 and 1691 and one each in 1692, 1694, 1695, 1697, 1701, and 1703.[63]

Meanwhile, the new provincial assembly had passed a bill condemning Sabbath-breaking (3 November 1685). It declared that the Lord's Day was profaned by unlawful traveling, shooting, racing and hunting horses, hunting, tippling, unlawful pastimes, and worldly employments, all of which were therefore prohibited. Any offender convicted before a justice of the peace would be fined six shillings and eightpence or committed to the stocks for two hours.[64]

The provincial assembly, however, was short-lived. The Duke of York, after becoming king in 1685, annulled the Charter of Liberties, thus depriving the people of a share in the supreme legislative power and creating great anxiety in what was now a royal province. But James was dethroned three years later, and in the confusion attending the Glorious Revolution the government of the colony fell into the hands of Jacob Leisler for two years. In 1691 he was hanged for treason and the assembly was restored.

During the administration of Governor Benjamin Fletcher (1692-1698) the quest for a new provincial statute on Sabbath observance was slowed by political considerations. On 23 August 1692, a week before Fletcher's arrival, it was ordered in the assembly "that a Bill may be drawn for the better Observation of the Lord's Day, and that each respective Town within this Province have a Minister or Reader, to read Divine Service."[65] This coupling of Sabbatarianism with ministerial maintenance indicates the existence of popular support for the former. Fletcher's commission authorized him to select the ministers for ecclesiastical appointments and his secret instructions implied that he was to develop the Anglican church. At the time there was not a single Anglican church in the colony nor an Anglican minister other than the chaplain of troops. The assembly, understanding that Fletcher's ultimate purpose was the maintenance of Anglican ministers, refused to accommodate him.[66]

In his inaugural address to the assembly two months later, Fletcher recommended that provision be made for the support of an able ministry and for strict observance of the Lord's Day. Again the chamber delayed, provoking from the governor at the opening of the next assembly on 22 March 1693 the complaint that representatives had ignored the ministry bill. Two weeks later Fletcher told the delegates that they were heady with the privileges of Englishmen and Magna Charta but had put the bill last, and the same law provided for the religion of the Church of England and against Sabbath-breaking. He hoped at the next session they would do something effectual.[67]

In September a ministry bill of limited scope and character finally passed. It applied only to six districts in four of the ten counties of the province—New York, Westchester, Queens, and Richmond (Staten Island)—where most of the English-speaking people not in eastern Long Island were located. The bill, unsectarian, gave no preference to any one Protestant religious body and refrained from giving the governor authority to induct and suspend ministers. Fletcher, however, interpreted it so as to leave the impression that it established the Anglican church in New York.[68]

This enactment cleared the way for adoption of "An Act against Profanation of the Lords Day, called Sunday," which sped through the assembly and was signed by Fletcher on 22 October 1695. It did not require sanctification of the Sabbath but prohibited its desecration by traveling, working in servile occupations, shooting, fishing, sporting, playing, racing horses, frequenting of tippling houses, or engaging in unlawful pastimes on Sunday on penalty of six shillings or three hours in the stocks. Slaves and servants unable to pay were to get thirteen lashes.

Exceptions to the ban on traveling were permitted if required by an act of necessity or to attend public worship, provided the journey not exceed twenty miles, for postmen and others engaged in official duties, and for persons sent to obtain a physician or midwife. On Fletcher's recommendation, the law did not apply to Indians not professing the Christian religion. The 1695 law, like those of Maryland and Rhode Island at similar stages, went as far as circumstances allowed to safeguard the special character of the Lord's Day.[69]

At the opening of the eighteenth century, therefore, the institution of the Sabbath was an important force for civilization in the colony of New York. Little if any vocal opposition to the theory underlying the law was heard, though anti-Sabbatarians, Quakers, and Anabaptists were present in the jurisdiction. In 1703, however, it was alleged that Jonathan Whitehead, justice of the peace in Queens County, had defended his traveling on the Sabbath on the ground that there should be no distinction between days. If Thursday observance were ordered, he reportedly said, within a century that day would be as religiously kept as the Sabbath was. Whitehead denied the charge.[70]

Evidence strongly suggests growing support for the idea that the Lord's Day was set apart from other days. Most communities in the province enforced the local ordinances and the provincial law on Sabbath observance. Caleb Heathcote was especially active. An Englishman who migrated to New York in 1692, Heathcote settled in Westchester, where he prospered as a merchant and served as a militia colonel and a judge. A devoted churchman, he complained that the province was unsurpassably heathenish. Sundays, he declared, were "the only time sett apart by [people] for all manner of vain sports and lewd diversions, and they were grown to such a degree of rudeness, that it was intolerable." Heathcote may have exaggerated, but he threatened his militia with hard Sunday drill unless they spent the Sabbath in worship. Moreover, the Westchester County court of sessions on which he sat ordered that a person be employed to read sermons on Sunday forenoons and afternoons and forbade breach of the Lord's Day on penalty of twenty shillings for each offense.[71]

Few non-Puritans were as zealous as Heathcote, but in the early eighteenth century the King's County court of sessions ordered constables to search suspected places for Sabbath-profaners or face fine for neglect of duty, Huntington adopted a similar policy, Brooklyn prohibited Sabbath travel except as permitted by the 1695 law, Southampton levied fines for Sunday violations, the rector at Rye complained of much Sabbath-breaking, the Ulster County court of sessions apparently made an order against breach of the Sabbath, and the common council of Albany issued ordinances in 1724 and 1726 which provided stiff penalties for desecrating the weekly rest day.[72] The list could be extended.

New York City, which contained about five thousand residents around 1700 and ranked after Boston as the largest town in the colonies, followed the same path. The grand jury presented Sabbath-breakers to the Supreme Court of Judicature, which had cognizance in all civil and criminal cases and sat quarterly. Jacob Teller and Philip Schuyler were presented on 6 April 1696 "for playing at deys on the Sabbath," and Francis Hulin for entertaining them at play in his house. A warrant was issued for taking the men into custody, but the disposition of the case is not recorded. Violations of the Lord's Day were not uncommon in the thriving seaport with its diverse population, and there was a constant effort to suppress such crimes. One finds several grand jury presentments against the City of New York for failure on the part of its officials in the performance of their duty to enforce existing laws in the period from 1697 to 1713. One reads: "The Bench having sent for the Mayr and Aldermen did cause to be read . . . an Addresse from the Grand Jury setting forth a Genll breach of the Lords day and urged their diligence in causing the constables [to] go about during divine service."[73]

By the early eighteenth century the colony of New York had developed its own peculiar pattern of Sabbatarianism. Sunday was neither largely disregarded as in early New Netherland nor God's day of state as in New England. But the Sabbath in New York resembled that of New England more than the first Dutch settlers of the province would have thought possible. Sarah Knight, a native Bostonian, departed from home in October 1704 on a journey which took her by way of New Haven to New York City, where she remained a fortnight. A keen observer, Madam Knight wrote that "they are not strict in keeping the Sabbath as in Boston and other places where I had bin, But seem to deal with great exactness as farr as I see or Deall with."[74] Her comment accurately reflects conditions in the colony, which at that time contained a population of over nineteen thousand souls, three-quarters of whom lived on Manhattan Island and Long Island. Both the theory and practice of the Sabbath in New York changed remarkably little before the end of the eighteenth century.

10

The Restoration
Colonies: I

DURING THE RESTORATION (1660-1685), in addition to New York, England laid the foundations of five American colonies. The two Carolinas, New Jersey, Pennsylvania, and Delaware all originated during the reign of Charles II. Here, as elsewhere, Sabbatarianism resulted from interaction between intellectual and socioeconomic forces, and fresh forces were at work.

New attitudes toward the Lord's Day emerged in post-Restoration England. Puritanism reached its apogee during the Interregnum. The government imposed strict Sabbath observance upon the nation, and excesses in these years created revulsion against the septennial institution which manifested itself immediately after the king returned. People suddenly used Sunday less as a day of rest and more for activities of various sorts— work, travel, and recreation. Contemporary diarists such as Samuel Pepys in London and Ralph Josselin in the country described the changes. Pepys personally rejected some Puritan taboos and observed that others did likewise. Josselin, a vicar in Essex, deplored the sudden transformation of the Sabbath into "the sport and pleasure day of the generall rout of people."[1]

The reaction was brief, for Puritanism had left a deep imprint on the nation. Gradually the pendulum came to rest somewhere near the middle of its arc. The result was the emergence by 1700 of the peculiar English Sunday which prevailed for more than two centuries. Actually two schools of thought on the keeping of Sunday developed. One, which retained a Puritan viewpoint and observed the day with much severity, included most Nonconformists—Presbyterians, Independents, and Baptists—and many Anglicans. The adherents of the other, which treated the day as a Christian festival rather than a Jewish fast, were members of the Church of England. Between these extremes were many varieties of opinion.[2]

A reconstruction of theology underlay the new departure. Prior to 1660 (except for transferring the obligation to Sunday), Puritans had regarded the Fourth Commandment as an immutable moral law, whereas Anglicans viewed Lord's Day observance as an appointment of the Church. After the Restoration, churchmen continued to distinguish between the Jewish Sabbath and the Christian Lord's Day. Jeremy Taylor (1613-1667), Edward Stillingfleet (1635-1699), and others insisted that Christians, unlike Jews, had no divine commandment for their holy day. Christians observed the Lord's Day because the Apostles had established a practice which the Church had always followed. Anglican theologians, however, did emphasize the value of Sunday observance for the Christian life. "The religious observation of the Lord's Day is no novelty started by some late sects and parties among us," Bishop Stillingfleet wrote in 1696, "but . . . it hath been the general sense of the best part of the Christian world."[3] To contrast Stillingfleet with the Anglican Thomas Rogers, who in 1607 called Sabbatarian doctrine anti-Christian, shows the extent of Puritan influence during the seventeenth century.

Leading Puritan theologians of the post-Restoration period substantially modified the teachings of their predecessors. John Owen (1616-1683) continued to emphasize the divine authority and moral nature of the Christian Sabbath, but his chief writing on the subject, published in 1671, emphasized Heb. 4:3-11 rather than the Fourth Commandment as a basis for the institution. John Lightfoot (1602-1675), master of Catherine Hall, Cambridge, treated the matter in a sermon on Exod. 20:11. He made the Gospel precede the institution of the Sabbath and argued that the obligation to keep it holy rests both on the law of nature and on evangelical revelation. Richard Baxter (1615-1691) addressed the issue in *The Divine Appointment of the Lord's Day* (1671). Discarding the Fourth Commandment as the foundation of the weekly festival, he traced its origin to the example of the Apostles and made a New Testament ordinance the basis for the observance.[4]

This narrowing of theoretical differences went hand in hand with new governmental attitudes. Charles II wisely refrained from republishing the Book of Sports. In 1662 he urged the clergy to admonish people against profaning the Lord's Day and a year later issued a proclamation requiring church attendance and prohibiting sitting in inns during divine service and selling of wares, except milk before or after services. The royal proclamation declared that the English church excelled any other Reformed church in its zeal for proper Sabbath observance.[5] Meanwhile, Parliament was struggling with many bills designed to reflect the emerging consensus on the subject. One of these mysteriously disappeared after passing both houses and never became law. Additional effort finally yielded the Sunday Observance Act of 1677. This statute required everyone to exercise religious duties publicly and privately on the Lord's Day and prohibited ordinary labor, trade, and travel on Sunday on penalty of five shillings. The law was silent on sports and recreations, leaving that vexed area of activity to be regulated by earlier acts.[6]

Thus, while allowing for a wide range of practice, the rules laid down by church and state required a common code of behavior. Sunday was reserved for rest and worship. People were to abstain from servile labor and to subordinate rest to worship by attending church. Beyond this central core of belief, however, opinions differed. More permissive Anglicans allowed lawful and convenient recreations on Sunday and viewed the refreshment of the natural man as appropriate to the occasion. According to the foreign visitor Henri Misson, "one of the good *English* Customs on the Sabbath Day, is to feast as nobly as possible, and especially not to forget the Pudding."[7]

Dissenters and Anglicans of the more restrictive school made Sunday a Jewish fast, though not uniformly. One finds some strict notions as to what constitutes a work of necessity, with the basis for the distinctions not always clear. Sir Matthew Hale allowed stopping the breach of a seawall, milking cows, setting a broken bone, and dressing meat but prohibited the quenching of fire in a hayrack and carrying cut corn out of the rain on Sunday. This school forbade all recreations on the Sabbath, limiting pastimes to reading the Bible and theological books. Baxter, however, did not oppose walking in the fields, and both he and Owen approved of moderate Sunday feasting. John Wells (d. 1696), a Nonconformist minister and author of *The Practical Sabbatarian* (1668), may have been more typical. His long and tedious volume called for a burdensome round of Mosaic Sabbath duties, and a whole chapter recounted horrid stories of divine vengeance visited upon violators of the Lord's Day. A London broadside entitled *Divine Examples of God's Severe Judgments upon Sabbath Breakers* called itself "a fit Monument for our present Times." The rhetorical convention of attributing one's own downfall to breach of the Lord's Day apparently dates from this period. Misson, commenting on England's strict observance of the Sabbath, "particularly in the printed

Confessions of Persons that are hang'd,'' observed that "Sabbath break-ing is the Crime the poor Wretches always begin with. If they kill'd Father and Mother, they would not mention that Article, till after having pro-fess'd how often they had broke the Sabbath.'' [8]

The character of the new English Sunday was fairly well set under the later Stuarts, and after the Glorious Revolution there was a return to Puri-tan severity. The key to the evangelical vigor is found in the moral refor-mation of 1688 and the renewed vitality of the Church of England. Wil-liam and Mary set a good example. In 1689 the King ordered the clergy to preach frequently against vice, including profanation of the Lord's Day, and a year later the Queen forbade hackney carriages and horses to work on Sundays. Mary also had constables stationed at streetcorners to capture puddings on their way to bakers' ovens on the holy day! The Anglican church exhibited a zeal for reform. Societies for the Reformation of Man-ners, formed in 1692 by some young men to deepen their spiritual life, sought to check immorality. They spurred civil officials to prosecute Sab-bath-offenders, and by 1702 more than twenty thousand persons in and about London had been convicted of swearing, cursing, and profaning the Lord's Day. The Society for the Propagation of the Gospel in Foreign Parts was formed in 1701 to promote the Gospel throughout the foreign possessions of the British Empire. The new climate of opinion insured that Anglican missionaries would carry the doctrine of the well-kept Sab-bath across the Atlantic. [9]

Two other attitudes toward the holy day which influenced the colonies arose out of the disintegration of the compound of Puritanism during the Civil War and Commonwealth. They were in a real sense the opposite sides of the same coin. During the early seventeenth century Puritanism had embraced divergent tendencies. One of its distinguishing principles was the centrality of the conversion experience. Puritans stressed the need for a personal rebirth, and inherent in the doctrine of preparation devised by the brotherhood of spiritual preachers was a degree of tension between the Law and the Gospel. Some clergy and laity emphasized the duty of man to prepare himself for redemption by keeping God's command-ments; others insisted that salvation came by grace through faith in Christ. Another distinguishing principle of Puritanism was millennial-ism. John Foxe and later writers taught that the kingdom of Chirst was to be realized in England, and Puritans believed they were divinely commis-sioned to reconstruct church and state in accordance with the Bible.

But the prophets differed in their vision of the coming Jerusalem. The collapse of authority after 1640 liberated centrifugal tendencies which splintered the Puritan movement. A renewal of intense religious zeal stimulated the growth of the main Puritan churches and led to the emergence of not only the Quakers but also a heterogeneous assortment of radical religious sects.[10] Two tendencies significant for the Sabbath emerged out of the confusion: one stressed the Letter, the other the Spirit. The former led to Seventh-Day Sabbatarianism, the latter to the obliteration of all distinction between days.

A literal interpretation of Scripture had tempted a few persons like John Traske and Theophilus Brabourne into observing the Saturday Sabbath before 1640, and now this inclination gathered momentum. In a time of uncertainty religious men searched the Bible for a key to the future, emphasizing the apocalyptical books of Daniel and Revelation. The Fifth Monarchy movement emerged out of such a context in the days of triumphant Puritanism. This politico-religious sect gathered around a few Puritan preachers and army officers. The Fifth Monarchy men based their beliefs primarily on a literal interpretation of the seventh chapter of the Book of Daniel. They believed that the four beasts described there were the four great empires of history. The fourth and last of these, the Roman empire, had been shattered in 1649 with the beheading of the king and would shortly be replaced by a Fifth, the monarchy of Christ. Meanwhile, the duty of the saints was to prepare for the Day of the Lord by bringing all things into line with Scripture.

The sectarian visionaries hoped for the fruition of their plans in 1653. The Nominated Parliament which met that year was constituted by selecting those persons who were judged most fit to rule for God, and Fifth Monarchists led the radical contingent. Their program of social reconstruction concentrated on the abolition of tithes and legal reform. Fifth Monarchy men in general wanted no other laws except those of the Bible, and the criminal code proposed by William Aspinwall prescribed capital punishment for twelve offenses, including willful profanation of the Sabbath.

The eschatological hopes of Fifth Monarchists were shattered in December 1653 when Parliament was dissolved and Cromwell became Lord Protector. New calculations based on Bible chronology inspired a belief that the millennium would come in 1656. But when that year passed uneventfully and Cromwell was offered the kingship, armed fanatics determined to usher in the reign of the saints by the sword. Thomas Venner, a London cooper who had lived in Massachusetts from 1638 to 1651, led an armed insurrection to dethrone the beast in April 1657. It was easily suppressed.[11]

The failure of the Venner Rising marks a turning point in the development of Seventh-Day Sabbatarianism for two reasons. First, a close connection had existed between Fifth Monarchists and Baptists. The prime recruiting ground of the Fifth Monarchy sect was the Baptist societies. The English Baptist community arose out of Separatism, the left wing of the Puritan movement, with the General or Arminian Baptists, founded in 1612, the earliest to organize. The Particular or Calvinist Baptist church was formed between 1633 and 1638. Both were "gathered" churches, based on believers' baptism, and both were pioneers in the battle for liberty of conscience. The Baptists sided with Parliament during the Civil War, and their numbers grew rapidly during the Commonwealth period. Some Baptists were millenarians, and many became Fifth Monarchy men. The leading Fifth Monarchy preachers, Christopher Feake, John Rogers, and Vavasor Powell, were Baptists. The biblicism associated with millennialist enthusiasm led members of both groups into Saturday Sabbatarianism during the 1650s. About 1651 a General Baptist congregation in Lothbury, London, went over to Seventh-Day views under the leadership of Dr. Peter Chamberlen (1601-1683), a physician and eccentric social reformer. It organized as the Mill Yard Church a year later and was the only Baptist society as a whole to endorse Fifth Monarchism. John Belcher, a bricklayer and Fifth Monarchy man closely associated for a time with Venner, was the leading preacher in a Particular Seventh-Day Baptist church in London.[12]

Second, in 1657, when Venner's abortive stroke manifested the error in calculating the beginning of saintly rule, the millenarian enthusiasm declined, the literalist temper remained, and with attention focused on the Fourth Commandment, passive Fifth Monarchists were rapidly transformed into Seventh-Day Baptists. The change of thought can be traced in several Fifth Monarchy pamphleteers: John Spittlehouse published *The Unchangeable Morality of the Seventh Day Sabbath* (1657); William Aspinwall, apparently changing his views, replied with *The Abrogation of the Jewish Sabbath* (1657); and Thomas Tillam, a Baptist minister in Colchester, refuted Aspinwall in a work whose title vividly illustrates the tie between millenarianism and Saturday Sabbatarianism: *The Seventh-Day Sabbath Sought Out and Celebrated: Or, The Saints Last Design upon the Man of Sin, with Their Advance of Gods First Institution to Its Primitive Perfection, Being a Clear Discovery of that Black Character in the Head of the Little Horn, Dan. 7.25. The Change of Times and Laws. With the Christians Glorious Conquest over that Mark of the Beast, and Recovery of the Long-Slighted Seventh Day, to Its Antient Glory, wherein Mr. Aspinwall May Receive Full Answer to His Late Piece against the Sabbath* (1657).[13]

The Fifth Monarchy movement declined rapidly after the Restoration.

The sects of "fanatics" fell under deep suspicion, and in October 1660 the government executed two Fifth Monarchist military men. Venner, leading an armed party, threw London into panic by striking another blow for King Jesus in January 1661. The rebels were killed or captured and Venner was hanged and quartered. Chiliastic sectarianism as a political force was ended, and a general imprisonment of radical sectarians followed. In November 1661 authorities made an example of John James, a Fifth Monarchy preacher and Seventh-Day Baptist, sentencing him to death for preaching that bordered on sedition. Savage repression forced Fifth Monarchists to choose between submission or flight and hastened the transformation of passive Fifth Monarchy men into peaceful propagators of either the millenarian or the Seventh-Day faith.[14]

Saturday Sabbatarians were usually but not exclusively found in Baptist churches in post-Restoration England. General and Particular Baptists observed the practice, maintaining on the basis of Gen. 2:2-3 and the Fourth Commandment that the Creator had sanctified Saturday forever. The sect had about nine or ten churches in late seventeenth-century England. About 1672 Francis Bampfield (c. 1615-1684), a former prebendary of Exeter Cathedral and royalist in politics, adopted Seventh-Day views; four years later he organized Pinner's Hall, a Seventh-Day Baptist church in London. He won his brother Thomas Bampfield, Speaker of the House of Commons in 1659, to his tenets. The Seventh-Day Baptists attracted a few men of superior social status after the Restoration, and Joseph Davis, a linen merchant, strengthened the body by building a meetinghouse in the Mill Yard and endowing it with a manor. Nevertheless, Seventh-Day Baptism was a by-product of the intense biblicism of the age. The numbers were always small and after a generation the sect dwindled into insignificance. By the mid-eighteenth century the Seventh-Day Baptist Church had virtually disappeared in England. But the idea crossed the ocean and sank tenacious roots in American soil.[15]

A spiritual approach to religion became common after 1640. Left-wing Puritans in their search for inward experience had for years stressed the operations of the Holy Spirit, and when the Puritan compound disintegrated those who failed to find assurance in intellectual acceptance or strict external observance replaced Scripture with inner authority. The result was the rise of a Spiritual movement which included Spiritual Puritans, Seekers, Waiters, Familists, Ranters, Quakers, and other mystical groups.[16] These sects had their own milder forms of millenarianism. They believed their mission was to inaugurate the new creation, wherein the dispensation of Moses would give way to that of Christ and the Spirit. The conviction that man was totally dependent upon the direct leading of the Holy Spirit in worship and conduct inspired a radical assault on the Sabbath. The Ranters, for example, denounced all meetings for worship as useless.

Quakerism was a part of the Spiritual movement which gradually developed a character of its own. George Fox (1624-1691), the great prophet of the new faith, experienced a religious "opening" in 1647 and immediately began to proclaim the Day of the Lord. His mission was to lead people from legal Christianity to true worship. His social teaching included a puritanical condemnation of wakes and revels, sports and games, and other forms of vanity and looseness. The early Quakers— Children of the Light or Friends in Truth they called themselves—fed an unsatisfied craving for inner religious experience, and the sect grew rapidly during the Interregnum. Quakerism became a movement in the north in 1652, with many recruits coming out of fellowship in Seeker societies. Aggressive "Publishers of Truth" then spread the Quaker message to the rest of the nation and overseas, meeting their best reception in London and Bristol. The Quakers, who constituted a distinctive and isolated element within society, regarded themselves as the people of God and entertained eschatological hopes for England. In 1660 their numbers were an estimated thirty to forty thousand men, women, and children. After the Restoration their rate of growth was slowed by persecution, and in meeting the internal challenge of an unfettered individualism a spontaneous movement was transformed into an organized religious sect, the Society of Friends. Quakers gradually abandoned their apocalyptical visions and adjusted to the realities around them.[17]

Fox had no consistent philosophical framework in which to fit his religious intuitions, and the task of systematizing Quaker thought fell to Restoration Friends, three of whom deserve special notice. Isaac Penington (1616-1679), a Puritan who found peace for his troubled soul by publicly becoming a Quaker in 1658, subsequently dedicated his considerable intellectual powers to disseminating Quaker teachings to the world. His collected writings were published in 1681. Robert Barclay (1648-1690), a gifted Scot bred in Calvinism, was sent to Paris to be educated in a Roman Catholic college before he was called home in 1663 on his mother's death. He converted to Quakerism in 1666 and vindicated its doctrines in various writings. Barclay's *Apology for the True Christian Divinity*, which appeared in Latin in 1676 and in English two years later, is the most systematic formulation of the Quaker faith. It directly challenged the Westminster Confession in a somewhat scholastic exposition of twelve theological principles. William Penn (1644-1718) became a Quaker in 1667 and thereafter devoted himself to establishing the ideas of the Society of

Friends in England and America. His collected writings were first published in 1726.

Scholars differ over the extent to which Quaker theological thought
developed during the seventeenth century, but the evidence furnished by
Fox, Penington, Barclay, and Penn indicates that Friends were in basic
and continuing accord on the Sabbath question.[18] Fox records his opposition to the Puritan Sabbath in his *Journal* and in more sustained form in
other writings. His most controversial work, *The Great Mystery of the
Great Whore Unfolded* (1659), replied to over a hundred pamphlets
directed against Friends and included "An Answer to Thomas Tillam's
Book Called, 'The Seventh-Day Sabbath.' " Fox fought the Ranter spirit
within Quakerism in the early 1660s when John Perrot, denying the validity of all human arrangements in religious worship, came out against
meeting at set times and places.[19] "Concerning Worship," the eleventh
proposition of Barclay's *Apology*, is an extended discussion of Quaker
views on the subject. Penington and Penn treated the matter at various
places in their works.[20]

The Quaker view of the Sabbath followed from their main theological
propositions. According to the Friends' doctrine of the Inner Light, a
divine seed or light in every man was capable of working redemption in
the human heart. Conversion was treated in terms of a radical dualism
between the human and the divine. Man was depraved and totally dependent on God for redemption; hence it was vain to seek relief by external observance or legal righteousness. Christ came to put an end to the
Law with its base and beggarly Jewish ceremonies and to teach people by
his Spirit. While accepting the Bible as authoritative, Quakers considered
it neither the touchstone by which to try all doctrines nor the primary
means to a knowledge of God. Firsthand religious experience depended
on possession of Christ, the promised seed. Quakers made the Spirit, the
Light within that enlightened every man, the only firm foundation of the
Christian faith.

These beliefs repudiated Sabbath observance. According to Friends,
who frequently cited Gal. 4:9-11 to support their position, Sabbath-
keeping was a Jewish ceremony from which Christ had freed men. The
Fourth Commandment imposed no obligation upon Christians because
the New Covenant had abrogated the Old. All holy days and Sabbaths
had ended; they were shadows of which the substance is Christ. Sabbath-
breaking was no evil because no Sabbath existed to be broken.[21] During
the Commonwealth and after the Restoration, Quakers were actively persecuted for acting out these convictions.[22]

The formulators of the faith also held positive views on the subject.

Quaker theory spiritualized the Sabbath and allowed no distinction between days. "All days are alike holy in the sight of God," wrote Barclay, and Penn added, "we utterly renounce all special and moral Holiness in Times and Days." The theory regarded the Sabbath rest not as a weekly cessation from servile labor but as a heavenly rest for the people of God. Penn said, "all People must now come to keep God's *Great Sabbath.*" Because God's spirit is not tied to times and places and all true and acceptable worship is spiritual or inward, the Gospel Sabbath should be spiritual and invisible. Legal worship consists in external observance performed by man's own will and natural strength, but the Spirit is not at man's beck and call, and spiritual worship cannot be conducted on a fixed schedule.[23]

Despite this radical theory, Quaker practice fell into the tracks of an ancient institution. The result was "Quaker Sabbatarianism." Friends recognized the practical necessity of setting apart some time for rest and worship and chose Sunday for these purposes. Some primitive Quakers worked on the Lord's Day, perhaps to prove their emancipation from legalism. But Fox disapproved of Sunday labor, and Thomas Ellwood recounted without censure the story of a poor Quaker cobbler cruelly whipped by authorities in 1662 for continuing on Sunday some work he could not finish late Saturday. Penn, stung by the criticism that Quakers followed their usual trades on the Lord's Day, replied that the whole world knows better.[24] He protested too much, but the trend was in that direction. Many Quakers, including Penn, traveled on the Sabbath for reasons other than attending meetings.[25] From the beginning, however, Sunday was the main Quaker day of worship. Reason and expediency rather than divine commandment justified the choice. Barclay and Penn both emphasized that they did not recognize the Sabbath as a moral institution, but they defended the use of Sunday by citing the example of the Apostles and the primitive Christians, "without superstitiously straining the scriptures for another reason."[26] Quakers, who very early replaced the "heathen" names of days and months with numerical names, referred to Sunday as the First Day.[27]

The message was social as well as religious, and the moral puritanism of the Society of Friends was highly conducive to "Quaker Sabbatarianism." Products of a Puritan culture, Friends believed that man has but a few days and must therefore use every minute wisely. Redeem the time! Penn and others advised. "Time is what we want most, but what, alas! we use worst," he wrote, "and for which God will certainly most strictly reckon with us, when Time shall be no more."[28] Quakers took for granted the Puritan doctrine of the calling; Fox advised Friends to labor diligently in some lawful employment, and Penn declared that "the Perfection of Christian Life extends to every honest Labour or Traffic used among Men."[29] They took up Fox's cry against all forms of pride, frivolity, and indulgence. *No Cross, No Crown,* Penn's outstanding work on the subject, denounced vain recreations, including drinking, feasting, gaming, dancing, sports, music, and like pastimes: "the Best Recreation is to do Good."[30] The Quaker pattern of life called for six days of disciplined industry followed by a day of rest and worship.

In addition to new attitudes toward the use of time, other English intellectual advances affected Sabbatarianism in the colonies. The impulse toward religious toleration and liberty of conscience matured slowly in seventeenth-century England. The proliferation of sects during the Commonwealth period demonstrated the practical value of mutual forbearance, while Penn along with some of the keenest intellects of the age championed the concept in later years. The growth of this idea in the Restoration colonies precluded the imposition of a uniform pattern of Sabbatarianism. Political and civil rights also advanced. The theory of government by consent of the governed was established after a century of conflict, and the rights of Englishmen received formal protection after the Glorious Revolution. The application of these principles meant that any religious establishment would be arrived at through political process, with due regard for the rights of the individual.

Social and economic considerations influenced the development of Sabbatarianism in late seventeenth-century America. Besides thin settlement of the people, ethnic and religious diversity was influential in molding the area. The powerful attraction of the Promised Land was partly responsible for the heterogeneity of the population. The Restoration colonies were proprietary. The Crown granted royal favorites vast tracts in the New World, and proprietors wanted money from their holdings. To enlist colonists they offered cheap land and often religious freedom and political rights as well. New Jersey, Pennsylvania, and Delaware, embodying the principle of liberty of conscience in their fundamental law, became an asylum for people of different faiths. Of the original thirteen colonies, they, along with Rhode Island, were the only ones which never had an established church.

The repulsion of Europe was the other factor instrumental in producing a people of mixed national and religious origins. The post-Restoration attempt to form the basis for a comprehensive English church failed, and in the interest of securing religious uniformity and suppressing dissent the government made religious persecution its policy for a whole generation. The Clarendon Code, the name applied to the Corporation

Act (1661), the Act of Uniformity (1662), the Conventicle Act (1664), and the Five Mile Act (1665), was a flexible instrument of repression. The Conventicle Act of 1670 renewed the earlier one, which imposed punishment for attendance at worship not in Anglican forms, with milder penalties but new incentives to enforcement. It aimed at ruining offenders by fines, which could be distrained, rather than imprisonment, with penalties going in thirds to the king, the poor, and the informer. Informers stood to gain in direct relation to their zeal in reporting conventicles, an odious system that earned the contempt of all decent people. Moreover, justices were permitted to break into suspect houses. The persecution caused untold suffering. Puritans sustained losses estimated at from two to fourteen thousand pounds sterling and thousands in prison. But Quakers bore the brunt of it. Over fifteen thousand Friends were jailed in England and Wales, four hundred and fifty of whom died. The Act of Toleration (1689) provided that the laws against religious nonconformists no longer applied to those who took the oaths of supremacy and allegiance, but by that time thousands of refugees from England, Wales, Scotland, and Ireland had sought asylum in America. New England added to the migration to the Restoration colonies. Some Puritans left in order to resist change; and some non-Puritans departed to escape religious intolerance.[31] Palatine Germans, poor and oppressed by state churches, constituted the largest single Continental immigrant group in the period studied.

THE CAROLINAS HAD a common origin in the letters patent which Charles II granted a group of eight English merchants and courtier-promoters on 24 March 1663. The King made these men the true and absolute lords proprietors of a region lying between the thirty-sixth and thirty-first degrees of northern latitude and extending westward to the Pacific Ocean, and gave them feudal powers equal to those possessed by the Bishop of Durham. The laws promulgated by the proprietors were to be enacted with the assent of the freemen, so long as they were reasonable and agreeable to the laws of England. The charter also envisioned establishment of the Church of England, though the proprietors were authorized to permit all religious groups to enjoy liberty of worship, provided they conform to the beliefs and practices of the Anglican church.[32]

To attract colonists and provide a formal plan of government for a group going from Barbados to plant in the Cape Fear region, the proprietors adopted the Concessions and Agreement in 1665. It provided for dividing Carolina into three counties, granted extensive power to a popular assembly, and guaranteed liberty of conscience. But the Concessions and Agreement was obsolete after the settlement at Cape Fear ended in 1667.[33]

As a substitute the proprietors devised the Fundamental Constitutions in 1669. To what extent John Locke, secretary to Anthony Ashley Cooper (later the Earl of Shaftesbury), the most active promoter among the proprietors, contributed to its composition is a question on which historians differ. This Grand Model, intended to create a feudal system in government, economics, and society, provided for a local nobility, freemen, leet-men with no voice in the government, and slaves subject to their masters in all respects except religion. The proprietors retained ultimate governmental control. They and the local nobility (landgraves and caciques) were to exercise executive, legislative, and judicial jurisdiction through the palatine's court, seven proprietor's courts, and a grand council. Parliament—consisting of the proprietors or their deputies; the local nobility; and one freeholder elected by the freeholders of each precinct, of which there were four per county—lacked the legislative initiative and its actions required ratification by the palatine (the eldest proprietor) and three other proprietors.[34]

No man was to be admitted a freeman or have an estate or habitation within Carolina who did not acknowledge that God is to be solemnly and publicly worshipped. The Church of England was to be established; yet toleration was to be shown to all inhabitants, including slaves, and any seven or more persons "agreeing in any religion, shall constitute a church or profession." In every such association three particulars of belief were declared essential: that there is a God; that God is publicly to be worshipped; and that every church declare the external way "whereby they witness a truth as in the presence of God." No person above seventeen could have any benefit or protection of law or hold any place of profit or honor who was not recorded as a member of some church.[35]

Though never fully implemented, the Fundamental Constitutions left its imprint on life in Carolina. It remained a disturbing factor for three decades, with the proprietors often revising and the people strongly opposing the aristocratic plan. During these years separate settlements sprang up in the northern and southern parts of the province, but the attempt to combine them was never realized. The names North Carolina and South Carolina were in common use before they were legally adopted.

The most successful attempt to colonize South Carolina was set in motion by Lord Ashley just after adoption of the Fundamental Constitutions. A party of one hundred and forty sailed from England in August 1669 and settled the following year on the Ashley River, about twenty-five miles from the sea. In 1680 they removed to a site at the junction of the Ashley and Cooper rivers, which they named Charles Town (renamed Charleston in 1783). Population increased rapidly, with many immigrants arriving from the West Indies, and by 1700 the colony contained between five and six thousand whites plus a larger number of Indian and Negro slaves. Settlers laid out plantations in the environs, but because of danger from the Spaniards and the Indians they hesitated to venture many miles beyond the community stronghold. A brisk trade in furs and slaves developed, and South Carolina enjoyed a substantial town life. Charles Town was the most important population center south of Philadelphia during the colonial period.[36]

Conflict between the proprietors and the people troubled the early years. The governors sent over were often of poor quality. Though Parliament was erected in 1671, the Grand Council was the most important instrument of government for some time, and the Assembly did not gain the right to initiate legislation until 1694. Religious differences exacerbated political controversy. Anglicans were originally most numerous, but many English dissenters—Presbyterians, Baptists, and Quakers—emigrated to South Carolina, as did Huguenot refugees, especially after revocation of the Edict of Nantes in 1685. According to an estimate of 1710, Anglicans constituted 42 percent of the population; Presbyterians, including the French Protestants who retained their separate organization, and Congregationalists, 45 percent; Baptists 10 percent; and Quakers 0.25 percent.[37]

The Anglican church was established by law, though not without a struggle. An act of 1698 regarding ministerial maintenance virtually gave it a privileged position, but the Exclusion Act of 1704 legally created the religious establishment, which was formally organized by the Church Act of 1710. That measure provided for ten parishes, for building churches and parish houses in six of them, and for supporting the clergy by taxation.[38]

The respect for religion of the first colonists was the basis of social order in the infancy of the plantation. Most of them undoubtedly were attached to Sabbatarianism of the type found among Anglicans and Puritans in post-Restoration England. But the dearth of ministers and churches weakened the restraints of religion, occasioning regression, so the government came to its aid. The very first act of assembly, in May 1682, dealt with observation of the Sabbath, though the original is missing. Another Sunday law was passed on 11 December 1691. Complaining that "many idle, loose and disorderly people doe wilfully profane the [Lord's Day] in tipling, shooteing, gameing, and many other vicious exercises, pastimes and meetings, whereby ignorance prevails" and God's judgments might be expected, the statute ordered all persons to observe the Lord's Day by exercises of piety and religion. Public worship was not required, but a number of Sunday activities were banned. The law prohibited ordinary labor for persons sixteen or older, the sale of any kind of goods, travel (except for necessity or public worship), and sale of alcoholic liquors in taverns—all on fine of five shillings for each offense. No slave was permitted to work on the Sabbath on the same penalty to the owner. Persons found drunk (apparently at any time) were to pay a like amount, while those who swore profanely were to be fined sevenpence-halfpenny for each offense. Constables could distrain goods to satisfy penalties, and a third of the fines recovered went to informers. The law made exceptions for preparing food in families, preparing and selling food in public houses, and the sale of milk before 9 A.M. and after 4 P.M. In June 1692 the Grand Council prohibited the frequenting of punch- or tippling-houses during divine service on sentence of twenty-four hours in prison. And the next October the assembly passed another act for better observance of the Lord's Day (whose original is also missing).[39]

Nevertheless, at the turn of the century Sabbath observance in South Carolina was poor. The number of clergymen was simply inadequate to the need. Charles Town was best supplied with ministers and churches. Episcopalians could attend St. Philip's Church, perhaps the oldest organized religious society in the province and the first to erect a building (not before 1682). Others could attend the dissenters' church located on what became Meeting Street—John Cotton, Jr., briefly served as its minister in 1699—and the Quakers had their own meeting. For a time the only Episcopal clergymen beyond Charles Town were the Reverend Samuel Thomas at Goose Creek and a Mr. Williams southward near the Edisto River. A group of Congregationalists at Dorchester, up the Ashley River some twenty miles from Charles Town, had the Reverend Joseph Lord as minister. These Puritans, who arrived in late 1695 from Dorchester, Massachusetts, stayed together as a distinct community until 1752, when they removed to Georgia. There were said to be six Presbyterian churches south of Charles Town in 1710, but probably there were not as many ministers to serve them.[40]

Many colonists succumbed to the temptation to work and play on the Sabbath. Samuel Thomas, the first missionary sent to South Carolina by the Society for the Propagation of the Gospel in Foreign Parts, set his face against these abuses, and other clergy may have done the same. Thomas arrived in 1702 and settled at the home of Governor Sir Nathanael Johnson on the Cooper River in St. James's Parish at Goose Creek. He found "an ignorant but well inclined people," who lived at a great distance from each other and had never enjoyed a settled minister.[41] "A great number of people for want of spiritual guides were gone over to the Anabaptists and to other Sectaries," he wrote, "and which is yet worse many of 'em had almost laid aside the profession of religion and forgot that they were Christians by name, the Lord's day was almost universally profaned, and many scandalous irregularities abounded." The frontier had brought the inhabitants close to heathenism. Though he could minister to each of his widely scattered congregations but one Lord's Day in three, this Anglican missionary labored hard for improved Sabbath observance. In 1705 he acquainted the SPG with "the great abuse of employing the Negroes and other Slaves in their usual labours on the Lord's day," and the Society ordered the matter laid before the Bishop of London. Thomas met some success before his death in 1706. He "prevail'd with the greatest part of the people to a religious care in sanctifying the Lord's day," and blessed God that he saw "a visible abatement of immorality and profaneness in the Parish."[42]

In 1712 the political leaders of South Carolina again resorted to law to improve Sabbath observance. "The holy keeping of the Lord's Day is a principle part of the true service of God," declared this enactment, which drew heavily upon statutes passed during the reigns of Elizabeth I, Charles I, and Charles II. The one significant new feature ordered all persons to attend some lawful assembly for public worship on the Lord's Day upon penalty of five shillings. The remainder of the act followed the lines of the 1691 law. It forbade worldly labor for persons fifteen or older (reduced from sixteen); the sale of goods; travel; sports and pastimes; and entertainment of guests, except lodgers and travelers, in public houses on Sundays. No servants or slaves were to work on the weekly rest day. The penalty was five shillings for each offense, and the same exceptions were made as previously. Nothing was said about paying informers, but a provision was added that no writ, process, or warrant was to be served on the Lord's Day except for treason, felony, or breach of the peace.[43]

The 1712 statute long remained the basic law on the subject in that jurisdiction. It was revised neither when South Carolina became a royal province in 1719 nor when the colony became a state during the American Revolution, and it was still South Carolina's Sunday law in 1880.[44] A statute that remains unchanged for so many years presumably is not a vital force in the community.

Law, however, is but one agency of social betterment, and an occasional clergyman spoke for proper Sabbath observance as a means of promoting religious and moral welfare. In a pastoral letter of 1727, Edmund Gibson, Bishop of London, exhorted colonists and missionaries in English plantations abroad to encourage the instruction of their slaves in the Christian faith, inveighing against permitting or compelling them to labor on the Lord's Day, because Christianity teaches that God has given one day in seven to be a day of rest. Masters had a duty to see that all persons under their government keep the Sabbath holy and should set a good example of the Christian life by doing the same. A 1740 act governing Negroes and other slaves prohibited their employment in any work or labor on Sunday, works of absolute necessity and ''the necessary occasions of the family'' excepted, on fine of five pounds.[45]

Thus, the Sabbatarian ideal exerted a humane and beneficial influence in South Carolina, and other voices were raised in its behalf as population spread into the backcountry. In the early 1740s, for example, the Reverend John Giessendanner, Jr., offended some Sabbath-breakers at Orangeburg by publicly rebuking their ''great Irregularities and disorders,'' and the Welsh Neck and Cashaway Baptist churches in the Pedee section kept a strong hold on their members, requiring attendance on Sunday.[46] Nevertheless, a low standard of Sabbath observance had developed in South Carolina by 1740, and that pattern persisted during the remainder of the colonial period.[47]

THE EARLY HISTORY of North Carolina is largely identified with the northeastern part of the colony, that region between the Chowan River and Currituck Inlet. Virginians migrated there before 1663, and the province of Albemarle was settled the following year. Albemarle County was for long the only organized government in northern Carolina. But the proprietors neglected the jurisdiction, and the local assembly quarreled with a series of ineffective governors over control of the government. In 1691 the history of North Carolina, as distinct from Albemarle province, began with the appointment of a new deputy governor for the settlement (the nominal governor was at Charles Town).[48]

North Carolina differed from South Carolina fundamentally. The colony was dedicated to agriculture rather than trade and enjoyed few contacts with the outside world. There was no town life. The inhabitants, who in 1700 numbered between four and five thousand whites, excluding Indians and Negroes, were widely scattered on plantations along the rivers and shores of Albemarle Sound. North Carolina was originally a refuge for the poor and oppressed. The people possessed the greatest degree of freedom but were without religious instruction and the restraining influence of community life, and religious conditions were deplorable. William Edmundson (1627-1712), the Anglo-Irish Quaker missionary and first minister to preach in the colony, visited in 1671. ''Many

People came," he wrote of the first meeting he held there, "but they had little or no Religion, for they came, and sat down in the Meeting smoking their Pipes." Captain Henderson Walker, president of the Council, wrote in 1703 that North Carolina had been settled for fifty years and for the most part of twenty-one years it had been "without priest or altar" and before that "much worse."[49]

The early settlers represented a diversity of religious beliefs. By the turn of the century there were Anglicans, Quakers, Presbyterians, and Baptists, besides the irreligious. The Anglicans, according to John Blair, an SPG missionary, were "fewest in number, but the better sort of people." Quakers were numerous. After Edmundson's first trip, George Fox visited North Carolina in 1672 and Edmundson returned in 1676. They made converts, immigrants swelled the number of Friends, and a monthly meeting was organized by 1680. John Archdale, a Quaker convert, was appointed governor in 1694. The last quarter of the seventeenth century has been called "the golden age of Quakerism in North Carolina."[50]

A religious establishment was the most troublesome issue in the early eighteenth century. Anglicans generally favored it, while the other groups were united and vociferous in their disapproval. The church was established by law in 1701. Dissenters and liberal churchmen were against the enactment, which the proprietors disallowed. In 1703, however, despite a large Quaker representation in the Assembly, the Episcopal governor secured passage of a new Vestry Act. Opposition to the unclear measure resulted in great confusion and culminated in the Cary Rebellion, and a new church law was adopted in 1715.[51]

North Carolina undoubtedly had the poorest Sabbath observance of any colony founded in the seventeenth century, as evidenced by reports of SPG missionaries. John Blair, who traveled constantly to minister to his scattered flock and could be in only one place on Sunday, found his parishioners "won't spare time of another day" to hear sermons or have their children baptized; his comment suggests that they rested on the Sabbath. John Urmstone, finding that his congregation often failed to meet him on Sunday, complained that "every body would have a Church by his own door every Sunday or not at all." But he was the worst of the missionaries sent to North Carolina, and the people had little use for him. He departed in 1721, declaring that he would rather be "Vicar to the Bear Garden than Bishop of North Carolina."[52]

The state first tried to regulate Sabbath observance in 1715. By that time the population numbered seventy-five hundred whites and thirty-seven hundred blacks, and the colony was entering a new era of growth and progress. North Carolina had become an independent province in

1712; the authority of the central government was strengthened after the colony obtained its own governor; and the Indian menace was removed with defeat of the Tuscaroras in 1713. Poised on the brink of a period of prosperity and quietness, the legislature of 1715 decided to revise and codify all the earlier laws, and it was only natural to supply one regulating religious and moral conduct.

The law of 1715 regulated the observance of Sunday and of three holy days and also suppressed profaneness, immorality, and other crimes. It ordered all persons to observe the Lord's Day "by exercising themselves publickly and privately in the required duties of Piety and true Religion," but without requiring attendance at public worship; and it banned all worldly labor as well as hunting and fishing by persons fourteen or older on penalty of ten shillings. The statute established three new memorial days: 30 January, the day Charles I was executed, and 22 September, the day of the Tuscarora Massacre in 1711, were declared days of humiliation; and 29 May, the birth and restoration date of Charles II, a holy day. Any person gaming, drinking, or working on the first two or failing to celebrate the latter appropriately was to be fined five shillings. Servants and slaves were prohibited from working on the Lord's Day on payment of the same amount by the master. Trade and travel on Sunday and the sale of alcoholic liquor on that day and on the two fast days were banned on penalty of ten shillings. Drunkenness on Sunday and on the same two days was finable at a like amount, and on any other day at five shillings. Authorities could distrain goods on nonpayment of fines or put the offender in the stocks for three hours. Half of all fines recovered were to go to informers, a regressive feature, and half to the parish poor. Exceptions were made for preparing food in families and preparing and selling it in public houses on Sundays. The act also provided fines for profane swearing and cursing, sexual immorality, and living together as man and wife when not lawfully married. Every minister was to read the statute twice a year immediately after divine service.[53]

At least a few persons were prosecuted under the 1715 law. A grand jury presented seven individuals for Sabbath-breaking at a General Court for Chowan Precinct on 29 October 1719. Four men named Spivy were named on an information by Mary Chappell; and Henry Pendleton, Emmanuel Low, and Benjamin West on an information by James Bell. Low, if the man of that name who was John Archer's son-in-law, was a former secretary of the province and probably a Quaker. He and West were charged with allowing their Negroes to work on the Sabbath. All seven were bound over. The disposition of the case against the Spivys, who were also charged with hog stealing, is tangled and obscure. Apparently two of them were finally penalized for Sabbath-breaking, and the other persons were ordered to pay the legal fine for their crimes and discharged.[54]

North Carolina became a royal colony in 1729, and the best picture of Sabbath observance in the province on the eve of the transformation came from William Byrd (1674-1744) in his account of the surveying of the line dividing Virginia and North Carolina. These colonies had disputed the area between them ever since the 1665 charter had extended the Carolina boundary thirty minutes north of the thirty-sixth parallel provided for in the 1663 charter, but it was not until George II prepared to buy the shares of the Carolina proprietors that a survey of this area, the most densely populated part of North Carolina, was finally conducted. Four commissioners were appointed by each colony; they met with their surveyors and assistants at Currituck Inlet on 5 March 1728. The joint expedition consumed one month in the spring and two in the autumn. Byrd, head of the Virginia commission, described his experiences in *The History of the Dividing Line betwixt Virginia and North Carolina,* a classic in American literature first published in 1841, and in *The Secret History of the Line,* a briefer and much franker work which disguised the names of the participants. It was first published in 1929.[55]

Byrd's perspective in these accounts is that of an urbane and sophisticated Virginia aristocrat, educated in England and familiar with the best learning of the ages. He found much to criticize. His observations are satirical and amusing but never malicious. His commentary on the laziness of the people of Lubberland, where the men imposed all the work on the women and were "slothful in everything but getting of children," is often cited. He also charged the government with the unneighborly policy of sheltering runaway slaves, debtors, and criminals.[56]

A devoted Anglican and Sabbath-keeper, Byrd had a keen eye for religious conditions. Preparing to pass through "an ungodly country where they should find neither church nor minister," the Virginia commissioners upon Byrd's recommendation appointed the Reverend Peter Fontaine their chaplain and wrote to inform the North Carolina commissioners that they would come with a chaplain to make Christians of the "many gentiles on your frontier." For this purpose they intended to rest in camp every Sunday to afford leisure for the good work. The joint expedition was indeed punctilious in observing the weekly festival. "The Sabbath happened very opportunely," Byrd wrote of the first Sunday, "to give some ease to our jaded people, who rested religiously from every work but that of cooking the kettle." Sunday also provided an opportunity for worship. "Our chaplain . . . rubbed us up with a seasonable sermon," said Byrd of the expedition's second Sunday. "This was quite a new thing to our brethren of North Carolina, who live in a climate where no clergy-man can breathe, any more than spiders in Ireland.'' He charged that the North Carolinians ''do not know Sunday from any other day, any more than Robinson Crusoe did, which would give them a great advantage were they given to be industrious. But they keep so many Sabbaths every week that their disregard of the seventh day has no manner of cruelty in it, either to servants or cattle.'' The next Sunday North Carolinians flocked from all parts to hear the sermon, ''partly out of curiosity and partly out of devotion.'' A week later, however, their ''zeal was not warm enough to bring them through the rain to church, especially now their curiosity was satisfied.''[57]

Meanwhile, the chaplain had gone to preach in nearby Edenton, a town of forty or fifty small houses which Byrd thought was ''the only metropolis in the Christian or Mahometan world where there is neither church, chapel, mosque, synagogue or any other place of public worship of any sect or religion whatsoever.'' Speaking of the SPG missionaries, he noted that ''unfortunately, the priest has been too lewd for the people, or, which oftener happens, they too lewd for the priest.'' Hence ''these reverend gentlemen have always left their flocks as arrant heathen as they found them.'' To Byrd the North Carolinians, untroubled by religion, were the least superstitious of any people living. When the Virginians went home for the summer, ''we . . . congratulated one another upon our return into Christendom.''[58]

The same pattern of rest and worship was repeated in the fall. But the two commissions had never worked in harmony, and on Saturday, 5 October, controversy erupted over how far to extend the line. The North Carolinians were unwilling to continue or to have the Virginians proceed without them, whereas Byrd wanted to finish the task before the weather worsened. He agreed that the surveyors should make a plat of the distance run together, provided it was done by Monday noon. Though the surveyors had to work on Sunday, he viewed this as a work of necessity and therefore pardonable, all the more so because the surveyors attended prayers before going to work. ''Our pious friends of Carolina assisted in this work with some seeming scruple, pretending it was a violation of the Sabbath, which we were the more surprised at because it happened to be the first qualm of conscience they had ever been troubled with during the whole journey.'' They had stayed away from prayers to hammer out an unnecessary protest, and after divine service ''an unusual fit of godliness made them fancy that finishing the plats, which was now matter of necessity, was a profanation of the day.''[59]

The Virginians pushed on by themselves after this rupture, and in early

November first quarreled over whether to travel on the Sabbath. Byrd, the most scrupulous, argued for remaining in camp to give the horses needed rest and because of "the duty of the day." He was unwilling to do evil that good might come of it. The others feared the animals might starve for want of forage, and the chaplain, casuistically according to Byrd, held that necessity "would excuse a small violation of the Fourth Commandment." A week later when provisions were short the chaplain "pronounced it lawful to make bold with the Sabbath and send a party out a-hunting."[60]

Byrd never explicitly correlates the laziness of the Lubberlanders with their disregard for the Sabbath, but his comments reveal the deplorable state of religion in North Carolina at the time. Conditions did not quickly change, though the Crown instructed the royal governors to establish the Anglican church on a sound footing and grant religious toleration to all Protestants. Repeated efforts to obtain a new Vestry Act succeeded only in 1765. Meanwhile, after 1730 the dissenting sects grew and spread in the colony, and in revising the laws in 1741 the Assembly passed a new act for better observation of the Lord's Day and more effectual suppression of vice and immorality. This bill directed that all persons shall on Sunday "carefully apply themselves to the Duties of Religion and Piety." It prohibited all works of ordinary labor; hunting, fishing, or fowling; and any game, sport, or play on the Sabbath on penalty of ten shillings for persons fourteen and over. The fine for drunkenness was five shillings on the Lord's Day and half as much on weekdays. In addition, cursing, fornication, and the begetting of bastards were made punishable. The fines were to go in halves to the informer and the parish where the offense occurred.[61] This measure brought to an end the formative period in the development of the Sabbath in the province, and the 1741 statute long remained North Carolina's basic enactment on the subject.

11

The Restoration
Colonies: II

SABBATARIANISM IN NEW JERSEY was shaped by a complicated set of forces. The political situation was tangled and the region was even more varied religiously than ethnically. In March 1664 the Duke of York received a charter for the territory between the Connecticut and Delaware rivers, and in June he awarded the region between the Hudson and Delaware to two of the Carolina proprietors, Sir John Berkeley and Sir George Carteret. A decade later, after a brief Dutch repossession of New Netherland, the ownership changed and Carteret was granted the eastern part of New Jersey. Berkeley sold his interest in the province to John Fenwick, who was acting in behalf of Edward Byllynge. Both were Quakers, and the latter became a bankrupt whose affairs were put in the hands of William Penn and two other Friends. They persuaded Carteret to partition the province into East and West New Jersey, and a deed of 1676 effected a division which lasted until New Jersey was reunited as a royal colony in 1702.[1]

Although their indenture gave them only ownership of the soil, Berkeley and Carteret developed New Jersey as if they possessed political authority as well. In February 1665 they issued their Concessions and Agreement to promote settlement. This instrument, a somewhat shortened and altered version of the Concessions for Carolina, was a frame of government and a guarantee of rights. It provided for a governor represent-

244

ing the proprietors and a general assembly consisting of the governor, members of the council, and elected representatives. The Concessions guaranteed liberty of conscience, provided it was not used to foster licentiousness or disturb the civil peace, and the charter also authorized the assembly to appoint and maintain ministers, giving liberty to others to maintain whatever ministers they wished. Neither the proprietors nor the assembly could infringe upon the liberty of conscience guaranteed by the fundamental law.[2]

Captain Philip Carteret, sent to govern the province, landed at Elizabethtown in August 1665. Cheap land and liberty of conscience were powerful magnets, and eastern New Jersey experienced rapid population growth during the ensuing decade. The immigrants, largely from New England and the Yankee settlements on Long Island, imparted a Puritan character to the area. As in New England, Sabbatarianism originally rested on custom rather than written law. Newark was founded in 1668 by strict Puritans from New Haven colony who departed to avoid the Half-Way Covenant and impending absorption by Connecticut colony. At the outset twenty-three heads of families adopted fundamental orders, agreeing that residents must accept the religion of the majority and govern themselves by such orders as they had in their former home. Abraham Pierson, formerly of Southampton and Branford, was the spiritual leader of this flock. The first settlers of Elizabethtown, mainly Long Island Puritans of more moderate views, upheld the Puritan Sabbath by prohibiting unnecessary travel and labor on the Lord's Day. Woodbridge, Piscataway, Middletown, and Shrewsbury were cast in a similar mold.[3]

The province as well as the towns relied on custom to govern Sabbath observance in early years. When the General Assembly first met at Elizabethtown, in May 1668, delegates from the six towns enacted a legal code with a decidedly Old Testament flavor. They made a number of crimes capital and closely regulated personal conduct, but made no mention of the Lord's Day. Despite statutes intended to promote morality, the diversity of the people, their pecuniary interest, the guarantee of liberty of conscience, and a shortage of ministers resulted in a lack of religious zeal. Several parts of East Jersey were without clergymen and regular religious services until later.[4]

When the assembly again met at Elizabethtown, in late 1675, the province had its own identity. The state came to the aid of religion when deputies enacted the first Sabbath ordinance. Unable to require attendance at public worship, they prohibited profanation of the Lord's Day by servile work (works of mercy and necessity excepted), unlawful recreations, unnecessary travel, and disturbance of ministers during divine service, all on punishment of fine, imprisonment, or corporally at the judgment of the local court. The last provision was designed to prevent Ranters from disturbing Quaker meetings. Two years later the assembly banned tavern-keepers from allowing disorderly drinking on the Lord's Day on penalty of ten shillings for the first offense, twenty for the second, and the like. Constables, if informed, were to seek out wrongdoers and set them in the stocks for two hours. Informers were to receive a third of the fines recovered, the remainder going to the poor.[5] These laws reflect the Puritan character of East Jersey in the formative period.

Important changes occurred after the death of Sir George Carteret in 1680. Two years later the trustees of his estate sold East Jersey to William Penn and eleven English associates, all Quakers except one. These twelve doubled their number, among others adding two non-Quakers, two Dublin men, and six Scots to the ranks. Despite the diversity of the Twenty-Four Proprietors and the Puritan character of East Jersey, Penn and several colleagues wished to transform the settlement into a haven for Quaker coreligionists and designed the Fundamental Constitutions of 1683 for this purpose. It guaranteed liberty of conscience to all believers and stated that no one was to be compelled ''to frequent and maintain any religious worship, place or ministry whatsoever.'' However, faith in Jesus Christ was required to hold public office. Puritan scruples were honored by a statement that nothing in the document was intended to sanction atheism, irreligion, cursing, swearing, drunkenness, profaneness, whoring, adultery, murder, violence, stage plays, masques, revels, or similar abuses.[6] The assembly, however, rejected this cumbersome fundamental law. The Scots took over active management of the province, and a large influx of English and Scottish immigrants arrived in following years, bringing Anglicanism and Presbyterianism to East Jersey.

Robert Barclay the Apologist, one of the Twenty-Four Proprietors, was appointed governor for life. He exercised authority by a deputy, and when the first General Assembly under the new regime met at Elizabethtown on 1 March 1683, it mitigated the severity of the earlier Puritan code. Penn sat as a member of the Council and influenced the revision. A section on the Sabbath blending Puritan and Quaker thought was introduced. ''That according to the good example of the premitive Christians, and for the ease of the creation,'' it stated, ''every first day of the week, called the Lord's day, people shall abstain from their common daily labour, that they may the better dispose themselves to worship God according to their understanding.'' Recreations despised by Puritans and Quakers alike—stage plays, revels, and dissipations that excite people to ''rudeness, cruelty, looseness, and irreligion''—were also declared punishable.[7]

Provisions against profaning the Sabbath emerged after a sharp exchange between a Puritan-Quaker assembly and an Anglican council. The deputies sent up a bill which required everyone to worship in public or private or pay a fivepence fine. Members of the council argued that the law just enacted prohibiting daily labor on Sunday sufficed. Compulsory worship, they added, was false worship, an "Abomination to the wholy God." The council also objected that "it seemes unreasonable to take witnes for privat worship." According to John E. Pomfret, "this strong antagonism against using informers was typically American." Moreover, the council thought the deputies were assuming that the Lord's Day was holier than other days, whereas Scripture, Rom. 14:5-6, states that the Lord "has no profane Dayes." Finally, the council concluded, "Lib'ty of Concience ought to be preferred and Licenciousness punished."[8]

As enacted, the law was silent on attending church. It dealt only with Sabbath profanations, prohibiting travel (except for worship and necessity), riding to hunt horses or beasts, working or trading, drinking in an ordinary, playing at games, sports, and plays, and "any other exercise, than sober and religious exercise," works of necessity excepted. The penalty was five shillings for the first and ten for each additional offense, and no provision was made for informers, a forward step.[9]

The 1683 law served East Jersey for more than two decades. The Court of Common Pleas sitting at Perth Amboy used it to prosecute offenders. In 1687 Israel Thornell of Woodbridge was convicted for fishing on the Lord's Day and a levy on his property was ordered in the sum of five shillings and costs. Jonathan Donham, an attorney, was presented a decade later for "breach of the Saboth"; the disposition of his case is unrecorded. Numerous indictments for violating the Sunday law were made at the local level. The Piscataway town records, for example, show several presentments in the 1690s for working and traveling on the Sabbath. And when Jeremiah Basse became governor in 1698, at which time East Jersey contained ten towns and about six or eight thousand souls, he issued a proclamation for the suppression of vice and immorality which particularly charged officials to enforce the law against breach of the Sabbath.[10]

Lewis Morris (1671-1746), a prominent resident and later the outstanding political figure in New Jersey, cast light on the subject in a memorial of 1700. An active Anglican, he may have exaggerated the defects of the Presbyterians, Congregationalists, Dutch Reformed, Lutherans, Quakers, and Baptists in East Jersey. Of Middletown he wrote, "there is no such thing as Church or Religion amongst them, they are p'haps the most ignorant and wicked People in the world, their meetings on Sundays is at the Public house, where they get their fill of Rum, and go to fighting and running of races which are Practices much in use that day all the Province over." Describing Shrewsbury, site of the first Quaker meeting in the middle colonies, Morris said that "the [Quaker?] Youth of the whole Province are very debauch'd and very ignorant, and the Sabbath day seems there to be set apart for Rioting and Drunkenness."[11]

The Seventh-Day Baptist Church in New Jersey originated in Piscataway, a town settled mainly by descendants of Plymouth colony Pilgrims, some of whom had briefly lived in the Piscataqua region of New England. Six Baptists, including Edmund Dunham and Hezekiah Bonham, apparently took the initiative in the religious organization of the community. With the help of Thomas Killingsworth, a Baptist minister recently arrived on Cohansey Creek (Salem) from Norwich, Connecticut, they established the Baptist church of Piscataway about 1690; the Sabbath question caused a schism within the congregation a decade later. As the story is told, Dunham, a lay preacher in the Piscataway church, admonished Bonham for working on Sunday, whereupon Bonham challenged his brother-in-law to prove that the first day was holy by divine institution. Dunham, after carefully studying the subject, concluded that the true Sabbath fell on the seventh day. In all likelihood, however, Dunham had come under the influence of Seventh-Day Baptist ideas. Seventeen persons closely related by blood and marriage sided with Dunham, who went in 1705 to Westerly, Rhode Island, and was ordained by the Reverend William Gibson. Two years later the schismatics organized the Seventh-Day Baptist Church, and Dunham ministered to it until his death in 1735. Other congregations of this denomination came into existence at Shiloh (1737) and Squan (1745).[12]

With the division of New Jersey, the western part, then a wilderness except for a few Swedes, Dutch, and Finns on the lower Delaware, came into the possession of Friends. After Fenwick bought Berkeley's interest in the province for Byllynge in 1674, Byllynge transferred his rights to three other Quakers, including Penn. These trustees wished to plant a Quaker commonwealth in the New World. A small party under Fenwick laid the beginnings of Salem in 1675, and Penn was chiefly responsible for sending out eight hundred colonists in 1677-78. They founded Burlington, which became the chief town in West Jersey. Over a thousand persons were living in the province by 1680. Most were English Quakers, who established meetings for worship soon after landing.

The Quaker trustees adopted the Concessions and Agreements of 1677 to provide a government for their province. Though Penn has long been regarded as the principal author, Byllynge probably had a greater hand in preparing the document which laid the basis for a free commonwealth. A general assembly, to be elected by universal suffrage, was given complete authority over taxation and legislation within the limits of the fundamental law. The Concessions provided for an executive consisting of ten commissioners and guaranteed trial by jury, freedom from oppression and slavery, liberty of conscience, and religious equality. But this noble constitution was never adopted. In 1680 the Duke of York vested the government solely in Byllynge, who proclaimed himself governor in place of the hydra-headed executive.[13]

The Quaker experiment in self-government and individual rights nevertheless went forward, with religion the cohesive force during the colonial period. An assembly, meeting at Burlington in 1681, established the principle of the Concessions by making it impossible for the governor lawfully to execute his office without popular consent or against the liberties of the people. This legislative body also adopted a penal code which exhibited "a prudent reserve in naming crimes, and a humane forbearance in their punishment." The Quakers of West Jersey were willing to legislate to promote morality, especially in sexual matters, but not regarding the Sabbath.[14] Thus, legislation on the subject was relatively late in emerging.

The earliest law on the matter came in 1693, by which time many important changes had occurred in the colony. Byllynge died in 1685, and the man who purchased his proprietary rights could not manage the whole vast enterprise singlehandedly. In 1692 he sold out to the West Jersey Society, most of whose forty-eight stockholders were members of the Church of England. A substantial non-Quaker migration occurred after 1685, and an Anglican minority gradually assumed disproportionate political influence. In October 1693 the assembly passed the colony's first Sabbath legislation. This enactment declared that "it hath been the practice of all societies of Christian professors to set a part one day in the week for the worship and service of God, and that it hath been and is the antient law of England (according to the practice of the primitive Christians) to set a part the first day of the week to that end," adding that this good practice had been neglected in West Jersey. Redress of the evil rested on reason and experience rather than the Word of God. The statute prohibited unnecessary servile labor and travel on "the Lord's Day, or first day," except for religious worship or necessity, as well as tippling, sporting, and gaming. Persons convicted were to pay six shillings for every offense, as were publicans who entertained tipplers on the First Day.[15]

Prosecution of Sabbath-breakers in the court of sessions at Burlington coincided with non-Quaker control of that tribunal. Prior to 1687 Friends held all but two places on the bench, but in the 1690s John Tatham and

Nathaniel Westland, Burlington merchants, became justices and headed an anti-Quaker party which seized control of the court. Tatham served as its president in 1698 and 1699, during which time presentments under the 1693 law occurred. At the 8 August 1698 session the bench instructed the grand jury to inquire whether any had profaned the Sabbath by "fetching up wild horses thereon." The grand jury reported that it could find no one guilty. At the 3 November session Lawrence Morris, a Quaker presented "for that he with 2 Negro's on the Lords Day being the 25th of September last came up the River with a float of Loggs or timber," was discharged after showing that he acted out of necessity. On 20 February 1699 James Antram, the Quaker constable of Mansfield, presented Richard Francis, a non-Quaker, and Edward Andrews, a Quaker, "for that each of them carried a gun on the Lords Day." On 15 March the court ordered the license taken away from Nathaniel Petit, a non-Quaker, convicted with his wife of keeping bad order in their tavern, "as keeping persons drunk and breaking the Sabbath and other Misdemeanors."[16]

The proprietary period in New Jersey came to an end in April 1702. With their authority disintegrating, the proprietors "surrendered" their pretended legislative power, the "right" to exercise governmental jurisdiction which had never been valid under English law, while retaining title to the soil. Political authority was transferred to the Crown, which combined the two Jerseys into a single royal province. The British bureaucracy appointed a royal governor to administer the province (New Jersey had the same governor as New York until 1738), curtailed self-government, and created a single legislature meeting alternately at Perth Amboy and Burlington. The governmental structure established by these and other changes lasted until the Revolution.

Though New Jersey under the proprietors had a heterogeneous population and a wide variety of religious beliefs, a single pattern of Sabbatarianism took early root in both provinces. In East Jersey, with its strong Puritan leaven and more compact population, and in West Jersey, where Quaker ideals dominated a rural society until 1702, the belief that the First Day should be devoted to rest and worship shaped the life and character of the community even before it was translated into law. This background made it easy for the legislature under the first royal governor to pass a Sabbath law for the united province. It was part of a statute for the suppression of vice and immorality enacted in 1704. Although it did not require attendance at church, the act provided penalties for drunkenness, cursing and swearing, and sexual offenses, and prohibited breaking the Lord's Day by ordinary work on fine of six shillings or four hours in the stocks. Keepers of public houses were not to serve drinks on Sunday, especially during time of public worship, on penalty of six shillings. The legislation of 1704 set a legal standard which remained in force in New Jersey until 1790.[17]

WHEN PENN BECAME a Quaker in 1667, Friends were beginning to lose confidence in their capacity to usher in the millennium. Nevertheless, the optimistic young convert began an active career designed to transform the world. But a decade of hardscrabble effort dampened his eschatological hopes for England. Convinced by 1679 that it was impossible to change the country by direct action, Penn turned to America as the place in which to establish an essentially Quaker colony and make money. In 1680 he petitioned the Crown, and the following year Charles II discharged an old debt by issuing a charter granting Penn a vast tract west of New Jersey and north of Maryland and making him true and absolute proprietor of Pennsylvania.[18]

In 1682 Penn drew up two documents for the "holy experiment" in which Quakers were to set an example to the nations. The Frame of Government was based on the theory that government, instituted because of the Fall, existed to terrify the wicked and encourage the good. Although for Penn the quality of the people outweighed any system of laws, he established a governmental structure consisting of a governor, council, assembly, and courts. The popularly elected assembly was merely to affirm or negate proposals submitted by the governor and council. According to the Frame, no business was to be transacted on the First Day. The Laws Agreed Upon in England contained forty provisions for the colony, including articles on liberty of conscience and abstention from labor on the First Day which laid the basis for legislation in the settlement.[19]

Penn accomplished a good deal during the twenty-two months of his first visit to Pennsylvania. Landing at Chester in late October 1682, he called the assembly and council to meet there in December. Delegates came from Pennsylvania and Delaware.[20] At the time the northern province had about three thousand white inhabitants and the lower counties on the Delaware perhaps a third of that number; many were Swedes, together with some Finns and Dutch traders. After brief debate the assembly and council adopted the proprietor's Frame of Government and the Great Law, which embraced most of the Laws Agreed Upon in England and some others later added. The first chapter, combining two articles submitted by Penn, guaranteed liberty of conscience to all monotheists and forbade ordinary labor on the Lord's Day so that all "may the better dispose themselves to read the Scriptures of truth at home, or frequent such meetings of religious worship abroad, as may best sute their respective persuasions." The code provided that the days and months be called "as in Scripture, and not by Heathen names." It imposed penalties for swearing, cursing, sexual offenses, drunkenness, and various recreations including stage-plays, masques, revels, bullbaiting, cockfighting, cards, dice, and lotteries.[21] The Sabbath law was stiffened the following year when delegates from the three counties in each province unanimously agreed on a fine of five shillings for breach of the Lord's Day and double for every repeated offense.[22] This statute remained in force until 1705.

"Quaker Sabbatarianism" took root during the early decades when the province was rapidly developing. Settlers arrived by the hundreds—English, Scottish, Irish, Welsh, Dutch, and German—and Philadelphia became a busy port. Quaker meetings were established in various places in the colony, and Friends occupied positions of control in the government. Here as elsewhere Sunday differed from the rest of the week, and authorities enforced the law regulating Sabbath observance.[23] At a court held in Philadelphia in March 1683 the grand jury presented a ship for firing guns on the First Day. Governor John Blackwell, in 1689, bitterly denounced the avarice of the Pennsylvania Quakers, "each praying with his neighbor on First Days and then preying upon him the other six!"[24] A few years later the governor and council, to prevent "tumultuous gatherings" of Negroes in the city on Sundays, ordered that any "gadding abroad" then without permission were to be jailed for the night and given thirty-nine lashes at a cost of fifteen pence to their masters.[25] In Delaware County a grand jury presented a man in 1688 for traveling on the First Day "with a yoke of oxen and a wayne, and a horse or more before them," and the following year Haunce Urine was indicted in the Chester County court for working on Sunday. In 1696 the latter tribunal fined two young men five shillings each for running a horse race on the First Day, and John Radley was fined twenty shillings for working on that day.[26]

Penn returned to Pennsylvania in 1699 for two years, his last visit to the province. The colony had grown appreciably during his absence. Philadelphia was a city of a good five thousand, and in 1700 the estimated population of Pennsylvania was eighteen thousand. Continuing factionalism had wracked the colony, however, and a Second Frame of Government (1683) had been superseded by a Third (1696). Life in England had been difficult for the proprietor, whose friendship with James II proved costly after the Glorious Revolution. Penn was removed from the governorship of the colony in 1692 and not restored until 1694. Now he landed at Chester on 1 December, laid over briefly, and then proceeded to Philadelphia via water on a Sunday, timing his arrival so as to impress the Quakers at worship near the landing. Governor William Markham, a non-Quaker and absent from the meeting, was caught by surprise. He had not thought the Quaker leader would travel on the First Day.[27] Before departing, Penn issued a new charter which established the political system under which Pennsylvania was governed until the Revolution. It perpetuated the guarantee of liberty of conscience and freedom from compulsion to maintain any religious worship or ministry.

Prosecutions for breach of the Sabbath mirror the morals of the time and the role of the state in advancing private and public welfare. In remote Kent County, Delaware, at a court held in early 1702 the grand jury presented Thomas Nickolls for "frequently Imployinge his Servant on the Sabbath day." The servant was probably Susannah Johnson, a nine-year-old bound to service after her parents, a free Negro and an Englishwoman, ran away. In Philadelphia at the same time the grand jury presented "men's sons and servants" who robbed orchards and committed many unruly actions on First Days. It also noted the great abuse of Negroes gathering in a tumultuous manner on the streets on Sundays. A year later four Philadelphia barbers were presented for trimming customers on First Days. Examples could be multiplied.[28]

A new Sabbath law was enacted in late 1705. The assembly met in Philadelphia under Governor John Evans, who informed members of objections to several Pennsylvania statutes by the attorney general in England. The house therefore revised the code.[29] It amended the chapter on liberty of conscience, restricting the protection to Trinitarian Christians and dropping the clause enjoining observance of the Sabbath. For the latter it substituted "An Act to Restrain People from Labour on the First Day of the Week." This rehearsed the value of weekly rest in familiar language and raised the penalty for worldly work on the Lord's Day from five to twenty shillings. Exceptions were made for householders preparing food, watermen landing passengers, butchers killing and selling meat, fishermen vending fish in summer months, and the sale of milk before 9 A.M. or after 5 P.M. No legal process was to be served or executed on Sunday. Drinking in taverns on First Days was prohibited on penalty of one shilling sixpence, and tavern-keepers convicted of countenancing Sunday tippling were to pay ten shillings for each offense. Another act prevented Negroes from meeting in great numbers on Sundays or at any other times. Offenders, above four in number and upon no lawful business of their masters, could be publicly whipped, not exceeding thirty-nine lashes.[30]

The impulse behind this enactment was the changing character of the province. A tide of German, Swiss, Huguenot, and Scotch-Irish immigration was reducing the Friends to a minority and introducing wide diversity in religious observance. By 1705 Pennsylvania had strict First Dayers, strict Seventh Dayers, and many shades of opinion between these extremes. The law therefore attempted to insure the original Quaker ideal, a day devoted to rest, worship, and peaceful inactivity, at the time it was coming under great pressure. The influx of immigrants into the land of religious freedom resulted in unsettlement of religious convictions, and Seventh-Day Sabbatarianism in particular flourished. British colonists apparently introduced the idea into the province, Quakers took it up following a schism within the Society of Friends, and some German immigrants enthusiastically adopted the practice, giving a moribund British notion a new lease on life in the American wilderness.

Pennsylvania had a strong attraction for oppressed British Baptists. They established the first church of their denomination there in 1684, and more permanent societies developed later. Some Baptist families from Wales, together with an Irish and an English Baptist, arriving on the banks of the Pennepek near Philadelphia about 1686, organized a church two years later. The Baptist church of Philadelphia traces its origins to 1687, when services were held there under the auspices of the Pennepek residents, but it was not formally organized until 1698, after a number of English Baptists took up residence.[31]

Seventh-Day Baptist societies resulted from a local dispute within Quakerism. George Keith (1638-1716), a Scottish Quaker and colleague of Fox, Barclay, and Penn, led the schism. He emigrated to East Jersey as surveyor-general in 1685 and removed to Philadelphia four years later. Finding spiritual laxness in the New World, especially among the younger generation of Friends, Keith wanted to steer his coreligionists in orderly paths by a systematic formulation of the faith; and he criticized Friends in the Ministry for serving as civil magistrates in the province. These views brought him into conflict with the authorities. At issue was the sufficiency of the Light within for salvation. Keith contended that faith in Christ was also essential. The dispute erupted at the Philadelphia-Burlington Yearly Meeting in September 1691 and became increasingly bitter the next year. In 1692 the Yearly Meeting disowned Keith and his followers. The schism affected a fourth of the members of that body and sixteen out of thirty-two Meetings of the Philadelphia-Burlington Yearly Meeting.[32]

After Keith returned to England in 1693, the leaderless "Christian Quakers" scattered. Some returned to Quakerism, some went to Anglicanism—Keith was ordained priest in 1700—or Baptism, and some persisted in separatism, notably the "Keithian Quakers" at Upper Providence, Southampton, Philadelphia, and Lower Dublin. These congregations resigned themselves to the guidance of Scripture, and their determination to practice accordingly ultimately carried many to the Saturday Sabbath and to baptism of adult believers by immersion. The most forward society in these matters met at the house of Thomas Powell in Upper Providence, southwest of Philadelphia. Its forwardness was owing to Abel Noble, the apostle of the Saturday Sabbath in Pennsylvania. Reliable information on Noble is scanty. Most writers agree that he was born in England, brought up as a Quaker, and came to Philadelphia in 1684. He became a Keithian, then a Baptist, and finally a Seventh-Day Baptist. The Reverend Thomas Killingsworth of New Jersey baptized him in 1696, after which he became absorbed in preaching Baptist doctrine, especially the sacred observance of the original Sabbath.[33] How and when he completed this evolution is not known for certain, although it has been said that while on a tour in East Jersey, Noble was introduced to the Saturday Sabbath by William Gillette, a Saturday-keeping Huguenot refugee, physician, and minister of Connecticut.[34]

Noble labored at Upper Providence among people whose religious convictions lacked stability. In January 1697 in Ridley Creek he baptized Thomas Martin, a public Friend who had been active in the Chester Quaker Meeting. Martin baptized sixteen other Quakers; and together with a New Jersey Baptist they organized a church in October 1697. Martin was chosen pastor by lot. In 1700 a division over the Sabbath broke up the society. The Seventh-Day people from Upper Providence moved to Newtown and established the first church of their sect in Pennsylvania.[35]

While the Keithian Quakers at Southampton in Bucks County merit no further attention here, those at the other places indicated underwent a transformation similar to the one just described. At Philadelphia a number of Keithians joined Heinrich B. Köster, a German immigrant who began in 1695 to preach Lutheran doctrine among English settlers in Germantown and Philadelphia, in debates with orthodox Friends. About 1697 Köster baptized nine Keithian followers and birthright Quakers, including the former Quaker ministers Thomas Rutter (d. 1729) and William Davis (1663-1745). Morgan Edwards says that both were baptized in 1697 by Thomas Killingsworth, a Baptist minister of New Jersey, which would have been a second baptism for the two. In any event, both Rutter and Davis became prominent Seventh-Day Baptist preachers. Rutter became the minister of a church formed in Philadelphia in 1698 by the nine

Keithians baptized by Köster, and this congregation later became the Seventh-Day Baptist Church of Philadelphia.[36]

The Keithians in Lower Dublin met at the house of Andrew Pratt. William Davis, a native of Wales forced to leave Oxford University on becoming a Quaker, joined this group. He arrived in Philadelphia in 1684, followed Keith in separation, and after baptism by Killingsworth joined the Pennepek Baptist Church. In February 1698 he was expelled for heretical views concerning the nature of Christ and joined the Keithians at Andrew Pratt's home. Some members of that circle formed a Baptist church at Upper Providence in 1699 with Davis as minister. Davis learned of the binding force of the original Seventh Day from Abel Noble, and his congregation divided over the issue. A few families under Davis established a Seventh-Day Baptist church in the southwestern corner of Chester County around Oxford and Nottingham.

Thus, by about 1700 British Seventh-Day Baptist societies existed at Newtown, Philadelphia, and Oxford-Nottingham. A fourth came into being in 1726 when some English and Welsh families withdrew from the regular Baptist church in Tredyffryn township and established a Seventh-Day Baptist meeting on French Creek in western Chester County.[37]

The Jewish Sabbath exerted a strong appeal in Pennsylvania at the turn of the century. In 1697 the Lutheran minister Jonas Auren (d. 1713) arrived from Sweden and settled at Gloria Dei Church in Philadelphia. His intercourse with Seventh-Day adherents convinced him that Saturday was the true Sabbath, a doctrine he advocated in *Noah's Dove,* said to have been published in 1700 in Philadelphia.[38] Erick T. Biorck (Bjoerk; d. 1740), a Swedish Lutheran clergyman who arrived with Auren and became pastor of Holy Trinity Church in Wilmington, countered his compatriot with *A Little Olive Leaf Put in the Mouth of that (So Called) Noah's Dove* (New York, 1704). Biorck, noting that the colonists were easily swayed by dangerous doctrines, argued that the New Testament as well as the example of the Apostles and the Fathers furnished ground for observing the Lord's Day.

Certain German immigrants proved especially susceptible to the idea of the Saturday Sabbath. In 1694 a party of German Pietists under Johannes Kelpius (1673-1708) landed in Pennsylvania. A product of the religious enthusiasm that swept over seventeenth-century Germany, inspired largely by the writings of Jacob Böhme (1575-1624), these mystics settled on the banks of the Wissahickon near Germantown and erected an eremetical Chapter of Perfection, also known (based on Rev. 12:6) as The Woman in the Wilderness. Abel Noble visited the members, who combined mystical doctrines with millennialism, and they divided over the

Sabbath question. Kelpius is said to have adopted the observance of Saturday, though the evidence is fragmentary. As we have seen, his deputy, Heinrich Köster, picked up the idea during his ministrations in Philadelphia. But according to Julius F. Sachse, Köster returned to Europe in 1699, after concluding that his usefulness among the English colonists required him to join the Saturday-Sabbath movement, which he refused to do.[39]

The trickle of German immigration widened into a flood in the eighteenth century, bringing Lutherans, Reformed, Mennonites, Baptists, and others to the religiously pluralistic and intellectually plastic province. German Baptist Brethren, in particular the followers of Johann Conrad Beissel (1690-1768), found the faith and practice of the original Sabbath irresistible. This religious organization arose at Schwarzenau in 1708 when Alexander Mack (1679-1735), a prosperous miller, and seven others, all reared in the Reformed faith except for one Lutheran, baptized each other and formed a church that followed the guidance of the New Testament.[40]

Religious persecution drove many Dunkers, so-called because they "dunked" or baptized by trine immersion, out of the Palatinate. Peter Becker (1687-1758) guided the first of these sectarians, a party of twenty families, to Pennsylvania in 1719; they settled at Germantown. Beissel arrived a year later. Born after the death of his father, a drunken baker, he was orphaned at eight, grew up without supervision, and in turn became a baker. The young man exhibited a remarkable natural gift for music, and revealing strong mystic and pietistic tendencies—he apparently came under the influence of Böhmist thought at this time—gave himself to religion at twenty-five. After a brief sojourn at Schwarzenau he transferred to Germantown.

After a year studying the weaver's trade with Becker, Beissel moved to the sparsely settled Conestoga Valley, where he and three companions decided to live together in seclusion from society on Mill Creek in Lancaster County. Here he became convinced that duty required observance of the last day of the week. The teachings of Böhme impressed him with the glory of the Sabbath, but the immediate stimulus may have been the influence of English settlers in neighboring Chester County. His friends soon departed, and in 1724 the solitary was joined at Swedes Spring by Michael Wohlfahrt (1687-1741), a native of Memel on the Baltic (in present Lithuania) who had associated in early life with mystics and was at the time "in pretty close agreement with the Inspirationists."[41]

These religious visionaries kept the Saturday Sabbath in the forest for some time before first propagating the doctrine. Their solitude was broken by the revival from 1722 to 1725 which stimulated the German Brethren in Pennsylvania to form religious societies. In December 1723 the Baptists at Germantown organized the first church of their denomination (Church of the Brethren) in America, with Becker as elder. He and other Dunkers then evangelized among the scattered Germans in the province, and during divine services held in the Pequea Valley on 12 November 1724 at which Beissel and Wohlfahrt were present, religious enthusiasm rose to a high pitch. Beissel, humbling his pride, allowed Becker to baptize him. He and six others who received the sacrament formed the Conestoga Baptist Church with Beissel their acknowledged leader.

Religion excited lively discussion among German settlers at the time, and the Sabbath question was engrossing. The Germantown Dunkers feared the spread of Beissel's views, and the Conestoga Baptists divided over the subject. Beissel directed the numerically stronger Saturday-keepers, while Johannes Hildebrand, backed by Becker, headed the Lord's Day observers. An event already described now aided Beissel and Wohlfahrt. In 1726 British Seventh-Day Baptists established a church nearby at French Creek. Abel Noble visited them frequently and extended his visits to the enthusiasts in Earl Township, who in turn attended meetings of the Saturday-keepers in Nantmeal.

Thus encouraged, the Conestoga mystics became apostles of the Seventh-Day Sabbath among the German-speaking population in the province. They disseminated their views by both the spoken and printed word. Wohlfahrt, or Welfare as the English called him, headed the most successful of the missionary teams. He spread the message west of the Schuylkill and in Philadelphia, where he expounded his doctrines in Quaker and Baptist meetings and denounced contemporary evils in the marketplace. Perhaps the first German-language book published in America was "a little book on the Sabbath" written by Beissel.[42] It appeared in Philadelphia in 1728, but no copy survives.

Beissel published another treatise on the subject in the same year, the only extant version of which is an English translation by Wohlfahrt, *Mystyrion Anomias: The Mystery of Lawlessness* (Philadelphia, 1729). After quoting Scripture to prove the abiding character of the Law, the author devotes half of the treatise to defense of the seventh-day Sabbath as opposed to the every-day Sabbath and the first-day Sabbath. By means of a father and son dialogue he purged himself of doubts which preceded his active propagation of the doctrine of the original Sabbath. His position is that the Sabbath is a blessing rather than a curse. The seventh-day observance was instituted as "a Distinction . . . between holy and unholy." It flows from God's love, is not a commandment caused by sin (which was not yet in the world when God established the rest day), and abides till the whole creation is again freed from the penalties of sin. The external Sabbath is not an Old Testament institution abolished by Christ. Sin, not the Law, was annihilated. Christ came to fulfill rather than destroy the Law, and the seventh-day Sabbath remains. The Christian is not free from the Law, for those who love God keep His commandments. Establishment of the New Covenant neither writes the Law upon man's heart nor abrogates it. In the New Covenant Christ enables men to keep the Law out of pleasure rather than necessity.

The last half of the tract is rich with apocalyptical speculation. Beissel assigns the wedding day of the Lamb (Rev. 19:7-9) and the seventh-day Sabbath to the seventh time (Rev. 10:7, 11:15, 16:17). Adam and Wisdom originally inhabited one body, but the bond was dissolved when Adam fell. At the marriage supper this union, the pure image of God, will be reconstituted, but the delights of the Sabbath will be vouchsafed only to the Bride and her companions, not to the entire universe. The true Sabbath was observed from the beginning until people neglected it, for which the papacy is blamed. God gives man the Sabbath to remind him of the Eternal Rest which is to come. We cannot attain to the rest of eternity without spiritual struggle. One may keep the first day in addition to but not in place of the seventh day, for God commands observance of the latter but nowhere in the Bible are we commanded to keep the former. Some mystical numerology and blows at the papal Antichrist follow, and the treatise ends with the quotation of Rev. 14:8-12.[43]

This pamphlet is indebted to two different intellectual sources. One is the mystical doctrine of the Pietists as expounded by Jacob Böhme. Beissel was deeply influenced by the German philosopher's thought and well acquainted with passages in which his master praised the Sabbath. Böhme treats the rest day as an end of all labor and strife. The Sabbath was the abode of Celestial Wisdom, "the true image of God," fashioned by the Lord eternally as a representation of His inexpressible repose. The observance of the Sabbath was enjoined upon the Jews so that their day of rest might typify the "inner, holy, eternal Sabbath." Böhme spiritualized the Sabbath as a type of the Eternal Rest in the world to come. Beissel remained faithful to that viewpoint, while assimilating the views of the Seventh Day Sabbatarians who surrounded him. *Mystyrion Anomias* relates his doctrine of the Sabbath to his theology of redemption and salvation. No doubt many who were unable to follow his spiritual interpretation and apocalyptical speculation were convinced by the literalistic argument that God gives man an unalterable command to keep the seventh-day Sabbath.[44]

In addition to translating Beissel's tract, Wohlfahrt published *The Naked Truth Standing against All Painted and Disguised Lies, Deceit, and Falsehood: Or, the Lord's Seventh-Day Sabbath Standing as a Mountain Immoveable Forever* (Philadelphia, 1729). This slight work cites three "witnesses" in favor of the seventh and against the first day. The first is God himself, who rested on the seventh day and commanded his people to worship on *the* (not *a*) Sabbath. The second is Christ, who went into the synagogue on the Sabbath and never commanded another day. The third is the acts of the Apostles and the early Christians. The author mentions a few scriptural references to buttress his position and reinforces the argument by contending that worship on the first day is like worship of the golden image mentioned in the Book of Daniel. The popes established the first-day observance, and so-called men of reason have aided them in perverting Scripture. But the time is coming when those who worship false images will be punished.

This aggressive crusade for the Saturday Sabbath had important consequences. After Beissel brought out his little book on the Sabbath, the Conestoga Baptist Church publicly adopted the original Sabbath for divine service. (It had previously held meetings on Sunday and quietly observed Saturday.) The result was a schism within the Church of the Brethren. In 1728 the Germantown and Conestoga congregations separated, and a year later the German Baptists at Conestoga split into two distinct organizations, chiefly over the Sabbath question.

About this time the Saturday-keepers began to be persecuted by civil authorities. Julius F. Sachse argued that the growth in numbers and importance of the sect led to fear that the Seventh Dayers, if not promptly checked, might in time gain the upper hand and change the province's day of worship. He exaggerated the danger, but considerable tension did exist. The provincial law of 1705 prohibited Sunday labor, and in Lancaster County, created in 1729, an aroused citizenry supported local officials who imposed fines upon offenders. This harassment merely stiffened the backs of true believers.[45]

Orthodoxy in Pennsylvania mounted a counteroffensive. As early as 1723 James Logan, a leading Quaker official who came to America in 1699 as Penn's secretary, listed breach of the Christian Sabbath or Lord's Day as a crime against God. Perhaps the pressure of events in the New World accounts for this radical departure from early Quaker theology. John Meredith answered the pamphlets by Beissel and Wohlfahrt in *A Short Discourse Proving that the Jewish or Seventh-Day Sabbath is Abrogated and Repealed* (Philadelphia, 1729). He argued more conventionally than his adversaries, but all the Pennsylvania treatises on the subject are either intellectually inferior to or of an entirely different order from their New England counterparts. In 1732 David Evans, the Presbyterian minister at Tredyffryn, sought to counter erroneous doctrines by issuing a catechism based upon the Westminster Assembly's Shorter Catechism. Somewhat later Benjamin Franklin, whose first Philadelphia employer, the printer Samuel Keimer, kept the Seventh Day, criticized Jedidiah Andrews, the Presbyterian minister in the city, for a sermon on the fourth chapter of Philippians that stressed five points dear to Puritans, the first of which was the need to keep the (Sunday) Sabbath holy.[46] The inability to transpose that text into a higher key suggests that Andrews, a native of Massachusetts, was reacting against the danger raised by Abel Noble, Conrad Beissel, and their followers.

The Ephrata Cloister is the most interesting of the Seventh-Day Baptist societies in Pennsylvania. Its line of descent has been traced to the time of Beissel's voluntary withdrawal in 1732 from the church of his sect in Lancaster County to live in seclusion on Cocalico Creek nearby. Some followers joined him, forming the nucleus of one of the earliest utopian communities in America. During a great revival in 1735 Beissel organized a pilgrimage to the Tulpehocken Valley in Berks County, where he won some notable recruits. One was Peter Miller (1710-1796), who had been ordained by Philadelphia Presbyterians after arriving from the Palatinate in 1730. Minister to two congregations on the frontier, he now publicly renounced the Reformed church and was rebaptized. Several individuals and families followed Miller to Ephrata, including the Indian interpreter Conrad Weiser (1696-1760), a Lutheran by birth and chief elder in Miller's church at Tulpehocken when the two came under Beissel's influence. Ephrata gained fresh accessions from Germantown. Alexander Mack, patriarch of the Schwarzenau movement, had come there in 1729 hoping to restore unity among the German Baptist Brethren in Pennsylvania. This was impossible, and after Mack's death in 1735 two factions developed at Germantown, with the chief controversy being the true Sabbath. German Baptists who favored strict observance of Christian duties joined Beissel on the Cocalico.[47]

The Ephrata Cloister took shape in the autumn of 1735. Beissel—Father Friedsam to the faithful—exercised spiritual and temporal control over the settlement, which was organized into monastic orders for both sexes and a secular group that retained the married state and lived with their families. The brothers and the sisters, each with their own convent, supported themselves by laboring at agriculture, handicrafts, and a variety of other pursuits. The Ephrata Dunkers were famous for their printing press, the high quality of their music, and ornamented hymn books. The weakness was a lack of centrality, for the three parts of the commune had little connection except through the binding force of their distinctive principles, of which Saturday Sabbatarianism and a particular mode of baptism were supremely important. Beissel had the temperament of a fanatic, but his genius was to combine these and other disparate elements together and to convince fellow enthusiasts that a new era of Christianity could be inaugurated on such improbable foundations.

Religious eclecticism flourished at Ephrata. A cloistered community of Protestant monks and nuns observed the Jewish Sabbath and also engaged in the love-feasts, midnight watches, kiss of peace, and foot-washing of the primitive church. The brothers, bearded, barefooted, and often tonsured, and sisters sought redemption by living an ascetic life: they ate a spare diet, dressed in medieval garb, slept on boards, and vowed chastity. Though they read Scripture, especially the Old Testament, they also believed themselves to be possessed by an Inner Light. Hence they used no prayers in their worship, preached sermons inspired by the outpouring of the Holy Spirit, and despised outward institutions except for the Sabbath.[48] They taught their youth on the rest day, introducing the concept of the Sunday school long before it took hold in the larger society, and began their day at sunset. Israel Acrelius, provost of the Swedish Lutheran churches in America, visited the community in 1753. He wrote that Beissel's conduct during divine service "appeared rather ridiculous than devotional" and that the Vorsteher or Superintendent did not know what he believed. Acrelius thought most of the members, numbering at the time about sixty brothers and sisters (at its height the community contained fewer than three hundred persons), were "very stupid." Though Miller's powers of mind were superior to those of Beissel, Acrelius considered theological discussion with him unprofitable. Ephrata was in large part indebted to Beissel's magnetic personality and originality. On his death in 1768, Miller succeeded him as head of Ephrata, but twilight had already set in on the Brotherhood of Zion and the Order of Virgins.[49]

IN SUMMARY, A variety of types of Sabbath observance existed in Pennsylvania by the early eighteenth century. "Quaker Sabbatarianism," which had developed in England by the time Penn obtained his charter, shaped the life of the colony during its formative years and long continued to influence the Pennsylvania Quakers. A second pattern, essentially the Puritan Sabbath as reconstructed in the post-Restoration period, was that of the orthodox Protestants. Anglicans, Presbyterians, regular Baptists, and Lutherans normally took "higher" doctrinal ground on the theory of the day than Quakers, and their observance was likely to be stricter than that of Friends. But for practical purposes Quakers and Protestants were in agreement, and the official embodiment of their outlook was the Sabbath law of 1705. That enactment remained the basic legislation on the subject in Pennsylvania until 1779. The third pattern was that of the Seventh-Day Baptists. English immigrants brought the doctrine and practice to Pennsylvania (whence it spread southward into the Virginia and Carolina backcountry), and German sectarians breathed new life into an idea spawned by the religious ferment of the Commonwealth period in England.[50] The Seventh-Day Baptists were the first society in Pennsylvania to claim the right to worship after the dictates of their own conscience under the charter provision granting liberty of conscience to all men. Their exercise of religious liberty created civil strife, a harbinger of problems the United States would face in later years.

12

New England's Glory

THE SABBATH WAS well established in New England at the time of the Stuart Restoration in 1660, and it remained entrenched during the late seventeenth century when vast changes swept over the area and produced a spiritual crisis. A loss of certainty about the role of American Puritans in the regeneration of mankind was one source of that crisis. Restoration policy called for tighter control of the colonies and for reducing the power and independence Massachusetts had acquired. That policy, which treated the Bay colony as the equal of others in an imperial system, undermined the belief that the Puritans were the people of God engaged in furthering the providential plan of carrying the Reformation to completion in a virgin land.

A general sense of religious deterioration was another source of New England's spiritual crisis. The region enjoyed physical security and rising prosperity between the Restoration and King Philip's War, but with the passing of the pioneers there was danger lest the children lose the faith of the fathers. The rate of conversions slowed, and the churches devised the Half-Way Covenant to insure a continual supply of members. Clerical and lay leaders, fearing that growing materialism threatened the power of godliness, castigated the people for failure to keep the terms of the covenant made with God at the time of settlement. The jeremiad became the characteristic form of literary expression as the new generation assumed responsibility for defining the Puritan mission.[1]

These forces were felt primarily after 1675 and affected opinionmakers far more than the common man. Most residents continued to set high standards of Sabbath observance, as a few representative examples demonstrate. Michael Wigglesworth's *Day of Doom* placed Sabbath-polluters along with other sinners on God's left hand on the dreadful day of judgment. These were to suffer eternal hell-fire because they "cast off aw[e] of Gods strict Law." This poem, published in 1662, became a best seller. John Eliot, the apostle to the Indians, was so zealous about the Lord's Day that he objected in writing when, in a treatise published in 1671, the English theologian John Owen warned against loading the Sabbath with a burdensome round of duties. John Hull, a prosperous Boston merchant who died in 1683, ordered his captains to see that the Sabbath was sanctified on his ships so that the Lord's blessing might be with them.[2] Nathaniel Mather, aged sixteen, recorded in 1685 that when very young he went astray from God and was taken with vanities and follies. "Of the manifold Sins which then I was guilty of," he confessed, "none so sticks upon me, as that being very young, I was *whitling on the Sabbath-day;* and for fear of being seen, I did it behind the door. A great Reproach of God! A Specimen of that *Atheism* that I brought into the World with me!" Mrs. Mary Rowlandson, seized by the Indians during King Philip's War, remembered on her first Sabbath in captivity her previous carelessness with God's holy time and many misspent Sabbaths and easily saw how righteous it would be for God to cut off the thread of her life. But on a later Sabbath while held for ransom she remembered the Sabbath as a day of delight, a time when people went "to the house of God, to have their Souls refresht; and then home, and their bodies also."[3]

Jasper Danckaerts, the Labadist, visited Boston for a month in 1680 and recorded an impression which summarizes the practice of the region. "All their religion," he wrote, "consists in observing Sunday, by not working or going into the taverns that day; but the houses are worse than the taverns. No stranger or traveller can therefore be entertained on a Sunday, which begins at sunset on Saturday, and continues until the same time on Sunday. At these two hours you see all their countenances change."[4] The Sabbath was New England's glory. Its observance required duty, but the day of rest and worship brought physical and spiritual refreshment and was an occasion of great joy.

After 1660 New England resumed its struggle to maintain strict Sabbaths, and a distinguishing feature of this effort to 1675 was its continuity with the past. Attendance at the established Congregational church on Sundays was a prime concern, and Massachusetts, with a population of eighty thousand souls, took the lead in securing it. A statutory revision of the colony laws in November 1660 reaffirmed compulsory attendance, and a month later the General Court declared in an address to the king, "Wee could not live without the publicke worship of God."[5]

This policy brought Massachusetts into conflict with the Restoration government. The colony began to punish Friends again, using its Sabbatarian laws and passing fresh legislation. When Charles II learned of the sufferings of Massachusetts Quakers, he ordered that Friends under sentence of corporal punishment or death be sent to England for trial. The General Court thereupon suspended the harsher anti-Quaker laws and sought an adjustment with England. When the king confirmed the colony's charter in June 1662, he commanded that all free men of competent estate and religious orthodoxy be granted the franchise and that liberty of conscience be allowed. Massachusetts refused to comply. Late in 1663 the court directed that all persons who refused to attend public worship should be incapable of voting in civil assemblies.[6]

The authorities continued to harass Quakers for failure to attend church. About twenty of the sixty persons indicted in Essex County for this offense during the 1660s were repeaters. They were fined according to law, with levies of five pounds and ten pounds being common. Ten persons were once amerced thirteen pounds each for fifty-two absences. Eliakim Wardall and Philip Verin were forward in insisting that the state lacked authority to force attendance at religious worship, although few non-Quakers were convicted for this offense through 1675. Judges dismissed many presentments for lack of evidence or on grounds of mental or physical incapacity. Yet when Henry Batchiler and wife were presented at Ipswich, in 1661, for absence from divine service, Essex County officials obtained permission from the General Court to make such disposition of the persons and estate of the couple as was judged most conducive to their own good. Courts usually admonished occasional neglect, as with George Fairebank in Suffolk County in 1673, and dealt more harshly with frequent offenders. But in 1675 the court merely admonished and exacted costs from two Hull men who confessed long absences.[7]

The churches as well as the state disciplined members for not attending worship. At Charlestown in the middle 1660s the First Church excommunicated Thomas Gould, Thomas Osborne, and the latter's wife for persistent refusal to attend Lord's Day worship. Civil authorities subsequently punished Gould and others for lengthy neglect of the ordinances and other religious offenses, though the accused, founding members of the first Baptist church in Massachusetts, insisted that they had attended worship in a church founded in accordance with the Gospel.[8]

Profanations of the Lord's Day remained a serious problem. Sports and recreations had not yet made appreciable inroads, and Augustine's dictum better to plow than to dance on Sunday was accepted truth—though it was forbidden to plow on the Sabbath. In 1662, when Henry Phelps, a Salem Quaker, was complained of for forcing his son John to carry dung and mend a hogshead on the Lord's Day, the magistrates ordered that John be placed in some religious family as an apprentice. And Walter Fairfield was haled into court at Ipswich twice in 1673 for either detaining his servant from the Sabbath meeting or not requiring him to attend.[9] The state was moving forward by using its authority to prevent the exploitation of labor on Sunday.

Sabbath labor and travel were growing concerns. The basic law on the subject dated from 1646 and authorized constables to suppress all manner of Sabbath profanations. It fixed no penalty, but courts usually imposed five shillings. In October 1668 the General Court expressly prohibited all servile work on the Sabbath on penalty of ten shillings for the first offense and double for every subsequent infraction, and if the crime were "circumstanced with prophaness or high handed presumption," the punishment could be augmented at the discretion of the judges. Travel on the Sabbath was forbidden by the same penalties.[10]

Although presentments indicate zeal, courts showed restraint in administering the law. At Salem in the early 1670s the quarterly court admonished Goodwife Brabrook for carrying half a bushel of corn or peas with her when she went to the Sabbath meeting and John Gamage for fetching a horse before sunset. Suffolk County courts fined two men ten shillings each plus fees for breach of the Sabbath and admonished and imposed costs on two Boston butchers on a first conviction for selling meat after dark on a Sabbath eve. In 1675, however, the court ordered the gates on Boston Neck locked at sunset on Saturday to stop traffic between Boston and Roxbury.[11]

A general loosening of morals and manners occurred after 1660, especially among young people, as evidenced by play and rudeness on the evenings of the Lord's Day, disturbances during religious services, and singing, dancing, and reveling in public houses. At Springfield in 1661, for example, Samuel Harmon tickled and squeezed Jonathan Morgan during the sermon until Morgan cried, and he fought with Joseph Leonard outside the meetinghouse. The frontier court fined Harmon and Leonard five shillings each. A number of towns appointed officials to prevent similar disorders.[12]

The records of Plymouth colony, whose population in 1675 has been estimated at less than seventy-five hundred inhabitants, show that, apart from Quakers, only two men were convicted for neglect of public worship in the decade after 1660. Both were ordered to pay the legal fine of ten shillings. Though statutory revision in 1671 emphasized the need for official encouragement of religion, the code relaxed the requirement for Sabbath observance. Henceforth *frequent* neglect of approved public worship, especially for negligence, idleness, or profaneness of spirit, was to incur a penalty of ten shillings. In the only recorded case by 1675, the court ordered three men who lived in heathen isolation from good society to attend public worship or depart from the colony.[13]

New Plymouth, however, dealt severely with profanations of the Lord's Day. Although in 1663 a court fined John Shilley twenty shillings for playing cards on the Sabbath, most of the convictions during the 1660s were for servile labor or travel, with magistrates ordering penalties of ten shillings for such offenses as trimming the hair of a servant, carrying wood, and unnecessary journeys. In 1670 the General Court raised the penalty for Sabbath labor to forty shillings or a public whipping, and for travel or bearing a burden on Sunday to twenty shillings or four hours in the stocks. The revised code of 1671 applied the forty-shilling amercement to both work and travel and also to sports and recreations; and if the sin was committed proudly, presumptuously, and with a high hand against the authority of God, offenders could be put to death or grievously punished. In 1671 four men were fined thirty shillings each for sailing from Yarmouth to Boston on the Lord's Day, and subsequently others were ordered to pay forty shillings for profaning the Sabbath by servile labor or in other ways. In dealing with Sabbath burglary in its 1671 revision, Plymouth drew on the codes of Massachusetts and Connecticut. It provided branding on the right and left hand for the first and second offenses respectively, and on the forehead with the letter *B* for a third violation.[14]

In 1662 Plymouth prohibited the dispensing of wine and liquor on Sundays except to guests in inns. But then people misbehaved outside the Sabbath meetings rather than going inside, so authorities ordered constables to present offenders. Finally, in 1670, the court directed selectmen and constables to visit any suspected place and present persons that "slothfully doe lurke att hom or gett together in companies to neglect the publicke worship of God or prophane the Lords day."[15]

After the Restoration, Connecticut obtained a royal charter which enabled it to absorb the jurisdiction of New Haven in 1665. Three years later the united colony, numbering eight or nine thousand inhabitants, enacted a law regulating Sabbath observance. The statute of May 1668 provided that anyone who profaned the Sabbath by unnecessary travel or play or who remained out of the meetinghouse when there was room inside pay five shillings or sit in the stocks an hour. That October the legislature added that persons charged with breach of the law were to be judged guilty unless they demonstrated that they had attended the public worship or were necessarily detained.[16]

In New London in 1667 the county court fined Matthew Waller and Goodwife Willey each five shillings for not attending the ministry of the Word; Goody Willey had also failed to bring her children to church. And in 1670, when Norwich residents complained of John Pease for living alone, for idleness, and for not attending public worship, the court ordered the town to see that he be lodged with a suitable family and employ himself in some lawful calling. One could easily multiply examples.[17]

Connecticut, like Plymouth, was zealous to prevent breaches of the Sabbath. At New Haven in 1662 a court reproached Goodwife Bassett for speaking sinful words to another woman on the Sabbath on the grounds that she broke the rule of the Fourth Commandment. Soon thereafter the town fathers appointed a man to see that employees at the ironworks, where the furnaces were allowed to burn on Sunday, attended worship. In 1665 magistrates ordered Thomas Sewell to be severely whipped and make double restitution for feigning sickness so he could absent himself from church and commit burglary on Sunday. (Indeed, Sabbath burglary was so frequent that many residents, including John Davenport, feared leaving their houses unattended during worship.) At New London in 1673 the county court imposed fines of five shillings for working on the Lord's Day, twenty shillings for driving cattle then, and forty shillings for sailing to Norwich on the Sabbath. John Lewis and Sarah Chapman were presented "for sitting together on the Lord's day, under an apple tree, in Goodman Chapman's orchard." The authorities may have had reason to be concerned, for Lewis was also brought up "for absenting himself at unseasonable hours of the night, to the great grief of his parents."[18]

In 1663 New Haven discovered that a number of youths fell into vain ways immediately after the Sabbath by singing, dancing, and playing cards. The court fined these apprentices and young persons and the couple that entertained them without the permission of their masters and parents; a year later the town empowered constables to see that the orders regulating the Sabbath and night meetings be carefully attended.[19]

Efforts to extend Christianity and the Sabbath to the Indians went forward after 1660. Missionaries continued to preach and publish to instruct them in sound principles and lead them from barbarism to civilization.

Eliot's translation of the Bible into Indian appeared in 1663; it was the first Bible published in any language on the North American continent. Among his other translations was Bishop Bayly's *Practise of Piety*, printed in 1665. By 1674 there were fourteen towns of "praying Indians" and eleven hundred native converts in Massachusetts, eight communities of "praying Indians" and perhaps a larger number obedient to the Gospel in New Plymouth, and others on Martha's Vineyard and in Connecticut. And the civilized and religious Indians kept the Sabbath. But the Indian war which erupted in 1675 scattered the Christian natives and reduced the number of their towns.[20]

Sabbatarianism tightened its grip on the northeastern frontier after 1660. New Hampshire remained under the jurisdiction of Massachusetts through 1679, so religious observance was regulated by Bay colony laws. Local courts made what seems to be a halfhearted effort at enforcement. For failure to attend authorized worship, several Quakers were heavily fined in the early 1660s; of the dozen non-Quakers subsequently presented, one of whom was charged with not permitting his servant to attend church, some were admonished, most were fined, and a few did not appear. For profaning the Sabbath—most presentments for this crime involved excessive drinking and attendant evils, not servile labor or travel—fines of ten shillings were common.[21]

After the Crown turned New Hampshire into a royal province in 1680, the new government drafted its own legislation. The Cutt Code was disallowed in England, however, and the body of laws adopted under Cranfield in 1682 became operative. This code, though not requiring attendance at public worship, provided stiff penalties for speaking contemptuously of the Scriptures and for behaving contemptuously toward the Word of God preached. To suppress profanations of the Lord's Day, an article imposed a fine of ten shillings or an hour in the stocks for unnecessary servile labor, travel, sports, frequenting of ordinaries during time of church, or loitering ("idly straggling abroad") on the Sabbath. Constables were to search for offenders during time of public worship. This remained the basic legislation on the subject for a century. New Hampshire court records are less informative than those of other New England jurisdictions, but local authorities apparently demonstrated little zeal in securing strict Sabbaths.[22]

Although Massachusetts completed its annexation of Maine in 1658, the Restoration government removed its control east of the Piscataqua during the early 1660s, and it was not regained unil 1668. A decade later Massachusetts purchased the province from Gorges' heirs and in 1680 established a government for the area under the Gorges charter of 1639.

The charter of 1691 gave Massachusetts the whole of Maine to the St. Croix, and until 1760 the province of Maine was the county of York.

After 1660 Maine leaders struggled to civilize their frontier society. Religion, specifically Puritanism, was an important agency. Puritan culture was extended through the introduction of Massachusetts law and the establishment of a court system based on that of the Bay colony. The General Assembly of Maine was the legislative body of the province, its acts being subject to the veto of the Massachusetts General Court. No attempt was made, however, to draw up a code of laws. Various local courts, meeting ordinarily at York or Wells, heard criminal cases and administered certain aspects of public business. Their dockets reflected the continuing influence of the Puritan moral and social code. Sabbath offenses were one of the chief items dealt with through the early eighteenth century, ranking perhaps second after sexual misdeeds.

Concern for public worship was intense. Although Maine was not compactly settled, courts ordered towns to provide for edification on the Lord's Day; meanwhile, residents were to meet at a private house to sanctify the Sabbath or attend church in a neighboring community. Towns were frequently presented for not appointing a place for public worship and for not having a minister, "whereby many persons take lyberty to neglect if not profayne the sabboth."[23] To miss church was to risk punishment. Since Anglicans were considered orthodox and Baptists were few in number, Quakers constituted the only significant group to absent themselves out of principle. Many Friends, particularly at Kittery, were convicted for neglect of public worship during the 1660s and later. Although open expressions of defiance are rare in the records, in 1671 Moses Collins disowned constituted worship as "false and Idolitrous," a view shared by Sarah Mills; and in 1675 Adam Gudding denied the morality of the Fourth Commandment.[24] Many Quakers, repeated offenders and guilty of long absences, were only admonished; others were fined and whipped, though much less severely than in Massachusetts.

William Screven of Kittery, a Baptist, was presented in 1675 for not frequenting the public meeting on the Lord's Day, but he was remitted because he usually attended Joshua Moodey's meeting in Portsmouth. A Kittery magistrate threatened local residents with penalties for attending Baptist meetings. Screven was baptized in the Baptist church in Boston in July 1681 and licensed to preach the following January. Returning to Maine, he was accused of speaking against baptism and ordered not to keep public exercises on the Lord's Day any place in the province and to observe public worship. In June he was brought before the General Assembly for violating the decree; unwilling to obey it, he agreed to leave

Maine. A Baptist church was organized at Kittery on 25 September 1682, and Screven remained in the jurisdiction until 1695. (He removed to South Carolina by December 1696 and later founded the Baptist church in Charleston.)[25]

Many failed to attend church out of profane neglect, and presentments often link idleness with absence from worship. John Josselyn, the brother of Henry Jocelyn, was presented at York on 15 September 1668 for neglect of public worship. He later denounced the Massachusetts Sabbath laws in *An Account of Two Voyages to New England* (1674). William Hilton, bound in a bond of ten pounds in 1682 to attend Lord's Day services, was indicted in 1691 for not coming to church. Courts were selective in imposing sentences, acquitting some, admonishing many (including repeated offenders who had promised to reform), and fining others. The number of presentments for not coming to church and the moderation in dealing with wrongdoers are impressive, although judicial determination to enforce the law appears to have been weakening by the turn of the century. Nevertheless, Maine courts were quick to cite for contempt persons who did not appear to answer charges of nonattendance, and their patience knew limits. Nicholas Turbut, a repeated offender, promised to attend church but failed, and finally, in 1708, the judges ordered him to pay fines and fees and be whipped ten stripes.[26]

While emphasizing church attendance, officials also attempted tirelessly to suppress profanations of the Lord's Day. Servile labor and unnecessary travel were the major offenses, and the presentments—for driving cattle, selling a horse, carrying a load of hay, putting to sea, and traveling on worldly business—reflect the activities of a farming and fishing community. A presentment for loading staves on the evening before the Lord's Day indicates when the Sabbath began in Maine. Some cases of disorderly behavior involved excessive drinking, but far less often than in New Hampshire. At York in 1669 a man was presented for disorder and music in his house on the Sabbath. At Kittery in 1691 three men were fined twenty shillings each for shooting and killing a deer on the Sabbath, but sport is not mentioned. In 1697 a Kittery man who struck and abused his wife several times on the Lord's Day was fined twenty shillings for the blows and five for breach of the Sabbath. At Wells in 1700 two men were ordered to pay five shillings and costs each for riding and running their horses and shouting in a disorderly manner on the Lord's Day. And in 1705 the court of sessions at York declared that adultery was aggravated because committed on the Sabbath.[27] The Puritan Sabbath had become an integral part of the Maine way of life.

A NEW TONE is discernible after 1675, when New England's spiritual crisis became acute. In addition to the changed relations with the mother country and the perceived loss of religious vitality, new adversities troubled the area. King Philip's War began in June and took a devastating toll in lives and property before running its course. A year later Edward Randolph, agent for the Lords of Trade and Plantations, arrived in Boston and began a systematic attack on the general policy and leading public men of Massachusetts which culminated in 1684 in abrogation of the charter. Various natural disasters occurring after the Indian war—fire, shipwreck, drought, pestilence, and plague—were perceived as visitations of God's wrath. Leaders redoubled their efforts to convince themselves that the Puritans were still God's elect engaged in a divine mission. A new conservatism inspired an effort to save the past, and the new science was used in a search for empirical proofs of God's favor toward his people.

Whether breaches of the moral code in general and of the Sabbath in particular were more numerous after 1675 than before is open to question, but officials embarked on reform as a means of ending God's controversy with New England. Massachusetts passed a law on 3 November 1675 which included provisions for supervising young people in order to curb disturbances during worship and special measures to prevent the sin of idleness. And on 24 May 1677 the court enacted legislation enjoining ministers twice a year on the Lord's Day to read and urge compliance with all laws regulating Sabbath observance. John Higginson, minister at Salem, objected on the grounds that it was unsuitable for a minister's calling to do so and that it might set a precedent for imposing worse duties upon the clergy. So the court repealed the bill in October 1679 and ordered town constables or clerks to read the statutes once a year.[28]

Another mechanism for maintaining strict Sabbaths was the tythingman. The office was established when such traditional agencies as the family, the church, and the apprentice system proved ineffective in preserving discipline. The tythingman was made responsible for supervising the morals of ten or twelve families in his neighborhood. The Sabbath law of May 1677 ordered him, in the absence of constables, to apprehend all Sabbath-breakers and persons who permitted disorders in public houses on the Sabbath. It directed tythingmen to take offenders to Boston or a designated county seat and put them in a cage in the marketplace pending prosecution. In October, moreover, the court authorized tythingmen to inspect public licensed houses of entertainment as well as private unlicensed ones, to enter such places to prevent Sabbath abuses—in 1659 a Puritan Parliament had rejected a similar proposal as a dangerous invasion of liberty—and to act in precincts beyond their own. The tythingmen were a flexible instrument for subjecting the entire community to the obligations of the Sabbath.[29]

The age of the Mathers was dawning, and Increase Mather, minister of the North Church in Boston, thought still more public reformation was needed. He had much to do with calling an assembly of churches for the purpose. The reforming Synod of 1679 considered what evils provoked God's judgments on New England and what could be done to correct them. Mather drew up the result, *The Necessity of Reformation,* and the General Court ordered it published. This jeremiad declared that religion had become subservient to worldly interests, and it gave Sabbath-breaking a prominent place in its catalogue of thirteen contemporary evils. According to Mather, multitudes profanely absent themselves from public worship and ''many under pretence of differing Apprehensions about the beginning of the Sabbath, do not keep a seventh part of time holy to the Lord, as the fourth Commandment requireth.'' Travel and work as well as worldly discourses were common on the Sabbath, and some sanctified the day in a heartless manner if they did not wholly neglect it. All these evils would bring ''Wrath, Fires and other Judgments upon a professing People.''[30]

Taking its cue from the Synod, the court enacted two laws to halt degeneracy and revive the faith of the fathers. One ordered the keeping of a ward on Boston Neck and as needed in other incorporated towns from sunset to 9 P.M. on Saturday to prevent travel at that time. The other strengthened the power of tythingmen by authorizing them to present those whose course of life by omission of family government and instruction of children and servants, or by idleness, profligate, uncivil or rude practices of any sort, tended toward irreligion or profaneness.[31]

The demand for public reformation may have stimulated harsher penalties for Sabbath offenses, but the evidence makes this doubtful. Essex and Suffolk county courts apparently punished neglect of public worship after 1675 much as before. The latter awarded Samuel Rigbee twenty shillings or ten stripes for failure to attend church in 1677 and Paul Gifford forty shillings or fifteen stripes for this offense in 1685, but Rigbee's crime was compounded by drunkenness, swearing, and idleness, and Gifford's by cursing and lying.[32]

Punishments for profaning the Sabbath were no harsher after 1675, but the law continued to be enforced. In Suffolk County, Eliphalet Stretton was fined ten shillings plus costs for doing servile work with a needle on the Sabbath, but Stretton was a Quaker who frequently failed to attend authorized worship. At Salem a father and son, admonished for neglecting the public ordinances, also were suspected of walking abroad after the meeting. An Essex County court fined Thomas Maule for working in his account books on Sunday after his Irish-Catholic maidservant, forced to labor on the Sabbath, informed on him. For Sabbath burglary in 1685, an Indian of Martha's Vineyard was sentenced to be branded on the forehead with the letter *B,* have one of his ears cut off, and pay fifteen shillings to his victim. Plymouth courts ordered various residents to pay forty shillings each for breach of the Lord's Day.[33]

Tythingmen, usually working in pairs, inspected suspected places on Saturday evenings and Sunday mornings. At Salem in 1679 two roundsmen of the Lord warned a servant to go to meeting or be reported, and upon complaint they awakened Mary Meds on the Sabbath after long pounding at her door to question her about constant neglect of public worship. She told them to look after rude boys, for she "cold not nor wold not goe to metting for none of them all." At Watertown in 1684 a tythingman complained of two men for profaning the Sabbath "by sitinge as thay went Home from the publick wurship," and the men were admonished. During these years various towns renewed orders to put an end to walking abroad during worship and to see that no one departed from church until the entire service was finished.[34]

In 1680 Nehemiah Partridge and Robert Pike discovered a determination to require observance of the full duration of the Sabbath. They realized on a Saturday evening that if they waited until Monday morning to start their journey from Salisbury, New Hampshire, to Boston, spring thaws would delay them. Because the Sabbath had already begun, they decided to remain in Salisbury until sunset on Sunday, and then go that night as far as Newbury, where they could use the bridge and ferry. They set out all too eagerly late the next day, Partridge saying he could see no sun, Pike that he saw light where the sun had set. Alas, the sun had set in a cloud, and Ephraim Winsley testified that the men rode by when the sun was still a half-hour high. Pike was fined for profaning the Sabbath.[35]

New Plymouth was especially troubled by travel on the Lord's Day. Authorities laid much of the responsibility on the influence of Pocasset (now in Tiverton), which was south of Taunton and contained many Quakers. George Shove, the minister at Taunton, informed Governor Hinckley in 1682 that the case was desperate, and if the latter could prevent Sabbath profanations "it will much conduce to the securing of religion and the turning-away of God's wrath from us, which else will undoubtedly kindle a fire upon us not to be quenched." So the General Court devised a system whereby each town was to choose an official who would grant a ticket permitting travel in case of impending death or similar necessity, without which Sunday travelers could be fined forty shillings.[36]

Strict Sabbaths remained the general rule in Massachusetts after 1675, and colony leaders were determined to keep it that way. Edward Randolph, reporting to the Board of Trade on the state of New England in 1676, described the Massachusetts laws which were most contradictory to those of England. According to him, the Bay statutes were founded on the Word of God rather than the laws of England, and among the specifically objectionable enactments were one penalizing observance of Christmas and other holy days of the Church of England and another requiring attendance at Congregational worship on the Lord's Day and on appointed fast and thanksgiving days.[37]

The attorney general and solicitor general agreed, adding that the penalty for walking streets or fields and for children playing on the Sabbath was also objectionable; and if the Word of God meant the Mosaic Law, it could not be reconciled with the colony charter, citing as an example "to make it death to gather sticks on the Sabbath, and many others." These English officials said that the Massachusetts agents, William Stoughton and Peter Bulkeley, were "in a manner ashamed" of many objectionable laws, "only as regards that concerning the observation of the Lord's day they seemed somewhat tenacious." The Lords of Trade advised the King to direct Massachusetts to abolish its repugnant laws, and on 27 May 1681 the General Court indicated that because of pressure from the Crown it would change those relating to highway robbery, treason, and heresy by Quakers, and even the law on the observance of Christmas. But of the Sabbath law it would permit "no alteration."[38]

Significantly, Increase Mather included no example of divine wrath visited upon Sabbath-breakers in *An Essay for the Recording of Illustrious Providences* (1684), though he sought such information while preparing that book, a scientific account of the workings of Providence in New England. John Bishop of Stamford replied in 1682 to a query about some young men who allegedly died after racing on the Sabbath that it was hard to come at truths of this nature "whereby God in His Judgemts might be glorified." Bishop asked Mather not to use the material until it could be verified, and Mather was cautious because he was scientific.[39]

Although the New England clergy responded to contemporary intellectual advances more quickly than did the laity, they were conservative in defending the Sabbath.[40] One of the three sermons preached before James Morgan, a convicted murderer, before his execution in Boston on 11 March 1686 affords an example. Joshua Moodey, the minister at Portsmouth and a Harvard graduate, preached to Morgan on the Sabbath afternoon before his hanging the following Thursday. "You seem to bewail your Sin of Sabbath-breaking," he told Morgan. "Well, know that you shall never have another Sabbath to break." Then, addressing himself to the congregation of nearly five thousand people, Moodey added, "Sabbath-breaking is likewise a growing Evil among you, and therefore to be testified against. Hear this poor condemned Person telling you, That he feels this sin now lying as an insupportable Load upon him: And all that are guilty of this Sin, shall find it sooner or later alike burdensome to them. It hath been observed of old, that Religion lives and dies with the Sabbath. And you now hear this Dying Man bewail his Sabbath-breaking."[41] This sermon may have been the first use in New England of the rhetorical convention of attributing a doomed man's destruction to abuse of the Lord's Day.

Connecticut as well as Massachusetts believed that the Indian war and other adversities were tokens of divine displeasure for religious relapse, one example of which was a slighting of Sabbath obligations. In May 1676 the General Court sought to effect reform. A new law prohibited sporting in the streets or fields and drinking in houses of public entertainment or elsewhere on the evening preceding or following the Sabbath upon penalty of ten shillings. It forbade servile labor and all "prophane discourse" and "rude or unreverent behaviore" on the Sabbath. If such labor were committed with high-handed presumption and profaneness, the punishment could be increased from ten shillings at the discretion of the judges. This first written enactment regulating worldly employment on the rest day in Connecticut silently reduced the death penalty for presumptuous labor on the Sabbath authorized by the New Haven code of 1650.[42]

Connecticut punished violators of its reformatory laws. At New London in 1682, for example, two men were ordered to pay fifteen shillings for neglect of public worship and two others were fined for fishing on the Sabbath. Yet in May 1684 the General Court concluded that the laws had not achieved the desired effect for lack of enforcement. It therefore ordered that the statutes of 1676 be published and directed constables and jurymen to present offenders once a month or be fined ten shillings for neglect. (Connecticut did not appoint tythingmen until 1721.) And in October 1686 the court enjoined local authorities to be particularly zealous in apprehending Sabbath-breakers.[43]

IN THESE SAME years the Rogerene church came into existence and aggressively challenged the institution of the Sabbath. John Rogers (1648-1721), founder of this singular sect, was a pioneer of religious freedom. He was one of seven children of James Rogers, who settled at New London about 1660 and became one of the richest landowners of the colony, and Elizabeth Rowland Rogers. In 1670 John married Elizabeth, daughter of Matthew Griswold of Lyme, and granddaughter of Henry Wolcott, both prominent Connecticut men. The young couple settled down in comfort on a farm near New London and were soon the parents of a daughter and son.[44]

Rogers strongly supported Congregational orthodoxy until 1674, when he was converted by the Seventh-Day Baptists of Rhode Island. Through the efforts of Stephen Mumford, an English immigrant, several members of the regular Baptist church of Newport embraced the original Sabbath in the spring of 1665. But friction arose in 1669 when the first-day elders of the Newport society charged the seventh-day people with leaving Christ and going to Moses. So in December 1671 seven Saturday-keepers withdrew from the regular Baptist church, and on 3 January 1672 they organized the Seventh-Day Baptist church, the first in America. By 1673 four residents of Westerly were Saturday Sabbatarians and affiliated with their brethren at Newport. The idea of the "true" Sabbath spread to New London, twenty miles distant, through visits exchanged by residents of the neighboring towns.[45]

Rogers began ministering to a small circle of family members, servants, and neighbors in 1674. A year later the Rogerenes told the visiting Quaker missionary William Edmundson that they kept the seventh day holy because it was strictly commanded in the Old Testament and that its observance was more required than the remainder of the Mosaic Law. Probably this tiny group (estimated at ten persons in 1678) would have met little trouble had they followed the dictates of conscience quietly. But Rogers found the first-day Sabbath nowhere commanded in Scripture, and he bitterly opposed the union of church and state as manifested in laws compelling attendance at public worship and proper observance of the Lord's Day. So he launched a bold and relentless crusade against the New England Sabbath, and for his efforts suffered heavy penalties.[46]

Rogers' wife left him when he cast his lot with the Seventh-Day Baptists. She returned with the two children to her father and applied for a divorce on the grounds of John's heterodoxy and alleged sexual immoralities. He had confessed certain wrongs to her during his religious conversion, and others accused him of revolting vices.[47] The General Court granted a divorce in October 1676 without offering any reason, a strange procedure but perhaps understandable in light of her family's influence. A year later, in awarding Mrs. Rogers custody of the children, the legislature explained that Rogers had openly renounced the visible wor-

ship of New England and called the Christian Sabbath a "meere invention." It is hard to avoid the conclusion that Rogers lost his wife and children primarily for espousing the Saturday Sabbath.[48]

In addition, civil and ecclesiastical authorities prosecuted Rogers and
his followers. In September 1676 John Rogers and his father James and
brothers James and Jonathan, whom he had converted, were presented to
the county court for profaning the Sabbath, "which is the first day of the
week," and for declaring that they would not refrain from servile labor
on that day. Each was fined ten shillings and put under bond of ten
pounds for good behavior. But the Rogerenes were fanatically devoted to
the truth as they perceived it, and members of the sect were repeatedly
fined and imprisoned for neglect of public worship, openly laboring on
the Lord's Day, blasphemy in calling the Christian Sabbath an idol, and
disturbing authorized worship by invading meetinghouses and publicly
charging ministers with lies and false doctrine. John Rogers was sentenced
to prison for a total of fifteen years for opposing what he called the "Red
Dragon" of false worship, and he was whipped twice, on one occasion receiving sixty-six stripes (the biblical limit was thirty-nine) on a charge of
blasphemy.[49]

The rise of the Rogerenes caused great anxiety in Connecticut. Writing
to Increase Mather in 1681, Simon Bradstreet, minister of the church in
New London, expressed the opinion that far more persons opposed the
Christian Sabbath than his correspondent realized. According to Bradstreet, most Baptists either questioned or denied the institution, and not
one in a hundred good Christians would be able to maintain its underlying doctrine with any strength.[50] About this time, it appears, Governor
William Leete propounded several questions to Rogers on the subject,
and James Fitch, the English-born minister at Norwich, was so alarmed
that he published A Brief Discourse Proving that the First Day of the
Week is the Christian Sabbath (1683). Rogers held that Jesus was not
Lord of the Sabbath, that the work of redemption was not as great as the
work of creation, and that the seventh day, being commanded in the
Decalogue, was unalterable. Fitch based his case primarily on Rev. 1:10
and the contention that the Lord's Day was settled upon by the Apostles
and had been observed in all churches since primitive times. The Lord's
Day was the Christian Sabbath by divine institution, and God would
humble the people of Connecticut for profaning the holy day.[51]

Shortly after these events Rogers struck out in a new direction. Fitch
and other critics charged that he had abandoned his earlier beliefs and
adopted mainly Quaker principles, whereas Rogerene writers maintained
that the founder of the sect was constant in his principles except on one is-

sue. Rogers consistently maintained that baptism by immersion in water, the Lord's Supper, and the laying on of hands were useful religious ordinances; although he publicly confuted leading Quaker doctrines, he moved toward spiritual religion without ever embracing Quakerism. Rogers was independent of mind and his religion was a unique blend of somewhat disparate elements which he defended in more than a dozen treatises.[52]

The one issue on which he radically changed his views was the Sabbath. After receiving the new light vouchsafed him, Rogers denounced Seventh-Day Baptist teaching on the validity of the original Sabbath and adopted a spiritual interpretation of the septennial institution. Now he held that the Old Covenant contained a temporal Sabbath, a shadow of the substance to come, whereas the New Covenant contained the Sabbath itself, a rest to the soul which remains to the people of God. Observance of the external Sabbath was of no account in the life of believers. The Rogerenes usually met for worship on the Lord's Day, but they declared labor on that day to be lawful and made a point of working then.[53]

THE MASSACHUSETTS CHARTER was finally abrogated in 1684, and in late 1686 Sir Edmund Andros arrived in Boston to govern the Dominion of New England. He was instructed to see that liberty of conscience was allowed to all and that the Church of England receive particular encouragement, a charge that spelled the end of the Puritan era in New England. On 8 March 1687 the Council passed a bill which probably liberalized the law on compulsory attendance at worship, although its exact provisions are not known. In any event, James II's Declaration of Indulgence, read before Andros and the Council on 21 May and published the following August, determined the matter. The King granted the free exercise of religion and full liberty of public worship. But the Dominion of New England collapsed before New England was forced to scrap its compulsory-attendance law. Andros was overthrown when the news reached Boston that William and Mary had assumed the throne, and to blacken the hated governor's name, Massachusetts charged him, among other offenses, with Sabbath-breaking.[54]

The people of New England put themselves back under the covenant immediately after the Glorious Revolution. In 1690 the Massachusetts General Court ordered that the laws against vice, particularly Sabbath-breaking, idleness, and other impieties, be vigorously executed; and the Connecticut legislature directed that the laws of 1676 suppressing Sabbath profanations and other religious offenses be enforced so that government might be a "teror to evill doers as in o[u]r first times, and the Lord may yet tak pleasure in us as his people."[55]

Reversion to reform was well under way when Massachusetts received a new charter in 1691. This organic law required that liberty of conscience be granted all Christians except Roman Catholics, but it neither established nor gave special status to any religious denomination. Hence the General Court attempted to reconstruct as much of the old ecclesiastical system as possible.[56] Taxation for religious purposes and Sabbatarianism were two leading issues before the legislature. Compulsory maintenance, though a source of conflict for decades, was less important than compulsory attendance and proper Lord's Day observance, for Puritans still believed that religion fared according to the Sabbath.

In October 1692, therefore, the General Court enacted a new law for the better observance of the Lord's Day. The first section was artfully contrived to imply that everyone had to attend church as well as refrain from certain activities on the Sabbath. "All and every person and persons whatsoever, shall, on that day," it read, "carefully apply themselves to duties of religion and piety, publickly and privately; and that no tradesman, artificer, labourer or other person whatsoever, shall, upon the land or water, do or exercise any labour, business or work of their ordinary callings, nor use any game, sport, play or recreation on the Lord's Day, or any part thereof (works of necessity and charity only excepted), upon pain that every person so offending shall forfeit five shillings." The statute also prohibited travel on the Sabbath on penalty of ten shillings, and it enjoined masters and heads of families to prevent transgressions by those under them. Constables and tythingmen were directed to enforce the measure and to prohibit swimming or walking in the streets or fields from Saturday evening to Monday morning.[57]

The question as to how far New England had declined from the ideals of the fathers became acute after 1675, when various adversities led to the conviction that God had a controversy with his covenant people. A belief developed that a close correlation existed between abuse of the Sabbath and the calamities that befell New England. Sabbath reform became important and superstitions regarding the use of the holy day deepened. Yet, as the century closed, strict Sabbaths remained New England's garland of glory.

13

An Enduring Sign

THE PURITAN THEORY of the Sabbath was formulated when the medieval world-picture still shaped the Western mind, and the controversy it engendered in the seventeenth century occurred within the limits of the inherited perception of reality. Sharing a theocentric outlook, the disputants quarreled over biblical interpretation and the primacy of the Word written in Scripture as opposed to the Word written on the heart. Meanwhile, intellectual advances in Europe were occasioning a vast reconstruction of thought. The scientific revolution culminating in the seventeenth century was instrumental in effecting a new intellectual model. Empirically verifiable laws of nature became the preferred means of explaining the operations of the physical universe, and the old image of reality was discarded.[1]

The New England clergy generally accepted the new learning with alacrity, but they stubbornly adhered to the old doctrine of the Sabbath. Nevertheless, the familiar Puritan theory came under attack after 1700; the Rogerenes resumed the assault, and Jeremiah Dummer questioned the rationale for the septennial institution. Yet Sabbath observance in New England remained on a high level well into the eighteenth century.

LEADING NEW ENGLAND theologians defended traditional Sabbatarian doctrine in these years. Samuel Willard (1640-1707) graduated from Harvard College in 1659, was ordained minister at Groton in 1663, and served at the Third (Old South) Church in Boston from 1678 until his death. In 1701 he was called to preside over Harvard as vice-president, which he did without relinquishing his pastoral charge. His great work, *A Compleat Body of Divinity* (1726), consists of two hundred and fifty monthly lectures on the Westminster Assembly's Shorter Catechism, delivered between January 1668 and April 1707. These sermons represent the theology of New England at the time.[2]

Willard emphasized the rational strain prominent in Puritanism. He reached the Fourth Commandment in his one hundred and sixty-seventh sermon in January 1702 and devoted nine months to its exposition. At the outset he strove to establish the morality of the rest day, believing that to regard the Sabbath as of human rather than divine appointment was fatal to religion. If Christians were released from sabbatical obligations, one could bid farewell to religion, since experience indicates "that the Power of Religion will always fare among a People, as the Sabbath doth."[3] The Fourth Commandment was part of God's moral law; its obligations conformed to the law of nature and the dictates of human reason. But though the law of nature gave man a moral reason for reserving a specific time for religious duties, its light was incapable of informing man as to how much time should be separated to holy purposes. Designation of the Sabbath for the purpose depended on positive institution and was an exercise of divine prerogative. In appointing the time, God required one complete period of twenty-four hours in every seven days. Willard argued that Scripture commences the Sabbath on Saturday evening. His sermons gave fresh currency to an old point of view.

John Rogers changed his opinions on the Sabbath about 1684, but little is known about his conflict with the established order during the next two decades. James Fitch remained his antagonist, and Gurdon Saltonstall, who was ordained minister of the church at New London in 1691 and became a bitter foe, attempted to crush the Rogerenes. The five writings Rogers claimed to have published before 1705, none of which can now be located, apparently date from these years. One was probably the book denounced on 13 May 1697 by the Connecticut General Court as "scandalous and hereticall."[4] Another was undoubtedly *An Impartial Relation of an Open and Publick Dispute Agreed upon between Gurdon Saltonstall . . . and John Rogers* (Philadelphia, 1701). Rogers arranged for its publication on one of his trips to Pennsylvania to consult with Kelpius and the mystical community known as The Woman in the Wilderness. Although Sachse wrote that "the only point in which they approached agreement was with regard to the keeping of the seventh day," Rogers was at the time no longer a Saturday-keeper. Perhaps their point of agreement was opposition to the sanctity of the First Day.[5]

In 1705 Rogers published *A Mid-Night Cry from the Temple of God to the Ten Virgins*. He relates his sufferings for "prophaining the Dragons Sabbath, which they ignorantly call Gods Sabbath," and adds that while in jail in March 1694 he decided to make war against his enemies. So he wrote and hung out of the prison window a proclamation of war against the Red Dragon (Satan), the Beast he empowers (the powers of this world), the false church that rides on the Beast, and the false prophets established by the Beast (the clergy). Later that month Rogers was arrested for blasphemy, fined five pounds for reproaching the ministry, ordered to sit on the gallows for a quarter of an hour, and directed to give bond of fifty pounds not to disturb the church. Since he refused to pay, he was imprisoned for nearly four years, during which time he was whipped sixty-six stripes. Rogers then describes at some length his own unique religious beliefs. His section on the Sabbath, an explication of Heb. 4:4, offers a spiritual interpretation of the institution. *A Mid-Night Cry* was presumably one of the two works sent to the Massachusetts legislature by John Rogers and his son which that body in December 1705 ordered to be burned by the common hangman near the whipping post in Boston.[6]

John Rogers continued to trouble authorities until his death in 1721, and then John Rogers, Jr. (1674-1753) and John Bolles (1677-1767) led the battle against the Dragon's Sabbath. They wrote numerous tracts, and the Rogerenes were frequently fined and imprisoned for violating provincial laws requiring attendance at worship and nonprofanation of the holy day and for disturbing the meetings of others. John Rogers boldly followed the truth vouchsafed to him, arousing fierce and highly personal opposition. He emphasized Deut. 5:12-15 rather than the favorite Puritan text, Exod. 20:8-11, in discussing the Sabbath, and this enabled him to view it in terms of the creation of a people rather than the creation of the world. The Sabbath was the sign between God and Israel of the latter's deliverance from bondage in Egypt. Just as the deliverance was from a temporal condition, so too was the Sabbath the sign of a temporal condition. The seven-day rest was a sign to the Jews of a rest from the oppression of enemies until Christ came.[7]

ROGERS POSED A significant threat to the Puritan doctrine of the Sabbath, but he existed on the fringes of power and his actions probably deflected attention from his theories. Jeremiah Dummer offered the sharpest challenge to orthodox Sabbatarian thought in a Latin treatise published early in the century. Born in 1681 to a prominent Boston family, he graduated from Harvard College at the head of his class in 1699. He remained in residence at Harvard until 1701 and then went to Holland to continue his theological education, enrolling first at the University of Leyden, where he wrote two treatises under Professor Herman Witsius and won praise for his learning and modesty. Dummer later transferred to the University of Utrecht, where he received master's and doctor's degrees in 1703.[8]

The Sabbath question was still being agitated when Dummer arrived in the Netherlands, and Witsius was in the thick of it. A Calvinist renowned for opposing Arminianism, he attempted to mediate between the followers of Cocceius and Voetius. Through Witsius, Dummer came in touch with scholars who made philology their main tool in investigating theological issues. They tried to prove their faith by science, reducing Scripture to historical fact by testing words, comparing texts, and removing unwarranted accretions. This methodology enabled Dummer to transcend the limitations of his Harvard education, and in Holland he liberated himself from the authority of Aristotle and the Schoolmen. Dummer's religious faith remained essentially unimpaired as his intellectual horizons widened, but he embraced views on the Sabbath which shocked New England.[9]

Dummer's *De Jure Judaeorum Sabbati,* written under the direction of Witsius and dedicated to four Massachusetts ministers, was published in Leyden in 1703. In considering the foundation of the institution, the author admits that the Fourth Commandment contains a moral element. Reason binds all men to worship God publicly at a fixed and perpetually recurring time; and if worship ceases piety will weaken, opening a door to wickedness. Dummer nevertheless asserts that the Fourth Commandment is not grounded in nature, but is a ceremonial observance depending on the free determination of God's arbitrary will. Rejecting the primeval origin of the Sabbath, Dummer maintains that God sanctified the day of rest only by anticipation when he completed the work of creation. The Lord later joined the Fourth Commandment, which was entirely ceremonial, to the other nine moral precepts in the Decalogue to prevent the Jews from rushing headlong into idolatry, which they were about to do.[10]

The Fourth Commandment is therefore temporary and mutable, not a perpetually binding moral law. Since rigid observance belongs to the ceremonial aspects of the Fourth Commandment, the "Judaizing Christians of today who urge the observance of the Lord's Day with a more than iron rigidity are worthy of the censorial rod. They command that twenty-four hours, precisely measured by the clock, must to be given over to sacred exercises without any relaxation of mind. I judge all these people to smell more of Jewish superstition than of Christian religion.''

Dummer does not, however, oppose freeing the whole of the Sabbath from evening to evening for religious exercises if it is done without superstition and without censuring others.[11]

The remainder of the treatise is devoted to proving that the obligation of the Sabbath rests on positive law rather than on moral or natural law. History shows that one searches in vain for traces of the Jewish Sabbath among ancient nations. Indeed, "they must deceive themselves strongly who believe a great number of Romans or other nations revered the Sabbath. For far the greatest part not only neglected and scorned it, but also considered it a joke." Even if he concedes the primeval origin of the Sabbath, Dummer's position cannot be challenged, for sacrifices and circumcision were established before the Mosaic order, and yet these practices were so far from being part of the moral and eternal law that Paul himself taught that they availed nothing. If he errs in his argument, the author adds, he has the company of nearly all the leaders of the Jewish and Christian churches and many blamelessly orthodox recent theologians, including Calvin himself.[12]

The book concludes with a strong endorsement of New England's practical Sabbatarianism. Dummer does not oppose the seventh part of time as excessively large for God's service and would even accept a larger proportion. If superstition were excluded, he would unstintingly praise the zeal for the Lord's Day in which New England easily surpasses all other nations of Christendom.[13]

De Jure Judaeorum Sabbati exploded like a bombshell in New England. Dummer apparently sent a copy to Samuel Sewall, a leading public figure bound to him by family ties and personal affection. Judge Sewall regarded the morality of the Sabbath as the Ark of the New England Covenant. He chastised his young friend, citing a host of prominent theologians who controverted his opinions, wishing he had chosen another topic for his graduate paper, and reminding him that "these things . . . are of very great Consequence, because so much of practical Religion depends upon a due observation of the Sabbath."[14]

Sewall persuaded others to censure the Latin disquisition. At his urging, apparently, Cotton Mather preached on the subject, a sermon quickly published as *The Day Which the Lord Hath Made: A Discourse Concerning the Institution and Observation of the Lord's Day* (1703). A copy was given to every member of the General Court. According to the Boston preacher, God instituted the Sabbath at the beginning of the world with special regard to the work of creation and redemption. The Almighty appointed the time to be observed, and the Apostles as well as the Lord specified the memorial of the Resurrection as the day to be kept by Christians. Mather coupled a warning that nonobservance of the Lord's Day would bring horrible curses with a promise that observance would yield temporal blessings: "Our Shops, our Ships, our Fields, will all fare the better, for our Circumspection about the Sabbath." The warning enabled the minister to appear as the adversary of Dummer and the Saturday-keepers, while the promise revealed an instrumental attitude toward the Sabbath which was dangerous for a Puritan.[15]

Dummer arrived home hoping to enter the ministry. As the first Harvard graduate to return from the Continent with a Ph.D. and a man whose erudition excited both amazement and envy, he had reason to anticipate a bright future. He soon discovered, however, that *De Jure Judaeorum Sabbati* blocked every avenue to preferment. So the aspirant tried to prove his orthodoxy when an occasional pulpit opened to him, and Increase Mather cited the encomiums of the learned Witsius to help him obtain a church. But Dummer received no call.[16] As Sewall's correspondents reveal, Massachusetts considered him unreliable. James Keith, the minister at Bridgewater, criticized The Law of the Jewish Sabbath as "nothing but hay and stubble."[17] Edward Taylor, the poet and pastor of Westfield, Connecticut, described the Latin treatise as "a very Sorrowfull matter" and castigated the author for "Intollerable Pride" in pulling out "the very bowells of Practicall Piety" by writing that the Reformed Church of New England lay upon superficial foundations. Dummer's doctrine would destroy the work of the Reformation. To root out the holiness of the Sabbath opened a door to human invention as lawful and necessary to the worship of God. If God ordained worship but no time for it, who was to appoint the time, and what proof was there that the human conscience was obliged to keep it? For anyone thus to frolic with his own fancy and "bite away the Divine institution" of the Sabbath was "atheisticall Poison" likely to bring back saints' days.[18]

The orthodox establishment denied the renegade an opportunity to teach as well as to preach. Increase Mather tried to secure an appointment for Dummer as professor of philology at Harvard, but the latter's tract put it out of reach. By October 1704, his prospects dashed, Dummer prepared to depart for Europe. Mather, however, thought it not to New England's honor that such a well-qualified native son should flee for want of encouragement, and a scheme was devised to offer Dummer a Harvard position in return for written disavowal of the opinions expressed in his disquisition. Accordingly, he preached a sermon in Boston on 29 October which was published the following month as *A Discourse on the Holiness of the Sabbath Day*.[19]

Dummer used the occasion to clarify rather than repudiate his controversial views. He passes over the original institution of the Sabbath and its change from one day to another to discuss what he considers the real issue: is the seventh part of time reserved for worship a moral or a positive institution? The question enables him to emphasize the distinction between moral and positive laws. Moral laws partake of the very essence of the Lord's divinity. God cannot do other than command the moral precepts which are part of the nature of things, since to do so would be a stain on his purity (as, for example, to authorize any act forbidden by the moral law contained in the Decalogue). Such moral laws are discoverable by the light of nature. Positive laws depend entirely on God's will, which the Lord can exercise freely and despotically without dishonoring his attributes. He can demand for his worship any portion of time that he chooses. His determination of a seventh part rather than a sixth or eighth part is an act of his will. Hence the obligation to worship imposed by the Christian Sabbath rests on positive rather than moral law. Man could never discover that God requires one day in seven for worship without Revelation. As authorities on what precepts are moral, Dummer names Aristotle, Cicero, Selden, and Grotius, adding that the matter is philological rather than theological and turns on the meaning of "positive" and "moral." And nothing he might say would injure the Sabbath, since it would stand with equal authority by either the law of nature or the commandment of God. It casts no contempt on the Sabbath, Dummer observes—in a gross miscalculation—to dispute its morality. The sermon closes by describing how the Sabbath should be observed, and on this point Dummer would have pleased the strictest Puritan.[20]

Increase Mather wrote a preface designed to gain acceptance for the *Discourse*. Admitting that some passages in the Latin dissertation were not expressed as cautiously as possible, he thought that the sermon should clear Dummer from being considered opposed to the Christian Sabbath.[21] Despite Mather's plea, Dummer disappointed those who expected an affirmation of orthodoxy. Samuel Torrey, the aged minister at Weymouth, found the 1703 disquisition little if at all corrected by the 1704 sermon in its "most gravaminous" points. Dummer, he concluded, had not altered his belief that the original seventh day was no Sabbath but only a figurative promise that God would give the Jews a Sabbath twenty-five hundred years later. And if the Sabbath could be postponed from Adam to Moses, it could with as good reason be postponed again. On these premises the Sabbath was not written on the heart of man at the Creation or later. In deleting the Fourth Commandment from the Decalogue or moral law, Dummer inferred that God saw no need of the Sabbath to uphold his worship, his covenant, his church, and his religion.

"And now," Torrey queried, "who can look upon the face of this Opinion without Blushing?" Dummer's treatise was "never calculated for the Meridian of New-England," for the people "have been (whatever they are now) very jealous of, and zealous for the very strict observance of the fourth Command, and the Sabbath."[22]

Finding opportunities for employment in New England dim at best, Dummer decided to depart, and in the fall of 1708 arrived in London. His unforgivable fault lay in revealing the hidden rationalism in New England Puritanism. True, he discovered grounds for the Christian Sabbath in its positive appointment by the Lord, and he strongly endorsed proper observance of the holy day. Nevertheless, his denial of the morality of the Sabbath shook the foundations of practical religion and destroyed his usefulness in New England. As Perry Miller observed, Dummer's views on the Sabbath illustrate the Age of Reason emerging from the Age of Faith.[23] At a time when the new learning was challenging the old certainties, orthodox leaders feared such an attitude as a threat to the New England Way. Let the notion spread that the Fourth Commandment rested on the arbitrary will of God rather than on the moral law and right reason and the day would soon dawn when people would refuse to obey the precept on the grounds that it was unreasonable.

Dummer lived in England after 1708, serving both Massachusetts and Connecticut and earning a reputation as the greatest colonial agent before Benjamin Franklin. Although he experienced a spiritual crisis and became more of a rationalist, he never abandoned himself to infidelity.[24] The reaction to his treatise on the Sabbath haunted Dummer to the end of his days. Some New England residents visited him in England, and after the company grew merry with wine, Jeremiah Allen, who had an excellent memory, entertained the group by repeating verbatim some of the most striking passages from the *Discourse on the Holiness of the Sabbath Day*. As a witness reported, "Mr. D[ummer] was struck dumb with astonishment and unfitted for any further enjoyment that Eveng and the recollection of it worried him ever after."[25]

THOUGH ROGERS AND Dummer criticized the rationale for the Puritan Sabbath, leading New England theologians agreed with Willard. Cotton Mather wrote frequently on the subject. He portrayed strict keeping of the Lord's Day as part of New England's heritage in *Magnalia Christi Americana* (1702). His biographies of the governors and divines who laid the foundations for the kingdom of Christ in America praised their high regard for the Sabbath. He even fabricated stories to make his point, as when he wrote that Peter Bulkeley was so "exact a Sabbath-keeper, that if

290 THE AMERICAN EXPERIENCE

at any time he had been asked, Whether he had kept the Sabbath? He would have replied, *Christianus sum, intermittere non possum''* (I am a Christian; I cannot omit it).[26] In addition, he altered biographies in the *Magnalia* which had previously been published in *Johannes in Eremo* (1695) to make the Sabbath obligation more palatable to readers. One of these added to the life of John Cotton a stipulation that ministers could work on the Sabbath "if God's Providence have straitned [their] time in the Week-days before, by concurrence of other Business, not to be avoided."[27] With this rationalization the worldly could reconcile Sunday labor with the Word of God. Reaffirming the Puritan conviction that "religion is just as the Sabbath is," Mather's *Magnalia,* which went far in determining how Anglo-Americans viewed New England Puritanism in the eighteenth century, declared, "It has been truly and justly observed, That our whole Religion fares according to our Sabbaths, that poor Sabbaths make poor Christians, and that a Strictness in our Sabbaths inspires a Vigour into all our other Duties."[28]

Cotton Mather's reply to Jeremiah Dummer was used to reclaim the Indians from error. In October 1706 the Commissioners of the United Colonies, concluding that a number of Christianized red men were unhappily leavened with Saturday Sabbatarianism and that their numbers were in danger of increasing, directed Experience Mayhew to translate into the Indian language Mather's *The Day Which the Lord Hath Made* (1703). The Indian edition with the English and Indian titles on facing pages appeared under the original title in 1707.[29]

Benjamin Wadsworth (1670-1737), liberal minister at the First Church in Boston for over three decades before he became President of Harvard College in 1725, was entirely orthodox on the septennial institution. He briefly discussed it in *An Essay on the Decalogue* (1719) and at greater length in *The Lord's Day Proved to be the Christian Sabbath* (1720). The latter aimed at showing why the first rather than the seventh day of the week should be kept holy and indicates a continuing effort to counteract the Saturday Sabbath-keepers. Wadsworth declared that inferiors ought not obey superiors who directed them to do anything that profaned the Sabbath. The following year John Rogers answered point by point. He also responded to a pamphlet entitled *Thesis Concerning the Sabbath* about which little is known other than that it was printed in New London, and described his continuing quarrel with Connecticut authorities, especially Gurdon Saltonstall, who had been governor since 1707.[30]

Benjamin Colman (1673-1747), minister of the liberal Brattle Street Church (established in Boston in 1699) and a man of vigorous intellect, also expressed traditional views. In *The Doctrine and Law of the Holy*

Sabbath (1725) he argued on the basis of the Old Testament that the Sabbath was the first law given to man in Paradise. From the beginning God had threatened and executed dreadful punishments for its violation, and the holy prophets had insisted on sanctification of the day. Colman admitted that the Lord's Day was enjoined more by example than precept in the New Testament, but just as the original Sabbath was a sign to the Jews that God was their Creator, so too was the Lord's Day the sign to his people that God was their Redeemer. The Fourth Commandment stood as the most visible token of the covenant of grace and salvation through Christ. The form and the power of religion were retained by Sabbath observance, and New England should celebrate the festival as the badge and livery of its being the covenant people. Colman knew "no one Rule more compendious, comprehensive and effectual for the revival and perpetuity of Religion among us than this, that we keep the Lord's Sabbaths, as a Sign between Him and us thro' out our Generations, that He is the Lord that doth sanctify us."[31]

A decade later Benjamin Colton, minister of a church at Hartford, published a sermon that treated the change of the Sabbath from the seventh to the first day of the week.[32] His effort was probably aimed at correcting Saturday-keepers and Rogerenes in the area. In the period to 1740, therefore, New England divines maintained the traditional Puritan doctrine of the Sabbath.

Despite the tenacity of the theory, practice was not entirely satisfactory in the early eighteenth century. Doctrinal controversy probably contributed to the result. The spread of Dummer's opinions apparently touched off a wave of Sabbath-breaking, and on 29 October 1705 the *Boston News Letter* published a warning "to let People know, That Open Profanation of the Lord's Day, will not pass Unpunished."[33] Judge Sewall strove mightily to uphold strict Sabbaths. He pleaded with the governor to prevent illuminations in Boston on Sunday to celebrate an English naval victory, sought to keep the colors from being flown at Castle William on the Lord's Day, cried out "Down Sabbath, Up St. George" when guns were fired on a Sunday in honor of Coronation Day, joined constables in patrolling Boston to prevent disturbances on a Sabbath Eve that fell on Guy Fawkes Day, argued that a license should not be granted to a ship's captain to work on his vessel on Sunday, reported revelers in a tavern on a Saturday night, and caused shops to be shut when he found them open at that time. Yet Sewall did not scruple to entertain friends and to visit and dine out on the Sabbath.[34]

The Boston of Sewall and the Mathers was also the Boston of Benjamin Franklin. The clever son of pious but humble parents was ambitious and harnessed the Lord's Day in the service of self-improvement. His time for literary exercises—he used the *Spectator* as a model to perfect his writing—and for reading was in the margins of weekly workdays and on Sundays. He contrived to be in his brother's print shop alone on the Sabbath, "evading as much as I could the common Attendance on publick Worship, which my Father used to exact of me when I was under his Care: And which indeed I still thought a Duty; tho' I could not, as it seemed to me, afford the Time to practise it."[35] With Franklin the Sabbath is no longer a day of prayer but a day of study, and Puritanism gives way to the Enlightenment.

Travel on the Sabbath continued to cause difficulties. Most New Englanders went no further than a mile or two to attend church on the Lord's Day, and they interrupted any long journeys by stopping from Saturday evening to Monday morning.[36] In 1712 Increase Mather wondered if New England should not have, as Scotland did, a law prohibiting ships from departing on Sunday even though the wind was good then and might be poor on Monday. Four years later Judge Sewall was willing to excuse two Ipswich merchants for traveling on the Lord's Day in return for a written promise not to repeat the offense; they preferred to pay a fine of forty shillings. Sewall also thought that the only thing recommending a Newbury man for appointment as justice of the peace was that his residence on a neck of land might enable him to check travel on the Sabbath. The town of Boston repeatedly provided watches and wards on the neck leading to Roxbury to prevent that evil in the early eighteenth century.[37]

Use of the evening before and after the Lord's Day presented special problems. The opening of stores on Saturday evenings led the Boston town meeting in 1701 to prohibit all business at that time as well as on the Sabbath Day.[38] Tension existed over the duration of the Sabbath, with some urging that the day be kept from midnight to midnight rather than evening to evening, and others putting the Lord's Day evening to worldly entertainment. New England was gaining a reputation for the licentiousness of its Sunday evenings, and Cotton Mather concluded that more wickedness was done at that time than on all weekday evenings combined.[39] He preached on the subject before the General Court, and the lower house asked him to publish his sermon. *A Good Evening for the Best of Dayes* (1708) held that the holy day ran from evening to evening, and the author insisted upon a religious observance of Sunday evening without getting into polemical argument between contending groups. Those who kept Saturday evening should not offend those who observed Sunday evening by disporting themselves at that time, and vice versa.

Godly immigrants would be confused about New England opinion on the duration of the Sabbath if they saw parents on rambles, children in revels, and servants in cabals on Lord's Day evenings.[40]

Sabbath superstitions enjoyed a vogue in the years after 1700, and many ministers catered to it. Cotton Mather described how passengers on a ship that put into New Haven in 1697 learned on their long and famine-stricken voyage that they could catch one dolphin every day, two on Saturdays, but none at all on Sundays; so "with an Holy Blush at last they left off trying to do anything on the Lord's Days," trusting the Lord to feed them as He did Israel with his manna.[41] In *The Fisher-Mans Calling* (1712) Mather tells of some fishermen on the Isles of Shoals who agreed to devote the Lord's Day and one other day a month to religion. One such day, however, they wanted to go to sea to make up for days lost because of foul weather. Their minister, John Brock, told them if they would tarry and worship they would catch fish until weary later. Thirty went and five remained; the thirty caught four fish, whereas the five subsequently took five hundred.[42]

Meanwhile, a broadside entitled *Divine Examples of Gods Severe Judgments upon Sabbath Breakers* was published in Boston in 1708. Its woodcuts were originally executed between 1675 and 1680 by John Foster, a Boston engraver and printer, who copied verbatim a broadside of the same title printed in London in 1671. This publication, with four pictures showing people dying as a punishment for unlawful Sunday sports and labor, was reprinted as "a fit Monument for our present Times."[43] Increase Mather interpreted the fire in Boston on the night of 2 October 1711 as a sign of God's wrath against a professing people who profaned the Sabbath. The Puritan leader had seen burdens carried through the streets on the Lord's Day and bakers, carpenters, and smiths employed in servile labor; in a sermon on Jer. 17:27 he asked if the Lord had not "kindled a *Fire* which has *devoured our Palaces?*"[44] When an earthquake shook New England in October 1727, James Allin, the credulous minister of Brookline, queried in *Thunder and Earthquake* (1727) whether a God jealous of his Sabbaths had not demonstrated his abhorrence of the evil of profaning the day?[45]

Since the rationale for good Sabbaths remained intact and practice fell short of the ideal, the state attempted to close the gap. In Connecticut a 1708 law extended the English Toleration Act of 1689 to the province. Everyone was still taxed to support the established ministry and compelled to attend religious assemblies regularly, but individuals could now worship in the church of their choice. This statute, however, was of no help to Quakers or Rogerenes, whose principles forbade them to take the required oath of allegiance. Some Rogerenes were arrested in 1716 for disturbing the congregation at New London during time of worship.[46]

Connecticut adopted additional regulations for the rest day. One forbade persons from gathering in companies on Sunday evenings on penalty of five shillings or up to two hours in the stocks, and it imposed a fine of fifty shillings on publicans who allowed such meetings. Another law ordered that anyone presented for neglect of public worship was to pay five shillings unless he could prove attendance or gave sufficient reason for being absent.[47] In 1714 the General Court asked the General Association of Congregational churches to direct the ministry of each particular association to inquire into the state of religion in each parish to see if public worship on the Lord's Day was neglected and what other evils provoked God. A year later the legislature prohibited vessels from sailing or weighing anchor (except to attend church) within two miles of any place where public worship was held between dawn and dusk on the Lord's Day on forfeiture of forty shillings.[48]

To remedy the defects of earlier laws Connecticut passed an important new statute in May 1721. It ordered everyone to frequent the service of God on the Lord's Day in some congregation or suffer the usual penalty, and it provided a fine of five shillings for anyone who left his place of residence on the Sabbath except to attend authorized services or do a work of necessity. This legislation was profoundly influential in securing the stillness of the Sabbath in eighteenth-century Connecticut. In addition, it forbade rude and unlawful behavior which disturbed the public worship of others on punishment of forty shillings—a provision aimed at the Rogerenes. No person convicted under the statute was to have liberty to appeal, and refusal to pay fines levied could lead to a month of forced labor (a penalty changed in October to a public whipping with up to twenty stripes). Two years later, following trouble with religious dissenters, the state raised the penalty for neglect of approved public worship to twenty shillings.[49]

Massachusetts perfected its Sabbath laws in these same years. A statute of 1712 directed that all found disporting themselves in towns on the "good evening for the best of days" pay five shillings or be jailed or set in the stocks. Four years later the General Court revised the Lord's Day legislation of 1692. The 1716 statute provided that anyone who neglected public worship for a full month was to pay twenty shillings. While the fine remained at the former rate of five shillings per absence, the requirement of weekly attendance was substantially relaxed. In addition, working or playing on the Lord's Day was to be fined ten shillings and travel twenty;

for a second offense the penalties were doubled and the offender bound over to the next session of the court with sureties for good behavior.[50]

A 1727 statute revised the earlier acts in the light of experience. The emphasis was now on prohibiting profanations. Penalties for engaging in servile labor or sports on the Sabbath were raised to fifteen shillings for a first offense and double that for a second, while the amercement for travel went from thirty shillings for an initial infraction to three pounds for a subsequent one. Although funerals were conducted in Massachusetts on the Sabbath in the early eighteenth century, the act of 1727 forbade attendance at funerals on the Lord's Day or the following evening except in extraordinary cases and after obtaining permission. The stated reason was to avoid disorders caused when children and servants congregated in the streets to view the dread solemnities. The law was to be enforced by fining funeral directors forty shillings and gravediggers and sextons half that amount. The enactment also dealt with use of the evening preceding and following the holy day by forbidding swimming, unnecessary walking or riding in the streets or common fields, engaging in secular business, and keeping shops or warehouses open during the designated periods on penalty of ten shillings for a first violation and double for a second.[51]

The statutes enacted by Connecticut in 1721 and Massachusetts in 1727 lasted in their essential outlines until after the American Revolution. They continued to require attendance at public worship and proper Sabbath observance, and such revisions as occurred tended to increase the penalties for profanation of the holy day.[52] Not until 1792, after the government of the new nation was operating on the basis of the federal Constitution, did Massachusetts relax its law, making churchgoing compulsory only once every three months.[53]

New England demonstrated great solicitude for the Sabbath at the end of the period covered by this book. In 1739 Governor Jonathan Belcher of Massachusetts issued a proclamation which declared that strict observance of the Lord's Day had been a laudable concern of the government since the first settlement of the colony, but that bold and open violation of the laws relating to the Sabbath manifested decay in religion and exposed the people to God's judgments. He commanded rigorous compliance with and enforcement of the Sabbath laws.[54] The same year a broadside published at Boston lamented that

My holy Sabbaths which
your Fathers highly priz'd
Are dreadfully prophan'd by you
and wickedly despiss'd.[55]

Despite apprehensions, strict Sabbath observance remained characteristic of the New England Way. Authorities continued to enforce the laws
vigorously. In 1725 eight Rogerenes, one a woman, journeying to a religious meeting at Lebanon, Connecticut, were arrested on a charge of traveling on the Sabbath. They were imprisoned at New London until Monday, and then tried, convicted, and sentenced in the court of Joseph
Backus. They chose to be whipped rather than pay the twenty-shilling
fine, whereupon Deputy Governor Joseph Jenks of Rhode Island issued
an indignant proclamation. Backus defended the punishment on the
grounds that the Rogerenes knew that their travel was contrary to law and
would offend those who religiously observed the Sabbath. They contemptuously chose to travel on Sunday to attend a baptism scheduled on
a weekday to express their "Malicious Abhorrence" of the rest day. Authorities had to act lest they "tamely resign up the sacredness of the Sabbath."[56] Two years later Connecticut magistrates sentenced William Wat-
kins, a Sabbath burglar, to branding on the forehead and cropping of his
right ear in addition to restoring the stolen goods and paying the owner
twice its value.[57] That year the Bishop of London urged the Privy Council
to secure and enforce in Massachusetts and the royal provinces laws prohibiting profanation of the Sabbath and other vices.[58] It was ironic, and a
great tribute to the religious and moral influence of Puritanism, that
Laud's successor promoted good Sabbath observance in the colonies. At
Harvard College, where future leaders of America were being trained, the
Sabbath was upheld in its purity. The rules ordered students to attend
public worship on the Lord's Day on penalty of a fine of three shillings or
punishment by admonition, degradation, or expulsion, and the rules
treated Saturday evening as part of the holy day. Though Ben Franklin,
the printer's apprentice, made Sunday his "Studying-Day," Harvard
students understood that the Sabbath was for worship and spiritual edification.[59] The rising generation in New England was brought up in the
belief that good Sabbath observance was the foundation of practical religion. Phebe Bartlett, the four-year-old whom Jonathan Edwards described
on the eve of the Great Awakening, may have been an unusual child, but
her outlook on the Sabbath was typical. "She has been very strict upon
the Sabbath"; Edwards wrote, "and seems to long for the Sabbath day
before it comes, and will often in the week time be inquiring how long it
is to the Sabbath day, and must have the days particularly counted over
that are between, before she will be contented."[60]

An Englishman named Bennett testified to this effect upon visiting
New England in 1740: "Their observation of the sabbath . . . is the strictest kept that ever I yet saw anywhere, . . . On that day, no man, woman,

or child is permitted to go out of town on any pretence whatsoever; nor can any that are out of town come in on the Lord's Day.'' Even if they could, ''it wouldn't answer their end: for the same care is taken, all the country over, to prevent travelling on Sundays.'' Throughout New England they are ''diligent in detecting . . . offenders of this sort, . . . and those that are of the Independent persuasion refrain . . . in point of conscience. And as they will by no means admit of trading on Sundays, so they are equally tenacious about preserving good order in the town on the Lord's Day.'' This obscure traveler noted that they will not permit anyone to walk down to the waterside, though some of the houses adjoin the wharfs, ''nor, even in the hottest days of summer, will they admit of any one to take the air on the Common.'' ''If two or three people, who meet one another in the street by accident, stand talking together,—if they do not disperse immediately upon the first notice, they are liable to fine and imprisonment,'' and are sure to feel the penalty. What Bennett found ''most extraordinary is, that they commence the sabbath from the setting of the sun on the Saturday evening; and, in conformity to that, all trade and business ceases, and every shop in the town is shut up: even a barber is finable for shaving after that time.'' No tavern is permitted to entertain company, lest the house and every person found therein be fined. ''I don't mention this strict observation of the Lord's Day as intended rather to keep people within the bounds of decency and good order than to be strictly complied with, or that the appointment of this duty was only by some primary law since grown obsolete,'' Bennett concluded, ''but that it is now in full force and vigor, and that the justices, attended with a posse of constables, go about every week to compel obedience to this law.''[61]

This evaluation would have struck a responsive chord in the region described. While lamenting the lapses that did occur, prominent Puritans of the early eighteenth century took pride in believing that their country enjoyed the best Lord's Days in the world. Both Increase Mather and Benjamin Wadsworth expressed this conviction, and Cotton Mather rejoiced that ''New-England having obtained Help from God, continues to have unto this very Day, the Best Sabbaths of any Countrey under the Cope of Heaven.''[62]

Hence the Sabbath, which had been considered at the time of the founding of New England a sign of the covenant between God and his chosen people, remained more than a century later a ''Sign between Him and us thro' out our Generations.''[63]

Epilogue

THE PURITAN SABBATH was the product of a combination of forces which underlay the transition from the late medieval to the early modern period in Western civilization. Reformed theology in alliance with covenant theology prepared the soil out of which the theory arose, but it was only in England that these intellectual tendencies converged with political, economic, and social developments to create Sabbatarianism. The doctrine of the Sabbath formulated by spiritual preachers in the late sixteenth century was refreshingly novel, and yet its roots extended far back into antiquity. According to Puritan spokesmen, the Sabbath was established at the Creation and renewed at Mount Sinai, and its observance was later transferred from the seventh to the first day of the week as a memorial of the Resurrection. The duty to keep the Lord's Day holy was part of the moral law and binding upon mankind forever.

Sabbatarian doctrine was a unique and significant contribution to modern culture, and it made deep and lasting inroads upon England. After the teaching was first enunciated, it won increasing favor with a majority of middle-class Englishmen until theory and practice precipitated controversy, and then Sabbatarianism became closely identified with Puritanism. Strict observance of the day reached its peak during the Interregnum, but after the Restoration a reaction against the Judeo-Christian institution occurred. By 1700, however, a modified form of the Puri-

tan Sabbath became part of the national life, and the English Sunday retained its hold on the kingdom for another two centuries.

In Europe the innovative doctrine had to make its way against established modes of conduct, whereas the New World offered a fluid and
plastic environment. During the seventeenth century the theory and
practice of the septennial institution were carried to the American colonies, and the Puritan Sabbath made the most profound impact on the incipient nation. The distinctive teaching expressed a dominant aspiration
of American society in the formative stage of its development. In varying
degree, the colonies all shared the conviction that religion was central to
the good life and the foundation of a strong state, and proper Sabbath
observance was considered the palladium of religion.

The imported theory was quickly translated into political action and
social organization along the Atlantic seaboard. Laws reflect the basic values of a community, and everywhere the state used its power to regulate
observance of the weekly day of rest and worship. These statutes coincided
with the ethical imperatives contained in the divine or moral law, with
the result that violations of the Sabbath were branded crimes as well as
sins. The degree of commitment to the Puritan theory varied from place
to place depending on such variables as the locus of political authority,
the character of the population, the time of settlement, and the material
environment. In the first half of the seventeenth century immigrants
brought the rationale for the septennial institution from England, directly in every case except that of New Netherland, where it came indirectly by way of Holland. In the last half of the century England was the
source from which an attenuated theory of the Puritan Sabbath as well as
Quaker and Seventh-Day Sabbatarian views on the subject flowed to
the colonies, while New England preserved and dispensed Sabbatarian
doctrine in its pristine splendor.

Sabbatarianism planted roots in all the coastal settlements from Maine
to South Carolina in the seventeenth century, and that development illustrates the pervasive influence of Puritanism in early American culture.
New England exhibited the keenest attachment to the Sabbath. Massachusetts especially regarded the institution as an enduring sign of the covenant between God and his chosen people. Authorities there crushed
those who challenged the institution—Roger Williams and the Antinomians in the 1630s, the Quakers in the 1650s and after, and the Rogerenes
and Jeremiah Dummer in the early eighteenth century. These occurrences
illustrate that theory played a prominent part in shaping the character of
the people and the societies in the infancy of the future nation. The conflict over the Sabbath makes it hard to agree with Daniel Boorstin that

"during the great days of New England Puritanism there was not a single important dispute which was primarily theological."[1] The evolution of the Sabbath also provides important evidence on the nature of Puritanism. Some scholars have contended that this historical phenomenon was so diverse that it cannot properly be treated as a whole. Puritanism was indeed varied and complex, but the Sabbath was a common denominator and a unifying element in Anglo-American Puritanism, perhaps the leading one.

Sabbatarianism went far in determining the quality of life in early America, and by about 1740 a pattern of observance had arisen which was remarkably similar from colony to colony (at least legally) and which remained highly stable throughout the rest of the century. The strengths and weaknesses of the Puritan doctrine and practice were manifest by this time. The Puritan Sabbath taught people to put the purposes of God first, to obey the absolute moral imperatives of the Judeo-Christian ethic. In insisting that men and women reserve time at periodical intervals for worship and spiritual edification, Sabbatarianism guaranteed that man would cultivate the better side of his nature. Wherever the septennial festival flourished, human beings did not sink into the slough of materialism and barbarism. Well might Thomas Shepard say of the Sabbath, "keep this, keep all; lose this, lose all."[2]

Sabbatarianism was also significant in conditioning attitudes toward economic life. The Puritan teaching sanctified enterprise and proscribed idleness by enjoining men to work six days a week and rest on the seventh. Thus, Sabbatarianism was an important stimulus to the growth of capitalistic and industrial society, but the ethical component of the theory held that life meant far more than personal or social success. In reality the doctrine of the Sabbath was socially progressive. The strong social case for the enforcement of the Sabbath rest has been obscured by historians who repeat anti-Puritan propaganda about blue laws and the killjoy side of Sabbatarianism.[3]

Yet the weekly rest day had the defects of its virtues. Strict adherence to the stern ethical demand of the ancient Mosaic tradition made for legalism. The Puritan doctrine emphasized a literal approach to Scripture which denied both that Christ had freed believers from the Law and also the operations of the Holy Spirit. Moreover, the stress on keeping external commandments revived the repudiated Roman Catholic emphasis on the earning of salvation by suggesting that sanctification did count toward justification or that security lay in activity. Closely related was the sharp distinction between sacred and secular time. The repeated affirmation that six days were for work and one for worship tended to separate religion from the rest of life. Compulsory public worship made churchgoing a social ideal in early America, and the consequence was often a stultifying formalism. Benjamin Franklin, for example, continued going to church throughout his life. He liked to attend services not only to meet people and exchange ideas but also to maintain his prestige as a serious man and his reputation as a Christian. In a letter of 1764, he urged his daughter to continue attending church, because if she failed to do so his political enemies would inflate her indiscretions into crimes to wound and afflict him.[4]

Sabbatarianism denied the compound nature of man by appealing only to the rational and serious element in his makeup. While the Puritans were not always opposed to sports and recreations as such, for all practical purposes this appeared to be the case, because they feared and prohibited recreations and entertainments that touched the irrational springs of man's nature, those that catered to the sensual appetites, and those that took place on the Lord's Day. Hence Sabbatarianism suppressed the sportive, playful, and aesthetic element in American culture in the formative years.

Nevertheless, the history of this Puritan institution hardly supports the assertion that "the Calvinistic, orthodox tenets of the seventeenth and eighteenth centuries constituted nothing more nor less than an outrage on human nature productive in all probability of no beneficial results whatever."[5] A religious establishment and forced worship went far under existing conditions to advance individual and social welfare. Compulsory attendance at the weekly school of God served as a vital agency in promoting piety and civilization. The Sabbath rest countered the dangerous tendency to relapse into primitivism inherent in the settlement of the wilderness. The conviction that religion fared in accordance with the Sabbath instilled in the American character a strength and simplicity dependent on the severity of an unwavering religious discipline.

Voltaire, the apostle of the Enlightenment, voiced what was surely the common understanding on the subject in the colonies when he said, "If you wish to destroy the Christian religion you must first destroy the Christian Sunday."[6] By the early nineteenth century Americans viewed the Sabbath as the safeguard of the republic, believing that a nation founded on a substratum of infidelity has but a short existence. Peter S. DuPonceau (1760-1844), a French immigrant and a prominent lawyer and scholar of Philadelphia, noted the continuing importance of the Puritan institution in his adopted land. According to him, "of all we claimed as characteristic, our observance of the Sabbath is the only one truly national and American; and for this cause, if for no other, he trusted it would never lose its hold on our affections and our patriotism.''[7] Several decades later G. Stanley Hall (1844-1924), a native of Massachusetts on the threshold of a prominent career in psychology and philosophy, wrote that ''the American, perhaps, even more than the English, Sunday might almost be called a philosophical institution. A day of rest, of family life and introspection, it not only gives seriousness and poise to character and brings the saving fore-, after-, and over-thought into the midst of a hurrying objective and material life, . . . but it teaches self-control, self-knowledge, self-respect, as the highest results of every intellectual motive and aspiration.''[8] This statement testified to the deeper reasonableness of an ancient inheritance which the Puritans reshaped and which came into full flower in America, where the Sabbath demonstrated the force of theory and of idealism in molding thought and culture.

Notes
Bibliographical Essay
Index

ABBREVIATIONS

Andrews, *Colonial Period*
 Charles M. Andrews, *The Colonial Period of American History*. 4 vols. New Haven, Yale University Press, 1934-1938.

Brigham, *Laws of Plymouth*
 William Brigham, ed., *The Compact with the Charter and Laws of the Colony of New Plymouth*. Boston, 1836.

CMHS
 Collections of the Massachusetts Historical Society.

Conn. Col. Recs.
 J. Hammond Trumbull and Charles J. Hoadly, eds., *The Public Records of the Colony of Connecticut, 1636-1776*. 15 vols. Hartford, 1850-1890.

DAB
 Allen Johnson and Dumas Malone, eds., *Dictionary of American Biography*. 20 vols. New York, Charles Scribner's Sons, 1928-1936.

DNB
 Leslie Stephen and Sidney Lee, eds., *Dictionary of National Biography*. 63 vols. New York, Macmillan and Co., 1885-1900.

Essex Court Recs.
 [George F. Dow], ed., *Records and Files of the Quarterly Courts of Essex County, Massachusetts, [1636-1683]*. 8 vols. Salem, Essex Institute, 1911-1921.

Mass. Bay Recs.
 Nathaniel B. Shurtleff, ed., *Records of the Governor and Company of the Massachusetts Bay in New England*. 5 vols. in 6. Boston, 1853-1854.

New Haven Col. Recs.
 Charles J. Hoadly, ed., *Records of the Colony and Plantation of New Haven from 1638 to 1649* [Vol. 1]; *Records of the Colony or Jurisdiction of New Haven from May 1653 to the Union* [1665] [Vol. 2]. Hartford, 1857-1858.

New Haven Town Recs.
 Franklin B. Dexter and Zara J. Powers, eds., *Ancient Town Records, New Haven Town Records, 1649-1769*. 3 vols. New Haven, New Haven Colony Historical Society, 1917-1962.

Ply. Col. Recs.
 Nathaniel B. Shurtleff and David Pulsifer, eds., *Records of the Colony of New Plymouth in New England*. 12 vols. in 10. Boston, 1855-1861.

PMHS
 Proceedings of the Massachusetts Historical Society.

PCSM
 Publications of the Colonial Society of Massachusetts.

Winthrop, *Journal*
 John Winthrop, *The History of New England from 1630 to 1649*. Edited by James Savage. New 2 vol. ed. Boston, 1853.

Winthrop Papers
 Winthrop Papers. 5 vols. [Boston], Massachusetts Historical Society, 1929-1947.

Notes

Prologue

1. *God's Plot: The Paradoxes of Puritan Piety, Being the Autobiography and Journal of Thomas Shepard,* ed. Michael McGiffert ([Amherst], The University of Massachusetts Press, 1972), p. 61. Shepard's first attempt at flight failed, and he did not reach Massachusetts until October 1635.

2. Thomas Shepard, *Theses Sabbaticae: Or, The Doctrine of the Sabbath* (London, 1649), preface, sig. A2 [p. 4]. The work was republished in 1650 and 1655, and again in *The Works of Thomas Shepard,* ed. John A. Albro, 3 vols. (Boston, 1853), 3:7-271.

3. Shepard, *Theses Sabbaticae,* preface, sig. B [p. 7].

4. For an admirable survey of the doctrines on which the following account draws, see James A. Hessey, *Sunday: Its Origin, History, and Present Obligation,* 3d ed. (London, 1866), pp. 4-12 and *passim.*

5. Shepard, *Theses Sabbaticae,* preface, sig. A2, B [pp. 6, 7].

6. E. W. Hengstenberg, *The Lord's Day,* trans. James Martin (London, 1853), p. 7.

1. The Judeo-Christian Inheritance

1. James A. Hessey, *Sunday: Its Origin, History, and Present Obligation,* pp. 104-107.

2. S. R. Driver, *The Book of Genesis,* 10th ed. (London, Methuen & Co.,

1916), p. 35; see also idem, "Sabbath," in James Hastings, ed., *A Dictionary of the Bible,* 4 vols. (New York, C. Scribner's Sons, 1898-1902), 4:319-320.

    3. B. Davie Napier, *Song of the Vineyard: A Theological Introduction to the Old Testament* (New York, Harper and Row, 1962), pp. 45-49.

    4. On this and the next two paragraphs, ibid., pp. 65-78, and G. Ernest Wright, *The Old Testament against Its Environment* (London, SCM Press, 1950), pp. 46-68.

    5. Bernhard W. Anderson, *The Living World of the Old Testament,* 2d ed. (London, Longman, 1967), pp. 60-63 (quotation p. 62).

    6. For examples, see Exod. 31:12-17, 35:2; Ezek. 20:12-26; Num. 15:32-36; Jer. 17:27.

    7. Driver, "Sabbath," in Hastings, *Dictionary of the Bible*, 4:320.

    8. Mark 2:27-28; see also Matt. 12:8.

    9. This and the next four paragraphs draw upon Frederic W. Farrar, *History of Interpretation* (London, 1886), passim; Robert H. Pfeiffer, *Introduction to the Old Testament* (New York, Harper and Brothers, 1948), pp. 3-10, 41-49, and passim; Robert M. Grant, *The Bible in the Church: A Short History of Interpretation* (New York, Macmillan Co., 1954), passim; Bernhard W. Anderson, ed., *The Old Testament and Christian Faith: A Theological Discussion* (New York, Harper and Row, 1963), pp. 1-7; and Emil G. Kraeling, *The Old Testament Since the Reformation* (London, Lutterworth Press, 1955), pp. 7-8.

    10. W. B. Trevelyan, *Sunday* (London, Longmans, Green, and Co., 1902), pp. 14-19; Hessey, *Sunday,* pp. 14-15, 23-50; Gregory Dix, *The Shape of the Liturgy* (Westminster, Eng., Dacre Press, 1945), pp. 335-341; and Edward V. Neale, *Feasts and Fasts: An Essay on the Rise, Progress, and Present State of the Laws Relating to Sundays and Other Holidays* (London, 1845), pp. 88-90.

    11. Quoted in Hessey, *Sunday,* p. 58.

    12. Ibid., pp. 59-66; Neale, *Feasts and Fasts,* pp. 17-19.

    13. Dix, *Shape of the Liturgy,* pp. 333-336; Hessey, *Sunday,* pp. 67-87; and Trevelyan, *Sunday,* pp. 25-33.

    14. Hessey, *Sunday,* pp. 67-87; Neale, *Feasts and Fasts*, pp. 19-24.

    15. B[enjamin] Thorpe, ed., *Ancient Laws and Institutes of England,* 2 vols. ([London], 1840), 1:105; 2:161; Neale, *Feasts and Fasts,* pp. 103-105.

    16. Hessey, *Sunday,* p. 90.

    17. J. L. Cate, "The English Mission of Eustace of Flay (1200-1201)," in *Études d'Histoire Dédiées a la Mémoire de Henri Pirenne* (Brussels, Nouvelle Société d'Éditions, 1937), pp. 67-89.

    18. Hessey, *Sunday,* pp. 91-92.

    19. Ibid., pp. 95-96; A. G. Dickens, *Lollards and Protestants in the Diocese of York, 1509-1558* (London, Oxford University Press, 1959), pp. 9, 242-244.

    20. *Luther's Works,* ed. Jaroslav Pelikan and Helmut T. Lehmann, 55 vols. (St. Louis, Concordia Publishing House and Philadelphia, Fortress Press, 1955-1973), 35: 164-168, 173-174; 54:51-52; 50:92-94, 98; 22:141; Kraeling, *Old Testament,* pp. 9-20; Gerhard O. Forde, *The Law-Gospel Debate: An Interpretation of Its Historical*

Development (Minneapolis, Augsburg Publishing House, 1969), pp. viii, 175-199.

21. George H. Williams, *The Radical Reformation* (Philadelphia, Westminster Press, 1962), pp. xxiii-xxxi, 28, 38-58, 81-84, 815-865, and passim; George H. Williams and Angel M. Mergal, eds., *Spiritual and Anabaptist Writers,* Library of Christian Classics, 25 (London, SCM Press, 1947), pp. 22-31; *Luther's Works,* 40:79-223; Roland H. Bainton, *The Reformation of the Sixteenth Century* (Boston, Beacon Press, 1952), pp. 95-109, 123-140; idem, *Here I Stand: A Life of Martin Luther* (New York, Abingdon-Cokesbury Press, 1950), pp. 207-209, 258-261; Gordon Rupp, "Word and Spirit in the First Years of the Reformation," *Archiv für Reformationsgeschichte,* 49 (1958), 13-26; A. G. Dickens, *Reformation and Society in Sixteenth-Century Europe* (London, Thames and Hudson, 1966), pp. 125-150.

22. John Calvin, *Institutes of the Christian Religion,* ed. John T. McNeill, trans. Ford L. Battles, 2 vols. (Philadelphia, Westminster Press, 1960), passim, esp. 1:394-401 (II, viii, 28-34; here and hereafter parenthetical references are to the book, chapter, and section in the *Institutes*); James Mackinnon, *Calvin and the Reformation* (London, Longmans, Green and Co., 1936), pp. 214-270; Kraeling, *Old Testament,* pp. 21-32.

23. *Luther's Works,* 34:54; 64:55, 71; 53:23; 40:93-94, 91; 2:361-362; 3:77; 7:152; 23:236-239, 241; 61:29n; 54:51-52; Hessey, *Sunday,* p. 166 (the source of the quotation, taken from a part of Luther's *Table Talk* that is not in the American [Pelikan and Lehmann] edition of *Luther's Works*).

24. *Luther's Works,* 1:79-82; 12:25; 44:54-80; 51:143-145, 261-265, 333-334; 53:23; Theodore G. Tappert, trans. and ed., *The Book of Concord: The Confessions of the Evangelical Lutheran Church* (Philadelphia, Muhlenberg Press, 1959), pp. 375-379. Philip Schaff, *The Creeds of Christendom,* 4th ed., rev. and enlarged, 3 vols. (New York, 1899), 3:74-75, 16, 20-26, 42-49, 58-72.

25. Williams, *Radical Reformation,* pp. 848, 408-410, 229, 252, 257, 512, 675, 726, 732; Anthony A. Hoekema, *The Four Major Cults: Christian Science, Jehovah's Witnesses, Mormonism, Seventh-Day Adventism* (Grand Rapids, Mich., Wm. B. Eerdmans Publishing Co., 1963), pp. 89-100, 161-169.

26. Williams and Mergal, *Spiritual and Anabaptist Writers,* pp. 28-35, 149, 152, 154, 191, 253; Dickens, *Lollards and Protestants,* pp. 19, 20; and A. G. Dickens, *The English Reformation* (New York, Schocken Books, 1964), p. 34.

27. Calvin, *Institutes,* 1:400 (II, viii, 34). See also Kraeling, *Old Testament,* pp. 25-32; Mackinnon, *Calvin and the Reformation,* pp. 214-220, 236-239; Georgia Harkness, *John Calvin: The Man and His Ethics* (New York, Henry Holt and Co., 1931), pp. 118-122.

28. Calvin, *Institutes,* 1:399 (II, viii, 33).

29. John T. McNeill, *The History and Character of Calvinism* (New York, Oxford University Press, 1954), pp. 135, 165-168, 184-190; Douglas Campbell, *The Puritan in Holland, England and America,* 4th ed. rev.; 2 vols. (New York, Harper and Brothers, 1902), 2:157; Schaff, *Creeds of Christendom,* 1:435.

30. Schaff, *Creeds of Christendom,* 1:533-535; 540-549; 3:345.

31. Ibid., 1:360-384, 417; 3:233-306, 831-909; *The Decades of Henry Bul-*

linger, ed. Thomas Harding, The Parker Society, 4 vols. (Cambridge, 1849-1852), 1:253-267; Christopher Hill, *Society and Puritanism in Pre-Revolutionary England* (London, Secker and Warburg, 1964), pp. 171-172.

32. R. Douglas Brackenridge, "The Development of Sabbatarianism in Scotland, 1560-1650," *Journal of Presbyterian History,* 42 (September 1964), 150-155; Schaff, *Creeds of Christendom,* 3:454; Hessey, *Sunday,* p. 200.

33. Williams, *Radical Reformation,* pp. xxiv-xxvi, xxviii, xxx, 832-833, 846, 854, 857-865; Williams and Mergal, *Spiritual and Anabaptist Writers,* pp. 21-22; Bainton, *Reformation of the Sixteenth Century,* pp. 95-109, 140; Peter Y. De Jong, *The Covenant Idea in New England Theology, 1620-1847* (Grand Rapids, Mich., Wm. B. Eerdmans Publishing Co., 1945), p. 2.

34. Bainton, *Here I Stand,* pp. 311-312; William A. Mueller, *Church and State in Luther and Calvin: A Comparative Study* (Nashville, Tenn., Broadman Press, 1954), pp. 2-70.

35. Williams, *Radical Reformation,* p. xxiv and passim.

36. Schaff, *Creeds of Christendom,* 3:382; Mackinnon, *Calvin and the Reformation,* pp. 251-255; Mueller, *Church and State,* pp. 71-160.

37. William A. Clebsch, *England's Earliest Protestants, 1520-1535* (New Haven, Yale University Press, 1964), pp. 45, 121-122, 158, 162; E. G. Rupp, *Studies in the Making of the English Protestant Tradition* (Cambridge, University Press, 1949), p. 39 (first quotation); Hessey, *Sunday,* p. 198; William Tyndale, *An Answer to Sir Thomas More's Dialogue,* ed. Henry Walter, The Parker Society (Cambridge, 1850), pp. 97-98 (second quotation). Also see William Tyndale, *Doctrinal Treatises and Introductions to Different Portions of the Holy Scriptures,* ed. Henry Walter, the Parker Society (Cambridge, 1848), pp. 226, 351-352.

38. John Northbrooke, *A Treatise wherein Dicing, Dauncing, Vaine Playes, or Enterluds, with Other Idle Pastimes, etc. Commonly Used on the Sabboth Day, Are Reproved* (London [1577?]), ed. [John P. Collier], The Shakespeare Society, IV, no. 1 (London, 1843), p. 44; Henry M. Dexter, *The Congregationalism of the Last Three Hundred Years* (New York, 1880), p. 26.

39. Quoted in Dickens, *English Reformation,* pp. 113-114; see also Henry Gee and William J. Hardy, eds., *Documents Illustrative of English Church History* (London, Macmillan and Co., 1910), pp. 150, 172-173, 271; Dexter, *Congregationalism,* pp. 26-27; and Hill, *Society and Puritanism,* p. 146.

40. Charles Lloyd, ed., *Formularies of Faith Put Forth by Authority During the Reign of Henry VIII* (Oxford, 1856), pp. 142-148, 306-311 (quotation pp. 308-309). See also the useful introduction in T. A. Lacey, ed., *The King's Book: Or, a Necessary Doctrine and Erudition for any Christian Man* (London, S.P.C.K., 1932).

41. Clebsch, *England's Earliest Protestants,* p. 316 and passim; Leonard J. Trinterud, "The Origins of Puritanism," *Church History,* 20 (March 1951), 37-43.

42. Clebsch, *England's Earliest Protestants,* pp. 137-204, 313-318, 9 (quotation). See also Jens G. Møller, "The Beginnings of Puritan Covenant Theology," *Journal of Ecclesiastical History,* 14 (April 1963), 50-54.

43. Gee and Hardy, *Documents Illustrative,* pp. 369-370.

44. Edward Cardwell, ed., *Documentary Annals of the Reformed Church of England,* 2 vols. (Oxford, 1844), 1:15-16.

45. Ibid., p. 92.

46. Most gainfully employed Americans have at least 112 nonwork days annually. This includes 2 free days a week, usually Saturday and Sunday (104 days); 7 familiar national holidays of a religious or civil character; and Columbus Day. Regional, state, or local celebrations often add more leisure time.

47. Gee and Hardy, *Documents Illustrative,* pp. 379, 382; W. B. Whitaker, *Sunday in Tudor and Stuart Times* (London, Houghton Publishing Co., 1933), pp. 23-24; Walter H. Frere and William M. Kennedy, eds., *Visitation Articles and Injunctions of the Period of the Reformation,* Alcuin Club Publications, 3 vols. (London, Longmans, Green and Co., 1910), 2:348, 351, 366-367.

48. Christina H. Garrett, *The Marian Exiles: A Study in the Origins of Elizabethan Puritanism* (Cambridge, University Press, 1938), pp. 1-59; M. M. Knappen, *Tudor Puritanism: A Chapter in the History of Idealism* (Chicago, University of Chicago Press, 1939), chaps. 6-8; W. M. Southgate, "The Marian Exiles and the Influence of John Calvin," *History,* 27 (September 1942), 148-152.

2. The Puritan Sabbath

1. Christopher Hill, *Society and Puritanism in Pre-Revolutionary England,* pp. 206-208. Hill's view is narrower than mine. "The reasons for the peculiar British Sunday are to be sought," he writes at p. 208, "in the peculiar economic and political development of England." However valid, this obscures the force of religious and moral factors. As Hill himself argues in discussing the relation of English intellectual history after 1588 to the events that led to the seventeenth-century crisis, "Puritanism was perhaps the most important complex of ideas that prepared men's minds for revolution, but it was not the only one"; see Hill, *Intellectual Origins of the English Revolution* (Oxford, Clarendon Press, 1965), p. 6. Puritanism deserves equal if not greater emphasis in accounting for the rise of Sabbatarianism.

2. J. E. Neale, *Elizabeth I and Her Parliaments, 1559-1581* (New York, St. Martin's Press, 1958), pp. 28-29, 33-35; William Haller, *Foxe's Book of Martyrs and the Elect Nation* (London, Jonathan Cape, 1963), pp. 16-18.

3. Neale, *Elizabeth I and Her Parliaments, 1559-1581,* pp. 51-84. For the text of the two acts of April 1559, see Henry Gee and William J. Hardy, eds., *Documents Illustrative of English Church History,* pp. 442-467.

4. Pre-Elizabethan Puritanism has been treated above in relation to William Tyndale. After 1660, English Puritanism lived on as a moral force and a spiritual temper and, institutionally, in alliance with Pietism. For a sampling of the literature, see Hill, *Society and Puritanism,* pp. 13-29; and Jerald C. Brauer, "Reflections on the Nature of English Puritanism," *Church History,* 23 (June 1954), 99-108.

5. Edward Cardwell, *A History of Conferences and Other Proceedings Connected with the Revision of the Book of Common Prayer, 1558-1690* (Oxford, 1840), pp. 39-41, 117-120; John Strype, *Annals of the Reformation,* new ed., 4 vols. in 7

(Oxford, 1824), 1:pt. 1, 470-505, 518-532. Other reform proposals called for ministers to face the people during common prayer, omission of the sign of the cross in baptism, optional kneeling during holy communion, use of the surplice by ministers in time of divine service as sufficient, and the removal of organs.

6. W. H. Frere and C. E. Douglas, eds., *Puritan Manifestoes: A Study of the Origins of the Puritan Revolt* (London, S.P.C.K., 1907), p. x; Gee and Hardy, *Documents Illustrative*, pp. 467-475.

7. Champlin Burrage, *The Early English Dissenters in the Light of Recent Research (1550-1641)*, 2 vols. (Cambridge, University Press, 1912), 1:passim; 2:16-17, 23, 294-295; David Little, *Religion, Order, and Law: A Study in Pre-Revolutionary England* (New York, Harper and Row, 1969), pp. 81-95.

8. A. F. Scott Pearson, *Thomas Cartwright and Elizabethan Puritanism, 1553-1603* (Cambridge, University Press, 1925), pp. 25-46; Neale, *Elizabeth I and Her Parliaments, 1559-1581*, pp. 295-297; Frere and Douglas, *Puritan Manifestoes*, p. 8 (quotation); Patrick Collinson, "John Field and Elizabethan Puritanism," in S. T. Bindoff et al., eds., *Elizabethan Government and Society: Essays Presented to Sir John Neale* (London, The Athlone Press, 1961), pp. 127-162.

9. Donald J. McGinn, *The Admonition Controversy* (New Brunswick, N.J., Rutgers University Press, 1949), pp. 64-93; A. F. Scott Pearson, *Church and State: Political Aspects of Sixteenth Century Puritanism* (Cambridge, University Press, 1928), p. 124; *The Works of John Whitgift*, ed. John Ayre, The Parker Society, 3 vols. (Cambridge, 1851-1853), 1:175.

10. Pearson, *Thomas Cartwright*, pp. 236-240, 244-250, 252-262; Frere and Douglas, *Puritan Manifestoes*, pp. 107-109; Albert Peel, ed., *The Seconde Parte of a Register*, 2 vols. (Cambridge, University Press, 1915), 1:14.

11. Powel Mills Dawley, *John Whitgift and the English Reformation* (New York, Charles Scribner's Sons, 1954), pp. 161-191; Stuart B. Babbage, *Puritanism and Richard Bancroft* (London, S.P.C.K., 1962), pp. 18-42; Roland G. Usher, *The Reconstruction of the English Church*, 2 vols. (New York, D. Appleton and Co., 1910), 1:42-67; and Patrick Collinson, *The Elizabethan Puritan Movement* (Berkeley and Los Angeles, University of California Press, 1967).

12. William Haller, *The Rise of Puritanism: Or, The Way to the New Jerusalem as Set Forth in Pulpit and Press from Thomas Cartwright to John Lilburne and John Milton, 1570-1643* (New York, Columbia University Press, 1938), pp. 3-82.

13. Haller, *Foxe's Book of Martyrs*, passim; J. F. Mozley, *John Foxe and His Book* (London, S.P.C.K., 1940), passim. Foxe had published Latin editions of what became his Book of Martyrs in 1554 and 1559. The 1570 English edition was the most influential in shaping the minds of Anglo-Americans in succeeding generations. See also Herschel Baker, *The Wars of Truth: Studies in the Decay of Christian Humanism in the Earlier Seventeenth Century* (Cambridge, Mass., Harvard University Press, 1952), pp. 12-25; Roger L. Shinn, *Christianity and the Problem of History* (New York, Charles Scribner's Sons, 1953), pp. 29-97; Ernest L. Tuveson, *Millennium and Utopia: A Study in the Background of the Idea of Progress* (Berkeley and Los Angeles, University of California Press, 1949); idem, *Redeemer Nation: The Idea of America's Millennial Role* (Chicago, University of Chicago Press, 1968), chaps. 1-2; and C. A.

Patrides, *The Phoenix and the Ladder: The Rise and Decline of the Christian View of History* (Berkeley and Los Angeles, University of California Press, 1964).

14. Edward Cardwell, *Documentary Annals of the Reformed Church of England*, 1:220-221; *Certaine Sermons or Homilies Appointed to Be Read in Churches in the Time of the Late Queen Elizabeth of Famous Memory* (London, 1623), p. 126.

15. Walter H. Frere and William M. Kennedy, *Visitation Articles and Injunctions of the Period of the Reformation*, 3:passim; W. P. M. Kennedy, *Elizabethan Episcopal Administration: An Essay in Sociology and Politics,* Alcuin Club Collections, 3 vols. (London, A. R. Mowbray and Co., 1924), 1:cxx, cxxxvi, and passim; Millar MacLure, *The Paul's Cross Sermons, 1534-1642* (Toronto, University of Toronto Press, 1958), pp. 200-225; William H. Hale, *A Series of Precedents and Proceedings in Criminal Causes . . . 1475 to 1640; Extracted from Act-Books of Ecclesiastical Courts in the Diocese of London, Illustrative of the Discipline of the Church of England* (London, 1847), pp. i-lxiii and passim; Hubert Hall, "Some Elizabethan Penances in the Diocese of Ely," *Transactions of the Royal Historical Society,* 3d ser., 1 (1907), 263-277.

16. *Certaine Sermons or Homilies,* p. 126.

17. Peel, *Seconde Parte,* 2:54.

18. A. K. Wikgren, "The English Versions of the Bible," in Matthew Black and H. H. Rowley, eds., *Peake's Commentary on the Bible* (London, Thomas Nelson and Sons, 1962), pp. 24-26; John T. McNeill, *The History and Character of Calvinism,* p. 312; and Haller, *Foxe's Book of Martyrs,* pp. 50-54, 73-76 (quotation p. 74).

19. Quoted in Michael Walzer, *The Revolution of the Saints: A Study in the Origins of Radical Politics* (Cambridge, Mass., Harvard University Press, 1965), p. 187.

20. J. R. Green, *A Short History of the English People* (New York, 1886), p. 457.

21. John F. H. New, *Anglican and Puritan: The Basis of Their Opposition, 1558-1640* (Stanford, Stanford University Press, 1964), passim.

22. Article VII reads: "The Old Testament is not contrary to the New, . . . Although the Law given from God by Moses, as touching Ceremonies and Rites, do not bind Christian men, nor the civil precepts thereof ought of necessity to be received in any commonwealth: yet notwithstanding, no Christian man whatsoever is free from the obedience of the Commandments which are called Moral." E. Tyrrell Green, *The Thirty-Nine Articles and the Age of the Reformation* (London, 1896), p. 53.

23. Charles H. George and Katherine George, *The Protestant Mind of the English Reformation, 1570-1640* (Princeton, Princeton University Press, 1961), pp. 232-233; Little, *Religion, Order, and Law,* pp. 101-104, 124-126.

24. John Strype, *The History of the Life and Acts of . . . Edmund Grindal* (Oxford, 1821), pp. 168-177; *The Remains of Edmund Grindal,* ed. William Nicholson, The Parker Society (Cambridge, 1843), p. 215 (quotation).

25. John Northbrooke, *A Treatise wherein Dicing, Dauncing, Vaine Playes, or Enterluds, with Other Idle Pastimes, etc. Commonly used on the Sabboth Day, Are Reproved,* p. 66.

26. Strype, *Annals of the Reformation,* 3:pt. 1, 495-497.

27. Pearson, *Church and State,* p. 125.

28. On this and the next paragraph, see Alan Simpson, *Puritanism in Old and New England* (Chicago, University of Chicago Press, 1955), pp. 2, 5-6, 17-18, 21, 106; Brauer, "Reflections on the Nature of English Puritanism," pp. 100-104; William Perkins, *The Workes of That Famous and Worthy Minister of Christ in the University of Cambridge, Mr. William Perkins,* 3 vols. (London, 1616-1618), 1:421-438 (hereafter Perkins' *Works* are cited by volume and page number, with the title of the treatise given where appropriate; in this instance, *A Case of Conscience*); Robert Middlekauff, "Piety and Intellect in Puritanism," *William and Mary Quarterly,* 3d ser., 22 (July 1965), 457-470; John von Rohr, "Covenant and Assurance in Early English Puritanism," *Church History,* 34 (June 1965), 195-203.

29. Louis Berkhof, *Reformed Dogmatics: Historical* (Grand Rapids, Mich., Wm. B. Eerdmans Publishing Co., 1937), pp. 68, 150, 207-213; B. A. Gerrish, *Grace and Reason: A Study in the Theology of Luther* (Oxford, Clarendon Press, 1962), pp. 114-137.

30. Gerrish, *Grace and Reason,* passim; Gordon Rupp, *The Righteousness of God: Luther Studies* (New York, Philosophical Library, 1953), pp. 81-256.

31. Peter Y. De Jong, *The Covenant Idea in New England Theology, 1620-1847,* pp. 18-49; Leonard J. Trinterud, "The Origins of Puritanism," pp. 37-57; Anthony A. Hoekema, "The Covenant of Grace in Calvin's Teaching," *Calvin Theological Journal,* 2 (November 1967), 133-136.

32. For a detailed treatment, see Heinrich Heppe, *Reformed Dogmatics Set Out and Illustrated from the Sources,* rev. and ed. Ernst Bizer, trans. G. T. Thomson (London, George Allen & Unwin, 1950; first published 1861), pp. 281-409.

33. On this and the next paragraph, see Trinterud, "The Origins of Puritanism," pp. 39-45; Jens G. Møller, "The Beginnings of Puritan Covenant Theology," pp. 50-54; William A. Clebsch, *England's Earliest Protestants,* pp. 137-204.

34. Quoted in Møller, "The Beginnings of Puritan Covenant Theology," p. 53.

35. The following four paragraphs draw on Calvin, *Institutes;* Von Rohr, "Covenant and Assurance in Early English Puritanism," pp. 195-203; Hoekema, "The Covenant of Grace in Calvin's Teaching," pp. 133-161; and Møller, "The Beginnings of Puritan Covenant Theology," pp. 46-67.

36. Calvin, *Institutes,* 1:822 (III, xviii, 2).

37. Møller, "The Beginnings of Puritan Covenant Theology," p. 67.

38. Calvin, *Institutes,* 2:1503 (IV, xx, 15); see also 1:348n.

39. Ibid., 1:354-366 (II, vii, 6-17). See also Gal. 3:24. The second use of the Law was by the civil magistrate to protect the community from evildoers and unbelievers.

40. Calvin, *Institutes,* 1:361 (II, vii, 12); Møller, "The Beginnings of Puritan Covenant Theology," p. 50.

41. Perry Miller, *The New England Mind: The Seventeenth Century* (Cambridge, Mass., Harvard University Press, 1953; first published 1939), pp. 365-397; and idem, "The Marrow of Puritan Divinity," in *Errand into the Wilderness* (Cambridge, Mass., Harvard University Press, 1956), pp. 48-98.

42. Many of the articles previously cited in this section are critiques of Miller on

Puritan covenant thought. See also Everett H. Emerson, "Calvin and Covenant Theology," *Church History,* 25 (June 1956), 136-144; and George M. Marsden, "Perry Miller's Rehabilitation of the Puritans: A Critique," *Church History,* 39 (March 1970), 91-105.

43. Norman Pettit, *The Heart Prepared: Grace and Conversion in Puritan Spiritual Life* (New Haven, Yale University Press, 1966), pp. 1-85.

44. David Hall, "Understanding the Puritans," in Herbert J. Bass, ed., *The State of American History* (Chicago, Quadrangle Books, 1970), p. 338.

45. Perkins, *Works,* 2:1-152 (*The Whole Treatise of the Cases of Conscience*); Pettit, *Heart Prepared,* pp. 48-85; Møller, "The Beginnings of Puritan Covenant Theology," pp. 56-67; Edmund S. Morgan, *Visible Saints: The History of a Puritan Idea* ([New York], New York University Press, 1963), pp. 67-71.

46. Max Weber, *The Protestant Ethic and the Spirit of Capitalism,* trans. Talcott Parsons (New York, Charles Scribner's Sons, 1958). Weber's essay was first published in a German periodical in 1904-1905 and reprinted in 1920. An English translation by Talcott Parsons was published in London by G. Allen & Unwin in 1930.

47. The literature of controversy on the Weber thesis is voluminous. For an introduction, see Robert W. Green, ed., *Protestantism and Capitalism: The Weber Thesis and Its Critics* (Lexington, Mass., D. C. Heath and Co., 1959). Next to Weber, R. H. Tawney had the widest influence on Anglo-American thought. His *Religion and the Rise of Capitalism: A Historical Study* (London, John Murray, 1926), was published four years before an English translation of *The Protestant Ethic and the Spirit of Capitalism* appeared. Opinions differ as to whether one may accurately speak of a Weber-Tawney thesis. A valuable appraisal is Winthrop Hudson, "The Weber Thesis Re-examined," *Church History,* 30 (March 1961), 88-99.

48. On this and the next paragraph, see Roger Lockyer, *Tudor and Stuart Britain, 1471-1714* (New York, St. Martin's Press, 1964), pp. 1-15, 132-154; Frederick C. Dietz, *An Economic History of England* (New York, Henry Holt and Co., 1942), pp. 103-119, 137-156; H. M. Robertson, *Aspects of the Rise of Economic Individualism: A Criticism of Max Weber and His School* (Cambridge, Cambridge University Press, 1933), pp. 168-206; Amintore Fanfani, *Catholicism, Protestantism and Capitalism* (London, Sheed and Ward, 1935), pp. 164-167.

49. John Nef, *The Conquest of the Material World* (Chicago, University of Chicago Press, 1964), pp. 215-239 and passim. See also Nef's *Cultural Foundations of Industrial Civilization* (Cambridge, University Press, 1958).

50. D. C. Coleman, "Industrial Growth and Industrial Revolutions," *Economica,* n.s., 23 (February 1956), 1-22. I owe this reference to Professor Antoni Maczak of the University of Warsaw. See also Phyllis Deane, *The First Industrial Revolution* (Cambridge, Cambridge University Press, 1965), pp. 1-5.

51. J. U. Nef, "The Progress of Technology and the Growth of Large-Scale Industry in Great Britain, 1540-1640," *Economic History Review,* 5 (October 1934), 3-24; reprinted in Nef, *Conquest of the Material World,* pp. 121-143 (quotation p. 140).

52. Roberston, *Rise of Economic Individualism,* pp. 1-15 (quotation p. 6). See

also Albert Hyma, *Christianity, Capitalism and Communism: A Historical Analysis* (Ann Arbor, Mich., George Wahr, 1937), pp. 31, 149.

53. For Perkins on the calling, see his *Works*, 1:747-779. Although Perkins scattered references to the Sabbath throughout his writings, he gave it sustained treatment as follows: 1:46-49 (*A Golden Chaine*); 2:105-112 (*The Whole Treatise of the Cases of Conscience*); 2:285-286 (*A Commentarie . . . Upon . . . Galatians*); 3:238-242 (an exposition of Revelation 1:10: "And I was ravished in the spirit on the Lord's Day.") See also Louis B. Wright, "William Perkins: Elizabethan Apostle of 'Practical Divinity,' " *Huntington Library Quarterly*, 3 (January 1940), 171-196.

54. Perkins, *Works*, 1:750, 752, 754.

55. Ibid., pp. 754, 757.

56. Kemper Fullerton, "Calvinism and Capitalism," *Harvard Theological Review*, 21 (July 1928), 163-195; Charles George and Katherine George, "Protestantism and Capitalism in Pre-Revolutionary England," *Church History*, 27 (December 1958), 351-371; George and George, *Protestant Mind*, pp. 126-143; Karl H. Hertz, "Max Weber and American Puritanism," *Journal for the Scientific Study of Religion*, 1 (Spring 1962), 193.

57. Perkins, *Works*, 1:752. Paul uses the phrase twice. Advising Christians on daily life, he urges them in Eph. 5:16 to walk as children of the light, "Redeeming the time, because the days are evil." He entreats Christians in Col. 4:5 to "Walk in wisdom toward them that are without, redeeming the time." These quotations are from the Authorized Version. The Revised Standard Version speaks of "making the most of the time." On the Puritan attitude toward time, also see George and George, *Protestant Mind*, pp. 133-134.

58. Perkins, *Works*, 1:755-756.

59. On this issue Puritan and Anglican were in fundamental disagreement, a fact which vitiates the otherwise valuable article by Timothy H. Breen, "The Non-Existent Controversy: Puritan and Anglican Attitudes on Work and Wealth, 1600-1640," *Church History*, 35 (September 1966), 273-287.

60. Reformers also tried to get Parliament to enact a Lord's Day observance law in 1563. Dean Alexander Nowell urged such a bill in a sermon at the opening of Parliament. In all likelihood a Puritan drafted the measure, which prohibited fairs, markets, the opening of certain kinds of shops, and unnecessary work by servants on Sundays and holy days. Parliament ignored the request. Neale, *Elizabeth I and Her Parliaments, 1559-1581*, passim.

61. Frere and Douglas, *Puritan Manifestoes*, p. 24; Whitgift, *Works*, 2:565-595 (second quotation p. 587). Perkins said that the Fourth Commandment not only permits but enjoins labor on six days. *Works*, 1:755. See also Little, *Religion, Order, and Law*, pp. 96-100.

62. Walzer, *Revolution of the Saints*, pp. 210, 199, 211, 211n, and passim.

63. Perkins, *Works*, 1:755; Tawney, *Religion and the Rise of Capitalism*, p. 253. Walzer's point is part of his thesis that Puritanism derived from Calvin an ideology for a radical politics and a repressive social system, a view which rests on his conviction that Calvin was more an innovator in political thought than in theology. For valuable perspective on Walzer, see David Little, "Max Weber Revisited: The 'Protestant

Ethic' and the Puritan Experience of Order,'' *Harvard Theological Review*, 59 (October 1966), 415-428; and Little, *Religion, Order, and Law,* pp. 105-226.

64. Nef, *Conquest of the Material World,* pp. 229, 235; Fanfani, *Catholicism, Protestantism and Capitalism,* pp. 53-72. Though Whitgift wanted to preserve holy days, he was also interested in rationalizing time; see his *Works,* 2:579. On quantitative precision, see Nef, *Cultural Foundations,* passim.

65. Winthrop Hudson, "Puritanism and the Spirit of Capitalism," *Church History,* 18 (March 1949), 3-17; Roland G. Usher, ed., *The Presbyterian Movement in the Reign of Queen Elizabeth as Illustrated by the Minute Book of the Dedham Classis, 1582-1589* (London, Royal Historical Society, 1905), p. 53; Hill, *Society and Puritanism,* pp. 165-166.

66. Northbrooke, *A Treatise,* p. 96.

67. Johan Huizinga, *Homo Ludens: A Study of the Play-Element in Culture* (Boston, The Beacon Press, 1955), pp. 1-27, 46-75, and passim.

68. E. O. James, *Seasonal Feasts and Festivals* (New York, Barnes and Noble, 1961), passim; Huizinga, *Homo Ludens,* pp. 13-27, 46-75.

69. James, *Seasonal Feasts,* pp. 228-232, 292-299, 272-280; T. F. Thistelton-Dyer, *British Popular Customs, Present and Past* (London, 1876), pp. 20-21; A. R. Wright, *British Calendar Customs: England. II: Fixed Festivals, January-May, Inclusive,* ed. T. E. Lones (London, The Folk-Lore Society, 1938), pp. 85-87; Clement A. Miles, *Christmas in Ritual and Tradition: Christian and Pagan* (London, T. Fisher Unwin, 1912), pp. 297-308, 345-346.

70. James, *Seasonal Feasts,* pp. 298-299; Miles, *Christmas,* pp. 347-348; Wright, *British Calendar Customs,* 2:88-90; A. R. Wright, *British Calendar Customs: England. I: Movable Festivals,* ed. T. E. Lones (London, The Folk-Lore Society, 1936), pp. 22-28; Thistelton-Dyer, *British Popular Customs,* pp. 65-69.

71. James, *Seasonal Feasts,* pp. 309-311; Wright, *British Calendar Customs,* 2:200-215; Thistelton-Dyer, *British Popular Customs,* pp. 223-273; Phillip Stubbes, *The Anatomie of Abuses,* ed. Frederick J. Furnivall, The New Shakespeare Society, Series 6, nos. 4 and 6 (London, 1877-1879), p. 149.

72. Wright, *British Calendar Customs,* 1:148-161; Thistelton-Dyer, *British Popular Customs,* pp. 278-282 and passim; A. L. Rowse, *The Elizabethan Renaissance: The Life of the Society* (New York, Charles Scribner's Sons, 1971), p. 239; Miles, *Christmas,* pp. 185, 357-360.

73. For descriptions of Elizabethan sports I have drawn on works dealing with seasonal festivals, many of which are cited in the preceding notes; Puritan literature cited below; Dennis Brailsford, *Sport and Society: Elizabeth to Anne* (London, Routledge & Kegan Paul, 1969), chaps. 1-4; and Rowse, *Elizabethan Renaissance,* chaps. 7-8. There is much valuable material on "Sports and Pastimes" in *Shakespeare's England: An Account of the Life and Manners of His Age,* 2 vols. (Oxford, Clarendon Press, 1916), chap. 27.

74. Brailsford, *Sport and Society,* pp. 38-41; Stubbes, *Anatomie of Abuses,* pp. 88, 52, 60-61 (in the prefatory material); x-xii, 21. Stubbes's chapter on the Sabbath makes him one of the earliest writers to adumbrate the new theory.

75. Compare Percy A. Scholes, *The Puritans and Music in England and New*

England: A Contribution to the Cultural History of Two Nations ([1934], New York, Russell and Russell, 1962), pp. 309, 312-313, and passim, who argues that there was no special Puritan attitude to recreation.

76. Huizinga, *Homo Ludens,* p. 13; Perkins, *Works,* 1:774-775 *(Treatise of Vocations);* Stubbes, *Anatomie of Abuses,* pp. xi, 174, 157. See also Brailsford, *Sport and Society,* pp. 123-133.

77. Stubbes, *Anatomie of Abuses,* p. 147.

78. Ibid., pp. 184, 180, 177-178; Brailsford, *Sport and Society,* pp. 53-54; Rowse, *Elizabethan Renaissance,* pp. 215, 218-219; *Robert Laneham's Letter: Describing a Part of the Entertainment unto Queen Elizabeth at the Castle of Kenilworth in 1575,* ed. F. J. Furnivall, The Shakespeare Library [Series 6, no. 14] (London, Chatto and Windus, 1907), p. 16.

79. Allardyce Nicoll, ed., *The Elizabethans* (Cambridge, University Press, 1957), p. 122; Rowse, *Elizabethan Renaissance,* pp. 247-251; and Stubbes, *Anatomie of Abuses,* p. 155 (quotation). See also Northbrooke, *A Treatise,* p. 175.

80. J. W. Allen, *English Political Thought, 1603-1660. Vol. 1, 1603-1644* (London, Methuen & Co., 1938), p. 299.

81. Stubbes, *Anatomie of Abuses,* p. 180; Hill, *Society and Puritanism,* p. 160.

82. Brailsford, *Sport and Society,* pp. 124, 25-33; Hill, *Society and Puritanism,* p. 191; and idem, "Puritans and the 'Dark Corners of the Land,' " *Transactions of the Royal Historical Society,* 5th ser., 13 (1963), 97.

83. *Robert Laneham's Letter,* pp. 12-13, 20-33; T. C. Mendenhall, *The Shrewsbury Drapers and the Welsh Wool Trade in the Sixteenth and Seventeenth Centuries* (London, Oxford University Press, 1953), p. 44.

84. E. K. Chambers, *The Elizabethan Stage,* 4 vols. (Oxford, Clarendon Press, 1923), 1:passim; M. C. Bradbrook, *The Rise of the Common Player: A Study of Actor and Society in Shakespeare's England* (Cambridge, Mass., Harvard University Press, 1964), passim; Allen, *English Political Thought,* pp. 282-283.

85. MacLure, *Paul's Cross Sermons,* pp. 210-211; Chambers, *Elizabethan Stage,* 4:208-212.

86. Sibbes is quoted in Geoffrey F. Nuttall, *The Holy Spirit in Puritan Faith and Experience* (Oxford, Basil Blackwell, 1947), p. 146, but see Calvin, *Institutes,* 1:58 (I, v, 5); Stubbes, *Anatomie of Abuses,* p. 142.

87. From a sermon of 24 August 1578 quoted in Chambers, *Elizabethan Stage,* 4:199.

88. Northbrooke, *A Treatise,* p. 96.

89. Bradbrook, *Common Player,* pp. 48-49, 51, 102-108, 111-115, 117; Chambers, *Elizabethan Stage,* 1:329; 4:appendix E; F. P. Wilson, *The Plague in Shakespeare's London* (Oxford, Clarendon Press, 1927), pp. 15-16, 50-54; J. F. D. Shrewsbury, *A History of Bubonic Plague in the British Isles* (Cambridge, University Press, 1970), pp. 189-206, 212-255.

90. Northbrooke, *A Treatise,* p. 92; Carl Bridenbaugh, *Vexed and Troubled Englishmen, 1590-1642* (New York, Oxford University Press, 1968), pp. 199-200; Rowse, *English Renaissance,* pp. 171-172; Stephen Gosson, *The School of Abuse* (London, 1579), ed. [John P. Collier], The Shakespeare Society, vol. 4, no. 2 (London, 1841), p. 25; Stubbes, *Anatomie of Abuses,* p. 145.

91. Chambers, *Elizabethan Stage,* 1:255; Elbert N. S. Thompson, *The Controversy between the Puritans and the Stage* (New York, Henry Holt and Co., 1903), pp. 39-40.

92. Henry A. Kelly, *Divine Providence in the England of Shakespeare's Histories* (Cambridge, Mass., Harvard University Press, 1970), pp. 1-5; Strype, *Annals of the Reformation,* 2:pt. 2, 401-403; Chambers, *Elizabethan Stage,* 4:208; John Field, *A Godly Exhortation, by Occasion of the Late Judgement of God, Shewed at Parris-Garden* (London, [1583]); *Divine Examples of God's Severe Judgments upon Sabbath-Breakers, in Their Unlawful Sports, Collected out of Several Divine Subjects, viz. Mr. H. B. Mr. Beard, and the Practice of Piety* (London, 1671), a broadside. The quoted verse, from the broadside, may actually date from a later period. C. L. Kingsford, "Paris Garden and the Bear-baiting," *Archaeologia,* 70 (1920), 155-178, conclusively demonstrates that the bearbaiting took place at the Bear Garden on the Bankside and not the Paris Garden. Since spectators crossed the Thames and commonly landed at the Paris Garden Stairs nearby, the site was referred to as Paris Garden.

93. J. E. Neale, *Elizabeth I and Her Parliaments, 1584-1601* (London, Jonathan Cape, 1957), pp. 48-83, 95-101.

94. M. M. Knappen, "The Early Puritanism of Lancelot Andrewes," *Church History,* 2 (June 1933), 95-104; John H. Overton, "Lancelot Andrewes," *DNB;* but cf. Paul A. Welsby, *Lancelot Andrewes, 1555-1626* (London, S.P.C.K., 1958), pp. 3-39, and Peter Heylyn, *Extraneus Vapulans* (London, 1656), p. 126. A 1630 edition of Andrewes' lectures, based on students' notes and expanded in 1641, was reprinted in Andrewes, *A Pattern of Catechistical Doctrine,* Library of Anglo-Catholic Theology, 7 (Oxford, 1846), 152-169. The 1642 edition entitled *The Morall Law Expounded* is the best on the Fourth Commandment. The 1650 edition entitled *The Pattern of Catechistical Doctrine* is the most reliable except on the Sabbath, which the editor altered to harmonize with Andrewes' later beliefs. See Welsby, *Lancelot Andrewes,* pp. 22-23.

95. Charles H. Cooper and Thompson Cooper, *Athenae Cantabrigienses,* 2 vols. (Cambridge, 1861), 2:143-144; Alexander Gordon, "Richard Greenham or Grenham," *DNB;* Haller, *Rise of Puritanism,* pp. 26-35. Greenham may have been the first to publish on the subject, as undocumented statements by both Fuller, the seventeenth-century historian, and Marsden may be read to imply. (Thomas Fuller, *The Church History of Britain,* new 3-vol. ed. (London, 1837; first published 1655), 3:132-134; J. B. Marsden, *The History of the Early Puritans,* 2d ed. (London, 1853), p. 246.) Christopher Hill states (*Society and Puritanism,* p. 170) that Greenham published in 1592. Alexander Gordon said that Greenham's discourse "had been in many hands for many years" before Holland, who found three copies and edited the best, included it in Greenham's published works. (Gordon, "Lancelot Andrewes," *DNB.*) The first edition of Greenham's published works appeared in 1599 (although the fifth edition says 1601). I have used *The Workes of the Reverend and Faithful Servant of Jesus Christ, M. Richard Greenham,* ed. H[enry] H[olland], 5th ed. (London, 1612), pp. 128-171.

96. Thompson Cooper, "Nicholas Bownde or Bound," *DNB.* Bownde wrote several other religious works after 1595 which emphasize pastoral theology.

97. Nicolas [*sic*] Bownde, *The Doctrine of the Sabbath* (London, 1595). The author dedicated the work to the Puritan Robert Devereux, Earl of Essex, then a popular favorite and well regarded at court. He accounts for his relations with Greenham and his preparation of the book in a prefatory note, where he also observed that 1595 was the year after God's heavy judgments by a variety of outrages of weather.

98. Andrewes, *Pattern*, pp. 152-155; Greenham, *Works*, pp. 128-155. Bownde's *Doctrine of the Sabbath* ran to 286 pages; pages are available in several British libraries and at the Folger Shakespeare Library, Washington, D.C. He expanded this, publishing a 479-page treatise, *Sabbathum Veteris et Novi Testamenti: Or the True Doctrine of the Sabbath* (London, 1606). The references following are to the 1606 edition, where Bownde treats the theory from pp. 1-121. Greenham devoted a much larger proportion of his work to theoretical considerations than did Andrewes or Bownde.

99. Bownde, *Sabbathum Veteris*, p. 124.

100. Ibid., pp. 135-189 (quotation p. 148); Andrewes, *Pattern*, pp. 155-160; Greenham, *Works*, pp. 162-167; Northbrooke, *A Treatise*, p. 65; Perkins, *Works*, 2:110 (*The Whole Treatise of the Cases of Conscience*).

101. Bownde, *Sabbathum Veteris*, pp. 189-235.

102. Ibid., pp. 262-283; Andrewes, *Pattern*, p. 160; Greenham, *Works*, pp. 168-170.

103. Bownde, *Sabbathum Veteris*, pp. 285-479; Andrewes, *Pattern*, pp. 160-165; Greenham, *Works*, pp. 156-160.

104. M. M. Knappen, *Tudor Puritanism: A Chapter in the History of Idealism*, p. 442.

105. Bownde, *Doctrine of the Sabbath*, p. 234 and *Sabbathum Veteris*, p. 417. Bownde was quoting Calvin, who had written in a sermon on Deut. 5 that "the Sunday therefore ought to serve us, for a tower to mount on high to view the workes of God from afarre, when wee are neither hindred nor occupied with any thing."

3. Good Sabbaths Make Good Christians

1. J. W. Allen, *English Political Thought . . . 1603-1644*, p. 269.

2. Quoted in Cotton Mather, *Magnalia Christi Americana: Or The Ecclesiastical History of New England* (London, 1702), bk. 3, p. 178; Christopher Hill, *Society and Puritanism in Pre-Revolutionary England*, pp. 209, 206.

3. Thomas Fuller, *The Church History of Britain*, 3:143-144.

4. Quoted from a London petition of 1640 in H. Hensley Henson, *Studies in English Religion in the Seventeenth Century* (London, John Murray, 1903), pp. 44-45n.

5. Edgar S. Furniss, *The Position of the Laborer in a System of Nationalism: A Study in the Labor Theories of the Later English Mercantilists* (Boston, Houghton Mifflin Co., 1920), p. 44; Margaret James, *Social Problems and Policy during the Puritan Revolution, 1640-1660* (London, G. Routledge & Sons, 1930), p. 22.

6. Fuller, *Church History*, 3:144.

7. A. W. Pollard and G. R. Redgrave, *A Short-Title Catalogue of Books Printed in England, Scotland, and Ireland, 1475-1640* (London, The Bibliographical Society, 1926), list three known copies, but Miss Katharine F. Pantzer, who is revising the STC, finds ten in Britain, and there is one in the United States.

8. Henry Gee and William J. Hardy, *Documents Illustrative of English Church History,* p. 509.

9. James L. Lindsay, 26th Earl of Crawford, *Tudor and Stuart Proclamations, 1485-1714,* calendared by Robert Steele, 2 vols. (Oxford, Clarendon Press, 1910), 1:108 (no. 944); W. B. Whitaker, *Sunday in Tudor and Stuart Times,* pp. 69-70.

10. William Barlow, *The Summe and Substance of the Conference . . . at Hampton Court* (London, 1604), pp. 82-83.

11. Charles H. McIlwaine, ed., *The Political Works of James I* (Cambridge, Mass., Harvard University Press, 1918), pp. xv-lxxx, xc-xci; John D. Eusden, *Puritans, Lawyers, and Politics in Early Seventeenth-Century England* (New Haven, Yale University Press, 1958), chaps. 1-3.

12. Stuart B. Babbage, *Puritanism and Richard Bancroft* (London, S.P.C.K., 1962), chaps. 3, 4-7; Henry A. Wilson, ed., *Constitutions and Canons Ecclesiastical, 1604* (Oxford, Clarendon Press, 1923), E verso-E2; and Whitaker, *Sunday,* pp. 70-71.

13. Thomas Rogers, *The Catholic Doctrine of the Church of England: An Exposition of the Thirty-Nine Articles,* ed. J. J. S. Perowne, The Parker Society (Cambridge, 1854), pp. 18-20. This work was originally published as *The Faith, Doctrine, and Religion, Professed, and Protected in the Realme of England . . . Expressed in Thirty-Nine Articles* (Cambridge, 1607).

14. Quoted in Geoffrey F. Nuttall, *Visible Saints: The Congregational Way, 1640-1660* (Oxford, Basil Blackwell, 1957), p. 133.

15. J. E. Neale, *Elizabeth I and Her Parliaments, 1584-1601,* pp. 394-405; *Journals of the House of Lords* (n.p., n.d.), 2:248, 251 (hereafter cited as *Lords Journals*); Whitaker, *Sunday,* p. 107.

16. *Journals of the House of Commons* (n.p., 1803-) 1:260, 261, 267, 268-269 (hereafter cited as *Commons Journals*); *Lords Journals,* 2:375, 384, 400, 444; Whitaker, *Sunday,* pp. 103-104.

17. Thomas L. Moir, *The Addled Parliament of 1614* (Oxford, Clarendon Press, 1958), p. 69; *Commons Journals,* 1:467, 468, 476, 483, 492; *Lords Journals,* 2:706, 707, 710, 713, 714; Whitaker, *Sunday,* pp. 105-106.

18. Richard Byfield, *The Doctrine of the Sabbath Vindicated* (London, 1631), p. 181; Millar MacLure, *The Paul's Cross Sermons, 1534-1642,* pp. 229, 231, 233, 235, 236, 237, 238.

19. [Lewis Bayly], *The Practise of Pietie: Directing a Christian How to Walke That He May Please God,* 3d ed. (London, 1613), pp. 513-515. The date of the first published edition is not known.

20. Roland G. Usher, *The Reconstruction of the English Church,* 2:34-35, 39.

21. Sidney A. Peyton, ed., *The Churchwardens' Presentments in the Oxfordshire Peculiars of Dorchester, Thame and Banbury,* Oxfordshire Record Society Series, 10 (Oxford, The Society, 1928), passim; [Claude] Jenkins, ed., "Act Book of the Archdeacon of Taunton," Somerset Record Society, *Collectanea,* II, 43 (1928), 23;

Hill, *Society and Puritanism,* pp. 151-159; H. A. Doubleday and William Page, eds., *The Victoria History of the County of Bedford,* 3 vols. (Westminster, Archibald Constable & Co., 1904-1912), 1:336n; E. R. Brinkworth, "The Study and Use of Archdeacons' Court Records: Illustrated from the Oxford Records (1566-1759)," *Transactions of the Royal Historical Society,* 4th ser., 25 (1943), 105; W. J. Hardy, comp., *Hertford County Records. Notes and Extracts from the Sessions Rolls, 1581-1894,* 3 vols. (Hertford, C. E. Longmore, 1905-1910), 1:xx, 34. See also Sumner Chilton Powell, *Puritan Village: The Formation of a New England Town* (Middletown, Conn., Wesleyan University Press, 1963), p. 44.

22. Jenkins, "Act Book of the Archdeacon of Taunton," pp. 26-27, 25 (quotation); William Page and J. Horace Round, eds., *The Victoria History of the County of Essex* (London, Archibald Constable & Co., 1907), 2:46; Hill, *Society and Puritanism,* p. 155n; Whitaker, *Sunday,* pp. 73-76.

23. Brinkworth, "The Study and Use of Archdeacons' Court Records," p. 105.

24. Hill, *Society and Puritanism,* pp. 183-194; Whitaker, *Sunday,* pp. 76-77.

25. *Diary of Lady Margaret Hoby, 1599-1605,* ed. Dorothy M. Meads (Boston, Houghton Mifflin Co., 1930), pp. 47, 62.

26. Edward Brerewood, *A Learned Treatise of the Sabaoth, Written . . . to Mr Nicholas Byfield, Preacher in Chester. With Mr Byfields Answere and Mr Brerewoods Reply* (Oxford, 1630), pp. 1-4. Brerewood dated his letter to Byfield 16 May 1611; his reply 15 July 1611.

27. Hill, *Society and Puritanism,* p. 176. See also Christopher Hill, *Intellectual Origins of the English Revolution,* pp. 51-52.

28. Nicholas Byfield answered Edward Brerewood curtly and somewhat haughtily (see note 26 above), citing Greenham as having already refuted Brerewood's tenets and declining to enter into further controversy with a stranger. Professor Brerewood replied with considerable heat during the summer of 1611 and at greater length before his death in 1613. Richard Byfield responded with *The Doctrine of the Sabbath Vindicated* (1631) after a publisher brought out Brerewood's first treatise in 1630. Brerewood's *Second Treatise of the Sabbath: Or, An Explication of the Fourth Commandment* was published posthumously at Oxford in 1632.

29. "Mr Byfields Answere," in Brerewood, *Learned Treatise,* pp. 81-82; Byfield, *The Sabbath Vindicated,* pp. 185-186, 188-190.

30. Brerewood, *Learned Treatise,* pp. 5-53 (quotation p. 53).

31. Byfield, *The Sabbath Vindicated,* pp. 75-77, 6-7, 104-108, 181-182, 45, A2 verso.

32. Hill, *Society and Puritanism,* pp. 178-179; Whitaker, *Sunday,* p. 80.

33. *Winthrop Papers,* 1:155, 157, 162, 168, 158.

34. Ibid., p. 198. The metaphor of the Sabbath as God's market day was popular throughout the seventeenth century. Bishop Bayly used it about the time Winthrop did. Thomas Gataker wrote in 1637: "As frequenting of markets maketh a rich man, so keeping of Sabbaths maketh a rich Christian. And as we count him a bad husband that followeth games on the market-day, so may we as well count him a spiritual unthrift that spendeth the Sabbath in that sort" (quoted in Hill, *Society and Puritan-*

ism, p. 145). Roger Crabb (1621-1680), for a time a hatter and the man who probably inspired the phrase "mad as a hatter," was a religious perfectionist who viewed the Sabbath as an abominable idol. He spoke of the church as "the old jade," and to keep the Sabbath was "to observe her Market-Day." John Mason (1646-1694), whose career was orthodox until about 1690, once praised the Sabbath as "England's Glory" and wrote that "this Market-Day doth Saints enrich." See Christopher Hill, *Puritanism and Revolution: Studies in Interpretation of the English Revolution of the Seventeenth Century* (London, Secker & Warburg, 1958), pp. 318, 328.

35. *Winthrop Papers,* 1:208, 215, 236.

36. W. P. Baker, "The Observance of Sunday," in Reginald Lennard, ed., *Englishmen at Rest and Play: Some Phases of English Leisure, 1558-1714* (Oxford, Clarendon Press, 1931), pp. 113-114.

37. *God's Plot: The Paradoxes of Puritan Piety, Being the Autobiography and Journal of Thomas Shepard,* pp. 40, 38; *The Autobiography of Richard Baxter,* ed. J. M. Lloyd Thomas (London, J. M. Dent & Sons, 1931), pp. 3-4; *Winthrop Papers,* 1:187.

38. Samuel R. Gardiner, *History of England from the Accession of James I to the Outbreak of the Civil War, 1603-1642,* new ed., 10 vols. (London, 1895-1899), 3:248; cf. Hill, *Society and Puritanism,* p. 194.

39. Gardiner, *History of England,* 3:248-249; Robert Halley, *Lancashire: Its Puritanism and Nonconformity,* 2 vols. (Manchester, 1869), 1:129, 147-148; James Tait, "The Declaration of Sports for Lancashire (1617)," *English Historical Review,* 32 (October 1917), 561-568; Ernest Axon, ed., "Manchester Sessions, Notes of Proceedings before . . . Magistrates I:1616-1622/23," *The Record Society for the Publication of Original Documents Relating to Lancashire and Cheshire,* 42 (1901), 15-17.

40. Edward Cardwell, *Documentary Annals of the Reformed Church of England,* 2:188n.

41. Tait, "The Declaration of Sports for Lancashire (1617)," pp. 562-564; *The Journal of Nicholas Assheton of Downham in the County of Lancashire,* ed. F. R. Raines, The Chetham Society, 14 (1848), 34 (quotation), 40-45; *Manchester Sessions,* pp. xxiv-xxvi (text of the Declaration for Lancashire).

42. *The Kings Majesties Declaration to His Subjects Concerning Lawful Sports to Be Used* (London, 1618). The text has often been reprinted—once by an American manufacturer of sporting goods—and is usually found together with the Declaration of Sports issued by Charles I in 1633. The quotations here are from the text given in Cardwell, *Documentary Annals,* 2:188-193.

43. This and the next two paragraphs draw on Whitaker, *Sunday,* pp. 95-100; Gardiner, *History of England,* 3:251; and Henson, *English Religion,* p. 46.

44. Peter Heylyn, *The History of the Sabbath,* 2d ed. rev. (London, 1636), bk. 2, p. 261.

45. Fuller, *Church History,* 3:270-273; Gardiner, *History of England,* 3:251-252; Mary A. E. Green, ed., *Calendar of State Papers, Domestic Series . . . James I,* 5 vols. (London, 1857-1872), 2:164; 3:72-73, 78, 128-129, 188, 276 (quotation).

46. Eusden, *Puritans, Lawyers, and Politics,* p. 82. Eusden believes "it is im-

322   NOTES TO PAGES 74-77

probable that corroborative precedents could be found" for the claims James made. I

322   NOTES TO PAGES 74-77

probable that corroborative precedents could be found" for the claims James made. I disagree for reasons made clear in my text. In any case, the fear of the prerogative was a real one.

47. *Commons Journals*, 1:511, 514 (first quotation), 521-522, 524; Wallace Notestein, Frances Helen Relf, and Hartley Simpson, eds., *Commons Debates, 1621*, 7 vols. (New Haven, Yale University Press, 1935), 2:82; 4:52-53 (second quotation p. 53); 5:255, 467; 6:376-377.

48. *Commons Journals*, 1:524-525; Notestein, Relf, and Simpson, *Commons Debates*, 2:104-105; 4:53; 5:467-468; 6:450-451.

49. *Commons Journals*, 1:628, 630; Notestein, Relf, and Simpson, *Commons Debates*, 2:150, 164, 397; 3:297, 298-299, 324; 4:75-76, 377-378; 5:16, 176, 257; 6:361-372; *Lords Journals*, 3:36, 38, 130, 138, 139, 140-141.

50. *Commons Journals*, 1:671, 673, 678; *Lords Journals*, 3:248, 249, 252; *Cal. S. P. Dom.*, 4:260 (the quotation is in a letter of 28 May 1624 from Edward Nicholas to John Nicholas). See also Whitaker, *Sunday*, pp. 109-110.

51. As quoted in Gardiner, *History of England*, 7:75. On Laud, see H. R. Trevor-Roper, *Archbishop Laud, 1573-1645* (London, Macmillan and Co., 1940).

52. Whitaker, *Sunday*, pp. 116-117, 110-113; *Commons Journals*, 1:799, 800; *Lords Journals*, 3:444, 450, 451, 465; and Alexander Luders et al., eds., *The Statutes of the Realm [1101-1713]*, 9 vols. in 11 (London, 1810-1824), 5:1 (1 Car. I, c. 1).

53. The act of 1627 seems to have passed both houses a year earlier, but it did not become law. See *Commons Journals*, 1:825, 827, 840, 842, 846; *Lords Journals*, 3:567, 569, 575. For the 1627 act as passed see *Commons Journals*, 1:877, 880, 894, 903; *Lords Journals*, 3:788, 794, 809, 810; *Statutes of the Realm*, 5:25 (3 Car. I, c. 2).

54. Whitaker, *Sunday*, pp. 117-120; P[eter] Heylyn, *Cyprianus Anglicus: Or, The History of the Life and Death of the Most Reverend and Renowned Prelate William by Divine Providence, Lord Archbishop of Canterbury* (London, 1671), p. 242; William Prynne, *Canterburies Doome* (London, 1646), pp. 132-134; Trevor-Roper, *Laud*, p. 5.

55. Gardiner, *History of England*, 7:319-321; Heylyn, *Cyprianus Anglicus*, pp. 241-243; Prynne, *Canterburies Doome*, pp. 128, 134, 141-142, 151-154 (irregular pagination in original). The text of the Declaration of Sports (London, 1633) is in Cardwell, *Documentary Annals*, 2:188-193.

56. Fuller, *Church History*, 3:377-378; *The Works of . . . William Laud*, 7 vols. in 9 (Oxford, 1847-1860), 4:251-256; Heylyn, *Cyprianus Anglicus*, p. 148; Henson, *English Religion*, p. 49.

57. Gardiner, *History of England*, 7:317-318. On this subject, see also Nellis M. Crouse, "Causes of the Great Migration, 1630-1640," *New England Quarterly*, 5 (January 1932), 3-36; Allen French, *Charles I and the Puritan Upheaval: A Study of the Causes of the Great Migration* (Boston, Houghton Mifflin, 1955); and Carl Bridenbaugh, *Vexed and Troubled Englishmen, 1590-1642*.

58. About 120 books and pamphlets appeared in the century that followed. See Baker, "Observance of Sunday," p. 97; and Robert Cox, *The Literature of the Sabbath Question*, 2 vols. (Edinburgh, 1865).

59. James Gairdner and James Spedding, *Studies in English History* (Edinburgh, 1881), p. 305.

60. Heylyn's presentation copy (of the second edition, published in 1636 as was the first edition) to Thomas, Viscount Wentworth, Lord Deputy of Ireland, became the property of Charles Sumner of Massachusetts. Sumner gave it to Harvard University, where it is in the Houghton Library.

61. Henson, *English Religion,* pp. 63-64.

62. Fuller, *Church History,* 3:274; Hill, *Society and Puritanism,* pp. 202-205; Cox, *Sabbath Question,* 1:152-153; Notestein, Relf, and Simpson, *Commons Debates,* 2:96n, 397; 3:298-299, 324; 4:377-378.

63. Fuller, *Church History,* 3:372-373; Cox, *Sabbath Question,* 1:157-158; Hill, *Society and Puritanism,* pp. 210-213.

64. Samuel Clark[e], *The Lives of Sundry Eminent Persons in this Later Age* (London, 1683), p. 7; see also idem, *A Generall Martyrologie* (London, 1651), pp. 387-388.

65. Nehemiah Wallington, *Historical Notices of Events Occurring Chiefly in the Reign of Charles I,* ed. R[osamond] Webb, 2 vols. (London, 1869), 1:53-54. *God's Judgements* was ultimately incorporated in this book.

66. The first edition has been attributed to William Prynne, though it was undoubtedly written by Burton, whose name appears on the title page of the 1641 edition. See also Cox, *Sabbath Question,* 1:187-188.

67. Corymboeus [Richard Brathwaite], *Barnabae Itinerarium, or Barnabees Journall* ([London, 1638]), sig. B 4; quoted in Douglas Bush, *English Literature in the Earlier Seventeenth Century, 1600-1660,* 2d ed., rev. (Oxford, Clarendon Press, 1962), p. 47.

68. *The Works of George Herbert,* ed. F. E. Hutchinson (Oxford, Clarendon Press, 1941), p. 75.

69. Quoted in Hill, *Society and Puritanism,* p. 169n.

70. *Works of George Herbert,* p. 196.

4. The Chesapeake Colonies

1. Perry Miller, "Religion and Society in the Early Literature of Virginia," in *Errand into the Wilderness,* p. 101. Thomas Nelson Page made essentially the same point in *The Old Dominion: Her Making and Her Manners* (New York, Charles Scribner's Sons, 1914), p. 364, lamenting the attempt of many historians to explain the settlement of Virginia as only for gain, whereas "the planting of Virginia had its origin in the religious zeal of the people of England."

2. William Waller Hening, ed., *The Statutes at Large, Being a Collection of All the Laws of Virginia,* 13 vols. (New York, 1823), 1:69 (hereafter cited as *Va. Statutes*); Elizabeth Davidson, *The Establishment of the English Church in the Continental American Colonies* (Durham, Duke University Press, 1936), pp. 11-24; William Seiler, "The Church of England as the Established Church in Seventeenth-Century Virginia," *Journal of Southern History,* 15 (November 1949), 481.

3. *Travels and Works of Captain John Smith, President of Virginia, and Admiral of New England, 1580-1631,* ed. Edward Arber; new ed. A. G. Bradley, 2 vols. (Edinburgh, John Grant, 1910), 2:957-958; Edward L. Goodwin, *The Colonial Church in Virginia* (Milwaukee, Morehouse Publishing Co., 1927), p. 97.

4. Edward Maria Wingfield, "A Discourse of Virginia" (1608), ed. Charles Deane, *Transactions and Collections of the American Antiquarian Society: Archaeologia Americana,* 4 (1860), 98-99.

5. Alexander Brown, *The Genesis of the United States,* 2 vols. (Boston, 1890), 1:371.

6. London, 1612. A photostatic copy of the original in the Massachusetts Historical Society has been published; references here are to that (hereafter cited as *Laws*). The text is also in Peter Force, ed., *Tracts and Other Papers, Relating Principally to the Origin, Settlement, and Progress of the Colonies in North America,* 4 vols. (Washington, 1836-1846), 3:no. 2.

7. Walter F. Prince, "The First Criminal Code of Virginia," *Annual Report of the American Historical Association for the Year 1899,* 2 vols. (Washington, 1900), 1:328.

8. Strachey, *Laws*, pp. 3-19.

9. Ibid., pp. 3-4.

10. Ibid., pp. 54, 34.

11. Ibid., pp. 4-5, 53, 55.

12. William Strachey, "A most dreadfull Tempest . . ." in J[ohn] H[enry] Le-Froy, *Memorials of the Discovery and Early Settlement of the Bermudas or Somers Islands, 1515-1685,* 2 vols. (London, 1877), 1:41, 47.

13. [Robert Johnson], *The New Life of Virginea* (London, 1612), in Force, *Tracts,* 1:no. 7, pp. 4, 13.

14. Prince, "The First Criminal Code of Virginia," p. 313.

15. Ralph Hamor, *A True Discourse of the Present State of Virginia* (London, 1615), p. 27. Hamor added that "more [persons] deserved death in those daies" when the "severe and strict imprinted booke of Articles" took effect "then do now the least punishment, so as if the law should not have restrained by execution, I see not how the utter subversion and ruine of the Colony should have bin prevented."

16. On the iron discipline and severe punishments imposed during Dale's regime, and on population, see Thomas H. Wynne and W. S. Gilman, eds. *Colonial Records of Virginia* (Richmond, 1874), p. 74; Lyon G. Tyler, ed., *Narratives of Early Virginia, 1606-1625* (New York, Charles Scribner's Sons, 1907), pp. 420-423, 433.

17. Susan Myra Kingsbury, ed., *The Records of the Virginia Company of London*, 4 vols. (Washington, Government Printing Office, 1906-1935), 3:93 (hereafter cited as *Recs. Va. Co.*); Prince, "The First Criminal Code of Virginia," pp. 356-359.

18. *Recs. Va. Co.,* 3:173; Richard L. Morton, *Colonial Virginia, I: The Tidewater Period, 1607-1710* (Chapel Hill, University of North Carolina Press, 1960), p. 93; George M. Brydon, *Virginia's Mother Church and the Political Conditions Under Which It Grew . . . 1607-1814,* 2 vols. (Richmond, Virginia Historical Society, 1947-1952), 1:147.

19. *Recs. Va. Co.,* 3:208.

20. *Va. Statutes,* 1:122-123.

21. H. R. McIlwaine, ed., *Minutes of the Council and General Court of Colonial Virginia* (Richmond, The Colonial Press, 1924), p. 104; *Va. Statutes,* 1:144.

22. *Recs. Va. Co.,* 4:581. However, the assembly ordered that whenever two holidays fell together between the Annunciation and Michaelmas (which was the growing season from 25 March to 29 September), only the first was to be observed, "by reason of our necessities."

23. *Va. Statutes,* 1:155-156.

24. McIlwaine, *Minutes*, pp. 33, 39, 107-108, 194.

25. Susie M. Ames, ed., *County Court Records of Accomack-Northampton, Virginia, 1632-1640,* American Legal Records, 7 (Washington, American Historical Association, 1954), pp. xv, 128-129 (quotation); and idem, ed., *County Court Records of Accomack-Northampton, Virginia, 1640-1645* (Charlottesville, The Virginia Historical Society, 1973), pp. 179, 182-185. See also idem, *Studies of the Virginia Eastern Shore in the Seventeenth Century* (Richmond, The Dietz Press, 1940).

26. *Va. Statutes,* 1:261, 263.

27. Philip Alexander Bruce, *Institutional History of Virginia in the Seventeenth Century,* 2 vols. (New York, G. P. Putnam's Sons, 1910), 1:65; Brydon, *Virginia's Mother Church,* 1:91-93; *Va. Statutes,* 1:240; 2:51; 1:309.

28. Bruce, *Institutional History,* 1:29-30, 31; Beverly Fleet, ed., *Virginia County Abstracts,* 1st ser., 34 vols. (Richmond, n.d.), 31:69.

29. *Va. Statutes,* 1:311, 433, 434. The 1646 act used the word "Sabbath" in the title and "Lord's Day" in the text. This is the first usage of "Lord's Day" in Virginia statutes. Bruce, *Institutional History,* 1:31.

30. Ames, *Ct. Recs. of Accomack, 1632-1640,* p. xvii.

31. Joseph B. Felt, *The Ecclesiastical History of New England,* 2 vols. (Boston, 1855-1862), 1:471-472; Bruce, *Institutional History,* 1:30-31.

32. Bruce, *Institutional History,* 1:258.

33. Ibid., 1:31, 32, 34, 235, 238-239; *Va. Statutes,* 1:532-533; 2:48.

34. Edward Eggleston, *The Beginners of a Nation* (New York, 1897), p. 242. Eggleston portrays Calvert as covertly seeking to further Catholicism; see bk. 3, chap. 1.

35. William T. Russell, *Maryland, the Land of Sanctuary: A History of Religious Toleration in Maryland from the First Settlement until the American Revolution* (Baltimore, J. H. Furst Co., 1907).

36. J. Thomas Scharf, *History of Maryland,* 3 vols. (Baltimore, 1879), 1:54 (Article 4), 59 (Article 22).

37. William H. Browne et al., eds., *Archives of Maryland,* 72 vols. (Baltimore, 1883-1972), 5:267-268 (hereafter cited as *Md. Arch.*).

38. Andrews, *Colonial Period,* 2:288-289; *The Calvert Papers,* no. 1. Maryland Historical Society, Fund-Publication No. 28 (Baltimore, 1889), p. 132.

39. This must be remembered in using the words "freedom" or "liberty" in connection with "religion" or "conscience" as applied to early Maryland. In actual fact, there were Jews in Maryland before the 1649 "Act concerning Religion," and they apparently suffered no hardship owing to belief. See Matthew Page Andrews, *The*

Founding of Maryland (Baltimore, Williams & Wilkins Co., 1933), pp. 154, 156.

40. Thomas O'Brien Hanley, *Their Rights and Liberties: The Beginnings of Religious and Political Freedom in Maryland* (Westminster, Md., Newman Press, 1959), pp. 79-108.

41. Scharf, *History of Maryland,* 1:54 (Article 7).

42. *Md. Arch.,* 1:53.

43. Ibid., p. 33.

44. Winthrop, *Journal*, 2:180; Bradley T. Johnson, *The Foundation of Maryland and the Origin of the Act concerning Religion of April 21, 1649.* Maryland Historical Society, Fund-Publication No. 18 (Baltimore, 1883), pp. 95-122.

45. Eggleston noticed the strange anomaly of Puritans seeking refuge under a "proprietary who was a papist and who practiced toleration—two things almost equally hateful to the Puritans"; *Beginnings of a Nation,* p. 253.

46. Johnson, *Foundation of Maryland,* pp. 126-130; Andrews, *Colonial Period,* 2:310.

47. George Lynn-Lachlan Davis, *The Day-Star of American Freedom: Or, The Birth and Early Growth of Toleration, in the Province of Maryland* (New York, 1855), pp. 128-141. The question is more complicated than Davis indicates.

48. *Md. Arch.,* 1:246; Andrews, *Colonial Period,* 2:310-311.

49. *Md. Arch.,* 1:244-246. Among other wrongs made punishable by the Act were publishing or maintaining that the moral law of God contained in the Ten Commandments was no rule of Christian life, and that observation of the Lord's Day as enjoined by ordinances and laws of England was not according to or was contrary to the Word of God.

50. *Md. Arch.,* 1:119; 4:35-38; Lawrence C. Wroth, "The First Sixty Years of the Church of England in Maryland, 1632-1692," *Maryland Historical Magazine,* 11 (March 1916), 12-13, 16, 18 (hereafter cited as "Church of England in Maryland").

51. *Md. Arch.,* 1:343-344.

52. Ibid., 54:27, 41, 59, 78, 193 (quotation), 195. Also see Raphael Semmes, *Crime and Punishment in Early Maryland* (Baltimore, Johns Hopkins Press, 1938), pp. 163-165.

53. Ibid., 1:83; 41:144-146, 566-567; Wroth, "Church of England in Maryland," p. 12. As for the ordinance of 1639, the proprietor had initially proposed "that Holy Church within this Province shall have all her rights liberties and immunities safe whole and inviolable in all things." The assembly had changed the language to read as quoted above. *Md. Arch.,* 1:40. On this subject see also Andrews, *Colonial Period,* 1:40-83; Matthew Page Andrews, *History of Maryland: Province and State* (Garden City, Doubleday, Doran & Co., 1929), pp. 107-108; Hanley, *Rights and Liberties,* pp. 100-108, and Eggleston, *Beginnings of a Nation,* p. 251.

54. *Md. Arch.,* 2:414-415; 7:51-53.

55. Philip Alexander Bruce, *Social Life of Virginia in the Seventeenth Century* (Richmond, Whittet & Shepperson, 1907), pp. 235, 218-222, 194-210, 241-244. Carl Bridenbaugh, *Myths and Realities: Societies of the Colonial South* (Baton Rouge, Louisiana State University Press, 1952), and Jane Carson, *Colonial Virginians at Play*

(Charlottesville, Colonial Williamsburg, 1965) deal primarily with the eighteenth century, but they also illuminate the earlier period.

56. Goodwin, *Colonial Church in Virginia,* pp. 90-91.

57. *Va. Statutes,* 1:457; 2:86; *Md. Arch.,* 2:413; 68:42.

58. H. R. McIlwaine, ed., *Executive Journals of the Council of Colonial Virginia, 1680-1739,* 4 vols. (Richmond, Virginia State Library, 1925-1930), 1:269.

59. Brydon, *Virginia's Mother Church,* 1:173, 174, 180, 190. In 1697, however, there were twenty-two ministers in fifty parishes; Ames, *Virginia Eastern Shore,* p. 218.

60. *Va. Statutes,* 1:290; 2:48, 204; Brydon, *Virginia's Mother Church,* 1:184-186. Two of the holy days commemorated deliverance from Indian massacres, one fast recalled the execution of Charles I, and a feast celebrated the Restoration of Charles II. Other holy days were established after 1662.

61. Bruce, *Institutional History,* 1:32, 35-36; Thomas Jefferson Wertenbaker, *The First Americans, 1607-1690* (New York, Macmillan Co., 1927), p. 270; Ames, *Virginia Eastern Shore,* pp. 184-185.

62. John B. Boddie, *Colonial Surrey* (Richmond, The Dietz Press, 1948), pp. 84-85; Bruce, *Institutional History,* 1:13, 32, 34, 242; Leonard W. Labaree, ed., *Royal Instructions to British Colonial Governors, 1670-1776,* 2 vols. (New York, D. Appleton-Century Co., 1935), 2:495 (quotation).

63. Quoted in Bruce, *Institutional History,* 1:33; Mary N. Stanard, *Colonial Virginia: Its People and Customs* (Philadelphia, J. P. Lippincott and Co., 1917), p. 328.

64. Brydon, *Virginia's Mother Church,* 1:279-287; *Va. Statutes,* 3:71-72.

65. Although details are lacking, the legislative history of the enactment can be followed in official records. The dispute between the Council and the House seems not to have turned on provisions regarding the Sabbath but upon punishment of fornication, adultery, and blasphemy, all of which were to be made to conform to instructions of the Crown and the law of England. H. R. McIlwaine, ed., *Journals of the House of Burgesses of Virginia,* [1619-1702], 3 vols. (Richmond, Virginia State Library, 1913-1915), 2:350, 353, 354, 359-360; H. R. McIlwaine, ed., *Legislative Journals of the Council of Colonial Virginia,* 3 vols. (Richmond, The Colonial Press, 1918-1919), 1:141. Yet the act as passed does not agree with what the Council seems to have demanded and got. Hening, *Va. Statutes,* 3:71-75.

66. McIlwaine, *Jnls. of House of Burgesses,* 2:460, 461, 478; McIlwaine, *Jnls. of Council,* 1:195, 196, 199. These records indicate that the House of Burgesses and the Council agreed on a new Sabbath law in 1693 which omitted reference to fornication and adultery as well as blasphemy, but no such enactment appears in the *Va. Statutes* for that year. In 1696, however, the General Assembly included provisions relative to the Lord's Day in a statute entitled "An act for punishment of fornication and seaverall other sins and offences." *Va. Statutes,* 3:137-140. See also Bruce, *Institutional History,* 1:34.

67. Bruce, *Social Life,* p. 196; H. R. McIlwaine, ed., *Jnls. of House of Burgesses,* 3:66, 158.

68. *Va. Statutes*, 3:170-171. The English law required that all persons frequent divine service on the Lord's Day in an approved assembly of religious worship. Bruce, *Institutional History,* 1:35, says that in 1699, "the General Assembly adopted a law which provided that any adult failing to be present at some form of religious services should be fined." His implication is that attendance every Sunday is demanded; but the important words of the Virginia statute (*Va. Statutes,* 3:170) are "refuse to resort . . . once in two monthes to heare devine service upon the sabbath day," words which clearly differ from both the English statute and Bruce's interpretation of the Virginia statute.

69. Seiler, "The Church of England as the Established Church in Seventeenth-Century Virginia," p. 497.

70. McIlwaine, *Jnls. of House of Burgesses,* 3:163, 164, 166, 178, 179, 181, 183; McIlwaine, *Jnls. of Council,* 1:264, 265, 266, 267, 269, 276.

71. *Va. Statutes,* 3:360-361.

72. Wroth, "Church of England in Maryland," pp. 25-34.

73. *Md. Arch.,* 5:130-132 (quotation p. 131).

74. Ibid., pp. 133-134, 252-253.

75. Wroth, "Church of England in Maryland," pp. 24.

76. *Md. Arch.,* 13:147-150.

77. Wroth, "Church of England in Maryland," p. 35.

78. Ibid., p. 38; Theodore C. Gambrall, *Studies in the Civil, Social and Ecclesiastical History of Early Maryland* (New York, 1893), p. 131; Davidson, *Establishment of the English Church,* pp. 25-36.

79. *Md. Arch.,* 13:425-427.

80. The king disallowed laws of 1696 and 1700 on legal technicalities, with the result that the church was temporarily disestablished from 1696 until 1703. See Wroth, "Church of England in Maryland," p. 36.

81. Gambrall, *History of Early Maryland,* p. 133. At least seven churches were existent in 1692. Wroth, "The First Sixty Years of the Church of England in Maryland," p. 39. Wroth (p. 16) says that 49 clergymen officiated at various times prior to 1700, and of these 22 had been in Maryland before 1692. Presumably he speaks only of ministers of the Church of England.

82. *Md. Arch.,* 19:419-420; 34:736.

83. Ibid., 26:435 (quotation); 34:735.

5. A Light to the Nation

1. The writings of the Puritans themselves offer the best evidence of their views on these matters. Among helpful secondary works are Giorgio Spini, *Autobiografia della Giovane America: La Storiografia Americana dai Padri Pellegrini all' Indepedenza* (Autobiography of early America: American historiography from the Pilgrim Fathers to Independence; Turin, Giulio Einaudi, 1968), pp. 5-94; the works by Haller, Baker, and Tuveson cited in Chapter 2, n. 13; Perry Miller, *The New England Mind: From Colony to Providence* (Cambridge, Mass., Harvard University Press, 1953); and Robert Middlekauff, *The Mathers: Three Generations of Puritan Intellectuals, 1596-1728* (New York, Oxford University Press, 1971).

2. William Bradford, *History of Plymouth Plantation, 1620-1647,* ed. W. C. Ford et al., 2 vols. (Boston, Houghton Mifflin Co., 1912), 2:329; 1:446-447. The quotation combines two separate phrases in a way that is entirely consonant with Bradford's outlook. Bradford's *History,* first published in 1856, was written between 1630 and 1650.

3. Ibid., 2:330 and passim.

4. John Cotton, *Gods Promise to His Plantations* (London, 1630), Old South Leaflets, 3, no. 53 (Boston, 1894), p. 5 (italics omitted). See also Edwin D. Mead, "John Cotton's Farewell Sermon to Winthrop's Company at Southampton," *PMHS,* 3d ser., 1 (1908), 101-115; Winthrop, *Journal,* 1:400.

5. [Edward Johnson], *Johnson's Wonder-Working Providence, 1628-1651,* ed. J. Franklin Jameson (New York, Charles Scribner's Sons, 1910), pp. 23-25 (italics omitted). For material on Johnson and his History, see Jameson's Introduction; Samuel E. Morison in the *DAB;* Sacvan Bercovitch, "The Historiography of Johnson's *Wonder-Working Providence,*" *Essex Institute Historical Collections,* 104 (April 1968), 138-161, and Charles E. Banks, *The Planters of the Commonwealth* ([1930], reprt. Baltimore, Genealogical Publishing Co., 1967), p. 188. Johnson's book was originally published late in 1653 but under the date of 1654 with the title *A History of New-England, from the English Planting in the Yeere 1628 untill the Yeere 1652.*

6. For the larger context, see George L. Haskins, *Law and Authority in Early Massachusetts: A Study in Tradition and Design* (New York, Macmillan Co., 1960); and Alexander M. Bickel, "Much More than Law Is Needed," *New York Times Magazine,* 9 August 1964.

7. William Bradford and Nathaniel Morton, "History of the Plymouth Church, 1620-1680," in *Plymouth Church Records, 1620-1859,* 2 vols. (New York, The University Press, 1920-1923), 1:92-107 (quotation p. 107). These records are also printed in the *PCSM,* 22-23 (1920-1923).

8. Winthrop, *Journal,* 2:412.

9. Compare Louis B. Wright, *Middle-Class Culture in Elizabethan England* (Chapel Hill, University of North Carolina Press, 1935), p. 462, who argues that the taste for literature of warning flourished with renewed vigor as the American Puritans pondered the wrath of an avenging deity. Such a sweeping judgment fails to distinguish between early and late Puritanism in America.

10. Increase Mather, "To the Reader," in Cotton Mather, *A Good Evening for the Best of Dayes* (Boston, 1708). On Cotton's influence in America, see Cotton Mather, *Magnalia Christi Americana,* bk. 3, p. 27.

11. The original of this manuscript of three and a half folio pages of crabbed handwriting is in the Emmanuel College Library, Cambridge University. Chester N. Greenough in *PCSM,* 19 (1918), 366-367, and Julius H. Tuttle, "Writings of Rev. John Cotton," in *Bibliographical Essays, A Tribute to Wilberforce Eames* (Cambridge, Mass., Harvard University Press, 1924), p. 365, both noted its existence. My edition of the text, to be published by the Colonial Society of Massachusetts, will make the document itself available for the first time.

12. William Pynchon, *A Treatise of the Sabbath . . . Whereunto Is Annexed a Treatise of Holy Time* (London, 1655 [1654]). Pynchon also wrote *The Time When the First Sabbath Was Ordained* (London, 1654).

13. Bradford, *Plymouth Plantation*, 1:176; *Mass. Bay Recs.*, 1:395; Winthrop, *Journal*, 1:130-131 (italics mine).

14. See D. de Sola Pool, "Hebrew Learning among the Puritans of New England Prior to 1700," *Publications of the American Jewish Historical Society*, 20 (1911), 31-83; Kenneth B. Murdock, "The Puritans and the New Testament," *PCSM*, 25 (1924), 239-243; Clifford K. Shipton, "The Hebraic Background of Puritanism," *Publications of the American Jewish Historical Society*, 47 (March 1958), 140-153 (quotation p. 141); and Eugene R. Fingerhut, "Were the Massachusetts Puritans Hebraic?" *New England Quarterly*, 40 (December 1967), 521-531.

15. A reprint, with a Preface by Samuel J. McCormick, was published in New York, 1877; see pp. 57-61.

16. Ibid., p. 59; Walter F. Prince, "An Examination of Peters's 'Blue Laws,' " *Annual Report of the American Historical Association for the Year 1898* (Washington, 1899), pp. 97-138. A prominent target of Prince's criticism was J. Hammond Trumbull, ed., *The True-Blue Laws of Connecticut and New Haven and the False Blue-Laws Invented by the Rev. Samuel Peters* (Hartford, 1876).

17. Edw[ard] Winslow, *New England's Salamander* (London, 1647), pp. 23-24.

18. *Plymouth Church Records*, 1:106.

19. Charles Francis Adams, "Some Phases of Sexual Morality and Church Discipline in Colonial New England," *PMHS*, 2d ser., 6 (1891), 494; Daniel Wait Howe, *The Puritan Republic of the Massachusetts Bay in New England* (Indianapolis, 1899), p. 163; Samuel Adams Drake, *History of Middlesex County, Massachusetts*, 2 vols. (Boston, 1880), 2:371.

20. Bradford, *Plymouth Plantation*, 1:244, 245-246.

21. See W. DeLoss Love, Jr., *The Fast and Thanksgiving Days of New England* (Boston, 1895).

22. Bradford, *Plymouth Plantation*, 1:230-231, briefly mentions the event. The best account is in Henry Martyn Dexter, ed., *Mourt's Relation, or Journal of the Plantation at Plymouth* (Boston, 1865), p. 133 (source of quotation). The bulk of this work was written by William Bradford and Edward Winslow.

23. George D. Langdon, Jr., *Pilgrim Colony: A History of New Plymouth, 1620-1691* (New Haven, Yale University Press, 1966), is the most recent general account; older valuable histories include Roland G. Usher, *The Pilgrims and their History* (New York, Macmillan Co., 1918); Henry M. Dexter and Morton Dexter, *The England and Holland of the Pilgrims* (Boston, Houghton, Mifflin and Co., 1906), and Edward Arber, ed., *The Story of the Pilgrim Fathers, 1606-1623* (London, 1897).

24. Johnson, *Wonder-Working Providence*, p. 59.

25. *The Letters from and to Sir Dudley Carleton, Knt. during His Embassy in Holland*, [ed. Philip Yorke], 3d ed. (London, 1780), p. 380. The letter was written on 22 July 1619.

26. Petrus J. Blok, *History of the People of the Netherlands*, trans. Oscar A. Bierstadt and Ruth Putnam, 5 vols. (New York, G. Putnam's Sons, 1898-1912), 3:chap. 14; Herbert D. Foster, "Liberal Calvinism," in *Collected Papers* (n.p., privately printed, 1929), pp. 106-146; Philip Schaff, *The Creeds of Christendom*, 1:509-515; John Hales, *Golden Remains* (London, 1659), pp. 3-4.

27. Bradford, *Plymouth Plantation*, 1:53-55 (quotation p. 55). I have put Bradford's third point last. Though Bradford feared that incessant labor induced premature aging, the leaders were relatively young by present standards: in 1620, Brewster was 56; Robinson, 45; Bradford, 32; and Winslow, 26.

28. Ed. Howard M. Chapin (Providence, Club for Colonial Reprints, 1916), p. 89.

29. Ed. Howard J. Hall (New York, Scholars' Facsimiles & Reprints, 1937), p. 3.

30. *Mourt's Relation*, pp. 80, 82-83, 90, 97.

31. Edmund S. Morgan, *Visible Saints: The History of a Puritan Idea*, pp. 11-63; *Plymouth Church Records*, 1:64.

32. *Ply. Col. Recs.*, 11:3-5. See also Brigham, *Laws of Plymouth*, pp. 28-35, for some additional laws of the early years, and *Plymouth Church Records*, 1:109. The needs of defense and agriculture also dictated the pattern of settlement. The fort built on Burial Hill in 1622 was used for worship until a meetinghouse was constructed in 1648.

33. *Mourt's Relation*, pp. 83-89 (quotation p. 89).

34. Ibid., pp. 98-111 (quotations pp. 109, 111). Wretched conditions in the Indian village contributed to speeding the emissaries home.

35. Scarcely 50 of the 101 persons who landed at Plymouth in December 1620 were alive the following April, and more died before the first ship arrived in November 1621. See also Bradford, *Plymouth Plantation*, 1:407n, 317, 325-327.

36. Ibid., pp. 362-363.

37. Ibid., pp. 380-397, 399 (first quotation), 402 (second quotation).

38. Ibid., pp. 384, 384n.

39. *Governor William Bradford's Letter Book* (Boston, Massachusetts Society of Mayflower Descendants, 1906), p. 13.

40. Quoted in William Bradford, *Of Plymouth Plantation, 1620-1647*, ed. Samuel Eliot Morison (New York, Alfred A. Knopf, 1959), p. 204n. On Morton and Merrymount, see Charles Francis Adams, *Three Episodes of Massachusetts History*, 2 vols. (Boston, 1892), chaps. 10-11, 13; and Thomas Morton, *The New English Canaan*, ed. Charles Francis Adams, Jr., The Prince Society (Boston, 1883), pp. 1-98.

41. Morton, *New English Canaan*, p. 279.

42. Bradford, *Plymouth Plantation*, 2:48.

43. J. Franklin Jameson, ed., *Narratives of New Netherland, 1609-1664* (New York, Charles Scribner's Sons, 1909), p. 122.

44. Bradford, *Plymouth Plantation*, 2:152.

45. Ibid., p. 152n.

46. London, 1634, ed. C[harles] D[eane], The Prince Society (Boston, 1865), p. 14.

47. Bradford, *Plymouth Plantation*, 2:152.

48. Ibid., p. 153; Reyner and Brewster to the Rev. Brethren of the Church of Christ in Boston, 5 August 1639. Cotton Papers, Boston Public Library. Also in Bradford, *Plymouth Plantation*, 2:275n-276n.

49. *Ply. Col. Recs.*, 11:18; also in Brigham, *Laws of Plymouth*, p. 48.

50. *Ply. Col. Recs.*, 1:44; Brigham, *Laws of Plymouth,* p. 61.

51. *Ply. Col. Recs.*, 1:75, 87, 92, 74; 2:4, 140, 156.

52. Ibid., p. 44; Bradford, *Plymouth Plantation,* 2:328-330.

53. Bradford, *Plymouth Plantation,* 2:369.

54. Joseph B. Felt, *The Ecclesiastical History of New England,* 2:459; Robert E. Wall, Jr., *Massachusetts Bay: The Crucial Decade, 1640-1650* (New Haven, Yale University Press, 1972), chap. 4.

55. *Winthrop Papers,* 5:56.

56. *Ply. Col. Recs.*, 11:57-58.

57. One hundred Cambridge men and another 32 from Oxford emigrated to Massachusetts between 1629 and 1645. The proportion of university graduates to families was high, ranging from one to either 32 or 44 families, depending upon which total population estimates are used. By contrast, Plymouth Colony was impoverished intellectually. See Samuel Eliot Morison, *The Founding of Harvard College* (Cambridge, Mass., Harvard University Press, 1935), pp. 40, 118, 141n, 359-361; Bradford, *Plymouth Plantation,* 1:134n.

58. This and the following three paragraphs draw on Frances Rose-Troup, *The Massachusetts Bay Company and Its Predecessors* (New York, The Grafton Press, 1930); idem, *John White, the Patriarch of Dorchester [Dorset] and the Founder of Massachusetts, 1575-1648* (New York, G. P. Putnam's Sons, 1930); and Andrews, *Colonial Period,* 1:344-374.

59. Andrews, *Colonial Period,* 1:346.

60. Ibid., p. 360.

61. The charter is printed in *Mass. Bay Recs.,* 1:3-20, and more recently in *PMHS,* 62 (1930), 251-273. Also see the *Winthrop Papers,* 1:295-310; 2:106-149.

62. Charles E. Banks, *The Winthrop Fleet of 1630* (Boston, Houghton Mifflin Co., 1930), pp. 46-53; Darrett B. Rutman, *Winthrop's Boston: Portrait of a Puritan Town, 1630-1649* (Chapel Hill, University of North Carolina Press, 1965), p. 136.

63: Banks, *Winthrop Fleet,* pp. 33-45. The white population of New England increased from less than a thousand souls in 1630 to something between seventeen and twenty-five thousand in 1640. See Morison, *Founding of Harvard College,* pp. 253, 360-361; and Andrews, *Colonial Period,* 1:497.

64. *Winthrop Papers,* 2:282-295 (quotations pp. 292, 293, 294).

65. Ibid., p. 295.

66. Rutman, *Winthrop's Boston,* pp. 23-40, 280-283; Andrews, *Colonial Period,* 1:500.

67. This and the next three paragraphs draw upon Edmund S. Morgan, *The Puritan Dilemma: The Story of John Winthrop* (Boston, Little, Brown and Co., 1958), pp. 84-100; Haskins, *Law and Authority,* pp. 25-65; and Arthur H. Buffinton, "The Massachusetts Experiment of 1630," *PCSM,* 32 (1937), 308-320.

68. Eleven assistants emigrated to Massachusetts in 1630, but two returned to England very shortly and one died, leaving only eight assistants in the colony by October 1630. There appears to have been only one freeman in the colony in addition to the governor, deputy governor, and the assistants; Haskins, *Law and Authority,* p. 238n.

69. *Mass. Bay Recs.*, 1:79, 74, 87. On 23 August 1630 the Court of Assistants appointed the governor, deputy governor, and four assistants justices of the peace and gave them power like their English counterparts to reform abuses and punish offenders.

70. *Mass. Bay Recs.*, 1:79-80, 366. Haskins estimates the proportion as not much more than 7 or 8 percent. *Law and Authority*, p. 29.

71. For this and the next paragraph, see especially Morgan, *Visible Saints*, chaps. 1-3. Also see Charles E. Park, "Two Ruling Elders of the First Church in Boston: Thomas Leverett and Thomas Oliver," *PCSM*, 13 (1912), 82-95.

72. Edward Howes to John Winthrop, Jr., *Winthrop Papers*, 3:100-101.

73. Charles E. Park, "Excommunication in Colonial Churches," *PCSM*, 12 (1911), 321-332. Also see George L. Haskins, "Ecclesiastical Antecedents of Criminal Punishment in Early Massachusetts," *PMHS*, 72 (1963), 21-35.

74. Emil Oberholzer, Jr., *Delinquent Saints: Disciplinary Action in the Early Congregational Churches of Massachusetts* (New York, Columbia University Press, 1956), pp. 43-77, 3.

75. Larzer Ziff, "The Social Bond of Church Covenant," *American Quarterly*, 10 (Winter 1958), 456; Park, "Excommunication in Colonial Churches," p. 330.

76. Richard D. Pierce, ed., "The Records of the First Church in Boston, 1630-1868," *PCSM*, 39-41 (1961), 1:52, 54. On Mattocke, see also ibid., pp. 26-27, 53-55.

77. *Mass. Bay Recs.*, 1:405, 109.

78. John Winthrop, Jr., to Henry Oldenberg, Hartford, 12 November 1668, *PMHS*, [16] (1878), 237.

79. Wells to Wallington, 1633, in the N[ehemiah] Wallington Papers, Sloane Manuscripts, Library of Congress. Wells is not identifiable in the *Mass. Bay Recs.* or in other books on the early planters of Massachusetts Bay.

80. *Mass. Bay Recs.*, 1:82, 369; Charles E. Banks, *Topographical Dictionary of 2885 English Emigrants to New England, 1620-1650* (Philadelphia, Elijah E. Brownell, 1937), p. 119; idem, *Winthrop Fleet*, p. 59 (which errs on a date).

81. *Bradford's Letter Book*, p. 57. See also *Winthrop Papers*, 2:309, 312, 314, 320.

82. Alexander Young, ed., *Chronicles of the First Planters of the Colony of Massachusetts Bay* (Boston, 1846), p. 385; see also pp. 311-319.

83. *Mass. Bay Recs.*, 1:106.

84. Ibid., pp. 140, 142-143.

85. The background material on Connecticut in this and the next three paragraphs is drawn from Andrews, *Colonial Period*, 2:67-143; idem, "The Beginnings of the Connecticut Towns," *Annals of the American Academy of Political and Social Science*, 1 (October 1890), 165-191; Dorothy Deming, *The Settlement of the Connecticut Towns*, Tercentenary Commission of the State of Connecticut, Committee on Historical Publications, no. 6 (n.p., n.d.), 1-75; and Franklin B. Dexter, "The History of Connecticut, as Illustrated by the Names of Her Towns," *Proceedings of the American Antiquarian Society*, n.s., 3 (1885), 421-448.

86. John M. Taylor, *Roger Ludlow: The Colonial Lawmaker* (New York, G. P. Putnam's, 1900), pp. 57-65; *Conn. Col. Recs.*, 1:20, 21.

87. Several diaries in the Henry E. Huntington Library, San Marino, California, demonstrate the point.

88. *Conn. Col. Recs.*, 1:73, 95, 96, 150. Also see "Hartford Town Votes, I: 1635-1716," *Collections of the Connecticut Historical Society*, 6 (1897), 2, 12, 57.

89. "Hartford Town Votes," pp. 65-66.

90. Isabel M. Calder, *The New Haven Colony* (New Haven, Yale University Press, 1934), chaps. 1-3; Andrews, *Colonial Period*, 2:144-194.

91. Edward E. Atwater, *History of the Colony of New Haven* (New Haven, 1881), pp. 72-73; Calder, *New Haven Colony*, p. 82.

92. *New Haven Town Recs.*, 1:392-397 (quotations p. 393). Davenport's remarks date from 1652, but he and Eaton undoubtedly thought the same way in 1638.

93. *New Haven Col. Recs.*, 1:12; Calder, *New Haven Colony*, pp. 40-44, 48, 106-129.

94. *New Haven Col. Recs.*, 1:12, 13-17, 20-21.

6. Roger Williams and the Antinomians

1. *Mass. Bay Recs.*, 1:95, 117-119.

2. Winthrop, *Journal*, 1:389; 2:67; 1:388, 191.

3. *Mass. Bay Recs.*, 1:137, 147; Winthrop, *Journal*, 1:191, 211.

4. Winthrop, *Journal*, 1:211-214 (quotation p. 212).

5. *Mass. Bay Recs.*, 1:174.

6. Winthrop, *Journal*, 1:240-241. On Cotton's code see Worthington C. Ford, "Cotton's 'Moses his Judicials,' " *PMHS*, 2d ser., 16 (1903), 274-284; and Isabel M. Calder, "John Cotton's 'Moses His Judicials,' " *PCSM*, 28 (1935), 86-94.

7. [John Cotton], "An Abstract of the Laws of New England," in [Thomas Hutchinson], ed., *A Collection of Original Papers Relative to the History of the Colony of Massachusetts-Bay* (Boston, 1769), p. 179. Reprinted by William H. Whitmore and William S. Appleton, eds., [*The Thomas*] *Hutchinson Papers*, 2 vols., The Prince Society (Albany, 1865). In both, the Cotton code (pp. 161-179 and 1:183-205 respectively) has all the marginal citations of Scripture. Many of these references are lacking in the *Abstract* printed in *CMHS*, 1st ser., 5 (1798; reprinted 1835), 173-187.

8. Hutchinson, *Original Papers*, pp. 168, 173.

9. Ford, "Cotton's 'Moses his Judicials,' " pp. 281, 284 (quotation).

10. Winthrop, *Journal*, 2:253; also see *Mass. Bay Recs.*, 2:93.

11. Quoted in W[illem] Schenk, *The Concern for Social Justice in the Puritan Revolution* (London, Longmans, Green and Co., 1948), p. 136. On Aspinwall, see Thomas Hutchinson, *The History of the Colony and Province of Massachusetts-Bay*, ed. Lawrence S. Mayo, 3 vols. (Cambridge, Mass., Harvard University Press, 1936), 1:61n; see also ibid., p. 373n. In 1642, however, Massachusetts provided the death penalty for a third crime of Sabbath burglary or robbery if done presumptuously.

12. Williams to Major Mason, Providence, 22 June 1670, in *The Complete Writings of Roger Williams*, 7 vols. (New York, Russell & Russell, 1963), 6:347. The first six volumes of the *Complete Writings* are a reprint of Williams' works as originally issued in the *Publications of the Narragansett Club*, 1st ser. (Providence, 1866-1874). Hereafter Williams' writings and John Cotton's exchange with him in the

Complete Writings will be cited by title, with the date of each piece given on the first entry, followed by volume and page references.

13. On Williams, see Mauro Calamandrei, "Neglected Aspects of Roger Williams' Thought," *Church History*, 21 (September 1952), 239-258; Perry Miller, *Roger Williams: His Contribution to the American Tradition* (Indianapolis, Bobbs-Merrill Co., 1953); Ola E. Winslow, *Master Roger Williams: A Biography* (New York, Macmillan Co., 1957), which contains many inaccuracies and some erroneous assertions about Williams and the Sabbath; and Edmund S. Morgan, *Roger Williams: The Church and the State* (New York, Harcourt, Brace & World, 1967).

14. Williams to John Cotton (son of Williams' antagonist), Providence, 25 March 1671, 6:356; Winthrop, *Journal,* 1:63.

15. Williams, "Mr. Cottons Letter . . . Examined and Answered" (1644), 1:321.

16. Winthrop, *Journal,* 1:188, 194.

17. Cotton, "John Cotton's Answer to Roger Williams" (1647), 2:106; Winthrop, *Journal,* 1:204; Williams, "Mr. Cottons Letter . . . Examined and Answered," 1:323.

18. *Mass. Bay Recs.,* 1:160-161; Winthrop, *Journal,* 1:204. The only entry in the *Mass. Bay Recs.* relative to the trial and sentence is that cited. The charter empowered the Massachusetts Bay Company to "expulse" all who attempted its detriment or annoyance, and Massachusetts Bay banished nineteen persons before Williams, five for villainy or dishonesty, the others for acts or speech endangering civil or ecclesiastical order.

19. As stated in "The Bloudy Tenent Washed" (1647), 2:164n-165n.

20. *Mass. Bay Recs.,* 1:140, 142-143; Winthrop, *Journal,* 1:193-194.

21. Cotton, "A Letter of Mr. John Cottons . . . to Mr. Williams" (1643), 1:297.

22. Miller, *Roger Williams,* pp. 33-38; idem, "Roger Williams," *Complete Writings,* 7:10-19.

23. Williams, "Mr. Cottons Letter . . . Examined and Answered," 1:392 (quotation), 356-358; Williams, "The Bloudy Tenent of Persecution" (1644), 3:174, 184, 200, 316, 317-380.

24. Cotton, "A Letter of Mr. John Cottons . . . to Mr. Williams," 1:299-311, 344-396; Cotton, "John Cotton's Answer to Roger Williams," 2:92-237.

25. Cotton, "John Cotton's Answer to Roger Williams," 2:158.

26. Cotton, "A Letter of Mr. John Cottons . . . to Mr. Williams," 1:303.

27. Williams, "The Bloudy Tenent of Persecution," 3:66-67.

28. Williams, "Mr. Cottons Letter . . . Examined and Answered," 1:329-334; Cotton, "John Cotton's Answer to Roger Williams," 2:66-233; Williams, "The Hireling Ministry None of Christs" (1652), 7:149-187; Williams, "George Fox Digg'd out of His Burrowes" (1676), 5:102-104.

29. Williams, "Mr. Cottons Letter . . . Examined and Answered," 1:326-327, 328 (quotation), 335.

30. Williams, "The Bloudy Tenent of Persecution," 3:90-128, 146-175, 223-290, 333-352.

31. Williams, "Mr. Cottons Letter . . . Examined and Answered," 1:335; Wil-

liams, "Queries of Highest Consideration" (1644), 2:259-260; Williams, "The Bloudy Tenent of Persecution," 3:146-175, 214, 249-250, 258-259.

32. Williams, "Queries of Highest Consideration," 2:260; Williams, "The Bloudy Tenent of Persecution," 3:289-290.

33. Williams, "The Bloudy Tenent of Persecution," 3:237 (quotation); Williams, "Queries of Highest Consideration," 2:266.

34. Cotton, "John Cotton's Answer to Roger Williams," 2:19.

35. See William Gammell, *Life of Roger Williams* (Boston, 1846), pp. 38-39, and Irving B. Richman, *Rhode Island: Its Making and Its Meaning,* 2d ed., 2 vols. in 1 (New York, G. P. Putnam's Sons, 1908), p. 17.

36. John Winthrop, "A Short Story of the Rise, Reign, and Ruine of the Antinomians, Familists and Libertines" (1644), in David D. Hall, ed., *The Antinomian Controversy, 1636-1638: A Documentary History* (Middletown, Conn., Wesleyan University Press, 1968), pp. 262, 310.

37. Emery Battis, *Saints and Sectaries: Anne Hutchinson and the Antinomian Controversy in the Massachusetts Bay Colony* (Chapel Hill, University of North Carolina Press, 1962), treats the life of Anne Hutchinson. This book is trustworthy as to the facts but questionable in some of its interpretations.

38. Winthrop, "A Short Story" (1644), in Hall, *Antinomian Controversy,* pp. 263-264, 267-269; "The Examination of Mrs. Anne Hutchinson at the Court at Newtown" (1637), in Hall, *Antinomian Controversy,* pp. 314-318.

39. Winthrop, *Journal,* 1:239; Hall, *Antinomian Controversy,* pp. 3-20.

40. Tiziano Bonazzi, *Il Sacro Esperimento: Teologia e Politica nell' America Puritana* (The holy experiment: Theology and politics in Puritan America; Bologna, Il Mulino, 1970); Norman Pettit, *The Heart Prepared: Grace and Conversion in Puritan Spiritual Life,* chap. 5; Hall, *Antinomian Controversy,* pp. 10-20; Winthrop, *Journal,* 1:255, 281-282.

41. Winthrop, "A Short Story," pp. 269-270; "The Examination of Mrs. Anne Hutchinson at the Court at Newtown," pp. 317-326.

42. Winthrop, *Journal,* 1:240.

43. Ibid., pp. 241-243, 246, 252-253.

44. John Cotton, "Sixteene Questions of Serious and Necessary Consequence" (1644), "The Elders Reply" (1637?), and "Mr. Cottons Rejoynder" (1637?), in Hall, *Antinomian Controversy,* pp. 43-151.

45. Winthrop, *Journal,* 1:247-250 (quotations pp. 247, 250).

46. Ibid., pp. 256, 255.

47. Ibid., p. 255.

48. *Mass. Bay Recs.,* 1:189; Winthrop, *Journal,* 1:257 (quotation).

49. Winthrop, *Journal,* 1:262, 265; *Mass. Bay Recs.,* 1:196.

50. Winthrop, "A Short Story," pp. 220, 221, 222, 231, 237-238 (Errors and Confutations nos. 4-5, 9, 13, 44, 69).

51. Ibid., pp. 227, 228 (first quotation), 229, 232, 234 (second quotation), 235, 237, 239 (Errors and Confutations nos. 33, 36, 38, 48, 57, 59, 67, 72).

52. Ibid., pp. 230-231 (Errors and Confutations nos. 40, 42, 43).

53. [Edward Johnson], *Johnson's Wonder-Working Providence, 1628-1651,* pp. 134-135.

54. Winthrop, *Journal,* 1:291-296; *Mass. Bay Recs.,* 1:205-212.

55. "The Examination of Mrs. Anne Hutchinson at the Court at Newtown," pp. 311-348.

56. "A Report of the Trial of Mrs. Anne Hutchinson before the Church in Boston" (1638), in Hall, *Antinomian Controversy,* pp. 349-388.

57. See, for example, Winthrop, "A Short Story," pp. 203-204, 264. But cf. *God's Plot: The Paradoxes of Puritan Piety, Being the Autobiography and Journal of Thomas Shepard,* p. 25n.

58. Winthrop, *Journal,* 1:304. See also Winthrop, "A Short Story," p. 216.

7. The Letter and the Spirit

1. *Mass. Bay Recs.,* 1:222, 279, 346; Winthrop, *Journal,* 1:388; and Isabel Calder, "John Cotton's 'Moses His Judicials,' " pp. 88-91. On Ward, see Janette Bohi, "Nathaniel Ward, A Sage of Old Ipswich," *Essex Institute Historical Collections,* 99 (January 1963), 3-32.

2. *Mass. Bay Recs.,* 1:344; F. C. Gray, "Remarks on the Early Laws of Massachusetts Bay; with the Code Adopted in 1641, and Called The Body of Liberties," *CMHS,* 3d ser., 8 (1843), 191-237.

3. Thomas Shepard, *Theses Sabbaticae: Or, The Doctrine of the Sabbath,* preface, sig. b 2 [pp. 12-13].

4. Ibid., pp. 4-10 (quotation p. 4).

5. English correspondents, often writing pseudonymously or anonymously because of the controversial nature of their subject, kept John Winthrop informed about the fresh agitation of the Sabbath question stirred up by Bishop White's book, the response by Richard Byfield, *The Lords Day, the Sabbath Day* ([London?], 1636; also attributed to William Prynne), and other works. These letters, dated from September 1636 to about May 1637, are in the *Winthrop Papers,* 3:298-306, 355-363, 369-371, 380-381, 397-402.

6. Samuel Eliot Morison, *The Founding of Harvard College,* pp. 208-209; Andrew McF. Davis, "A Few Words about the Writings of Thomas Shepard," *Proceedings of the Cambridge Historical Society,* 3 (1908), 79-89. For examples of books refuted see Shepard, *Theses Sabbaticae,* pt. 1, pp. 53, 59, 87, 89 (Theses 80, 88, 116, 117).

7. John Allen of Dedham, John Cotton of Boston, Thomas Cobbett of Lynn, Thomas Hooker of Hartford, and Richard Mather of Dorchester all wrote to Shepard on the subject between 1646 and 1648. See the Index to the Hutchinson Collection, Massachusetts Archives, *s.v.* "Thomas Shepard," p. 474. The letters are in Mass. Arch., 240:103-103a, 107-108, 129, 137-140, 160-161 (Richard Mather's critique). Also see Joseph B. Felt, *The Ecclesiastical History of New England,* 1:569, 614.

8. Shepard, *Theses Sabbaticae,* pt. 1, pp. 4-21 (Theses 10-30); (quotations p. 21).

9. Ibid., pp. 21-31 (Theses 31-46).

10. Ibid., pp. 31-54 (Theses 47-80); (quotations pp. 51 and 53 respectively).

11. Ibid., pp. 54-62 (Theses 81-92).

12. Ibid., pp. 62-99 (Theses 93-119).

13. Ibid., pp. 99-151 (Theses 120-207).

14. Ibid., pt. 2 (Theses 1-44).

15. Ibid., pt. 3 (Theses 1-102). John Allen differed slightly as to the precise time when the Christian Sabbath begins; see Hutchinson Collection, Massachusetts Archives, 240:107-108.

16. Shepard, *Theses Sabbaticae,* pt. 4 (Theses 1-20); (quotation p. 48).

17. C. H. Firth and R. S. Rait, eds., *Acts and Ordinances of the Interregnum, 1642-1660,* 3 vols. (London, H. M. Stationery Office, 1911), 1:420-422; W. B. Whitaker, *Sunday in Tudor and Stuart Times,* pp. 144-153.

18. Firth and Rait, *Acts and Ordinances,* 1:598-599, 607-608, 954; Whitaker, *Sunday,* pp. 153-158.

19. Philip Schaff, *The Creeds of Christendom,* 3:648-649; Robert Cox, *The Literature of the Sabbath Question,* 1:237-244.

20. *Mass. Bay Recs.,* 3:11; Max Farrand, ed., *The Laws and Liberties of Massachusetts* (Cambridge, Mass., Harvard University Press, 1929).

21. *Laws and Liberties of Massachusetts,* pp. vii-viii.

22. Ibid., pp. 20 (Article "Ecclesiastical," sect. 14); 24 (Article "Heresie"); 13 (Article "Constables"); 4-5 (Article "Burglarie and Theft").

23. *Mass. Bay Recs.,* 1:140, 221.

24. For three presentments between 1639 and 1643, see *Mass. Bay Recs.,* 1:234, 265 (Katherine Finch), and *Essex Court Recs.,* 1:10, 51 (Jane Verin and Robert Norman, Jr.).

25. Winthrop, *Journal,* 2:36, 93, 336 (quotations).

26. Samuel Gorton, "Simplicity's Defence against Seven-Headed Policy" (London, 1646), ed. William R. Staples, *Collections [of the] Rhode Island Historical Society,* 2 (1835), 10. On Gorton, see Robert E. Wall, Jr., *Massachusetts Bay: The Crucial Decade, 1640-1650,* chap. 4.

27. Gorton, *Simplicity's Defence,* pp. 51-52, 68 (quotations), 113-114, and passim; Edward Winslow, *Hypocrisie Unmasked: A True Relation of the Proceedings of the Governor and Company of the Massachusetts against Samuel Gorton of Rhode Island,* ed. Howard M. Chapin (Providence, Club for Colonial Reprints, 1916), pp. 1-5, 33, 42, 55, and passim; Winthrop, *Journal,* 2:69-71, 102, 144-149, 165-169, 171-179, 188-189; *Mass. Bay Recs.,* 2:38, 40-41, 44, 51, 52, 53, 57.

28. *Mass. Bay Recs.,* 2:85; William H. Whitmore and William S. Appleton, eds., *[The Thomas] Hutchinson Papers,* 1:220. For the magistrates' response see ibid., pp. 243-244. Also see Wall, *Crucial Decade,* chap. 5.

29. Felt, *History of New England,* 1:580; also see Winthrop, *Journal,* 2:212-214.

30. *Mass. Bay Recs.,* 2:177-178 (Journal of the upper house); 3:99 (Journal of the lower house).

31. *Essex Court Recs.,* 1:114, 134, 158, 159, 275.

32. *Mass. Bay Recs.*, 2:177 (Journal of the upper house); 3:98-99 (Journal of the lower house).

33. *Essex Court Recs.*, 1:138. Bound to good behavior, Mary Oliver refused to give bond in 1648 and was ordered sent to Boston jail.

34. *Laws and Liberties of Massachusetts*, p. 24.

35. *Mass. Bay Recs.*, 1:209.

36. *Essex Court Recs.*, 1:50, 51, 75, 99 (quotation), 110, 135, 138; Winthrop, *Journal*, 2:52; George F. Dow, *Domestic Life in New England in the Seventeenth Century* (Topsfield, Mass., Perkins Press, 1925), p. 27.

37. Winthrop, *Journal*, 1:366. James Savage, Winthrop's nineteenth-century editor, remarked that such instances of traveling on Sunday "are now almost unknown."

38. Ibid., 2:96; Gorton, "Simplicity's Defence," pp. 113-114; *Mass. Bay Recs.*, 1:248, 336, 344; *Essex Court Recs.*, 1:133.

39. *Mass. Bay Recs.*, 1:109, 203; Everett H. Emerson, *John Cotton* (New York, Twayne Publishers, 1965), p. 92.

40. *Essex Court Recs.*, 1:10, 13, 113, 115, 134.

41. Winthrop, *Journal*, 2:54-58; *Mass. Bay Recs.*, 1:344; 2:12-13.

42. *Mass. Bay Recs.*, 2:151; *Laws and Liberties of Massachusetts*, p. 13.

43. Winthrop, *Journal*, 1:216-217; *Essex Court Recs.*, 1:18, 20; *Mass. Bay Recs.*, 1:297 (quotation); Winthrop, *Papers*, 4:247.

44. *Mass. Bay Recs.*, 2:22; *Essex Court Recs.*, 1:44, 60; *Laws and Liberties of Massachusetts*, pp. 4-5.

45. Williston Walker, *The Creeds and Platforms of Congregationalism* (New York, 1893), pp. 159-237 (text of the Platform included here); *Mass. Bay Recs.*, 3:70-72; 4:pt. 1, pp. 57-58.

46. William Greenleaf and Samuel Mather spoke for New England in asserting that "where there are no law sermons, there will be few gospel lives." See their preface to "Subjection to Christ" in *The Works of Thomas Shepard*, 3:278.

8. The New England Way

1. C. H. Firth and R. S. Rait, eds., *Acts and Ordinances of the Interregnum, 1642-1660*, 2:383-387, 423-425, 1162-1170.

2. W. B. Whitaker, *Sunday in Tudor and Stuart Times*, pp. 158-165.

3. *Diary of Thomas Burton, Esq., Member in the Parliaments of Oliver and Richard Cromwell, from 1656 to 1659*, ed. John T. Rutt, 4 vols. (London, 1828), 2:229, 260-268 (quotations p. 264).

4. Increase Mather, "To the Reader," in Cotton Mather, *A Good Evening for the Best of Dayes*, sig. A 2 [p. 2].

5. Charles Chauncy, *Gods Mercy Shewed to His People in Giving Them a Faithful Ministry and Schooles of Learning for the Continual Supplyes Thereof* (Cambridge, Mass., 1655), pp. 15-16.

6. *The Diary of Michael Wigglesworth, 1653-1657: The Conscience of a Puritan*, ed. Edmund S. Morgan (Gloucester, Mass., Peter Smith, 1970), pp. 38, 44, 66,

69-70, and passim. The *Diary* was first published in *PCSM,* 35 (1951), 311-444.

7. *Mass. Bay Recs.,* 4:pt. 1, pp. 366-367.

8. *Essex Court Recs.,* 1:174, 183, 184, 258, 360, 414, 244-245, 258.

9. Ibid., pp. 174, 184, 225, 273, 387; 2:3, 11, 39, 48.

10. Alice Morse Earle, *The Sabbath in Puritan New England* (New York, 1891), p. 247; Sidney Gunn, "Sarah Kemble Knight," *DAB;* John Josselyn, *An Account of Two Voyages to New-England* (London, 1674), p. 178.

11. *Mass. Bay Recs.,* 3:316-317.

12. Second Report of the Record Commissioners of the City of Boston, *Boston Town Records, [1634-1661]* (Boston, 1877), p. 131.

13. *Mass. Bay Recs.,* 4:pt. 1, p. 347. The 1653 and 1658 laws were combined in the Massachusetts code of 1658 under the heading "Sunday," which may be the first official use of this pagan word in New England.

14. Rufus M. Jones, *The Quakers in the American Colonies* (London, Macmillan and Co., 1911), is still useful, though it will soon be replaced by three volumes by as many different hands.

15. George Bishop, *New-England Judged, By the Spirit of the Lord,* 2 pts. (London, 1702-1703; first published 1661-1667), pp. 7, 9 (italics omitted).

16. *Mass. Bay Recs.,* 4:pt. 1, pp. 277-278.

17. Jones, *Quakers in the American Colonies,* pp. 45-54.

18. *Essex Court Recs.,* 2:49; Bishop, *New England Judged,* pp. 50-53; Jones, *Quakers in the American Colonies,* pp. 64-65.

19. *Mass. Bay Recs.,* 4:pt. 1, pp. 308-309.

20. Bishop, *New England Judged,* pp. 54-56; *Essex Court Recs.,* 2:103, 109; *Mass. Bay Recs.,* 4:pt. 1, p. 321.

21. Bishop, *New England Judged,* pp. 62-66, 69; *Essex Court Recs.,* 2:103-105; Joseph B. Felt, *The Ecclesiastical History of New England,* 2:208.

22. *Essex Court Recs.,* 2:106-107, 118; Bishop, *New England Judged,* pp. 74-85, 71.

23. Bishop, *New England Judged,* pp. 85-87; *Mass. Bay Recs.,* 4:pt. 1, pp. 345-349. Nicholas Phelps had somehow replaced Samuel Gaskin as one of the imprisoned Quakers.

24. Bishop, *New England Judged,* p. 88; *Essex Court Recs.,* 2:135, 151.

25. *Mass. Bay Recs.,* 4:pt. 1, pp. 367; Bishop, *New England Judged,* pp. 100-104; and Samuel Adams Drake, *A Book of New England Legends and Folk Lore,* rev. ed. (Boston, Little, Brown and Co., 1901), p. 185.

26. John Norton, *The Heart of N[ew]-England Rent at the Blasphemies of the Present Generation: Or a Brief Tractate Concerning the Doctrine of the Quakers* (Cambridge, Mass., 1659).

27. Jones, *Quakers in the American Colonies,* pp. 79-89 (quotations pp. 84, 87); *Mass. Bay Recs.,* 4:pt. 1, pp. 383-384, 385-390.

28. *Essex Court Recs.,* 2:193.

29. *New Haven Col. Recs.,* 1:26, 28 (quotation), 46, 56, 84. It is more likely that Isaiah's fine was five shillings.

30. Isabel M. Calder, *The New Haven Colony,* pp. 170-171, 232-233; *New Haven Col. Recs.,* 1:115, 130.

31. *New Haven Col. Recs.,* 1:397, 399-400, 261.

32. Ibid., pp. 324-325, 109, 120, 337-338.

33. Ibid., p. 358.

34. *New Haven Town Recs.,* 1:258, 247, 220.

35. *New Haven Col. Recs.,* 2:146-147, 154-155, 186: text of code pp. 559-616.

36. Ibid., pp. 587-588, 605, 573.

37. Bernard C. Steiner,*A History of the Plantation of Menunkatuck and of the Original Town of Guilford, Connecticut* (Baltimore, 1897), pp. 86, 88.

38. *New Haven Town Recs.,* 1:17, 339-343.

39. *New Haven Col. Recs.,* 2:242-247.

40. *Conn. Col. Recs.,* 1:523-524, 522, 513-514, 247; text of code pp. 509-563.

41. "Records of the Particular Court of Connecticut, 1639-1663," *Collections of the Connecticut Historical Society,* 22 (1928), 130, 169, 88, 103, 191, 128, 124.

42. *Conn. Col. Recs.,* 1:283-284, 303, 308, 324, 311-312.

43. "Hartford Town Votes, I: 1635-1716," p. 129; Samuel Orcutt, *A History of the Old Town of Stratford and the City of Bridgeport, Connecticut,* 2 vols. (New Haven, 1886), 1:167.

44. *Ply. Col. Recs.,* 11:57-58; Brigham, *Laws of Plymouth,* pp. 92-93.

45. *Ply. Col. Recs.,* 2:165, 3:52, 47.

46. Ibid., 2:173-174; 3:150, 5 (quotation), 10, 124, 224.

47. Ibid., 2:162; Francis Baylies, *An Historical Memoir of the Colony of New Plymouth, 1608-1692,* 2 vols. (Boston, 1866), 2:210; Felt, *History of New England,* 2:26-27.

48. *Ply. Col. Recs.,* 2:172-173; 3:4, 74 (quotation).

49. Ibid., 3:111, 112, 113, 124-126, 129-130; Jones, *Quakers in the American Colonies,* pp. 40-41; Frederick Freeman, *The History of Cape Cod,* 2 vols. (Boston, 1860-1869), 1:221.

50. *Ply. Col. Recs.,* 11:100-101; Brigham, *Laws of Plymouth,* pp. 103-104.

51. Brigham,*Laws of Plymouth,* pp. ix, 113-114;*Ply. Col. Recs.,* 11:100-101.

52. Quoted in Felt,*History of New England,* 2:239-240;*Ply. Col. Recs.,* 3:167-168, 183, 189.

53. Felt, *History of New England,* 2:240; Freeman, *History of Cape Cod,* 2:265;*Ply. Col. Recs.,* 3:passim; 8:95-100.

54. On this subject, see Roy H. Pearce, "The 'Ruines of Mankind': The Indian and the Puritan Mind,"*Journal of the History of Ideas,* 13 (April 1952), 200-217; William Kellaway,*The New England Company, 1649-1776: Missionary Society to the American Indians* (New York, Barnes and Noble, 1961); and Alden Vaughan, *New England Frontier: Puritans and Indians, 1620-1675* (Boston, Little, Brown and Co., 1965), chaps. 9-11.

55. *Mass. Bay Recs.,* 1:209; 3:6-7. Connecticut passed a similar law in 1652; *Conn. Col. Recs.,* 1:235. *Mass. Bay Recs.,* 2:84, 134 (Journal of the upper house); 3:56-57 (Journal of the lower house).

56. Ibid., 2:178-179.

57. These three Indian tracts and four others mentioned in this paragraph are in the *CMHS,* 3d ser., 4 (1834). References to individual works follow.

58. Kellaway, *The New England Company*, chaps. 1-2, 4.

59. "The Day-Breaking, If Not the Sun-Rising of the Gospell with the Indians in New-England" (1647), *CMHS*, 3d ser., 4 (1834), 4, 22-23. Eliot's sermon was published anonymously. See also John Dunton, *Letters Written from New England, A.D. 1686,* ed. W. H. Whitmore, The Prince Society (Boston, 1867), pp. 231-232.

60. *Mass. Bay Recs.,* 4:pt. 2, p. 199.

61. See Eliot's letters in Henry Whitfield, "The Light Appearing More and More Towards the Perfect Day: Or, A Farther Discovery of the Present State of the Indians in New-England" (1651), *CMHS,* 3d ser., 4 (1834), 126-128; and Whitfield, "Strength out of Weaknesse: Or, A Glorious Manifestation of the Further Progresse of the Gospel among the Indians in New-England" (1652), ibid., pp. 171-172. See also John Eliot, *The Christian Commonwealth: Or, the Civil Policy of the Rising Kingdom of Jesus Christ* (London, [1659]).

62. *Mass. Bay Recs.,* 2:188-189 (quotation); 3:105-106; 4:pt. 1, p. 334.

63. Thomas Shepard, "The Clear Sun-shine of the Gospel Breaking Forth upon the Indians in New-England" (1648), *CMHS,* 3d ser., 4 (1834), 40; John Eliot and Thomas Mayhew, "Tears of Repentance: Or, a Further Narrative of the Progress of the Gospel amongst the Indians in New-England" (1653), ibid., p. 246.

64. Winthrop, *Journal,* 2:147; also reported in *Mass. Bay Recs.,* 2:56.

65. Edward Winslow, "The Glorious Progress of the Gospel, Amongst the Indians in New England" (1649), *CMHS*, 3d ser., 4 (1834), 86; Eliot and Mayhew, "Tears of Repentance" (1653), ibid., pp. 250-251.

66. Brigham, *Laws of Plymouth,* pp. 96, 100; *Ply. Col. Recs.,* 10:142; *Conn. Col. Recs.,* 2:61.

67. *Mass. Bay Recs.,* 2:177; Eliot and Mayhew, "Tears of Repentance," p. 251; John Eliot, *Indian Dialogues* (Cambridge, Mass., 1671), p. 14; John Eliot, *The Dying Speeches of Several Indians* (Cambridge, Mass., [1685?]), p. 9.

68. On general developments the most recent work is Charles E. Clark, *The Eastern Frontier: The Settlement of Northern New England, 1610-1763* (New York, Alfred A. Knopf, 1969), but more useful for my purposes are Andrews, *Colonial Period,* 1:chaps. 4, 15-16, 19; Frank B. Sanborn, *New Hampshire: An Epitome of Popular Government* (Boston, Houghton Mifflin Co., 1904), Jeremy Belknap, *The History of New Hampshire,* 2 vols. (New York, Johnson Reprint Corp., 1970; originally published 1812), vol. 1; and William D. Williamson, *The History of the State of Maine,* 2 vols. (Hallowell, Me., 1832), vol. 1.

69. *Mass. Bay Recs.,* 1:342-343; 2:43.

70. Otis G. Hammond, ed., *New Hampshire Court Records, 1640-1692,* Nathaniel Bouton et al., eds., *New Hampshire Provincial and State Papers,* vol. 40 (Concord, State of New Hampshire, 1943), pp. 11-12, 48, 122.

71. Ibid., pp. 17, 83, 131, 42, 84, 88, 130, 145, 133-134, 140, 111.

72. [Charles T. Libby, Robert E. Moody, and Neal W. Allen, Jr.], eds., *Prov-

ince and Court Records of Maine, 5 vols. (Portland, Maine Historical Society, 1928-1964), 1:76, 87-88 (hereafter cited as *Maine Recs.*).

73. Ibid., pp. 133, 136.

74. Ibid., pp. 135, 146, 160, 180 (quotation).

75. Ibid., 2:2, 12, 13, 23, 25, 30, 32, 43, 44, 52, 53, 81-82, 90-91.

76. *Ply. Col. Recs.,* 3:144.

77. Williamson, *History of Maine,* 1:390; *Maine Recs.,* 2:67, 80-81, 87.

78. William D. Williamson, "Sketches of the Lives of Early Maine Ministers," *Collections and Proceedings of the Maine Historical Society,* 2d ser., 4 (1893), 73.

79. John R. Bartlett, ed., *Records of the Colony of Rhode Island and Providence Plantations,* 10 vols. (Providence, 1856-1865), 1:22 (hereafter cited as *R.I. Col. Recs.*).

80. "Testimony of Roger Williams" (1658), in *The Complete Writings of Roger Williams,* 6:305.

81. Winthrop, *Journal,* 1:340; *R.I. Col. Recs.,* 1:14. On general developments in the colony, see Irving B. Richman, *Rhode Island: Its Making and Its Meaning;* and Howard M. Chapin, ed., *Documentary History of Rhode Island,* 2 vols. (Providence, Preston and Rounds Co., 1916-1919), vol. 1.

82. *R.I. Col. Recs.,* 1:16.

83. *Winthrop Papers,* 4:31, 61; Winthrop, *Journal,* 1:340-341.

84. *Winthrop Papers,* 4:59, 57; Samuel Gorton, "Simplicity's Defence against Seven-Headed Policy," pp. 50-52. Unfortunately Williams does not indicate the time when the Lord's Day was over.

85. Thomas Shepard, "The Clear Sun-shine of the Gospel Breaking Forth upon the Indians in New-England" (1648), p. 61. Shepard quoted the sachem to show that loose observation of the Sabbath was a stumbling block to all religion.

86. The reasons for Williams' views are discussed in Chapter 6. For a specific statement, see Williams, "A Key into the Language of America" (1643), *Complete Writings,* 1:160-161. *Ply. Col. Recs.,* 10:288.

87. *R.I. Col. Recs.,* 1:52-54; Chapin, *Documentary History,* 2:35-36; John Clark [*sic*], "Ill Newes from New-England" (London, 1652), *CMHS,* 4th ser., 2 (1854), 23-25.

88. Chapin, *Documentary History,* 2:94; Richman, *Rhode Island,* p. 139; *R.I. Col. Recs.,* 1:112-113, 118.

89. Chapin, *Documentary History,* 2:82; Clarke, "Ill Newes from New-England."

90. Henry Whitfield, "The Light Appearing More and More towards the Perfect Day: Or, A Farther Discovery of the Present State of the Indians in New-England," pp. 135-137.

91. *R.I. Col. Recs.,* 1:190; the entire code is at pp. 147-190.

92. Ibid., pp. 279-280.

93. Williams, *Complete Writings,* 6:278-279.

94. *R.I. Col. Recs.,* 2:5-6; the entire patent is at pp. 3-21.

95. Williams, *Complete Writings,* 6:346-347.

96. *R.I. Col. Recs.,* 2:503-504.

97. Henry Clarke, *A History of the Sabbatarians or Seventh Day Baptists in America* (Utica, N.Y., 1811), pp. 8-9, 18; Isaac Backus, *A History of New England with Particular Reference to the Denomination of Christians Called Baptists,* 2d ed. with notes by David Weston, 2 vols. (Newton, Mass., 1871), 1:324-327; Samuel G. Arnold, *History of the State of Rhode Island and Providence Plantations,* 2 vols. (New York, 1859-1860), 1:427.

98. *R.I. Col. Recs.,* 3:30-31.

99. Ibid., pp. 234-235, 240, 244; *Acts and Laws of His Majesty's Colony of Rhode Island and Providence Plantations* (Newport, R.I., 1745), p. 156.

100. Arthur E. Wilson, *Paddy Wilson's Meeting-House in Providence Plantations, 1791-1839* (Boston, Pilgrim Press, 1950), p. 193.

101. Mather, *Magnalia Christi Americana,* bk. 7, p. 20; Arnold, *History of Rhode Island,* 2:80.

102. *Acts and Laws of His Majesty's Colony of Rhode Island and Providence Plantations, 1745-1752* (Newport, R.I., 1752), p. 83. But money had depreciated in value; see Arnold, *History of Rhode Island,* 2:180.

9. New Netherland and New York

1. Ellis L. Raesly, *Portrait of New Netherland* (New York, Columbia University Press, 1945), p. 332.

2. This and the next two paragraphs draw upon John R. Brodhead, *History of the State of New York, 1609-1691,* 2 vols. (New York, 1853-1871), 1:passim; G. Edmundson, "The Dutch Republic," in A. W. Ward et al., eds., *The Cambridge Modern History* (Cambridge, University Press, 1907), 3:chap. 19; and T. M. Parker, "Protestantism and Confessional Strife," in R. B. Wernham, ed., *The New Cambridge Modern History* (Cambridge, University Press, 1968), 3:chap. 4.

3. Philip Schaff, *The Creeds of Christendom,* 1:502-508, 529-554; 3:345. See also E. W. Hengstenberg, *The Lord's Day,* p. 65.

4. Benjamin Hanbury, *Historical Memorials Relating to the Independents, or Congregationalists,* 3 vols. (London, 1839-1844), 3:581; John W. Beardslee, III, ed., *Reformed Dogmatics: J. Wollebius, G. Voetius, F. Turretin* (New York, Oxford University Press, 1965), pp. 3-23; Hengstenberg, *Lord's Day,* p. 69; James Gilfillan, *The Sabbath Viewed in the Light of Reason, Revelation, and History* (Edinburgh, 1861), pp. 90-93. Dutch names take many forms in the literature in English because of variant spellings and because Dutch clergymen ordinarily Latinized their names. In this chapter Dutch names are given as they are most frequently found in the best sources. Mr. M. O. Woelders, Deputy Librarian, Bibliotheek der Rijksuniversiteit te Leiden, and an unnamed correspondent in the Royal Library, The Hague, kindly furnished bibliographical information on Dutch and Latin works published in the Netherlands in the seventeenth century.

5. Gerard Brandt, *The History of the Reformation and Other Ecclesiastical Transactions in and about the Low Countries . . . to the Famous Synod of Dort,* 4 vols. (London, 1720-1723), 3:28-29, 289-290, 320; Petrus J. Blok, *History of the People of*

the Netherlands, 3:chap. 14; Herbert D. Foster, "Liberal Calvinism," pp. 106-146; Schaff, *Creeds of Christendom,* 1:509-515.

6. Gilfillan, *The Sabbath,* pp. 91-92, 94-95; Samuel M. Jackson, ed., *The New Schaff-Herzog Encyclopedia of Religious Knowledge,* 13 vols. (New York, Funk and Wagnals, 1908-1914), *s.v.* Teellinck; Willem J. M. Engleberts, *William Teellinck* (Amsterdam, 1898), pp. 9-10, 52.

7. William Ames, *The Marrow of Theology,* trans. and ed. John D. Eusden (Boston, Pilgrim Press, 1968), pp. 1-3, 8, 19, 287-300; Douglas Horton, trans., *William Ames by Matthew Nethenus, Hugo Visscher, and Karl Reuter* (Cambridge, Mass., Harvard Divinity School, 1965); and Keith L. Sprunger, *The Learned Doctor William Ames: Dutch Backgrounds of English and American Puritanism* (Urbana, University of Illinois Press, 1972).

8. Gilfillan, *The Sabbath,* pp. 95-97, 98-99; Engelberts, *Willem Teellinck,* p. 68. Burs's work was entitled *Threnos ofte Weeclaghe Aenwijsende de Oorsaken des Jammerlijcken Staats van het Land de Ontheyliginge des Sabbathdaeghs* (Threnos or Lamentation Showing the Causes of the Pitiful Condition of the Country and the Desecration of the Sabbath). Teellinck's work was entitled *Noodwendigh Vertoogh Aengaende den Tegenwoordigen Bedroefden Staet van Gods Volck* (A Necessary Demonstration concerning the Present Afflicted State of God's People; Middelburg, 1627).

9. Gilfillan, *The Sabbath,* pp. 99-106; *The New Schaff-Herzog Encyclopedia,* *s.v.* authors' names; Robert Cox, *The Literature of the Sabbath Question;* and the work by Eaton described in the next paragraph. Though Gomarus defended the theory that the Fourth Commandment was binding only upon the Jews, he also pleaded for better practical observance of the Christian Sabbath.

10. Samuel E. Morison, *The Founding of Harvard College,* pp. 200-201, 377. Ames dealt with the Sabbath in bk. 4, chap. 33.

11. Eaton, *Inquisitio;* Ames, *Marrow of Theology,* pp. 287-300; Horton, *Ames by Visscher,* pp. 133-140.

12. The *Inquisitio* appeared in William Ames, *Opera Omnia* (Amsterdam, 1658), vol. 2, last item, with separate title page and separate pagination (54 pages). The title page reads: Guilielmi Amesi, *Sententia de Origine Sabbati et Die Dominico, Quam ex ipsius mente Concepit scripto et publice disputavit.* Nathanael Eatonus, Angl. Amstelodami, 1658. Although the title page and a preface (dated 1653 by the Julian calendar) by Schotanus indicate that the opinions are those of Ames and that Eaton was his reporter, the work was by Eaton; despite assertions to the contrary, Ames wrote no tract bearing this title.

13. Gilfillan, *The Sabbath,* pp. 107-111; and appropriate entries in *The New Schaff-Herzog Encyclopedia* and Cox, *Sabbath Question.* A fourth stage in the controversy over the Sabbath arose in late seventeenth-century Holland and resulted in books of inordinate length. One ran to 1,196 pages, another to 1,769 pages, whereas the longest English book on the subject was 1,150 pages. See Cox, *Sabbath Question,* 1:237-238; 2:137, 448.

14. Henry C. Murphy, ed. *Journal of a Voyage to New York and a Tour in Several of the American Colonies in 1679-80, by Jaspar Dankers and Peter Sluyter* (Brooklyn, 1867), p. xi.

15. This and the three paragraphs following draw on Brodhead, *History of New York,* vol. 1; J. Franklin Jameson, *Naratives of New Netherland, 1609-1664;* Andrews, *Colonial Period,* 3:70-96; and David M. Ellis et al., *A Short History of New York State* (Ithaca, Cornell University Press, 1957), chap. 2. A. J. F. van Laer, trans. and ed., *Van Rensselaer Bowier Manuscripts: Being the Letters of Kiliaen van Rensselaer, 1630-1643* (Albany, University of the State of New York, 1908), contains the Charter of the Dutch West Indies Company (pp. 86-115); the Charter of Freedoms and Exemptions of 1629 (pp. 136-152), and other documents relating to the colony of Rensselaerswyck. The 1640 charter is printed in E. B. O'Callaghan and B. Fernow, eds., *Documents Relating to the Colonial History of the State of New York,* 15 vols. (Albany, 1853-1887), 1:119-123 (hereafter cited as *N.Y. Col. Docs.*).

16. E. B. O'Callaghan, ed., *The Documentary History of the State of New York,* 4 vols. (Albany, 1849-1851), 4:21-22 (hereafter cited as *Doc. Hist. N.Y.*).

17. A. J. F. van Laer, ed., *Documents Relating to New Netherland, 1624-1626* (San Marino, Calif., Henry E. Huntington Library, 1924), pp. 2, 5, 36. The 1640 charter declared: "No other Religion shall be publicly admitted in New Netherland except the Reformed, as it is at present preached and practiced by public authority in the United Netherlands," *N.Y. Col. Docs.,* 1:123.

18. E. T. Corwin, ed., *Ecclesiastical Records, State of New York,* 7 vols. (Albany, James B. Lyon, 1901-1916), 1:38-39 (hereafter cited as *Eccl. Recs. N.Y.*); Frederick J. Zwierlein, *Religion in New Netherland: A History of the Development of the Religious Conditions in the Province of New Netherland, 1623-1664* (Rochester, N.Y., John P. Smith Printing Co., 1910), pp. 39-43.

19. Zwierlein, *Religion,* pp. 61-62; Albert Eekhof, *Jonas Michaelius: Founder of the Church in New Netherland* (Leyden, A. W. Sijthoff's Publishing Co., 1926), pp. 1-6.

20. Van Laer, *Documents Relating to New Netherland,* pp. 187, 207.

21. Jameson, *Narratives of New Netherland,* p. 113.

22. Eekhof, *Jonas Michaelius,* pp. 129, 67-69. For biographical detail (not always accurate) on the clergy mentioned in this chapter, see Frederick L. Weis, "The Colonial Clergy of the Middle Colonies: New York, New Jersey, and Pennsylvania, 1628-1776," *Proceedings of the American Antiquarian Society,* 66 (1957), 167-351.

23. Zwierlein, *Religion,* pp. 67-70; Van Laer, *Van Rensselaer Bowier Manuscripts,* pp. 271, 267; Raesly, *Portrait,* pp. 74, 206-208; *Eccl. Recs. N.Y.,* vol. 1.

24. E. B. O'Callaghan, ed., *Laws and Ordinances of New Netherland, 1638-1674* (Albany, 1868), p. 25 (hereafter cited as *Laws of New Netherland*); Brodhead, *History of New York,* 1:chaps. 9-11; Zwierlein, *Religion,* pp. 70-72, 78-82; Raesly, *Portrait,* pp. 206-208.

25. Van Laer, *Van Rensselaer Bowier Manuscripts,* pp. 208, 251, 418, 404, 423, 431, 686, 694.

26. The biography by Victor H. Paltsits in the *DAB* is balanced and excellent. Henry H. Kessler and Eugene Rachlis, *Peter Stuyvesant and His New York* (New York, Random House, 1959), is a lively account with new and highly valuable facts about Stuyvesant's date of birth (see esp. pp. 285-287).

27. *Laws of New Netherland,* pp. 60-62. See B[erthold] Fernow, ed., *The Records of New Amsterdam, 1653 to 1674,* 7 vols. (New York, 1897), 1:1-2, for a somewhat different translation of this ordinance. Hereafter cited as *Recs. N. Amst.*

28. Older historians valued the guilder at forty cents, recent ones at sixty-five cents, but it is of course impossible to translate the value of seventeenth-century Dutch money into twentieth-century equivalents with any precision. See Van Laer, *Van Rensselaer Bowier Manuscripts,* p. 847, and Kessler and Rachlis, *Peter Stuyvesant,* p. 282. The fine of six guilders was 6 percent of the monthly salary of the minister at New Amsterdam at this time, and equivalent to the price of thirty one-pound loaves of white bread at official rates in 1656. See *Eccl. Recs. N.Y.,* 1:217, 254; *Laws of New Netherland,* p. 261.

29. *Eccl. Recs. N.Y.,* 1:236; *Laws of New Netherland,* pp. 93-96, 98-99, 89; cf. *Recs. N. Amst.,* 1:5-6, 8-9. The penalty for Sunday trading was redemption of forfeited wares by payment of twenty-five florins plus a fine of one pound Flemish.

30. A.J. F. van Laer, ed., *Minutes of the Court of Rensselaerswyck, 1648-1652* (Albany, The University of the State of New York, 1922), pp. 7-24, 112, 139. For the events leading up to Kettelheym's sentence, see pp. 61-62, 108. Biographical sketches of many of the settlers of Rensselaerswyck are found in van Laer, *Van Rensselaer Bowier Manuscripts,* pp. 805-846.

31. A.J. F. van Laer, ed., *Minutes of the Court of Fort Orange and Beverwyck, 1652-1670,* 2 vols. (Albany, The University of the State of New York, 1920-1923), 1:56, 57-58, 108, 235, 239, 240, 241, 244-245; 2:64-67, 298-299. Some men were also presented for playing ice hockey on an officially proclaimed day of prayer; see 2:23.

32. *Laws of New Netherland,* pp. 415-416; "The Dutch Records of Kingston, Ulster County, New York, Part I, May 31, 1658-November 18, 1664," trans. Samuel Oppenheim, in *Proceedings of the New York State Historical Association,* 11 (1912), 11, 79, 81-85, 91.

33. Isabel M. Calder, "John Cotton's 'Moses His Judicials,' " p. 92; *Records of the Town of Southampton,* 6 vols. (Sag-Harbor, N.Y., J. H. Hunt, 1874-1915), 1:vi, 18-20, 37-38; 2:30. See also James Truslow Adams, *History of the Town of Southampton* (Bridgehampton, N.Y., Hampton Press, 1918), p. 106.

34. Bernice Schultz, *Colonial Hempstead* (Lynbrook, N.Y., The Review-Star Press, 1937), pp. 3-13, 14-16, 53-54, 177-179; Benjamin D. Hicks, ed., *Records of the Towns of North and South Hempstead, Long Island, N.Y.,* 8 vols. (Jamaica, N.Y., Long Island Farmer Print, 1896-1904), 1:56-57; *Eccl. Recs. N.Y.,* 1:396.

35. Henry Onderdonk, Jr., *The Annals of Hempstead, 1643 to 1832* (Hempstead, N.Y., 1878), pp. 16, 18; Schultz, *Colonial Hempstead,* pp. 203-215; Kessler and Rachlis, *Peter Stuyvesant,* pp. 186-196.

36. *Doc. Hist. N.Y.,* 3:922.

37. Jameson, *Narratives of New Netherland,* p. 291; *Eccl. Recs. N.Y.,* vol. 1; Zwierlein, *Religion,* chaps. 5-8; John W. Pratt, *Religion, Politics, and Diversity: The Church-State Theme in New York History* (Ithaca, Cornell University Press, 1967), pp. 11-25.

38. *Recs. N. Amst.,* 1:290-291. The first Jew to settle permanently on Manhat-

tan, Jacob Barsimon, arrived in August 1653; and twenty-three Jewish refugees from Brazil landed in September 1654. Kessler and Rachlis, *Peter Stuyvesant,* pp. 176-186.

39. *Eccl. Recs. N.Y.,* 1:335-336; *Recs. N. Amst.,* 2:396, 397.

40. Ibid., 1:24-27. Compare *Laws of New Netherland,* pp. 258-263, 310-314.

41. E. B. O'Callaghan, ed., *Calendar of Historical Manuscripts,* 2 vols. (Albany, 1865-1866), 1:198, 226, 241, 252, 261, 262-263.

42. *Recs. N. Amst.,* 5:46, 48, 64, 93 (quotation); I. N. Phelps Stokes, *The Iconography of Manhattan Island, 1498-1909,* 6 vols. (New York, Robert H. Dodd, 1915-1928), 1:101.

43. *Laws of New Netherland,* pp. 448-449 (but cf. *Recs. N. Amst.,* 4:301-302, where the ordinance is dated 15 September 1663); *Recs. N. Amst.,* 5:39.

44. According to Edward T. Corwin, "The Ecclesiastical Condition of New York at the Opening of the Eighteenth Century," *Papers of the American Society of Church History,* 2d ser., 3 (1912), 82-83, 106-107, there were a total of twenty-one churches in New Netherland during Dutch rule. About a dozen were Dutch Reformed, including one each in New Jersey and Delaware; the remainder were Presbyterian or Congregational, all of which were located on Long Island, including the eastern portion, except for one in Westchester County. These churches had been served by twenty-four ministers, sixteen of whom were Dutch Reformed. In 1664 about twelve ministers remained in service, of whom seven were Dutch Reformed.

45. Ellis, *New York State,* pp. 29-38 (also the source of background material for later paragraphs); Wesley F. Craven, *New Jersey and the English Colonization of North America* (Princeton, D. Van Nostrand Co., 1964), p. 47.

46. Corwin, "Ecclesiastical Condition of New York," pp. 83-85; Thomas F. O'Connor, "Religious Toleration in New York, 1664-1700," *New York History,* 17 (October 1936), 391-410; Ira Rosenwaike, *Population History of New York City* (Syracuse, Syracuse University Press, 1972), pp. 6-13.

47. Albert E. McKinley, "The Transition from Dutch to English Rule in New York: A Study in Political Imitation," *American Historical Review,* 6 (July 1901), 717; A. J. F. van Laer, ed., *Minutes of the Court of Albany, Rensselaerswyck and Schenectady, 1668-1685,* 3 vols. (Albany, The University of the State of New York, 1926-1932), 1:7-9, 96, 281; 2:389. See also 1:69, 148.

48. McKinley, "The Transition from Dutch to English Rule in New York," pp. 705-717. The Duke's Laws are printed in *Collections of the New York Historical Society,* 1 (1811), 305-397.

49. Ibid., pp. 333, 334, 338.

50. *Recs. N. Amst.,* 6:405-406; *Laws of New Netherland,* pp. 476-480, 482, 492-507.

51. [Herbert L. Osgood, ed.], *Minutes of the Common Council of the City of New York, 1675-1776,* 8 vols. (New York, Dodd, Mead and Co., 1905), 1:27 (hereafter cited as *Common Council of N.Y.C.*).

52. Van Laer, *Court of Albany, Rensselaerswyck and Schenectady,* 2:36, 46, 95, 278, 322-323, 381, 400.

53. Ibid., pp. 187-188; 2:402; 3:16, 74-79, 139, 140, 186, 205.

54. Ibid., 2:292, 374. See 2:447 and 3:278, 478, 529, for other examples.

55. Ibid., 2:394-395; 3:147-148, 251-252, 461-462, 545; Alice Morse Earle, "Sunday in New Netherland and Old New York," *Atlantic Monthly*, 78 (October 1896), 547.

56. Peter Ross, *A History of Long Island from Its Earliest Settlement to the Present Time*, 3 vols. (New York, The Lewis Publishing Co., 1902), 1:117.

57. *Doc. Hist. N.Y.*, 3:212-213.

58. Charles R. Street, ed., *Huntington Town Records, Including Babylon, Long Island, N.Y., 1653-1873*, 3 vols. (Huntington, N.Y., 1887-1889), 1:369.

59. *Journal of Jasper Danckaerts, 1679-1680*, ed. Bartlett B. James and J. Franklin Jameson (New York, Charles Scribner's Sons, 1913), pp. 44-47, 58-59, 68, 166, 170, 189-196 (quotations pp. 47, 59, 196).

60. The Charter is printed in *The Colonial Laws of New York from the Year 1664 to the Revolution*, 5 vols. (Albany, 1894), 1:111-116 (quotation p. 116). See also Corwin, "Ecclesiastical Condition of New York," p. 85.

61. *Common Council of N.Y.C.*, 1:133-134.

62. *Doc. Hist. N.Y.*, 1:186.

63. *Common Council of N.Y.C.*, 1:212, 224, 247, 276-277, 371, 392; 2:21, 183, 223.

64. *Col. Laws of N.Y.*, 1:173-174.

65. *Journal of the Votes and Proceedings of the General Assembly of the Colony of New York, April 9, 1691-September 27, 1743* (New York, 1744), p. 21.

66. Corwin, "Ecclesiastical Condition of New York," pp. 87-88.

67. *Journal of the Legislative Council of the Colony of New York, 1691-1775*, 2 vols. (Albany, 1861), 1:25, 35, 39.

68. Ibid., 1:42, 47, 48; Corwin, "Ecclesiastical Condition of New York," pp. 89-91; R. Townsend Henshaw, "The New York Ministry Act of 1693," *Historical Magazine of the Protestant Episcopal Church*, 2 (December 1933), 199-204; Elizabeth H. Davidson, *The Establishment of the English Church in the Continental American Colonies*, pp. 37-46.

69. *Jnl. of Leg. Council of Col. of N.Y.*, 1:84; *Col. Laws of N.Y.*, 1:356-357.

70. *Doc. Hist. N.Y.*, 3:200-201.

71. Dixon Ryan Fox, *Caleb Heathcote, Gentleman Colonist: The Story of a Career in the Province of New York, 1692-1721* (New York, Charles Scribner's Sons, 1926), pp. 202, 203-204; Dixon Ryan Fox, ed., "The Minutes of the Court of Sessions (1657-1696), Westchester County, New York," *Publications of the Westchester County Historical Society*, 2 (1924), 81-84.

72. Benjamin F. Thompson, *History of Long Island from Its Discovery and Settlement to the Present Time*, 3d rev. ed., 3 vols. (New York, Robert H. Dodd, 1918), 2:78; *Huntington Town Records*, 2:170; Ross, *History of Long Island*, 1:117; Adams, *History of Southampton*, p. 106; *Eccl. Recs. N.Y.*, 3:1695, 2215; 4:2366; Julius Goebel, Jr. and T. Raymond Naughton, *Law Enforcement in Colonial New York: A Study in Criminal Procedure (1664-1776)* (New York, The Commonwealth Fund, 1944), p. 40n.

73. "Minutes of the Supreme Court of Judicature, April 4, 1693 to April 1, 1701," *Collections of the New York Historical Society*, 45 (1913), 93, 128-129; see

also pp. 159, 192; and Paul M. Hamlin and Charles E. Baker, eds., "Supreme Court of Judicature of the Province of New York, 1691-1704," *Collections of the New York Historical Society,* 78-80 (1952-1959), 2:103; 3:68.

74. Sarah Knight, *The Journal of Madam Knight,* ed. Malcolm Freiberg ([1825], Boston, David R. Godine, 1972), p. 30.

10. The Restoration Colonies: I

1. W. P. Baker, "The Observance of Sunday," in Reginald Lennard, ed., *Englishmen at Rest and Play: Some Phases of English Leisure, 1558-1714,* pp. 126-131; *The Diary of the Rev. Ralph Josselin, 1618-1683,* ed. Ernest Hockliffe (London, Camden Society, 1908) p. 145; see also pp. 135, 137, 139, 140, 142.

2. J. Wickham Legg, *English Church Life from the Restoration to the Tractarian Movement* (London, Longmans, Green and Co., 1914), p. 232.

3. Quoted in Robert Cox, *The Literature of the Sabbath Question,* 2:9; see also pp. 10-12; and J. H. Overton, *Life in the English Church (1660-1714)* (London, 1885), pp. 316-317.

4. H. Hensley Henson, *Studies in English Religion in the Seventeenth Century,* pp. 64-71; Cox, *Sabbath Question,* 2:19-35.

5. Edward Cardwell, ed., *Documentary Annals of the Reformed Church of England,* 2:309; James L. Lindsay, 26th Earl of Crawford, ed., *Tudor and Stuart Proclamations, 1485-1714,* 1:408.

6. W. B. Whitaker, *Sunday in Tudor and Stuart Times,* pp. 187-194.

7. Quoted in John Ashton, *Social Life in the Reign of Queen Anne,* 2 vols. (London, 1882), 2:121. See also Overton, *English Church,* pp. 317-319; Legg, *English Church Life,* pp. 234-235; and Cox, *Sabbath Question,* 2:13.

8. Legg, *English Church Life,* pp. 232-233; Cox, *Sabbath Question,* 2:25-28, 33-34, 13-17; William E. A. Axon, *Lancashire Gleanings* (Manchester, 1883), pp. 67-68; and Ashton, *Social Life,* 2:121 (quotation). The London broadside appeared in 1671.

9. Dudley W. R. Bahlman, *The Moral Revolution of 1688* (New Haven, Yale University Press, 1957); Cardwell, *Documentary Annals,* 2:376; Overton, *English Church,* pp. 320, 213-214, 218-222.

10. Two contemporary works on the subject, both of which touch on the Sabbath question, are Ephraim Pagitt, *Heresiography* (London, 1645), and Thomas Edwards, *Gangraena* (London, 1646). Also see Robert Barclay, *The Inner Life of the Religious Societies of the Commonwealth,* 3d ed. (London, 1879), and C. E. Whiting, *Studies in English Puritanism from the Restoration to the Revolution, 1660-1688* ([London], S.P.C.K., 1931), chap. 6. Robert Barclay of Reigate, author of *The Inner Life,* is not to be confused with Robert Barclay of Ury, the Quaker Apologist.

11. Louise F. Brown, *The Political Activities of the Baptists and Fifth Monarchy Men in England during the Interregnum* (Washington, American Historical Association, 1912), chaps. 1-4; W[illem] Schenk, *The Concern for Social Justice in the Puritan Revolution,* chap. 8, and P. G. Rogers, *The Fifth Monarchy Men* (London, Oxford University Press, 1966), chaps. 1-6.

12. Brown, *Baptists and Fifth Monarchy Men;* A. C. Underwood, *A History of the English Baptists* (London, Kingsgate Press, 1947), chaps. 2-5.

13. W. T. Whitley, *A History of British Baptists,* 2d rev. ed. (London, The Kingsgate Press, 1932), pp. 84-86. All works listed were published in London.

14. Rogers, *Fifth Monarchy Men,* chaps. 7-9; Whitley, *British Baptists,* p. 110; Underwood, *English Baptists,* chap. 5.

15. Underwood, *English Baptists,* pp. 112-115, 147-148; Cox, *Sabbath Question,* 1:267; Whitley, *British Baptists,* pp. 133-134, 172, 176, 183, 313. See also J. L. Gamble and C. H. Greene, "Seventh Day Baptists in the British Isles," in *Seventh Day Baptists in Europe and America,* 2 vols. (Plainfield, N.J., The American Sabbath Tract Society, 1910), 1:19-115. In the mid-twentieth century the Mill Yard Church was being kept alive with the aid of American Seventh-Day Baptists.

16. Geoffrey F. Nuttall, *The Holy Spirit in Puritan Faith and Experience.*

17. The standard authority is William C. Braithwaite, *The Beginnings of Quakerism,* 2d ed. rev. by Henry J. Cadbury (Cambridge, University Press, 1955), and idem, *The Second Period of Quakerism,* 2d ed. rev. by Henry J. Cadbury (Cambridge, University Press, 1961). I also used Hugh Barbour, *The Quakers in Puritan England* (New Haven, Yale University Press, 1964).

18. See Melvin B. Endy, Jr., *William Penn and Early Quakerism* (Princeton, Princeton University Press, 1973).

19. *The Journal of George Fox,* rev. ed. by John L. Nickalls (Cambridge, University Press, 1952). Also see Fox's paper of 1677 on observing days in *The Journal of George Fox,* 8th (bicentenary) ed., 2 vols. (London, Friends' Tract Association, 1901), 2:301-310; *The Works of George Fox,* 8 vols. (Philadelphia, 1831), 3:314-337; Braithwaite, *Second Period of Quakerism,* pp. 228-241.

20. The suggestion has been made that Penn learned while studying with Moïse Amyraut, an anti-Calvinist professor of theology at the Huguenot Academy in Saumur, France, that the observance of the Sabbath must not be made a burden and that some portion of it could be devoted to healthful recreation. This view apparently originated with Mabel R. Brailsford, *The Making of William Penn* (London, Longmans, Green and Co., 1930), p. 123, and later writers have perpetuated it. But Penn differed from Amyraut, and this book should make it clear that there are no convincing grounds for the notion that Penn derived his attitude toward the Sabbath from Amyraut.

21. For illustrative examples of Quaker views of the Sabbath, see Fox, *Journal,* ed. Nickalls, pp. 36, 38, 317-318, 332; George Fox, "The Protestant Christian Quaker," *Works,* 6:92-105; "Several Treatises Worthy of Every True Christian's Serious Consideration," *Works,* 6:463-472; Isaac Penington, "An Epistle to All Such as Observe the Seventh Day of the Week for the Sabbath of the Lord," in *The Works of . . . Isaac Penington* (London, 1681), pp. 258-259; Penington, "The New Covenant of the Gospel Distinguished from the Old Covenant of the Law, and the Rest or Sabbath of Believers, from the Rest or Sabbath of the Jews" (1660), *Works,* pp. 260-295; Robert Barclay, "Truth Clear'd of Calumnies" (1670), in Robert Barclay, *Truth Triumphant through the Spiritual Warfare, Christian Labours, and Writings of Robert Barclay,* 3 vols. (London, 1718), 1:70-75.

22. Norman Penney, ed., "*The First Publishers of Truth*" (London, Headley

Brothers, 1907), pp. 64, 101-102, 280, 319; Braithwaite, *Beginnings of Quakerism,* pp. 444-451, and *Second Period of Quakerism,* chaps. 1-4.

23. Robert Barclay, *An Apology for the True Christian Divinity* (New York, 1827), pp. 344-409 (quotation p. 349, italics omitted); Barclay, "William Mitchell Unmasked" (1671), *Truth Triumphant,* 1:169-173; William Penn, "A Serious Apology for the Principles and Practices of the People Call'd Quakers" (1671; written in collaboration with George Whitehead), in *A Collection of the Works of William Penn,* 2 vols. (London, 1726), 2:51 (first Penn quotation); "Travels in Holland and Germany" (1677), *Works,* 1:93. See also Isaac Penington, *The Way to the Sabbath of Rest: Or, The Souls Progresse in the Work of Regeneration* (London, 1655), for another spiritual interpretation of the Sabbath. This title is not in Penington's *Works.*

24. *The Journal of George Fox,* ed. Norman Penney, 2 vols. (Cambridge, University Press, 1911), 2:314, 461n.6; *The History of the Life of Thomas Ellwood,* ed. C. G. Crump (New York, G. P. Putnam's Sons, 1900), pp. 102-103; "Wisdom Justified of Her Children" (1673), *Works,* 2:479.

25. Fox, *Journal,* ed. Nickalls, pp. 669, 751; *The Short Journal and Itinerary Journals of George Fox,* ed. Norman Penney (Cambridge, University Press, 1925), pp. 108, 310n; *Life of Thomas Ellwood,* pp. 43-48; Fox, *Journal,* ed. Penney, 2:482n.; Brailsford, *William Penn,* p. 143.

26. Braithwaite, *Beginnings of Quakerism,* pp. 141, 184, 312, 315; Barclay, *Apology,* pp. 350 (quotation); Penn, "Wisdom Justified of Her Children," 2:479-480.

27. For examples in 1649, see Fox, *Journal,* ed. Nickalls, pp. 41, 44, 46; also see Braithwaite, *Beginnings of Quakerism,* p. 139.

28. "No Cross, No Crown" (1682, not 1668 as indicated in Penn's *Works*), *Works,* 1:356; "Some Fruits of Solitude" (1693), *Works,* 1:819 (quotation).

29. Frederick B. Tolles, *Meeting House and Counting House: The Quaker Merchants of Colonial Philadelphia, 1682-1763* (Chapel Hill, University of North Carolina Press, 1948), p. 55; "No Cross, No Crown," *Works,* 1:295.

30. "No Cross, No Crown," *Works,* 1:355 (italics omitted).

31. On religious persecution in late seventeenth-century Britain see, among others, G. N. Clark, *The Later Stuarts, 1660-1714* (Oxford, Clarendon Press, 1934); Gerald R. Cragg, *Puritanism in the Period of the Great Persecution, 1660-1688* (Cambridge, University Press, 1957); and Braithwaite, *Second Period of Quakerism,* chaps. 1-7.

32. For a good general treatment of the beginnings and later years of the two Carolinas, on which the present account draws, see Andrews, *Colonial Period,* 3:chaps. 5-6. The text of the charter is in William L. Saunders, ed., *The Colonial Records of North Carolina,* 10 vols. (Goldsboro, 1886-1890), 1:20-33 (hereafter cited as *N.C. Col. Recs.*). For a more recent edition see Mattie E. E. Parker, ed., *North Carolina Charters and Constitutions, 1578-1698* (Raleigh, Carolina Charter Tercentenary Commission, 1963), pp. 74-89 (hereafter cited as *N.C. Charters*). A second charter in 1665 pushed the boundaries northward to approximately the present line between North Carolina and Virginia and southward a hundred miles below the present line between Georgia and Florida.

33. *N.C. Col. Recs.*, 1:75-92; *N.C. Charters*, pp. 107-127.

34. *N.C. Col. Recs.*, 1:187-206; *N.C. Charters*, pp. 128-185.

35. *N.C. Col. Recs.*, 1:202-203; *N.C. Charters*, pp. 181-182.

36. Besides Andrews, for basic information on early South Carolina consult David D. Wallace, *South Carolina: A Short History, 1520-1948* (Columbia, University of South Carolina Press, 1966), chaps. 4-15, 23.

37. Wallace, *South Carolina*, p. 61.

38. Elizabeth H. Davidson, *The Establishment of the English Church in the Continental American Colonies*, pp. 58-66.

39. David Ramsay, *History of South Carolina*, 2 vols. in 1 (Newberry, S.C., 1858), 2:3; Thomas Cooper and David J. McCord, *The Statutes at Large of South Carolina*, 10 vols. (Columbia, 1836-1841), 2:68-70 (hereafter cited as *S.C. Statutes*); A. S. Salley, Jr., ed., *Journal of the Grand Council of South Carolina, 1671-1692*, 2 vols. (Columbia, The Historical Commission of South Carolina, 1907), 2:44; *S. C. Statutes*, 2:74.

40. Wallace, *South Carolina*, pp. 58-60; "Letters of Rev. Samuel Thomas, 1702-[1706]," *South Carolina Historical and Genealogical Magazine*, 4 (1903), 283; Edward McCrady, *The History of South Carolina under the Proprietary Government, 1670-1719* ([1897]; reprinted New York, Russell & Russell, 1969), pp. 326-327; Frederick L. Weis, *The Colonial Clergy of Virginia, North Carolina and South Carolina* (Boston, Society of the Descendants of the Colonial Clergy, 1955), p. 91.

41. "Letters of Rev. Samuel Thomas," p. 226; see also pp. 279, 283.

42. "Documents Concerning Rev. Samuel Thomas, 1702-1707," *South Carolina Historical and Genealogical Magazine*, 5 (1904), 44-45, 26, 46.

43. *S. C. Statutes*, 2:396-399. On the Engish precedents, see John F. Grimké, *The Public Laws of the State of South Carolina* (Philadelphia, 1790), pp. 19-20.

44. Henry E. Young, "Sunday Laws," in *Report of the Third Annual Meeting of the American Bar Association* (Philadelphia, 1880), p. 138.

45. Frederick Dalcho, *An Historical Account of the Protestant Episcopal Church in South Carolina* (Charleston, 1820), pp. 107, 111-112; Grimké, *Public Laws of South Carolina*, p. 168.

46. Quoted in Gilbert P. Voight, "Religious Conditions among German-Speaking Settlers in South Carolina, 1732-1774," *South Carolina Historical Magazine*, 56 (April 1955), 60; Robert L. Meriwether, *The Expansion of South Carolina, 1729-1765* (Kingsport, Tenn., Southern Publishers, 1940), pp. 96-97.

47. See, for example, Charles Woodmason, *The Carolina Backcountry on the Eve of the Revolution*, ed. Richard J. Hooker (Chapel Hill, University of North Carolina Press, 1953), pp. 47, 53, 95-98; and Young, "Sunday Laws," p. 139.

48. Besides Andrews, *Colonial Period*, 3:chaps. 5-6, good background material is found in Hugh T. Lefler and Albert R. Newsome, *North Carolina: The History of a Southern State* (Chapel Hill, University of North Carolina Press, 1954), chaps. 3-9.

49. William Edmundson, *A Journal of the Life, Travels, Sufferings, and Labour of Love in the Work of the Ministry*, ed. John Stoddardt (Dublin, 1715), p. 59. On Quaker missionary activity, see Rufus M. Jones, *The Quakers in the American Colonies*, pp. 283-287. *N.C. Col. Recs.*, 1:571-572. On religion in early North Caro-

lina, also see Francis L. Hawks, *History of North Carolina,* 2 vols. (Fayetteville, N.C., 1858-1859), 2:335-370.

50. *N.C. Col. Recs.,* 2:602; Stephen B. Weeks, *The Religious Development in the Province of North Carolina* (Baltimore, 1892), p. 32.

51. Weeks, *Religious Development,* pp. 32-38; idem, *Church and State in North Carolina* (Baltimore, 1893), chaps. 1-2; and Davidson, *Establishment of the English Church,* pp. 47-57.

52. *N.C. Col. Recs.,* 1:603, 765; 2:374.

53. William L. Saunders and Walter Clark, eds., *The State Records of North Carolina,* 16 vols. (Goldsboro, 1886-1907), 23:3-6 (hereafter cited as *N.C. State Recs.*). This set continues the *N.C. Col. Recs.* and the first volume is numbered 11.

54. *N.C. Col. Recs.,* 2:365, 404-405, 411.

55. The best editions of both are in *The Prose Works of William Byrd of Westover,* ed. Louis B. Wright (Cambridge, Mass., Harvard University Press, 1966).

56. Ibid., pp. 204-205, 192 (quotation), 312, 212.

57. Ibid., pp. 42, 44, 184, 194, 195, 72, 77. Daniel Defoe's *Robinson Crusoe* was published in 1719.

58. Ibid., pp. 207, 82-83; see also p. 195.

59. Ibid., pp. 105-108, 236-237 (quotations p. 237).

60. Ibid., pp. 134-135, 283, 139, 299.

61. Lefler and Newsome, *North Carolina,* pp. 122-132; *N.C. State Recs.,* 23:173-175.

11. The Restoration Colonies: II

1. The present account draws upon Andrews, *Colonial Period,* 3:chap. 4; John E. Pomfret, *The Province of East New Jersey, 1609-1702: The Rebellious Proprietary* (Princeton, Princeton University Press, 1962); idem, *The Province of West New Jersey, 1609-1702: A History of the Origins of an American Colony* (Princeton, Princeton University Press, 1956); and Richard P. McCormick, *New Jersey from Colony to State, 1609-1789* (Princeton, D. Van Nostrand Co., 1964).

2. The text is in Aaron Leaming and Jacob Spicer, eds., *The Grants, Concessions, and Original Constitutions of the Province of New Jersey* (Philadelphia, [1756]), pp. 12-26 (hereafter cited as *Consts. of N.J.*). For a more recent edition see Julian P. Boyd. ed., *Fundamental Laws and Constitutions of New Jersey, 1664-1964* (Princeton, D. Van Nostrand Co., 1964), pp. 51-66.

3. Isabel M. Calder, *The New Haven Colony,* pp. 251-256; "Records of the Town of Newark, New Jersey," *Collections of the New Jersey Historical Society,* 6 (1864), 2-4, 10, 11; Theodore Thayer, *As We Were: The Story of Old Elizabethtown* (Elizabeth, N.J., The New Jersey Historical Society, 1964), p. 28.

4. *Consts. of N.J.,* pp. 77-84; William A. Whitehead, *East Jersey under the Proprietary Governments* (New York, 1846), p. 168; also see Nelson R. Burr, "The Religious History of New Jersey before 1702," *Proceedings of the New Jersey Historical Society,* 56 (July 1938), 169-190; (October 1938), 243-266.

5. *Consts. of N.J.,* pp. 98-99, 124. Ranters disturbed the meeting William Ed-

mundson held in East Jersey about this time; see William Edmundson, *A Journal of the Life, Travels, Sufferings, and Labour of Love in the Work of the Ministry*, p. 92.

6. *Consts. of N.J.*, pp. 153-166 (quotation p. 162). Also in Boyd, *Fundamental Laws of N.J.*, pp. 109-125.

7. *Consts. of N.J.*, p. 237.

8. William A. Whitehead et al., eds., *Documents Relating to the Colonial History of the State of New Jersey*, 1st ser., 42 vols. (Newark, 1880-1949), 13:36-37 (hereafter cited as *N.J. Archives*); Pomfret, *East New Jersey*, p. 174.

9. *Consts. of N.J.*, pp. 245-246.

10. Preston W. Edsall, ed. *Journal of the Courts of Common Right and Chancery of East New Jersey, 1683-1702* (Philadelphia, American Legal History Society, 1937), pp. 226-227, 228, 310; Orra E. Monnette, *First Settlers of Ye Plantations of Piscataway and Woodbridge, Olde East New Jersey, 1664-1714*, 7 vols. (Los Angeles, The Leroy Carman Press, 1930-1935), 2:190; *N.J. Archives*, 13:238.

11. [Lewis Morris] , "The Memorial of Col. Morris Concerning the State of Religion in the Jerseys, 1700," *Proceedings of the New Jersey Historical Society*, 4 (1850), 119.

12. Morgan Edwards, *Materials towards a History of the Baptists in Jersey* (Philadelphia, 1792), p. 24; Monnette, *Piscataway and Woodbridge*, 2:180-193; see also 3:327; 4:588.

13. *Consts. of N.J.*, pp. 382-411. Also in Boyd, *Fundamental Laws of N.J.*, pp. 71-104. On the question of authorship, see John E. Pomfret, "The Problem of the West Jersey *Concessions* of 1676/7," *William and Mary Quarterly*, 3d ser., 5 (January 1948), 95-105.

14. *Consts. of N.J.*, pp. 423-437, 460, 527-528; quotation from the Quaker Thomas F. Gordon, *The History of New Jersey* (1834), in Whitehead, *East Jersey*, p. 164.

15. *Consts. of N.J.*, p. 519.

16. H. Clay Reed and George J. Miller, eds., *The Burlington Court Book: A Record of Quaker Jurisprudence in West New Jersey, 1680-1709*, American Legal Records, 5 (Washington, The American Historical Association, 1944), pp. li, 206, 209, 211, 212-213, 218.

17. *The Acts of the General Assembly of the Province of New Jersey . . . [1703-1732]* (Philadelphia, 1732), p. 3.

18. Melvin B. Endy, Jr., *William Penn and Early Quakerism*, pp. 126-141; Hannah Roach Benner, "The Planting of Pennsylvania: A Seventeenth Century Real Estate Development," *Pennsylvania Magazine of History and Biography*, 92 (January 1968), 9.

19. Staughton George et al., eds., *Charter to William Penn, and Laws of the Province of Pennsylvania, Passed between the Years 1682 and 1700, Preceded by Duke of York's Laws . . .* (Harrisburg, 1879), contains these early documents (quotation p. 103); hereafter cited as *Laws of Pa.*

20. The Duke of York deeded the lands on the lower Delaware River to Penn in August 1682, and at Chester in December an act of union annexed Delaware to Pennsylvania. On these early years, see Edwin B. Bronner, *William Penn's "Holy Experi-*

ment": The Founding of Pennsylvania, 1681-1701 (New York, Columbia University Press, 1962), and Joseph E. Illick, *William Penn the Politician: His Relations with the English Government* (Ithaca, Cornell University Press, 1965), chaps. 1-2, 6.

21. *Votes and Proceedings of the House of Representatives of the Province of Pennsylvania, 1682-1776,* 8 vols. (Philadelphia, 1752-1756), reprinted in *Pennsylvania Archives, Eighth Series* (Harrisburg, 1931-1936), 1:1-13 (hereafter cited as *Votes of Assembly*); *Laws of Pa.,* pp. 108, 116 (quotations).

22. *Votes of Assembly,* in *Pennsylvania Archives*, 8th ser., 1:33. This provision is not, so far as I have been able to determine, included in *Laws of Pa.*

23. A precedent existed for judicial protection of the Sabbath under the Duke of York's Laws, in force in the area from 1676 to 1682. A court held at New Castle in 1681, declaring that frequent shooting of partridges "doth much tend" to profane the Lord's Day, prohibited the hunting or shooting of all game on Sunday upon penalty of ten guilders for the first offense, twenty for the second, and loss of gun for the third; *Records of the Court of New Castle on Delaware, 1676-1681* (Lancaster, Pa., Wickersham Printing Co., 1904), p. 488.

24. John Watson, *Annals of Philadelphia and Pennsylvania in the Olden Time,* 2 vols. (Philadelphia, 1870), 1:300; quoted in Augustus C. Buell, *William Penn as the Founder of Two Commonwealths* (New York, D. Appleton and Co., 1904), p. 225.

25. *Minutes of the Provincial Council of Pennsylvania,* in *Colonial Records of Pennsylvania, 1683-1790,* 16 vols. (Philadelphia, 1852-1853), 1:380-381 (hereafter *Minutes of the Provincial Council).*

26. George Smith, *History of Delaware County, Pennsylvania* (Philadelphia, 1862), pp. 167, 194; *Record of the Courts of Chester County, Pennsylvania, 1681-1697* (Philadelphia, The Colonial Society of Pennsylvania, 1910), pp. 177, 380, 391.

27. Harry Emerson Wildes, *William Penn* (New York, Macmillan Publishing Co., 1974), pp. 302-304.

28. Leon deValinger, Jr., ed., *Court Records of Kent County, Delaware, 1680-1705,* American Legal Records, 8 (Washington, The American Historical Association, 1959), pp. 201, 151-152; "Presentments, Petitions, &c., between the Years 1702 and 1774," *Collections of the Historical Society of Pennsylvania,* 1 (1853), 259, 261; Watson, *Annals of Philadelphia and Pennsylvania,* 1:306, 308; Smith, *Delaware County,* p. 216.

29. *Votes of Assembly,* in *Pennsylvania Archives,* 8th ser., 1:502-503.

30. *Minutes of the Provincial Council,* in *Colonial Records,* 2:210-211; *Votes of Assembly,* in *Pennsylvania Archives,* 8th ser., 1:520-528, 563-564; *The Laws of the Province of Pennsilvania* (Philadelphia, 1714), pp. 32, 35-37, 77. The governor signed the act in January 1706.

31. Morgan Edwards, *Material towards a History of the Baptists in Pennsylvania* (Philadelphia, 1770), pp. 6-54.

32. Ethyn W. Kirby, *George Keith (1638-1716)* (New York, D. Appleton-Century Co., 1942).

33. Edwards, *Baptists in Pennsylvania,* p. 56. The assertion by Edwards that Noble was a Seventh-Day Baptist minister when he arrived is certainly erroneous. Noble was one of the forty-eight Keithian signers of *The Reasons of the Separation,* and

he was married at Darby Quaker Meeting in 1692. See Monnette, *Piscataway and Woodbridge,* 2:190.

34. *Seventh-Day Baptists in Europe and America,* 1:124-125, 132, 150. Compare Julius F. Sachse, *The German Pietists of Provincial Pennsylvania, 1694-1708* (Philadelphia, 1895), 125-126n.

35. Edwards, *Baptists in Pennsylvania,* pp. 57-58.

36. Sachse, *German Pietists,* pp. 260-277; Edwards, *Baptists in Pennsylvania,* p. 58; Frederick L. Weis, "The Colonial Clergy of the Middle Colonies: New York, New Jersey, and Pennsylvania, 1628-1776," p. 304.

37. Edwards, *Baptists in Pennsylvania,* pp. 59-60, 24-27; Corliss F. Randolph, *A History of the Seventh Day Baptists in West Virginia* (Plainfield, N.J., The American Sabbath Tract Society, 1905), pp. 1-8. The tempestuous and eccentric Davis went to Westerly, Rhode Island, in 1711.

38. No copy of this treatise has been found. Auren went so far as to lay the cornerstone of Holy Trinity Church in Wilmington on a Saturday in 1698, and he later preached to his Lutheran congregation in New Jersey on Sundays while he and his family observed Saturdays.

39. Sachse, *German Pietists,* pp. 128-138, 136-137, 159, 161-163, 276-277, 289; Andrew Steinmetz, "Kelpius: The Hermit of the Wissahickon," *American-German Review,* 7 (August 1941), 7-12; and E. Gordon Alderfer, "Johannes Kelpius and the Spiritual Ferment of the Seventeenth Century," *American-German Review,* 17 (August 1951), 3-6.

40. Edwards, *Baptists in Pennsylvania,* pp. 64-89; the valuable if not always careful study by Julius F. Sachse, *The German Sectarians of Pennsylvania, 1708-1800: A Critical and Legendary History of the Ephrata Cloister and the Dunkers,* 2 vols. (Philadelphia, 1899-1900); Martin G. Brumbaugh, *A History of the German Baptist Brethren in Europe and America,* 2d ed. (Elgin, Ill., Brethren Publishing House, 1910); and Walter C. Klein, *Johann Conrad Beissel: Mystic and Martinet, 1690-1768* (Philadelphia, University of Pennsylvania Press, 1942), pp. 1-35. Donald F. Durnbaugh, ed., *The Brethren in Colonial America* (Elgin, Ill., The Brethren Press, 1967), is a collection of original sources.

41. [Brothers] Lamech and Agrippa, *Chronicon Ephratense: A History of the Community of Seventh Day Baptists at Ephrata, Lancaster County, Penn'a,* trans. J. Max Hark (Lancaster, 1889), p. 140n. An indispensable but partisan souce, in effect an authorized biography of Beissel. Brother Agrippa was John Peter Miller, who is treated later in the text.

42. Ibid., p. 44.

43. Beissel, *Mystyrion Anomias,* p. 6 (quotation). Beissel follows his custom of quoting Scripture without reference, but the texts are identified in Klein, *Johann Conrad Beissel,* pp. 61-66.

44. Klein, *Johann Conrad Beissel,* pp. 188-189.

45. Sachse, *German Sectarians,* 1:179; *Chronicon Ephratense,* pp. 44-45. Years earlier Benjamin Furly (1636-1714), a close associate of Penn in promoting Quakerism on the Continent, had expressed concern not only for the religious liberty but also for the personal rights of prospective immigrants to Pennsylvania. He thought that the

1683 law enjoining all to abstain from labor on the First Day might prove "a vile snare" to the conscience of those for whom the Sabbath was of human rather than divine institution and who "may be pressed in spirit . . . sometimes to work upon that day"; William I. Hull, *William Penn and the Dutch Quaker Migration to Pennsylvania* (Swarthmore, Pa., Swarthmore College, 1935), pp. 342-343. Immediately after enactment of the 1705 Sunday law, the Saturday-keepers in the province petitioned the House for "Relief against the ill Use which may be made of the Law"; *Votes of Assembly,* in *Pennsylvania Archives,* 8th ser., 1:569. The prohibition of Sunday labor to Saturday-keepers, especially Jewish, was a persistent and pressing problem in the United States until the middle of the twentieth century.

46. James Logan, *The Charge Delivered from the Bench to the Grand-Jury, at the Court of Quarter Sessions, Held for the County of Philadelphia* (Philadelphia, 1723), p. 13; Sachse, *German Sectarians,* 1:201-202; *The Autobiography of Benjamin Franklin,* ed. Leonard W. Labaree et al. (New Haven, Yale University Press, 1964), pp. 147-148.

47. *Chronicon Ephratense,* chaps. 13, 15, 17; Paul A. W. Wallace, *Conrad Weiser, 1696-1760: Friend of Colonist and Mohawk* (Philadelphia, University of Pennsylvania Press, 1945), chaps. 7-8, 12-13; E. Gordon Alderfer, "Conrad Beissel and the Ephrata Experiment," *American-German Review,* 21 (August-September 1955), 23-25.

48. Yet Brother Agrippa (or Jabez) gave a spiritual interpretation to the Sabbath Day. See Julius F. Sachse, "A Unique Manuscript by Rev. Peter Miller," *Pennsylvania-German Society Proceedings,* 21 (1912), 40.

49. Israel Acrelius, *A History of New Sweden,* trans. William M. Reynolds, *Memoirs of the Historical Society of Pennsylvania,* 11 (1874), 373-401 (quotations pp. 388, 391). According to Edwards, *Baptists in Pennsylvania,* p. 75, the Ephrata Community numbered thirty-two brothers and sisters in 1770.

50. Klaus G. Wust, "German Mystics and Sabbatarians in Virginia, 1700-1746," *Virginia Mazazine of History and Biography,* 72 (July 1964), 330-347; Klein, *Johann Conrad Beissel,* pp. 157-160.

12. New England's Glory

1. Perry Miller, *The New England Mind: From Colony to Province,* is a classic account of the declension. But also see Giorgio Spini, *Autobiografia della Giovane America: La Storiografia Americana dai Padri Pellegrini all' Independenza,* pt. 2; and Robert Middlekauff, *The Mathers: Three Generations of Puritan Intellectuals, 1596-1728.*

2. Edited by Kenneth B. Murdock (New York, The Spiral Press, 1929), pp. 17, 40 (stanzas 31, 126); Cotton Mather, *Magnalia Christi Americana,* bk. 3, pp. 178-179; "The Diaries of John Hull," *Transactions and Collections of the American Antiquarian Society: Archaeologia Americana,* 3 (1857), 125; see also pp. 250-251.

3. Mather, *Magnalia,* bk. 4, p. 216; Mary Rowlandson, "Narrative of the Captivity of Mrs. Mary Rowlandson" (1682), in Charles H. Lincoln, ed., *Narratives of the Indian Wars, 1675-1699* (New York, Charles Scribner's Sons, 1913), pp. 124, 145.

4. *Journal of Jasper Danckaerts, 1679-1680,* p. 274.

5. *Mass. Bay Recs.,* 4:pt. 1, p. 452.

6. Ibid., pt. 2, pp. 164-166, 37, 88.

7. *Essex Court Recs.,* 2:202-249 passim; 3-5:passim. On Wardall and Verin, see ibid., 3:99-100, 111. *Mass. Bay Recs.,* 4:pt. 2, p. 7; Zechariah Chafee, Jr., and Samuel Eliot Morison, eds., "Records of the Suffolk County Court, 1671-1680," *PCSM,* 29-30 (1933), 1:256-257; 2:594-595.

8. "The First Record-Book of the First Church in Charlestown, Massachusetts," *New-England Historical and Genealogical Register,* 24 (1870), 10-12, 133; *Mass. Bay Recs.,* 4:pt. 2, pp. 290-291, 373-375.

9. *Essex Court Recs.,* 2:261-262; 5:221, 267.

10. *Mass. Bay Recs.,* 4:pt. 2, p. 395.

11. *Essex Court Recs.,* 5:38; 6:26; "Suffolk County Court," 1:125; 2:645, 646.

12. Joseph H. Smith, ed., *Colonial Justice in Western Massachusetts, 1639-1702: The Pynchon Court Record* (Cambridge, Mass., Harvard University Press, 1961), pp. 252-253; *The Records of the Town of Cambridge (Formerly Newtowne), Massachusetts, 1630-1703* (Cambridge, Mass., City Council, 1901), p. 178.

13. *Ply. Col. Recs.,* 4:42, 53; 5:169; Brigham, *Laws of Plymouth,* pp. 242-243, 269-270, 247.

14. *Ply. Col. Recs.,* 4:42, 29; 5:51; 11:176-177; Brigham, *Laws of Plymouth,* pp. 247; *Ply. Col. Recs.,* 5:53, 61, 87, 99, 152; Brigham, *Laws of Plymouth,* p. 246.

15. *Ply. Col. Recs.,* 11:137, 228.

16. *Conn. Col. Recs.,* 2:88, 102.

17. Frances M. Caulkins, *History of New London, Connecticut* (New London, 1895), pp. 250-251.

18. *New Haven Town Recs.,* 1:527-528; 2:1-2, 178, 140-141, 148-151; Caulkins, *New London,* pp. 251, 250 (quotations).

19. *New Haven Town Recs.,* 2:26-30, 42-43, 156.

20. William Kellaway, *The New England Company, 1649-1776: Missionary Society to the American Indians,* pp. 133-136; Daniel Gookin, "Historical Collections of the Indians in New England" (1674), *CMHS,* 1st ser., 1 (1792, reprinted 1806), 181-210.

21. Otis G. Hammond, ed., *New Hampshire Court Records, 1640-1692,* pp. 185-187, 189, 190, 203, 230, 254, 259, 272, 278, 286, 340, 341, 348, 169, 183, 203, 242, 265-266, 330, 346, 348, 349, 371, 377, 441.

22. Nathaniel Bouton et al., eds., *New Hampshire Provincial and State Papers,* 40 vols. (Concord, State of New Hampshire, 1867-1943), 1:446.

23. [Charles T. Libby, Robert E. Moody, and Neal W. Allen, Jr.], eds., *Province and Court Records of Maine,* 2:118, 101, 104 (quotation). This discussion is based on the abundant material in these records (hereafter cited as *Maine Recs.*), 1:236-338 passim; 2-5. References can be easily located by consulting the appropriate entries in the indexes *s.v. Crimes.* In what follows the only additional citations will be to specific individuals and events treated.

24. *Maine Recs.,* 2:225 (quotation), 306.

25. Ibid., 2:306-307; 3:xxxiv-xxxix, 165.

26. Ibid., 2:170; 3:165-302; 4:75, 77, 98, 105, 110, 249, 250, 296, 333, 334, 343.

27. Ibid., 2:433, 184; 3:301; 4:88, 91, 254, 255, 364.

28. *Mass. Bay Recs.*, 5:59-63, 133; Higginson to Increase Mather, Salem, 30 September 1678, "The Mather Papers," *CMHS*, 4th ser., 8 (1868), 278-279; *Mass. Bay Recs.*, 5:243.

29. *Mass. Bay Recs.*, 5:133, 155.

30. Quoted in Mather, *Magnalia*, bk. 5, p. 89. The Reforming Synod is also discussed in Williston Walker, *The Creeds and Platforms of Congregationalism*, pp. 409-439.

31. *Mass. Bay Recs.*, 5:239-240, 241.

32. "Suffolk County Court," 2:846; Historical Records Survey, Work Projects Administration, "Abstract and Index of the Inferiour Court of Pleas (Suffolk County Court) Held at Boston, 1680-1698," (mimeographed, Boston, 1940), p. 126.

33. "Suffolk County Court," 2:867, 868; *Essex Court Recs.*, 7:81; 8:222-226; *Inferiour Court of Pleas (Suffolk)*, p. 126; *Ply. Col. Recs.*, 5:253; 6:172.

34. *Essex Court Recs.*, 7:251; *Watertown Records*, 8 vols. in 7 (Watertown, Mass., Watertown Historical Society, 1894-1939), 2:17; see, for example, *Town Records of Salem, Massachusetts*, 3 vols. (Salem, The Essex Institute, 1868-1934), 2:238-239; 3:55.

35. *Essex Court Recs.*, 7:376.

36. Shove to Hinckley, Taunton, 23 February 1682, "The Hinckley Papers," *CMHS*, 4th ser., 5 (1861), 58; *Ply. Col. Recs.*, 5:234; 11:258; *Records of the Town of Plymouth, 1636-1783*, 3 vols. (Plymouth, Avery and Doten, 1889-1903), 1:171.

37. Robert N. Toppan, ed., *Edward Randolph . . . 1676-1703,* 5 vols., The Prince Society (Boston, 1898), 2:231-232; see also pp. 313, 318.

38. W. Noel Sainsbury and J. W. Fortescue, eds., *Calendar of State Papers, Colonial Series, . . . 1677-1680* (London, 1896), pp. 139-140, 141; *Mass. Bay Recs.*, 5:321-322.

39. Bishop to Mather, 16 September 1682, "The Mather Papers," *CMHS*, 4th ser., 8 (1868), 311-312.

40. See Clifford K. Shipton, "The New England Clergy of the 'Glacial Age,' " *PCSM*, 32 (1937), 24-54.

41. John Dunton, *Letters Written from New-England, A.D. 1686*, pp. 126, 127-128.

42. *Conn. Col. Recs.*, 2:280.

43. Caulkins, *New London*, p. 252; *Conn. Col. Recs.*, 3:147-148, 202-203.

44. Caulkins, *New London*, pp. 201-221; John R. Bolles and Anna B. Williams, *The Rogerenes: Some Hitherto Unpublished Annals Belonging to the Colonial History of Connecticut* (Boston, Stanhope Press, 1904); Corliss Fitz Randolph, "The Rogerenes," in *Seventh Day Baptists in Europe and America*, 2:1261-1281; Ellen S. Brinton, "The Rogerenes," *New England Quarterly*, 16 (March 1943), 3-19; idem, "Books by and about the Rogerenes," *Bulletin of the New York Public Library*, 49 (September 1945), 627-648; and Henry B. Parkes in the *DAB*.

45. Henry Clarke, *A History of the Sabbatarians or Seventh Day Baptists in America*, pp. 8-9, 18; William L. Burdick, "The Eastern Association," in *Seventh Day Baptists in Europe and America*, 2:589-601; Frederic Denison, *Westerly (Rhode Island) and Its Witnesses . . . 1626-1876* (Providence, 1878), pp. 59-60; *The First Hundred Years: Pawcatuck Seventh Day Baptist Church, Westerly, Rhode Island, 1840-1940* (Westerly, The Utter Co., 1940), p. 30.

46. William Edmundson, *A Journal of the Life, Travels, Sufferings, and Labour of Love in the Work of the Ministry*, pp. 83-84; Clarke, *History of the Sabbatarians*, p. 9; David Benedict, *A General History of the Baptist Denomination in America*, 2 vols. (Boston, 1813), 2:424; Caulkins, *New London*, p. 210.

47. Peter Pratt, *The Prey Taken from the Strong* (New London, 1725), contains an attack on the personal life of Rogers. Pratt was a former disciple of Rogers, and his father married Rogers' divorced wife. John Rogers, Jr., replied in *An Answer to a Book Lately Put forth by Peter Pratt, Entituled, The Prey Taken from the Strong* (New York, [1726]).

48. "Bradstreet's Journal, 1664-73," *New-England Historical and Genealogical Register*, 9 (January 1855), 47; *Conn. Col. Recs.*, 2:292, 326 (quotation); Bolles and Williams, *The Rogerenes*, pp. 127-129. The two children, Elizabeth and John Jr., voluntarily chose to live with their father when they became about fourteen.

49. Caulkins, *New London*, pp. 205-206, 251 (quotation); Bolles and Williams, *The Rogerenes*, pp. 142-155; John Rogers, *A Mid-Night-Cry from the Temple of God to the Ten Virgins Slumbering and Sleeping* ([New York, 1705?]), pp. 5-15; John Bolles, "To the Reader," in John Rogers, *A Mid-Night-Cry from the Temple of God to the Ten Virgins Slumbering and Sleeping*, 2d ed. (New London, [1722]), title page, verso.

50. Bradstreet to Mather, New London, 20 April 1681, "The Mather Papers," *CMHS*, 4th ser., 8 (1868), 477.

51. Fitch, *Brief Discourse* (n.p., 1683). This work is bound with Fitch, *An Explanation of the Solemn Advice . . . Respecting the Reformation of Those Evils Which Have Been the Procuring Cause of the Late Judgments upon New-England* (Boston, 1683), and occupies pp. 73-133. On Fitch, see William B. Sprague, *Annals of the American Pulpit*, 9 vols. (New York, 1859-1869), 1:180.

52. Fitch to Increase Mather, 1 July 1684, "The Mather Papers," *CMHS*, 4th ser., 8 (1868), 476. Brinton, "Books by and about the Rogerenes," pp. 633-637.

53. John Rogers, "To the Seventh-Day Baptists," in *An Epistle to the Churches of Christ call'd Quakers* (New York, 1705), pp. 37-58.

54. Viola F. Barnes, *The Dominion of New England: A Study in British Colonial Policy* (New Haven, Yale University Press, 1923); "Commission to Sir Edmund Andros," *CMHS*, 3d ser., 7 (1838), 139-149; Robert N. Toppan, "Andros Records," *Proceedings of the American Antiquarian Society*, n.s., 13 (1899), 260-261; (1900), 463, 475; *The Andros Tracts*, 3 vols., The Prince Society (Boston, 1868-1874).

55. Mather, *Magnalia*, bk. 5, p. 97; *Conn. Col. Recs.*, 4:29.

56. Susan M. Reed, *Church and State in Massachusetts, 1691-1740* (Urbana, University of Illinois Press, 1914), pp. 36-40.

57. [Ellis Ames et al.], eds., *The Acts and Resolves, Public and Private, of the Province of the Massachusetts Bay,* 21 vols. (Boston, 1869-1922), 1:58-59.

13. An Enduring Sign

1. E[ustace] M. W. Tillyard, *The Elizabethan World Picture* (London, Chatto & Windus, 1943); C. S. Lewis, *The Discarded Image: An Introduction to Medieval and Renaissance Literature* (Cambridge, University Press, 1964).

2. William B. Sprague, *Annals of the American Pulpit,* 1:166; John L. Sibley and Clifford K. Shipton, *Biographical Sketches of Graduates of Harvard University,* 16 vols. (Cambridge, Mass., C. W. Sever and Harvard University Press, and Boston, Massachusetts Historical Society, 1873-1972), 2:13-36 (hereafter cited as *Sibley's Harvard Graduates*); Perry Miller, *The New England Mind: From Colony to Province,* pp. 421, 450-451.

3. Samuel Willard, *A Compleat Body of Divinity* (Boston, 1726), pp. 648-597 (error in pagination; actually runs pp. 648-685), 649 (quotation).

4. John R. Bolles and Anna B. Williams, *The Rogerenes,* pp. 164, 173-193; Frances M. Caulkins, *History of New London, Connecticut,* pp. 212-214; John Rogers, *A Mid-Night-Cry from the Temple of God to the Ten Virgins Slumbering and Sleeping* ([New York, 1705?]), p. 16; Ellen Brinton, "Books by and about the Rogerenes," pp. 633-634; *Conn. Col. Recs.,* 4:201 (quotation).

5. Brinton, "Books by and about the Rogerenes," pp. 633-634; Julius F. Sachse, *The German Pietists of Provincial Pennsylvania, 1694-1708,* pp. 161-163 (quotation p. 161).

6. Rogers, *A Mid-Night-Cry,* pp. 5-16, 136-145; Brinton, "Books by and about the Rogerenes," p. 634.

7. John Rogers, "Concerning the Christian Sabbath," in *A Mid-Night-Cry,* pp. 136-145; see also "To the Seventh-Day Baptists," in *An Epistle to the Churches of Christ call'd Quakers,* pp. 37-58.

8. Shipton, *Sibley's Harvard Graduates,* 4:454-455; Charles L. Sanford, "The Days of Jeremy Dummer, Colonial Agent" (Ph.D. diss., Harvard University, 1952).

9. Sanford, "Jeremy Dummer," pp. 60-73; E. W. Hengstenberg, *The Lord's Day,* p. 70; Robert Cox, *The Literature of the Sabbath Question,* 2:1-5, 92-99.

10. Jer[emiah] Dummer, *De Jure Judaeorum Sabbati* (The Law of the Jewish Sabbath; Leyden, 1703), pp. 3-5 (par. 3-6). My translation is from the copy in the Boston Public Library, with citations to page (and numbered paragraph) in the Latin original.

11. Ibid., p. 6 (par. 7).

12. Ibid., pp. 11-20 (par. 16-25); (quotation p. 16, par. 22).

13. Ibid., p. 20 (par. 26).

14. Sewall to Dummer, 10 October 1704, "Letter-Book of Samuel Sewall," *CMHS,* 6th ser., 1-2 (1886-1888), 1:302-304 (quotation p. 303). Sewall took great interest in the Jews out of a millenarian hope of their speedy conversion to Christianity. On 12 March 1702 he had written asking his cousin Jeremy Dummer to "pleasure

me'' by sending word as to "whether the Jews in Holland and elsewhere doe begin their weekly Sabbath in the Evening''; ibid., p. 268.

15. Ibid., p. 304; "Diary of Cotton Mather," 2 vols., *CMHS,* 7th ser., 7-8 (1911-1912), 1:471-472; 474-475; Cotton Mather, *The Day Which the Lord Hath Made* (Boston, 1703), p. 41; italics omitted.

16. Sanford, "Jeremy Dummer," pp. 82, 89-91, 97; Shipton, *Sibley's Harvard Graduates,* 4:455.

17. Keith to Sewall, 17 April 1704, in the New England Historic Genealogical Society Library, Boston.

18. Taylor to Sewall, 17 November 1704, in the New England Historic Genealogical Society Library. Sanford, "Jeremy Dummer," pp. 83-85, directed me to the Keith and Taylor letters.

19. Shipton, *Sibley's Harvard Graduates,* 4:455-456; Sanford, "Jeremy Dummer," pp. 82, 92-93; Sewall to Dummer, 10 October 1704, "Letter-Book of Samuel Sewall," *CMHS,* 6th ser., 1-2 (1886-1888), 1:302, 304.

20. Jeremiah Dummer, *A Discourse on the Holiness of the Sabbath Day* (Boston, 1704).

21. Increase Mather, "Introduction" to Dummer, *A Discourse,* p. v.

22. Torrey to Dummer, 26 December 1704, "Letter-Book of Samuel Sewall," *CMHS,* 6th ser., 1-2 (1886-1888), 1:304-309.

23. Miller, *The New England Mind: From Colony to Province,* pp. 424-426, 429.

24. Sheldon S. Cohen, "The Diary of Jeremiah Dummer," *William and Mary Quarterly,* 3d ser., 24 (July 1967), 397-422; Shipton, *Sibley's Harvard Graduates,* 4:460, 465.

25. "Letter-Book of Samuel Sewall," *CMHS,* 6th ser., 1-2 (1886-1888), 1:305n.

26. Mather, *Magnalia,* bk. 3, p. 97; italics omitted in all but the Latin quotation. Also see R. E. Watters, "Biographical Technique in Cotton Mather's *Magnalia,*" *William and Mary Quarterly,* 3d ser., 2 (April 1945), 156.

27. Mather, *Magnalia,* bk. 3, p. 27; italics omitted. See also Peter H. Smith, "Politics and Sainthood: Biography by Cotton Mather," *William and Mary Quarterly,* 3d ser., 20 (April 1963), 203-204.

28. Mather, *Magnalia,* bk. 3, p. 178; italics omitted.

29. William Kellaway, *The New England Company, 1649-1776: Missionary Society to the American Indians,* pp. 148-149; J. Hammond Trumbull, "Books and Tracts in the Indian Language or Designed for the Use of the Indians, Printed at Cambridge and Boston, 1653-1721," *Proceedings of the American Antiquarian Society,* 1873 (1874), 58-59.

30. Benjamin Wadsworth, *The Lord's Day Proved to Be the Christian Sabbath* (Boston, 1720), pp. 55-56, 62; John Rogers, *An Answer to a Book Intituled, The Lords Day Proved to Be the Christian Sabbath . . . and Also an Answer to a Pamphlet Intituled Thesis Concerning the Sabbath* (Boston, 1721).

31. Benjamin Colman, *The Doctrine and Law of the Holy Sabbath* (Boston, 1725), p. iii; italics omitted.

32. Benjamin Colton, *Two Sermons Deliver'd at Hartford . . . The First Sermon Treats of the Change of the Sabbath from the Seventh to the First Day of the Week* (New London, 1735), pp. 1-36.

33. Quoted in Sanford, "Jeremy Dummer," p. 97; italics omitted.

34. "Diary of Samuel Sewall, 1674-1729," *CMHS*, 5th ser., 5-7 (1878-1882), 2:72-73, 83, 101, 267, 268-269, 276, 421; 3:50, 55, 169.

35. *The Autobiography of Benjamin Franklin*, p. 63.

36. For examples, see "Diary of Samuel Sewall," *CMHS*, 5th ser., 5-7 (1878-1882), 3:193; and Jonathan Edwards, *The Works of President Edwards*, 8 vols. (Worcester, Mass., 1808-1809), 1:40.

37. Increase Mather, *Meditations on the Sanctification of the Lord's Day* (Boston, 1712), pp. 24-25; A Report of the Record Commissioners of the City of Boston [Eleventh and Thirteenth Reports], *Records of Boston Selectmen, 1701-1736* (Boston, 1884-1885).

38. A Report of the Record Commissioners of the City of Boston [Eighth Report], *Boston Records from 1700 to 1708* (Boston, 1883), pp. 13-14.

39. Edward Ward, *A Trip to New England. With a Character of the Country and People* (London, 1699), was a malicious but entertaining account. A recent edition is Howard W. Troyer, ed., *Five Travel Scripts Commonly Attributed to Edward Ward* (New York, Columbia University Press, 1933). Cotton Mather considered Ward one of the "filthy men" who wrote evil of New England; see Mather's *The Terror of the Lord* (Boston, 1727), p. 21, and p. 15 in the work cited in the next note.

40. Cotton Mather, *A Good Evening for the Best of Dayes: An Essay to Manage an Action of Trespass against Those Who Mispend the Lord's Day Evening* (Boston, 1708).

41. Mather, *Magnalia*, bk. 6, p. 9; italics omitted.

42. Cotton Mather, *The Fisher-Mans Calling* (Boston, 1712), pp. 23-24.

43. The quotation is in the title of the broadside. See also Samuel A. Green, *John Foster, The Earliest American Engraver and the First Boston Printer* (Boston, Massachusetts Historical Society, 1909), pp. 13-15, 125.

44. Mather, *Meditations*, p. 46.

45. James Allin, *Thunder and Earthquake: A Loud and Awful Call to Reformation*, 2d ed. (Boston, 1727), pp. 33-34; Shipton, *Sibley's Harvard Graduates*, 5:508.

46. *Conn. Col. Recs.*, 5:505, 559; M[aria] Louise Greene, *The Development of Religious Liberty in Connecticut* (Boston, Houghton, Mifflin and Co., 1905), pp. 187-188; Bolles and Williams, *The Rogerenes*, pp. 214, 215, 227, 242.

47. *Conn. Col. Recs.*, 5:130, 317, 323.

48. *Acts and Laws of His Majesties Colony of Connecticut in New-England* (New London, 1715), pp. 206-207; *Conn. Col. Recs.*, 5:525.

49. *Conn. Col. Recs.*, 6:248-249, 277-278, 401.

50. [Ellis Ames et al.], eds., *The Acts and Resolves, Public and Private, of the Province of the Massachusetts Bay*, 1:679, 681; 2:58-59 (hereafter cited as *Acts and Resolves of Massachusetts*).

51. Ibid., 2:456-457. On funerals on the Sabbath in the period between 1693 and 1715, see "Diary of Samuel Sewall," *CMHS*, 5th ser., 5-7 (1878-1882), 1:374, 381, 391, 406, 488; 2:9, 14, 52, 111, 201, 251, 279, 321; 3:50, 53. In 1701, however,

the Boston town meeting ordered that no one dig a grave or make a coffin on the Lord's Day on penalty of twenty shillings. A Report of the Record Commissioners of the City of Boston [Eighth Report], *Boston Records from 1700 to 1708*, p. 13.

52. *Acts and Resolves of Massachusetts*, 2:1071; 3:270, 986; 4:416; *Acts and Laws of His Majesty's English Colony of Connecticut in New England in America* (New-London, 1750), p. 139.

53. *The Laws of the Commonwealth of Massachusetts Passed from the Year 1780 to the End of the Year 1800*, 2 vols. (Boston, 1801), p. 538.

54. Governor Jonathan Belcher, *A Proclamation for Preventing Disorders on the Lord's Day* (Boston, 1739). An original is in the Massachusetts Historical Society Library.

55. Ola E. Winslow, ed., *American Broadside Verse from Imprints of the Seventeenth and Eighteenth Centuries* (New Haven, Yale University Press, 1930), p. 181.

56. Joseph Backus, *The Proclamation of the Honourable Joseph Jenks, Dep. Governour, Answered: And the Proceedings of a Justice's Court Held at Norwich, July 26, 1725 therein Refer'd to, Vindicated* (New London, 1726), pp. 6, 5.

57. "Diary of Joshua Hempstead of New London, Connecticut, 1711-1758," in *Collections of the New London County Historical Society*, 1 (1901), 182.

58. Leonard W. Labaree, ed., *Royal Instructions to British Colonial Governors, 1670-1776*, 2:504-505.

59. "Harvard College Records," *PCSM*, 15-16 (1925), 136, 593; *The Autobiography of Benjamin Franklin*, p. 146.

60. Jonathan Edwards, *The Great Awakening*, ed. C. C. Goen (New Haven, Yale University Press, 1972), p. 202.

61. "Boston in 1740," *PMHS*, 5 (1862), 115-116.

62. Increase Mather, *Meditations*, p. ix; Wadsworth, *The Lord's Day*, pp. iii-iv; Cotton Mather, *A Good Evening for the Best of Dayes*, p. 8; italics omitted.

63. Colman, *Doctrine and Law*, p. iii.

Epilogue

1. Daniel J. Boorstin, *The Americans: The Colonial Experience* (New York, Random House, 1958), p. 6.

2. Thomas Shepard, *Theses Sabbaticae*, preface, sig. b 2 [p. 11].

3. Christopher Hill, *Society and Puritanism in Pre-Revolutionary England*, p. 165.

4. Herbert M. Morais, *Deism in Eighteenth Century America* (New York, Columbia University Press, 1934), p. 65.

5. Charles F. Adams, *Massachusetts: Its Historians and Its History* (Boston, 1893), p. 84.

6. Quoted in William Hodgkins, *Sunday: Christian and Social Significance* (London, Independent Press, 1960), p. v.

7. *The Bulletin of the New York Sabbath Committee*, 7 (August-September [1920]), 1.

8. G. Stanley Hall, "Philosophy in the United States," *Mind*, 4 (January 1879), 105.

Bibliographical Essay

THIS BOOK RESTS on a large variety and quantity of materials. Because the notes provide rather full documentation, a list of references cited, however valuable, would swell the size of the volume without adding appreciably to its scholarly merit. Hence I have added a selective rather than comprehensive Bibliographical Essay. It does not discuss theological and religious writings; ecclesiastical articles, canons, and codes; church records; civil statutes and codes; legislative and judicial proceedings; diaries, autobiographies, memoirs, and personal accounts; travel reports; and other kinds of primary sources consulted; nor does it discuss a large body of secondary sources used, including bibliographies, biographical dictionaries, reference works, and most church, town, and local histories. The Essay, intended as a critical guide to the secondary literature which proved most valuable in my research, includes several authorities not cited in the notes, but only a portion of the references consulted.

The Judeo-Christian Sabbath is a classic case of a persistent problem, one that a certain school of historians would call a problem of the "long duration." Few questions in Western civilization have provoked controversy over a greater span of time, and the septennial institution in early America cannot be properly comprehended apart from this background. Many general histories of the weekly festival from ancient to modern times have appeared in the modern era, but most of them defend a particular religious point of view and must be handled accordingly. The best statement of the Ecclesiastical or Dominical theory of the Lord's Day is James A. Hessey, *Sunday: Its Origin, History, and Present Obligation* (London, 1860). This learned and judicious book, originally the Bampton lectures at the University of Oxford, went through five editions by 1889, with the fourth being published in New York in 1880. I used the 3d ed. (London, 1866). Hessey describes the major theories concerning the Sabbath which were propounded in England after the Reformation and discusses the history of the Sabbath and Lord's Day question from antiquity to that time. Later Anglican clergymen popularized his enormously influential views. An example is W. B. Trevelyan, *Sunday* (London, Longmans, Green, and Co., 1912), which briefly treats the history to his own day and discusses the principles of Sunday observance.

Several modern authors defend the Sabbatarian theory of the Lord's Day. James A. Gilfillan, a Scottish clergyman, wrote *The Sabbath Viewed in the Light of Reason, Revelation, and History, with Sketches of Its Literature* (Edinburgh, 1861) before Hessey's book appeared. A valuable feature is its history of conflicts of opinion over the subject in various countries. The plates of this book were presented to the New York Sabbath Committee, which joined with the American Tract Society in publishing the work ([New York], n.d.). George S. Gray, *Eight Studies of the Lord's Day* (Cambridge, Mass., 1884) was intended chiefly as an antidote to Hessey. Wilbur F. Crafts, *The Sabbath for Man: A Study of the Origin, Obligation, History, Advantages and Present State of Sabbath Observance, with Special Reference to the Rights of Workingmen* (New York, 1885), occupies the same theoretical ground; its appendix includes a discussion of Sabbath literature. William DeLoss Love, an American Presbyterian, published several articles on the subject in *Bibliotheca Sacra* between 1879 and 1881 which were revised and issued as *Sabbath and Sunday* (Chicago, 1896).

Robert Cox, *The Literature of the Sabbath Question*, 2 vols. (Edinburgh, 1865), provides copious extracts from major writings on the subject from antiquity to the author's own day.

These volumes emphasize theological considerations. Another type of book takes a legal approach. Examples are Robert Cox, *Sabbath Laws and Sabbath Duties Considered in Relation to their Nature and Scriptural Grounds and to the Principles of Religious Liberty* (Edinburgh, 1853), and A. H. Lewis, *A Critical History of Sunday Legislation from 321 to 1888 A.D.* (New York, 1888).

On the Old Testament period and hermeneutics, the works I found most useful were S. R. Driver, *The Book of Genesis*, 10th ed. ([1904], London, Methuen & Co., 1916); Robert H. Pfeiffer, *Introduction to the*

Old Testament (New York, Harper and Brothers, 1948); G. Ernest Wright, *The Old Testament against Its Environment* (London, SCM Press, 1950); B. Davie Napier, *Song of the Vineyard: A Theological Introduction to the Old Testament* (New York, Harper and Row, 1962); Bernhard W. Anderson, *The Living World of the Old Testament,* 2d ed. (London, Longman, 1967); Frederic W. Farrar, *History of Interpretation* (London, 1866); Robert M. Grant, *The Bible in the Church: A Short History of Interpretation* (New York, Macmillan Co., 1954); and Emil G. Kraeling, *The Old Testament Since the Reformation* (London, Lutterworth Press, 1955).

Because the Reformation marked a turning point in the emergence of modern Sabbatarianism, I have attempted to relate the American Sabbath to its major manifestations. Of general histories, Philip A. Schaff, *The Creeds of Christendom,* 3 vols., 4th ed. rev. and enlarged ([1878], New York, 1899), rests on immense erudition; the first volume is a historical commentary, and documents follow. Two recent surveys, brief but excellent, are Roland H. Bainton, *The Reformation of the Sixteenth Century* (Boston, Beacon Press, 1952), and A. G. Dickens, *Reformation and Society in Sixteenth-Century Europe* (London, Thames and Hudson, 1966).

Roland H. Bainton, *Here I Stand: A Life of Martin Luther* (New York, Abingdon-Cokesbury Press, 1950), gives a lively introduction to the German reformer. More specialized studies are Gordon Rupp, *The Righteousness of God: Luther Studies* (New York, Philosophical Library, 1953), part 2 of which treats Luther's break with Catholicism and his emphasis on justification by faith; B. A. Gerrish, *Grace and Reason: A Study in the Theology of Luther* (Oxford, Clarendon Press, 1962), a revisionist book on Luther's criticism of reason; and Jaroslav Pelikan, *Luther the Expositor: Introduction to the Reformer's Exegetical Writings* (St. Louis, Concordia Publishing House, 1959), the first or companion volume to *Luther's Works,* ed. Jaroslav Pelikan and Helmut T. Lehmann, 55 vols. (St. Louis, Concordia Publishing House, and Philadelphia, Fortress Press, 1955-1973).

Calvin shaped the theological tradition out of which Anglo-American Sabbatarianism arose, and his *Institutes of the Christian Religion*, ed. John T. McNeill, trans. Ford L. Battles, 2 vols. (Philadelphia, Westminster Press, 1960) is basic. Other important studies include James Mackinnon, *Calvin and the Reformation* (London, Longmans, Green and Co., 1936); John T. McNeill, *The History and Character of Calvinism* (New York, Oxford University Press, 1954); Georgia Harkness, *John Calvin: The Man and His Ethics* (New York, Henry Holt and Co., 1931); T. R.

Torrance, *Calvin's Doctrine of Man* (London, Lutterworth Press, 1949); Wilhelm Niesel, *The Theology of Calvin,* trans. Harold Knight (Philadelphia, Westminster Press, 1956), a work at variance with other authorities on Calvin's legalism and his thought on the relation between the two Testaments; and Anthony A. Hoekema, "The Covenant of Grace in Calvin's Teaching," *Calvin Theological Journal,* 2 (November 1967), 133-161. William A. Mueller, *Church and State in Luther and Calvin: A Comparative Study* (Nashville, Broadman Press, 1954), treats the two leading reformers on an important subject.

George H. Williams, *The Radical Reformation* (Philadelphia, Westminster Press, 1962), presents a masterly synthesis of a diverse and sprawling movement that bears a minor but vital relation to the Anglo-American Sabbath.

Among recent accounts of religious reconstruction in England, A. G. Dickens, *The English Reformation* (New York, Schocken Books, 1964), and William A. Clebsch, *England's Earliest Protestants, 1520-1535* (New Haven, Yale University Press, 1964), are estimable. The latter convincingly argues that Tyndale introduced into England the type of Christianity called Puritan, a religion involving rewards for righteousness and punishments for unrighteousness. Leonard J. Trinterud, "The Origins of Puritanism," *Church History,* 20 (March 1951), 37-57, contends that the concept of the conditional covenant, imported from the Rhineland before 1558, decisively shaped Elizabethan Puritanism, but in my opinion the evidence does not support this thesis.

Much of the immense literature on Puritanism as a historical movement is essential in establishing the context in which Sabbatarianism emerged in England. Especially important for the late sixteenth century are M. M. Knappen, *Tudor Puritanism: A Chapter in the History of Idealism* (Chicago, University of Chicago Press, 1939), a splendid analysis of early nonconformity and the Puritan ethos, and William Haller, *The Rise of Puritanism: Or, The Way to the New Jerusalem As Set Forth in Pulpit and Press from Thomas Cartwright to John Lilburne and John Milton, 1570-1643* (New York, Columbia University Press, 1938), which describes the rise of the brotherhood of spiritual preachers and of a new spiritual climate. Patrick Collinson, *The Elizabethan Puritan Movement* (Berkeley and Los Angeles, University of California Press, 1967), emphasizes political and ecclesiastical organization within the Puritan movement. The older works of Henry M. Dexter, *The Congregationalism of the Last Three Hundred Years* (New York, 1880), and Champlin Burrage, *The Early English Dissenters in the Light of Recent Research (1550-1641),* 2 vols. (Cambridge, University Press, 1912), are still valuable.

Charles H. George and Katherine George, *The Puritan Mind of the English Reformation, 1570-1640* (Princeton, Princeton University Press, 1961), is useful, but it maintains that "Anglican" and "Puritan" thought were fundamentally similar until about 1625, an untenable thesis. John F. H. New, *Anglican and Puritan: The Basis of their Opposition, 1558-1640* (Stanford, Stanford University Press, 1964), demonstrates that theological as opposed to secular ideas were the basis of the differences in thought between the two groups, although New depreciates the importance of covenant theology. Everett H. Emerson, *English Puritanism from John Hooper to John Milton* (Durham, Duke University Press, 1968), introduces some Puritan writings.

Specialized studies include Charles D. Cremeans, *The Reception of Calvinistic Thought in England* (Urbana, University of Illinois Press, 1949); J. E. Neale, *Elizabeth I and Her Parliaments, 1559-1581* (New York, St. Martin's Press, 1958), and *Elizabeth I and Her Parliaments, 1584-1601* (London, Jonathan Cape, 1957); Donald J. McGinn, *The Admonition Controversy* (New Brunswick, N.J., Rutgers University Press, 1949); A. F. Scott Pearson, *Thomas Cartwright and Elizabethan Puritanism, 1535-1603* (Cambridge, University Press, 1925), and *Church and State: Political Aspects of Sixteenth Century Puritanism* (Cambridge, University Press, 1928); Powel Mills Dawley, *John Whitgift and the English Reformation* (New York, Charles Scribner's Sons, 1954); and Paul A. Welsby, *Lancelot Andrewes, 1555-1626* (London, S.P.C.K., 1958).

On the early seventeenth century, Samuel R. Gardiner, *History of England from the Accession of James I to the Outbreak of the Civil War, 1603-1642,* 10 vols., new ed. (London, 1895-1899), is a masterly synthesis, but I also drew on such recent and specialized works as John D. Eusden, *Puritans, Lawyers, and Politics in Early Seventeenth-Century England* (New Haven, Yale University Press, 1958); Stuart B. Babbage, *Puritanism and Richard Bancroft* (London, S.P.C.K., 1962); H. R. Trevor-Roper, *Archbishop Laud, 1573-1645* (London, Macmillan and Co., 1940); Louis B. Wright, *Middle-Class Culture in Elizabethan England* (Chapel Hill, University of North Carolina Press, 1935), which treats the period from 1558 to 1640; Wallace Notestein, *The English People on the Eve of Colonization, 1603-1630* (New York, Harper and Brothers, 1954); and Carl Bridenbaugh, *Vexed and Troubled Englishmen, 1590-1642* (New York, Oxford University Press, 1968).

Christopher Hill explores the economic, political, religious, and intellectual forces behind the seventeenth-century English revolution in various books, and I have consulted his *Economic Problems of the Church from Archbishop Whitgift to the Long Parliament* (Oxford, Clarendon

Press, 1956); *Puritanism and Revolution: Studies in the Interpretation of the English Revolution of the Seventeenth Century* (London, Secker & Warburg, 1958); *Intellectual Origins of the English Revolution* (Oxford, Clarendon Press, 1965); and especially *Society and Puritanism in Pre-Revolutionary England* (London, Secker & Warburg, 1964). The latter, a brilliant and provocative work, shows how the rising classes made moral and material use of the Puritan ethos, including Sabbatarianism. Professor Hill is especially interested in the relations between Puritanism and economic change, but his economic interpretation does not in my opinion accord with historical reality, and he fits the evidence into a framework of Marxian presuppositions.

Michael Walzer, *The Revolution of the Saints: A Study in the Origins of Radical Politics* (Cambridge, Mass., Harvard University Press, 1965), interprets English Puritanism as a new form of discipline, the product of acute social disorder. David Little offers a dissenting opinion in "Max Weber Revisited: The 'Protestant Ethic' and the Puritan Experience of Order," *Harvard Theological Review*, 59 (October 1966), 415-428, and he treats the basic problem from a wider perspective in *Religion, Order, and Law: A Study in Pre-Revolutionary England* (New York, Harper and Row, 1969).

Many writers discuss the English Sunday, but a few treat it with great skill. W. B. Whitaker, *Sunday in Tudor and Stuart Times* (London, Houghton Publishing Co., 1933), a perceptive analysis, traces the evolution of laws regulating Sabbath behavior; and W. P. Baker, "The Observance of Sunday," in Reginald Lennard, ed., *Englishmen at Rest and Play: Some Phases of English Leisure, 1558-1714* (Oxford, Clarendon Press, 1931), emphasizes social history. H. Hensley Henson, *Studies in English Religion in the Seventeenth Century* (London, John Murray, 1903), contains a penetrating chapter on the Sabbath, and political and constitutional aspects are treated in J. R. Tanner, *English Constitutional Conflicts of the Seventeenth Century, 1603-1689* (Cambridge, University Press, 1928), and in J. W. Allen, *English Political Thought, 1603-1660. Vol. 1, 1603-1644* (London, Methuen & Co., 1938), an excellent critical evaluation of Puritanism which stresses the importance of the Sabbath.

Because the notes to my account (in Chapter 2) of the interrelated forces that called the theory of the Sabbath into being are fairly full, this Essay need only supplement them. Perry Miller shaped the minds of a whole generation on American Puritanism and on covenant theology, but I had to emancipate myself from the limitations of his conclusions on the doctrine of covenant theology, which he initially stated in "The Marrow of Puritan Divinity," *Publications of the Colonial Society of Massachu-*

setts, 32 (1937), 247-300 (also in *Errand into the Wilderness* [Cambridge, Mass., Harvard University Press, 1956], 48-98), and in *The New England Mind: The Seventeenth Century* (Cambridge, Mass., Harvard University Press, 1939), a weighty book, but one that too often walks on stilts. Calvin's *Institutes* and the books and articles cited in the notes were of primary importance in shaping my own views on the subject.

The relation of Puritanism and Sabbatarianism to the new world of capitalism and industry is enormously complex. In addition to the authorities cited in the notes, my conclusions draw also on Werner Sombart, *The Quintessence of Capitalism: A Study of the History and Psychology of the Modern Business Man,* trans. M. Epstein (London, T. Fisher Unwin, 1915); Frank H. Knight, "Historical and Theoretical Issues in the Problem of Modern Capitalism," *Journal of Economic and Business History,* 1 (November 1928), 119-136; Sidney A. Burrell, "Calvinism, Capitalism, and the Middle Classes: Some Afterthoughts on an Old Problem," *Journal of Modern History,* 23 (June 1960), 129-141; Christopher Hill, "Protestantism and the Rise of Capitalism," in F. J. Fisher, ed., *Essays in the Economic and Social History of Tudor and Stuart England: In Honour of R. H. Tawney* (Cambridge, Cambridge University Press, 1961), 15-39; Kurt Samuelsson, *Religion and Economic Action: A Critique of Max Weber,* trans. E. Geoffrey French, ed. D. C. Coleman (New York, Harper and Row, 1961), and Edmund S. Morgan's review of Samuelsson in *William and Mary Quarterly,* 3d ser., 20 (January 1963), 135-140; Herbert Luethy, "Once Again: Calvinism and Capitalism," *Encounter,* 22 (January 1964), 26-38; S. N. Eisenstadt, ed., *The Protestant Ethic and Modernization: A Comparative View* (New York, Basic Books, 1968); and the first chapter in H. R. Trevor-Roper, *The Crisis of the Seventeenth Century: Religion, the Reformation, and Social Change* (New York, Harper and Row, 1968). Benjamin Nelson, *The Idea of Usury: From Tribal Brotherhood to Universal Otherhood,* 2d ed., enlarged (Chicago, University of Chicago Press, 1969), cites recent literature on the Weber hypothesis.

References in the notes indicate the relation of Puritanism to sports, recreations, the theater, and the theme of divine revenge visited upon impiety. Two studies that provide valuable perspective are Lily B. Campbell, *Shakespeare's Tragic Heroes: Slaves of Passion* (Cambridge, University Press, 1930), and Henry A. Kelly, *Divine Providence in the England of Shakespeare's Histories* (Cambridge, Mass., Harvard University Press, 1970).

My account of the Sabbath in early America is based primarily upon original sources, but I used many secondary studies to establish the historical context. Charles M. Andrews, *The Colonial Period of American History*, 4 vols. (New Haven, Yale University Press, 1934-1938), is the leading authority on the founding and settlement of the colonies in the seventeenth century. To supplement this classic I relied upon nineteenth-century studies, which often contain vital information passed over by later historians, and more recent works.

The literature on the Chesapeake colonies is uneven, but Virginia is better served than Maryland. Richard L. Morton, *Colonial Virginia. Vol. 1, The Tidewater Period, 1607-1710* (Chapel Hill, University of North Carolina Press, 1960), is balanced and excellent. Edward L. Goodwin, *The Colonial Church in Virginia* (Milwaukee, Morehouse Publishing Co., 1927), is detailed and judicious on the early years, but George M. Brydon superseded it in *Virginia's Mother Church and the Political Conditions under Which It Grew . . . 1607-1814*, 2 vols. (Richmond, Virginia Historical Society, 1947-1952), the first volume of which carries the story to 1727. Thomas Nelson Page, *The Old Dominion: Her Making and Her Manners* (New York, Charles Scribner's Sons, 1914), noted the religious impulse in the founding of Virginia, a point Perry Miller exaggerated in "Religion and Society in the Early Literature of Virginia," in *Errand into the Wilderness* (Cambridge, Mass., Harvard University Press, 1956), 99-140. Philip Alexander Bruce provides important data in *Social Life in Virginia in the Seventeenth Century* (Richmond, Whittet & Shepperson, 1907), and in *Institutional History of Virginia in the Seventeenth Century*, 2 vols. (New York, G. P. Putnam's Sons, 1910), but some of his interpretations are untenable in the light of later research. Mary N. Stanard, *Colonial Virginia: Its People and Customs* (Philadelphia, J. B. Lippincott Co., 1917), also treats social history, and Susie M. Ames, *Studies of the Eastern Shore in the Seventeenth Century* (Richmond, The Dietz Press, 1940), though limited in scope, is solid. Walter F. Prince, "The First Criminal Code of Virginia," *Annual Report of the American Historical Association for the Year 1899*, 2 vols. (Washington, 1900), 1:309-363, is indispensable.

The writing of Maryland history has long been marked by religious polemic. Edward Eggleston, *The Beginners of a Nation* (New York, 1897), is anti-Catholic, whereas William T. Russell, *Maryland, the Land of Sanctuary: The History of Religious Toleration in Maryland from the First Settlement until the American Revolution* (Baltimore, J. H. Furst Co., 1907), and J. Moss Ives, *The Ark and the Dove: The Beginning of Civil and Religious Liberties in America* (New York, Longmans, Green and Co., 1936), are pro-Catholic. More impartial accounts include Newton D. Mereness, *Maryland as a Proprietary Province* (New York, Macmillan Co., 1901); Matthew Page Andrews, *History of Maryland: Province and State* (Garden City, N.Y., Doubleday, Doran & Co., 1929), and *The Founding of Maryland* (Baltimore, Williams and Wilkins Co., 1933); and Thomas O'Brien Hanley, *Their Rights and Liberties: The Beginnings of Religious and Political Freedom in Maryland* (Westminster, Md., Newman Press, 1959). Theodore C. Gambrall, *Studies in the Civil, Social and Ecclesiastical History of Early Maryland* (New York, 1893), deserves praise, as does Lawrence C. Wroth, "The First Sixty Years of the Church of England in Maryland, 1632-1692," *Maryland Historical Magazine,* 11 (March 1916), 1-41. Raphael Semmes, *Crime and Punishment in Early Maryland* (Baltimore, Johns Hopkins Press, 1938), is based on the sources.

Useful older studies of the Chesapeake colonies include Alexander Brown, *The Genesis of the United States,* 2 vols. (Boston, 1890), and several works by Edward D. Neill, which, because they are often careless and inaccurate, are not mentioned by title.

Many studies contribute to understanding the Puritan mission in settling New England. These include Roger L. Shinn, *Christianity and the Problem of History* (New York, Charles Scribner's Sons, 1953); C. A. Patrides, *The Phoenix and the Ladder: The Rise and Decline of the Christian View of History* (Berkeley and Los Angeles, University of California Press, 1964); Ernest L. Tuveson, *Millennium and Utopia: A Study in the Background of the Idea of Progress* (Berkeley and Los Angeles, University of California Press, 1949), and *Redeemer Nation: The Idea of America's Millennial Role* (Chicago, University of Chicago Press, 1968), which is weak on seventeenth-century New England; Herschel Baker, *The Wars of Truth: Studies in the Decay of Christian Humanism in the Earlier Seventeenth Century* (Cambridge, Mass., Harvard University Press, 1952), which discusses the doctrine of Providence; John W. Beardslee, III, *Reformed Dogmatics: J. Wollebius, G. Voetius, F. Turretin* (New York, Oxford University Press, 1965), whose introduction treats Providence and predestination from Augustine through the seventeenth century; William Haller, *Foxe's Book of Martyrs and the Elect Nation* (London, Jonathan Cape, 1963), a central work in this context; Peter Gay, *A Loss of Mastery: Puritan Historians in Colonial New England* (Berkeley and Los Angeles, University of California Press, 1966), an interesting but overly simple account; and Giorgio Spini, *Autobiografia della Giovane America: La Storiografia Americana dai Padri Pellegrini all' Independenza* (Autobiography of early America: American historiography from the Pilgrim Fathers to Independence; Turin, Giulio Einaudi, 1968), a superlative study which deserves to be translated into English.

Some nineteenth-century accounts of early New England illuminate the Puritan Sabbath indirectly or directly. Joseph Felt, *The Ecclesiastical History of New England*, 2 vols. (Boston, 1855-1862), is based on close familiarity with the sources at a time when they were largely unpublished. George E. Ellis, *The Puritan Age and Rule in the Colony of the Massachusetts Bay, 1629-1685* (Boston, 1888), is genial and rewarding. W. DeLoss Love, Jr., *The Fast and Thanksgiving Days of New England* (Boston, 1895), casts light on the observance of days. Alice Morse Earle, *The Sabbath in Puritan New England* (New York, 1891), contains much useful information; this highly popular book went through eleven editions by 1913.

More recent studies include Frances Rose-Troup, *The Massachusetts Bay Company and Its Predecessors* (New York, Grafton Press, 1930), and *John White, The Patriarch of Dorchester [Dorset] and the Founder of Massachusetts, 1575-1648* (New York, G. P. Putnam's Sons, 1930); Perry Miller, *Orthodoxy in Massachusetts, 1630-1650: A Genetic Study* (Cambridge, Mass., Harvard University Press, 1933); Edmund S. Morgan, *The Puritan Dilemma: The Story of John Winthrop* (Boston, Little, Brown and Co., 1958), and *Visible Saints: The History of a Puritan Idea* ([New York], New York University Press, 1963); and George L. Haskins, *Law and Authority in Early Massachusetts: A Study in Tradition and Design* (New York, Macmillan Co., 1960). Darrett B. Rutman, *Winthrop's Boston: Portrait of a Puritan Town, 1630-1649* (Chapel Hill, University of North Carolina Press, 1965), traces the failure to realize Winthrop's vision of a holy commonwealth. Larzer Ziff, *The Career of John Cotton: Puritanism and the American Experience* (Princeton, Princeton University Press, 1962), and Everett H. Emerson, *John Cotton* (New York, Twayne Publishers, 1965), are brief biographies.

Charles F. Adams, *Three Episodes of Massachusetts History*, 2 vols. (Boston, 1892), treats the Antinomian Controversy from an unsympathetic perspective; Emery Battis, *Saints and Sectaries: Anne Hutchinson and the Antinomian Controversy in the Massachusetts Bay Colony* (Chapel Hill, University of North Carolina Press, 1962), is questionable in its interpretations; the introduction to David D. Hall, ed., *The Antinomian Controversy, 1636-1638: A Documentary History* (Middletown, Conn., Wesleyan University Press, 1968), is excellent. Tiziano Bonazzi, *Il Sacro Esperimento: Teologia e Politica nell' America Puritana* (The holy experiment: Theology and politics in Puritan America; Bologna, Il Mulino, 1970), seizes upon the Antinomian Controversy to make severe judgments about repression in American culture.

The book by Robert E. Wall, Jr., entitled *Massachusetts Bay: The Cru-*

cial Decade, 1640-1650 (New Haven, Yale University Press, 1972), carries the story forward, and Emil Oberholzer, Jr., *Delinquent Saints: Disciplinary Action in the Early Congregational Churches of Massachusetts* (New York, Columbia University Press, 1956), is comprehensive. The encounter between Puritans and Indians is analyzed in William Kellaway, *The New England Company, 1649-1776: Missionary Society to the American Indians* (New York, Barnes & Noble, 1962), and Alden Vaughan, *New England Frontier: Puritans and Indians, 1620-1675* (Boston, Little, Brown and Co., 1965), both solid, scholarly works.

As for the neighbors of Massachusetts, George D. Langdon, Jr., *Pilgrim Colony: A History of New Plymouth, 1620-1691* (New Haven, Yale University Press, 1966), the most recent study, is balanced and judicious. In addition to the books by Edward Arber, Henry M. Dexter and Morton Dexter, and Roland G. Usher mentioned in the notes, other informative works are Daniel Plooij, *The Pilgrim Fathers from a Dutch Point of View* (New York, New York University Press, 1932); Francis Baylies, *An Historical Memoir of the Colony of New Plymouth, . . . 1608-1692,* 2 vols. (Boston, 1866); Frederick Freeman, *The History of Cape Cod: The Annals of Barnstable County and of Its Several Towns,* 2 vols. (Boston, 1860-1869); and John A. Goodwin, *The Pilgrim Republic: An Historical Review of the Colony of New Plymouth* (Boston, 1888).

There are general histories of Connecticut, but none to compare with Isabel M. Calder's superb study of *The New Haven Colony* (New Haven, Yale University Press, 1934). Edward E. Atwater, *History of the Colony of New Haven to Its Absorption into Connecticut* (New Haven, 1881), and Charles H. Levermore, *The Republic of New Haven* (Baltimore, 1886), have merit. The so-called blue laws of New England are most closely associated with New Haven and Connecticut and have given rise to a considerable literature. Royal R. Hinman anonymously edited *The Blue Laws of New Haven Colony, Usually Called the Blue Laws of Connecticut* (Hartford, 1838), to which he added restrictive laws of other colonies and "other interesting and instructive antiquities." J. Hammond Trumbull, ed., *The True-Blue Laws of Connecticut and New Haven and the False Blue-Laws Invented by the Rev. Samuel Peters* (Hartford, 1876), defended the Puritans and denounced Peters. Walter F. Prince, "An Examination of Peters's 'Blue Laws,' " *Annual Report of the American Historical Association for the Year 1898* (Washington, 1899), a model of scholarship, went far to exonerate the Anglican clergyman of mendacity, but superficial and sensational books like Gustavus Myers, *Ye Olden Blue Laws* (New York, Century Co., 1921), popularized a myth that dies hard. Kenneth W. Cameron is sympathetic to Peters, whom he interprets as an unrivaled historical polemicist and a teller of tall tales, in the introduction to *The Works of Samuel Peters of Hebron, Connecticut: New-England Historian, Satirist, Folklorist, Anti-Patriot, and Anglican Clergyman (1735-1826)*, ed. Kenneth W. Cameron (Hartford, Transcendental Books, 1967).

A serviceable guide to the dissident New England colony is Irving B. Richman, *Rhode Island: Its Making and Its Meaning*, 2d ed., 2 vols. in 1 (New York, G. P. Putnam's Sons, 1908), but Samuel Greene Arnold, *History of the State of Rhode Island and Providence Plantations, 1636-1790*, 2 vols. (New York, 1859-1860), and Howard M. Chapin, ed., *Documentary History of Rhode Island*, 2 vols. (Providence, Preston and Rounds Co., 1916-1919), make contributions. Ola E. Winslow narrates the life of the founder in *Master Roger Williams: A Biography* (New York, Macmillan Co., 1957), but to understand his career one might better turn to Edmund S. Morgan, *Roger Williams: The Church and the State* (New York, Harcourt, Brace & World, 1967). Also recommended are Mauro Calamandrei, "Neglected Aspects of Roger Williams' Thought," *Church History*, 21 (September 1952), 239-258, and Perry Miller, "Roger Williams: An Essay in Interpretation," in *The Complete Writings of Roger Williams*, 7 vols. (New York, Russell & Russell, 1963), 7:5-25.

Charles E. Clark, *The Eastern Frontier: The Settlement of Northern New England, 1610-1763* (New York, Alfred A. Knopf, 1969), is thorough, but the author's contention that Massachusetts imposed Puritan culture upon the northeastern settlements overstates the case. Of older histories, William D. Williamson, *The History of the State of Maine*, 2 vols. (Hallowell, Me., 1832), is detailed and informative though occasionally inaccurate, and Frank B. Sanborn, *New Hampshire: An Epitome of Popular Government* (Boston, Houghton Mifflin Co., 1904), is brief but solid.

To understand the Dutch background to Sabbatarianism in New Netherland would have been easier had a history of Puritanism in seventeenth-century Holland been available. Lacking such a volume (which Professor Keith L. Sprunger is now preparing), I consulted a wide variety of references. Most are cited in Chapter 9, notes 2-14, but Raymond P. Stearns, *Congregationalism in the Dutch Netherlands: The Rise and Fall of the English Congregational Classis, 1621-1635* (Chicago, American Society of Church History, 1940), and Douglas Campbell, *The Puritan in Holland, England, and America*, 2 vols., 4th ed. rev. ([1892], New York, Harper & Brothers, 1902), also deserve mention.

Various secondary works helped shape my conclusions on New Netherland and New York. The general histories by John R. Brodhead, *History of the State of New York, 1609-1691,* 2 vols. (New York, 1853-1871), and David M. Ellis et al., *A Short History of New York State* (Ithaca, Cornell University Press, 1957), were illuminating. Ellis M. Raesly, *Portrait of New Netherland* (New York, Columbia University Press, 1945), primarily a cultural and intellectual history, is a lively evaluation. Frederick J. Zwierlein, *Religion in New Netherland: A History of the Development of the Religious Conditions in the Province of New Netherland, 1623-1664* (Rochester, N.Y., John P. Smith Printing Co., 1910), is comprehensive, and Albert Eekhof, *Jonas Michaelius: Founder of the Church in New Netherland* (Leyden, A. W. Sijthoff's Publishing Co., 1926), affords a close look at an important preacher. Samuel Oppenheim, "The Early History of the Jews in New York, 1654-1664: Some New Matter on the Subject," *Publications of the American Jewish Historical Society,* 18 (1909), 1-91 (also separately published [New York, American Jewish Historical Society, 1909]), discusses this subject. Henry H. Kessler and Eugene Rachlis, *Peter Stuyvesant and His New York* (New York, Random House, 1959), has vital new information on the date of Stuyvesant's birth. The articles by Albert E. McKinley, "The Transition from Dutch to English Rule in New York: A Study in Political Imitation," *American Historical Review,* 6 (July 1901), 693-724; Edward T. Corwin, "The Ecclesiastical Condition of New York at the Opening of the Eighteenth Century," *Papers of the American Society of Church History,* 2d ser., 3 (1912), 79-115; and Thomas F. O'Connor, "Religious Toleration in New York, 1664-1700," *New York History,* 17 (October 1936), 391-410, merit attention. John W. Pratt, *Religion, Politics, and Diversity: The Church-State Theme in New York History* (Ithaca, Cornell University Press, 1967), covers a long period. Mariana (Griswold) van Rensselaer (Mrs. Schuyler van Rensselaer), *History of the City of New York in the Seventeenth Century,* 2 vols. (New York, Macmillan Co., 1909), is strong on social history. I. N. Phelps Stokes, *The Iconography of Manhattan Island, 1498-1909,* 6 vols. (New York, Robert H. Dodd, 1915-1928), is a treasure trove of information.

The Restoration colonies were greatly influenced by English developments after 1660, and G. N. Clark, *The Later Stuarts, 1660-1714* (Oxford, Clarendon Press, 1934), is a sound history. The works by Reginald Baker, H. Hensley Henson, and W. P. Whitaker, all previously cited, treat religion and the Sabbath, and additional light is shed by J. H. Overton, *Life in the English Church (1660-1714)* (London, 1885), an informative book; J. Wickham Legg, *English Church Life from the Restoration to the Tractarian Movement* (London, Longmans, Green and Co., 1914); C.

E. Whiting, *Studies in English Puritanism from the Restoration to the Revolution, 1660-1688* ([London], S.P.C.K., 1931), a detailed study; Gerald R. Cragg, *Puritanism in the Period of the Great Persecution, 1660-1688* (Cambridge, University Press, 1957); and Dudley W. R. Bahlman, *The Moral Revolution of 1688* (New Haven, Yale University Press, 1957).

The forces contributing to legalistic religion in England can be approached from the Fifth Monarchy movement or British Baptism. The most recent book on the former is B. S. Capp, *The Fifth Monarchy Men: A Study in Seventeenth-Century English Millenarianism* (Totowa, N.J., Rowman and Littlefield, 1972), but a rich harvest can be gleaned from Louise F. Brown, *The Political Activities of the Baptists and Fifth Monarchy Men in England during the Interregnum* (Washington, American Historical Association, 1912); W[illem] Schenk, *The Concern for Social Justice in the Puritan Revolution* (London, Longmans, Green and Co., 1948); and P. G. Rogers, *The Fifth Monarchy Men* (London, Oxford University Press, 1966). Christopher Hill, *Antichrist in Seventeenth-Century England* (London, Oxford University Press, 1971), also treats the problem. The valuable article by J. F. Maclear, "New England and the Fifth Monarchy: The Quest for the Millennium in Early American Puritanism," *William and Mary Quarterly*, 3d ser., 32 (April 1975), 223-260, appeared too late to be of use at the time of writing. From the other perspective the most helpful works were W. T. Whitley, *A History of the British Baptists*, 2d (rev.) ed. (London, The Kingsgate Press, 1932), and A. C. Underwood, *A History of the British Baptists* (London, Kingsgate Press, 1947).

Spiritual religion is discussed in a large body of literature. Robert Barclay, *The Inner Life of the Religious Societies of the Commonwealth*, 3d ed. (London, 1879), considers an important phase of the movement, while Gertrude Huehns, *Antinomianism in English History, with Special Reference to the Period 1640-1660* (London, Cresset Press, 1951), shows how the search for truth can influence political action. The origins of Quakerism have been variously interpreted. Still indispensable, especially as updated in the light of recent research, is William C. Braithwaite, *The Beginnings of Quakerism*, 2d ed. rev. by Henry J. Cadbury (Cambridge, University Press, 1955), and *The Second Period of Quakerism*, 2d ed. rev. by Henry J. Cadbury (Cambridge, University Press, 1961). Geoffrey F. Nuttall, *The Holy Spirit in Puritan Faith and Experience* (Oxford, Basil Blackwell, 1947), emphasizes the close relationship between radical Puritanism and early Quakerism, and Hugh Barbour, *The Quakers in Puritan England* (New Haven, Yale University Press, 1964), examines the social and economic context in which the Society of Friends emerged. Melvin B.

Endy, Jr., *William Penn and Early Quakerism* (Princeton, Princeton University Press, 1973), stresses the spiritual ferment of the Interregnum. Howard Brinton, *Friends for 300 Years: The History and Beliefs of the Society of Friends Since George Fox Started the Quaker Movement* (New York, Harper and Brothers, 1952), puts Quaker principles in historical perspective.

Harry Emerson Wildes, *William Penn* (New York, Macmillan Publishing Co., 1974), is comprehensive but untrustworthy; an appendix lists more than twenty-five earlier studies of the Quaker leader most important for the American experience. Catherine Owens Peare, *William Penn: A Biography* (Philadelphia, J. B. Lippincott Co., 1957), is still worth consulting, and William I. Hull, *William Penn: A Topical Biography* (New York, Oxford University Press, 1937) is singular in its approach. Penn is difficult to capture in a biography, and to understand him one must turn to specialized studies such as Joseph E. Illick, *William Penn the Politician: His Relations with the English Government* (Ithaca, Cornell University Press, 1965), and Mary Maples Dunn, *William Penn: Politics and Conscience* (Princeton, Princeton University Press, 1967).

Wesley F. Craven, *The Colonies in Transition, 1660-1713* (New York, Harper and Row, 1968), surveys the entire American scene. The most recent general history of South Carolina is M. Eugene Sirmans, *Colonial South Carolina: A Political History, 1663-1763* (Chapel Hill, University of North Carolina Press, 1966), but David Ramsay, *History of South Carolina*, 2 vols. in 1 (Newberry, S.C., 1858); Edward McCrady, *The History of South Carolina under the Proprietary Government, 1670-1719* ([1897], New York, Russell & Russell, 1969); and David D. Wallace, *South Carolina: A Short History, 1520-1948* (Columbia, University of South Carolina Press, 1966), have something to offer. Frederick Dalcho, *An Historical Account of the Protestant Episcopal Church in South Carolina from the First Settlement of the Province to the War of the Revolution* (Charleston, 1820), is rewarding; another denominational history is Leah Townshend, *South Carolina Baptists, 1670-1805* (Florence, S.C., Florence Printing Co., 1935). Hugh T. Lefler and Albert R. Newsome, *North Carolina: The History of a Southern State* (Chapel Hill, University of North Carolina Press, 1954), was most helpful, but Francis L. Hawks, *History of North Carolina*, 2 vols. (Fayetteville, N.C., 1858-1859), which contains documents and a historical narrative, deals profitably with religious matters, and two works by Stephen B. Weeks, *The Religious Development in the Province of North Carolina* (Baltimore, Johns Hopkins Press, 1892), and *Church and State in North Carolina* (Baltimore, John Hopkins Press, 1893), are useful.

The tangled history of early New Jersey is analyzed by John E. Pomfret in *The Province of West New Jersey, 1609-1702: A History of the Origins of an American Colony* (Princeton, Princeton University Press, 1956), and in *The Province of East New Jersey, 1609-1702: The Rebellious Proprietary* (Princeton, Princeton University Press, 1962). Various volumes in the New Jersey Historical Series shed light on the politicas, economic, social, ethnic, and religious aspects of Sabbatarianism, notably Richard P. McCormick, *New Jersey from Colony to State, 1609-1789* (Princeton, D. Van Nostrand Co., 1964), and Julian P. Boyd, ed., *Fundamental Laws and Constitutions of New Jersey, 1664-1964* (Princeton, D. Van Nostrand Co., 1964), which contains an excellent introduction. William A. Whitehead, *East Jersey under the Proprietary Governments* (New York, 1846), rewards the reader, and Theodore Thayer, *As We Were: The Story of Old Elizabethtown* (Elizabeth, N.J., The New Jersey Historical Society, 1964), is a careful study. On religion, Morgan Edwards, *Materials towards a History of the Baptists in Jersey* (Philadelphia, 1792), is invaluable, and Nelson R. Burr, "The Religious History of New Jersey before 1702," *Proceedings of the New Jersey Historical Society,* 56 (July 1938), 169-190, and *The Anglican Church in New Jersey* (Philadelphia, Church Historical Society, 1954), are worthy. Orra E. Monnette, *First Settlers of Ye Plantations of Piscataway and Woodbridge, Olde East New Jersey, 1664-1714,* 7 vols. (Los Angeles, The Leroy Carman Press, 1930-1935), is a rich mine of local history.

Many diverse strands came together in Philadelphia, and among the general histories are Robert Proud, *The History of Pennsylvania . . . from 1681 till after the Year 1742,* 2 vols. (Philadelphia, 1797); George Smith, *History of Delaware County, Pennsylvania* (Philadelphia, 1862); John Watson, *Annals of Philadelphia and Pennsylvania in the Olden Time,* 2 vols. ([1830] Philadelphia, 1870); and J. Thomas Scharf and Thompson Westcott, *History of Philadelphia, 1609-1884,* 3 vols. (Philadelphia, 1884). Specialized studies possess greater utility, and a number are excellent, including Edwin B. Bronner, *William Penn's "Holy Experiment": The Founding of Pennsylvania, 1681-1701* (New York, Columbia University Press, 1962), and Gary B. Nash, *Quakers and Politics: Pennsylvania, 1681-1726* (Princeton, Princeton University Press, 1968). Frederick B. Tolles, *Meeting House and Counting House: The Quaker Merchants of Colonial Philadelphia, 1682-1763* (Chapel Hill, University of North Carolina Press, 1948), and *James Logan and the Culture of Provincial Pennsylvania* (Boston, Little, Brown and Co., 1957), are rewarding. Ethyn W. Kirby, *George Keith (1638-1716)* (New York, D. Appleton-Century Co., 1942), analyzes dissension within the Quaker community. Morgan Edwards, *Materials towards a History of the Baptists in Pennsyl-*

vania (Philadelphia, 1770) is again invaluable. Julius F. Sachse's two studies, *The German Pietists of Provincial Pennsylvania, 1694-1708* (Philadelphia, 1895), and *The German Sectarians of Pennsylvania, 1708-1800: A Critical and Legendary History of the Ephrata Cloister and the Dunkers,* 2 vols. (Philadelphia, 1899-1900), are important sources, though facts and interpretations are not always reliable. Martin G. Brumbaugh, *A History of the German Baptist Brethren in Europe and America,* 2d ed. (Elgin, Ill., Brethren Publishing House, 1910), is soberly responsible, and Walter C. Klein, *Johann Conrad Beissel: Mystic and Martinet, 1690-1768* (Philadelphia, University of Pennsylvania Press, 1942), offers a judicious evaluation.

As for New England after 1660, Perry Miller, *The New England Mind: From Colony to Province* (Cambridge, Mass., Harvard University Press, 1953); Robert Middlekauff, *The Mathers: Three Generations of Puritan Intellectuals, 1596-1728* (New York, Oxford University Press, 1971); and the work by Giorgio Spini cited previously are all basic. Hardly less important are Viola F. Barnes, *The Dominion of New England: A Study in British Colonial Policy* (New Haven, Yale University Press, 1923); Michael G. Hall, *Edward Randolph and the American Colonies, 1676-1703* (Chapel Hill, University of North Carolina Press, 1960); Robert G. Pope, *The Half-Way Covenant: Church Membership in Puritan New England* (Princeton, Princeton University Press, 1969); Richard L. Bushman, *From Puritan to Yankee: Character and the Social Order in Connecticut, 1690-1765* (Cambridge, Mass., Harvard University Press, 1967); Clifford K. Shipton, "A Plea for Puritanism," *American Historical Review,* 40 (April 1935), 460-467, and "The New England Clergy of the 'Glacial Age,' " *Publications of the Colonial Society of Massachusetts,* 32 (1937), 24-54; and Edmund S. Morgan, "New England Puritanism, Another Approach," *William and Mary Quarterly,* 3d ser., 18 (April 1961), 236-242. Companion studies are M[aria] Louise Greene, *The Development of Religious Liberty in Connecticut* (Boston, Houghton, Mifflin and Co., 1905), and Susan M. Reed, *Church and State in Massachusetts, 1691-1740* (Urbana, University of Illinois Press, 1914). Ellen S. Brinton, "Books by and about the Rogerenes," *Bulletin of the New York Public Library,* 49 (September 1945), 627-648, opens the door on a sect that deserves closer investigation. John R. Bolles and Anna B. Williams, *The Rogerenes: Some Hitherto Unpublished Annals Belonging to the Colonial History of Connecticut* (Boston, Stanhope Press, 1904), contains "A Vindication" by Bolles and a "History of the Rogerenes" by Williams. Charles L. Sanford, "The Days of Jeremy Dummer, Colonial Agent" (Ph.D. dissertation, Harvard University, 1952), discusses an important figure in the development of the Sabbath in New England.

Index

289; Colman on, 290-291. *See also* Decalogue; Fourth Commandment; Legalism
Law and Gospel: Luther on, 16; Calvin on, 17, 19; in English covenant thought, 36-40; in Antinomian Controversy, 144-151; Shepard on, 153-157; in English Commonwealth, 225-232
Laws Agreed Upon in England, 251-252
Laws and Liberties, 135, 152, 159-165
Laws of Ecclesiastical Polity (Hooker), 34
Learned Treatise of the Sabbath, A (Brerewood), 67
Leddra, William, 172, 174, 181
Legalism: Jewish, 9-10; Jesus Christ rejects, 10; Roman Catholic, 13-14; Luther rejects, 16, 17-18, 36; Carlstadt on, 17; Radical Reformation and, 17, 18, 36-40; in Reformed theology, 19, 36-39; Puritans and, 34-35, 39-40; Tyndale and, 37-38; Calvin and, 38-39; and Puritan Sabbatarian theory, 56-57, 60, 62-63; Winthrop and, 69; under Charles I, 78-79; Traske and, 79; Brabourne and, 79; in Cotton code, 134, 137-138; and Antinomian Controversy, 144-151 passim; Shepard and, 154-157; in Rhode Island, 195; Voetius and, 202-203; in New Netherland, 216; Wells and, 224; in English Civil War and Commonwealth, 225, 226-228; Fifth Monarchists and, 226-228; Seventh-Day Sabbatarians and, 226-228; Seventh-Day Baptists and, 248, 254-262 passim; in New Jersey, 248; in Pennsylvania, 254-263 passim; in Massachusetts, 276; Rogerenes and, 278-279; Dummer and, 285; influence in America, 300
Legal process, serving of on Sunday, 100, 215, 253
Leisler, Jacob, 218
Leonard, Joseph, 267
Lewis, John, 269
Lightfoot, John, 223
Literary controversy over Sabbath: in England, 62-63, 77-78, 223, 224, 227, 229-232, 337n; in New England, 110, 153-157, 277-280, 283-289; in Netherlands, 198, 203, 285
Literature of warning: medieval use of, 14;

under Elizabeth, 54; under Stuart rulers, 79, 224-225; in New England, 276-277, 293
Little Olive Leaf Put in the Mouth of that (So Called) Noah's Dove, A (Biorck), 256
Lloyd, Mrs. Elizabeth, 91
Locke, John, 234
Logan, James, 260
Lollards, 15
Long Island: English towns on, 133, 175, 209-210; Dutch towns on, 209
Lord of Misrule, 50, 120
Lord's Day, 56; theories of, 2-3, 15; origins of, 11-12, 13; and Jewish Sabbath, 12-13, 223. *See also* Names of weekly rest day
Lord's Day Proved to be the Christian Sabbath, The (Wadsworth), 290
Lord's Day, the Sabbath Day, The (Byfield), 78
Lord, Rev. Joseph, 236
Loring, Rev. Israel, 114
Low, Emmanuel, 240
Lubberland, 241, 243
Lucena, Abraham de, 211
Ludlow, Roger, 132
Ludwell, Col. Philip, 102
Lute, William, 279
Luther, Martin, 11, 15-22 passim, 24, 36
Lutheran church, 204, 217, 247, 257
Lyford, John, 119
Lygonia, 187, 189

Mack, Alexander, 257, 261
Magnalia Christi Americana (C. Mather), 289
Maine: origins of, 185-186; government of, 187-189, 270-271; Sabbath in, 188, 189-190, 271, 272; Plymouth colony in, 189; Lygonia, 189-190; public worship in, 271, 272; Baptists in, 271-272
Malbon, Richard, 176
Marbury, Francis, 144
Market of the soul, 69, 320n
Markham, William, 253
Martin, Henry, 101
Martin, Thomas, 255
Maryland, charter of and toleration in, 93-

Selyns, Henricus, 209

Separatism, 110; origins of, 29; and Sabbatarianism, 34-35; Scrooby-Leyden
Separatists, 115-117; in Plymouth, 117-
123 passim; and ecclesiastical polity,
128; Roger Williams and, 138-144 passim

Seventh-Day Baptists: first church in America, 195, 278; of Westerly, Rhode Island,
196; English origins of, 226-228; in East
Jersey, 248; in Pennsylvania, 254-263
passim; and Rogerenes, 278-280; refuted, 290, 291. *See also* Baptists; Saturday Sabbatarians

Seventh-Day Sabbatarians. *See* Saturday
Sabbatarians

*Seventh-Day Sabbath Sought Out and
Celebrated, The* (Tillam), 227

Sewall, Samuel, 286, 287, 291, 292

Sewell, Thomas, 269

Sexual offenses, 114, 122, 163-164, 172,
240, 243, 250, 252

Shattuck, Samuel, 171, 172

Shattuck, Mrs. Samuel, 173

Shaw, John, Jr., 122

Shepard, Thomas: quoted, 1-2, 300; emi-
grates to Massachusetts, 1, 77, 129, 305n;
Theses Sabbaticae, 3, 110, 153-157; and
spiritual brotherhood, 31; youth of, 70;
and Massachusetts law code, 136, 159; in
Antinomian Controversy, 147, 148;
defends Puritan Sabbath, 153-157; and
"Eliot tracts," 183

Shepherd, Thomas, 74-75

Sherley, James, 118

Shilley, John, 268

Shipton, Thomas, 67

Shooting of guns, prohibited or punished:
in Virginia, 91, 92; in Maryland, 97-98;
in Plymouth, 122; to Indians, 185; in
Rhode Island, 195; in New Netherland,
209, 212, 215; in New York, 218, 219; in
South Carolina, 235; in Maine, 272

"Short discourse of Mr. John Cotton, A,"
111-112

*Short Discourse Proving that the Jewish or
Seventh-Day Sabbath is Abrogated and
Repealed, A* (Meredith), 260

Shorter Catechism, Westminster Assem-

bly's, 261, 283

Shove, George, 275

Sibbes, Richard, 52

Sign, Sabbath as, 9, 37, 109, 284, 291, 297,
299

Sipse, James, 91

Skelton, Samuel, 129, 139

Sluyter, Peter, 217

Smith, John (scholar), 35

Smith, Capt. John (of Va.), 86

Smith, John, (of Mass.), 179

Smith, Miss Provided, 173

Smith, Mrs. John, 173

Smith, Rev. Ralph, 117

Societies for the Reformation of Manners,
225

Society for the Propagation of the Gospel in
Foreign Parts, 225, 236, 237

Society for the Propagation of the Gospel in
New England, 183

South Carolina: origins and settlement of,
233, 234-235; Grand Council, 235, 236;
religion and Sabbath, 235-238

Southwick, Cassandra, 171, 172

Southwick, Josiah, 171, 172

Southwick, Laurence, 171, 172

Sparkles of Glory (Saltmarsh), 154

Speene, John, 184

SPG, 225; missionaries of, 236-237, 237-
238, 239, 242

Spiritual brotherhood, 225; origins of and
doctrine of Sabbath, 30-31; and founding of Massachusetts, 123-124, 125;
influence in Holland, 199

Spiritual crisis, of New England, 264-265,
273-281 passim

Spiritual religion, 17, 170, 262; and Radical
Reformation, 16, 18-19; and English
Puritanism, 35-36, 40; and Antinomian
Controversy, 144-151 passim; Shepard
on, 153-157; in New England, 160-161;
in Plymouth, 180; in Rhode Island, 190-
196 passim; Gorton and, 191, 192-193;
Antinomians and, 192; in Netherlands,
198; in England, 225-226, 228-232; and
sects, 228; and Quakers, 229-232; Rogers
and, 280-284. *See also* Quakerism

Spittlehouse, John, 227

Spivys (North Carolinians), 240-241